MAKING the LAW

THE COURTS AND THE CONSTITUTION

EDITED BY

JOHN SAYWELL
YORK UNIVERSITY

GEORGE VEGH
ONTARIO BAR

Copp Clark Pitman Ltd.
A Longman Company
Toronto

ISBN 0-7730-5098-1

executive editor: Brian Henderson
editing: Melanie Sherwood
series design: Susan Hedley
cover design: Liz Nyman
typesetting: Marnie Morrissey
printing and binding: Webcom Limited

Canadian Cataloguing in Publication Data

Main entry under title:

Making the law: the courts and the constitution

Includes bibliographical references.
ISBN 0-7730-5098-1

1. Canada - Constitutional law - Cases. 2. Canada - Constitutional law - Interpretation and construction. 3. Courts - Canada. I. Saywell, John, 1929– II. Vegh, George.

KE4218.5.M33 1991   342.71   C90-095885-5
KF4482.M33 1991

Copp Clark Pitman Ltd.
2775 Matheson Blvd. East
Mississauga, Ontario
L4W 4P7

associated companies: *Longman Group Ltd. London .*
Longman Inc. New York · Longman Cheshire Pty., Melbourne ·
Longman Paul Pty., Auckland

Printed and bound in Canada.

1 2 3 4 5   5098-1   95 94 93 92 91

OTABIND

Bound to stay open

Publisher's Note

Otabind (Ota-bind). This book has been bound using the patented Otabind process. You can open this book at any page, gently run your finger down the spine, and the pages will lie flat.

FOREWORD

Canadians have spent endless years debating their constitution. Although the arcane meanings of sections 91 and 92 of the *British North America Act* were never the stuff of ordinary discourse, they were critically important. This collection of articles and cases makes that clear, as well as showing just how and in what ways the intentions of the Fathers of Confederation were altered—or not, depending on your point of view—by the British Jurists who sat on the Judicial Committee of the Privy Council, the highest appeal court of the Empire. After the abolition of appeals to the Judicial Committee in 1949, the Supreme Court of Canada became the court of last resort; after the inclusion of the *Charter of Rights and Freedoms* in the constitution in 1982, the Supreme Court had the crucial role of determining the Charter's meaning and application.

John Saywell, Professor of History at York University, and George Vegh of the Ontario Bar have collected the most important cases that bear on the development of Canada's constitution. Then they added the key scholarly articles, as well as some they have written especially for this collection. The result is a first-class compendium, a guide to understanding how Canada moved from the B.N.A. Act of 1867 to the Present *Constitution Act* and the *Charter of Rights and Freedoms*. We will all be spending more time in the 1990s discussing our constitution; this volume is simply indispensable for those who want to participate effectively.

J.L. Granatstein
General Editor

CONTENTS

○

INTRODUCTION

M *aking the Law* has been designed as an introduction to the role of the courts in shaping the evolution of the Canadian constitution. Until 1982, the courts were mainly concerned with the federal constitution— the distribution of powers between Ottawa and the provinces. With the Charter of Rights and Freedoms, the role of the courts, above all of the Supreme Court of Canada, became even more important. The courts became the final arbiter of the line dividing the power of the state and the rights and freedoms of the individual. In the 1980s, the decisions of nine men and women on the Supreme Court became front page news as they dealt with such controversial issues as language rights and abortion, and gave meaning to such phrases as "freedom of expression" and "principles of fundamental justice."

Until relatively recently, the study of judicial review was the preserve of the law schools and of a few specialists in political science and history in a few universities. But when the Court became an important actor during the heightened tension between Ottawa and the provinces in the 1970s, and when the prolonged and agonizing negotiations over the 1982 constitution began, a much earlier interest in judicial review was revived. There was a dramatic increase in the number of books and articles about the courts by scholars outside the law schools as well as within. Constitutional law, judicial review, and constitutional history slowly became a more important part of the university curricula.

Making the Law is a response to that revived interest. We have arranged the book historically, for it is a study of the evolution of the constitution. The book is divided into five sections: the distribution of powers in the 1867 constitution; the formative years of judicial review, 1874–1912, dominated by the decisions of Lord Watson of the Judicial Committee; the period 1912–1949 when federal power was severely restricted by the decisions of Lord Haldane in the 1920s, and by the Judicial Committee in the New Deal decisions in 1937; the postwar period when the Supreme Court, emancipated from the doctrine of the Judicial Committee, gradually and hesitantly imposed its own view of the federal constitution; and, finally, the role of the Supreme Court in providing substance to the Charter of Rights. We have provided a brief historical and contextual introduction to each section.

The judicial decisions are the core of the book. The extracts, in manageable form, are printed without editorial comment. We believe that only a close study of the texts themselves will compel the student to examine critically the process of judicial reasoning. Only an investigation of the decisions themselves will show if they conform to the language of the constitution as elaborated in section one, and reveal how the doctrine of precedent—the "building blocks" of judicial review—has led to the constitutional structure we now have. It is one thing to be told how this happened; it is another to go through the process of analysis and discovery.

The commentaries build on and provide a context for the decisions. They have been selected or written by the authors to raise fundamental questions about the nature of constitutional law, about the "objectivity" of those on the bench. They investigate the role of the courts as policy makers that allocate jurisdiction within a federal constitution or determine the nature and scope of state power and individual rights and freedoms. Articles on Watson and Haldane and the decisions of the postwar Supreme Court suggest that judges do not "discover" the law in a judicial vacuum but are profoundly influenced by their own view of the law, the state and of society. Limitations of space prevented us from including as many articles as we would have liked, but in our own commentaries we have presented the views, we hope fairly, of other scholars. A short bibliography provides a basis for further reading and research.

Making the Law has been written and edited with the undergraduate student in mind. This approach raises questions rather than provides textbook answers. It is best used as a volume of texts, not as a textbook. Ideally, both the decisions and the commentaries, above all the decisions, will provide the substance for a constant interaction in the classroom.

1

THE DISTRIBUTION
OF POWERS

o

READING SECTIONS 91 AND 92

JOHN SAYWELL AND GEORGE VEGH

o

Constitutional law, to a very large extent, has been created by the courts attempting to define the nature and scope of federal and provincial legislative authority. The *British North America Act* of 1867, now the *Constitution Act, 1867*, distributed power to legislate between the two levels of government. The Charter of Rights and Freedoms in the *Constitution Act, 1982*, has since placed limits on the legislative power of both levels of government.

Judicial review of statutes challenged on constitutional grounds imposes on the court the necessity to determine the "pith and substance" of the legislation in question in order to locate it within federal or provincial jurisdiction. It also involves an analysis of the structure and wording of the sections of the 1867 Act which set out the distribution of powers. The drafting history and the language of the 1867 constitutional statute, therefore, provide the necessary points of departure for anyone wishing to understand the role the courts have played in the evolution and shaping of the Canadian constitution. Practising lawyers have often dismissed such an analysis as too academic. In recent years, however, justices of the Supreme Court have displayed a willingness, indeed in some cases a determination, to look again at the 1867 Act rather than base their decision on the layers of judicial decisions alone.

Constitutions are not written in a vacuum, although arguments and decisions in court rooms sometimes suggest that language has no content. Certainly federal constitutions that distribute the power to legislate are drafted with clear policy objectives in mind; the language chosen is intended to convey legislative intent. The objectives of the state founders in 1867 were clear. They desired to create a government that would embrace the geographic expanse and provide the political foundations and constitutional framework for a Dominion within the British Empire. The creation of a new nation would, they hoped, ensure the political and economic survival of a British North America facing industrialisation and new technologies, confronting British adoption of the more profitable imperialism of free trade, and threatened by American expansion. Apparent necessity and political ambition may have suggested a legislative union of the colonies, but political and cultural realities made possible only a federal solution. Indeed, the dynamics of the federation movement were due in part to the failure of the French and English to live in a unitary state. Paradoxically, in fact, Confederation was a response to the demand for "self-government," a divorce and a re-marriage under the terms of a new contract, an earlier version of cultural independence and economic association. The opposition in Quebec and the Atlantic colonies has traditionally been cited to explain the impossibility of a legislative union. But in all probability, Ontario's experience with what was described as Quebec's "domination" would have precluded the possibility of a unitary state if one had been realistically proposed.[1]

The real question, then, was what kind of a federal system should be created. Given the dynamic leadership of the federation movement, particularly in Toronto and Montreal, and the economic and expansionist imperatives driving the union movement, the answer clearly was a highly centralised system that could be combined with the political necessity and desirability of maintaining viable local communities and governments. There was, of course, no formula for equilibrium, but friend and foe of the new federal constitution which emerged in 1867 agreed that the central government was so dominant that the provinces were indeed glorified municipalities, however pretentious their determination to retain parliamentary institutions. With the "true" American form of federalism before them, political scientists have labelled the Canadian system "quasi-federal."[2]

As the contemporary debates in all the colonies reveal, and as scholarship has confirmed, it was not the division of legislative power between the federal government and the provinces that led to the label of quasi-federal, and made some spokesmen despair of the survival of the provinces. Indeed, the division of legislative power was not a matter of long or heated debate. Far more controversial were the provisions giving the federal government the power to appoint senators, to *disallow* provincial legislation without constitutional limitation, to appoint provincial lieutenant-governors who were expected to act as federal officers and had the power to *reserve* provincial bills for the consideration of the federal government, and to unilaterally take over "works" within a province that were deemed to be for the general advantage of Canada or two or more provinces. These were the clauses that gave the central government unilateral powers inconsistent with jurisdictional equality that led to the label of "quasi-federal."

Politically, the instruments of federal dominance could not be sustained, and by the early twentieth century the power of disallowance and the utility of the lieutenant-governor as a federal agent in the provinces had been diminished, if not destroyed, by practice and convention. Slowly, but more surely, the federal constitution was being shaped in law as the courts undertook the task of determining the legislative authority given to the federal and provincial governments. Whether or not an attempt to determine the "intentions" or "objectives" of the authors of a constitutional statute, or any statute for that matter, should (or can) be part of the process of judicial review, it is the necessary and essential beginning for anyone wishing to understand the role of the courts in Canadian constitutional law.

At the Quebec Conference in October 1864, the delegates agreed on two lists of subjects within which the federal and provincial governments would have power to legislate. The sections seemed straightforward. The federal government was given the power to make laws for "the peace, welfare and good government of the Federated Provinces...and especially laws respecting the following subjects...." With a few exceptions the list itself survived almost intact, and appeared as the enumerations in section 91 of the *Constitution Act, 1867.* Because no list could exhaust all possibilities of laws for peace, welfare and good government, a final clause stated: "And generally respecting all matters of a general character, not specially and exclusively reserved for the Local Governments and Legislatures." The provinces were also provided with a list of subjects, very similar to those in section 92 of the Act, concluding with the clause: "And generally all matters of a private or local nature not assigned to the General Parliament." But they also realised that general and local matters could overlap, hence the qualification "reserved for" and "not assigned to" in the matching residuum at the end of each list. Moreover, in the sections dealing with provincial powers over property and civil rights and over the incorporation of companies, there was the explicit subtraction from these powers of matters within those broad subjects "assigned to the General Parliament."[3]

These lists of subjects survived almost intact in the final wording of the division of powers in the 1867 constitution. The intentions seem clear. As John A. Macdonald stated during the debate on the Resolutions:

> Any honourable member on examining the list of different subjects which are to be assigned to the General and Local legislatures respectively, will see that all the great questions which affect the general interests of the Confederacy as a whole, are confided to the General Parliament, while the local interests and local laws of each section are preserved intact, and entrusted to the care of the local bodies.[4]

A moment's reflection will reveal that there was an obvious difference between the two lists: the provinces were clearly given jurisdiction over matters that related to the social, cultural, and, to a large extent, business life of the local communities. The central government was given control over the economic development and management of the new nation, as well as the responsibility for criminal law. (In the United States this was given to the states.) The central government even held the power to "nationalise" laws relating to property and civil rights in the common law provinces if the provinces agreed.

The limitation on provincial jurisdiction over property and civil rights (and the unfulfilled ambition to render that law uniform in all the provinces but Quebec) was of fundamental importance. As Professor W.R. Lederman has explained, the phrase "property and civil rights" came to Canada in the *Quebec Act* of 1774. This act:

> provided that French law and custom were to obtain respecting property and civil rights in the royal colony of Quebec. This covered all law except English criminal law, and except the English public law that came to Quebec as necessary context for English colonial governmental institutions....Moreover, these words retained this very broad significance in Upper and Lower Canada between 1791 and 1841, and

in the United Province of Canada, 1841–1867. The Fathers of Confederation knew all about this—they lived with it every day—and naturally they took the broad scope of the phrase for granted.[5]

As a result they were determined to make clear that much of what might be considered property and civil rights (and matters of a local and private nature) were, in fact, among the powers assigned to the central government.

The historical evidence makes it very clear that the British government desired to strengthen, not weaken, the central government. As Lord Carnarvon, the Colonial Secretary, wrote to his predecessor:

> If with the acquiescence of the Delegates I could see my way to any reduction of the general powers granted...to the Local Legislatures I should be glad to do so with the view of adding strength to the central Government but this must depend upon them.[6]

This desire must have been made clear to Lord Thring and the draftsmen in the Colonial Office who were given the task of translating the Quebec Resolutions into proper statutory form. There is no reason to believe that in the translation, the protection of federal power would be in any way diminished; indeed, given the British concern that the centre would be too weak, the reverse would be more likely.

An early draft in London first introduced the now familiar phrase giving power to legislate "in relation to Matters coming within Classes of Subjects," and also transferred the federal residuum to the beginning of the Section outlining its legislative authority. The form, if not the objective of the residuum, however, was significantly altered as it became truly a grant of residual legislative authority. The draft read as follows:

> It shall be lawful for Her Majesty, Her Heirs and Successors, by and with the Advice and Consent of the Houses of Parliament of the United Colony, to make laws for the Peace, Order, and good Government of the United Colony and of the several Provinces, in relation to all Matters not coming within the Classes of Subjects by this Act assigned exclusively to Provincial Legislation; and for greater certainty, but not so as to restrict the Generality of the foregoing Terms of this Section, it is hereby declared that the Legislative Authority of the Parliament of the United Colony extends to all Matters coming within the Classes of Subjects next hereinafter enumerated; that is to say...[then followed the list largely as set out in the Quebec Resolutions].[7]

In the same draft, the qualification was removed from "property and civil rights" but reappeared in a different form at the end of the section outlining federal legislative authority:

> [A]ny Matter coming within any of the Classes of Subjects enumerated in this section shall not be deemed to come within the Subject of Property and Civil Rights comprised in the enumeration of the Classes of Subjects by this Act assigned exclusively to Provincial Legislation.

The limitation on the incorporation of provincial companies was now expressed in the words "with exclusively Provincial Objects." The provincial residual clause disappeared.

We do not have all the drafts of the emerging statute, or a full record of the discussions among the Canadians then in London, the Colonial Office officials and the draughtsmen. We do know that John A. Macdonald at one point anticipated "a good deal of difficulty with Mess. Cartier and Langevin on the proposed changes as to Property and Civil Rights,"[8] but the record is silent on what those proposed changes were or what occurred. We can assume, however, that it was an attempt to limit the scope of that section. Even so, the same wording as above apparently survived at least one more draft. When the statute finally emerged, however, there had been three significant changes in what became sections 91 and 92 of the Act.

It is impossible to believe that there is no connection among these three changes. First, the provincial "residual" clause reappears in section 92(16) as: "Generally all Matters of a merely local or private Nature within the Province." Second, the final words of section 91, which had been protecting federal power against unlimited provincial jurisdiction over property and civil rights, now in direct and explicit language refers to the new 92(16). Finally, the words "notwithstanding anything in this Act" have been added to section 91. Given the constant concern about property and civil rights, these words must have been intended to protect the exclusive power of the federal government to legislate on matters within the enumerated classes of subjects against the possible, or inevitable, wide scope of property and civil rights, as well as against all other provincial enumerations.

The language and structure of sections 91 and 92 of the *Constitution Act, 1867* may be broken down and summarised as follows:

1. The provincial governments are given *exclusive* authority to make laws "in relation to Matters coming within" a specific list of subjects. "Property and civil rights" is listed without any qualification except the phrase "within the Province." In addition, the provincial residuum has reappeared as 92(16): "Generally all Matters of a merely local or private Nature within the Province." The addition of the adjective "merely" suggests an obvious limiting purpose.

2. The grant of legislative authority to the central government, the *enacting clause*, is now expressed in section 91 as the power "to make laws for the Peace, Order and good Government of Canada, *in relation to all Matters not coming within the Classes of Subjects by this Act assigned exclusively to the Legislatures of the Provinces...*" (our italics). The "and for greater Certainty, but not so as to restrict the Generality of the foregoing Terms of this Section, it is hereby declared" phrase, (the *declaratory* phrase), which appeared in an earlier draft now has had added to it "notwithstanding anything in this Act." The *notwithstanding* clause clearly includes, and thus limits, the authority conferred on the provinces by section 92, including property and civil rights.

3. The final words of section 91, following 91(29)— "shall not be deemed..." (the *deeming* clause)—no longer refers to and limits property and civil rights, but in direct and explicit language refers to and limits 92(16).

4. The enumerated heads of power in section 91 are stated to be extensions of the power conferred in the enacting clause. Despite later commentary which

describes them as "illustrations" of an exclusive federal residual power, qualified only by section 92, the language of the Act does not so describe them. They are there—have always been there—as discreet and deliberate grants of power to make laws "in relation to all Matters not coming within the Classes of Subjects by this Act assigned exclusively to the Legislature of the Provinces" which are now protected by the notwithstanding clause against any encroachment of property and civil rights, and by the deeming clause against 92(16).

From his analysis of the drafting history, Professor Lederman reached much the same conclusion about the intent, logic and symmetry of sections 91 and 92:

> I infer from the comparison that the "notwithstanding" clause in the opening words of section 91 and the "deeming" clause in the closing words were designed to ensure that the twenty-nine specific categories in the original federal list were to be taken as withdrawn from the historic scope of the provincial property and civil rights clause, and withdrawn also from the new provincial category of things generally of a local or private nature in the province.
>
> In other words, the implication is plain that this double-listing was done because the Fathers of Confederation, the Colonial Secretary and the parliamentary draftsmen were all satisfied that it was necessary; that the rather long and particular federal list, supported by the "notwithstanding" clause and the "deeming" clause, was essential if terms like banking, marriage and divorce, copyright, connecting railways, and so on were to be within the power of the new federal Parliament, where they wanted them to be.
>
> Accordingly, it follows that the twenty-nine specific categories of federal parliamentary power originally listed in section 91 are not merely illustrations of what would have been embraced anyway by the federal general power to make laws in all matters not assigned to the provinces. For the reasons of historical fact that I have given about the phrase property and civil rights, the federal list was not just superfluous grammatical prudence, it was compelled by historical necessity and had independent standing. Many if not most of the twenty-nine enumerated heads in section 91 confer powers on the federal Parliament that would not have been attracted to that Parliament by the federal general power alone in single-handed competition with the historic property and civil rights clause.
>
> The result of this reasoning about the nature of section 91 may be recapitulated as follows. The twenty-nine more particular powers, the so-called enumerated powers, add greatly to the competence that would have been invested in the federal Parliament by the general power alone, though no doubt there is a modest amount of overlapping. On the other hand, the federal general power is no mere appendage to the twenty-nine enumerated powers, an appendage labelled for "emergencies only" [as Lord Haldane for the Judicial Committee would later suggest]. It covers considerable ground that the

enumerated powers do not cover. What then do we see when we look at the complete picture afforded by sections 91 and 92? I say we see a total system of power distribution wherein thirty heads of federal power, including a national general and residual power, compete with sixteen heads of provincial power, one of which is a local general and residuary power. The grammar and syntax of sections 91 and 92 are as consistent with this result as with any other, and the history of central British North America from 1774 to 1867 confirms this alternative as the correct picture of the system. This is why I describe Canadian power distribution as the total competition of thirty federal heads of power with sixteen provincial heads of power....The picture is indeed a complex one, but anything less is surely oversimplification.[9]

Complex indeed, as a century of judicial review has confirmed. Professor Lederman's recapitulation adds its own element of confusion, if not complexity. Many legal scholars will take strong exception to his "thirty heads of power, *including a national general and residual power.*" Equating the enacting clause (the residual power)—the only grant of power to the central government—with the enumerations is clearly not justified by the language of section 91 which declares that the residual power "extends" to all matters coming with the enumerated heads. That extension of the residual power was designed to place federal power to legislate in relation to matters coming within those enumerated heads beyond any shadow of a legislative or judicial doubt. In the Quebec Resolutions there were clearly two residual clauses, one general and one local. In the 1867 Act the residual power was firmly and powerfully located in section 91, and 92(16) has become an enumerated head of power designed to catch matters local and private that did not fit elsewhere. Some of the symmetry in the Quebec Resolutions disappeared in London, and while the exclusivity of provincial authority to legislate on matters specified was strengthened, so too was the authority of the federal government within its enumerated heads. It remained as the sole possessor of the residual power over all Matters that did not fall within any Class of Subjects.

Introducing the bill for the union of the colonies in the House of Lords, the Colonial Secretary, Lord Carnarvon, was the first of a long line of authorities who attempted to explain the federal distribution of powers:

> In this is, I think, comprised the main theory and constitution of Federal Government: on this depends the practical working of the new system; and here we navigate a sea of difficulties—there are rocks on the right hand and on the left. If, on the one hand, the Central Government is too strong, then there is risk it may absorb the local action and that wholesome self-government by the Provincial bodies, which it is a matter of both good faith and practical expediency to maintain; if, on the other hand, the Central Government is not strong enough, there arises a conflict of States' rights and pretensions, cohesion is destroyed and the effective rigour of the central authorities is encroached upon. The real object which we have in view is to give to the Central Government those high functions and almost sovereign powers by which general principles and uniformity of legislation may be secured in those questions that are of common import to all the

provinces; and, at the same time, to retain for each Province so ample a measure of municipal liberty and self-government as will allow, and indeed compel, them to exercise those local powers which they can exercise to great advantage to the community....[10]

Carnarvon emphasised the broad sweep of the federal government's economic and financial powers, including "all regulations with regard to trade and commerce," and an unlimited power of taxation, and its responsibility for the criminal law. Moreover, he concluded,

> just as the authority of the Central Parliament will prevail whenever it may come into conflict with the Local Legislatures, so the residue of legislation, if any, unprovided for in the specific classifications which I have explained will belong to the Central body. It will be seen under the 91st clause that the classification is not intended "to restrict the generality" of the powers previously given to the Central Parliament, and that those powers extend to all laws made for the peace, order and good government of the Confederation—terms which, according to all precedents, will, I understand, carry with them an ample measure of legislative authority.[11]

Such was not to be the case.

NOTES

1. Opposition to the centralised federal system established in 1867 emerged too quickly in Ontario to make credible the argument that Ontario would have accepted a unitary state. See Bruce W. Hodgins, "Disagreement at the Commencement: Divergent Ontario Views of Federalism," in *Oliver Mowat's Ontario*, ed. Donald Swainson (Toronto, 1972), 52–68; and Christopher Armstrong, *The Politics of Federalism: Ontario's Relations with the Federal Government, 1867–1942* (Toronto, 1981).

2. K. C. Wheare, *Federal Government* (London, 1963), 19.

3. *Quebec Resolutions,* section 43, subsections 14–15, cited in G. P. Browne, *Documents on the Confederation of British North America* (Toronto, 1969).

4. *Parliamentary Debates* on the subject of the Confederation of the British North America provinces (Quebec, 1965), 40.

5. W. R. Lederman, "Unity and Diversity in Canadian Federalism: Ideals and Methods of Moderation," *Can. Bar Rev.* 53 (1975): 601–602. On the scope of property and civil rights and on the construction of sections 91 and 92 see: K. Lysyk, "Constitutional Reform and the Introductory Clause of Section 91: Residual and Emergency Law-Making Authority," *Can. Bar Rev.* 57 (1979): 531–74.

6. Lord Carnarvon to Edward Cardwell, 20 July 1866, cited in Browne, *Documents*, 55.

7. Browne, *Documents*, 247ff. The same draft of 23 January 1867 gave the title of "Superintendent" to the provincial lieutenant-governors and gave provincial legislatures power to pass "Ordinances" apparently in an attempt to diminish their status.

8. Governor General Monck to Lord Carnarvon, 13 January 1967, cited in Browne, *Documents*, 230.

9. Lederman, "Unity and Diversity," 602–3.

10. *Hansard's Parliamentary Debates*, 3d ser., 185 (1867): 563–66.

11. Ibid., 563–66.

THE JUDICIAL COMMITTEE AND THE BRITISH NORTH AMERICA ACT◇

G. P. BROWNE

o

THE COMPARTMENT QUESTION AND THE THREE-COMPARTMENT VIEW

The British North America Act is also unusual in its enumerative character; instead of the normal residuary statement and enumerated list, it contains a "general" statement and two enumerated lists. Thus in section 91, the federal parliament is given power "to make laws for the Peace, Order, and good Government of Canada." Further on in this section, however, there is a list of thirty-one[1] enumerated "classes of subjects" (concerning which the federal parliament has "exclusive legislative authority"). And then, in section 92, there is a list of sixteen enumerated "classes of subjects" (concerning which the provincial legislatures may also "exclusively make laws")....

Section 91 accordingly consists of two "parts": the "Peace, Order, and good Government" clause (up to the first semi-colon in the "Introductory words"); and the thirty-one "heads" (introduced by the phrase "and for greater Certainty," and rounded off by the "deeming" paragraph, beginning "And any Matter"). The first problem in the interpretation of the British North America Act concerns the relationship between these parts. Is the first supplementary to the second, or is the second illustrative of the first? If the heads are supplementary, sections 91 and 92 would contain three "compartments"—the Peace, Order, and good Government clause, the heads of section 91, and section 92. Alternatively, if the second part of section 91 is illustrative, there would be only two "compartments"—section 91 (as a whole) and section 92.

◇Excerpted from G. P. Browne, *The Judicial Committee and the British North America Act* (University of Toronto Press, 1967), 36–42.

The three-compartment view is based on a pair of arguments: one derived from the introductory words of section 91, the other from the deeming paragraph. The legislative authority conferred on the federal parliament by the Peace, Order, and good Government clause is expressly confined to matters "not coming within the Classes of Subjects by this Act assigned exclusively to the Legislatures of the Provinces." But the federal parliament is also said to have an "exclusive" legislative authority, which "notwithstanding anything in this Act...extends to all Matters coming within the Classes of Subjects next herein-after enumerated." It follows that since these definitions would be incompatible unless they represented different "kinds" of powers, they must signify that the powers covered by the Peace, Order, and good Government clause are supplementary to those delimited by the heads— and that sections 91 and 92 contain three compartments.

As for the deeming paragraph, the question is whether the expression "Class of Matters of a local or private Nature" (which is "comprised in the Enumeration of the Classes of Subjects by this Act assigned exclusively to the Legislatures of the Provinces") refers to all the heads of section 92, or only to head 16 ("Generally all Matters of a merely local or private Nature in the Province"). If this expression refers to head 16 only, then the deeming paragraph would be no more than a safeguard against provincial "encroachments," under the authority of section 92(16), on the heads of section 91. On the other hand, if the expression "Class of Matters of a local or private Nature" refers to all the heads of section 92, then (because the deeming paragraph expressly applies to the heads of section 91 alone, and so excludes the Peace, Order, and good Government clause) three compartments must be entailed.

A supplementary interpretation of the heads of section 91 would involve an order of priority as well. Since the Peace, Order, and good Government clause is confined to matters "not coming within the Classes of Subjects by this Act assigned exclusively to the Legislatures of the Provinces," section 92 must be "prior" to that clause. However, since the heads of section 91 are modified by the *non obstante* clause ("notwithstanding anything in this Act"), they must be prior to section 92. An order of priority—according to which the heads of section 91 outrank section 92, which in turn outranks the Peace, Order, and good Government clause—is the result. Furthermore, if the deeming paragraph ensures that any matter coming within the heads of section 91 does not come within section 92, then (because section 92 outranks the Peace, Order, and good Government clause) the same order of priority ensues.

The next effect would be a three-step procedure for settling disputes over legislative competence. If an impugned law were held to be, "in pith and sub-stance," in relation to a matter coming within a subject enumerated in the heads of section 91, it would be assigned to the federal parliament. Similarly, if that law were held to be, "in pith and substance," in relation to a matter coming within a subject enumerated in section 92, it would be assigned to the provincial legislatures. But if the law were held not to be, "in pith and substance," in relation to a matter coming within a subject comprised in either the heads of section 91 or section 92, then (because of the Exhaustion Theory) it would come within the Peace, Order, and good Government clause, and so would be assigned to the federal parliament.[2]

Finally, in addition to imposing a three-compartment view, an order of priority among the three compartments, and a three-step procedure for settling disputes over legislative competence, a supplementary interpretation of the heads of section 91 would give the Peace, Order, and good Government clause a "residuary" character. For if that clause is supplementary to those heads, it would cover only the powers that were left over, or became "residuary," once the powers defined in the heads of section 91 and in section 92 had been distributed between the federal parliament and the provincial legislatures. In short, the Peace, Order, and good Government clause would be a mere catch-all for any legislative powers that were presumably included in the total grant of legislative authority, but which were not actually specified.

Such an interpretation could induce a tendency to regard the Peace, Order, and good Government clause in the light of a last resort—to be invoked only when it proved impossible to consign a law to one of the enumerated lists. If the court of final appeal tried to fit as much legislation as possible into those lists, however, it could enlarge the ambit of the subjects comprised within them. Indeed, since the "subject" most susceptible to such enlarging is probably the one described in head 13 of section 92 ("Property and Civil Rights in the Province"),[3] the ultimate effect could be an enlargement of the legislative sphere of the provinces, at the expense of the federal parliament. Nor would this effect be lessened if the court were also determined to safeguard the "federal" character of the Canadian Constitution—or at any rate, to establish the principle of "co-ordinate and independent authorities."

THE TWO- AND FOUR-COMPARTMENT VIEWS

While the two-compartment view is also based on a pair of arguments, in this case both arguments are derived from the introductory words of section 91.[4] In the second part of those words, the thirty-one enumerated classes of subjects are listed "for greater Certainty, but not so as to restrict the Generality of the foregoing Terms of this Section." As if to underline that explanation, this second part is then expressed in declaratory, rather than enacting terms ("it is hereby declared" and "extends," as opposed to "shall extend"). It would seem to follow that the heads of section 91 illustrate the ambit of the Peace, Order, and good Government clause; that the two "parts" of section 91 are not separate, but conjoined; and that sections 91 and 92 contain only two compartments—section 91 (as a whole) and section 92.

If section 91 is read as a whole, however, the *non obstante* clause (which in the three-compartment view, refers to the heads of section 91 only) must refer to the Peace, Order, and good Government clause as well. Section 91 must therefore be "prior," as a whole, to section 92. On the other hand, this priority need not imply that the legislative authority of the federal parliament must outrank that of the provincial legislatures. For the notion of exclusive legislative spheres, and hence the federal principle of "co-ordinate and independent authorities," can still be preserved: by defining the word "matter" so as to distinguish between "subject" and "scope." In other words, the federal parliament must have exclusive power to make laws concerning any "subject" providing those laws are of national "scope." And the provincial legislatures must have exclusive power to make laws concerning the "subjects" enumerated in section 92, providing those laws are of provincial "scope."

Disputes over legislative competence can now be settled by means of a two-step procedure. If an impugned law were held to be, "in pith and substance," in relation to a matter coming within a "subject" comprised in section 92—and if it were also of provincial "scope"—it would be assigned to the provincial legislatures. If that law were held to be, "in pith and substance," in relation to any matter of national "scope," then—regardless of "subject"—it would come within the Peace, Order, and good Government clause, and so would be assigned to the federal parliament.

Finally, in addition to imposing a two-compartment view, the priority of section 91 (as a whole) over section 92, and a two-step procedure for settling disputes over legislative competence, an illustrative interpretation of the heads of section 91 would give the Peace, Order and good Government clause a "general," rather than a "residuary" character. Instead of being a mere catch-all for residuary legislative powers, this clause would become the means of defining the legislative authority of the federal parliament. And this authority would enable that parliament to make laws concerning any "subject"—providing those laws were of national "scope."

Such an interpretation might well alarm the courts. The federal parliament would be able, and perhaps tempted, to infringe on the autonomy of the provincial legislatures. Moreover, the judiciary would be involved, not just in a particular political situation, but in the general political process. For the courts would be required to estimate both the intentions of the legislating bodies and the likely effects of their legislation. They would accordingly become the arbiters, if not the censors, of legislative actions. And they would probably tend to produce more "factual" decisions, which do not lend themselves easily to the establishment of precedents. The adoption of a two-compartment view could thus entail fundamental changes, not merely in the character of the judgments in appeal cases, but in the significance of the Rule of Precedent and the Theory of Judicial Restraint.

This is not to imply that the three-compartment procedure fails to allow for the consideration of "scope." On the contrary, the Dimensions and Emergency Doctrines[5] make it possible to accept the three-compartment view, and at the same time to ensure that laws concerned with "subjects" enumerated in section 92 (and not concerned with any "subjects" enumerated in the heads of section 91) are assigned to federal parliament.[6] The classification step would now be determined by the ranking of the three compartments; since the Peace, Order, and good Government clause is outranked by section 92, considerations of "subject" would normally carry more weight in the consignment process than those of "scope." In fact, given a concern for the principle of "co-ordinate and independent authorities," a solicitude for the legislative autonomy of the provinces, and an acceptance of the three-compartment view, the consideration of "scope" would probably require the presence of very exceptional circumstances.

Sections 91 and 92 have also been viewed as containing four compartments: the Peace, Order, and good Government clause; the heads of section 91; heads 1–15 (inclusive) of section 92; and section 92, head 16.[7] This view is derived from the general phrasing of section 92(16). In the *Local Prohibition* judgment[8] of 1896, Lord Watson observed that head 16 appears to have "the same office which the general enactment with respect to matters concerning the peace, order, and good government of Canada, so far as supplementary of the enumerated subjects, fulfils in s. 91." Accordingly, in the *Manitoba Liquor Act* judgment[9] of 1902, Lord Macnaghten proposed a corresponding order of priority, together with a four-step procedure for settling disputes over legislative authority.

Unfortunately, however, this view distorts the third-compartment status of the Peace, Order, and good Government clause. Whereas the status of that clause is based on the overall structure of sections 91 and 92, the fourth-compartment status of section 92(16) is derived from the phrasing of the head itself.[10] The latter reasoning is therefore basically different from the former, if not incompatible with it. Furthermore, since section 92(16) is on the same structural footing as the other heads of section 92, and since those heads (according to the supplementary interpretation of section 91) are all "prior" to the Peace, Order, and good Government clause, it is doubtful whether a fourth-compartment character can be ascribed to head 16 of section 92 at all. But in any case, it seems more meaningful to contrast the two-and three-compartment views. For the only explicit "authority" behind the four-compartment view is a construction proposed by Lord Macnaghten, on the basis of an observation made by Lord Watson, as to the "apparent" office of section 92(16). In contrast, both the determining feature of the Judicial Committee's interpretative scheme, and the burden of the textual debate over that scheme, are concerned with the interrelationship of the two "parts" of section 91.[11]

NOTES

1. The original number of twenty-nine was increased through the addition of heads 1 and 2a: the former (which caused the "Public Debt and Property" head to be re-numbered as head 1a) was added by the *British North America* (No. 2) *Act, 1949*, 13 Geo. VI, c. 81; the latter had been added earlier, by the *British North America Act, 1940*, 3-4 Geo. VI, c. 36.

2. In practice, the three-step procedure is short-circuited by first asking whether s. 92 applies, and only then inquiring whether the heads of s. 91 are also applicable. This shortened procedure was used by Lord Haldane in *Toronto Electric Commissioners v. Snider*, [1925] A.C. 396, at 406.

3. For reasons that are shown in chap. 6, sec. 2 and chap. 7, of Browne, *The Judicial Committee*.

4. The following account is based on O'Connor's Report, the thesis of which has been adopted almost universally, and sometimes literally: see Kennedy, (1943) 8 *Cambridge Law Journal* 146-60.

5. See Browne, *The Judicial Committee*, chap. 9, sec. 3; chap. 11; chap. 12, sec. 1.

6. For further discussion of this possibility, see Browne, *The Judicial Committee*, chap. 4, secs. 1 and 2; chap. 5, secs. 2 and 3; chap. 6, sec. 1; chap. 7, sec. 1; chap. 9, secs. 1 and 2; chap. 11; chap. 12, sec. 1.

7. See Clokie, *Canadian Government*, 210-16; also (though more implicitly) Clement, *Canadian Constitution, passim.*

8. *A.G. Ont. v. A.G. Can.*, [1896] A.C. 348, at 365. See Browne, *The Judicial Committee*, chap. 4, sec. 1.

9. *A.G. Man. v. Manitoba Licence Holders' Association*, [1902] A.C. 73, at 78. See Browne, *The Judicial Committee*, 48 and 88.

10. Compounded by the application of the "Paramountcy Doctrine," according to which federal legislation is said to "override" provincial legislation where neither is *ultra vires.*

11. The 32 major references to the introductory words of s.91, as well as the 16 to the deeming paragraph, are marked in col. D of the Analytical Table, in Browne, *The Judicial Committee*.

WHAT PEACE, ORDER AND GOOD GOVERNMENT?[◇]

A.S. ABEL

Often it is said that a fundamental difference between the Canadian federal structure and that of the United States is the location of the residual powers of government[1]—often and falsely. There the central government has only delegated powers; all others belong to the states. Here, it is suggested, the case is reversed with the provinces having only specified powers and the Dominion competent as to everything else. A very real distinction between the two schemes does exist, but not that. Instead, what differentiates them is that here there is no residue of powers. None whatever. Everything is distributed. Once that is seen and the dimensions of the distribution recognized, most of the vexed questions about the respective areas of authority answer themselves in a mutually satisfying manner with no need for writing a new Act, simply by deigning to read the old one.

The demonstration is not easy. The difficulty does not arise out of the text of the *British North America Act* which is plain enough. It lies in the accretion of obscurities which has arisen from not heeding its language. Put bluntly, if the word "of" had been read to mean "of" and not totally taken as being "in," confusion would have been avoided and the claims alike to federal and provincial hegemony seen as the false issues they in fact are. The burden of my remarks will be the elaboration of that utterance.

We can concentrate on sections 91 and 92. A few other sections, notably those immediately following the two, add further detail about central and provincial authority without however, altering the basic pattern. Section 91 gives the boundaries of Parliament's, that is, of the federal legislature's competence. Section 92 defines that of the provinces. Canadian constitutional discussion, in and out of the courts, has been largely preoccupied with their correlation.

Section 91 itemizes thirty-one classes of subjects for use in sorting out situations where there is exclusive legislative authority in Parliament, section 92 lists

◇ *Western Ontario Law Review* (1968), 1–17.

sixteen for Provincial legislatures. In each group, some are so particular as almost to be trivial—"Beacons, Buoys, Lighthouses and Sable Island," "The Management and Sale...of the Timber and Wood" on the land belonging to the provinces. Others cover a lot of ground—"Criminal Law," "Property and Civil Rights in the Province." But broad or narrow, individually, or altogether they have the appearance of furnishing a catalogue of potential legislative concerns from which the courts need only select the appropriate one, not without difficulty perhaps, to determine whether a law is *intra vires*. Constitutional adjudication becomes a matching game with the court placing the legislative specimen alongside the colour samples to make the closest identification that judicial optics permits with one of the thirty-one or of the sixteen.

The high visibility of the listed members readily explains why that approach was taken. They stand out so; there are so many of them; and some are so invitingly precise. It seems as though he who runs may read.

In fact, he who runs is almost certain to misread, not noticing as he races through the Act that the listed heads are not made the content of granted power. They are "classes of subjects." But authority is not given to legislate on classes of subjects. Parliament is not empowered to make laws on any class of subjects within section 92. What matters is "matters."[2] The provinces may make laws as to "matters" falling within classes of subjects specified in section 92, and Parliament laws for "the peace, order, and good government of Canada" which laws, if they are on "matters" falling within the classes of subjects specified in 91, have a special status allocated to them.

The role of the classes of subjects is thus much subtler than appears from a quick reading. Sections 91 and 92 are not equivalent to Article I, section 8, of the United States Constitution which forthrightly provides that "The Congress shall have Power to lay and collect Taxes...to regulate Commerce...to establish a uniform Rule of Naturalization" and all the rest.

The distinction may appear unduly refined. Nevertheless it is central to the Canadian federal scheme. Every law out of necessity will be on some "matter." But human prescience is incapable of articulating a list of classes of subjects such that every possible "matter" has some place there to go and very obviously it could not be done under such drafting circumstances as those of the *British North America Act* of 1867, an instrument fashioned by practical politicians to cope with problems they were encountering[3] and not a doctrinal dream child of political philosophers.

Then how does one deal with a law on a "matter" with no "class of subject" it can call home?

There are three conceivable approaches. One is to recognize some one's possession of the undefined residue of legislative power. That was how it was done in the United States, implicitly the framers felt, by giving the federal government only specified powers,[4] but in any case explicitly by the Tenth Amendment.[5] Another is to leave a legislative gap with no government authorized to make a law about a matter falling outside every named class of subjects. But, we have been told

> the powers distributed between the Dominion on the one hand and the
> provinces on the other hand cover the whole area of self government
> within the whole area of Canada. It would be subversive of the entire

scheme and policy of the Act to assume that any point of internal self government was withheld from Canada.[6]

The statement quite clearly excludes the second approach. There remains a third, to eliminate both residue and gap by allowing every "matter" to find a home somewhere but by searching the principles of placement elsewhere than in the listed classes of subjects. On my reading of it, this is the plan of the *British North America Act*—no gap, no residue, the matter of every possible law having its accommodation provided. But if not in the listed classes of subjects, where is one to look for the classifying principle? The answer to that is in the interplay of 91 and 92.

Section 91 is a structurally complex section. It contains four major components—first, a primary grant—to make laws for the "Peace, Order, and Good Government of Canada"; second, a general qualification of the primary grant, that they be "in relation to...Matters not coming within the classes of Subjects...assigned exclusively to the...Provinces"; third, an illustrative specification listing thirty-one classes of subject as exemplifying "far greater Certainty but not so as to restrict the Generality" of the scope of the "exclusive legislative authority of the Parliament" involved in the primary grant, and, fourthly, an admonition that no matter coming within the thirty-one classes of subjects shall "be deemed to come within the Class of Matters of a Local or Private Nature...assigned...the Provinces."

Section 92 is formally simpler. Basically, it is a pendant to 91; the second limb of which anticipated that exclusive legislative power on matters falling within some classes of subjects was to be assigned the Provinces and thereby taken out of the primary federal grant. That suggestion is fulfilled by section 92's listing of sixteen such classes of subjects as the area of provincial competence. The sixteenth, "Generally all Matters of a merely local or private Nature in the Province" echoes the phraseology of the fourth and final limb of 91. Of the sixteen, it alone is there singled out as a category which matters falling within the federal list of classes of subjects should be deemed not to come within. Why? Is there something special about it?

It is indeed very different. In certain respects it is the provincial equivalent of the "peace, order and good government" clause; and between them they eliminate any occasion for a residual grant in the Canadian federal system—or one might equally say, they effect a twin grant of residuary power, to the Dominion *and* to the provinces.

Here is the labyrinth to be threaded if we would come to an understanding of what the Act provided as to provincial and federal jurisdiction. Headlong dashes along inviting vistas of specific classes of subjects, the usual procedure in the past, have ended only in our getting deeper into the maze and out of breath. The more useful procedure would seem to be a step-by-step examination of each of the particular components mentioned.

A reasonable starting place is the grant of the federal power. That, to repeat, is to "make Laws for the Peace, Order, and good Government of Canada." The phrase is familiar, so much so that like many familiar things no one any longer sees it or looks at it. "Peace, order, and good government" has become a jingle eroded by time and repetition, like "give, devise and bequeath" or "love, honour and obey." It has had its ups and downs. Once upon a time the incapacity of a single

province to establish a uniform law throughout the Dominion was felt to bring it
into play,[7] which would have meant that it covered everything, what with every
province limited to governing "within the province." That reading rendered section
94's contingent authority to make uniform laws on property and civil rights in
Ontario, Nova Scotia and New Brunswick with the assent of those provinces as
redundant as it has in fact proved sterile.[8] It did not survive. There followed the
obscure birth and various fortunes of the emergency doctrine conveniently and
naturally invoked to validate federal wartime regulations,[9] but revealing itself as the
patched-up rationalization it was when it turned out that neither the union–
management struggles attending the industrialization of the country[10] nor the
marketing plight of the great national staple, wheat, in the 1920s[11] were emergencies, whilst "the evil of intemperance" in the late nineteenth century had "amounted
in Canada to an emergency, one so great and so general that at least for the period
it was a menace to the national life."[12] A doctrine of such whimsical incidence shed
only a fitful light and finally just (sort of) flickered out. There has followed a decade
or so of *ad hoc* ruling that specific matters—aeronautics,[13] telecommunications,[14]
atomic energy,[15] the national capital[16]—are for the federal government to regulate
as involving peace, order and good government. The characterisations have made
little pretence to analysis, prefigured in this by the decision which, momentarily
abandoning the emergency doctrine in its heyday for the older "gap" doctrine, had
supported the incorporation of Dominion companies.[17] The principal contribution
of the latest series of cases has probably been the tacit burial of the emergency
concept.

The inherent vice common to these approaches has been fixation on elucidat-
ing what constitutes "peace, order, and good government" as though it were some
sort of a package deal given in all its frightening (or appealing, as the case may be)
plenitude. But that is not what section 91 says. It gives power to make Laws for the
"Peace, Order, and good Government of Canada"—of Canada, mind you, not in
Canada. Had the words been said over slowly, not just rattled off, had the court
faced with a statute asked itself—does this involve the peace of Canada? the order
of Canada? the good government of Canada? rather that does it involve "peace,
order, and good government" the redirected emphasis may or may not have
produced more useful discussion.

To be sure, there has right along been a stream of subsidiary reference to the
"of Canada" element. The power, it was said early on, goes to "such matters as are
unquestionably of Canadian interest and importance,"[18] and much later, "the true
test must be found in the real subject matter of the legislation: if it is such that it
goes beyond local concerns or interests and must from its inherent nature be the
concern of the Dominion as a whole, then it will fall within the competence of the
Dominion Parliament as a matter affecting the peace, order, and good government
of Canada."[19] These leads were never consistently followed up, however. Indeed
they were viewed somewhat coldly in the Judicial Committee.[20] I do not read either
of them or "of Canada" in the text of the Act as requiring that the problem dealt
with be one of uniform and universal interest through the length and breadth of
the land.[21] It suffices that the peace of Canada, the order of Canada, the good
government of Canada be significantly at stake, that the matter be "unquestionably
of Canadian interest and importance," "the concern of the Dominion as a whole"—

a test which might well be satisfied by the Toronto Stock Exchange[22] or the Lakehead elevators,[23] localized though they are within a single province, with no doubt a rather more substantial impact there than in Halifax or Victoria—but a significant impact nevertheless throughout the whole of Canada. If the peace, the order, the good government of Canada in that sense be involved, there is no need to find a class of subjects in the listed thirty-one for the matter legislated on. Those are specimens, "for greater Certainty but not so as to restrict the Generality" of the granted power. The provincial list does have a bearing since it constitutes a qualification of the grant and we shall come to that in due time. But it is important first to insist on what it is that was granted—the power to make laws neither on matters coming within listed classes of subjects nor yet for peace, order, and good government but for the peace, order, and good government of Canada.

But, if not all, only some, peace, order, and good government fell within the federal grant, part must have been left out. What? and what provision was made as to legislation for that part? Peace, order, and good government abroad, to be sure; but no constitutional instrument professes to prescribe the government of foreign lands[24] so we can confine our inquiry to the Canadian scene. The answer on that basis to what was excluded is tautological but very important—the peace, order, and good government not of Canada, although in Canada, or in Lord Simon's formulation that which does not "(go) beyond local or provincial concerns or interests."

That formulation brings to mind the sixteenth item in the list of provincial legislative powers—"Generally all Matters of a merely local or private nature in the Province." That balances exactly the Dominion grant. Between them they encompass the whole possible range of legislation and there really was no need to have said more or to have elaborated either a federal or a provincial list.[25] They were elaborated of course and a little later on the object and consequences of that elaboration will be examined. At this point what deserves emphasis is that the last clause of section 92 is the counterpart of the opening part of 91 before 91 opens up the "for greater certainty" business.

Its character as such is revealed by an expression which has been as unduly overlooked as has the "of Canada" phrase in the peace, order, and good government clause. The expression is the word "Generally." That word which introduces item 16 is not used in connection with any listed item in 91 nor elsewhere in 92. If item 16 were only on a parity with the preceding fifteen, one would be driven to the inadmissible premise that the draftsmen of the Act inserted a word having no significance. The only escape is to recognize that here we have the real general grant of legislative power to the provinces, strictly equivalent to the Dominion power to make laws for the peace, order, and good government of Canada. This is the "Generality" for 92, as the peace, order, and good government of Canada is for 91, a Generality which in each case the accompanying specifics do not restrict but as to which they provide "greater Certainty."

Between them they accomplish what the abortive Sherman proposal presented to the 1787 constitutional convention in Philadelphia had in mind in proposing to empower Congress "to make laws binding on the people of the United States in all cases which may concern the common interests of the Union: but not to interfere with the government of the individual states in any matters of internal policy which respect the government of such states only, or wherein the general welfare of the United States is not concerned."[26] Sections 91 and 92 do seem to phrase the idea with more art than the Sherman proposals—with such an excess of art indeed, that the pattern got hidden. The peace, order, and good government of Canada is for the Parliament, matters of a local or private nature for the provinces—there is no room for a residue.

Collateral support for this line of thinking is provided by two of the specific grants. First, there is the singularly phrased clause 10 of section 92, dealing with works and undertakings which if purely local and not extending beyond a province are a provincial concern except those "for the general advantage of Canada or for the advantage of two or more of the Provinces." No doubt, that factor is to be authenticated in a designated way, namely, by a Parliamentary declaration—which declaration is not open to question[27]—but, assuming as one must, Parliamentary good faith in making it, the substantial distinction crops up again between things local and things with a general Canadian impact. The second extraordinary provision is section 95, respecting Laws about Agriculture and Immigration as to which both levels of government are authorized to legislate, Parliament's power being to make laws about agriculture "in any or all of the provinces" and immigration "into any or all of the provinces." Here Parliament is quite clearly being authorized to legislate even for particular localities freed of any tie with the "peace, order, and good government of Canada"; but note that where this is done the provision is embodied in a separate section expressing a true concurrent power outside the ambit of either 91 or 92 and their respective "generalities." What section 95 shows for present purposes is that when those who wrote the *British North America Act* thought the "local" versus "of Canada" distinction irrelevant, as when by exception they undertook to establish a fully concurrent power, they knew how to make their meaning plain.[28]

This conception of balancing grants to the federal and the provincial legislatures by the opening clause of section 91 and the closing clause of section 92 respectively, ingenious though it may be, confronts the hard fact that in each section an extensive list of specific items does appear. Does not their very presence establish that they have significance? and if the peace, order, and good government clause and the private and local clause provide exhaustively for the legislative competence of the two heads of government, does that not exclude any possibility of significance? The answer to the first question is yes but the answer to the second is no, and that negative answer destroys the spurious dilemma which may be responsible for judicial overemphasis of the specifics to the neglect of the sweeping grants. The specifics of both 91 and 92 in fact each have a double significance, one internal to the section wherein they appear and its general grant, again with relation to the companion section and *its* general grant. Each facet will be considered separately.

How the specifics of section 91 relate to the grant of power to make laws for the peace, order, and good government of Canada has already been commented on but bears repeating. The language of the Act is most explicit and quite conventional; classes of subjects are "hereinafter enumerated" "for greater Certainty, but not so as to restrict the Generality of the foregoing terms of this Section." This is a standard lawyers' formula, common in statutes and indeed in many other types of documents. It provides illustration: it removes doubts about the complete and unconditional inclusion of the named items in the class to which they relate: but it does not cut down the full natural content of the class. It is not merely that the formula negates the constructional principle of *noscitur a sociis*. It does do that and is a standard way of doing it, but it does not properly generate an implication of any restrictive construction whatever tending to confine the general language to a limited or exceptional operation. To treat the "peace, order, and good government of Canada" as in some way diminished by the enumeration of classes of subjects "for greater Certainty" was a construction heresy on the part of the Judicial Committee.

As the specifics of 91 are to the peace, order and good government clause, so are those of 92, paragraph 16, to the local and private clause. The "greater certainty" formula is not indeed repeated but the failure to do so proves nothing. Out of context, that can indeed be read as exhausting its function by prescribing relationships internal to 91 and such relationships only; but in the full context it equally admits of being regarded as indicative of an attitude regarding the effect to be ascribed to general grants, an attitude as relevant to 92 and its specifics as to 91. Lacking the express language, the interaction of the last paragraph of 92 and the preceding enumeration is more obscure; but parallel structure—a general grant accompanied by specification—partially takes over for the missing parallel language, in support of symmetrical application.

Still stronger and very nearly conclusive support derives from what the Act has to say about the effect of 91's specifics on the general grant of 92 and conversely of 92's specifics on the general grant in 91.

The final clause of 91 provides that "any matter coming within the Classes of Subjects enumerated in the Section shall not be deemed to come within the Class of Matters of a local or private Nature comprised in the Enumeration of the Classes of Subjects...assigned exclusively to the Legislatures of the Provinces." It will be noted that it does not provide that "any Matter coming within this section" but rather "within the Classes of Subjects enumerated" shall not be deemed and so forth. The unenumerated residue of section 91 is of course any legislation for the peace, order and good government of Canada that lies outside the enumerated classes. It will further be noted that what a matter coming within a class of subjects enumerated in 91 shall be deemed not to come within is "the Class of Matters of a Local or Private Nature" and not all the classes of subjects enumerated in section 92. It does not speak to the relation of the general clause of 91 to anything in 92. It does not speak to the relation of the specific clauses of section 91 to anything covered by the first fifteen clauses of 92. What it does do is exclude any claim that the general clause of section 92 shall ever be relevant to a matter following within a class of subjects enumerated in 91.[29]

The contours of the clause have attracted only casual judicial attention of a somewhat uncertain tenor[30] but if, as has been suggested, it has indeed been regarded as operating a limitation of Dominion powers, the criticism of such a treatment[31] is fully justified. The Dominion's power to make laws for the peace, order, and good government of Canada—or for that matter to make any laws at all—is wholly unaffected by it. The powers of the provinces under any head other than section 16 are wholly unaffected by it. What it does deal with and all it deals with is the scope of the provincial general power excluding its operation for legitimating laws as to any matters falling within a federal class of subjects enumerated in 91.[32]

But the second limb of the opening paragraph of section 91 makes provision identical in substance though stylistically different as to the interaction of the specifics of section 92 and the general clause of 91. That limb qualifies the grant of power to Parliament to make laws for the peace, order, and good government of Canada thus—"in relation to all matters not coming within the Classes of Subjects by this Act assigned exclusively to the Legislatures of the Provinces." On the face of it, that covers the general provincial grant as well but, reserving that for a moment, it certainly does say how the general power of 91 stands with respect to the enumerated provincial heads of power. What it says is that even though a law be for the peace, order, and good government of Canada, the federal power to make it does not exist as to matters falling within classes of subjects enumerated in 92.[33] It says it by qualification of the grant whereas the final clause of the section cuts down the provincial local and private clause by a deeming technique; but the result is the same—the competence of either level of government to legislate under its general power is ousted as to matters falling within the classes of subjects entrusted enumeratively to the other. The strict comparability of the two is once more in evidence.

Two points have yet to be covered—one, the relation between the two general powers, the other that of the enumerated powers in 91 with those in 92.

As was mentioned, the way that the qualification on the peace, order, and good government clause is phrased might conceivably extend to paragraph 16 as well as the fifteen preceding. Two considerations cast doubt on that approach. The first raises still another instance of overlooked language in the Act. The qualification on the federal grant reads, "in relation to all Matters not coming within the Classes of Subjects assigned exclusively to...the Province" and the responsive reading of the opening clause of section 92 is "In Each Province the Legislature may make laws in relation to Matters coming within the Classes of Subjects next hereinafter enumerated." Section 92 then proceeds to itemize fifteen categories descriptive of nominate areas of public concern but in paragraph 16 changes course and speaks in terms of "all Matters" of a merely local or private nature. The scheme of all the other enumerated heads, alike in 91 and in 92, was to empower the making of laws on what? Not on classes of subjects but on matters falling within classes of subjects. But in paragraph 16 of section 92, and only there the class of subjects is itself "Matters." Hence, as to it, the power is to make laws on matters falling within a class of subjects which itself is "Matters." How does one legislate on a matter falling within a class of subjects composed of "Matters" without legislating directly as to the matters of which that class of subjects is composed and which it is nothing else but. It would seem therefore that if under paragraph 16 the provincial legislature is permissibly legislating on matters, unmediated through a "class of subjects," that the qualifying branch of 91 which relates to "matters falling within classes of subjects" is not properly applicable.

This argument from the textual variation may be thought to be excessively ingenious. In any case it merely corroborates that which flows from the inherently reciprocal character of the two general grants. Any of the first fifteen heads of section 92 is such that some matters falling within it could potentially even if rarely be "unquestionably of Canadian interest and importance." To deal with that possibility, the qualifying clause was inserted to make plain that even so the grant of power to Parliament did not extend to it. But by no possibility can a matter involve the peace of Canada, the order of Canada, the good government of Canada yet be "of a merely local or private nature." They present true alternatives. A reservation from a grant exhausts its operation within the limits of what was granted and has no bearing on anything never included. Thus, where no enumerated power under either section is relevant and the result must rest on a naked confrontation of the two general powers, a court's task is simply to decide whether the statute deals with matters of national or merely local dimensions. That high responsibility cannot be evaded by recourse to either the qualifying or the "deemed" clauses of section 91, neither of which has any relevance.

Finally nothing in either of those clauses touches on how the enumerated heads in one section relate to those in the other. There was no need to define that.

> Neither the Dominion nor the provinces were given any authority or jurisdiction...over any *field of law*. Each, instead was given legislative authority to enact statutes *in relation to matters coming within* certain classifications...The law-making authority was not over the "field" or classification but over the matter (arising in the shape of concrete legislation) which "came within" and was assignable by the court to the class...The court, so the Fathers thought, could and would, as each statute, Dominion or provincial, came before it for judgment, ascertain to what class in section 91 or 92 the legislation in pith and substance belonged (i.e. came within) and could and would assign that statute to its proper class...[34]

A necessary premise of such an arrangement is that each member of the class of subjects is distinct and self-contained and that they are mutually exclusive. They need not be in the aggregate exhaustive of all possible legislative concerns, and that was recognized and allowed for by the elaborate provisions regarding the impact on the general grants of the enumerations; but, if they did not impinge on each other, there was no occasion to deal with the consequences of their mutual impact. This conception of them as isolated and the drafting precision employed to achieve it is evidenced clearly by paragraph 29 of section 91, particularly enumerating, as exclusively federal, legislation on matters falling within "Such Classes of Subjects as are expressly excepted in the Enumeration of the Classes of Subjects...assigned exclusively to the...Provinces" considered in connection with paragraphs 1, 7, and 10 of section 92, each with its fractional amputation from its class of subjects. The mention in section 92 would have independently sufficed to put the amputated portions in the unspecified residue to be legislated or by one or the other level of government according as the peace, order and good government of Canada or, conversely, matters of a merely local or private nature might be involved. Paragraph 29 would be redundant. Instead a separate class of subjects was established composed of the several fragments thus endowed with an artificial unity of their own.[35]

On the view taken as to the nature of the enumerated items, the matter to which a law related could not come simultaneously within more than one of these distinct self-contained classes of subjects. That is not to say that measures alike in content, even measures identically expressed, might not wind up variously and properly assigned to different classes of subjects. But that is because despite those resemblances the measures would be in relation to different "matters" and that involves the aspect doctrine.[36] A statute of limitations for suits on negotiable instruments may in one aspect relate to the "matter" of limitations of actions, in another to that of the rights and liabilities of parties to commercial paper. On the example given, once the "matter" is determined, it is fairly easy to find that it falls under the provincial class of subjects, "procedure in civil matters," or the federal class of subjects, "bills of exchange," as the case may be.[37] The whole trick is to find the matter to which the law relates and for that there is no formula. The proposition that "the matter depends upon the effect of the legislation not upon its purpose"[38] whatever its validity is not especially helpful. Talk in terms of pith and substance, with its suggestion that one seek the centre of gravity of the legislation whether a whole statute or a portion of statute which is being appraised, what conduct will be dominantly affected by its application and in what way, gives maybe as much guidance as one can hope for.[39] Once the "matter" to which the law relates is settled in whatever manner under whatever aspect is deemed relevant and found to fall under its appropriate class of subject—its sole and only appropriate class of subject—the circumstance that it may affect interests or relations which would fall under some other class of subjects may be disregarded.

Unfortunately this coherent conception of the status of the enumerated heads has become blurred in judicial and academic discourse—blurred by neglect of the distinction between "classes of subjects" which are the substance of the enumerations and "matters" through which any given law must be mediated,[40] blurred through subordination of the general grants whose relation to the scheme is so carefully stated to an undue concentration on the enumerations,[41] blurred through a prevalent tendency to lump classes of subjects in condemnation or support of an Act without troubling to distill out the "matter" to which it relates or assign that matter to the class of subjects under which it falls.[42] The result is that the carefully co-ordinated system of federalism spelled out in the Act has been so submerged that many now think what we need is a new allocation of competence when we have a perfectly good old one we never use.

There may well be good grounds for recasting the constitution—recasting it for example with respect to the composition and functions of the judiciary, with respect to the elimination of a host of moribund provisions, with respect to the provision of guarantees of certain personal rights, with respect to how federal subventions can be manipulated, with respect to the provision of an amending process.[43] None of these relates to the allocation of federal and provincial legislative powers. In the court of reason one can do what one cannot do in the courts of law and invoke the sponsor's explanation of the *British North America Act* when he introduced it:

The real object which we have in view is to give to the Central Government those high functions and almost sovereign powers by which uniformity of legislation may be secured in those questions that are of common importance to all the provinces; and, at the same time, to retain for each Province so ample a measure of municipal liberty and self government as will allow, and indeed compel, them to exercise those local powers which they can exercise with great advantage to the community.[44]

Sections 91 and 92 express and accomplish this. They compliment, they do not oppose each other. If all matters local and private to a particular province are within its control, how does that fall short of letting every province be *maître chez soi* to the full extent any of them has demanded—every province alike without need for any special status? If the Dominion has power to regulate whatever affects the peace of Canada, the order of Canada, the good government of Canada, wherein does it lack any authority as to which central direction is needed and appropriate, even though peace, order, and good government in but not of Canada being local and particular escapes it? There remain of course the enumerated powers with their specified relationship to the general grants which has already been sufficiently stated. But they should not be invoked in any case of challenged legislation until after and subsidiary to the basic question—does or does not the law involve that peace, order, and good government as to which Parliament may legislate—the peace, order, and good government of Canada. Upon the answer to that fundamentally rests the competence of the enacting government.[45]

NOTES

1. *Valin v. Langlois* (1879), 3 S.C.R. 1, 14; *A.G. Australia v. Colonial Sugar Refining Co.*, [1914] A.C. 237, 252. Cf. Kennedy, "Interpretation of the British North America Act," (1943) 8 *Cambridge Law Journal (Cam. L.J.)* 146, 155; Riddell, *The Canadian Constitution in Form and Fact* (1923), 5; Smith, *The Commerce Power in Canada and the United States* (1963), 23; Laskin, *Canadian Constitutional Law* 3d ed. (1966), 269 (hereafter cited as Laskin).

2. See Laskin, 85; O'Connor, *Report to the Senate of Canada on the B.N.A. Act 1939*, Annex, p. 40 (hereafter cited as O'Connor).

3. For the circumstances current at the time, see generally Waite, *The Life and Times of Confederation* (1962); Martin, *Foundations of Canadian Nationhood* (1955), c. 16.

4. See *The Federalist*, No. 84; *James Wilson, Works* 2 (1869), 56.

5. "The powers not delegated to the United States by The Constitution, nor prohibited by it to the States, are reserved to the States respectively, or to the people." Cf. The Commonwealth of Australia, *Constitution Act, 1900*, Section 107 ("Every power of the Parliament of a Colony which has become or becomes a State, shall, unless it is by this constitution exclusively vested in the Parliament of the Commonwealth or withdrawn from the Parliament of the State, continue as at the establishment of the Commonwealth, or as at the admission or establishment of the State, as the case may be.")

6. *A.G. Ontario v. A.G. Canada*, [1912] A.C. 571; *Murphy v. C.P.R.*, [1958] S.C.R. 626. For the suggestion of qualifications to this statement which may exist, see Laskin, 70 (3d ed.).

7. See *Russell v. The Queen* (1882), 7 A.C. 829.

8. For a discussion of this section see Scott, "Section 94 of the B.N.A. Act," (1942) 20 *Can. Bar Rev.* 525. The Judicial Committee, in *Citizens Insurance Co. v. Parsons* (1881), 7 A.C. 96 concluded that if section 94 were given a "narrow construction," "the dominion parliament could, under its general power legislate" for the whole dominion without regard to the limitations expressed by the section and that the section told against the existence of such an extensive federal power.

9. See, e.g. *Fort Francis Pulp & Power Co. Ltd. v. Manitoba Free Press Ltd.*, [1923] A.C. 695.

10. See *Toronto Electric Commissioners v. Snider*, [1925] A.C. 396.

11. Cf. *The King v. Eastern Terminal Elevator Co.* [1925] S.C.R. 434.

12. Per Haldane, in *Toronto Electric Commissioners v. Snider*, [1925] A.C. 396, 412. This "aspersion of the fair fame of Canada" was sturdily objected to by Anglin C.J. dissenting, in *The King v. Eastern Terminal Elevator Co.*, [1925] S.C.R. 434.

13. *Johannesson v. West St. Paul*, [1952] 1 S.C.R. 292; cf in *re Regulation and Control of Aeronautics in Canada*, [1931] A.C. 54.

14. *In re Regulation and Control of Radio Communication in Canada*, [1932] A.C. 304, 312 (alternative ground).

15. *Pronto Uranium Mines Ltd. v. Ontario Labour Relations Board*, [1956] O.R. 862, 5 D.L.R. (2d) 342.

16. *Munro v. National Capital Commission*, [1966] S.C.R. 663.

17. *John Deere Plow Co. Ltd. v. Wharton*, [1915] A.C. 330.

18. *A.G. Ontario v. A.G. Canada* [1896] A.C. 348, 360.

19. *A.G. Ontario v. Canada Temperence Federation*, [1946] A.C. 193, 205.

20. See e.g. *Canadian Federation of Agriculture v. A.G. Quebec*, [1951] A.C. 179.

21. When the argument that "an enactment [touching 'the peace, order, and good government of Canada'] must be one whose operation extends to the whole of Canada" was advanced in *Gold Seal, Ltd. v. Dominion Express Co.*, (1921) 62 S.C.R. 424, Duff J. expressed himself as "not prepared without further examination of the point to agree, that an enactment...confined in its operation to one province could not be sustained as relating to 'the peace, order and good government of Canada' " and, reserved opinion on the point. It will be noted that his formulation of the point reserved, operation in a single province is more extreme than the argument advanced, operation in a limited number of provinces but (1) the acceptance of declarations that works are for the general advantage of Canada though wholly internal to a province, see e.g. *Quebec Railway Light, Power Co. v. Beauport*, [1945] S.C.R. 16, and (2) the sustaining of federal statutes essentially non-uniform because in terms contemplating partial coverage, through making their operation, see, e.g. *A. G. Ontario v. Canada Temperance Federation*, [1946] A.C. 193 or their non-operation, see e.g. *Lord's Day Alliance of Canada v. A. G. British Columbia*, [1959] S.C.R. 497, depend on local action would seem to establish that limited coverage is not *per* se a constitutional objection.

22. The constitutionality of legislation addressed to the regulation of securities exchanges, seems never to have come up for decision, though regulation of securities dealers has been assumed to be for the provinces save in so far as affected by federal legislation under the criminal law power, see *Smith v. The Queen*, [1960] S.C.R. 776.

23. But cf. *The King v. Eastern Terminal Elevator Co.*, [1925] S.C.R. 434. Compare *Murphy v. C.P.R.*, [1958] S.C.R. 626.

24. This is not of course to deny that constitutional provisions may have extraterritorial operation, see *Reid v. Covert*, (1955) 354 U.S. 1, but only to recognize that the regulation of legal rights and internal government abroad are for those in authority within the territorial area concerned, cf., *Carl-Zeiss-Stiftung v. Rayner & Keeler Ltd.* No. 2, [1967] 1 A.C. 853.

25. In s. 92, No. 16 appears...to have the same office which the general enactment with respect to matters concerning the peace, order and good government of Canada, so far as supplementary to the enumerated subjects, fulfils in s. 91. It assigns to the provincial legislature all matters in a provincial sense local or private which have been omitted from the precedingenumeration, and although its terms are wide enough to cover, they were obviously not meant to include, provincial legislation in relation to the classes of subjects already enumerated.

A. G. Ontario v. A. G. Canada, [1896] A.C. 348, 365. "Head 16 contains what might be called the residuary power of the Province...(T)his points up the underlying division of the matters of legislation into those which are primarily of national and those of local import." *Reference re Farm Products Marketing Act*, [1957] S.C.R. 198 (per Rand J.).

26. Farrand, *The Records of the Federal Convention of 1787* 3 (1911), 616.

27. See *Luscar Collieries Ltd. v. McDonald*, [1925] S.C.R. 460, 480.

28. The courts have equally known how to annul it and to make section 95 a wholly illusory power alike for the Dominion and the provinces, see Laskin, 357–58.

29. See MacDonald, "The Constitution in a Changing World," (1948) 26 *Can. Bar Rev.* 21, 29 ("...The function of the concluding paragraph of section 91 was to require that any matter coming under any one of the...enumerated classes in section 91 and also appearing to come under the provincial residuary clause No. 16 ['Generally all matters of a merely *local or private nature* in The Province'] must be deemed to come under the former, thus resolving any apparent conflict in favour of the Dominion.")

30. As early as *Citizens Insurance Co. v. Parsons* (1881) 7 App. Cas. 96, 107, the limited ambit of the clause "in its grammatical construction" was noted.

A pretty positive dictum in *A. G. Ontario v. A. G. Canada*, [1896] A.C. 348, 359, however, characterising the "observation" as "not strictly accurate" but without proposing any textual analysis in justification of its reading the phrase "Class of Matters of a local and private nature" out of the Act, has been, equally without examination, accepted in later discussion, see e.g. *Great West Saddlery Ltd. v. The King*, [1921] 2 A.C. 91, 117, even though no such comment was necessary to the decision. This body of dicta exemplifies the "accretion of obscurities...from not heeding the language" referred to *supra*.

31. See O'Connor, 32.

32. The onus of showing that a matter comes within a class of subject enumerated in section 91, so as to prevent its being treated as local and private, falls on the party so asserting. *L'Union St.-Jacques de Montréal v. Belisle*, (1874) L.R. 6 P.C. 31, 36.

33. (W)hile for the purpose of dealing with a matter of interest to the whole Dominion in the sense of being a matter affecting and pertaining to the public order and good government of the whole Dominion...Parliament may legislate so long as its enactments are of such a character that they do not deal with matters from a provincial point of view within the specific classes of subjects enumerated in section 92 (that is the first fifteen heads), it is not within its power under the residuary clause to enact legislation which from the provincial point of view falls within any one of such classes.

In re The Board of Commerce Act, 60 S.C.R. 456, (per Duff J.). But cf. Kellock J. in *Johannesson v. West St. Paul*, [1952] 1 S.C.R. 292 ("Once the decision is made that a matter is of national interest and importance, so as to fall within the peace, order and good government clause, the Provinces cease to have any legislative jurisdiction with regard thereto and the Dominion jurisdiction is exclusive.")

34. O'Connor, 25.

35. Cf. *Commission du Salarie Minimum v. Bell Telephone Co. of Canada*, (1966) 59 D.L.R. (2d) 145.

36. For an early expression and application of this doctrine, see *Hodge v. The Queen* (1883) 9 App. Cas. 117; for a recent instance *Regina v. Clements*, (N.B. App. Div. 1967) 63 D.L.R. (2d) 513.

37. Cf. *Duplain v. Cameron*, [1961] S.C.R. 693 (sustaining provincial statute regulating dealers in "securities," defined to include *inter alia* "notes").

38. *A. G. Manitoba v. A. G. Canada*, [1929] A.C. 260, 269; *A. G. Canada v. Readers Digest Ass'n (Canada) Ltd.*, [1961] S.C.R. 775, 793.

39. Laskin, "Tests for the Validity of Legislation: *What's the 'Matter',*" 11 *Univ. of Tor. L. J.* 114 is a penetrating discussion of the problem.

40. Laskin, *Canadian Constitutional Law*, 85.

41. This misplaced emphasis as to the order of inquiry is revealed clearly, by *Russell v. The Queen*, (1892) 7 App. Cas. 829, ("...the *first question* to be determined is, whether the Act in question falls within any of the classes of subjects *enumerated* in sec. 92, and assigned exclusively to the Legislatures of the Provinces. If it does, then the further question would arise, viz, whether the subject of the Act does not also fall within any of the *enumerated classes* of subjects in sect. 91...").

42. Dozens of cases could be cited; by way of examples see the opinions in *Hodge v. The Queen*, (1883) 9 App. Cas. 117 (legislation sustained as "com(ing) within the heads 8, 15 and 16 of Sec. 92" and of Rinfret C.J. dissenting in *Reference re Validity of Sec. 5 (a) of the Dairy Industry Act*, [1949] S.C.R. 1 (supporting Act as falling within paragraphs 2 ("trade and commerce" and 27 ("criminal law") of sec. 91 and also within section 95, "agriculture").

43. The suggested matters substantially conform to those instanced by Marcel Faribault in an address to the Empire Club of Canada in Toronto on 1 December 1966, see *Empire Club Addresses 1966–67*, 113, save for the

omission of the first, residual power, as to which he makes the common and, I have undertaken to establish, mistaken assumption that it now belongs to the Dominion.

44. Speech of Lord Carnarvon in the House of Lords quoted in O'Connor, *Report* Annex 4 (1939), 76. The Hon. John A. Macdonald (as he then was) similarly said "I hope that we will have a strong central Government...and at the same time will preserve *for each Province its own identity—and will protect every local ambition*; and if we cannot do this we shall not be able to carry out the object we now have in view," (emphasis supplied). Whelan, ed. *The Union of the British Provinces* (1865) 44.

45. Even the authors of the Tremblay Report, in concluding, *Rapport de la Commission Royale sur les Problemes Constitutionelles* 1, (1956), 35 et seq. that "n'est vraie qu'en apparence" the principle that "tout ce qui etait d'intérêt général, a été confié au gouvernement fédéral, les provinces se réservant ce qui était d'intérêt régional ou local" on the ground that "en un sens tout *dans* un pays peut regarder l'intérêt général, et bien des choses, locales quand à leur situation ne servent pas moins le bien général de toute la communauté" have confused peace, order, and good government *in* Canada with that *of* Canada. It would indeed be hard to find a better concise statement of the two than theirs, *Rapport*, p. 38,

> En résumé on a confié au gouvernement central les grands services généraux, militaires, administratifs et techniques, mais on a réservé aux provinces tout-sauf les quelques exceptions mentionnées plus haut,—ce qui concerne l'organisation sociale, civile, familiale, scolaire, municipale, tout ce qui touche le plus à l'humain et influe d'advantage sur la manière de vivre du citoyen Canadien.

While the observation seems to have contemplated more particularly a characterisation of the respective enumerated powers, it seems even better calculated to describe the focus of the two residuary powers.

from *THE CONSTITUTION ACT, 1867*

Whereas the Provinces of Canada, Nova Scotia and New Brunswick have expressed their Desire to be federally united into One Dominion under the Crown of the United Kingdom of Great Britain and Ireland, with a Constitution similar in Principle to that of the United Kingdom:

And whereas such a Union would conduce to the Welfare of the Provinces and promote the Interests of the British Empire:

And whereas on the Establishment of the Union by Authority of Parliament it is expedient, not only that the Constitution of the Legislative Authority in the Dominion be provided for, but also that the Nature of the Executive Government therein be declared. . . .

III EXECUTIVE POWER

9. The Executive Government and Authority of and over Canada is hereby declared to continue and be vested in the Queen.

10. The Provisions of this Act referring to the Governor General extend and apply to the Governor General for the Time being of Canada, or other the Chief Executive Officer or Administrator for the Time being carrying on the Government of Canada on behalf and in the Name of the Queen, by whatever Title he is designated.

11. There shall be a Council to aid and advise in the Government of Canada, to be styled the Queen's Privy Council for Canada; and the Persons who are to be Members of that Council shall be from Time to Time chosen and summoned by the Governor General and sworn in as Privy Councilors, and Members thereof may be from Time to Time removed by the Governor General. . . .

13. The Provisions of the Act referring to the Governor General in Council shall be construed as referring to the Governor General acting by and with the Advice of the Queen's Privy Council for Canada. . . .

IV LEGISLATIVE POWER
Money Votes; Royal Assent

55. Where a Bill passed by the Houses of the Parliament is presented to the Governor General for the Queen's Assent, he shall declare, according to his Discretion, but subject to the Provisions of this Act and to Her Majesty's Instructions, either that he assents thereto in the Queen's Name, or that he withholds the Queen's Assent, or that he reserves the Bill for the Signification of the Queen's Pleasure.

56. Where the Governor General assents to a Bill in the Queen's Name, he shall by the first convenient Opportunity send an authentic Copy of the Act to one of Her Majesty's Principal Secretaries of State, and if the Queen in Council within Two Years after Receipt thereof by the Secretary of State thinks fit to disallow the Act, such Disallowance (with a Certificate of the Secretary of State of the Day on which the Act was received by him) being signified by the Governor General, by Speech or Message to each of the Houses of the Parliament or by Proclamation, shall annul the Act from and after the Day of such Signification.

57. A Bill reserved for the Signification of the Queen's Pleasure shall not have any Force unless and until, within Two Years from the Day on which it was presented to the Governor General for the Queen's Assent, the Governor General signifies, by Speech or Message to each of the Houses of the Parliament or by Proclamation, that it has received the Assent of the Queen in Council.

An Entry of every such Speech, Message, or Proclamation shall be made in the Journal of each House, and a Duplicate thereof duly attested shall be delivered to the proper Officer to be kept among the Records of Canada.

V PROVINCIAL CONSTITUTIONS
Executive Power

58. For each Province there shall be an Officer, styled the Lieutenant Governor, appointed by the Governor General in Council by Instrument under the Great Seal of Canada.

59. A Lieutenant Governor shall hold Office during the Pleasure of the Governor General; but any Lieutenant Governor appointed after the Commencement of the First Session of the Parliament of Canada shall not be removable within Five Years from his Appointment, except for Cause assigned, which shall be communicated to him in Writing within One Month after the Order for his Removal is made, and shall be communicated by Message to the Senate and to the House of Commons within One Week thereafter if the Parliament is then sitting, and if not then within One Week after the Commencement of the next Session of the Parliament.

60. The Salaries of the Lieutenant Governors shall be fixed and provided by the Parliament of Canada. . . .

Legislative Power

90. The following Provisions of this Act respecting the Parliament of Canada, namely,—the Provisions relating to Appropriation and Tax Bills, the Recommendation of Money Votes, the Assent to Bills, the Disallowance of Acts, and the Signification

of Pleasure on Bills reserved,—shall extend and apply to the Legislatures of the several Provinces as if those Provisions were here re-enacted and made applicable in Terms to the respective Provinces and the Legislatures thereof, with the Substitution of The Lieutenant Governor of the Province for the Governor General, of the Governor General for the Queen and for a Secretary of State, of One Year for Two Years, and of the Province for Canada.

VI DISTRIBUTION OF LEGISLATIVE POWERS

Powers of the Parliament

91. It shall be lawful for the Queen, by and with the Advice and Consent of the Senate and House of Commons, to make Laws for the Peace, Order, and good Government of Canada, in relation to all Matters not coming within the Classes of Subjects by this Act assigned exclusively to the Legislatures of the Provinces; and for greater Certainty, but not so as to restrict the Generality of the foregoing Terms of this Section, it is hereby declared that (notwithstanding anything in this Act) the exclusive Legislative Authority of the Parliament of Canada extends to all Matters coming within the Classes of Subjects next hereinafter enumerated; that is to say,—. . . .

1A. The Public Debt and Property. [Re-numbered 1949]

2. The Regulation of Trade and Commerce.

2A. Unemployment Insurance. [Added 1940]

3. The raising of Money by any Mode or System of Taxation.

4. The borrowing of Money on the Public Credit.

5. Postal Service.

6. The Census and Statistics.

7. Militia, Military and Naval Service, and Defence.

8. The fixing of and providing for the Salaries and Allowances of Civil and other Officers of the Government of Canada.

9. Beacons, Buoys, Lighthouses, and Sable Island.

10. Navigation and Shipping.

11. Quarantine and the Establishment and Maintenance of Marine Hospitals.

12. Sea Coast and Inland Fisheries.

13. Ferries between a Province and any British or Foreign Country or between Two Provinces.

14. Currency and Coinage.

15. Banking, Incorporation of Banks, and the Issue of Paper Money.

16. Savings Banks.

17. Weights and Measures.

18. Bills of Exchange and Promissory Notes.

19. Interest.

20. Legal tender.

21. Bankruptcy and insolvency.

22. Patents of Invention and Discovery.

23. Copyrights.

24. Indians and Lands reserved for the Indians.

25. Naturalization and Aliens.

26. Marriage and Divorce.

27. The Criminal Law, except the Constitution of Courts of Criminal Jurisdiction, but including the Procedure in Criminal Matters.

28. The Establishment, Maintenance, and Management of Penitentiaries.

29. Such Classes of Subjects as are expressly excepted in the Enumeration of the Classes of Subjects by this Act assigned exclusively to the Legislatures of the Provinces.

And any Matter coming within any of the Classes of Subjects enumerated in this section shall not be deemed to come within the Class of Matters of a local or private Nature comprised in the Enumeration of the Classes of Subjects by this Act assigned exclusively to the Legislatures of the Provinces.

Exclusive Powers of Provincial Legislatures

92. In each Province the Legislature may exclusively make Laws in relation to Matters coming within the Classes of Subject next hereinafter enumerated; that is to say,—

1. The Amendment from Time to Time, notwithstanding in this Act, of the Constitution of the Province, except as regards the Office of Lieutenant Governor. [Repealed 1982]

2. Direct Taxation within the Province in order to the raising of a Revenue for Provincial Purposes.

3. The borrowing of Money on the sole Credit of the Province.

4. The Establishment and Tenure of Provincial Offices and the Appointment and Payment of Provincial Officers.

5. The Management and Sale of the Public Lands belonging to the Province and of the Timber and Wood thereon.

6. The Establishment, Maintenance, and Management of Public and Reformatory Prisons in and for the Province.

7. The Establishment, Maintenance, and Management of Hospitals, Asylums, Charities, and Eleemosynery Institutions in and for the Province, other than Marine Hospitals.

8. Municipal Institutions in the Province.

9. Shop, Saloon, Tavern, Auctioneer, and other Licences in order to the raising of a Revenue for Provincial, Local, or Municipal Purposes.

10. Local Works and Undertakings other than such as are of the following Classes:—

(a) Lines of Steam or other Ships, Railways, Canals, Telegraphs, and other Works and Undertakings connecting the Province with any other or others of the Provinces, or extending beyond the Limits of the Province;

(b) Lines of Steam Ships between the Province and any British or Foreign Country;

(c) Such Works as, although wholly situate within the Province, are before or after their Execution declared by the Parliament of Canada to be for the general Advantage of Canada or for the Advantage of Two or more of the Provinces.

11. The Incorporation of Companies with Provincial Objects.

12. The Solemnization of Marriage in the Province.

13. Property and Civil Rights in the Province.

14. The Administration of Justice in the Province, including the constitution, Maintenance, and Organization of Provincial Courts, both of Civil and of Criminal Jurisdiction, and including Procedure in Civil Matters in those Courts.

15. The Imposition of Punishment by Fine, Penalty, or Imprisonment for enforcing any Law of the Province made in relation to any Matter coming within any of the Classes of Subjects enumerated in this Section.

16. Generally all Matters of a merely local or private Nature in the Province.

Education

93. In and for each Province the Legislature may exclusively make Laws in relation to Education, subject and according to the following Provisions:—

(1) Nothing in any such Law shall prejudicially affect any Right or Privilege with respect to Denominational Schools which any Class of Persons have by Law in the Province at the Union:

(2) All the Powers, Privileges, and Duties at the Union by Law conferred and imposed in Upper Canada on the Separate Schools and School Trustees of the Queen's Roman Catholic Subjects shall be and the same are hereby extended

to the Dissentient Schools of the Queen's Protestant and Roman Catholic Subjects in Quebec:

(3) Where in any Province a System of Separate or Dissentient Schools exists by Law at the Union or is thereafter established by the Legislature of the Province, an Appeal shall lie to the Governor General in Council from any Act or Decision of any Provincial Authority affecting any Right or Privilege of the Protestant or Roman Catholic Minority of the Queen's Subjects in relation to Education:

(4) In case any such Provincial Law as from Time to Time seems to the Governor General in Council requisite for the due Execution of the Provisions of this Section is not made, or in case any Decision of the Governor General in Council on any appeal under this Section is not duly executed by the proper Provincial Authority in that Behalf, then and in every such Case, and as far only as the Circumstances of each Case require, the Parliament of Canada may make remedial Laws for the due Execution of the Provisions of this Section and of any Decision of the Governor General in Council under this Section.

Uniformity of Laws in Ontario, Nova Scotia and New Brunswick

94. Notwithstanding anything in this Act, the Parliament of Canada may make Provision for the Uniformity of all or any of the Laws relative to Property and Civil Rights in Ontario, Nova Scotia, and New Brunswick, and of the Procedure of all or any of the Courts in Those Three Provinces, and from and after the passing of any Act in that Behalf the Power of the Parliament of Canada to make Laws in relation to any Matter comprised in any such Act shall, notwithstanding anything in this Act, be unrestricted; but any Act of the Parliament of Canada making Provision for such Uniformity shall not have effect in any Province unless and until it is adopted and enacted as Law by the Legislature thereof.

Agriculture and Immigration

95. In each Province the Legislature may make Laws in relation to Agriculture in the Province, and to Immigration into the Province; and it is hereby declared that the Parliament of Canada may from Time to Time make Laws in relation to Agriculture in all or any of the Provinces, and to Immigration into all or any of the Provinces; and any Law of the Legislature of a Province relative to Agriculture or to Immigration shall have effect in and for the Province as long and as far only as it is not repugnant to any Act of the Parliament of Canada....

VIII REVENUE, DEBITS; ASSETS; TAXATION

...

121. All Articles of the Growth, Produce, or Manufacture of any one of the Provinces shall, from and after the Union, be admitted free into each of the other Provinces....

IX MISCELLANEOUS PROVISIONS

General

...

132. The Parliament and Government of Canada shall have all Powers necessary or proper for performing the Obligations of Canada or of any Province thereof, as Part of the British Empire, towards Foreign Countries, arising under Treaties between the Empire and such Foreign Countries.

133. Either the English or the French Language may be used by any Person in the Debates of the Houses of the Parliament of Canada and of the Houses of the Legislature of Quebec; and both those Languages shall be used in the respective Records and Journals of those Houses; and either of those Languages may be used by any Person or in any Pleading or Process in or issuing from any Court of Canada established under this Act, and in or from all or any of the Courts of Quebec.

The Acts of Parliament of Canada and of the Legislature of Quebec shall be printed and published in both those Languages.

section

2

THE REAL CONSTITUTION
OF CANADA

1 8 6 7 - 1 9 1 2

o

T he origin and purpose of judicial review of the Canadian federal constitution is not as clear and obvious as we might expect, for we now take judicial review for granted. The Quebec Resolutions provided for the creation by the central government of a General Court of Appeal, a provision that emerged as section 101 of the 1867 Act. From the outset, however, the debates on the Resolutions make it clear that there was little agreement on exactly what that Court would do, and in particular whether it would be responsible for the judicial arbitration of disputes over federal and provincial jurisdiction.[1] Sir John A. Macdonald first contemplated a Court that would determine only the constitutional limitations of provincial governments. Oliver Mowat (Father of Confederation, Chancellor of Ontario, and future premier) observed that, given its powers to disallow provincial legislation and to appoint lieutenant-governors and judges of the superior courts in the provinces, any further protection of federal power seemed unnecessary.[2]

It was not until 1875 that the Liberal government introduced a bill to create the Supreme Court of Canada composed of six members, two of whom would be from Quebec and trained in the civil law. The Court was given appellate jurisdiction on all matters, civil and criminal. The Governor General in Council (the federal cabinet) was given power to refer "any matter" to the Court for its opinion. This opinion, said the Minister of Justice, was not a judgment but would carry considerable "moral weight." It was clear from the parliamentary debate that some believed that the Court was necessary to keep the provincial legislatures within bounds, for while the federal government had the power of disallowance, whether a provincial act was constitutional or not, disallowance was already under attack as an arbitrary, and often partisan, limitation on provincial rights.

The Minister of Justice agreed that disallowance was an unsatisfactory method. "What was needed," Jennifer Smith explains,

> was a tribunal whose decisions—especially adverse to the provinces—were acceptable to all parties. Apparently Fournier [Minister of Justice] viewed his "independent, neutral and impartial court" as an instrument of the central government. He contended that Ottawa needed "an institution of its own" in order to ensure proper execution of its laws because, however contrary to the spirit of Confederation, the time might come when "it would not be very safe for the Federal Government to be at the mercy of the tribunals of the Provinces."[3]

Although the Supreme Court would inevitably rule on the constitutionality of federal statutes as well, the more common view seemed to be that it would police provincial legislation. Since it could rule federal legislation, *ultra vires*, however, there was some concern that judicial review conflicted with the principles of parliamentary supremacy.

Whatever ambiguities surrounded the debate in Parliament, there was no hesitation on the part of the Supreme Court to assume responsibility for judicial review of both federal and provincial statutes. As Chief Justice Ritchie stated in one of the first cases to come before the Court:

In view of the great diversity of judicial opinion that has characterised the decisions of the provincial tribunals in some provinces, and the judges in all, while it would seem to justify the wisdom of the Dominion Parliament, in providing for the establishment of a Court of Appeal such as this, where such diversity shall be considered and an authoritative declaration of the law be enunciated, so it enhances the responsibility of those called upon in the midst of such conflict of opinion to declare authoritatively the principles by which both federal and local legislation are governed.[4]

Before the establishment of the Supreme Court, the final court of appeal in Canada was the Judicial Committee of the Privy Council, which was created in the early nineteenth century to hear appeals from colonial courts. The disposition of some Canadians was to end appeals to the Judicial Committee, and the 1875 Act made the judgment of the Supreme Court "final and conclusive" except for "any right which Her Majesty may be graciously pleased to exercise by virtue of Her Royal Prerogative." Although many Canadians were opposed to leaving the "final and conclusive" decision in constitutional cases to a federally appointed court, the matter became, for the time, academic when the British government refused to accept the abolition of appeals and persuaded the Canadian government to agree that the right of appeal remained. Not only could there be appeals from decisions of the Supreme Court of Canada, but litigants could, and did, also appeal directly to the Judicial Committee from provincial appeal courts and by-pass the Supreme Court. As Chief Justice Laskin commented, the Supreme Court "was left in the ambiguous position where it could not command appeals to it nor effectively control appeals from it."[5]

The Supreme Court was further weakened by the powerful doctrine of precedent (*stare decisis*), which means that lower courts are bound by the decisions of higher courts. Decisions of the Supreme Court were not "final and conclusive," but were subject to review by the Judicial Committee, whose decisions then became binding on the Supreme Court. By the turn of the century the Supreme Court was very much a "captive court" and, as Professor Hogg has stated, did not have "a decisive voice in the development of Canadian law, including constitutional law."[6] The power of precedent was made even greater because the Judicial Committee, whatever disagreements there may have been on the bench, reached a decision which was then delivered in a single judgment. The Supreme Court, on the other hand, adopted a practice whereby any, or every, judge could write a majority or minority decision or declare concurrence with a written decision. Although equally binding in theory, a 3 to 2 decision, based on perhaps three, four or five different opinions, was in fact much less persuasive than apparent unanimity.

By the turn of the century, the Supreme Court was not only a "captive" court, but a court diminished in prestige by the Judicial Committee's continuous rejection of its decisions. Specialists in constitutional law, including judges in the process of reaching their own decisions, have examined and re-examined the arguments behind the Judicial Committee's decisions, and many find the reasoning less than persuasive. In his article, Professor F. Murray Greenwood offers his explanation of a series of decisions which played an important role in altering the balance of power in the constitution. That Lord Watson, in particular, imposed his view of federalism on the constitution is the boast of Lord Haldane, who was himself to play a decisive role in the development of Canadian constitutional law.

As Greenwood notes, these decentralising tendencies were consonant with what appeared to be the general political mood of late nineteenth-century Canada. By the 1880s, strong provincial rights movements had emerged in most provinces in response to Macdonald's highly centralist economic and constitutional policy of nation-building. In Nova Scotia, opposition to the protective tariff fuelled a secessionist movement. A provincial rights movement emerged in Manitoba opposing the monopoly Macdonald had given to the Canadian Pacific Railway and his heavy-handed use of the power of disallowance to prevent Manitoba authorizing competing lines. In Quebec, a perceived lack of federal financial generosity and the execution of Louis Riel sparked a nationalist and autonomist movement. In Ontario, Oliver Mowat insisted on the constitutional equality of the provinces and challenged the unrestricted use of the power of disallowance. The statement of the provincial positions and of the explicit adoption of the compact theory as the basis of Canadian federalism (a theory which in effect argued that the 1867 constitution was the creation of the provinces and could only be altered by them) were contained in resolutions passed at the Interprovincial Conference of 1887. Macdonald dismissed the conference as a conspiracy of disgruntled Liberal premiers.[7]

The decisions of the Judicial Committee and the philosophy of federalism that seems to have determined Lord Watson's reading of the Act have come under severe academic criticism. But Alan Cairns has argued that however sound or unsound its decisions, the Judicial Committee should be applauded for decisions which complemented and reinforced the decentralising developments in the provinces. In a section of his article subtitled "Sociological Justification of the Judicial Committee," Cairns argues that from "the vantage point of a century of constitutional evolution the centralist emphasis of the Confederation settlement appears increasingly unrealistic."

The centralised federalism established in 1867, writes Cairns, "was inappropriate for the regional diversities of a land of vast extent and a large geographically concentrated, minority culture." The re-emergence of provincial loyalties, the basis of the regional pluralism that, in the 1960s and 1970s, Cairns posited as the reality that underlay the constitutional structure, was, he implies, as necessary as it was inevitable. "It is impossible to believe that a few elderly men in London deciding two or three constitutional cases a year precipitated, sustained and caused the development of Canada in a federalist direction the country would not otherwise have taken," Cairns states. Their decisions were "harmonious" with the trends within Canada. "Their great contribution, the injection of a decentralising impulse into a constitutional structure too centralist for the diversity it had to contain, and the placating of Quebec which was a consequence, was a positive influence in the evolution of Canadian federalism."

A critique of Cairns and his response are contained in the Commentary in Section Three. It is worth noting in passing, however, that in spite of the protest movements in the provinces, Macdonald and his Conservative Party secured healthy majorities in the elections of 1878, 1882, 1887 and 1891, even in the province of Ontario. In the election of 1887, for example, the year of the Interprovincial

Conference, the Conservatives won a majority in every province except Prince Edward Island which, with a Conservative government in office, did not send delegates. Generalisations about the mood of the public, on the constitutional implications of "provincial loyalties" or about "regional pluralism" must be treated with some scepticism.[8] So, too, should the argument that the courts are to be commended for decisions which seem to be in harmony with public opinion. A discussion of this issue more appropriately follows the examination of Lord Haldane's court, in Section Three.

NOTES

1. On the origins of the Supreme Court and judicial review see: Jennifer Smith, "The Origins of Judicial Review in Canada," *Canadian Journal of Political Science* (March 1983), 115–34; James G. Snell and Frederick Vaughan, *The Supreme Court of Canada* (Toronto, 1985).

2. Snell and Vaughan, *The Supreme Court of Canada*, 6–7

3. Smith, "Origins of Judicial Review," 125. The federal government appointed the judges of the provincial superior courts, but the administration of justice was in the hands of the provinces.

4. *Valin v. Langlois* (1879) 3 S.C.R. 529.

5. Bora Laskin, "The Supreme Court of Canada: The First One Hundred Years" *Canadian Bar Review* (1975), 459–61. Peter Russell has noted that 77 of the 159 constitutional decisions of the JCPC were on appeals from provincial courts. Peter H. Russell, *The Judiciary in Canada: The Third Branch of Government* (Toronto, 1987), 336.

6. Peter Hogg, *Constitutional Law of Canada* (Toronto, 1985), 167.

7. A convenient survey is Ramsay Cook, *Provincial Autonomy, Minority Rights and the Compact Theory 1867–1921,* no. 4, Studies of the Royal Commission on Bilingualism and Biculturalism (Ottawa, 1969). On the lieutenant-governor see John T. Saywell, *The Office of the Lieutenant-Governor* (Toronto, 1986). Watson's decision and Stephen Wexler's "two Crown" theory are discussed in the essay on Haldane in the Commentary in Section Three.

8. Alan C. Cairns, "The Judicial Committee and Its Critics," *Canadian Journal of Political Science* (September 1971), 301–45. The figures given in Beck, which differ somewhat from those in the *Parliamentary Guide* are Nova Scotia 14–7, New Brunswick 10–6, Quebec 33–32, Ontario 55–37, Manitoba 4–1. The Conservatives received 50.2 per cent of the popular vote and the Liberals 48.7 per cent. J.M. Beck *Pendulum of Power* (Toronto, 1968), 56.

SEVERN v. R.[*]

John Severn, a brewer, manufactured and sold liquor under licence of the federal government. He did not, as required by the province of Ontario, have a licence to do so and was charged with that offence. The provincial Act was challenged on the basis that it interfered with the exclusive federal power of "Trade and Commerce" — 92(2).

KNIGHT C.J.

In deciding important questions arising under the Act passed by the Imperial Parliament for federally uniting the Provinces of *Canada, Nova Scotia and New Brunswick,* and forming the Dominion of *Canada,* we must consider the circumstances under which that Statute was passed, the condition of the different Provinces themselves, their relation to one another, to the Mother Country, and the state of things existing in the great country adjoining *Canada,* as well as the systems of government which prevailed in these Provinces and countries. The framers of the Statute knew the difficulties which had arisen in the great Federal Republic, and no doubt wished to avoid them in the new government which it was intended to create under that Statute. They knew that the question of State rights as opposed to the authority of the General Government under their constitution was frequently raised, aggravating, if not causing, the difficulties arising out of their system of government, and they evidently wished to avoid these evils, under the new state of things about to be created here by the Confederation of the Provinces....

It is said this construction conflicts with the power of the Dominion Government to regulate trade and commerce, and the raising of money by any mode or system of taxation. All I can say in answer to that is, that so far, and so far only, as the raising of a revenue for provincial, municipal and local purposes is concerned, the *British North America Act,* in my opinion, gives to the Local Legislatures not an inconsistent but a concurrent power of taxation, and I fail to see any necessary conflict; certainly, no other or greater than would necessarily arise from the exercise of the power of direct taxation and the granting of shop and auctioneer licences specially vested in the local legislatures. It cannot be doubted, I apprehend, that both the Local Legislatures and Dominion Parliament may raise a revenue by direct taxation, and, if so, why may not both raise a revenue by means of licences? There need be no more conflict in the one case than in the other. The granting of shop and auctioneer licences necessarily interferes with trade and commerce, the former

---

[*][1878] 2 S.C.R. 70.

with retail trade, the latter with both wholesale and retail trade; for, in large business centres, auctioneers' sales on a wholesale scale are of daily occurrence.

Should at any time the burthen imposed by the Local Legislature, under this power, in fact conflict injuriously with the Dominion power to regulate trade and commerce, or with the Dominion power to raise money by any mode or system of taxation, the power vested in the Governor General of disallowing any such legislation, practically affords the means by which serious difficulty may be prevented. But I do not think we have any right to suppose for a moment that the Local Legislatures would legislate save for the legitimate purpose of raising a revenue, and not so as to interfere unnecessarily or injuriously with the legislation of the Dominion Parliament, still less, so as to destroy the very business from which the revenue is to be derived....

STRONG J. (dissenting):

That the regulation of trade and commerce in the Provinces, domestic and internal, as well as foreign and external, is, by the *British North America Act*, exclusively conferred upon the Parliament of the Dominion, calls for no demonstration, for the language of the Act is explicit....

I think, however, that in ascribing the power of the Legislature to pass this Statute to sub-section 9 of section 92, the learned counsel for the Crown put their case upon the true ground....

The imposition of licences authorized by this sub-section 9, is, it will be observed, confined to licences for the purposes of revenue, and it is not to be assumed that the Provincial Legislatures will abuse the power, or exercise it in such a way as to destroy any trade or occupation. Should it appear explicitly on the face of any Legislative Act that a licence tax was imposed with such an object, it would not be a tax authorized by this section, and it might be liable to be judicially pronounced *extra vires*. And however carefully the purpose or object of such an enactment might be veiled, the foresight of those who framed our constitutional Act led them to provide a remedy in the 90th section of the Act, by vesting the power of disallowance of Provincial Acts in the Executive Power of the Dominion, the Governor General in Council. There is, therefore, no room for the application of any argument *ab inconvenient:* sufficient to neutralize the rule of verbal construction already referred to.

HENRY J.:

Everything in the shape of legislation for the peace, order and good government of *Canada* is embraced, except as before mentioned. But sub-section twenty-nine goes further and provides for exceptions and reservations in regard to matters otherwise included in the power of legislation given to the Local Legislatures, and also provides that:

> Any matter coming within any of the classes of subjects enumerated *in this section* shall not be deemed to come within the class of matters of a local or private nature comprised in the enumeration of the classes of subjects by this Act assigned exclusively to the Legislatures of the Provinces.

"The regulation of trade and commerce" and "the raising of money by any mode or system of taxation" is, however, specially mentioned, and both include the right to make and have carried out all the provisions in the Dominion Act. This position has not been, and cannot be, successfully assailed. The subjects in all their details of which trade and commerce are composed, and the regulation of them, and the raising of revenue by indirect taxation, must, therefore, be matters referred to and included in the latter clause of sub-section 29....

Every constituent, therefore, of trade and commerce, and the subject of indirect taxation, is thus, as I submit, withdrawn from the consideration of the Local Legislatures, even if it should otherwise be *apparently* included. The Imperial Act fences in those twenty-eight subjects wholesale and in detail, and the Local Legislatures were intended to be, and are, kept out of the inclosure....

CITY OF FREDERICTON v. R.[◇]

The Canada Temperance Act, 1878 provided for the prohibition of the sale of intoxicating liquors where a municipal referendum to that effect had succeeded. The constitutionality of the Act was challenged by Thomas Barker, a Fredericton hotel owner whose application for a liquor licence was refused after that city had opted into the Act. The Supreme Court held, with one of the six judges dissenting, that the Act was *intra vires*.

RITCHIE C.J.:

If the Dominion Parliament legislates strictly within the powers conferred in relation to matters over which the *British North America Act* gives it exclusive legislative control, we have no right to enquire what motive induced Parliament to exercise its powers. The statute declares it shall be lawful for the Queen, by and with the advice and consent of the Senate and House of Commons, to make laws for the peace, order and good government of *Canada*, in relation to all matters not coming within the class of subjects by this act assigned exclusively to the legislatures of the Provinces, and, notwithstanding anything in the act, the exclusive legislative authority of the Parliament of *Canada* extends to all matters coming within the classes of subjects enumerated, of which the regulation of trade and commerce is one; and any matters coming within any of the classes of subjects enumerated shall not be deemed to come within the classes of matters of a local or private nature comprised in the enumeration of the classes of subjects by the act assigned exclusively to the legislatures of the Provinces. If then, Parliament, in its wisdom, deems it expedient for the peace, order and good government of *Canada* so to regulate trade and commerce as to restrict or prohibit the importation into, or exportation out of the Dominion, or the trade and traffic in, or dealing with, any articles in respect to which external or internal trade or commerce is carried on, it

---

◇[1880] 3. S.C.R. 505.

matters not, so far as we are judicially concerned, nor had we, in my opinion, the right to enquire whether such legislation is prompted by a desire to establish uniformity of legislation with respect to the traffic dealt with, or whether it be to increase or diminish the volume of such traffic, or to encourage native industry, or local manufacturers, or with a view to the diminution of crime or the promotion of temperance, or any other object which may, by regulating trade and commerce, or by any other enactments within the scope of the legislative powers confided to Parliament, tend to the peace, order and good government of *Canada*. The effect of a regulation of trade may be to aid the temperance cause, or it may tend to the prevention of crime, but surely this cannot make the legislation *ultra vires*, if the enactment is, in truth and fact, a regulation of trade and commerce, foreign or domestic....

With us the Government of the Province is one of enumerated powers, which are specified in the *B.N.A. Act*, and in this respect differs from the Constitution of the Dominion Parliament, which, as has been stated, is authorized "to make laws for the peace, order and good government of *Canada* in relation to all matters not coming within the classes of subjects by the Act assigned exclusively to the Legislatures of the Provinces";—and that "any matter coming within any of the classes of subjects enumerated shall not be deemed to come within the class of matters of a local or private nature comprised in the enumeration of the classes of subjects assigned exclusively to the Legislatures of the Provinces." Therefore "the regulation of trade and commerce," being one of the classes of subjects enumerated in sec. 91, is not to be deemed to come within any of the classes of a local or private nature assigned to the Legislatures of the Provinces....

HENRY J.:

The first, and, as I think, the only important consideration, is the extent to which effect should be given to the provision "The regulation of Trade and Commerce"; and, admitting for the moment the power of Parliament to pass the Act in reference to that subject, has it properly dealt with it? In deciding upon this question, our first inquiry is, whether Parliament intended the Act as a regulation of trade or commerce? It does not necessarily follow, that if one in the pursuit of one purpose or object does an unjustifiable Act, he can take shelter under a right he did not intend to assert or Act on. There are circumstances in which, in such a case, the party would not be held justified.

The preamble of an act will not, of course, by itself, give or take away jurisdiction to legislate. If, however, the legislature plainly shows by the preamble and provisions of the act that the legislation was directed, not in the pursuance of legitimate power, but in reference to a subject over which it had no jurisdiction, I am far from thinking it would be legitimate. We cannot assume any legislature would so act.

The preamble informs us that it was *"very desirable to promote temperance,"* and the Act is provided to be cited as *The Canada Temperance Act, 1878*. The object is therefore patent, but it is contended that the subsequent words in the preamble:

> And that there should be uniform legislation in all the Provinces respecting the traffic in intoxicating liquors—

makes a direct reference to *trade and commerce.* If the words last quoted stood alone, they would, to the extent they go, support the contention, but following the previous expression of the desire to *promote temperance,* we should construe them as only the expression of the idea, that *to promote temperance* uniform legislation respecting the traffic in spirituous liquors was deemed necessary as a means to the end, and not as at all intended as a regulation of trade and commerce.

GWYNNE J.:

The power to legislate upon every subject rests either in the Dominion Parliament, or in the Local Legislatures, and the Act is precise, that *all matters not exclusively assigned to the Local Legislatures* fall under the jurisdiction of the Dominion Parliament.

But to remove all doubts, in case the enactment under consideration should be of a nature to raise a doubt, whether it does or not deal with one or other of the matters particularly enumerated in the 92nd section, the second test may be applied, namely: "Does the enactment deal or interfere with any of the subjects particularly, and for greater certainty, enumerated in the 91st section? If it does, then, (notwithstanding that it otherwise might come within the class of subjects enumerated in the 92nd section), it is within the jurisdiction of the Dominion Parliament, for the plain meaning of the closing paragraph of the 91st section is that, notwithstanding any thing in the Act, any matter coming within any of the subjects enumerated in the 91st section shall not be deemed to come within the class of subjects enumerated in the 92nd section, however much they may appear to do so.

It was argued, that what was intended by this clause was to exclude the subjects enumerated in the 91st section from a portion only of the subjects enumerated in the 92nd section, namely: those only "of a local or private nature," the contention being that the 92nd section comprehends other subjects than those which come under the description of *"local or private,"* and so that, in effect, the intention was merely to declare, that none of the items enumerated in section 91 shall be deemed to come within item 16 of sec. 92. If this were the true construction of the class, it would make no difference in the result, nor would it effect any thing in aid of the contention in support of which the argument was used, for the previous part of the 91st section in the most precise and imperative terms declares, that, *"notwithstanding any thing in the Act,"* notwithstanding, therefore, any thing whether of a local or private nature, or of any other character, if there be anything of any other character enumerated in the 92nd section, the exclusive legislative authority of the Parliament of *Canada* extends to all matters coming within the class of subjects enumerated in the 91st section; but, in truth, all the items enumerated in the 92nd section are of a provincial and domestic, that is to say, of a "local or private" nature. The frame of the 92nd section differs from that of the 91st in its form. That of the 91st is general, of the 92nd particular; but this is precisely in character with the nature of the jurisdiction intended to be given to each....

Now, that the intemperate use of spirituous liquors is the fruitful cause of the greater part of the crime which is committed throughout the Dominion—that it is an evil of a national, rather than of a local or provincial character, will not, I apprehend, be denied. The adoption of any measures calculated to remove or diminish this evil is, therefore, a subject of national rather than of provincial import, and the devising and enacting such measures into law, as calculated to promote the peace, order, and good government of *Canada*, is a matter in which the Dominion at large and all its inhabitants are concerned....

Reading, therefore, the object of the Act to be as it was read in the Court below, namely: to endeavour to remove from the Dominion the national curse of intemperance, and observing that the means adopted to attain this end consist in the imposition of restraints upon the mode of carrying on a particular trade, namely: the trade in intoxicating liquors, it cannot admit of a doubt, that power to pass such an Act, or any Act, assuming to impose any restraint upon the traffic in intoxicating liquors, or to impose any rules or regulations, not merely for municipal or police purposes, to govern the persons engaged in that trade, and assuming to prohibit the sale of liquors, except under and subject to the conditions imposed by the Act, is not only not given *exclusively*, but is not *at all* given to the Provincial Legislatures.

o

THE CITIZENS' AND THE QUEEN INSURANCE COMPANY *v. PARSONS*◊

The three companies named in this suit were licensed by the federal government to carry on insurance business in Canada. The contracts issued by these companies to the above clients did not meet the statutory conditions prescribed by the province of Ontario.... In a 3 to 2 decision, the Supreme Court of Canada held that the province was competent to stipulate the conditions of an insurance contract as a matter of "Property and Civil Rights in the Province."

RITCHIE C.J.:

No one can dispute the general power of parliament to legislate as to "trade and commerce," and that where, over matters with which local legislatures have power to deal, local legislation conflicts with an Act passed by the Dominion parliament in the exercise of any of the general powers confided to it, the legislation of the local must yield to the supremacy of the Dominion parliament; in other words, that the provincial legislation in such a case must be subject to such regulations, for instance, as to trade and commerce of a commercial character, as the Dominion parliament may prescribe....

I think the power of the Dominion parliament to regulate trade and commerce ought not to be held to be necessarily inconsistent with those of the local legislatures to regulate property and civil rights in respect to all matters of a merely local and private nature, such as matters connected with the enjoyment and preservation of property in the province, or matters of contract between parties in relation to their property or dealings, although the exercise by the local legislatures of such powers may be said remotely to affect matters connected with trade and

◊[1880] 4 S.C.R. 215.

commerce, unless, indeed, the laws of the provincial legislatures should conflict with those of the Dominion parliament passed for the general regulation of trade and commerce. I do not think the local legislatures are to be deprived of all power to deal with property and civil rights, because parliament, in the plenary exercise of its power to regulate trade and commerce, may possibly pass laws inconsistent with the exercise by the local legislatures of their powers—the exercise of the powers of the local legislatures being in such a case subject to such regulations as the Dominion may lawfully prescribe.

The Act now under consideration is not, in my opinion, a regulation of trade and commerce; it deals with the contract of fire insurance, as between the insurer and the insured. That contract is simply a contract of indemnity against loss or damage by fire, whereby one party, in consideration of an immediate fixed payment, undertakes to pay or make good to the other any loss or damage by fire, which may happen during a fixed period to specified property, not exceeding the sum named as the limit of insurance....

GWYNNE J.:

...In so far as jurisdiction over "Property and Civil Rights," in every province may be deemed necessary for the perfect exercise of the exclusive jurisdiction given to the Dominion parliament over the several subjects enumerated in sec. 91, it is vested in the parliament, and what is vested in the local legislatures by item 13 of sec. 92, is only jurisdiction over so much of property and civil rights as may remain, after deducting so much of jurisdiction over those subjects as may be deemed necessary for securing to the parliament exclusive control over every one of the subjects enumerated in sec. 91, the residuum, in fact, not so absorbed by the jurisdiction conferred on the parliament....

Within this Dominion the right of exercise of National Sovereignty is vested solely in Her Majesty, the Supreme Sovereign Head of the State, and in the Parliament of which Her Majesty is an integral part; these powers are, within this Dominion, the sole administrators and guardians of the *Comity of Nations.* To prevent all possibility of the local legislatures creating any difficulties embarrassing to the Dominion Government, by presuming to interfere in any matter affecting trade and commerce, and by so doing violating, it might be, the Comity of Nations, all matters coming within those subjects are placed under the exclusive jurisdiction of the Dominion parliament; that the Act in question does usurp the jurisdiction of the Dominion parliament, I must say I entertain no doubt. The logical result of a contrary decision would afford just grounds to despair of the stability of the Dominion. The object of the *B.N.A. Act* was to lay in the Dominion Constitution the foundations of a nation, and not to give to provinces carved out of, and subordinated to, the Dominion, anything of the nature of a national or *quasi* national existence.

True it may be, that the Acts of the local legislatures affecting the particularly enumerated subjects placed by the *B.N.A. Act* under their exclusive control, if not disallowed by the Dominion Government, are supreme in the sense that they cannot be called in question in any court, but this supremacy is attributable solely to the authority of the *B.N.A Act,* which has placed those subjects under the exclusive control of the local legislatures, and is not, in any respect, enjoyed as an incident to national sovereignty.

To enjoy the supremacy so conferred by the *B.N.A. Act*, these local legislatures must be careful to confine the assumption of exercise of the powers conferred upon them, to the particular subjects expressly placed under their jurisdiction, and not to encroach upon subjects which, being of national importance, are for that reason placed under the exclusive control of the parliament.

o

L'UNION ST.-JACQUES DE MONTREAL v. DAME JULIE BELISLE$^\diamond$

L'Union St.-Jacques de Montréal benevolent society was facing financial difficulties; they arose primarily out of over generous pensions given to widows. At the society's request, the province of Quebec passed legislation allowing the former to pay two widows less than they were hitherto entitled. The legislation was challenged on the grounds that it dealt with a matter of federal jurisdiction, i.e.: 92(21) "Bankruptcy and Insolvency"....

LORD SELBOURNE:

Clearly this matter is private; clearly it is local, so far as locality is to be considered, because it is in the province and in the city of *Montreal*; and unless, therefore, the general effect of that head of sect. 92 is for this purpose qualified by something in sect. 91, it is a matter not only within the competency but within the exclusive competency of the provincial legislature. Now sect. 91 qualifies it undoubtedly, if it be within any one of the different classes of subjects there specially enumerated; because the last and concluding words of sect. 91 are: "And any matter coming within any of the classes of subjects enumerated in this section shall not be deemed to come within the class of matters of a local or private nature comprised in the enumeration of the classes of subjects by this Act assigned exclusively to the Legislatures of the provinces." But the *onus* is on the Respondent to shew that this, being of itself of a local or private nature, does also come within one or more of the classes of subjects specially enumerated in the 91st section.

o

CUSHING v. DUPUY$^{\diamond\diamond}$

The Canadian *Insolvency Act* provided that decisions of provincial courts of appeal were final in insolvency matters. Charles Cushing sought to challenge the finality of an order under this Act on the grounds that it violated property and civil rights.

$^\diamond$ [1874] 6 A.C. 31.
$^{\diamond\diamond}$[1880] 5 A.C. 409.

SIR MONTAGUE E. SMITH:

It was contended for the Appellant that the provisions of the *Insolvency Act* interfered with property and civil rights, and was therefore *ultra vires*. This objection was very faintly urged, but it was strongly contended that the Parliament of *Canada* could not take away the right of appeal to the Queen from final judgments of the Court of Queen's Bench, which, it was said, was part of the procedure in civil matters exclusively assigned to the Legislature of the Province.

The answer to these objections is obvious. It would be impossible to advance a step in the construction of a scheme for the administration of insolvent estates without interfering with and modifying some of the ordinary rights of property, and other civil rights, nor without providing some mode of special procedure for the vesting, realisation, and distribution of the estate, and the settlement of the liabilities of the insolvent. Procedure must necessarily form an essential part of any law dealing with insolvency. It is therefore to be presumed, indeed it is a necessary implication, that the Imperial statute, in assigning to the Dominion Parliament the subjects of bankruptcy and insolvency, intended to confer on it legislative power to interfere with property, civil rights, and procedure within the Provinces, so far as a general law relating to those subjects might affect them.

)

THE CITIZENS' AND THE QUEEN INSURANCE COMPANY v. PARSONS◇

SIR MONTAGUE E. SMITH:

The scheme of this legislation, as expressed in the first branch of sect. 91, is to give to the Dominion parliament authority to make laws for the good government of Canada in all matters not coming within the classes of subjects assigned exclusively to the provincial legislature. If the 91st section had stopped here, and if the classes of subjects enumerated in sect. 92 had been altogether distinct and different from those in sect. 91, no conflict of legislative authority could have arisen. The provincial legislatures would have had exclusive legislative power over the sixteen classes of subjects assigned to them, and the Dominion parliament exclusive power over all other matters relating to the good government of Canada. But it must have been foreseen that this sharp and definite distinction had not been and could not be attained, and that some of the classes of subjects assigned to the provincial legislatures unavoidably ran into and were embraced by some of the enumerated classes of subjects in sect. 91; hence an endeavour appears to have been made to provide for cases of apparent conflict; and it would seem that with this object it was declared in the second branch of the 91st section, "for greater certainty, but not so as to restrict the generality of the foregoing terms of this section" that (notwithstanding anything in the Act) the exclusive legislative authority of the parliament of Canada should extend to all matters coming within the classes of subjects enumerated in that section. With the same object, apparently, the paragraph at the

---

◇ [1881] 7 A.C. 96.

end of sect. 91 was introduced, though it may be observed that this paragraph applies in its grammatical construction only to No. 16 of sect. 92.

Notwithstanding this endeavour to give pre-eminence to the Dominion parliament in cases of a conflict of powers, it is obvious that in some cases where this apparent conflict exists, the legislature could not have intended that the powers exclusively assigned to the provincial legislature should be absorbed in those given to the Dominion parliament.... With regard to certain classes of subjects, therefore, generally described in sect. 91, legislative power may reside as to some matters falling within the general description of these subjects in the legislatures of the provinces. In these cases it is the duty of the Courts, however difficult it may be, to ascertain in what degree, and to what extent, authority to deal with matters falling within these classes of subjects exists in each legislature, and to define in the particular case before them the limits of their respective powers. It could not have been the intention that a conflict should exist; and, in order to prevent such a result, the two sections must be read together, and the language of one interpreted, and, where necessary, modified, by that of the other. In this way it may, in most cases, be found possible to arrive at a reasonable and practical construction of the language of the sections, so as to reconcile the respective powers they contain, and give effect to all of them. In performing this difficult duty, it will be a wise course for those on whom it is thrown, to decide each case which arises as best they can, without entering more largely upon an interpretation of the statute than is necessary for the decision of the particular question in hand.

The first question to be decided is, whether the Act impeached in the present appeals falls within any of the classes of subjects enumerated in sect. 92, and assigned exclusively to the legislatures of the provinces; for if it does not, it can be of no validity, and no other question would then arise. It is only when an Act of the provincial legislature *prima facie* falls within one of these classes of subjects that the further questions arise, viz., whether, notwithstanding this is so, the subject of the Act does not also fall within one of the enumerated classes of subjects in sect. 91, and whether the power of the provincial legislature is or is not thereby overborne ....

The next question for consideration is whether, assuming the Ontario Act to relate to the subject of property and civil rights, its enactments and provisions come within any of the classes of subjects enumerated in sect. 91. The only one which the Appellants suggested as expressly including the subject of the Ontario Act is No. 2, "the regulation of trade and commerce"....

The words "regulation of trade and commerce," in their unlimited sense are sufficiently wide, if uncontrolled by the context and other parts of the Act, to include every regulation of trade ranging from political arrangements in regard to trade with foreign governments, requiring the sanction of parliament, down to minute rules for regulating particular trades. But a consideration of the Act shews that the words were not used in this unlimited sense. In the first place the collocation of No. 2 with classes of subjects of national and general concern affords an indication that regulations relating to trade and commerce were in the mind of the legislature, when conferring this power on the Dominion parliament. If the words had been intended to have the full scope of which in their literal meaning they are susceptible, the specific mention of several of the other classes of subjects enumerated in sect. 91 would have been unnecessary; as, 15, banking; 17, weights and measures; 18, bills of exchange and promissory notes; 19, interest; and even 21, bankruptcy and insolvency.

"Regulation of trade and commerce" may have been used in some such sense as the words "regulations of trade" in the Act of Union between England and Scotland (6 Anne, c. 11), and as these words have been used in Acts of State relating to trade and commerce. Article V. of the Act of Union enacted that all the subjects of the United Kingdom should have "full freedom and intercourse of trade and navigation" to and from all places in the United Kingdom and the colonies; and Article VI. enacted that all parts of the United Kingdom from and after the Union should be under the *same* "prohibitions, restrictions, and *regulations of trade.*" Parliament has at various times since the Union passed laws affecting and regulating specific trades in one part of the United Kingdom only, without its being supposed that it thereby infringed the Articles of Union. Thus the Acts for regulating the sale of intoxicating liquors notoriously vary in the two kingdoms. So with regard to Acts relating to bankruptcy, and various other matters.

Construing therefore the words "regulation of trade and commerce" by the various aids to their interpretation above suggested, they would include political arrangements in regard to trade requiring the sanction of parliament, regulation of trade in matters of interprovincial concern, and it may be that they would include general regulation of trade affecting the whole Dominion. Their Lordships abstain on the present occasion from any attempt to define the limits of the authority of the Dominion parliament in this direction. It is enough for the decision of the present case to say that, in their view, its authority to legislate for the regulation of trade and commerce does not comprehend the power to regulate by legislation the contracts of a particular business or trade, such as the business of fire insurance in a single province, and therefore that its legislative authority does not in the present case conflict or compete with the power over property and civil rights assigned to the legislature of Ontario by No. 13 of sect. 92.

Having taken this view of the present case, it becomes unnecessary to consider the question how far the general power to make regulations of trade and commerce, when competently exercised by the Dominion parliament, might legally modify or affect property and civil rights in the provinces, or the legislative power of the provincial legislatures in relation to those subjects; questions of this kind, it may be observed, arose and were treated of by this Board in the cases of *L'Union St.-Jacques de Montréal v. Bélisle* [and] *Cushing v. Dupuy.*

ɔ

RUSSELL v. R. [◇]

Charles Russell was charged with unlawfully selling intoxicating liquors contrary to the *Canada Temperance Act, 1878*. The Supreme Court of Canada upheld the charge by reference to *City of Fredericton v. R.* The decision was appealed to the Judicial Committee of the Privy Council.

◇ [1882] 7 A.C. 829.

SIR MONTAGUE E. SMITH:

Next, their Lordships cannot think that the *Temperance Act* in question properly belongs to the class of subjects, "Property and Civil Rights." It has in its legal aspect an obvious and close similarity to laws which place restrictions on the sale or custody of poisonous drugs, or of dangerously explosive substances. These things, as well as intoxicating liquors, can, of course, be held as property, but a law placing restrictions on their sale, custody or removal, on the ground that the free sale or use of them is dangerous to public safety, and making it a criminal offence punishable by fine or imprisonment to violate these restrictions, cannot properly be deemed a law in relation to property in the sense in which those words are used in the 92nd section. What Parliament is dealing with in legislation of this kind is not a matter in relation to property and its rights, but one relating to public order and safety. That is the primary matter dealt with, and though incidentally the free use of things in which men may have property is interfered with, that incidental interference does not alter the character of the law. Upon the same considerations, the Act in question cannot be regarded as legislation in relation to civil rights. In however large a sense these words are used, it could not have been intended to prevent the Parliament of Canada from declaring and enacting certain uses of property, and certain acts in relation to property, to be criminal and wrongful. Laws which make it a criminal offence for a man wilfully to set fire to his own house on the ground that such an act endangers the public safety, or to overwork his horse on the ground of cruelty to the animal, though affecting in some sense property and the right of a man to do as he pleases with his own, cannot properly be regarded as legislation in relation to property or to civil rights. Nor could a law which prohibited or restricted the sale or exposure of cattle having a contagious disease be so regarded. Laws of this nature designed for the promotion of public order, safety, or morals, and which subject those who contravene them to criminal procedure and punishment, belong to the subject of public wrongs rather than to that of civil rights. They are of a nature which fall within the general authority of Parliament to make laws for the order and good government of Canada, and have direct relation to criminal law, which is one of the enumerated classes of subjects assigned exclusively to the Parliament of Canada. It was said in the course of the judgment of this Board in the case of the *Citizens Insurance Company of Canada v. Parsons*, that the two sections (91 and 92) must be read together, and the language of one interpreted, and, where necessary, modified by that of the other. Few, if any, laws could be made by Parliament for the peace, order, and good government of Canada which did not in some incidental way affect property and civil rights; and it could not have been intended, when assuring to the provinces exclusive legislative authority on the subjects of property and civil rights, to exclude the Parliament from the exercise of this general power whenever any such incidental interference would result from it. The true nature and character of the legislation in the particular instance under discussion must always be determined, in order to ascertain the class of subject to which it really belongs. In the present case it appears to their Lordships, for the reasons already given, that the matter of the Act in question does not properly belong to the class of subjects "Property and Civil Rights" within the meaning of sub-sect. 13....

The court then considered whether the "local option" aspect of the Act did not characterise it as a matter of local and private nature.

Their Lordships cannot concur in this view. The declared object of Parliament in passing the Act is that there should be uniform legislation in all the provinces respecting the traffic in intoxicating liquors, with a view to promote temperance in the Dominion. Parliament does not treat the promotion of temperance as desirable in one province more than in another, but as desirable everywhere throughout the Dominion. The Act as soon as it was passed became a law for the whole Dominion, and the enactments of the first part, relating to the machinery for bringing the second part into force, took effect and might be put in motion at once and everywhere within it. It is true that the prohibitory and penal parts of the Act are only to come into force in any county or city upon the adoption of a petition to that effect by a majority of electors, but this conditional application of these parts of the Act does not convert the Act itself into legislation in relation to a merely local matter. The objects and scope of the legislation are still general, viz., to promote temperance by means of a uniform law throughout the Dominion....

Their Lordships having come to the conclusion that the Act in question does not fall within any of the classes of subjects assigned exclusively to the Provincial Legislatures, it becomes unnecessary to discuss the further question whether its provisions also fall within any of the classes of subjects enumerated in sect. 91. In abstaining from this discussion, they must not be understood as intimating any dissent from the opinion of the Chief Justice of the Supreme Court of Canada and the other Judges, who held that the Act, as a general regulation of the traffic in intoxicating liquors throughout the Dominion, fell within the class of subject, "the regulation of trade and commerce," enumerated in that section, and was, on that ground, a valid exercise of the legislative power of the Parliament of Canada.

◌

HODGE v. R. ◆

The *Liquor Licence Act* of 1877 made provisions for the setting up of municipal commissions to regulate the conditions of liquor licences. Archibald Hodge, contrary to the regulations for the city of Toronto, allowed billiard playing in his tavern. The legislation was challenged on the grounds that the Provincial Legislature was not competent to legislate on liquor licensing.

LORD FITZGERALD:

The appellants contended that the legislature of Ontario had no power to pass any Act to regulate the liquor traffic; that the whole power to pass such an Act was conferred on the Dominion parliament, and consequently taken from the provincial legislature, by sect. 91 of the *British North America Act, 1867*; and that it did not

---

◆ [1883] 9 A.C. 117.

come within any of the classes of subjects assigned exclusively to the provincial legislatures by sect. 92. The class in sect. 91 which the *Liquor Licence Act, 1877,* was said to infringe was No. 2, "The Regulation of Trade and Commerce," and it was urged that the decision of this Board in *Russell v. Regina* was conclusive that the whole subject of the liquor traffic was given to the Dominion parliament, and consequently taken away from the provincial legislature. It appears to their Lordships, however, that the decision of this tribunal in that case has not the effect supposed, and that, when properly considered, it should be taken rather as an authority in support of the judgment of the Court of Appeal....

It appears to their Lordships that *Russell v. The Queen,* when properly understood, is not an authority in support of the appellant's contention, and their Lordships do not intend to vary or depart from the reasons expressed for their judgment in that case. The principle which that case and the case of the *Citizens Insurance Company* illustrate is, that subjects which in one aspect and for one purpose fall within sect. 92, may in another aspect and for another purpose fall within sect. 91....

Their Lordships consider that the powers intended to be conferred by the Act in question, when properly understood, are to make regulations in the nature of police or municipal regulations of a merely local character for the good government of taverns, &c., licensed for the sale of liquors by retail, and such as are calculated to preserve, in the municipality, peace and public decency, and repress drunkenness and disorderly and riotous conduct. As such they cannot be said to interfere with the general regulation of trade and commerce which belongs to the Dominion parliament, and do not conflict with the provisions of the *Canada Temperance Act,* which does not appear to have as yet been locally adopted.

BANK OF TORONTO v. LAMBE*

The Quebec Act imposed taxes on commercial industries carrying on business in that province. The Act was challenged by a number of banks and insurance companies on the grounds that it invaded federal jurisdiction over 92(2) "The Regulation of Trade and Commerce"; (3) "The Raising of Money by any Mode of Taxation" and (15) "Banking, Incorporation of Banks and the Issue of Paper Money." The challenge was upheld by the Supreme Court of Quebec; that decision was overruled by the Court of Queen's Bench.

LORD HOBHOUSE:

It has been earnestly contended that the taxation of banks would unduly cut down the powers of the parliament in relation to matters falling within class 2, viz. the regulation of trade and commerce; and within class 15, viz., banking, and the incorporation of banks. Their Lordships think that this contention gives far too wide an extent to the classes in question. They cannot see how the power of making

---

*[1887] 12 A.C. 575.

banks contribute to the public objects of the provinces where they carry on business can interfere at all with the power of making laws on the subject of banking, or with the power of incorporating banks. The words "regulation of trade and commerce" are indeed very wide, and in *Severn's Case* it was the view of the Supreme Court that they operated to invalidate the licence duty which was there in question. But since that case was decided the question has been more completely sifted before the Committee in *Parsons' Case*, and it was found absolutely necessary that the literal meaning of the words should be restricted, in order to afford scope for powers which are given exclusively to the provincial legislatures. It was there thrown out that the power of regulation given to the parliament meant some general or interprovincial regulations. No further attempt to define the subject need now be made, because their Lordships are clear that if they were to hold that this power of regulation prohibited any provincial taxation on the persons or things regulated, so far from restricting the expressions, as was found necessary in *Parsons' Case*, they would be straining them to their widest conceivable extent.

Then it is suggested that the legislature may lay on taxes so heavy as to crush a bank out of existence, and so to nullify the power of parliament to erect banks. But their Lordships cannot conceive that when the Imperial parliament conferred wide powers of local self-government on great countries such as Quebec, it intended to limit them on the speculation that they would be used in an injurious manner. People who are trusted with the great power of making laws for property and civil rights may well be trusted to levy taxes. There are obvious reasons for confining their power to direct taxes and licences, because the power of indirect taxation would be felt all over the Dominion. But whatever power falls within the legitimate meaning of classes 2 and 9, is, in their Lordships' judgment, what the Imperial parliament intended to give; and to place a limit on it because the power may be used unwisely, as all powers may, would be an error, and would lead to insuperable difficulties, in the construction of the Federation Act.

Their Lordships have been invited to take a very wide range on this part of the case, and to apply to the construction of the Federation Act the principles laid down for the United States by Chief Justice Marshall. Every one would gladly accept the guidance of that great judge in a parallel case. But he was dealing with the constitution of the United States. Under that constitution, as their Lordships understand, each state may make laws for itself, uncontrolled by the federal power, and subject only to the limits placed by law on the range of subjects within its jurisdiction. In such a constitution Chief Justice Marshall found one of those limits at the point at which the action of the state legislature came into conflict with the power vested in Congress. The appellant invokes that principle to support the conclusion that the Federation Act must be so construed as to allow no power to the provincial legislatures under sect. 92, which may by possibility, and if exercised in some extravagant way, interfere with the objects of the Dominion in exercising their powers under sect. 91. It is quite impossible to argue from the one case to the other. Their Lordships have to construe the express words of an Act of Parliament which makes an elaborate distribution of the whole field of legislative authority between two legislative bodies, and at the same time provides for the federated provinces a carefully balanced constitution, under which no one of the parts can pass laws for itself except under the control of the whole acting through the

Governor General. And the question they have to answer is whether the one body or the other has power to make a given law. If they find that on the due construction of the Act a legislative power falls within sect. 92, it would be quite wrong of them to deny its existence because by some possibility it may be abused, or may limit the range which otherwise would be open to the Dominion parliament.

o

THE LIQUIDATORS OF THE MARITIME BANK OF CANADA v. THE RECEIVER GENERAL OF NEW BRUNSWICK✧

The rights and privileges of the Crown's Prerogative demand that debts owing to it take precedence over simple contract debts. Thirty-five thousand dollars of the public money of the province of New Brunswick was deposited in the Maritime Bank of Canada. When that bank went into receivership, the province demanded priority payment over other creditors of the bank. Its claim relied on the prerogative of the Crown as vested in the Lieutenant-Governor. The liquidators of the bank claimed that only the Governor General possessed the prerogative rights of the Crown in Canada.

LORD WATSON:

The appellants...conceded that, until the passing of the *British North America Act, 1867,* there was precisely the same relation between the Crown and the province which now subsists between the Crown and the Dominion. But they maintained that the effect of the statute has been to sever all connection between the Crown and the provinces; to make the government of the Dominion the only government of Her Majesty in North America; and to reduce the provinces to the rank of independent municipal institutions. For these propositions, which contained the sum and substance of the arguments addressed to them in support of this appeal, their Lordships have been unable to find either principle or authority.

Their Lordships do not think it necessary to examine, in minute detail, the provisions of the Act of 1867, which nowhere profess to curtail in any respect the rights and privileges of the Crown, or to disturb the relations then subsisting between the Sovereign and the provinces. The object of the Act was neither to weld the provinces into one, nor to subordinate provincial governments to a central authority, but to create a federal government in which they should all be represented, entrusted with the exclusive administration of affairs in which they had a common interest, each province retaining its independence and autonomy. That object was accomplished by distributing, between the Dominion and the provinces, all powers executive and legislative, and all public property and revenues which had previously belonged to the provinces; so that the Dominion government should be vested with such of these powers, property, and revenues as were necessary for the due performance of its constitutional functions, and that the remainder should be retained by the provinces for the purposes of provincial government. But, in so far

---

✧[1892] A.C. 437.

as regards those matters which, by sect. 92, are specially reserved for provincial legislation, the legislation of each province continues to be free from the control of the Dominion, and as supreme as it was before the passing of the Act....

It is clear, therefore, that the provincial legislature of New Brunswick does not occupy the subordinate position which was ascribed to it in the argument of the appellants. It derives no authority from the Government of Canada, and its status is in no way analogous to that of a municipal institution, which is an authority constituted for purposes of local administration. It possesses powers, not of administration merely, but of legislation, in the strictest sense of that word; and, within the limits assigned by sect. 92 of the Act of 1867, these powers are exclusive and supreme. It would require very express language, such as is not to be found in the Act of 1867, to warrant the inference that the Imperial Legislature meant to vest in the provinces of Canada the right of exercising supreme legislative powers in which the British Sovereign was to have no share.

In asking their Lordship to draw that inference from the terms of the statute, the appellants mainly, if not wholly, relied upon the fact that, whereas the Governor General of Canada is directly appointed by the Queen, the Lieutenant-Governor of a province is appointed, not by Her Majesty, but by the Governor General, who has also the power of dismissal. If the Act had not committed to the Governor General the power of appointing and removing Lieutenant-Governors, there would have been no room for the argument, which, if pushed to its logical conclusion, would prove that the Governor General, and not the Queen, whose Viceroy he is, became the sovereign authority of the province whenever the Act of 1867 came into operation. But the argument ignores the fact that, by sect. 58, the appointment of a provincial governor is made by the "Governor General in Council by Instrument under the Great Seal of Canada," or, in other words, by the Executive Government of the Dominion, which is, by sect. 9, expressly declared "to continue and be vested in the Queen." There is no constitutional anomaly in an executive officer of the Crown receiving his appointment at the hands of a governing body who have no powers and no functions except as representatives of the Crown. The act of the Governor General and his Council in making the appointment is, within the meaning of the statute, the act of the Crown; and a Lieutenant-Governor, when appointed, is as much the representative of Her Majesty for all purposes of provincial government as the Governor General himself is for all purposes of Dominion government.

○

TENNANT v. UNION BANK OF CANADA◇

The Canadian *Bank Act* made receipts for undelivered goods valid in the hands of a third party for the receiving of goods. In a receivership dispute, the question arose as to whether the classification of receipts in the Act infringed on provincial jurisdiction over 91(13) "Property and Civil Rights in the Province."

◇[1894] A.C. 31.

LORD WATSON:

The appellant's plea against the legislative power of the Dominion parliament was accordingly made the subject of further argument; and, the point being one of general importance, their Lordships had the advantage of being assisted, in the hearing and consideration of it, by the Lord Chancellor and Lord Macnaghten. The question turns upon the construction of two clauses in the *British North America Act, 1867.* Sect. 91 gives the Parliament of Canada power to make laws in relation to all matters not coming within the classes of subjects by the Act exclusively assigned to the legislatures of the provinces, and also exclusive legislative authority in relation to certain enumerated subjects, the fifteenth of which is "Banking, Incorporation of Banks, and the Issue of Paper Money." Sect. 92 assigns to each provincial legislature the exclusive right to make laws in relation to the classes of subjects therein enumerated; and the thirteenth of the enumerated classes is "Property and Civil Rights in the Province."

Statutory regulations with respect to the form and legal effect, in Ontario, of warehouse receipts and other negotiable documents, which pass the property of goods without delivery, unquestionably relate to property and civil rights in that province; and the objection taken by the appellant to the provisions of the *Bank Act* would be unanswerable if it could be shown that, by the Act of 1867, the Parliament of Canada is absolutely debarred from trenching to any extent upon the matters assigned to the provincial legislature by sect. 92. But sect. 91 expressly declares that, "notwithstanding anything in this Act," the exclusive legislative authority of the Parliament of Canada shall extend to all matters coming within the enumerated classes; which plainly indicates that the legislation of that Parliament, so long as it strictly relates to these matters, is to be of paramount authority. To refuse effect to the declaration would render nugatory some of the legislative powers specially assigned to the Canadian Parliament. For example, among the enumerated classes of subjects in sect. 91, are "Patents of Invention and Discovery," and "Copyrights." It would be practically impossible for the Dominion parliament to legislate upon either of these subjects without affecting the property and civil rights of individuals in the provinces.

o

RE PROVINCIAL JURISDICTION TO PASS PROHIBITORY LIQUOR LAWS◆

The Supreme Court of Canada was asked to rule on the power of Ontario to pass prohibition legislation. The Court unanimously held that the matter was one of "Trade and Commerce" and thus within federal jurisdiction.

Justice Gwynne began his lengthy judgment by examining at length the statements made in the debates on Confederation at Quebec and in London and stated that "when a question should arise which should create any doubt" about where jurisdiction lay, "the doubt must be solved by endeavouring to ascertain the intention of the framers of the scheme and the parties to such treaty."

◆[1894] 24 S.C.R. 170.

GWYNNE J.:

It is true that their Lordships of the Privy Council in the *Citizens Insurance Company v. Parsons* upon a very different subject from that of prohibition of the exercise of the trade in intoxicating liquors threw out merely the suggestion that possibly the expression "the regulation of trade and commerce" in item No. 2 of sec. 91 may have been used in some such sense as the words "regulations of trade" in the Act of Union between England and Scotland, and as those words in the Acts of state relating to trade and commerce, but in construing expressions used in the *British North America Act, 1867*, we must never, as I have already observed, lose sight of the fact that those expressions are but the embodiment of the terms and provisions of the treaty prepared by the provincial statesmen assembled at Quebec by authority of Her Majesty the Queen, and concurred in by Her Majesty's Imperial Government, for the purpose of federally uniting the British North American provisions into one government, and we must always keep prominently present to our minds that the object of the framers of our constitution in framing its terms and provisions was, as abundantly appears from the above extracted passages from their speeches, to adopt the best features of the constitution of the United States of America, the only federal constitution with which they were familiar, and to which they would naturally look for light as to what they should adopt and what alter or reject, when engaged in the task of distributing the legislative powers between the Dominion parliament and the legislatures of the confederated provinces. Contemplating, as they were, the engrafting of what they considered the best features of the constitution of the United States of America upon the British constitution, for the purpose of framing a federal constitution for the union of the British North American provinces into a confederacy under one central government, it is, to my mind, with great deference I say it, altogether inconceivable that the framers of our constitution should have had present to their minds the Act of Anne, or any Act of state of the Imperial Government; neither the one nor the other of these could be expected to throw any light upon the subject in which they were engaged, namely, the distribution of legislative powers between the central or Dominion parliament and the legislatures of the provinces of the proposed confederacy, while, on the contrary, it was quite natural and to be expected that they should have had constantly present to their minds the constitution of the United States of America, the best features of which they desired to adopt, and to alter or reject those which did not seem to them to be desirable to be adopted. We must therefore, I submit, be excused if we confidently affirm that in making provision for the distribution of legislative powers between the Dominion parliament and the legislatures of the confederated provinces, and in such distribution making provision that the Dominion parliament should have exclusive jurisdiction in all matters coming within "the regulation of trade and commerce" in item No. 2 of sec. 91, neither was the Act of Union between England and Scotland, nor any Act of state of the Imperial Government relating to trade and commerce, ever present to the minds of the framers of our constitution, but that what in fact was so present was the constitution of the United States of America . . . and that what they intended by the particular expression under consideration was to place "fully and unrestrictedly" (to use the language of the late Mr. George Brown above extracted), unlimited and exclusive jurisdiction in the Dominion parliament over all matters of trade and commerce in every part of the Dominion, and that what they had in view in so doing was to strengthen the central parliament and to effect thereby an improvement in the constitution of the proposed confederacy over that of the United States of America, the central legislature of which has jurisdiction only over interstate trade and commerce and that with foreign countries. If the framers of our constitution had contemplated conferring upon the Dominion parliament only such a limited jurisdiction as that possessed by the Congress of the United States they would have had no difficulty, and doubtless would not have failed, in so expressing themselves; on the contrary the language they have used is of a most unlimited character and exhibits no intention of having such a limited construction. No argument in favour of such a limited construction can, I submit, be fairly drawn from the fact that jurisdiction is independently given by items 15, 18 and 19 of section 91, over banking, bills of exchange, interest and the like, which may be said to be matters coming within the classes of subjects coming under the terms "trade and commerce" for this repetition of powers involved in the enumeration of items appears to have been inserted for greater certainty, and there is, I think, an intention sufficiently manifested on the face of the Act, that the enumeration of particulars should not be construed so as to limit and restrict the operation and construction of general terms in which the particulars may be included.

SEDGEWICK J.:

Another principle of construction in regard to the *British North America Act* must be stated, viz., it being in effect a constitutional agreement or compact, or treaty, between three independent communities or commonwealths, each with its own parliamentary institutions and governments, effect must, as far as possible, be given to the intention of these communities, when entering into the compact to the words used as they understood them, and to the objects they had in view when they asked the Imperial Parliament to pass the Act. In other words, it must be viewed from a Canadian standpoint. Although an Imperial Act, to interpret it correctly reference may be had to the phraseology and nomenclature of pre-confederation Canadian legislation and jurisprudence, as well as to the history of the union movement and to the condition, sentiment and surroundings of the Canadian people at the time. In the *British North America Act* it was in a technical sense only that the Imperial Parliament spoke; it was there that in a real and substantial sense the Canadian people spoke, and it is to their language, as they understood it, that effect must be given....

Sedgewick then embarked on a lengthy analysis of the revised statutes of Canada of 1864 to determine what in effect came under "trade and commerce" in the fourth section of the consolidated statutes.

Now, we have here, I think, a clear indication of what at the time of confederation the Canadian people and legislatures understood to be included within the words "trade and commerce." They included, unquestionably, the carrying on of particular trades or businesses, and I think commercial law generally. The actual legislation under "trade and commerce" in regard to certain staple articles of commerce, such as bread, fish, coals, &c., indicates that any other legislation in the same line respecting any other article of commerce would come under the same description, so I take it that the regulation of the liquor traffic, whether by licensing it or prohibiting it altogether, has to do with "trade and commerce."

Such being the state of the existing legislation and the view that the different legislatures had of the all-inclusiveness of the phrases "trade and commerce" and "regulation of trade," what better collocation of words could be used for the purpose of making it clear that Parliament was to have exclusive jurisdiction in all matters relating to trade and relating to commerce, including the importation, manufacture and sale of all kinds of commodities, than that combination of the two phrases, the one from the sea board, the other from the inland provinces, to be found in sec. 91 "the regulation of trade and commerce"? And the words having that meaning, having been placed there for that object, are we not bound to give them the intended effect?

I am not attempting to even criticize the correctness of the conclusion to which their Lordships of the Privy Council came in *Citizens Ins. Co. v. Parsons.* I may be permitted, however, with all deference, to suggest that some of the considerations to which I have referred were not presented to their Lordships when the effect of the words under review was being discussed. All I suggest is that, inasmuch as the *British North America Act* was an Act materially affecting, modifying, repealing, pre-existing Canadian statute law, and revolutionizing the constitution of the component provinces, in interpreting that Act reference may and must be had to provincial statute law, rather than to imperial statute law, and that where, as in the present case, the constitutional Act uses a phrase which for years had had a well defined meaning in Canadian legislation, that is the meaning which should be given to it when used in that Act.

○

A.-G. ONTARIO v. A.-G. CANADA (LOCAL PROHIBITION)◇

The Supreme Court's decision was appealed to the Judicial Committee.

LORD WATSON:

In order to determine that issue, it becomes necessary to consider, in the first place, whether the Parliament of Canada had jurisdiction to enact the *Canada Temperance Act*; and, if so, to consider in the second place, whether, after that Act became the law of each province of the Dominion, there yet remained power with the Legislature of Ontario to enact the provisions of s. 18.

The authority of the Dominion parliament to make laws for the suppression of liquor traffic in the province is maintained, in the first place, upon the ground that such legislation deals with matters affecting "the peace, order, and good government of Canada," within the meaning of the introductory and general enactments of s. 91 of the *British North America Act*; and, in the second place, upon the ground that it concerns "the regulation of trade and commerce," being No. 2 of the

---

◇ [1896]A.C. 34.

enumerated classes of subjects which are placed under the exclusive jurisdiction of the Federal Parliament by that section. These sources of jurisdiction are in themselves distinct, and are to be found in different enactments.

It was apparently contemplated by the framers of the Imperial Act of 1867 that the due exercise of the enumerated powers conferred upon the Parliament of Canada by s. 91 might, occasionally and incidentally, involve legislation upon matters which are *prima facie* committed exclusively to the provincial legislatures by s. 92. In order to provide against that contingency, the concluding part of s. 91 enacts that "any matter coming within any of the classes of subjects enumerated in this section shall not be deemed to come within the class of matters of a local or private nature comprised in the enumeration of the classes of subjects by this Act assigned exclusively to the legislatures of the provinces." It was observed by this Board in *Citizens Insurance Co. of Canada v. Parsons* that the paragraph just quoted "applies in its grammatical construction only to No. 16 of s. 92." The observation was not material to the question arising in that case, and it does not appear to their Lordships to be strictly accurate. It appears to them that the language of the exception in s. 91 was meant to include and correctly describes all the matters enumerated in the sixteen heads of s. 92, as being, from a provincial point of view, of a local or private nature. It also appears to their Lordships that the exception was not meant to derogate from the legislative authority given to provincial legislatures by those sixteen sub-sections, save to the extent of enabling the Parliament of Canada to deal with matters local or private in those cases where such legislation is necessarily incidental to the exercise of the powers conferred upon it by the enumerative heads of clause 91. That view was stated and illustrated by Sir Montague Smith in *Citizens Insurance Co. of Canada v. Parsons* and in *Cushing v. Dupuy*, and it has been recognized by this Board in *Tennant v. Union Bank of Canada* and in *Attorney-General of Ontario v. Attorney-General for the Dominion.*

The general authority given to the Canadian parliament by the introductory enactments of s. 91 is "to make laws for the peace, order, and good government of Canada, in relation to all matters not coming within the classes of subjects by this Act assigned exclusively to the legislatures of the provinces"; and it is declared, but not so as to restrict the generality of these words, that the exclusive authority of the Canadian parliament extends to all matters coming within the classes of subjects which are enumerated in the clause. There may, therefore, be matters not included in the enumeration, upon which the Parliament of Canada has power to legislate, because they concern the peace, order, and good government of the Dominion. But to those matters which are not specified among the enumerated subjects of legislation, the exception from s. 92, which is enacted by the concluding words of s. 91, has no application; and, in legislating with regard to such matters, the Dominion parliament has no authority to encroach upon any class of subjects which is exclusively assigned to provincial legislatures by s. 92. These enactments appear to their Lordships to indicate that the exercise of legislative power by the Parliament of Canada, in regard to all matters not enumerated in s. 91, ought to be strictly confined to such matters as are unquestionably of Canadian interest and importance and ought not to trench upon provincial legislation with respect to any of the classes of subjects enumerated in s. 92. To attach any other construction to the general power which, in supplement of its enumerated powers, is conferred upon the

Parliament of Canada by s. 91, would, in their Lordships' opinion, not only be contrary to the intendment of the Act, but would practically destroy the autonomy of the provinces. If it were once conceded that the Parliament of Canada has authority to make laws applicable to the whole Dominion, in relation to matters which in each province are substantially of local or private interest, upon the assumption that these matters also concern the peace, order, and good government of the Dominion, there is hardly a subject enumerated in s. 92 upon which it might not legislate, to the exclusion of the provincial legislatures.

In construing the introductory enactments of s. 91, with respect to matters other than those enumerated, which concern the peace, order, and good government of Canada, it must be kept in view that s. 94, which empowers the Parliament of Canada to make provision for the uniformity of the laws relative to property and civil rights in Ontario, Nova Scotia, and New Brunswick does not extend to the province of Quebec; and also that the Dominion legislation thereby authorized is expressly declared to be of no effect unless and until it has been adopted and enacted by the provincial legislature. These enactments would be idle and abortive, if it were held that the Parliament of Canada derives jurisdiction from the introductory provisions of s. 91, to deal with any matter which is in substance local or provincial, and does not truly affect the interest of the Dominion as a whole. Their Lordships do not doubt that some matters, in their origin local and provincial, might attain such dimensions as to affect the body politic of the Dominion, and to justify the Canadian Parliament in passing laws for their regulation or abolition in the interest of the Dominion. But great caution must be observed in distinguishing between that which is local and provincial, and therefore within the jurisdiction of the provincial legislatures, and that which has ceased to be merely local or provincial, and has become matter of national concern, in such sense as to bring it within the jurisdiction of the Parliament of Canada. An Act restricting the right to carry weapons of offence, or their sale to young persons, within the province would be within the authority of the provincial legislature. But traffic in arms, or the possession of them under such circumstances as to raise a suspicion that they were to be used for seditious purposes, or against a foreign State, are matters which, their Lordships conceive, might be competently dealt with by the Parliament of the Dominion.

o

CITY OF MONTREAL v. MONTREAL STREET RAILWAY◇

The Canadian Board of Railway Commissioners ordered the Montreal Street Railway, which had shared a track with a federally controlled railway, to charge fees in accordance with a federal schedule. The Montreal Street Railway challenged the Board's jurisdiction to make such an order.

◇[1912] A.C. 333.

LORD ATKINSON:

It has accordingly been strongly urged on behalf of the respondents that if it be desirable in the interest of the Dominion to place the through traffic on a provincial line, such as the Street Railway, under the control of the Railway Commissioners, owing to its nature, character, or amount, the proper course for the Dominion parliament to take, and the only course it can legitimately take, is by statutory declaration to convert the provincial line into a federal line, thus removing it from the class of subjects placed under the control of the Legislature of the province, and placing it amongst the classes of subjects over which it has itself exclusive jurisdiction and control. And further, that there is nothing in the *British North America Act* to shew that such an invasion of the rights of the provincial legislature, as is necessarily involved in the establishment of this embarrassing dual control over their own provincial railways, was ever contemplated by the framers of the *British North America Act*. It has, no doubt, been many times decided by this Board that the two sections 91 and 92 are not mutually exclusive, that the provisions may overlap, and that where the legislation of the Dominion parliament comes into conflict with that of a provincial Legislature over a field of jurisdiction common to both the former must prevail; but, on the other hand, it was laid down in *Attorney-General of Ontario v. Attorney-General of the Dominion* (1) that the exception contained in s. 91, near its end, was not meant to derogate from the legislative authority given to provincial legislatures by the 16th sub-section of s. 92, save to the extent of enabling the Parliament of Canada to deal with matters, local or private, in those cases where such legislation is necessarily incidental to the exercise of the power conferred upon that Parliament under the heads enumerated in s. 91; (2) that to those matters which are not specified amongst the enumerated subjects of legislation in s. 91 the exception at its end has no application, and that in legislating with respect to matters not so enumerated the Dominion parliament has no authority to encroach upon any class of subjects which is exclusively assigned to the provincial legislature by s. 92; (3) that these enactments, ss. 91 and 92, indicate that the exercise of legislative power by the Parliament of Canada in regard to all matters not enumerated in s. 91 ought to be strictly confined to such matters as are unquestionably of Canadian interest and importance, and ought not to trench upon provincial legislation with respect to any classes of subjects enumerated in s. 92; (4) that to attach any other construction to the general powers which, in supplement of its enumerated powers, are conferred upon the Parliament of Canada by s. 91 would not only be contrary to the intendment of the Act, but would practically destroy the autonomy of the provinces; and, lastly, that if the Parliament of Canada had authority to make laws applicable to the whole Dominion in relation to matters which in each province are substantially of local or private interest, upon the assumption that these matters also concern the peace, order, and good government of the Dominion, there is hardly a subject upon which it might not legislate to the exclusion of provincial legislation. The same considerations appear to their Lordships to apply to two of the matters enumerated in s. 91, namely, the regulation of trade and commerce. Taken in their widest sense these words would authorize legislation by the Parliament of Canada in respect of several of the matters specifically enumerated in s. 92, and would seriously encroach upon the local autonomy of the province. In their Lordships' opinion these pronouncements have an important bearing on the question for decision in the present case, though the case itself in which they were made was wholly different from the present case, and the decision given in it has little if any application to the present case. They apparently established this, that the invasion of the rights of the province which the *Railway Act* and the Order of the Commissioners necessarily involve in respect of one of the matters enumerated in s. 92, namely, legislation touching local railways, cannot be justified on the ground that this Act and Order concern the peace, order, and good government of Canada nor upon the ground that they deal with the regulation of trade and commerce.

o

LORD WATSON[*]

R . B . H A L D A N E

o

... He was an Imperial judge of the very first order. The function of such a judge, sitting in the supreme tribunal of the Empire, is to do more than decide what abstract and familiar legal conceptions should be applied to particular cases. His function is to be a statesman as well as a jurist, to fill in the gaps which Parliament has deliberately left in the skeleton constitutions and laws that it has provided for the British Colonies. The Imperial legislature has taken the view that these constitutions and laws must, if they are to be acceptable, be in a large measure unwritten, elastic, and capable of being silently developed and even altered as the Colony develops and alters. This imposes a task of immense importance and difficulty upon the Privy Council judges, and it was this task which Lord Watson had to face when some fifteen years ago he found himself face to face with what threatened to be a critical period in the history of Canada. Lord Carnarvon's Confederation Act of 1867, which had given separate legislatures and executives to the Provinces, had by no means completely defined the relations of these legislatures and their Lieutenant-Governors to the Parliament and Governor General of the Dominion. Two views were being contended for. The one was that, excepting in such cases as were specially provided for, a general principle ought to be recognised which would tend to make the Government at Ottawa paramount, and the Governments of the Provinces subordinate. The other was that of federalism through and through, in executive as well as legislative concerns, whenever the contrary had not been expressly said by the Imperial Parliament. The Provincial Governments naturally pressed this latter view very strongly. The Supreme Court of Canada, however, which had been established under the Confederation Act, and was originally intended by all parties to be the practically final court of appeal for Canada, took the other view. Great unrest was the result, followed by a series of appeals to the Privy Council, which it was discovered still had power to give special leave for them,

[*] *The Juridical Review* 11 (1899): 278–81.

was commenced. I happened to be engaged in a number of these cases, and had to give such assistance as I could to the various Prime Ministers of the Provinces who came over to argue in person. Lord Watson made the business of laying down the new law that was necessary his own. He completely altered the tendency of the decisions of the Supreme Court, and established in the first place the sovereignty (subject to the power to interfere of the Imperial Parliament alone) of the legislatures of Ontario, Quebec and the other Provinces. He then worked out as a principle the direct relation, in point of exercise of the prerogative, of the Lieutenant-Governors to the Crown. In a series of masterly judgments he expounded and established the real constitution of Canada. The liquor laws, the Indian reserve lands, the title to regalia, including the precious metals, were brought before a Judicial Committee, in which he took the leading part, for consideration as to which of the rival claims to legislate ought to prevail. Nowhere is his memory likely to be more gratefully preserved than in those distant Canadian Provinces whose rights of self-government he placed on a basis that was both intelligible and firm....

... He was a great servant of the Empire. He did much to make stronger one of the real links which binds and unites its parts. Not many of those who talk glibly about Imperial Federation take the trouble to turn into the shabby doorway at the Whitehall end of Downing Street, and go up the worn, lead covered stair, through the faded red curtains into the plainly furnished room where the Supreme Tribunal of the Empire sits. Had they gone there any time during the last fifteen years, they would have beheld at his best one of the greatest lawyers that ever sat upon the British Bench, devoting his splendid powers to the spread throughout that Empire of faith in the justice of the Queen.

LORD WATSON, INSTITUTIONAL SELF-INTEREST, AND THE DECENTRALISATION OF CANADIAN FEDERALISM IN THE 1890s[*]

F. MURRAY GREENWOOD

>

In 1922, Viscount Haldane wrote that his late friend and predecessor on the Judicial Committee of the Privy Council, Lord Watson, had "put clothing upon the bones of the Constitution, and so covered them over with living flesh that the Constitution of Canada took a new form."[1] Indeed he had, by undermining the two essential propositions of Macdonald centralism: (1) that virtually all subjects of importance in the life of the country would fall under the Dominion's legislative power, and (2) that even acting within their limited jurisdiction the provinces, like colonies or municipalities, would be subject to the control of the federal government. Lord Watson achieved this result in two celebrated cases which were to affect profoundly the direction of Canadian federalism. In *The Liquidators of the Maritime Bank of Canada v. The Receiver-General of New Brunswick,* decided in 1892, Lord Watson delivered the Board's judgment that the Lieutenant-Governors were direct representatives of the Queen, asserted that Confederation had been created by a provincial compact, and declared that when acting within their jurisdiction the provinces were entitled to the fullest autonomy.[2] Four years later, in the *Local Prohibition* case,[3] Lord Watson in effect reversed the Board's earlier decision in *Russell v. The Queen*[4] and placed the Dominion's residual power in a position of subordination to provincial legislative jurisdiction. Section 91, he held, was divisible into two parts, each with a different potential to affect provincial matters. Acting under the enumerated heads, Parliament could encroach on provincial jurisdiction. Acting under the opening "Peace, Order, and good Government" clause it could not, except in extraordinary circumstances where the problem had attained "such

---

dimensions as to affect the body politic of the Dominion." This article offers an historical analysis of these two important decisions in the hope of shedding light on the longstanding controversy which continues concerning Lord Watson's motives for decentralising the constitution.[5] The author takes strong issue with the positivist thesis of G.P. Browne that the "federal principle" was not "imposed on the B.N.A. Act [by Lord Watson] but derived from it," and his further assertion that judges, like Themis, dispense justice free from extraneous ideological or political considerations.[6] According to Browne, Canadian constitutional law cannot be interpreted in the light of either "policy or history." The *Liquidators* and *Local Prohibition* cases, I contend, cannot be explained without recourse to both.

These cases marked the successful end of a long legal and political struggle for provincial rights waged by Ontario Liberals under the leadership of Premier Oliver Mowat.[7] Mowat's prime political aim was to embarrass the provincial Conservatives by attacking Tory centralism as a sell-out of Ontario. His constitutional objective was to substitute for Macdonald's system of subordination what came to be known as co-ordinate federalism, that is, a rough equality in legislative jurisdiction between Parliament and the provinces, and the right of the provinces to exercise their powers free from Dominion interference. During the 1880s and early 1890s, Mowat was strongly supported by such influential federal Liberals as party leader Edward Blake, his successor Wilfrid Laurier and the party's constitutional expert, David Mills. The Mowat version of the constitution was also seconded by the Liberal Premiers of Nova Scotia and New Brunswick, W.S. Fielding and A.G. Blair, the non-partisan Norquay government of Manitoba, its successor, the Greenway Liberal administration, and the Parti National Premier of Quebec, Honoré Mercier. The variety of particular interests which these politicians hoped to advance by using the provincial rights cry was almost endless and included increased federal subsidies for Nova Scotia, New Brunswick and Quebec, victory for Ontario in the dispute with Ottawa and Manitoba over the territory west of Fort William, increased powers for Quebec to protect French Canadian cultural particularity, an autonomous railway policy for Manitoba designed to break the C.P.R. monopoly, and additional sources of patronage.

Provincialists advanced these and other claims as necessary implications of a compact theory of Confederation according to which the B.N.A. Act was but an imperial ratification of an agreement worked out by the colonies, which had continued to exist as provinces after Confederation. As the provinces had been the creators of the federal system, it could not be presumed that they had voluntarily abandoned any powers or rights unless the text of the Act was perfectly unambiguous on the point. As David Mills put it in a speech to the House of Commons in 1875, Confederation was a union of "several independent and distinct sovereignties for certain definite purposes which have divested themselves of the original power of which they were possessed just in so far as these powers have been conferred upon a single or national Legislature."[8] From the compact theory provincialists deduced any number of specific conclusions: the unconstitutionality of federal disallowance, unless the provincial legislation was *ultra vires* or clearly detrimental to Canadians living outside the province in question; the obligation of the Lieutenant-Governor to exercise his executive discretion without consulting Ottawa; and the need for unanimous provincial consent to amendments. In the area of legislative competence provincialists, using the compact theory, often argued that in case of doubt, particularly where the problem had not been foreseen at Confederation, the matter should fall under provincial jurisdiction over "Property and Civil Rights" or "Matters of a merely local or private Nature" rather than "Peace, Order, and good Government." In other words, the provinces, like the American states, were vested with a residual "police" power which took precedence over federal jurisdiction.[9]

Provincialists were particularly insistent on one point: the Lieutenant-Governors were the equals, not the subordinates of the Governor General. They too represented the Queen and were therefore entitled to exercise Her Majesty's prerogative powers. Mowat was convinced that if such a royal and autonomous status were once accorded the executive heads of the provinces, all other provincial claims would naturally follow. Until the *Liquidators* case, however, he had little success in gaining his point with the Colonial Office, the Ministry of Justice, or the courts. Canadian judges tended to adopt one of two positions on the question.[10] One approach, based on sections of the B.N.A. Act suggesting that the Governor General, rather than the Queen, was the ultimate source of executive authority in the provinces, was simply to deny that the Lieutenant-Governors were the Queen's representatives. Royal prerogatives were therefore vested solely in the Governor General.[11] The second trend was to grant specific prerogative powers to the Lieutenant-Governors, either on the ground that they had at least a partial status as Her Majesty's representatives (as suggested by other sections in the Act, for example, sections 64 and 82), or as a general implication from the Act that executive authority was intended to parallel legislative jurisdiction.[12] Lord Watson, of course, swept away all such qualifications and held that as the Lieutenant Governors were appointed by the Governor General-in-Council and as the Governor General himself represented the Queen (sections 9, 10 and 58), the appointment was "the act of the Crown; and a Lieutenant-Governor, when appointed, is as much the representative of Her Majesty for all purposes of provincial government as the Governor General himself is for all purposes of Dominion Government."[13]

The Mowat–Watson conception of the B.N.A. Act was of course diametrically opposed to the centralist theory prevalent in Conservative circles and a segment of the legal profession. Confederation, centralists argued, could not be a compact; it was of necessity the work of the sovereign Imperial Parliament which had established new and insignificant bodies called provinces whose powers, like those of municipalities created by statute, should be restrictively interpreted.[14] It followed that the disallowance power was unrestricted and the Lieutenant-Governors were mere federal officials, politically responsible to the Dominion cabinet, and in no sense representatives of the Queen. It was also assumed that legislation of any importance on a topic which had not been foreseen by the Fathers, fell within the federal residual power.[15] More technically, centralists, applying the *Russell* case, contended that if federal legislation was not directly and primarily in relation to one of the matters in section 92, it was valid under "Peace, Order, and good Government." Under the conception, no question of encroachment or interference could logically arise and of course no division of section 91. While the centralist viewpoint on these and other matters tended to prevail in the Canadian courts, particularly in the Supreme Court, down to the end of the 1880s, it was rapidly ceasing to represent what might be called dominant Canadian political opinion on the nature of the federation.[16] Was it mere coincidence, as Browne would have us believe, that Lord Watson's major decentralising pronouncements were handed down at a time when the proponents of co-ordinate federalism had virtually won their case in the political arena?

THE BROWNE THESIS

Browne's positivist thesis does not deal directly with the *Liquidators* case, except in so far as he makes the general assertion that the federal principle derived from the Act and was not imposed on it. His aim is to justify Lord Watson's analysis of section 91 on the basis of what he calls a "three-compartment" view of legislative jurisdiction.[17] There is, Browne claims, a hierarchy of power in case of conflict, namely the enumerated heads of section 91, the enumerated heads of section 92, and lastly the "Peace, Order, and good Government" power. He supports this conception on the basis of Lord Watson's interpretation of the deeming clause, or preferably, on the basis of the *non obstante* clause ("notwithstanding anything in the Act") which introduces the enumeration in section 91. It is not my purpose to weigh the merits of the Watson–Browne view as opposed to that of O'Connor,[18] nor to judge the validity of Lord Watson's conception of the office of the Lieutenant-Governor. It is sufficient for my purposes that in each case alternative interpretations had been accepted by recognized jurists. The possibility of extra-legal influence cannot be eliminated simply by pointing out that there was some textual basis on which Lord Watson could rely to support his decisions. In order to rule out extra-legal factors it would be necessary to go further and demonstrate the law was so clear that any other interpretation was virtually out of the question.

The only other "proof" Browne advances to support his thesis is a recounting of instances in which members of the Judicial Committee and other British judges of the day described their procedure in positivist terms which emphasised adherence to precedent and the rules of statutory interpretation, and rigorous disregard of policy considerations. That all members of the Judicial Committee sitting on the two cases which interest us took this as their judicial philosophy may be conceded. But this fact, at most, only rules out two extra-legal possibilities; namely, that individual judges *purposely distorted what they took to be the law* in the interests of some policy consideration, or that the Board members, unclear as to the best legal interpretation, *openly agreed among themselves* to allow policy considerations to govern. But other possibilities remain. Individual judges, believing a number of legal interpretations to have been of equal merit, may have opted covertly for one of them on policy grounds. Equally possible, the members of the Board may have been unconsciously predisposed by policy or "value" considerations to accept a given interpretation as correct in law. There is a wealth of literature on the subject indicating that however positive the theory held by the participants, judicial decisions are often influenced by such considerations whenever the law is somewhat obscure, and politically or ideologically controversial questions are at stake.

Otherwise it would be difficult to explain how two members of the Judicial Committee and the House of Lords—Lord Davey, a radical Liberal and Lord Halsbury, an arch Conservative—could disagree so consistently in the 1890s and 1900s on questions involving trade unions.[19] It would be next to impossible to account for the remarkable reversals leading to the adoption of a *laissez-faire* philosophy by the United States Supreme Court in the 1890s.[20] Examples can also be drawn from the history of Canadian constitutional law. How would a positivist account for the diametrically opposed interpretation of the federal system by the centralist Gwynne J., a Macdonald appointee, and the decentralist Strong J. who had been appointed by the Liberals?[21] The positivist would also find it difficult to explain the differing attitudes to civil liberties among Anglophone and Francophone judges of the Supreme Court in the 1950s.[22] If in absolute terms the positivist thesis does not stand up, it is still possible that Browne was correct in applying it to the specific problem of Lord Watson's interpretation of the B.N.A. Act. The Board members may have done nothing more than apply their minds conscientiously to the law, remaining untouched, unconsciously or consciously, by policy influences. The facts, however, strongly suggest that this was not the case.

In the first place, Lord Watson and his colleagues do not seem to have approached these questions with open minds. The evidence indicates a definite predisposition to accept provincialist arguments without examining and weighing alternative interpretations very carefully. In the *Liquidators* case the texts relied on by centralists and moderates were largely ignored in the judgment. Nor did Lord Watson bother to deal with perhaps the strongest argument against accepting full co-ordinate status at the executive level (an argument which had been advanced by counsel for the Liquidators at the hearing[23]): that since the Lieutenant-Governors, unlike the Governor General (section 10), are described as acting in the Queen's name only in specified cases, such as summoning the legislature (section 82), the *expression unius* rule should apply. It followed that they did not act as the Queen's representatives in cases not specified, that is, in general. With similar disregard of contrary arguments, Lord Watson characterised the nature of Confederation in a manner which would have shocked most of the Fathers:

> The object of the Act was neither to weld the provinces into one, nor to subordinate provincial governments to a central authority, but to create a federal government in which they should all be represented, entrusted with the exclusive administration of affairs in which they had a common interest, each province retaining its independence and autonomy. That object was accomplished by distributing, between the Dominion and the provinces, all powers executive and legislative, and all public property and revenues which had previously belonged to the provinces; so that the Dominion Government should be vested with such of these powers, property, revenues as were necessary for the due performance of its constitutional functions, and that the remainder should be retained by the provinces for the purposes of provincial government. But, in so far as regards those matters which, by sect. 92, are specially

reserved for provincial legislation, the legislation of each province continues to be free from the control of the Dominion, and as supreme as it was before the passing of the Act.[24]

This analysis might have been written by David Mills, Edward Blake or Oliver Mowat. With its stress on the legal continuity of the colonies as provinces after 1867, and the assumption that the object was to grant the Dominion limited functions and the provinces residual powers, it amounted to an acceptance of the compact theory. This radical departure was achieved without even acknowledging there was another explanation of Confederation and without noticing that the B.N.A. Act in referring to the provinces, their boundaries and their constitutions, uses the future or enacting tense, which suggests that they were, in law, new creations. Lord Watson's statement is all the more remarkable when it is remembered that the Board had considered and, in effect, rejected a detailed "states' rights" interpretation of Confederation in the *Russell* case.[25] Lord Watson's declaration in favour of provincial autonomy flew in the face of sections 90, 92 (10) (c), 93 (4) and other provisions permitting federal interference in the exercise of what was normally provincial jurisdiction. True, the influential jurist, A.V. Dicey, had described state autonomy—such as found in the American constitution—as a fundamental principle of federalism, and had made the further general statement that the Canadian federal system was based on that of the United States.[26] This statement by Dicey, however, had been the target of much scholarly criticism, which pointed particularly to disallowance and the federal residual power to demonstrate that the Canadian Fathers had intended to establish a much more centralised federation than that of the United States.[27] The Judicial Committee itself (including three members who sat on the *Liquidators* case) had earlier contrasted the American and Canadian systems, and in so doing, had emphasised the absence of provincial autonomy. Whereas under the American constitution, Lord Hobhouse had written in *Bank of Toronto v. Lambe* "each state may make laws for itself, uncontrolled by the federal power," the B.N.A. Act "provides for the Federated provinces a carefully balanced constitution, under which no one of the parts can pass laws for itself except under the control of the whole acting through the Governor General."[28]

The same pattern was evident in the *Local Prohibition* case. Lord Watson completely ignored Gwynne J.'s lengthy historical and textual analysis designed to demonstrate the centralist intentions of the Fathers of Confederation.[29] He divided section 91 into two parts despite the almost unanimous view in Canadian legal circles that the enumerated heads were but examples of a single grant of jurisdiction.[30] Indeed, even the most unqualified provincialist interpretations had assumed (for their own purposes admittedly) that the enumeration and opening words were one and the same and subject to the same rules.[31] Nor did Lord Watson refer to Edward Blake's argument at the hearing that the phrase "Peace, Order, and good Government" was the traditional way in which British draftsmen referred to the totality of legislative power.[32] To support his novel interpretation of section 91, Lord Watson adopted an equally novel interpretation of the deeming clause at the end of section 91.[33] According to his Lordship, the deeming clause had been included to provide for and set limits to anticipated federal encroachments on matters normally dealt with by the provinces. Since it referred back only to the enumerated heads and not to "Peace, Order, and good Government," and applied not to section 92 (16) alone[34]—as had been stated in the *Parsons* case—but to all heads of section 92, the bifurcation of section 91 was warranted by the text. On the contrary, as O'Connor demonstrated at length, this interpretation, to say the least, is difficult to reconcile with the wording which refers to a single class of matters of a local or private nature within an enumeration of legislative subjects assigned to the provinces.[35] Lord Watson's application of the deeming clause to all heads of section 92 flew in the face of any number of scholarly analyses[36] and the assumption of the Board in four previous cases.[37] In the hearing of the *Local Prohibition* case itself two members of the Committee, Lords Davey and Herschell, had adopted the standard view that the clause applied only to section 92 (16).[38] Lord Watson's *tour de force* was accomplished, not by grammatical justification, but by a simple assertion that the comment in the *Parsons* case had been wrong:

> It was observed by this Board in *Citizens Insurance Co. of Canada v. Parsons* that the paragraph just quoted applies in its grammatical construction only to No. 16 of s. 92. The observation was not material to the question arising in that case, and does not appear to their Lordships to be strictly accurate. It appears to them that the language of the exception in s. 91 was meant to include and correctly describes all the matters enumerated in the sixteen heads of s. 92, as being, from a provincial point of view, of a local or private nature.[39]

If Lord Watson's disregard of contrary arguments suggests a definite bias toward the provincialist interpretation, so does his tendency to go far beyond what was necessary to decide the case at hand. The compact theory and the declaration in favour of provincial autonomy were clearly unnecessary for the disposition of the issue raised in the *Liquidators* case. In the *Local Prohibition* case, the decision might have been based simply on the double aspect doctrine, which Lord Herschell so obviously favoured during the hearing.[40] That is, where a subject—in this case liquor prohibition—fell outside the enumerated powers of sections 91 and 92, it could be dealt with by Parliament under "Peace, Order, and good Government," or in the absence of federal legislation, by the Provinces under their "residual" power, section 92 (16). In any case the validity of provincial legislation, actual and proposed, was in question and it is difficult to see why a general analysis of "Peace, Order, and good Government" was called for. It appears that Lord Watson was determined to enunciate as many wide-ranging provincialist interpretations as the nature of the cases would possibly allow.

In summary, Lord Watson's performance in the two cases was the very opposite of what one would expect if no extra-legal factors were operating. He might conceivably have reached many of the same conclusions had he proceeded as the pure juristic automaton of the positivist model; but surely there would be some indication that he had seriously explored the alternatives and some evidence of judicial self-restraint.

EXISTING SPECULATION ON LORD
WATSON'S MOTIVES

Referring to Lords Watson and Haldane, Professor Ronald Cheffins noted in his recent textbook on the constitution that "[a] great deal of speculation has been undertaken on why these particular men so favoured provincial legislative claims, but as yet no definite answer has appeared."[41] The statement is particularly apt with regard to Lord Watson. Lord Haldane at least has been the subject of a detailed study pointing to the influence of Hegelian philosophy on his desire to give Canadians a constitution tailored to what he understood to be their strong sense of regional identity.[42] J.R. Mallory has advanced a reasoned argument illustrating the impact of the *laissez-faire* conception of the state on the Haldane and Atkin Boards.[43] Except for Browne's thesis, no such detailed study has been done for the Committee in the 1890s. The many brief explanations of Lord Watson usually content themselves with a vague allusion to a provincialist bias or policy, although some go so far as to suggest deliberate manipulations of the law in the interests of policy—a possible but doubtful interpretation in view of the prevalence of positivism at the time.[44] Even in the case of the latter approach the nature of the policy is seldom spelled out. The most common motive alleged is not really a motive at all: that the Judicial Committee adhered to a decentralised "American" conception of Canadian federalism.[45] True, but the question remains why did it do so? Arthur Lower suggested that it was through the influence of Judah P. Benjamin, former Attorney General of the Confederacy and a leading member of the British Bar in the 1870s and early 1880s, that there "can be traced the stream of 'states' rights' arguments flowing through the London bar and Privy Council into the interpretation of the Canadian constitution."[46] This interesting hypothesis, however, has since been laid to rest.[47] Admittedly, one could point to some vague influences which may have predisposed a number of Judicial Committee members to favour decentralised government: sympathy among the British upper classes for states' rights during the American Civil War; Dicey's use of the American system as the true federal model; sympathy among Liberal members of the Committee[48] for Irish Home Rule[49] and strengthening municipal government;[50] and the possibility that Lord Davey, who had been very active as counsel for the provinces, had absorbed the constitutional viewpoint of his clients.[51] While these miscellaneous ideological factors may have played a minor role, it seems inherently unlikely that judges living in a unitary state would be deeply concerned about the question of centralisation versus decentralisation, particularly as applied to a distant colony.[52] Some other, stronger motive must be sought.

A few writers have offered distinctive, if very brief and unsupported explanations. Although his thesis deals primarily with the period between the wars, J.R. Mallory writes at times as if the desire to inhibit collectivism may also have influenced the Judicial Committee's interpretation of the B.N.A. Act in the nineteenth century. Professor Cheffins has suggested that a sympathetic attitude to Quebec influenced Lord Watson, in that he hoped to afford protection to the French Canadian minority by underwriting provincial autonomy.[53] Arthur Lower and F.R. Scott have hinted that Lord Watson's decisions were designed to weaken the central government and Parliament for the purpose of insuring the continuance of the Imperial tie: *"Divide et impera"* as Scott put it.[54] Are these hypotheses supported by the evidence?

In the period down to Lord Watson's death in 1899, the members of the Judicial Committee did not allow any concern they may have had about the growth of collectivist ideas to influence their handling of Canadian constitutional appeals. As these ideas gathered strength in Britain and Canada in the twentieth century one can indeed detect hostility on the part of the Committee which is reflected in a tendency to declare *ultra vires* federal or provincial attempts to regulate the economy or individual industries, to impose new forms of taxation and to protect segments of the population from the operation of the free market. It seems highly probable that from 1900 to 1939 the majority of the Judicial Committee's decisions relevant to the issue favoured *laissez-faire* over collectivism. This was not so, however, in the late nineteenth century. In the period 1879–1899, there were approximately thirteen decisions with a discernible effect, positive or negative, on business interests. At least eight had a negative effect and were decided against litigants engaged in business or representing business interests. Examples are *Bank of Toronto v. Lambe,*[55] which upheld a Quebec corporation tax, and the *Local Prohibition* case itself, which upheld provincial jurisdiction to prohibit the sale and manufacture of liquor.[56]

Thus, statistically speaking, no pro-business bias is evident before or during Lord Watson's period of activity on the Board. Nor can his conception of co-ordinate federalism be traced to such a bias. While it is true that many smaller businessmen in the 1880s and 1890s adopted "provincial rights" (for example construction contractors and railway promoters in Manitoba and sawmill operators in Ontario who sought, successfully (1897), a provincial ban on the export of pine), those at the commanding heights of the economy (financiers, C.P.R. directors and manufacturers with a national or international market) tended to be centralist. They wanted a strong, credit-worthy central government, with a near-monopoly of revenue, unchallenged authority to regulate trade, and power to curb provincial experiments detrimental to their interests. During the 1880s, this business élite applauded the repeated disallowance of Manitoba railway charters which threatened the C.P.R., expressed outrage when Macdonald refused to veto a Quebec tax on corporations, and prophesied doom if Mowat's conception of co-ordinate federalism should be implemented.[57] British investors in Canada, needless to say, were closely associated with this segment of the business community and, almost certainly, shared a like consitutional viewpoint.[58]

It must be admitted, of course, that in the long run Lord Watson's decentralisation of legislative jurisdiction—especially as extended by Lord Haldane—tended to inhibit collectivist legislation. For two decades between the Wars the provinces hesitated to penalize taxpayers or corporate investors by pioneering in such fields as minimum wages or unemployment insurance. This very real problem of states' or provincial rights, however, was barely perceived, if at all, in the 1890s. Those among the Fathers of the Australian federation who favoured collectivist legislation, for example, assumed that the states would and could take the initiative in this area. In the United States these questions were still largely unexplored by the end of the first decade of the twentieth century, while in Canada the problem was not the subject of comment in the *Canadian Law Times* until the eve of the First World War.[59] Moreover, in the late nineteenth century, legislation regulating wealth or industry in what was considered the public interest emanated from the provinces rather than Parliament. Where, for example, federal combines legislation was virtually non-existent, Quebec enacted a corporation tax in 1882. Ontario passed a Factory Act in 1884 restricting female and child labour, and a British Columbia statute of 1890 prohibited the employment of Chinese in the coal mines.[60] The situation was such, in other words, that a judge interested in preventing collectivist legislation would hardly have decided to decentralise legislative jurisdiction.

Lord Watson may well have sympathized with the minority situation of the French Canadians as Professor Cheffins suggests. Despite years of residence in London, he remained to the end, self consciously and proudly, a Scot among Englishmen, reading and re-reading Sir Walter Scott, his favourite author, and returning whenever possible to the Scottish countryside he so loved. In the House of Lords, his political speeches were devoted almost exclusively to the suitability—or as often as not the unsuitability—of legislation as it affected Scotland. As a judge he developed a reputation for maintaining well-established principles of the Scottish civil law—similar to that of Quebec—free from common law encroachment.[61] Thus, there may be something to Professor Cheffins's suggestion, but its importance should not be exaggerated. The constitutional struggle in the courts, after all, seldom involved Quebec; it was between an aggrieved Ontario and the federal government. Nor is there any reference to the particular needs of Quebec in Lord Watson's judgments on Canadian federalism, or in Lord Haldane's comments on those judgments. Finally, on the one constitutional issue directly involving French Canadian cultural survival—the Manitoba schools question—the Board, including Lord Watson, opted for cultural homogeneity rather than cultural pluralism.[62]

The Lower–Scott argument that Lord Watson was engaged in an imperialist scheme of "divide and rule" is almost impossible to test. The assumptions on which such an alleged motive was based are not spelled out, nor is any proof offered. One would have to attribute to Lord Watson, and other members of the Committee, an unusually long-range vision. Are we to believe that he thought along such lines as these: by increasing the role of the provinces in the constitution, the loyalties of Canadians would be focussed on their provinces and provincial governments rather than on Canada as a whole and the federal government, and this would inhibit the growth of a "national" feeling? This is perhaps conceivable, but even if the Board members did consider such a possibility, then they must also have wondered whether provincialism might at times endanger Imperial interests. While fostering provincial sentiment might help to maintain the Imperial connection, would it not also hamper the federal government if it should attempt to provide active support for Britain in wartime? Moreover, the "divide and rule" motive does not fit the political situation in Canada during the 1880s and first half of the 1890s. The centralist Conservatives in power in Ottawa posed no threat to the Imperial connection, whereas many prominent leaders of the provincialist Liberals, including Blake, Mills and Laurier, favoured decentralisation within the Empire as well as in

Canada. Why increase the prestige of the Liberals by sanctioning their interpretation of the constitution? Until these difficulties are resolved and some proof offered, the "divide and rule" thesis cannot be accepted.

INSTITUTIONAL SELF-INTEREST HYPOTHESIS

The most probable motivation influencing the Judicial Committee's interpretation of the Canadian federal system is hinted at in some observations Lord Haldane made in a series of addresses and essays published in 1902. Lord Watson, he wrote, "had rendered more services to the empire than many a distinguished statesman" as those "who have followed the recent history of Canada know." Lord Haldane went on to detail those services. The Supreme Court of Canada, he noted, had originally been intended as the final court of appeal for Canada, but had created alarm among Canadians by its one-sided, centralist approach to the B.N.A. Act. Lord Watson's judgments correcting this line of interpretation had established an equality between the provinces and the Dominion, thereby proving that the Judicial Committee, removed as it was from Canadian politics, was ideally suited to act as an "arbiter holding an absolutely even hand between...contending parties" even on the most explosive questions. The resulting satisfaction in Canada—where Lord Watson's name "will be long and gratefully remembered"—had, Lord Haldane implied, eliminated any desire to abolish appeals, and thus an important link of empire had been preserved. For Canadians, and indeed all colonial peoples, Lord Watson would long remain the embodiment of the best in British rule—"absolute freedom from partisanship and...a passionate love of justice."[63]

It is submitted that the main motivation influencing Lord Watson and his colleagues was a desire to preserve intact the appellate jurisdiction of the Judicial Committee. This institutional self-interest was undoubtedly sublimated into noble imperialism, for Lord Haldane's conception of the vital role of the Judicial Committee in the Empire was something of a commonplace in British legal circles and at the Colonial Office in the last quarter of the nineteenth century. Few would have disputed Lord Chancellor Selborne's statement in 1881 that the "business discharged by the Judicial Committee of the Privy Council was of the greatest possible importance. Upon it depended the contentment of Her Majesty's subjects in India and all the Colonies with the administration of justice."[64] Many would have agreed with G.D. Faber, former Registrar of the Judicial Committee, who claimed in 1900 that the "Privy Council appeal in the past has been the strongest bond of union between this country and the colonies."[65]

There are persuasive arguments and evidence to support the institutional self-interest hypothesis. First, it must be emphasised that Lord Haldane was in an excellent position to understand Lord Watson's thinking on Canadian constitutional cases. Lord Haldane had a large and varied practice before the Judicial Committee in the last two decades of the nineteenth century and appeared as counsel for Ontario in a number of appeals. More important, he was a close personal friend of Lord Watson. Many years later, he recalled that it was common for Lord Watson to invite him for a drink and a discussion of nice points of law which came before the Committee.[66]

Thus, one can legitimately infer from Lord Haldane's comments that Lord Watson was aware that correcting the Supreme Court's centralist interpretation of the constitution would be popular in Canada and would demonstrate the virtues of judicial imperialism.[67] Secondly, the situation was such that in the 1880s and 1890s a member of the Judicial Committee could not be entirely confident that Canada would remain content with judicial subordination.

Finally, the Board's behaviour on appeals from the Supreme Court indicates a definite bias against that Court. Lord Watson's decisions were but extreme examples of a tendency which can be discerned from the end of the 1870s when Supreme Court appeals were first heard by the Committee.

Prior to World War I, the abolition of appeals to the Judicial Committee probably never claimed the adherence of a majority of Canadians who were in a position to influence the issue. Nevertheless, from the vantage point of a member of the Judicial Committee in the 1880s and 1890s the possibility that Britain would be faced with an insistent demand from Canada to abolish or limit appeals must have appeared to be more than academic. When the Supreme Court had been established in 1875, the Liberal Minister of Justice, Télesphore Fournier, had stated his Government's preference for ultimately abolishing all appeals from the new Court to the Judicial Committee. An amendment designed as a step in that direction passed the House by the overwhelming vote of 112 to 40, despite Sir John A. Macdonald's opposition. Participants in the debate cited a variety of reasons for abolition, including national sentiment, the expense which favoured wealthier litigants, delay, and the alleged ignorance on the part of British judges of Canadian society and elements of Canadian law, such as the Quebec Civil Code. Fournier's successor, Edward Blake, went to London and engaged in an acrimonious dispute on the question with the Colonial Secretary, Lord Carnarvon. The latter, supported by Lord Chancellor Cairns and the law officers of the Crown, advanced the standard arguments—the importance of appeals in binding the Empire, the need to protect British investors in Canada, and the value of a court outside Canada to determine impartially "[q]uestions of great nicety...between the federal and provincial legislatures."[68] This opposition led to a retreat by the government, but did not altogether silence criticism of the Judicial Committee among influential Liberals. In 1880, for example, Blake, then Liberal leader, argued in the Commons for total abolition, not only on nationalist grounds, but also because, in his view, judges living in a unitary state would tend to adopt an overly centralised interpretation of Canadian federalism.[69] While the Macdonald government in the 1880s was decidedly opposed to abolition in general, it did undertake in 1888 to eliminate appeals in criminal cases.[70] Writing in the prestigious British law journal, the *Juridical Review*, John G. Bourninot, one of Canada's better known jurists, viewed this step as a forerunner to further limitation:

> But the general sense of the people is tending more and more to make the Supreme Court, as far as practicable, the ultimate Court of Appeal in all cases involving constitutional issues. It is felt that men, versed in the constitutional law of Canada and of the United States, and acquainted with the history and methods of government [i.e. federalism], as well as with the political conditions of the

country at large, are most likely to meet satisfactorily the difficulties of the cases as they arise, than European judges who are trained to move in the narrower paths of ordinary statutes. A remarkable assertion of the judicial independence of Canada can be seen in the Act passed by Parliament of the Dominion in 1888, which enacts that "notwithstanding any royal prerogative" no appeal shall be brought in any criminal case from any judgment or order of any court of Canada, to any Court of Appeal or authority by which, in the United Kingdom, appeals to Her Majesty in Council may be heard.[71]

Given this situation, a member of the Judicial Committee could not reasonably have thought that the appellate jurisdiction in Canadian cases was immune from successful attack. This possible danger of limitation must have become even more apparent in the 1890s when several of the politicians negotiating the new Australian constitution made known their view that appeals to the Privy Council from the Australian courts should be severely curtailed or abolished entirely.[72] The concern of the British government and members of the Judicial Committee with strengthening the latter's image in the eyes of colonial politicians was apparent in the reform of 1895, which allowed senior Dominion judges to sit on the Committee.[73]

If, as postulated, the motive of institutional self-interest was important, one would expect it to be statistically reflected in the Judicial Committee's handling of appeals from the Supreme Court of Canada. One would expect a high rate of reversal or repudiation. Regular affirmation of Supreme Court decisions and doctrines would not only enhance the latter's prestige in Canadian eyes, but would also run the risk that Canadian lawyers, scholars, politicians and journalists would begin to look upon the Judicial Committee as quite superfluous. Why retain an expensive, tardy appeal procedure, if the justices of the Supreme Court were obviously capable of accurate interpretation of the most complex legal problems? For similar reasons one should be able to detect in the Judicial Committee's decisions in the controversial field of constitutional law an easily grasped "philosophy" which was clearly distinct from that of the Supreme Court. Finally, one would anticipate that such a philosophy would be attractive to the predominant Canadian opinion on the constitution and would be one which appeared consistent with the oft-claimed virtue of Imperial impartiality rising above political squabbles in the colonies. The analysis which follows demonstrates that all these expectations are correct.

As early as 1884, the tendency of the Judicial Committee to reverse or ignore decisions of the Supreme Court was so pronounced that it provoked an outburst by Strong J. who complained in open court that "[o]ur judgments will not make any difference there; as a matter of fact, they never do. They do not appear to be read or considered there, and if they are alluded to it is only for the purpose of offensive criticism"[74] Table 1 suggests that there was substance to Strong J.'s allegation.

While half of the decisions appealed from the Supreme Court were reversed, only about one in three from other courts in the self-governing colonies met that fate and only one in four from other Canadian courts. It would require extreme pessimism as to the competence of the Supreme Court judges to conclude that they

TABLE 1   *COMPARATIVE FATE OF COLONIAL COURT DECISIONS*
            APPEALED TO THE JUDICIAL COMMITTEE, 1879-99 [+]

From	Decisions Appealed	Affirmed	Reversed	Percentage Reversed
Supreme Court of Canada	36	18	18[++]	50
All other Canadian courts	67	50	17	25
All courts in the self-governing colonies except the Supreme Court of Canada	211	142	69	33

[+] The table is compiled from the reported decisions in the Appeal Cases. Cases dealing with evidentiary or procedural matters were excluded. In case of doubt whether a decision had been substantially reversed or affirmed, the allocation of costs was used as the test. A few borderline cases were omitted (less than five per cent of the sample). Colonies with responsible government were chosen as the control group because they shared certain characteristics which were not present in many other parts of the Empire. The main function of the courts in the self-governing colonies was to apply European law to a population of European origin and the judges were appointed by local politicians rather than by the Colonial Office. The colonies included were Canada and its provinces, New South Wales, South Australia, Western Australia after 1890, Tasmania, Victoria, Queensland, Cape Colony, Natal after 1893, New Zealand and Newfoundland. If all courts in the Empire (except the Supreme Court of Canada), are included in the comparison, the reversal rate (286 cases) works out to 39 per cent.

[++] Includes the *McCarthy Act Reference* case (see tables 2 and 3 below).

were simply much less able to interpret the law than their confrères in New South Wales, Cape Colony, or New Zealand. It would stretch credulity to suggest that the judges of the Supreme Court were vastly inferior in interpreting the same laws as appeal court judges in the Canadian provinces, who were, after all, appointed by the same politicians who made Supreme Court appointments. Bias against the Supreme Court seems a less far fetched explanation of the statistics, and is supported by other proof.

The Judicial Committee's bias against the Supreme Court emerges clearly from a comparison of their handling of federal–provincial issues. Table 2 provides a statistical description of the Supreme Court's interpretation of Canadian federalism in the period to 1896, when it is generally agreed, it had lost most of its freedom to manoeuvre. The table includes only cases which raised an issue or issues of constitutional law on which there could be some serious doubt, shown by the fact that the court was not unanimous on the point or, if unanimous, was reversed on appeal. All issues dealt with questions of title to property, legislative jurisdiction, or the powers of the Lieutenant-Governors. A centralist position was defined as one which upheld a questioned Dominion right or power, or which rejected a claimed provincial right or power. A provincialist position was defined *mutatis mutandis.* In a few cases, which are indicated by an asterisk, the minority did not express a view on the constitutional point but decided the case on other grounds.

If conclusions were to be based on table 2 alone, it would be difficult to accept the common view that the Supreme Court was centralist in its early years. Only Gwynne J., was a thoroughgoing exponent of subordinate federalism, and from the beginning his view had been countered by Strong J., who appears to have inclined to some version of co-ordinate sovereignty. The statistics indicate that the votes of the other judges and the votes overall were about evenly for and against a centralist position. In terms of issues, ten were decided in a pro-centralist manner; nine were provincialist. Taken at face value, however, the statistics are misleading. Several decisions, namely numbers 8 (1), 11, 12, 15 and 16, were strongly influenced by previous decisions of the Judicial Committee.[75] Subtracting these decisions from the sample, the degree of centralism in the Court, *when left to its own devices*, can be described and estimated. When what might be called the "open" issues are isolated, the statistics reveal that not only Gwynne J., but Taschereau. J. as well, were decidedly centralist.[76] Only Strong J. was consistently provincialist, while the other judges oscillated without any discernible pattern. The numerical result is that 10 of 14 issues (or 71 per cent) were decided in a pre-centralist manner, and of the 76 individual votes cast, 45 (or nearly 60 per cent) were centralist. By way of contrast, the Judicial Committee heard 18 cases involving 20 federal–provincial issues during the period ending in 1896 after the Supreme Court made its centralist tendency clear during 1878–80. Fifteen issues, including six reversals of the Supreme Court, were decided in favour of the provinces (75 per cent).[77] While this statistical contrast is impressive enough, it does not begin to approximate the full measure of the Judicial Committee's dissociation from the constitutional position of the Supreme Court. Table 3 demonstrates that every major centralist doctrine of the Court—either as laid down by a majority in one or more decisions, or as adopted by several individual judges—was repudiated by the Committee.

The Judicial Committee had nothing to lose and everything to gain by its actions. Its continual disapprobation of the decisions of the Supreme Court avoided the risk of being labelled superfluous. The doctrine of co-ordinate federalism, most explicitly developed by Lord Watson, seemed almost tailor-made to that end. An easily remembered concept which served admirably to underline this divergence from the Supreme Court view, the stress on equality between contending levels of government, was entirely consistent with the vaunted impartiality of this Imperial body. It would, in addition, give the lie to the charge that the judges living in a unitary state could not understand federalism. Decentralisation, furthermore, was in accordance with the drift of constitutional opinion in Canada. During the 1880s and 1890s it must have been clear even to the most casual observer that subordinate federalism—unsuitable for a strongly regionalized and ethnically plural society— was in rapid decline. The federal government itself was becoming reluctant to use the disallowance power when no obvious national interest was at stake, and Parliament had yielded a number of legislative fields—factory regulation and insolvency for example—to the provinces. In 1887, an Interprovincial Conference, involving the Premiers of five of the seven provinces met at Quebec City and passed a series of resolutions favouring co-ordinate federalism. In the last two decades of the nineteenth century, the majority of scholarly and polemical studies published on the constitution attacked one or more features of Macdonald centralism and many of them made use of the compact theory.[78] The members of the Judicial Committee must have been impressed also by the fact that some of the Premiers, Mowat particularly, took a personal interest in a number of constitutional cases, while neither the Canadian Prime Minister nor the Minister of Justice ever appeared before the Board.[79] Finally, it might be noted that decentralisation could not hurt the cause with reference to appeals from Australia, for almost to a man the politicians negotiating that federation were confirmed states' rightists.[80]

TABLE 2   STATISTICAL DESCRIPTION OF THE SUPREME COURT OF CANADA'S INTERPRETATION OF CANADIAN FEDERALISM, 1878–1896

Case	Holding	Centralist (C) or Provincialist (P) Decision	Affirmed (A), Reversed (R) or Later Repudiated (REP) by the Judicial Committee	Individual Judgments						
				Gwynne	Taschereau	Henry	Ritchie	Fournier	Strong	Others
Severn v. The Queen (1878) 2 S.C.R. 70.	Held *ultra vires* an Ontario Statute requiring a licence of liquor wholesalers.	C	REP	–	C	C	P	C	P	Richards C. J. (C)
Lenoir v. Ritchie (1879) 3 S.C.R. 575.	Held ultra vires a N.S. statute granting precedence in the provincial courts to provincially appointed Q.C.	C	REP	C	C	C	–	P‡	P‡	–
City of Fredericton v. R. (1880) 3 S.C.R. 505.	Upheld the *Canada Temperance Act* under s. 91 (2).	C	REP	C	C	C	C	C	–	–
The Citizens Insurance Co. v. Parsons (1880) 4 S.C.R. 215.	Upheld an Ontario statute regulating fire insurance contracts (under s. 92 (13)).	P	A	C	C	P	P	P	P	–
Mercer v. A. G. Ontario (1881) 5 S.C.R. 538.	Held the L.-G. does not represent the Crown for the purposes of escheat.	C	R	C	C	C	P	C	P	–

TABLE 2 *continued*

Case	Holding	Centralist (C) or Provincialist (P) Decision	Affirmed (A), Reversed (R) or Later Repudiated (REP) by the Judicial Committee	Gwynne	Taschereau	Henry	Ritchie	Fournier	Strong	Others
						Individual Judgments				
Read v. A. G. Quebec (1883) 8 S.C.R. 408.	Held *ultra vires* a Quebec tax on exhibits filed in court.	C	A	C	P	C	C	C	P	–
Poulin v. The Corporation of Quebec (1884) 9 S.C.R. 185.	Three judges upheld provincial jurisdiction to regulate the hours of taverns; three judges refused to deal with the constitutional issue.	–	–	C†	C†	C†	P	P	P	–
McCarthy Act Reference (1885), Canada, Sessional Papers, 1885, no. 85a.	Issue No. 1: held *ultra vires* the Dominion *Liquor Licence Act* in so far as it dealt with retail licensing.	P	A	Reasons not reported						
	Issue No. 2: upheld the provisions of the Act dealing with wholesale licensing.	C	R	Reasons not reported						
St. Catherines Milling and Lumber Co. v. R. (1887) 13 S.C.R. 577.	Held the beneficial interest in certain Indian lands was vested in Ontario, not the Dominion	P	A	C	P	P	P	P	C	–

Case	Holding	Centralist (C) or Provincialist (P) Decision	Affirmed (A), Reversed (R) or Later Repudiated (REP) by the Judicial Committee	Individual Judgments						
				Gwynne	Taschereau	Henry	Ritchie	Fournier	Strong	Others
A. G. British Columbia v. A. G. Canada (1887) 14 S.C.R. 345.	Held that British Columbia's grant to the Dominion of land to further the construction of the CPR included mineral rights.	C	R	C	C	P	C	P	–	–
Molson v. Lambe (1888) 15 S.C.R. 253.	Upheld a Quebec liquor licensing statute.	P	–	C‡	C‡	P	P	P	P	–
Liquidators case (1889) 20 S.C.R. 695.	Held that the prerogative of prior payment in an insolvency was vested in the Crown in right of New Brunswick.	P	A	C	P	–	–	P	P	Patterson (P)
Lynch v. The Canada North-West Land Company (1891) 19 S.C.R. 204.	Upheld a Manitoba statute imposing a 10% penalty for late payment of municipal taxes.	P	–	C	P	–	P	–	P	Patterson (C)

TABLE 2 *continued*

Case	Holding	Centralist (C) or Provincialist (P) Decision	Affirmed (A), Reversed (R) or Later Repudiated (REP) by the Judicial Committee	Individual Judgments						
				Gwynne	Taschereau	Henry	Ritchie	Fournier	Strong	Others
Barrett v. The City of Winnipeg (1891) 19 S.C.R. 374.	Held *ultra vires* a Manitoba statute taxing Roman Catholic separate school supporters for the purpose of financing a common school system.	C	R	–	C	–	C	C	C	Patterson (P)
In Re Certain Statutes of the Province of Manitoba Relating to Education (1894) 22 S.C.R. 577.	Held that Roman Catholic separate school supporters had no right to appeal to the Dominion for remedial legislation restoring their exemption from taxation.	P	R	P	P	–	–	C	P	King (C)
A. G. Canada v. A. G. Ontario (1894) 23 S.C.R. 458.	Held that the Lieutenant Governor can exercise the royal prerogative of pardoning offenders against provincial laws.	P	–	C	P	–	–	P	P	King (P)

Case	Holding	Centralist (C) or Provincialist (P) Decision	Affirmed (A), Reversed (R) or Later Repudiated (REP) by the Judicial Committee	Individual Judgments						
				Gwynne	Taschereau	Henry	Ritchie	Fournier	Strong	Others
Huson v. South Norwich (1895) 24 S.C.R. 145.	Upheld provincial jurisdiction to prohibit retail sale of liquor by means of the local option technique.‡	P	A	C	P	–	–	P	P	Sedgewick (C)
Local Prohibition case (1895) 24 S.C.R. 170.	Issue No. 1: held that the provinces could not prohibit the retail sale of liquor, either outright or by means of the local option technique.‡	C	R	C	–	–	–	P	P	King (C) Sedgewick (C)
	Issue No. 2: held that the provinces could not prohibit the wholesale or manufacture of liquor.	C	R	C	–	–	–	C	C	King (C) Sedgewick (C)
Totals		10C/9P	6A/7R/3REP	15C/1P	9C/7P	5C/5P	4C/7P	7C/10P	3C/13P	8C/3P
Total of Individual Judgments		51C 46P								

‡ These diametrically opposed decisions were delivered on the same day by differently constituted benches, much to the outrage of the *Ottawa Citizen* (17 Jan. 1895) which charged that the court had made itself "a cause of mockery and ridicule with the public." When Lord Watson heard of the muddle he remarked laconically, "They must have been right once": *Liquor Prohibition Appeal*, 31.

TABLE 3   FATE OF CENTRALIST DOCTRINES ENUNCIATED IN THE SUPREME COURT, 1878–1896

Doctrine	Upheld by a Supreme Court Majority	Enunciated by Individual Judges	Fate
Federal Power to Regulate Trade and Commerce under s. 91 (2). S. 91 (2) includes intraprovincial trade and commerce.†	*Severn v. The Queen, McCarthy Act Reference* and the *Local Prohibition* case.		Repudiated by the Judicial Committee in the *Parsons* case, *Bank of Toronto v. Lambe* and the *Local Prohibition* case.
"Regulation" includes the power to prohibit a trade altogether.	*Fredericton v. The Queen* and the *Local Prohibition* case.		Repudiated by the Judicial Committee in the *Local Prohibition* case.
Status of Lieutenant-Governor The Lieutenant-Governor is not the direct representative of the Crown and cannot exercise Her Majesty's prerogative powers.‡‡	*Lenoir v. Ritchie* and the *Mercer* case.	per Gwynne J. in the *Liquidators* case.	Repudiated in the *Liquidators* case.
Residual Power If a matter does not clearly come within section 92, it falls within "Peace, Order, and good Government."*		per Henry J. in *Severn v. The Queen*, Taschereau and Gwynne JJ. in *Fredericton v. The Queen*, and Sedgewick and King JJ. in the *Local Prohibition* case.	Adopted in *Russell v. The Queen*, but repudiated in the *Local Prohibition* case.
General Nature of Confederation The general intention of the Fathers of Confederation was to create a highly centralised federal system, particularly by comparison to the United States' constitution.**		per Richards C.J., Fournier and Henry JJ. in *Severn v. The Queen*, Gwynne J. in *Fredericton v. The Queen*, Taschereau J. in the *Parsons* case, Gwynne and Sedgewick JJ. in the *Local Prohibition* case.	Adopted in *Bank of Toronto v. Lambe*, but repudiated in the *Liquidators* and *Local Prohibition* cases.

Doctrine	Upheld by a Supreme Court Majority	Enunciated by Individual Judges	Fate
Minority Rights The Manitoba Legislature had no authority to abolish separate school rights (particularly the right of exemption from taxes for the support of common schools) enjoyed in practice by Roman Catholics at the time of union.	*Barrett v. City of Winnipeg* (1892) 9 S.C.R. 374.		This unanimous Supreme Court decision was reversed on appeal to the Judicial Committee: (1892) A.C. 445.

⁺ This doctrine was laid down by all six judges in the *Severn* case including Henry J., who had attended the Quebec and London Conferences as a delegate from Nova Scotia and had helped prepare the initial draft of the B.N.A. Act. In the *McCarthy Act* and *Local Prohibition* cases the majority qualified this doctrine by excluding the regulation of retail trade from the ambit of federal power, obviously in deference to the holding in *Hodge v. The Queen*. Even Strong, the most extreme provincialist on the Court, accepted that regulation of intraprovincial trade was, in general, a federal responsibility. See Smith, *Commerce Power*, 31–32, 54–55.

⁺⁺ Typical of the majority view in these early cases was the statement by Taschereau J. in the former (at p. 263) that "Their office, as heads of the Province, is a very honourable one indeed, but they are not Her Majesty's representatives."

* Under this conception, no question of "encroaching" could logically arise and was therefore not mentioned by the judges cited.

** While this was by far the most common view, the compact theory was occasionally referred to. See e.g., Henry J. in *Fredericton v. The Queen* at p. 548.

The foregoing analysis, it is hoped, has demonstrated that the Judicial Committee's behaviour on Canadian appeals is entirely consistent with the institutional self-interest hypothesis. But, it may be asked, is there any evidence, aside from Lord Haldane's observations, that might serve to link the Committee directly with the motives postulated? A search for such material has uncovered one interesting item of proof. It appears that Lord Watson's revolutionary analysis of section 91 in the *Local Prohibition* case owed a great deal to a polemical study of the constitution written by an obscure New Brunswick lawyer, Jeremiah Travis, entitled *A Law Treatise on the Constitutional Powers of Parliament and of the Local Legislatures, Under the British North America Act, 1867.*[81] One purpose of the book was to heap ridicule on the Judicial Committee's decision in *Russell v. The Queen,* which Travis misinterpreted to mean that whenever Parliament desired to provide for the uniformity of law in any field, it could do so under the "Peace, Order, and good Government" clause, even to the point of legislating directly and primarily on matters listed in section 92.[82] Such rampant and wrong-headed centralism raised Travis's nationalist dander, and he concluded that the Judicial Committee was unfit to try questions involving the division of powers:

> Such questions are not more difficult than many other questions of law...and under the intelligent leadership of the able head of the Supreme Court of Canada, WILL BE MORE INTELLIGENTLY DEALT WITH by that Dominion Court, with one of the ablest lawyers in America at its head [Sir William Ritchie], than by a body, incapable as it seems, of doing better...than delivering such ridiculous judgments as [that]...in Russell v. The Queen;—THE JUDICIAL COMMITTEE OF THE PRIVY COUNCIL OF ENGLAND, who when they hear appeals from the Supreme Court of Canada, hear them not as of right, but in a kind of illegitimate way, called *'as of favour!'*[83]

Although generally speaking the book met with disfavour in Canadian legal circles,[84] it was reviewed in the British journal, *The Law Magazine and Law Review,* as an important contribution to a most complicated problem. To help spread the enlightenment, Travis, a man of monumental ego, sent a copy to at least nine members of the Judicial Committee, including two who later sat on the *Local Prohibition* case, Sir Richard Couch and more important, Lord Watson.[85] According to Travis, Edward Blake who had acted as counsel for Ontario in the *McCarthy Act Reference,* thought the book had influenced the Judicial Committee's decision in that case.[86] Whatever truth there is to that claim, it is almost beyond question that Lord Watson derived his interpretation of section 91 from Travis. Lord Watson seems to have shared Travis's erroneous view that *Russell v. The Queen* permitted Parliament to legislate on section 92 matters, whenever it claimed that the "Peace, Order, and good Government" of Canada required a uniform law throughout the country. His Lordship made it clear that he thought the *Russell* case had been wrongly decided,[87] and the justification he offered for his own judgment indicates what he believed was the issue:

> To attach any other construction to the general power which, in supplement of its enumerated powers, is conferred upon the Parliament

of Canada by s. 91, would, in their Lordships' opinion, not only be contrary to the intendment of the Act, but would practically destroy the autonomy of the provinces. If it were once conceded that the Parliament of Canada has authority to make laws applicable to the whole Dominion, in relation to matters which in each province are substantially of local or private interest, upon the assumption that these matters also concern the peace, order, and good government of the Dominion, there is hardly a subject enumerated in s. 92 upon which it might not legislate, to the exclusion of the provincial legislatures.[88]

Like Travis, Lord Watson pointed specifically to section 94 as being incompatible with any general power to enact uniform legislation in provincial fields of jurisdiction:

These enactments would be idle and abortive, if it were held that the Parliament of Canada derives jurisdiction from the introductory provisions of s. 91, to deal with any matter which is in substance local or provincial, and does not truly affect the interest of the Dominion as a whole.[89]

Alone among legal scholars, Travis divided section 91 into two parts with differing encroachment potentials, which was precisely the conception adopted by Lord Watson.[90] Travis assumed he had proved this contention by showing that the deeming clause applied to the whole of section 92 and not, as the Judicial Committee had incorrectly stated in the *Parsons* case, to section 92 (16) alone.[91] Travis's main argument on this point was the same as that of Lord Watson—that all matters in section 92 were of a local or private nature:

The whole first fifteen subjects relate to local or private matters '*in* the Province,' or '*to* the Province,' or '*of* the Province,' or '*for* the Province,'...the closing clause of the 91st section...[refers] *to the whole of the fifteen clauses*...And, grammatically, this is very clear. It is not—'the class of matters *contained in the 16th clause*',[92] but is 'the class of matters of a local or private nature, *comprised in the enumeration of the classes of subjects*...The class of matters, etc, comprised *in the enumeration of the classes; that is, in the whole sixteen classes of subjects of a local or private nature enumerated in that section.*

Thus in all material particulars, it appears that Lord Watson's novel interpretation of section 91 was derived from Travis's book, a work which condemned the centralism of the Judicial Committee in the *Russell* case and suggested that constitutional appeals would be better disposed of by the Supreme Court of Canada.

EPILOGUE

The *Liquidators* and *Local Prohibition* cases helped clarify and reinforce the strong drift toward provincial rights in late nineteenth century Canada, by providing legal sanction for the compact theory and co-ordinate federalism, concepts which were, by and large, to govern the federal system until the Second World War.[93] More specifically, the *Liquidators* case played a role in the demise (during the late 1890s and the first decade of the twentieth century) of the disallowance power in that vague but potentially unlimited area of provincial legislation which had been characterised variously as "unwise," "unjust" or "contrary to the first principles of legislation."[94] Such statutes, however vicious in principle the federal authorities thought them to be, would henceforth be left to be dealt with by the provincial legislatures and electorates. The case also helped undermine another of the essential techniques of Macdonald's subordinate federalism by making it politically next to impossible to insist on Ottawa's right to instruct the Lieutenant-Governors in the exercise of executive discretion.[95] These direct representatives of the Queen, governing provinces entitled to the fullest autonomy, would henceforth (and with the occasional, covert exception) exercise such political prerogatives as appointing or dismissing a premier, refusing a dissolution, signing or refusing to sign Orders in Council and so on without reference to the Federal Cabinet. As is well known, Lord Watson's subordination of "Peace, Order, and good Government" to section 92 in the *Local Prohibition* case was adopted and extended by Lord Haldane. His admiration for Lord Watson during this period was unbounded, and it is not surprising to discover that as early as 1900 Lord Haldane was referring to "Property and Civil Rights" as the true residential power in the Canadian constitution.[96] As the dominant member of the Judicial Committee from 1912 to 1925, Lord Haldane applied this notion in numerous cases, and in so doing, turned "Peace, Order, and good Government" into an emergency power. This remained the approach most frequently taken by the Board in dealing with legislative jurisdiction until the termination of appeals in 1949. The resulting nullification of federal initiatives in insurance, labour relations and combines regulation are too well known to require comment.

As for judicial imperialism after Lord Watson's landmark decisions, its triumph was complete for a half-century. By 1900, the Committee had developed a reputation for sagacity and fairness in Canadian legal circles.[97] Typical of comment was the contention of J.M. Clark, K.C. that the Judicial Committee had wisely understood that the decisions of the Supreme Court "would have rendered our Constitution quite unworkable."[98] The final irony was Lord Macnaghton's description in 1904 of the now captive Supreme Court as "an august and independent tribunal."[99] Gone were the days when the court included an acknowledged abolitionist such as Fournier J., a judge like Stone J. who would complain openly and bitterly of the Judicial Committee's arrogance, or a battler like Gwynne J. who would challenge at length what he believed to be an erroneous understanding of Confederation. In 1914, the Chief Justice of the "august and independent tribunal," Sir Charles Fitzpatrick, could write in the *Canadian Law Times* that "amongst lawyers and Judges competent to speak on the subject, there is but one voice, that where constitutional questions are concerned, an appeal to the Judicial Committee must be retained."[100]

NOTES

1. "The Work for the Empire of the Judicial Committee of the Privy Council" (1921–23) 1 *Camb. L.J.* 143, at 150. It is entirely proper that Lord Haldane and the large majority of scholars have pointed to Lord Watson as the predominant influence behind the Judicial Committee's interpretation of the Canadian constitution in the 1890s. From 1889, when he first took an active interest in this field, until his death in 1899, Lord Watson participated in all seventeen Canadian constitutional appeals and wrote the judgment in ten of them. His nearest rivals in point of activity in this period were Lord Macnaghten and Sir Richard Couch who sat on eleven and twelve cases respectively. The only members, other than Lord Watson, to write judgments were Lords Herschell (4), Halsbury (2) and Macnaghten (1). See I Olmsted, *Decisions of the Judicial Committee of the Privy Council Relating to the British North America Act, 1867 and the Canadian Constitution 1867–1954* (1954) 236–454.

2. [1892] A.C. 437 (P.C.).

3. *A.-G. Ontario v. A.-G. for the Dominion and the Distillers and Brewers' Association of Ontario* [1896] A.C. 348 (P.C.).

4. (1882) 7 App. Cas. 829 (P.C.).

5. See Alan C. Cairns, "The Judicial Committee and its Critics" (1971) 4 *Can. J. Pol. Sci.* 301–45, *passim.*

6. *The Judicial Committee and the British North America Act* (1967) v, 29–32.

7. See J.C. Morrison, *Oliver Mowat and the Development of Provincial Rights in Ontario: A Study in Dominion Provincial Relations, 1867–96* (Published under the auspices of the Ontario Department of Public Records and Archives, n.d.); John T. Saywell, *The Office of Lieutenant-Governor* (1957); Ramsay Cook, *Provincial Autonomy, Minority Rights and the Compact Theory, 1867–1921* (1969).

8. *Parl. Deb.* H.C., 1875, at 400.

9. See e.g., a speech by Mills, *Parl. Deb.* H.C., Vol. II, 1885, at 882.

10. See the review of authorities in James McI. Hendry, *Memorandum on the Office of Lieutenant-Governor of a Province* (1955) 6–12.

11. This had been the majority holding in two Supreme Court decisions: *Lenoir v. Ritchie* (1879) 3 S.C.R. 575 (re Queen's Counsel); *Mercer v. A.-G. Ontario* (1881) 5 S.C.R. 538 (re escheat). The *Mercer* decision was reversed on appeal but the Judicial Committee did not discuss the status issue: (1883) 8 App. Cas. 767 (P.C.). Gwynne J., dissenting, adopted the centralist position in the Supreme Court decision in the *Liquidators* case (1889) 20 S.C.R. 696, at 698–706. The sections of the B.N.A. Act usually cited by centralists were ss. 58–61; 17, 69, 71; 55 and 90.

12. This moderate trend in one or other of its versions was adopted by the majority in the Supreme Court of Canada decision. See also the decision in the New Brunswick Supreme Court (1888) 27 N.B.R. 379.

13. [1892] A.C. 437 at 443.

14. See e.g., John H. Gray (a New Brunswick delegate to the Quebec Conference), *Confederation* (1872) 56; John Fennings Taylor, *Are Legislatures Parliaments?* (1879) 15–17, 198–99; *The City of Fredericton v. The Queen* (1880) 3 S.C.R. 505, at 560–64, per Gwynne J.; (1887) 3 C.L.T. 279 at 281–83; D.A. O'Sullivan, *A Manual of Government in Canada* (1879) 119.

15. See, e.g., the speech of Sir Alexander Campbell, Minister of Justice, on a proposed Factory Act (1882): Eugene Forsey, "A Note on the Dominion Factory Bills of the Eighteen-Eighties" (1947) 13 *Can. J. Econ.* 581. See also John G. Bourinot, *The Federal Constitution of Canada* (1890) 2 *Jurid. Rev.* 131 at 209–13; Anon., *The Constitution of Canada* (1891) 7 C.L.T. 122, and table 3.

96 THE REAL CONSTITUTION OF CANADA

16. This is treated in detail below.

17. *The Judicial Committee and the British North America Act v,* 36–39 and 47–72.

18. I O'Connor, *Report to the Senate of Canada on the British North America Act* (1939) 18–78.

19. See the article on Davey in II *Concise Dictionary of National Biography.*

20. Arnold M. Paul, *Conservative Crisis and the Rule of Law: Attitudes of Bar and Bench, 1887–1895* 2d ed. (1969), is a rewarding in-depth study of this question and provides a useful biography. See also Walter F. Murphy and C. Herman Pritchett, eds., *Courts, Judges and Politics* (1961).

21. See table 2. The constant conflict between Gwynne J. and Strong J.—at least in the 1890s—probably owed something to personal animosity as well as differing conceptions of federalism. Strong, then Chief Justice, complained to the Minister of Justice in 1895 of Gwynne J.'s,

> senile irritability and constant attacks upon myself even in Court. Further, he has refused to attend conferences and his method of doing his work is to write his judgments without any consultation and then call on the other judges to agree with him, showing wrath if they venture to differ. I am afraid he and I cannot fit in together and if he will not or cannot be made to give way I am afraid I must.

(Strong C.J. to C.H. Tupper, 19 February 1895, Sir Charles Hibbert Tupper Papers, at 1387, University of British Columbia Library.)

22. Peter H. Russell, *The Supreme Court of Canada as a Bilingual and Bicultural Institution* (1969) 130–46, 188–206.

23. [1892] A.C. 437 at 438.

24. Ibid., at 441–42.

25. Claudius O. Johnson, "Did Judah P. Benjamin Plant the 'States' Rights' Doctrine in the Interpretation of the *British North America Act?*" (1967) 45 *Can. B. Rev.* 454, at 468–74.

26. *Introduction to the Study of the Law of the Constitution,* 6th ed. (1902, originally published in 1885), 136, 162.

27. See e.g., H. Jenkyns, "Remarks on Certain Points in Mr. Dicey's 'Law of the Constitution' " (1887) 3 *Law Q. Rev.* 204, at 206–7; John G. Bourinot, "The Federal Constitution of Canada" (1890) 2 *Jurid. Rev.* 131, at 135–36.

28. [1887] 12 App. Cas. 575, at 587 (P.C.). Lords Hobhouse and Macnaghten and Sir Richard Couch sat on both the *Lambe* and *Liquidators* cases.

29. In the judgment appealed from: *In re Provincial Jurisdiction to Pass Prohibitory Liquor Laws* (1895) 24 S.C.R. 170, at 204–30.

30. See e.g., Bourinot, "The Federal Constitution," at 209–13; Anon., *The Constitution of Canada.*

31. See, e.g., David Mills, *The Federal Constitution of Canada* (typescript lectures delivered at the University of Toronto in the early 1890s), David Mills Papers, University of Western Ontario Library; and the argument of Horace Davey (later Lord Davey), Counsel for Ontario, Quebec, New Brunswick and Nova Scotia in the McCarthy Act Reference case: Report of the Proceedings before the Judicial Committee of the Privy Council on the Hearing of the Petition of the Governor General of Canada in Relation to the Dominion Licence Acts of 1883 and 1884 (Typescript), Supreme Court of Canada Library, at 166. Arguing that the enumerated heads were mere examples of "Peace, Order, and good Government" and that from the latter, s. 92 matters were expressly excepted, Mills and Davey managed to deduce that provincial legislative jurisdiction *always* took precedence over federal powers whenever the two appeared to conflict.

32. *The Liquor Prohibition Appeal, 1895* (1895), 227–29. Blake represented the Ontario Distillers and Brewers' Association, which opposed provincial jurisdiction to enact prohibition.

33. "And any Matter coming within any of the Classes of Subjects enumerated in this Section shall not be deemed to come within the Class of Matters of a local or private Nature comprised in the Enumeration of the Classes of Subjects by this Act assigned exclusively to the Legislatures of the Provinces."

34. "Generally all Matters of a merely local or private Nature in the Province."

35. See I O'Connor, *Report*, 43–45; Browne, *The Judicial Committee* suggests that Lord Watson's reading of the deeming clause could conceivably be supported if "'comprised in' meant 'consisting of' (rather than 'included within')." The wording, however, refers to a class of matters "comprised in," not "comprised *of*" section 92. That the draftsman in using the word "comprised" was thinking of a single item on a list of legislative powers rather than the list itself is confirmed by an earlier draft, the "deeming clause" of which refers to the "Subject of Property and Civil Rights comprised in the enumeration," etc. S. 37(13) read "Property and Civil Rights in the Province": Joseph Pope, ed., *Confederation: Being a Series of Hitherto Unpublished Documents Bearing on the British North America Act* (1895) 152–54.

36. See e.g., P.B. Mignault, *Manuel de Droit Parlementaire* (1889) 315 n. J.E.C. Munro, *The Constitution of Canada* (1889) 257; W.H.P. Clement, *The Law of the Canadian Constitution* (1892) 484. Clement had offered a most convincing explanation of the function of the deeming clause. Considering the stress the Fathers of Confederation had laid on the "general" as opposed to the "local" nature of federal legislative powers, it was obviously prudent for the draftsman to make very clear that Parliament was not to be hampered by tests of geographical generality, but could validly legislate in relation to a single penitentiary in New Brunswick, a single sea coast in Nova Scotia, one marine hospital in Quebec, and one bank in Ontario.

37. *L'Union St.-Jacques de Montréal v. Bélisle* (1874) L.R. 6 P.C. 31, at 35–36; *Dow v. Black* (1875) L.R. 6 P.C. 272, at 282; *The Citizens Insurance Company of Canada v. Parsons* (1881) 7 App. Cas. 96, at 108 (P.C.); argument in *Hodge v. The Queen*, Canada, *Sessional Papers*, 1884, vol. 17, no. 30, 29 per Lord Hobhouse.

38. *The Liquor Prohibition Appeal*, 142, 185 and 195. This assumption by Lords Davey and Herschell reinforces the point made in "The Work for the Empire" that Lord Watson was the dominating influence on the Board.

39. *A.-G. Ontario v. A.-G. for the Dominion and the Distillers and Brewers' Association of Ontario*, at 359.

40. *The Liquor Prohibition Appeal, passim.*

41. *The Constitutional Process in Canada* (1969) 130.

42. Jonathan Robinson, "Lord Haldane and the *British North America Act*" (1970) 20 *U. Toronto L.J.* 55.

43. "The Courts and the Sovereignty of the Canadian Parliament" (1944) 10 *Can. J. Econ.* 165–78; *Social Credit and the Federal Power in Canada* (1955), chap. 3; *The Structure of Canadian Government* (1971) 335–48.

44. See, e.g., Bora Laskin, "'Peace, Order, and Good Government' Re-examined" (1947) 25 *Can. B. Rev.* 1054, at 1086.

45. See Cairns, "The Judicial Committee and Its Critics," at 312–13. Of course, there have always been commentators who, like Browne, assume that the Judicial Committee merely laid down the law. See, e.g., V. Evan Gray, "'The O'Connor Report' on the *British North America Act*, 1867" (1939) 17 *Can. B. Rev.* 309; R.F. McWilliams, "The Privy Council and the Constitution," at 579–82; L.P. Pigeon, "The Meaning of Provincial Autonomy" (1951) 29 *Can. B. Rev.* 1127. A more recent example is the compact theorist, G.F.G. Stanley, *A Short History of the Canadian*

Constitution (1969), who refers to the Judicial Committee's "careful and unprejudiced approach to Canadian problems," Stanley attributes this to the supposed fact—which was a staple argument used by nineteenth century legal imperialists in Britain—that the Board was "uninfluenced by local sympathies or party affiliations" (at 142).

46. "Theories of Canadian Federalism—Yesterday and Today," in *Evolving Canadian Federalism*, ed. Lower, Scott, et al. (1958) 1, at 29.

47. Johnson, "Did Judah P. Benjamin." The only case Benjamin pleaded which resulted in an important decentralist pronouncement was the *Parsons* case, and in this instance he was representing the centralist side of the argument. The "states' rights" interpretation he offered in the *Russell* case was ignored by the Board.

48. The political allegiance of the Board in the two cases was as follows: the *Liquidators* case—Liberals, Lords Hobhouse and Shand, and Conservatives, Lords Macnaghten, Morris and Watson; the *Local Prohibition* case—Liberals, Lords Herschell and Davey, and Conservatives, Lords Watson and Halsbury. The political allegiance, if any, of Sir Richard Couch, who sat on both cases, is unknown. Because of the political division on the Board, and the dominant role played by Lord Watson, an active supporter of Disraeli prior to his appointment, the outcome of the two cases cannot possibly be attributed to the direct influence of party politics.

49. Speaking as Liberal Chancellor in the House of Lords debate on Irish Home Rule, Lord Herschell defended Gladstone's policy and referred with approval to the fact that all over the world "there has been another principle, which side by side with this national [consolidation] principle has been more and more coming into force and operation, and that is the principle of decentralisation, of local autonomy": 17 *Parl. Deb.* (4th ser.) 586 (1893) [1892–1908].

50. Lord Hobhouse, for example, was active in municipal politics and local government reform even after his appointment to the Judicial Committee.

51. Representing the New Brunswick Government in the *Liquidators* case, Davey and fellow counsel argued (at 439) that the provinces "are not made in any way subordinate to the legislature and government of the Dominion. The intention was that the Dominion and the provinces should have co-ordinate authority within their respective spheres...." See also Davey, *Report* of the Proceedings.

52. It must be remembered, too, that certain members of the Board were probably opposed to decentralised government as a general principle: e.g., Lords Macnaghten, Morris and Halsbury who, as politicians, had been outspoken opponents of Irish Home Rule.

53. Cheffins, *The Constitutional Process in Canada*.

54. "Theories of Canadian Federalism" at 38; F.R. Scott, "French-Canadian and Canadian Federalism," *Evolving Canadian Federalism*, at 71–72.

55. [1887] 12 App. Cas. 575, at 587.

56. The other decisions which appear unfavourable to business may be found in I Olmsted, *Decisions of the Judicial Committee*, 66, 154, 184, 263, 402 and 436. Decisions favourable to business are found in ibid., 19, 30, 203, 443 and 451. There are some decisions which are ambiguous in their effect, that is, they would have benefited some sections of the business community but would have run contrary to the interests of other segments (e.g., ibid., 94, 287 and 304).

57. See, e.g., *The Journal of Commerce—Finance and Insurance Review*, 12 January and 16 March 1883; *The Monetary Times*, 14 and 28 October, and 11 November 1887; Social Credit and the Federal Power 14–16; C. Armstrong and V. Nelles, "Private Property in Peril: Ontario

Businessmen and the Federal System, 1898–1911" (1973) 47 *Bus. Hist. Rev.* 158.

58. See, e.g., the unfavourable reports of the Interprovincial Conference of 1887 in the *Canadian Gazette* (a trade review published in London) for that year.

59. Gordon Greenwood, *The Future of Australian Federalism* (1946) 47–49; Stephen Leacock, "The Limitations of Federal Government" [1909] *Am. Pol. Sci. Ass'n. Proc.* 37; A.H.F. Lefroy, "Points of Special Interest in Canada's Federal Constitution (1913) 33 C.L.T. 898.

60. 1882, 45 Vict., c. 22 (Que.); 1884, 47 Vict., c. 39 (Ont.); 1890, 53 Vict., c. 33, S. 1 (B.C.).

61. The material on Lord Watson is based mainly on British Parliamentary sessional debates, 1880–1899, and obituary notices in the 1899 issues of the *Judicial Review*, at 269–81 and the *Scottish Law Review*, at 229–43.

62. *City of Winnipeg v. Barrett* [1892] A.C. 445 (P.C.), upholding Manitoba's abolition of separate school rights.

63. *Education and Empire* (1902) 111–14 and 136–39.

64. 257 *Parl. Deb.* (3d ser.) 153–54 (1881) [1837–1891].

65. 83 *Parl. Deb.* (4th ser.) 85 (1900) [1892–1908]. For a typical example of the stress on impartiality, see Lord Davey's speech opposing a limitation of appeals from Australia: *Parl. Deb.* at 26–33. See also (1885) 1 *Law Q. Rev.* 278; (1889) 1 *Jurid. Rev.* 111; Frank MacKinnon, "The Establishment of the Supreme Court of Canada" (1946) 27 *Can. Hist. Rev.* 258, at 264–66; Cairns, "The Judicial Committee and Its Critics" at 314 n. 58. The Cairns and MacKinnon articles suggest that it was also a common assumption that the existence of the appeal acted as a protection for British investors in the colonies.

66. "The Work for the Empire," at 149–50.

67. The evidence is not sufficient to decide conclusively whether Lord Watson, believing the law to be unclear, purposely adopted a decentralist interpretation or was unconsciously predisposed to such an interpretation (or was perhaps influenced by some combination). However, Lord Haldane's many descriptions of Lord Watson as the perfect example of the statesman-judge needed on the Judicial Committee suggests an element of conscious purpose. Lord Haldane described such a jurist as one endowed with the "outlook that makes him remember that with a growing constitution things are always changing and developing, and you cannot be sure that what was right ten years ago will be right today." "The Work for the Empire," at 148.

68. MacKinnon, "The Establishment of the Supreme Court of Canada," at 267.

69. *Parl. Deb.* H.C., 1880, at 253–54.

70. 1888, 51 Vict., c. 43 (held *ultra vires* by the Judicial Committee in 1926).

71. Bourinot, "The Federal Constitution of Canada," at 216–17.

72. A.B. Weston, "The Privy Council and Constitutional Appeals: An Historical Retrospect" (1948–50) 1 *U.W. Aust'l. L. Rev.* 255.

73. 1895, 58 Vict. c. 44. This statute was enacted in response to mounting evidence of Australian dissatisfaction with appeals to the Judicial Committee. See Prime Minister Rosebery's speech on the bill in 41 *Parl. Deb.* (4th ser.) 331–33 (1895) [1892–1908]. Lord Halsbury, then shadow Lord Chancellor, supported the bill on the sole ground "that he thought it would be a great advantage to the Judicial Committee...that it should insure the increased confidence of the Colonies." Ibid., at 334.

74. Quoted in Alexander Smith, *The Commerce Power in Canada and the United States* (1963) 50 n. 8.

75. The Judicial Committee's decision in *Hodge v. The Queen*, (1883–84) 9 App. Cas. 117, that the regulation of retail trade was a provincial

responsibility had a clear impact on the Supreme Court decisions in no. 8(I) and II. In no. 15, two judges of the majority were of the opinion that the Judicial Committee's decision in the *Barrett* case had determined the question. No. 16 was a mere application of the Judicial Committee's decision in the *Liquidators* case. Eliminating the Supreme Court's decision in the *Liquidators* case itself requires more comment. Taschereau J.'s reversal of the position he took in the *Lenoir* case (see table 2, note 3) may well have owed something to the Judicial Committee's decision on appeal in the *Mercer* case, (1853) 8 App. Cas. 767. Moreover, Patterson J., with whom Fournier J. concurred, cited a number of statements made in passing by the Judicial Committee which implied that the Lieutenant-Governor was a representative of the Queen.

76. On open issues Taschereau J.'s votes were eight for a centralist and four for a decentralist position.

77. Two cases, the *McCarthy Act Reference* and the *Local Prohibition* case involved at least two distinguishable issues (see table 2). The other cases are found in I Olmsted, *Decisions of the Judicial Committee* 94, 145, 171, 184, 203, 216, 222, 236, 251, 263, 272, 287, 304, 316, 367 and 373. The only centralist position of consequence was the *Russell* case, which was in effect reversed in the *Local Prohibition* case.

78. See Cook, *Provincial Autonomy* 29–31, 43, and 66–67 for examples. The growth of Canadian sentiment in favour of the compact theory was noted in the 1890 issue of the *Juridical Review* (at 381). A detailed argument supporting the theory was presented to the Board at the very outset of Lord Watson's active career on Canadian constitutional appeals: *Jurid. Rev., The St. Catharine's Milling and Lumber Company v. The Queen: The Argument of Mr. Blake of Counsel for Ontario* (1888).

79. Mowat represented Ontario as counsel in the *Mercer* and *St. Catherine's Milling* cases and attended the hearing of the *Local Prohibition* case. A.G. Blair, Liberal Premier and Attorney General, represented the New Brunswick Government in the *Liquidators* case.

80. See Greenwood, *The Future of Australian Federalism*.

81. (1884).

82. Travis, *A Law Treatise* but particularly at 153–67.

83. Ibid., at 180–81.

84. See, e.g., the review in (1884) 4 C.L.T. 436 and A.H.F. Lefroy, "Prohibition: The Late Privy Council Decision" (1896) 16 C.L.T. 130. The book was indeed unorganized self-congratulatory, and in its comment on the *Russell* decision was attacking a straw man (see note 88).

85. I Travis, *Commentaries on the Law of Sales and Collateral Subjects* (1892), Introduction, at x. I am indebted to a former student of mine David Elliott, for this reference.

86. Travis, *Commentaries.*

87. *A.-G. Ontario v. A.-G. for the Dominion and the Distillers and Brewers' Association of Ontario,* at 362.

88. Ibid., at 361. The Travis-Watson reading of the *Russell* decision makes little sense. Sir Montague E. Smith's reference in that case [(1882) 7 App. Cas. 829, 4 at 840–41] to the Dominion desire for uniform legislation was made solely in answer to the contention that Parliament in adopting the local option technique was dealing with temperance as a municipal or local matter within the meaning of s. 92(16). Smith's judgment (at 838–40) made very clear that the test was not desired geographical uniformity but the nature or aim of the impugned federal legislation. The act in question, the *Canada Temperance Act, 1878,* regulated public morals, and did not,

except incidentally, deal with property relations. Had it had as its primary aim the regulation of property rights, no amount of desired "uniformity" would have saved it. Canadian judges, almost unanimously, had also denied the simple uniformity test: see Lefroy, "Prohibition" at 129 n. *r*.

89. *A.-G. Ontario v. A.-G. for the Dominion and the Distillers and Brewers' Association of Ontario*, at 361. Referring to Parliament's supposed power to enact uniform law on s. 92 matters, Travis asks rhetorically, "Is it not a *little singular* that a special power should be found necessary to enable Parliament to do that for three of the provinces [in the field of civil law]...as is specially provided in section 94 of the B.N.A. Act?" Travis, *A Law Treatise on the Constitutional Powers of Parliament and of the Local Legislatures, Under the British North America Act, 1867* (1884), 167.

90. Travis, *A Law Treatise*, 153–67.

91. Travis, *A Law Treatise*, 9–10, 118–23 and 176–79.

92. Travis, *A Law Treatise*. This argument is weak. The B.N.A. Act (and earlier drafts) uses descriptive rather than numerical cross-references throughout (e.g., ss. 90, 91(29), 92(1) and 147). Presumably the draftsman wished to avoid changing several numerical references with every new draft.

93. Both Lords Haldane and Atkin adhered to the compact theory. See e.g., *Attorney-General of the Commonwealth of Australia v. Colonial Sugar Refining Co.* [1914] A.C. 237, at 252 (P.C.); *A.-G. Canada v. A.-G. Ontario* [1937] A.C. 326, at 351 (P.C.).

94. That is, legislation which although thought to have no significant impact outside the province in question was considered detrimental to portions of the public in that province. This paternalistic use of the disallowance power was of the influence in this area of the autonomy declaration in the *Liquidators* case, see the report of

Allen Aylesworth (Minister of Justice) to the Governor General-in-Council, 29 March 1910, Francis H. Gisborne and Arthur A. Fraser, eds., *Correspondence, Reports to the Minster of Justice and Orders in Council upon the Subject of the Provincial Legislation, 1896–1920 (1922)* 95–96 (*re refusal to veto Ontario's nationalization of hydro*).

95. Even leading representatives of the once centralist Conservative party accepted co-ordinate federalism on this point after the *Liquidators* case. See, e.g., *Parl. Deb.* H.C. vol. 1, 1895, at 817–18 per Thomas Daly, Minister of the Interior; *Parl. Deb.* H.C. vol. 1, 1906–7, at 26–7, per Robert Borden, Leader of the Opposition.

96. 83 *Parl. Deb.* (4th ser.) 98 (1900) [1892–1908].

97. Cairns, "The Judicial Committee and Its Critics," at 316–17.

98. (1909) 29 C.L.T. 348. By 1900, Edward Blake, then a Member of the British House of Commons, had completely reversed his stand:

I know that in the country whence I come...it was found with us that where bitter controversies had been excited, where political passions had been engendered, where considerable disputations had prevailed, where men eminent in power and politics had ranged themselves on opposite sides, it was no disadvantage, but a great advantage to have an opportunity of appealing to an external tribunal such as the Judicial Committee, for the interpretation of the Constitution on such matters.

This statement is quoted by MacKinnon, "The Establishment of the Supreme Court of Canada," at 267.

99. *Daily Telegraph Newspaper Company Limited v. McLaughlin* [1904] A.C. 776, at 778 (P.C.).

100. Quoted in Cairns, "The Judicial Committee and Its Critics," at 317.

section

3

INVENTION AND
CONSOLIDATION

1 9 1 6 - 1 9 4 7

T he decades from the end of the first world war through the second tested the Canadian federal system almost to its limits. By the turn of the century Canada was in the process of becoming "a nation transformed" by massive migration to western Canada, by the explosion in manufacturing, and by the exploitation of natural resources. Rapid industrialisation and urbanisation brought new problems, and in time made imperative the intervention of the state in the economic and social life of the country. The form of that intervention would be decided in the realm of policy and politics. In Canada, however, state intervention, whether in the form of programs or of regulation, was complicated by the constitutional division of jurisdiction. Throughout the inter-war years, despite the grave postwar recession and the destructive collapse of the economy in the 1930s, the courts effectively prevented attempts by the federal government to implement remedial legislation. In almost every case, the federal powers over trade and commerce and criminal law, or its residual power, could not sustain legislation which was challenged as encroaching on the provincial power over property and civil rights.[1]

Lord Haldane was the dominant figure on the Judicial Committee from the time of his appointment as Lord Chancellor in 1911, to his death in 1927. He delivered decisions in half of the fifty Canadian constitutional cases that came before the court. While he followed faithfully in his mentor's footsteps, hardening the co-ordinate federalism structure Watson had placed on the Act, he also invented new and unique limitations on federal powers (some of which were later rejected by his own court). Haldane's view of the law and the constitution is discussed in the Commentary.

For a few years after Haldane's death a succession of decisions seemed to open up federal powers as the Judicial Committee appeared to take a more liberal, "living tree," view of the constitution. The regulation of combines, radio and aeronautics found their place in the criminal law, in the treaty power, and in the residual clause (which, it appeared, could house "new matters"). But the door was soon closed when the federal government belatedly attempted to come to grips with an industrial nation's economic and social problems starkly revealed by the Depression.

On the eve of the 1935 election, R.B. Bennett suddenly produced his "New Deal," a package of legislation which sought to regulate unfair competition and the marketing of natural products, set minimum wages and hours of work, and provide a national unemployment insurance scheme. The legislation passed, but Bennett was defeated in the election. Mackenzie King, who had argued that much if not all of the New Deal was unconstitutional, referred the acts to the Supreme Court, hoping that he could escape the responsibility of either implementing or shelving them. The arguments of federal counsel were generally regarded as unpersuasive, perhaps even half-hearted. Previous decisions had effectively destroyed the trade and commerce power. So strong was the doctrine of precedent that federal counsel made little or no attempt to argue that massive unemployment was a new "matter" demanding national remedies and should not have to be measured against property and civil rights. As a result, they adopted a "shotgun" approach hoping that one of the enumerated heads, or the treaty power, or the residual power might be capable of supporting the legislation. The arguments were not convincing.

Even so, the captive court only rejected unemployment insurance in a 4 to 2 decision and was equally divided on upholding the labour legislation as the fulfilment of a treaty obligation. Chief Justice Duff, an ardent judicial and political champion of provincial autonomy, accepted both as *intra vires*. As in the *Board of Commerce* case after the war, some members of the Court including Duff, appeared to be caught in the tension between the obvious necessity of remedial action and the limitations imposed by precedent.[2]

The Judicial Committee felt no such tension, at least in the written decisions. But years later one member of the Judicial Committee who sat on the New Deal cases stated explicitly, perhaps indiscreetly, that the decision on the Labour Conventions reference may have been wrong and implied that he, at least, may have reached a different decision. In the final written decision the ghosts of Smith (at least as the *Parsons* case had been read), Watson and Haldane lurked over the Judicial Committee. The attempts by the federal government to manage or regulate the economy could find no support in the enumerated heads of power or, despite the gravity of the crisis, in the power to legislate for the peace, order, and good government in Canada. Whatever the limitations on "property and civil rights" had been intended in the 1867 Act, that power was by now, as Haldane put it, "unreservedly," possessed by the provinces.[3]

The New Deal decisions aroused widespread public and scholarly criticism. Legal scholars subjected the work of Smith, Watson, Haldane and others to a searching historical and jurisprudential analysis, and found them wanting. And many Canadians concluded that the time had come to locate the final court of appeal firmly in Canada.[4]

NOTES

1. On regulation see: Carman D. Baggaley, *The Emergence of the Regulatory State in Canada, 1867–1939*, Technical Report no. 15, Economic Council of Canada (Ottawa, 1981).

2. See the excellent review of the New Deal cases by W.H. McConnell, "The Judicial Review of Prime Minister Bennett's 'New Deal,'" *Osgoode Hall Law Journal* (1968): 39–86. The best study of Duff is Gerald Le Dain, "Sir Lyman Duff and the Constitution," *Osgoode Hall Law Journal* 12, 2 (1974): 261–338.

3. Canadian Bar Review (1955), 1123–28. Lord Wright suggested that in finding the labour legislation valid under the treaty power, Duff was reaching a decision consistent with the *Radio* and *Aeronautics* decisions and in anticipation of the words of Lord Simon in *A. G. of Ontario v. Canada Temperance Federation* [1946] that the

> true test...must be found in the real subject matter of the legislation: if it is such that it goes beyond provincial or local concern or interests and must from its inherent nature be the concern of the Dominion as a whole...then it will fall within the competence of the Dominion Parliament as a matter affecting the peace, order and good

government of Canada, though it may in another aspect touch on matters specially reserved to the provincial legislatures.

Wright also seemed to be sympathetic to Duff's attempt to find the unemployment insurance legislation valid, although not necessarily for the same reasons. The subject matter, wrote Wright, seemed remote from ordinary insurance, which fell within property and civil rights. He believed "the pith and substance" of this matter "would seem to be the nation-wide system of social insurance." Duff's decisions, he concluded, "justify Sir Lyman's practical sense, and it may be his legal sense, of what was the correct construction and effect of the legislative measures involved."

4. See for example the exhaustive study by W.F. O'Connor: Canada, Senate *Report* Pursuant to Resolution of the Senate to the Honourable Speaker by the Parliamentary Counsel Relating to The Enactment of the *British North America Act, 1867*, any lack of consonance between its terms and judicial construction of them and cognate matters (Ottawa, 1939). See also Bora Laskin, "'Peace, Order, and good Government' Re-examined," *Canadian Bar Review* 25 (1947): 1054–87.

JOHN DEERE PLOW
COMPANY v. WHARTON◇

The John Deere Plow company was incorporated under the *Companies Act of Canada* which regulated the extent and limits of a company's power. *The Companies Act of British Columbia* required companies not incorporated in that province to be licensed or registered; in the absence thereof, a company could not carry on business or form enforceable contracts. The provincial Act was challenged as an infringement on federal jurisdiction over 91(2) "The Regulation of Trade and Commerce."

VISCOUNT HALDANE:

. . . Before proceeding to consider the question whether the provisions already referred to of the *British Columbia Companies Act,* imposing restrictions on the operations of a Dominion company which has failed to obtain a provincial licence, are valid, it is necessary to realise the relation to each other of ss. 91 and 92 and the character of the expressions used in them. The language of these sections and of the various heads which they contain obviously cannot be construed as having been intended to embody the exact disjunctions of a perfect logical scheme. The draftsman had to work on the terms of a political agreement, terms which were mainly to be sought for in the resolutions passed at Quebec in October, 1864. To these resolutions and the sections founded on them the remark applies which was made by this Board about the *Australian Commonwealth Act* in a recent case *(Attorney-General for the Commonwealth v. Colonial Sugar Refining Co.),* that if there is at points obscurity in language, this may be taken to be due, not to uncertainty about general principle, but to that difficulty in obtaining ready agreement about phrases which attends the drafting of legislative measures by large assemblages. It may be added that the form in which provisions in terms overlapping each other have been placed side by side shows that those who passed the Confederation Act intended to leave the working out and interpretation of these provisions to practice and to judicial decision.

The structure of ss. 91 and 92, and the degree to which the connotation of the expressions used overlaps, render it, in their Lordships' opinion, unwise on this or any other occasion to attempt exhaustive definitions of the meaning and scope of these expressions. Such definitions, in the case of language used under the condi-

---

◇[1915] A.C. 330.

tions in which a constitution such as that under consideration was framed, must almost certainly miscarry. It is in many cases only by confining decisions to concrete questions which have actually arisen in circumstances the whole of which are before the tribunal that injustice to future suitors can be avoided. . . . The wisdom of adhering to this rule appears to their Lordships to be of especial importance when putting a construction on the scope of the words "civil rights" in particular cases. An abstract logical definition of their scope is not only, having regard to the context of ss. 91 and 92 of the Act, impracticable, but is certain, if attempted, to cause embarrassment and possible injustice in future cases. It must be borne in mind in construing the two sections, that matters which in a special aspect and for a particular purpose may fall within one of them may, in a different aspect and for a different purpose, fall within the other. In such cases the nature and scope of the legislative attempt of the Dominion or the Province, as the case may be, have to be examined with reference to the actual facts if it is to be possible to determine under which set of powers it falls in substance and in reality. This may not be difficult to determine in actual and concrete cases. But it may well be impossible to give abstract answers to general questions as to the meaning of the words, or to lay down any interpretation based on their literal scope apart from their context.

Turning to the appeal before them, the first observation which their Lordships desire to make is that the power of the provincial legislature to make laws in relation to matters coming within the class of subject forming No. 11 of s. 92, the incorporation of companies with provincial objects, cannot extend to a company such as the appellant company, the objects of which are not provincial. Nor is this defect of power aided by the power given by No. 13, Property and Civil Rights. Unless these two heads are read disjunctively the limitation in No. 11 would be nugatory. The expression "civil rights in the Province" is a very wide one, extending, if interpreted literally, to much of the field of the other heads of s. 92 and also to much of the field of s. 91. But the expression cannot be so interpreted, and it must be regarded as excluding cases expressly dealt with elsewhere in the two sections, notwithstanding the generality of the words. If this be so, then the power of legislating with reference to the incorporation of companies with other than provincial objects must belong exclusively to the Dominion parliament, for the matter is one "not coming within the classes of subjects . . . assigned exclusively to the Legislatures of the Provinces," within the meaning of the initial words of s. 91, and may be properly regarded as a matter affecting the Dominion generally and covered by the expression "the peace, order, and good government of Canada."

Their Lordships find themselves in agreement with the interpretation put by the Judicial Committee in *Citizens Insurance Co. v. Parsons* on head 2 of s. 91, which confers exclusive power on the Dominion parliament to make laws regulating trade. This head must, like the expression, "Property and Civil Rights in the Province," in s. 92, receive a limited interpretation. But they think that the power to regulate trade and commerce at all events enables the Parliament of Canada to prescribe to what extent the powers of companies the objects of which extend to the entire Dominion should be exercisable, and what limitations should be placed on such powers. For if it be established that the Dominion parliament can create such companies, then it becomes a question of general interest throughout the

Dominion in what fashion they should be permitted to trade. Their Lordships are therefore of the opinion that the Parliament of Canada had power to enact the sections relied on in this case in the *Dominion Companies Act* and the *Interpretation Act*. They do not desire to be understood as suggesting that because the status of a Dominion company enables it to trade in a province and thereby confers on it civil rights to some extent, the power to regulate trade and commerce can be exercised in such a way as to trench, in the case of such companies, on the exclusive jurisdiction of the provincial Legislatures over civil rights in general. No doubt this jurisdiction would conflict with that of the Province if civil rights were to be read as an expression of unlimited scope. But, as has already been pointed out, the expression must be construed consistently with various powers conferred by ss. 91 and 92, which restrict its lateral scope. It is enough for present purposes to say that the Province cannot legislate so as to deprive a Dominion company of its status and powers. This does not mean that these powers can be exercised in contravention of the laws of the Province restricting the rights of the public in the Province generally. What it does mean is that the status and powers of a Dominion company as such cannot be destroyed by provincial legislation.

o

A.-G. CANADA v. A.-G. ALBERTA AND OTHERS◇

Section 4 of the *Insurance Act, 1910* prohibited the making of insurance contracts without licence from the federal government. It was found to be *ultra vires* the federal government, on a reference to the Supreme Court of Canada, Chief Justice Davies dissenting, and appealed to the Judicial Committee.

VISCOUNT HALDANE:

It must be taken to be now settled that the general authority to make laws for the peace, order, and good government of Canada, which the initial part of s. 91 of the *British North America Act* confers, does not, unless the subject matter of legislation falls within some one of the enumerated heads which follow, enable the Dominion parliament to trench on the subject matter entrusted to the provincial Legislatures by the enumeration in s. 92. There is only one case, outside the heads enumerated in s. 91, in which the Dominion parliament can legislate effectively as regards a province, and that is where the subject matter lies outside all of the subject matters enumeratively entrusted to the province under s. 92. *Russell v. The Queen* is an instance of such a case. There the Court considered that the particular subject matter in question lay outside the provincial powers. What has been said in subsequent cases before this Board makes it clear that it was on this ground alone, and not on the ground that the *Canada Temperance Act* was considered to be authorized as legislation for the regulation of trade and commerce, that the Judicial

◇[1916] 1 A.C. 588.

Committee thought that it should be held that there was constitutional authority for Dominion legislation which imposed conditions of a prohibitory character on the liquor traffic throughout the Dominion. No doubt the *Canada Temperance Act* contemplated in certain events the use of different licensing boards and regulations in different districts and to this extent legislated in relation to local institutions. But the Judicial Committee appears to have thought that this purpose was subordinate to a still wider and legitimate purpose of establishing a uniform system of legislation for prohibiting the liquor traffic throughout Canada excepting under restrictive conditions. The case must therefore be regarded as illustrating the principle which is now well established, but none the less ought to be applied only with great caution, that subjects which in one aspect and for one purpose fall within the jurisdiction of the provincial legislatures may in another aspect and for another purpose fall within Dominion legislative jurisdiction. There was a good deal in the Ontario *Liquor Licence Act*, and the powers of regulation which it entrusted to local authorities in the province, which seems to cover part of the field of legislation recognized as belonging to the Dominion in *Russell v. The Queen*. But in *Hodge v. The Queen* the Judicial Committee had no difficulty in coming to the conclusion that the local licensing system which the Ontario statute sought to set up was within provincial powers. It was only the converse of this proposition to hold, as was done subsequently by this Board, though without giving reasons, that the Dominion licensing statute, known as the *McCarthy Act*, which sought to establish a local licensing system for the liquor traffic throughout Canada, was beyond the powers conferred on the Dominion parliament by s. 91. Their Lordships think that as the result of these decisions it must now be taken that the authority to legislate for the regulation of trade and commerce does not extend to the regulation by a licensing system of a particular trade in which Canadians would otherwise be free to engage in the provinces. Sect. 4 of the statute under consideration cannot, in their opinion, be justified under this head. Nor do they think that it can be justified for any such reasons as appear to have prevailed in *Russell v. The Queen*. No doubt the business of insurance is a very important one, which has attained to great dimensions in Canada. But this is equally true of other highly important and extensive forms of business in Canada which are to-day freely transacted under provincial authority. Where the *British North America Act* has taken such forms of business out of provincial jurisdiction, as in the case of banking, it has done so by express words which would have been unnecessary had the argument for the Dominion government addressed to the Board from the Bar been well founded. Where a company is incorporated to carry on the business of insurance throughout Canada, and desires to possess rights and powers to that effect operative apart from further authority, the Dominion government can incorporate it with such rights and powers, to the full extent explained by the decision in the *John Deere Plow Co. v. Wharton*. But if a company seeks only provincial rights and powers, and is content to trust for the extension of these in other provinces to the Governments of those provinces, it can at least derive capacity to accept such rights and powers in other provinces from the province of its incorporation, as has been explained in the case of the *Bonanza Company*.

Their Lordships are therefore of the opinion that the majority in the Supreme Court were right in answering the first of the two questions referred to them in the affirmative.

›

RE THE BOARD OF COMMERCE ACT AND THE COMBINES AND FAIR PRICES ACT OF 1919◇

The Board of Commerce Act and *The Combines and Fair Prices Act* were federal legislation attempting to prevent the hoarding and the over-pricing of "necessaries of life." The Board was empowered to enquire into and prohibit the making of unfair profits; any order of the Board could be made a rule, order or decree of the Exchequer Court or of any Superior Court of any province of Canada. In this reference case, the Supreme Court of Canada divided evenly (3–3) over whether the federal government—under its jurisdiction over "the Regulation of Trade and Commerce" and for "the Peace, Order, and good Government of Canada"—had the authority to pass this legislation.

Delivering the judgment of the Chief Justice and Mignault J., Mr. Justice Anglin first reviewed some of the decisions relating to the trade and commerce power, and concluded that whatever meaning might have been given to earlier decisions, the effect of the decision in *John Deere* was that 91 (2)

> retains its place and office as an enumerative head of Federal legislative jurisdiction and that legislation authorized by its terms, properly construed, is not subject to the restrictions imposed on Dominion legislation that depends solely on the general "peace, order, and good government" clause, but, on the contrary, is effective although it invades some field of jurisdiction conferred on the Provinces by an enumerative head of sec. 92.

ANGLIN J.:

Probably the test by which it must be determined whether a given subject matter of legislation *prima facie* ascribable to either properly falls under sec. 91 (2) or sec. 92 (13) is this: Is it as primarily dealt with, in its true nature and character, in its pith and substance (in the language of Viscount Haldane's judgment just quoted), "a question of general interest throughout the Dominion," or is it (in Lord Watson's words in the *Local Prohibition* case), "from a provincial point of view of a local or private nature?"

In order to be proper subjects of Dominion legislation under "the regulation of trade and commerce" it may well be that the matters dealt with must not only be such as would ordinarily fall within that description, but, if the legislation would

---

◇[1920] 60 S.C.R. 456.

otherwise invade the provincial field, must also be "of general interest throughout the Dominion," or, in the language used by Lord Watson in the *Local Prohibition* case, in regard to legislation under the peace, order, and good government clause upon matters not enumerated in sec. 91, must be "unquestionably of Canadian interest and importance."

The regulation of the quantities of "necessaries of life" that may be accumulated and withheld from sale and the compelling of the sale and disposition of them at reasonable prices throughout Canada is regulation of trade and commerce using those words in an ordinary sense. While the making of contracts for the sale and purchase of commodities is primarily purely a matter of "property and civil rights," and legislation restricting or controlling it must necessarily affect matters ordinarily subject to Provincial legislative jurisdiction, the regulation of prices of necessaries of life—and to that the legislation under consideration is restricted—may under certain circumstances well be a matter of national concern and importance—may well affect the body politic of the entire Dominion. Moreover, "necessaries of life" may be produced in one Province and sold in another. In the case of manufactured goods the raw material may be grown in or obtained from one Province, may be manufactured in a second Province and may be sold in several other Provinces.

Effective control and regulation of prices so as to meet and overcome in any one Province what is generally recognized to be an evil—"profiteering"—an evil so prevalent and so insidious that in the opinion of many persons it threatens to-day the moral and social well-being of the Dominion—may thus necessitate investigation, inquiry and control in other Provinces. It may be necessary to deal with the prices and the profits of the growers or other producers of raw material, the manufacturers, the middlemen and the retailers. No one Provincial legislature could legislate so as to cope effectively with such a matter and concurrent legislation of all the Provinces interested is fraught with so many difficulties in its enactment, and its administration and enforcement that to deal with the situation at all adequately by that means is in my opinion quite impracticable.

Viewed in this light it would seem that the impugned statutory provisions may be supported, without bringing them under any of the enumerative heads of sec. 91, as laws made for the peace, order, and good government of Canada in relation to matters not coming within any of the classes of subjects assigned exclusively to the Legislatures of the Provinces, since, in so far as they deal with property and civil rights, they do so in an aspect which is not "from a provincial point of view local or private" and therefore not exclusively under provincial control.

Anglin and his colleagues concluded that the "true aspect and real purpose" of the Act related to "public order, safety or morals, affects the body politics of the Dominion and is a matter of national concern" so that it could be supported under the "good government" provision. But in view of Watson's cautionary warning in 1896, repeated by Haldane in 1916, about the need to give a narrow construction to this provision, he went further.

I think it is better that legislation such as that with which we are now dealing, which undoubtedly affects what would ordinarily be subject matters of Provincial jurisdiction, should, if possible, be ascribed to one of the enumerative heads of sec. 91. I prefer, therefore, to rest my opinion upholding its constitutional validity on the power of the Dominion parliament to legislate for "the regulation of Trade and Commerce" as well as on its power "to make laws for the peace, order, and good government of Canada," in regard to matters which, though not referable to any of the enumerative heads of sec. 91, should, having regard to the aspect in which and the purpose for which they are dealt with, properly be held not to fall within any of the enumerative heads of sec. 92—to "lie outside all the subject matters" thereby "entrusted to the Provinces."

The carrying out of the Act now in question, as I have endeavoured to point out, will, in some of its phases, affect the inter-provincial trade and the foreign trade in necessaries of life throughout the Dominion. It would therefore seem to fall within the jurisdiction conferred by head No. 2 as indicated in *Citizens Ins. Co. v. Parsons.*

DUFF J.:

Having regard then to the scope of sec. 18, the authority conferred upon the Board to interfere with the proprietary rights of producers, holders and consumers of any of the articles to which the Act applies, and the authority to interfere with the management of local works and undertakings, and to prescribe the conditions of contracts relating to such articles and to the manner in which the Act takes effect, I conclude that it is not an enactment in relation to trade and commerce within sec. 91, sub-sec. 2.

The second question is whether sec. 18 can be sustained as an exercise of the power of the Dominion under the introductory clause of sec. 91 to "make laws for the peace, order, and good government of Canada." Two conditions govern the legitimate exercise of this power. First—it is essential that the matter dealt with shall be one of unquestioned Canadian interest and importance as distinguished from matters merely local in one of the Provinces, and, secondly, that the legislation shall not trench upon the authority of the Province in respect of the matters enumerated in sec. 92. . . .

It is true that in *Russell v. The Queen* (1882), the *Canada Temperance Act* was held to be validly enacted under this general power and that in *Local Option Reference,* (1896) and in the *Manitoba Licence Holders'* case, [1902], the enactment of similar legislation was held to be competent to a local Legislature, the legislation being, of course, limited in its operation to the Province; but it is I think impossible to draw from these authorities on the "drink" legislation any general principle which can serve as a guide in passing upon the validity of the statutes before us . . . .

But it must be remembered that *Russell's* case was in great part an unargued case. Mr. Benjamin who appeared for the appellant—the Provinces were not represented upon the argument—conceded the authority of Parliament to enact legislation containing the provisions of the *Canada Temperance Act* to come into force at the same time throughout the whole of Canada and this Lord Herschell said, in a subsequent case, was a "very large admission." The Judicial Committee proceeded upon the view that legislation containing the provisions of the *Canada Temperance Act* was not, from a provincial point of view, legislation relating to "property and civil rights" within the Province; it was, they said, legislation dealing rather with public wrongs, having a close relation to criminal law and on this ground they held that the subject matter of it did not fall within the exceptions to the introductory clause. . . .

There is no case of which I am aware in which a Dominion statute not referable to one of the classes of legislation included in the enumerated heads of sec. 91 and being of such a character that from a provincial point of view, it should be considered legislation dealing with "property and civil rights," has been held competent to the Dominion under the introductory clause. . . .

"Property and civil rights," of course, taken in the most comprehensive sense, is a phrase of very wide application and like the words "Trade and Commerce," it must be restricted by reference to the context and the other provisions of secs. 91 and 92. But my view is that where a subject matter is from a provincial point of view comprehended within the class of subjects falling under "property and civil rights," properly construed *(ex hypothesi* such matter could not fall strictly within any of the classes of subjects enumerated in sec. 91) it is incompetent to the Dominion in exercise of the authority given by the introductory clause to legislate upon that matter either alone or together with subjects over which the Dominion has undoubted jurisdiction as falling neither within sec. 92 nor within the enumerated heads of sec. 91; and legislation which in effect has this operation cannot be legitimised by framing it in comprehensive terms embracing matters over which the Dominion has jurisdiction as well as matters in which the jurisdiction is committed exclusively to the Provinces.

Nor do I think it matters in the least that the legislation is enacted with the view of providing a remedy uniformly applicable to the whole of Canada in relation to a situation of general importance to the Dominion. The ultimate social, economic or political aims of the legislator cannot I think determine the category into which the matters dealt with fall in order to determine the question whether the jurisdiction to enact it is given by sec. 91 or sec. 92. The immediate operation and effect of the legislation, or the effect the legislation is calculated immediately to produce must alone, I think, be considered. I repeat that if, tested by reference to such operation and effect, the legislation does deal with matters which from a provincial point of view are within any of the first fifteen heads of sec. 92, it is incompetent to the Dominion unless it can be supported as ancillary to legislation under one of the enumerated heads of sec. 91. . . .

The consequences of this proposed view of the residuary clause, can be illustrated by the present legislation. The scarcity of necessaries of life, the high cost of them, the evils of excessive profit taking, are matters affecting nearly every individual in the community and affecting the inhabitants of every locality and every Province collectively as well as the Dominion as a whole. The legislative remedy attempted by sec. 18 is one of many remedies which might be suggested. One could conceive, for example, a proposal that there should be a general restriction of credits, and that the business of money lending should be regulated by a commission appointed by the Dominion government with powers conferred by Parliament. Measures to increase production might conceivably be proposed and to that end nationalisation of certain industries and even compulsory allotment of labour. In truth, if this legislation can be sustained under the residuary clause, it is not easy to put a limit to the extent to which Parliament through the instrumentality of commissions (having a large discretion in assigning the limits of their own jurisdiction, see sec. 16), may from time to time in the vicissitudes of national trade, times of high prices, times of stagnation and low prices and so on, supersede the authority of the Provincial legislatures. I am not convinced that it is a proper application of the drink legislation, to draw from it conclusions which would justify Parliament in any conceivable circumstance forcing upon a Province a system of nationalisation of industry.

o

RE THE BOARD OF COMMERCE ACT AND THE COMBINES AND FAIR PRACTICES ACT OF 1919⬦

The decision of the Supreme Court was appealed to the Judicial Committee.

VISCOUNT HALDANE:

The first question to be answered is whether the Dominion parliament could validly enact such a law. Their Lordships observe that the law is not one enacted to meet special conditions in wartime. It was passed in 1919, after peace had been declared, and it is not confined to any temporary purpose, but is to continue without limit in time, and to apply throughout Canada. No doubt the initial words of s. 91 of the *British North America Act* confer on the Parliament of Canada power to deal with subjects which concern the Dominion generally, provided that they are not withheld from the powers of that Parliament to legislate, by any of the express heads in s. 92, untrammelled by the enumeration of special heads in s. 91. It may well be that the subjects of undue combination and hoarding are matters in which the Dominion has a great practical interest. In special circumstances, such as those of a great war, such an interest might conceivably become of such paramount and overriding importance as to amount to what lies outside the heads in s. 92, and is not covered by them. The decision in *Russell v. The Queen* appears to recognize this as constitutionally possible, even in time of peace; but it is quite another matter to say that under normal circumstances general Canadian policy can justify interference, on such a scale as the statutes in controversy involve, with the property and civil rights of the inhabitants of the Provinces. It is to the legislatures of the Provinces that the regulation and restriction of their civil rights have in general been exclusively confided, and as to these the Provincial Legislatures possess quasi-sovereign authority. It can, therefore, be only under necessity in highly exceptional circumstances, such as cannot be assumed to exist in the present case, that the liberty of the inhabitants of the Provinces may be restricted by the Parliament of Canada,

---

⬦[1922] 1 A.C. 191.

and that the Dominion can intervene in the interests of Canada as a whole in questions such as the present one. For, normally, the subject matter to be dealt with in the case would be one falling within s. 92. Nor do the words in s. 91, the "Regulation of trade and commerce," if taken by themselves, assist the present Dominion contention. It may well be, if the Parliament of Canada had, by reason of an altogether exceptional situation, capacity to interfere, that these words would apply so as to enable that Parliament to oust the exclusive character of the Provincial powers under s. 92. . . .

For analogous reasons the words of head 27 of s. 91 do not assist the argument for the Dominion. It is one thing to construe the words "the criminal law, except the constitution of courts of criminal jurisdiction, but including the procedure in criminal matters," as enabling the Dominion parliament to exercise exclusive legislative power where the subject matter is one which by its very nature belongs to the domain of criminal jurisprudence. A general law, to take an example, making incest a crime, belongs to this class. It is quite another thing, first to attempt to interfere with a class of subject committed exclusively to the Provincial legislature, and then to justify this by enacting ancillary provisions, designated as new phases of Dominion criminal law which require a title to so interfere as basis of their application. . . .

Legislation setting up a Board of Commerce with such powers appears to their Lordships to be beyond the powers conferred by s. 91. They find confirmation of this view in s. 41 of the *Board of Commerce Act*, which enables the Dominion Executive to review and alter the decisions of the Board. It has already been observed that circumstances are conceivable, such as those of war or famine, when the peace, order, and good government of the Dominion might be imperilled under conditions so exceptional that they require legislation of a character in reality beyond anything provided for by the enumerated heads in either s. 92 or s. 91 itself. Such a case, if it were to arise would have to be considered closely before the conclusion could properly be reached that it was one which could not be treated as falling under any of the heads enumerated. Still, it is a conceivable case, and although great caution is required in referring to it, even in general terms, it ought not, in the view their Lordships take of the *British North America Act*, read as a whole, to be excluded from what is possible. For throughout the provisions of that Act there is apparent the recognition that subjects which would normally belong exclusively to a specially assigned class of subject may, under different circumstances and in another aspect, assume a further significance. Such an aspect may conceivably become of paramount importance, and of dimensions that give rise to other aspects. This is a principle which, although recognized in earlier decisions, such as that of *Russell v. The Queen*, both here and in the Courts of Canada, has always been applied with reluctance, and its recognition as relevant can be justified only after scrutiny sufficient to render it clear that the circumstances are abnormal. In the case before them, however important it may seem to the Parliament of Canada that some such policy as that adopted in the two Acts in question should be made general throughout Canada, their Lordships do not find any evidence that the standard of necessity referred to has been reached, or that the attainment of the end sought is practicable, in view of the distribution of legislative powers enacted by the Constitution Act, without the co-operation of the Provincial legislatures.

FORT FRANCES PULP AND POWER COMPANY, LTD. *v.* MANITOBA FREE PRESS COMPANY, LTD., AND OTHERS[*]

The Manitoba *Free Press* brought an action against the Fort Frances Pulp and Power Company to recover money paid to the company in 1919. The price of paper was then regulated by the federal government under the provisions of the *War Measures Act*, 1914. The Paper Control Tribunal, set up to settle disputes in this area, had ruled that the company had overcharged in supplying paper to the newspaper. The company responded that the tribunal had no authority to order it to refund the money.

VISCOUNT HALDANE:

It is clear that in normal circumstances the Dominion parliament could not have so legislated as to set up the machinery of control over the paper manufacturers which is now in question. The recent decision of the Judicial Committee in the *Board of Commerce Case*, as well as earlier decisions, show that as the Dominion Parliament cannot ordinarily legislate so as to interfere with property and civil rights in the Provinces, it could not have done what the two statutes under consideration purport to do had the situation been normal. But it does not follow that in a very different case, such as that of sudden danger fo social order arising from the outbreak of a great war, the Parliament of the Dominion cannot act under other powers which may well be implied in the constitution. The reasons given in the *Board of Commerce* case recognize exceptional cases where such a power may be implied.

In the event of war, when the national life may require for its preservation the employment of very exceptional means, the provision of peace, order and good government for the country as a whole may involve effort on behalf of the whole nation, in which the interests of individuals may have to be subordinated to that of the community in a fashion which requires s. 91 to be interpreted as providing for such an emergency. The general control of property and civil rights for normal purposes remains with the Provincial legislatures. But questions may arise by reason of the special circumstances of the national emergency which concern nothing short of the peace, order and good government of Canada as a whole.

The overriding powers enumerated in s. 91, as well as the general words at the commencement of the section, may then become applicable to new and special aspects which they cover of subjects assigned otherwise exclusively to the Provinces. It may be, for example, impossible to deal adequately with the new questions which arise without the imposition of special regulations on trade and commerce of a kind that only the situation created by the emergency places within the competency of the Dominion Parliament. It is proprietary and civil rights in new relations, which they do not present in normal times, that have to be dealt with; and these relations, which affect Canada as an entirety, fall within s. 91, because in their fullness they extend beyond what s. 92 can really cover. The kind of power adequate for dealing

[*] [1923] A.C. 695.

with them is only to be found in that part of the constitution which establishes power in the State as a whole. For it is not one that can be reliably provided for by depending on collective action of the Legislatures of the individual Provinces agreeing for the purpose. That the basic instrument on which the character of the entire constitution depends should be construed as providing for such centralised power in an emergency situation follows from the manifestation in the language of the Act of the principle that the instrument has among its purposes to provide for the State regarded as a whole, and for the expression and influence of its public opinion as such. This principle of a power so implied has received effect also in countries with a written and apparently rigid constitution such as the United States, where the strictly federal character of the national basic agreement has retained the residuary powers not expressly conferred on the Federal Government for the component States. The operation of the scheme of interpretation is all the more to be looked for in a constitution such as that established by the *British North America Act*, where the residuary powers are given to the Dominion Central Government; and the preamble of the statute declares the intention to be that the Dominion should have a constitution similar in principle to that of the United Kingdom.

Their Lordships, therefore, entertain no doubt that however the wordings of ss. 91 and 92 may have laid down a framework under which, as a general principle, the Dominion parliament is to be excluded from trenching on property and civil rights in the Provinces of Canada, yet in a sufficiently great emergency such as that arising out of war, there is implied the power to deal adequately with that emergency for the safety of the Dominion as a whole. The enumeration in s. 92 is not in any way repealed in the event of such an occurrence, but a new aspect of the business of Government is recognized as emerging, an aspect which is not covered or precluded by the general words in which powers are assigned to the Legislatures of the Provinces as individual units. Where an exact line of demarcation will lie in such cases it may not be easy to lay down a priori, nor is it necessary. For in the solution of the problem regard must be had to the broadened field covered, in case of exceptional necessity, by the language of s. 91, in which the interests of the Dominion generally are protected. As to these interests the Dominion government, which in its Parliament represents the people as a whole, must be deemed to be left with considerable freedom to judge.

The other point which arises is whether such exceptional necessity as must be taken to have existed when the war broke out, and almost of necessity for some period subsequent to its outbreak, continued through the whole of the time within which the questions in the present case arose.

When war has broken out it may be requisite to make special provision to ensure the maintenance of law and order in a country, even when it is in no immediate danger of invasion. Public opinion may become excitable, and one of the causes of this may conceivably be want of uninterrupted information in newspapers. Steps may have to be taken to ensure supplies of these and to avoid shortage, and the effect of the economic and other disturbances occasioned originally by the war may thus continue for some time after it is terminated. The question of the extent to which provision for circumstances such as these may have to be maintained is one on which a Court of law is loath to enter. No authority other than the central Government is in a position to deal with a problem which is essentially one of statesmanship. It may be that it has become clear that the crisis which arose is wholly at an end and that there is no justification for the continued exercise of an exceptional interference which becomes *ultra vires* when it is no longer called for. In such a case the law as laid down for distribution of powers in the ruling instrument would have to be invoked. But very clear evidence that the crisis has wholly passed away would be required to justify the judiciary, even when the question raised was one of *ultra vires* which it had to decide, in overruling the decision of the Government that exceptional measures were still requisite.

o

A.-G. ONTARIO v. RECIPROCAL INSURERS AND OTHERS AND A.-G. CANADA◇

Section 508 of the Criminal Code of Canada made it an offence to carry on the business of insurance in Canada except on behalf of a company or association licensed under the *Insurance Act, 1917* of Canada. Insurers would otherwise be able to carry on their business in Ontario if licensed under the provision of *The Reciprocal Insurers Act, 1922* of Ontario. Mr. Justice Duff sat on the Judicial Committee and delivered the decision.

MR. JUSTICE DUFF:

It is not seriously disputed that the purpose and effect of the amendment in question are to give compulsory force to the regulative measures of the *Insurance Act*, and their Lordships think it not open to controversy that in purpose and effect s. 508*c* is a measure regulating the exercise of civil rights. But, on behalf of the Dominion, it is argued that, although such be the true character of the legislation, the jurisdiction of Parliament, in relation to the criminal law, is unlimited, in the sense, that in execution of its powers over that subject matter, the Dominion has authority to declare any act a crime, either in itself or by reference to the manner or the conditions in which the act is done, and consequently that s. 508*c*, being by its terms limited to the creation of criminal offenses, falls within the jurisdiction of the Dominion.

The power which this argument attributes to the Dominion is, of course, a far-reaching one. Indeed, the claim now advanced is nothing less than this, that the Parliament of Canada can assume exclusive control over the exercise of any class of civil rights within the Provinces, in respect of which exclusive jurisdiction is given to the Provinces under s. 92, by the device of declaring those persons to be guilty of a criminal offence who in the exercise of such rights do not observe the conditions imposed by the Dominion. Obviously the principle contended for ascribes to the Dominion the power, in execution of its authority under s. 91, head 27, to promulgate and to enforce regulations controlling such matters as, for example, the solemnization of marriage, the practice of the learned professions and other

◇[1924] A.C. 328.

occupations, municipal institutions, the operation of local works and undertakings, the incorporation of companies with exclusively Provincial objects—and superseding Provincial authority in relation thereto. Indeed, it would be difficult to assign limits to the measure in which, by a procedure strictly analogous to that followed in this instance, the Dominion might dictate the working of Provincial institutions, and circumscribe or supersede the legislative and administrative authority of the Provinces.

Such a procedure cannot, their Lordships think, be justified, consistently with the governing principles of the Canadian Constitution, as enunciated and established by the judgments of this Board.

·>

TORONTO ELECTRIC COMMISSIONERS v. SNIDER[◇]

The *Industrial Disputes Investigations Act* was passed by the federal government in 1907. It prohibited strikes and lock-outs in certain public industries pending the report of a tripartite committee of labour, management and the state of an industrial dispute. The committee had authority to inspect the employer's premises and compel evidence on oath; it also had the power to demand the parties to produce what the committee considered to be relevant documents. The Toronto Electric Commissioners were appointed by the city to manage its municipal electric system. The Commission brought action against the Committee (consisting of Snider et. al.) to the Ontario Supreme Court where a 4–1 majority, Hodgins J., dissenting, held that the federal government had the authority to pass this legislation in relation to its jurisdiction over "Trade and Commerce" and "Criminal Law."

VISCOUNT HALDANE:

Whatever else may be the effect of this enactment, it is clear that it is one which could have been passed, so far as any Province was concerned, by the Provincial legislature under the powers conferred by s. 92 of the *British North America Act*. For its provisions were concerned directly with the civil rights of both employers and employed in the Province. It set up a Board of Inquiry which could summon them before it, administer to them oaths, call for their papers and enter their premises. It did no more than what a Provincial legislature could have done under head 15 of s. 92, when it imposed punishment by way of penalty in order to enforce the new restrictions on civil rights. It interfered further with civil rights when, by s. 56, it suspended liberty to lock-out or strike during a reference to a Board. It does not appear that there is anything in the Dominion Act which could not have been enacted by the Legislature of Ontario, excepting one provision. The field for the operation of the Act was made the whole of Canada. . . .

[◇] [1925] A.C. 396.

The power of the Dominion parliament to legislate in relation to criminal law, under head 27 of s. 91, was also considered to apply.

Before referring to these grounds of judgment their Lordships, without repeating at length what has been laid down by them in earlier cases, desire to refer briefly to the construction which, in their opinion, has been authoritatively put on ss. 91 and 92 by the more recent decisions of the Judicial Committee. . . .

Applying this principle, does the subject of the legislation in controversy fall fully within s. 92? For the reasons already given their Lordships think that it clearly does. If so, is the exclusive power *prima facie* conferred on the Province trenched on by any of the over-riding powers set out specifically in s. 91? It was, among other things, contended in the argument that the Dominion Act now challenged was authorized under head 27, "the Criminal Law, except the Constitution of Courts of Criminal Jurisdiction, but including the Procedure in Criminal Matters." It was further suggested in the argument that the power so conferred is aided by the power conferred on the Parliament of Canada to establish additional Courts for the better administration of the laws of Canada.

But their Lordships are unable to accede to these contentions. They think that they cannot now be maintained successfully, in view of a series of decisions in which this Board has laid down the interpretation of s. 91, head 27, in the *British North America Act* on the point. . . .

Nor does the invocation of the specific power in s. 91 to regulate trade and commerce assist the Dominion contention. In *Citizens Insurance Co. v. Parsons* it was laid down that the collocation of this head (No. 2 of s. 91), with classes of subjects enumerated of national and general concern, indicates that what was in the mind of the Imperial Legislature when this power was conferred in 1867 was regulation relating to general trade and commerce. Any other construction would, it was pointed out, have rendered unnecessary the specific mention of certain other heads dealing with banking, bills of exchange and promissory notes, as to which it had been significantly deemed necessary to insert a specific mention. The contracts of a particular trade or business could not, therefore, be dealt with by Dominion legislation so as to conflict with the powers assigned to the Provinces over property and civil rights relating to the regulation of trade and commerce. The Dominion power has a really definite effect when applied in aid of what the Dominion government are specifically enabled to do independently of the general regulation of trade and commerce, for instance, in the creation of Dominion companies with power to trade throughout the whole of Canada. This was shown in the decision in *John Deere Plow Co. v. Wharton.* The same thing is true of the exercise of an emergency power required, as on the occasion of war, in the interest of Canada as a whole, a power which may operate outside the specific enumerations in both ss. 91 and 92. And it was observed in *Attorney General for Canada v. Attorney General for Alberta*, in reference to attempted Dominion legislation about insurance, that it must now be taken that the authority to legislate for the regulation of trade and commerce does not extend to the regulation, for instance, by a licensing system, of a particular trade in which Canadians would otherwise be free to engage in the Provinces. It is, in their Lordships' opinion, now clear that, excepting so far as the power can be invoked in aid of capacity conferred independently under other words in s. 91, the power to regulate trade and commerce cannot be relied on as enabling the Dominion Parliament to regulate civil rights in the Provinces. A more difficult question arises with reference to the initial words of s. 91, which enable the parliament of Canada to make laws for the peace, order and good government of Canada in matters falling outside the Provincial powers specifically conferred by s. 92. For *Russell v. The Queen* was a decision in which the Judicial Committee said that it was within the competency of the Dominion parliament to establish a uniform system for prohibiting the liquor traffic throughout Canada excepting under restrictive conditions. It has been observed subsequently by this Committee that it is now clear that it was on the ground that the subject matter lay outside Provincial powers, and not on the ground that it was authorized as legislation for the regulation of trade and commerce, that the *Canada Temperance Act* was sustained: see *Attorney General for Canada v. Attorney General for Alberta*. But even on this footing it is not easy to reconcile the decision in *Russell v. The Queen* with the subsequent decision in *Hodge v. The Queen* that the Ontario *Liquor Licence Act*, with the powers of regulation which it entrusted to local authorities in the Province, was *intra vires* of the Ontario legislature. Still more difficult is it to reconcile *Russell v. The Queen* with the decision given later by the Judicial Committee that the Dominion licensing statute, known as the *McCarthy Act*, which sought to establish a local licensing system for the liquor traffic throughout the Dominion, was *ultra vires* of the Dominion parliament. As to this last decision it is not without significance that the strong Board which delivered it abstained from giving any reasons for their conclusion. . . .

It appears to their Lordships that it is not now open to them to treat *Russell v. The Queen* as having established the general principle that the mere fact that Dominion legislation is for the general advantage of Canada, or is such that it will meet a mere want which is felt throughout the Dominion, renders it competent if it cannot be brought within the heads enumerated specifically in s. 91. Unless this is so, if the subject matter falls within any of the enumerated heads in s. 92, such legislation belongs exclusively to Provincial competency. No doubt there may be cases arising out of some extraordinary peril to the national life of Canada, as a whole, such as the cases arising out of war, where legislation is required of an order that passes beyond the heads of exclusive Provincial competency. Such cases may be dealt with under the words at the commencement of s. 91, conferring general powers in relation to peace, order and good government, simply because such cases are not otherwise provided for. But instances of this, as was pointed out in the judgment of *Fort Frances Pulp and Power Co. v. Manitoba Free Press* are highly exceptional. Their Lordships think that the decision *Russell v. The Queen* can only be supported to-day, not on the footing of having laid down an interpretation, such as has sometimes been invoked of the general words at the beginning of s. 91, but on the assumption of the Board, apparently made at the time of deciding the case of *Russell v. The Queen,* that the evil of intemperance at that time amounted in Canada to one so great and so general that at least for the period it was a menace to the national life of Canada so serious and pressing that the National Parliament was called on to intervene to protect the nation from disaster. An epidemic of pestilence might conceivably have been regarded as analogous. It is plain from the decision in the *Board of Commerce* case that the evil of profiteering could not have been so invoked, for Provincial powers, if exercised, were adequate to it. Their

Lordships find it difficult to explain the decision in *Russell v. The Queen* as more than a decision of this order upon facts, considered to have been established at its date rather than upon general law.

o

EDWARDS *v*. A.-G. CANADA[◇]

The Supreme Court of Canada, in a reference case, unanimously decided that "qualified persons," as stated in section 24 of the *British North America Act*, did not include women; as such, women could not be appointed to the Canadian Senate. Duff J., came to that conclusion from the text of the Act—Section 23, which lists qualifications, refers to the applicant as "he." The rest of the Court came to its conclusion because of the common law disability of women to hold public office. This decision was appealed to the Judicial Committee.

LORD SANKEY:

The British North America Act planted in Canada a living tree capable of growth and expansion within its natural limits . . . .

Their Lordships do not conceive it to be the duty of this Board—it is certainly not their desire—to cut down the provisions of the Act by a narrow and technical construction, but rather to give it a large and liberal interpretation so that the Dominion to a great extent, but within certain fixed limits, may be mistress in her own house, as the Provinces to a great extent, but within certain fixed limited, are mistresses in theirs.

> The Privy Council, indeed, has laid down that Courts of law must treat the provisions of the *British North America Act* by the same methods of the construction and exposition which they apply to other statutes. But there are statutes and statutes; and the strict construction deemed proper in the case, for example, of a penal or taxing statute or one passed to regulate the affairs of an English parish, would be often subversive of Parliament's real intent if applied to an Act passed to ensure the peace, order and good government of a British Colony: see Clement's *Canadian Constitution*, 3rd ed., p. 347...

It must be remembered, too, that their Lordships are not here considering the question of the legislative competence either of the Dominion or its Provinces which arise under sections 91 and 92 of the Act providing for the distribution of legislative powers and assigning to the Dominion and its Provinces their respective spheres of Government. Their Lordships are concerned with the interpretation of an Imperial Act, but an Imperial Act which creates a constitution for a new country. Nor are their Lordships deciding any question as to the rights of women but only a question as to their eligibility for a particular position. No one, either male or

---

◇[1930] A.C. 124.

female, has a right to be summoned to the Senate. The real point at issue is whether the Governor General has a right to summon women to the Senate ....

A heavy burden lies on an appellant who seeks to set aside a unanimous judgment of the Supreme Court, and this Board will only set aside such a decision after convincing argument and anxious consideration, but having regard: (1) To the object of the Act—namely, to provide a constitution for Canada, a responsible and developing State; (2) that the word "person" is ambiguous, and may include members of either sex; (3) that there are sections in the Act above referred to which show that in some cases the word "person" must include females; (4) that in some sections the words "male person" are expressly used when it is desired to confine the matter in issue to males; and (5) to the provisions of the *Interpretation Act*, their Lordships have come to the conclusion that the word "persons" in section 24 includes members both of the male and female sex, and that, therefore, the question propounded by the Governor General should be answered in the affirmative, and that women are eligible to be summoned to and become members of the Senate of Canada, and they will humbly advise His Majesty accordingly.

o

PROPRIETARY ARTICLES TRADE ASSOCIATION v. A.-G. CANADA◇

Section 36 of the *Combines Investigation Act* made it an indictable offence to be a party to the formation or operation of a combine considered to be a detriment to the public or injurious to trade and commerce. Inquiries were made by a commission empowered by that Act to examine books, demand returns and summon witnesses. Likewise, Section 498 of the Criminal Code made it an indictable offence to "conspire, combine, or agree unduly to limit transportation facilities, restrain commerce, or lessen manufacture or competition." The Supreme Court unanimously held both Acts to be *intra vires* the federal government [1929] S.C.R. 409.

LORD ATKIN:

In their Lordships' opinion section 498 of the Criminal Code and the greater part of the provisions of the *Combines Investigation Act* fall within the power of the Dominion parliament to legislate as to matters falling within the class of subjects, "the criminal law including the procedure in criminal matters" (section 91, head 27). The substance of the Act is by section 2 to define, and by section 32 to make criminal combines which the legislatures in the public interest intends to prohibit. The definition is wide, and may cover activities which have not hitherto been considered to be criminal. But only those combines are affected "which have operated or are likely to operate to the detriment or against the interest of the

◇[1931] A.C. 310.

public, whether consumers, producers, or others"; and if Parliament genuinely determines that commercial activities which can be so described are to be suppressed in the public interest, their Lordships see no reason why Parliament should not make them crimes. "Criminal law" means the "criminal law in its widest sense": *Attorney General for Ontario v. Hamilton Street Ry. Co.* It certainly is not confined to what was criminal by the law of England or of any Province in 1867. The power must extend to legislation to make new crimes. Criminal law connotes only the quality of such acts or omissions as are prohibited under appropriate penal provisions by authority of the State. The criminal quality of an act cannot be discerned by intuition; nor can it be discovered by reference to any standard but one: Is the act prohibited with penal consequences? Morality and criminality are far from co-extensive; nor is the sphere of criminality necessarily part of a more extensive field covered by morality—unless the moral code necessarily disapproves all acts prohibited by the State, in which case the argument moves in a circle. It appears to their Lordships to be of little value to seek to confine crimes to a category of acts which by their very nature belong to the domain of "criminal jurisprudence"; for the domain of criminal jurisprudence can only be ascertained by examining what acts at any particular period are declared by the State to be crimes, and the only common nature they will be found to possess is that they are prohibited by the State and that those who commit them are punished. . . .

It is, however, not enough for Parliament to rely solely on the powers to legislate as to the criminal law for support of the whole Act. The remedies given under sections 29 and 30 reducing customs duty and revoking patents have no necessary connection with the criminal law and must be justified on other grounds. Their Lordships have no doubt that they can both be supported as being reasonably ancillary to the powers given respectively under section 91, head 3, and affirmed by section 122,"the raising of money by any mode or system of taxation," and under section 91, head 22, "patents of invention and discovery." It is unfortunately beyond dispute that in a country where a general protective tariff exists persons may be found to take advantage of the protection, and within its walls form combinations that may work to the public disadvantage. It is an elementary point of self-preservation that the legislature which creates the protection should arm the executive with powers of withdrawing or relaxing the protection if abused. The same reasoning applies to grants of monopolies under any system of patents.

The view that their Lordships have expressed makes it unnecessary to discuss the further ground upon which the legislation has been supported by reference to the power to legislate under section 91, head 2, for the "The regulation of trade and commerce." Their Lordships merely propose to disassociate themselves from the construction suggested in argument of a passage in the judgment in the *Board of Commerce* case under which it was contended that the power to regulate trade and commerce could be invoked only in furtherance of a general power which Parliament possessed independently of it. No such restriction is properly to be inferred from that judgment. The words of the statute must receive their proper construction where they stand as giving an independent authority to Parliament over the particular subject matter. But following the second principle noticed in the beginning of this judgment their Lordships in the present case forbear from defining the extent of that authority. They desire, however, to guard themselves from being supposed to lay down that the present legislation could not be supported on that ground.

If then the legislation in question is authorized under one or other of the heads specifically enumerated in section 91, it is not to the purpose to say that it affects property and civil rights in the Provinces. Most of the specific subjects in section 91 do affect property and civil rights but so far as the legislation of Parliament in pith and substance is operating within the enumerated powers there is constitutional authority to interfere with property and civil rights.

᳇

RE THE REGULATION AND CONTROL OF AERONAUTICS IN CANADA◇

The Supreme Court of Canada unanimously answered the following question in the negative: "Have the Parliament and Government of Canada exclusive legislative and executive authority for performing the obligations of Canada or any Province thereof, under the Convention entitled "Convention relating to the regulation of Aerial Navigation?" The Convention was drafted at the Paris Peace Conference and implemented on behalf of the British Empire by the British Parliament. Its substance essentially made up the *Aeronautics Act, 1927* and the *Air Regulations, 1920.*

LORD SANKEY:

Before discussing the several questions individually, it is desirable to make some general observations upon sections 91 and 92, and 132.

With regard to sections 91 and 92, the cases which have been decided on the provisions of these sections are legion. Many inquests have been held upon them, and many great lawyers have from time to time dissected them.

Under our system decided cases effectively construe the words of an Act of Parliament and establish principles and rules whereby its scope and effect may be interpreted. But there is always a danger that in the course of this process the terms of the statute may come to be unduly extended and attention may be derived from what has been enacted to what has been judicially said about the enactment.

To borrow an analogy; there may be a range of sixty colours, each of which is so little different from its neighbour that it is difficult to make any distinction between the two, and yet at the one end of the range the colour may be white and at the other end of the range black. Great care must therefore be taken to consider each decision in the light of the circumstances of the case in view of which it was pronounced, especially in the interpretation of an Act such as the *British North America Act,* which was a great constitutional charter, and not to allow general phrases to obscure the underlying object of the Act, which was to establish a system of government upon essentially federal principles. Useful as decided cases are, it is

---

◇[1932] A.C. 54.

always advisable to get back to the words of the Act itself and to remember the object with which it was passed.

Inasmuch as the Act embodies a compromise under which the original Provinces agreed to federate, it is important to keep in mind that the preservation of the rights of minorities was a condition on which such minorities entered into the federation, and the foundation upon which the whole structure was subsequently erected. The process of interpretation as the years go on ought not to be allowed to dim or to whittle down the provisions of the original contract upon which the federation was founded, nor is it legitimate that any judicial construction of the provisions of sections 91 and 92 should impose a new and different contract upon the federating bodies.

But while the Courts should be jealous in upholding the charter of the Provinces as enacted in section 92 it must no less be borne in mind that the real object of the Act was to give the central Government those high functions and almost sovereign powers by which uniformity of legislation might be secured to all the Provinces and members of a constituent whole. . . .

During the course of the argument, learned counsel on either side endeavoured respectively to bring the subject of aeronautics within section 91 or section 92. Thus, the apellant referred to section 91, item 2 (the regulation of trade and commerce); item 5 (postal services); item 9 (beacons); item 10 (navigation ad shipping). Their Lordships do not think that aeronautics can be brought within the subject navigation and shipping, although undoubtedly to a large extent, and in some respects, it might be brought under the regulation of trade and commerce, or the postal services. On the other hand, the respondents contended that aeronautics as a class of subject came within item 13 of section 92 (property and civil rights in the Provinces) or item 16 (generally all matters of a merely local or private nature in the Provinces). Their Lordships do not think that aeronautics is a class of subject within property and civil rights in the Provinces, although here again, ingenious arguments may show that some small part of it might be so included.

In their Lordships' view, transport as a subject is dealt with in certain branches both of section 91 and of section 92, but neither of those sections deals specially with that branch of transport which is concerned with aeronautics.

Their Lordships are of opinion that it is proper to take a broader view of the matter rather than to rely on forced analogies or piecemeal analysis. They consider the governing section to be section 132, which gives to the Parliament and Government of Canada all powers necessary or proper for performing the obligations towards foreign countries arising under treaties between the Empire and such foreign countries. As far as section 132 is concerned, their Lordships are not aware of any decided case which is of assistance on the present occasion. It will be observed, however, from the very definite words of the section, that it is the Parliament and Government of Canada who are to have all powers necessary or proper for performing the obligations of Canada, or any Province thereof. It would, therefore appear to follow that any Convention of the charter under discussion necessitates Dominion legislation in order that it may be carried out. It is only necessary to look at the Convention itself to see what wide powers are necessary for performing the obligations arising thereunder. By article 1 the high contracting parties recognize that every Power (which includes Canada) has complete and exclusive sovereignty over the air space above its territory; by article 40, the British Dominions and India are deemed to be States for the purpose of the Convention. . . .

To sum up, having regard (a) to the terms of section 132; (b) to the terms of the Convention which covers almost every conceivable matter relating to aerial navigation; and (c) to the fact that further legislative powers in relation to aerial navigation reside in the Parliament of Canada by virtue of section 91, items 2, 5 and 7, it would appear that substantially the whole field of legislation in regard to aerial navigation belongs to the Dominion. There may be a small portion of the field which is not by virtue of specific words in the *British North America Act* vested in the Dominion; but neither is it vested by specific words in the Provinces. As to that small portion it appears to the Board that it must necessarily belong to the Dominion under its power to make laws for the peace, order and good government of Canada. Further, their Lordships are influenced by the facts that the subject of aerial navigation and the fulfilment of Canadian obligations under section 132 are matters of national interest and importance; and that aerial navigation is a class of subject which has attained such dimensions as to affect the body politic of the Dominion.

›

RE REGULATION AND CONTROL OF RADIO COMMUNICATION IN CANADA◇

Canada had independently entered into *The International Radio–Telegraph Convention, 1927.* By Article 2 of that Convention: (1) The Contracting Governments undertake to apply the provisions of the present convention in all radio communication stations established or operated by the contracting Governments, and open to the international service of public correspondence... (2) They undertake, in addition, to adopt or to propose to their respective legislatures the measures necessary to impose the observance of the provisions of the present convention and the regulations annexed thereto upon individual persons and enterprises authorized to establish and operate radio communication stations for international service, whether or not the stations are open to public correspondence. The Supreme Court of Canada was asked, by way of a reference, whether parliament had authority to regulate radio transmission in Canada. Anglin C.J., Newcombe P. and Smith J. held that it did. Rinfret J. and Lamont J. dissented; they decided that Parliament's jurisdiction over radio communication was limited and not exclusive.

VISCOUNT DUNEDIN:

The learned Chief Justice and Rinfret J. expressed their regret that at the time of delivering judgment they had not had the advantage of knowing what was the

◇[1932] A.C. 304.

conclusion reached by this Board on the question referred as to aviation. It is, however, unnecessary to speculate as to what would have been the result had the learned judges known as we know now that the judgment of the Board *(In re Regulation and Control of Aeronautics in Canada* delivered on October 22, 1931) settled that the regulation of aviation was matter for the Dominion. It would certainly only have confirmed the majority in their opinions. And as to the minority, though it is true that reference is made in their opinions to the fact that as the case then stood aviation had been decided not to fall within the exclusive jurisdiction of the Dominion, yet had they known the eventual judgment it is doubtful whether that fact would have altered their opinion. For this must at once be admitted; the leading consideration in the judgment of the Board was that the subject fell within the provisions of section 132 of the *British North America Act, 1867*...And it is said with truth that, while as regards aviation there was a treaty, the convention here is not a treaty between the Empire as such and foreign countries, for Great Britain does not sign as representing the Colonies and Dominions. She only confirms the assent which had been signified by the Colonies and Dominions who were separately represented at the meetings which drafted the convention. But while this is so, the aviation case in their Lordships' judgment cannot be put on one side.

Counsel for the Province felt this and sought to avoid any general deduction by admitting that many of the things provided by the convention and the regulations thereof fell within various special heads of section 91. For example, provisions as to beacon signals he would refer to head 10 of section 91—navigation and shipping. It is unnecessary to multiply instances, because the real point to be considered is this manner of dealing with the subject. In other words the argument of the Province comes to this: Go through all the stipulations of the convention and each one you can pick out which fairly falls within one of the enumerated heads of section 91, that can be held to be appropriate for Dominion legislation; but the residue belongs to the Province under the head either of head 13 of section 92—property and civil rights, or head 16—matters of a merely local or private nature in the Province.

Their Lordships cannot agree that the matter should be so dealt with. Canada as a Dominion is one of the signatories to the convention. In a question with foreign powers the persons who might infringe some of the stipulations in the convention would not be the Dominion of Canada as a whole but would be individual persons residing in Canada. These persons must, so to speak, be kept in order by legislation and the only legislation that can deal with them all at once is Dominion legislation. This idea of Canada as a Dominion being bound by a convention equivalent to a treaty with foreign powers was quite unthought of in 1867. It is the outcome of the gradual development of the position of Canada vis-à-vis to the mother country, Great Britain, which is found in these later days expressed in the Statute of Westminster. It is not, therefore, to be expected that such a matter should be dealt with in explicit words in either section 91 or section 92. The only class of treaty which would bind Canada was thought of as a treaty by Great Britain, and that was provided for by section 132. Being, therefore, not mentioned explicitly in either section 91 or section 92, such legislation falls within the general words at the opening of section 91 which assign to the Government of the Dominion the power to make laws "for the peace, order, and good government of Canada in relation to all matters not coming within the classes of subjects by this Act assigned exclusively to the legislatures of the Provinces." In fine, though agreeing that the Convention was not such a treaty as is defined in section 132, their Lordships think that it comes to the same thing. On August 11, 1927, the Privy Council of Canada with the approval of the Governor General chose a body to attend the meeting of all the powers to settle international agreements as to wireless. The Canadian body attended and took part in deliberations. The deliberations ended in the convention with general regulations appended being signed at Washington on November 24, 1927, by the representatives of all the powers who had taken part in the conference, and this convention was ratified by the Canadian Government on July 12, 1928.

The result is in their Lordships' opinion clear. It is Canada as a whole which is amenable to the other powers for the proper carrying out of the convention; and to prevent individuals in Canada infringing the stipulations of the convention it is necessary that the Dominion should pass legislation which should apply to all the dwellers in Canada.

o

A.-G. BRITISH COLUMBIA v. A.-G. CANADA◊

Section 498A *(a)* of the criminal code made it an indictable offence for anyone who is "a party or privy to, or assists in, any transaction of sale which discriminates, to his knowledge, against competitors of the purchases... " through the use of a discount, rebate or allowance not open to all competitors "in respect of a sale of goods of like quality and quantity." Sections *(b)* and *(c)* made it a criminal offence to underprice goods for the purposes of destroying competition. The Supreme Court held the legislation to be *intra vires* the federal parliament, Cannon and Crockett JJ. dissenting as to part *(a)*. The decision was appealed to the Judicial Committee.

LORD ATKIN:

Their Lordships agree with the Chief Justice that his case is covered by the decision of the Judicial Committee in the *Proprietary Articles* case (1931). The decision in that case seems to be inconsistent with the ground of dissent of Crockett J. that subsection (a) lacks "the characteristic feature of crime, viz. the intent to do wrong." The basis of that decision is that there is no other criterion of "wrongness" than the intention of the legislature in the public interest to prohibit the act or omission made criminal. Cannon J. was of opinion that the prohibition cannot have been made in the public interest because it has in view only the protection of the individual competitors of the vendor. This appears to narrow unduly the discretion of the Dominion legislature in considering the public interest. The only limitation of the plenary power of the Dominion to determine what shall or shall not be criminal is the condition that Parliament shall not in the guise of enacting criminal legislation in truth and in substance encroach on any of the classes of subjects

◊[1937] A.C. 368.

enumerated in section 92. It is no objection that it does in fact affect them. If a genuine attempt to amend the criminal law, it may obviously affect previously existing civil rights. The object of an amendment of the criminal law as a rule is to deprive the citizen of the right to do that which apart from the amendment he could lawfully do. No doubt the plenary power given by section 91 (27) does not deprive the Provinces of their right under section 92 (15) of affixing penal sanctions to their own competent legislation. On the other hand there seems to be nothing to prevent the Dominion, if it thinks fit in the public interest, from applying the criminal law generally to acts and omissions which so far are only covered by provincial enactments. In the present case, there seems to be no reason for supposing that the Dominion are [sic] using the criminal law as a pretence or pretext or that the legislature is in pith and substance only interfering with civil rights in the Province. Counsel for New Brunswick called the attention of the Board to the Report of the Royal Commission on Price Spreads, which is referred to in the order of reference. It probably would not be contended that the statement of the Minister in the order of reference that the section was enacted to give effect to the recommendations of the Royal Commission bound the Provinces or must necessarily be treated as conclusive by the Board. But when the suggestion is made that the legislation was not in truth criminal legislation, but was in substance merely an encroachment on the provincial field, the existence of the report appears to be a material circumstance. Their Lordships are in agreement with the decision of the majority of the Supreme Court. They are of opinion that no part of the section is *ultra vires*, and they will humbly advise His Majesty that this appeal should be dismissed.

o

A.-G. BRITISH COLUMBIA v. A.-G. CANADA (NATURAL PRODUCTS MARKETING ACT)◇

This Act authorized the setting up of the Dominion Marketing Board to regulate the marketing of natural products—animals, vegetables, lumber, etc. The Board was empowered to regulate the time, place and the way in which these articles would be bought, sold, shipped, stored, etc. The marketing of such materials included international, interprovincial and intraprovincial trade. The Supreme Court unanimously held the Act to be *ultra vires* the federal government. The Judicial Committee of the Privy Council upheld the decision.

LORD ATKIN:

There can be no doubt that the provisions of the Act cover transactions in any natural product which are completed within the province, and have no connection with interprovincial or export trade. It is, therefore, plain that the Act purports to affect property and civil rights in the province, and if not brought within one of the enumerated classes of subjects in section 91 must be beyond the competence of the Dominion legislature. It was sought to bring the Act within the class (2) of section

◇[1937] A.C. 377.

91, namely "The Regulation of Trade and Commerce." Emphasis was laid upon those parts of the Act which deal with interprovincial and export trade. But the regulation of trade and commerce does not permit the regulation of individual forms of trade or commerce confined to the province. . . .

There was a further attempt to support the Act upon the general powers to legislate for the peace, order, and good government of Canada. Their Lordships have already dealt with this matter in their previous judgments in this series and need not repeat what is there said. The judgment of the Chief Justice in this case is conclusive against the claim for validity on this ground. In the result, therefore, there is no answer to the contention that the Act in substance invades the provincial field and is invalid. . . .

The Board were given to understand that some of the Provinces attach much importance to the existence of marketing schemes such as might be set up under this legislation: and their attention was called to the existence of provincial legislation setting up provincial schemes for various provincial products. It was said that as the Provinces and the Dominion between them possess a totality of complete legislative authority, it must be possible to combine Dominion and provincial legislation so that each within its own sphere could in co-operation with the other achieve the complete power of regulation which is desired. Their Lordships appreciate the importance of the desired aim. Unless and until a change is made in the respective legislative functions of Dominion and Province it may well be that satisfactory results for both can only be obtained by co-operation. But the legislation will have to be carefully framed, and will not be achieved by either party leaving its own sphere and encroaching upon that of the other. In the present case their Lordships are unable to support the Dominion legislation as it stands. They will, therefore, humbly advise His Majesty that this appeal be dismissed. . . .

o

A.-G. CANADA v. A.-G. ONTARIO (EMPLOYMENT AND SOCIAL SECURITY ACT)◇

The Supreme Court in a 4 to 2 decision, Duff C.J. and Davis J. dissenting, held the Act, which created an unemployment insurance fund through contributions of employers and employees to be *ultra vires* the federal government. The decision was upheld on appeal to the Judicial Committee. The preamble to the Act reads as follows:

> Whereas the Dominion of Canada was a signatory, as Part of the British Empire, to the Treaty of Peace made between the Allied and Associated Powers and Germany, signed at Versailles, on the 18th day of June, 1919; and whereas the said Treaty of Peace was confirmed by *The Treaties of Peace Act 1919*; and whereas, by

◇[1937] A.C. 355.

Article 23 of the said Treaty, each of the signatories thereto agreed that they would endeavour to secure and maintain fair and humane conditions of labour for men, women and children, both in their own countries and in all countries to which their commercial and industrial relations extend, and by Article 427 of the said Treaty declared that the well-being, physical, moral and intellectual, of industrial wage-earners is of supreme international importance; and whereas it is desirable to discharge the obligations to Canadian Labour assumed under the provisions of the said Treaty; and whereas it is essential for the peace, order, and good government of Canada to provide for a National Employment Service and Insurance and for the purpose of maintaining on equitable terms, interprovincial and international trade, and to authorize the creation of a National Fund out of which benefits to unemployed persons throughout Canada will be payable and to provide for levying contributions from employers and workers for the maintaining of the said Fund and for contributions thereto by the Dominion: Therefore, His Majesty, by and with the advice and consent of the Senate and House of Commons of Canada, enacts as follows:—

LORD ATKIN:

There can be no doubt that *prima facie* provisions as to insurance of this kind, especially where they affect the contract of employment, fall within the class of property and civil rights in the Province, and would be within the exclusive competence of the Provincial legislature. It was sought, however, to justify the validity of Dominion legislation on grounds which their Lordships on consideration feel compelled to reject. Counsel did not seek to uphold the legislation on the ground of the treaty-making power. There was no treaty or labour convention which imposed any obligation upon Canada to pass this legislation, and the decision on this question in the reference on the three labour Acts does not apply. A strong appeal, however, was made on the ground of the special importance of unemployment insurance in Canada at the time of and for some time previous to the passing of the Act. On this point it becomes unnecessary to do more than to refer to the judgment of this Board in the reference on the three labour Acts and to the judgment of the Chief Justice in the *Natural Products Marketing Act* which on this matter the Board have approved and adopted. It is sufficient to say that the present Act does not purport to deal with any special emergency. It founds itself in the preamble on general world-wide conditions referred to in the Treaty of Peace: it is an Act whose operation is intended to be permanent: and there is agreement between all the members of the Supreme Court that it could not be supported upon the suggested existence of any special emergency. Their Lordships find themselves unable to differ from this view.

It only remains to deal with the argument which found favour with the Chief Justice and Davis J. that the legislation can be supported under the enumerated heads, 1 and 3 of section 91 of the B.N.A. Act, 1867. (1) The public debt and property, namely (3) The raising of money by any mode or system of taxation. Shortly stated the argument is that the obligation imposed upon employers and persons employed is a mode of taxation; that the money so raised becomes public property and that the money so raised, together with assistance from money raised by general taxation, shall be applied in forming an insurance fund and generally in accordance with the provision of the Act.

That the Dominion may impose taxation for the purpose of creating a fund for special purposes and may apply that fund for making contributions in the public interest to individuals, corporations, or public authorities, could not as a general proposition be denied. Whether in such an Act as the present, compulsion applied to an employed person to make a contribution to an insurance fund out of which he will receive benefit for a period proportionate to the number of his contributions is in fact taxation, it is not necessary finally to decide. It might seem difficult to discern how it differs from a form of compulsory insurance or what the difference is between a statutory obligation to pay insurance premiums to the State, or to an insurance company. But assuming that the Dominion has collected by means of taxation a fund, it by no means follows that any legislation which disposes of it is necessarily within Dominion competence.

It may still be legislation affecting the classes of subjects enumerated in section 92, and, if so, would be *ultra vires*. In other words, Dominion legislation, even though it deals with Dominion property, may yet be so framed as to invade civil rights within the Province: or encroach upon the classes of subjects which are reserved to provincial competence. It is not necessary that it should be a colourable device, or a pretence. If on the true view of the legislation it is found that in reality in pith and substance the legislation invades civil rights within the Province or in respect of other classes of subjects otherwise encroaches upon the provincial field, the legislation will be invalid. To hold otherwise would afford the Dominion an easy passage into the provincial domain. In the present case their Lordships agree with the majority of the Supreme Court in holding that in pith and substance this Act is an insurance Act affecting the civil rights of employers and employed in each Province, and as such is invalid. The other parts of the Act are so inextricably mixed up with the insurance provisions of Part III that is impossible to sever them. It seems obvious also that in its truncated form, apart from Part III, the Act would never have come into existence. If follows that the whole Act must be pronounced *ultra vires*, and in accordance with the view of the majority of the Supreme Court their Lordships will humbly advise His Majesty that this special appeal be dismissed.

o

A.-G. CANADA v. A.-G. ONTARIO
(LABOUR CONVENTIONS REFERENCE)◇

In 1935 the government of Canada ratified three conventions which had been adopted by the International Labour Organization (of which Canada was a member) in 1919, 1921, and 1928, and later in the session passed the implementing statutes. In 1925 the Supreme Court had been asked whether Parliament was competent to give force to the convention regarding the hours of

---

◇[1937] A.C. 327.

labour and Mr. Justice Duff, for the court, held that it was not, as the subject matter of the convention fell within provincial jurisdiction. However, the decisions in the *Radio* and *Aeronautics* cases suggested that the legislation might be upheld under the treaty power, and federal counsel so argued. The Supreme Court divided 3 to 3 with Chief Justice Duff upholding the statutes and reversing his earlier decision in the light of the intervening decisions.

LORD ATKIN:

The first ground upon which counsel for the Dominion sought to base the validity of the legislation was section 132. So far as it is sought to apply this section to the conventions when ratified the answer is plain. The obligations are not obligations of Canada as part of the British Empire, but of Canada, by virtue of her new status as an international person, and do not arise under a treaty between the British Empire and foreign countries. This was clearly established by the decision in the *Radio* case ([1932] A.C. 304), and their Lordships do not think that the proposition admits of any doubt. It is unnecessary, therefore, to dwell upon the distinction between legislative powers given to the Dominion to perform obligations imposed upon Canada as part of the Empire by an Imperial executive responsible to and controlled by the Imperial Parliament, and the legislative power of the Dominion to perform obligations created by the Dominion executive responsible to and controlled by the Dominion parliament. While it is true, as was pointed out in the *Radio* case ... that it was not contemplated in 1867 that the Dominion would possess treaty-making powers, it is impossible to strain the section so as to cover the uncontemplated event. A further attempt to apply the section was made by the suggestion that while it does not apply to the conventions, yet it clearly applies to the Treaty of Versailles itself, and the obligations to perform the conventions arise "under" that treaty because of the stipulations in Part XIII. It is impossible to accept this view. No obligation to legislate in respect of any of the matters in question arose until the Canadian executive, left with an unfettered discretion, of their own volition acceded to the conventions, a *novus actus* not determined by the treaty. For the purposes of this legislation the obligation arose under the conventions alone. It appears that all the members of the Supreme Court rejected the contention based on section 132, and their Lordships are in full agreement with them.

If, therefore, section 132 is out of the way, the validity of the legislation can only depend upon sections 91 and 92. Now it had to be admitted that normally this legislation came within the classes of subjects by section 92 assigned exclusively to the Legislatures of the Provinces, namely—property and civil rights in the Province. This was, in fact, expressly decided in respect of these same conventions by the Supreme Court in 1925. How, then, can the legislation be within the legislative powers given by section 91 to the Dominion parliament? It is not within the enumerated classes of subjects in section 91: and it appears to be expressly excluded from the general powers given by the first words of the section. It appears highly probable that none of the members of the Supreme Court would have departed from their decision in 1925 had it not been for the opinion of the Chief Justice that the judgments of the Judicial Committee in the *Aeronautics* case ([1932] A.C. 54) and the *Radio* case ... constrained them to hold that jurisdiction to legislate for the purpose of performing the obligation of a treaty resides exclusively in the Parliament of Canada. Their Lordships cannot take this view of those decisions. The *Aeronautics* case . . . concerned legislation to perform obligations imposed by a treaty between the Empire and foreign countries. Section 132, therefore, clearly applied, and but for a remark at the end of the judgment, which in view of the stated ground of the decision was clearly *obiter*, the case could not be said to be an authority on the matter now under discussion. The judgment in the *Radio* case . . . appears to present more difficulty. But when that case is examined it will be found that the true ground of the decision was that the convention in that case dealt with classes of matters which did not fall within the enumerated classes of subjects in section 92, or even within the enumerated classes in section 91. Part of the subject matter of the convention, namely—broadcasting, might come under an enumerated class, but as so it was under a heading "Interprovincial Telegraphs," expressly excluded form section 92. Their Lordships are satisfied that neither case affords a warrant for holding that legislation to perform a Canadian treaty is exclusively within the Dominion legislative power.

For the purposes of sections 91 and 92, i.e., the distribution of legislative powers between the Dominion and the Provinces, there is no such thing as treaty legislation as such. The distribution is based on classes of subjects; and as a treaty deals with a particular class of subjects so will the legislative power of performing it be ascertained . . . . It would be remarkable that while the Dominion could not initiate legislation, however desirable, which affected civil rights in the Provinces, yet its Government not responsible to the Provinces nor controlled by Provincial parliaments need only agree with a foreign country to enact such legislation, and its Parliament would be forthwith clothed with authority to affect Provincial rights to the full extent of such agreement. Such a result would appear to undermine the constitutional safeguards of Provincial constitutional autonomy.

It follows from what has been said that no further legislative competence is obtained by the Dominion from its accession to international status, and the consequent increase in the scope of its executive functions. It is true, as pointed out in the judgment of the Chief Justice, that as the executive is now clothed with the powers of making treaties so the Parliament of Canada, to which the executive is responsible, has imposed upon it responsibilities in connection with such treaties, for if it were to disapprove of them they would either not be made or the Ministers would meet their constitutional fate. But this is true of all executive functions in their relation to Parliament. There is no existing constitutional ground for stretching the competence of the Dominion parliament so that it becomes enlarged to keep pace with enlarged functions of the Dominion executive. If the new functions affect the classes of subjects enumerated in section 92, legislation to support the new functions is in the competence of the Provincial legislatures only. If they do not, the competence of the Dominion legislatures is declared by section 91 and existed *ab origine*. In other words, the Dominion cannot, merely by making promises to foreign countries, clothe itself with legislative authority inconsistent with the constitution which gave it birth.

But the validity of the legislation under the general words of section 91 was sought to be established not in relation to the treaty-making power alone, but also as being concerned with matters of such general importance as to have attained "such dimensions as to affect the body politic," and to have "ceased to be merely local or provincial," and to have "become matter of national concern." . . . The law of Canada on this branch of constitutional law has been stated with such force and clarity by the Chief Justice in his judgment in the reference concerning the *Natural Products Marketing Act* ([1937] A.C. 377) dealing with the six Acts there referred to, that their Lordships abstain from sitting it afresh. The Chief Justice, naturally from his point of view, excepted legislation to fulfil treaties. On this their Lordships have expressed their opinion. But subject to this, they agree with and adopt what was there said. They consider that the law is finally settled by the current of cases cited by the Chief Justice on the principles declared by him. It is only necessary to call attention to the phrases in the various cases, "abnormal circumstances," "exceptional conditions," "standard necessity" *(Board of Commerce* case . . .), to show how far the present case is from the conditions which may override the normal distribution of powers in sections 91 and 92. The few pages of the Chief Justice's judgment will, it is to be hoped, form the *locus classicus* of the law on this point, and preclude further disputes.

It must not be thought that the result of this decision is that Canada is incompetent to legislate in performance of treaty obligations. In totality of legislative powers, Dominion and Provincial together, she is fully equipped. But the legislative powers remain distributed, and if in the exercise of her new functions derived from her new international status Canada incurs obligations they must, so far as legislation be concerned, when they deal with Provincial classes of subjects, be dealt with by the totality of powers, in other words by co-operation between the Dominion and the Provinces. While the ship of state now sails on larger ventures and into foreign waters she still retains the watertight compartments which are an essential part of her original structure. The Supreme Court was equally divided and, therefore, the formal judgment could only state the opinions of the three judges on either side. Their Lordships are of opinion that the answer to the three questions should be that the Act in each case is *ultra vires* of the Parliament of Canada, and they will humbly advise His Majesty accordingly.

o

A.-G. ONTARIO v. CANADA TEMPERANCE FEDERATION◇

The province of Ontario referred the "local option" provisions of the *Canada Temperance Act* to the Court of Appeal of that province. That Court held, Henderson J., dissenting, the Act to be *intra vires* the federal government.

VISCOUNT SIMON:

The Act having been passed in 1878, its constitutional validity was challenged in 1882 in *Russell*'s case, which arose out of a conviction of the appellant Russell for unlawfully selling intoxicating liquor contrary to the provisions of Part II of the Act. It was argued in that case that the Act was *ultra vires* of the Dominion parliament

---

◇[1946] A.C. 193.

on the ground that the matter was one which fell within section 92 of the *British North America Act* and was, therefore, within the exclusive jurisdiction of the provincial legislatures. The Board, however, held that the Act did not deal with any of the matters exclusively reserved to the provinces and upheld the validity of the statute on the ground that it related to the peace, order and good government of Canada. This decision has stood unreversed for sixty-three years. . . .

But in 1925 *Russell*'s case was commented on in a judgment of the Judicial Committee delivered by Lord Haldane in *Toronto Electric Commissioners v. Snider* and it is on this comment that the present appellants largely rely in support of their contention that it was wrongly decided. . . .

The first observation which their Lordships would make on this explanation of *Russell*'s case is that the *British North America Act* nowhere gives power to the Dominion parliament to legislate in matters which are properly to be regarded as exclusively within the competence of the provincial legislatures merely because of the existence of an emergency. Secondly, they can find nothing in the judgment of the Board in 1882 which suggests that it proceeded on the ground of emergency; there was certainly no evidence before that Board that one existed. The Act of 1878 was a permanent, not a temporary, Act, and no objection was raised to it on that account. In their Lordships' opinion, the true test must be found in the real subject matter of the legislation: if it is such that it goes beyond local or provincial concern or interests and must from its inherent nature be the concern of the Dominion as a whole (as, for example, in the *Aeronautics* case and the *Radio* case), then it will fall within the competence of the Dominion parliament as a matter affecting the peace, order and good government of Canada, though it may in another aspect touch on matters specially reserved to the provincial legislatures. War and pestilence, no doubt, are instances; so, too, may be the drink or drug traffic, or the carrying of arms. In *Russell v. The Queen*, Sir Montague Smith gave as an instance of valid Dominion legislation a law which prohibited or restricted the sale or exposure of cattle having a contagious disease. Nor is the validity of the legislation, when due to its inherent nature, affected because there may still be room for enactments by a provincial legislature dealing with an aspect of the same subject in so far as it specially affects that province.

It is to be noticed that the Board in *Snider*'s case nowhere said that *Russell v. The Queen* was wrongly decided. What it did was to put forward an explanation of what it considered was the ground of the decision, but in their Lordships' opinion the explanation is too narrowly expressed. True it is that an emergency may be the occasion which calls for the legislation, but it is the nature of the legislation itself, and not the existence of emergency, that must determine whether it is valid or not.

The appellants' first contention is that *Russell*'s case was wrongly decided and ought to be overruled. Their Lordships do not doubt that in tendering humbler advice to His Majesty they are not absolutely bound by previous decisions of the Board, as is the House of Lords by its own judgments. In ecclesiastical appeals, for instance, on more than one occasion, the Board has tendered advice contrary to that given in a previous case, which further historical research has shown to have been wrong. But on constitutional questions it must be seldom indeed that the Board would depart from a previous decision which it may be assumed will have been acted on both by governments and subjects. In the present case the decision now sought to be overruled has stood for over sixty years; the Act has been put into operation for varying periods in many places in the Dominion; under its provisions businesses must have been closed, fines and imprisonments for breaches of the Act have been imposed and suffered. Time and again the occasion has arisen when the Board could have overruled the decision had it thought it wrong. Accordingly, in the opinion of their Lordships, the decision must be regarded as firmly embedded in the constitutional law of Canada, and it is impossible now to depart from it. Their Lordships have no intention, in deciding the present appeal, of embarking on a fresh disquisition as to relations between sections 91 and 92 of the *British North America Act*, which have been expounded in so many reported cases; so far as the *Canada Temperance Act, 1878,* is concerned the question must be considered as settled once and for all.

o

BEYOND THE LAW: LORD HALDANE AND THE CANADIAN CONSTITUTION

JOHN SAYWELL AND GEORGE VEGH

o

Although Lord Watson, who imposed an enduring structure on sections 91 and 92 of the *Constitution Act, 1867,* may have had a more fundamental impact on the history of Canadian federalism than Haldane, Lord Haldane's decisions have aroused more historical interest. With few exceptions Watson wrote as if he were rendering a technical reading of the Act, one exception being his *obiter dicta* on the intentions of the Fathers in *Liquidators.* Haldane, on the other hand, while professing to remain faithful to the language of the Act, made no secret of his view that the Judicial Committee, and the judiciary generally, had a role more magnificent than giving mere technical renderings of the words of a constitutional statute, or any statute for that matter. Legal scholars and philosophers have discussed the philosophical and/or political position or bias that underlay his view of the role of judicial review and his interpretation of the Canadian federal constitution.[1]

HALDANE AND THE CONSTITUTION

Although Haldane always intended to be a lawyer, his student days were spent studying philosophy in Scotland and Germany. By the 1880s he had established a legal practice in London, and soon was engaged as counsel in a number of Canadian cases, usually for the provinces. As counsel for Ontario and at Watson's bar, Haldane unquestionably adopted the Watson/Mowat view of Canadian federalism, and perhaps, Mowat's view of the Canadian state. "Ontario gave me its general retainer," he wrote later, "and I appeared for the Prime Minister, Sir Oliver Mowat, throughout his struggles with Sir John MacDonald [sic], the Prime Minister of Canada, for the right of the Province to pass its own legislation." It was a strange comment for a man trained in the law.[2]

It was a strange comment as well from a man who had revealed on occasion that he understood the structure and logic of Canadian federalism as set out in 1867. His fullest statement when not dealing with a Canadian appeal came in a judgment he delivered in an Australian case. The question of *ultra vires*, he observed, could only be determined by examining the scheme of the Act of 1900 which established the Commonwealth Constitution:

> About the fundamental principle of that Constitution there can be no doubt. It is federal in the strict sense of the term, as a reference to what was established on a different footing in Canada shews. The *British North America Act* of 1867 commences with the preamble that the then Provinces [sic] had expressed their desire to be federally united into one Dominion with a Constitution similar in principle to that of the United Kingdom. In a loose sense the word "federal" may be used, as it is there used, to describe any arrangement under which self-contained States agree to delegate their powers to a common Government with a view to entirely new Constitutions even of the States themselves. But the natural and literal interpretation of the word confines its application to cases in which these States, while agreeing on a measure of delegation, yet in the main continue to preserve their original Constitutions. Now, as regards Canada, the second of the resolutions, passed at Quebec in October, 1864, on which the *British North America Act* was founded, shows that what was in the minds of those who agreed on the resolutions was a general Government charged with matters of common interest, and new and merely local Governments for the Provinces. The Provinces were to have fresh and much restricted Constitutions, their Governments being entirely remodelled. This plan was carried out by the Imperial statute of 1867. By the 91st section a general power was given to the new Parliament of Canada to make laws for the peace, order, and good government of Canada without restriction to specific subjects, and excepting only the subjects specifically and exclusively assigned to the Provincial Legislatures by s. 92. There followed an enumeration of subjects which were to be dealt with by the Dominion Parliament, but this enumeration was not to restrict the generality of the power conferred on it. The Act, therefore, departs widely from the true federal model adopted in the Constitution of the United States, the tenth amendment to which declares that the powers not delegated to the United States by the Constitution, nor prohibited by it to the States, are reserved to the States respectively or to their people. Of the Canadian Constitution the true view appears, therefore, to be that, although it was founded on the Quebec Resolutions and so must be accepted as a treaty of union among the then Provinces, yet when once enacted by the Imperial Parliament it constituted a fresh departure, and established new Dominion and Provincial Governments with defined powers and duties both derived from the Act of the Imperial Parliament which was their legal source.[3]

Although Haldane revealed a technical knowledge of the structure of the 1867 Act, it seems clear from his rendering that he did not like it; it was "loose" and not "natural." Years before, when discussing the Australian federation in the Commons, Haldane was even more revealing. Unlike Australia, he observed, in

> Canada the general powers of legislation are reserved to the Dominion Parliament. But the latter have among these specified powers the widest capacity for dealing unrestrictedly with property and civil rights. Therefore rather technically than in substance is there a difference between the Provincial Legislatures of Canada and those of Australia.[4]

The truth is that Haldane's view of Canadian federalism was fully formed before he sat on the Judicial Committee in 1912. He made that clear in his article on Watson, and on another occasion suggested that it was the Supreme Court of Canada that was responsible for giving the federal constitution a centralised appearance which the Judicial Committee had to counter. Once again praising Watson's services to Canada and the Empire, he wrote:

> In 1867 Lord Carnarvon passed his Confederation Act in accordance with resolutions passed in the various parts of Canada. Under this Constitution there was to be a Central Parliament and Executive at Ottawa to deal with the general affairs of Canada, and parliaments and executives in the provinces which should deal with provincial matters. The people of the Colony, who were suspicious of interference from Downing Street, also obtained power to create a Supreme Court for Canada, which should settle any constitutional questions that might arise, the intention being to get rid as far as possible of the Privy Council as a Canadian Court of Appeal. This Court was not set up for some years, but when it was, it began to produce a very different effect in the Colony from that which was intended. The judges took, or were suppose to take, the view that the meaning of the Confederation Act was that the largest interpretation was to be put upon the powers of the Central or Dominion Government, and the smallest on those of the Provinces. About twenty years ago a series of decisions were given by the Supreme Court of Canada which certainly gave colour to this view. There was alarm in the provinces, and the result was a succession of appeals to the Queen, for which special leave was obtained from the Privy Council. I well remember the circumstances of these cases, for it so happened that, when a junior, I was taken into them on behalf of Ontario, which bore the brunt of the struggle with the Dominion before the Privy Council . . . . Almost from the first Lord Watson took the lead in the decision of these appeals. He worked out a different view of the Canadian Constitution from that which had been foreshadowed by the Canadian Courts. He filled in the skeleton which the Confederation Act had established, and in large measure shaped the growth of the fibre which grew round it. He established the independence of the provinces and their executives . . . . His name will be long and gratefully remembered by Canadian statesmen.

The error of the Supreme Court decisions, wrote Haldane, was that they "laid down principles which, if accepted, would have placed the Provinces in the position of subordinate governments." But in the end the Judicial Committee,

> holding an absolutely even hand between the contending parties... settled that the true view of the Act was that it established a federal distribution of not only legislative but executive powers, and that in matters delegated to them the Provincial Governments had an authority as high as that of the Central Government. The relationship was, in other words, held to be one of strict co-ordination, and that in executive as well as legislative matters. On this principle one burning conflict after another was stilled.[5]

Lord Haldane came to the Judicial Committee as the champion of the provinces, the legal guardian of the doctrine of "strict co-ordination," determined to carry on the work for Canada and the Empire so nobly begun by Lord Watson.

Stephen Wexler has argued that the explanation of Haldane's commitment to provincial rights and co-ordinate federalism is to be found not in his view of the law of the constitution but in his two "first principles": his idealistic vision of the Empire and his commitment to Irish Home Rule. As an idealist, Haldane was given to reshaping reality to conform to his own sense of "the deeper or higher meanings of things." Although not an Imperialist of the Rudyard Kipling or Joseph Chamberlain school, he believed unquestioningly in the value, the unity and the destiny of the British Empire. And the Judicial Committee was one of those "silken bands" that held it together and whose value was appreciated wherever the Union Jack flew. "As showing the faith in this body which has been inspired into our distant peoples," he said on more than one occasion,

> it is told of a traveller who had penetrated into a remote part of India that he found the natives offering up a sacrifice to a far-off but powerful god who had just restored to the tribe the land which the Government of the day had taken from it. He asked the name of the god. The reply was: "We know nothing of him but that he is a good god, and that his name is the Judicial Committee of the Privy Council." The sense of the presence of sure and effective justice which this body has come to inspire is something which we as Britons may boast of.[6]

The Canadian tribe, too, had reason to be grateful for the "sure and effective justice" rendered by the Judicial Committee which had "established the independence of the provinces and their executives" and given them a federal constitution somewhat different from that intended.

Wexler argues that Haldane's imperialism forced him to diminish the central government and the Supreme Court, much as Greenwood argued in his article on Lord Watson. In Canada, it was Ottawa that epitomised the "national focus" that threatened the imperial connection. It was the Laurier government which cavilled at sending troops to South Africa in 1899 until an aroused public opinion demanded it. It was the Supreme Court that had championed the power of the central government and had to be overruled. Likewise, his passionate commitment to home rule for Ireland, Wexler suggests, echoed his statement that Mowat was engaged in a struggle "for the right of the province to pass its own legislation." Just as Ireland should be free to pass its own legislation, so too should the provinces of Canada "whose 'champion' he was, as if they were struggling for freedom." In short, the national government had to be diminished. "The major effect of Haldane's judgments was to deny sovereignty to the Canadian federal government," Wexler writes, "and undercutting the sovereign status of the federal government was a way to keep Canada from coming between Imperial Britain and the Canadian subjects of the Empire."

Stephen Wexler has argued that it was by inventing the "two Crowns" that Haldane was able to deny sovereignty to the central government and diminish its authority. Wexler found Haldane's "two Crowns" in his statement in *Re Initiative and Referendum Act* that the "scheme of the Act passed in 1867 was . . . not . . . to subordinate Provincial Governments to a central authority . . . . [E]ach Province was to retain its independence and autonomy and to be directly under the Crown as its head."[7] The statement, Wexler says,

> is clearly false in terms of the language of the Act. The *Constitution Act, 1867* does not envision the provincial governments as being "directly under the Crown." The Act very clearly envisions Canadian government as having this structure:

The Queen
Federal Government
Province A   Province B

> Haldane misread the Act as regards sovereignty and said it gave Canadian government this structure:

The Queen
Federal Government   Province A   Province B[8]

The Act does not "in *any* reading, give the two levels of government equal status, or make them both sovereign," argues Wexler. The *Constitution Act, 1867* divides up the *power* to govern, but it does not divide up *sovereignty*. In dividing up sovereignty, he continues, Haldane virtually destroyed the power to legislate for "Peace, Order, and good Government" which power, in his judgment, is sovereignty and alone linked the Queen to the legislative authority of governments in Canada. The result was that Haldane saw no coherence or logic in sections 91 and 92, but simply saw two lists of powers given to two governments, equal in status and differing only in function. Although Wexler insists that the enumerated heads in section 91 are "expressly said to be illustrative," which one can argue they are not, his conclusion that Haldane treated 91 and 92 "as lists of disembodied powers, rather than as a concerted division of powers" seems supported by Haldane's Canadian decisions, if not by his analysis in *Colonial Sugar Refining*.

The two Crowns, the basis for the theory of co-ordinate federalism, was the creation of the Judicial Committee, but Haldane only followed where Watson had tread. Before Confederation the lieutenant-governors of the smaller colonies and the governor general of Canada were appointed directly by the Crown and, while junior in rank, the lieutenant-governors were in no way subordinate to the governor general and reported directly to the Colonial Office. The 1867 Act, however, provided that the provincial lieutenant-governor was to be appointed by the governor general in council, that is by the federal government, and was to be paid and be dismissed by the federal government. The officer was also empowered to reserve provincial legislation for the consideration of the federal government, presumably on instructions from Ottawa. The "Executive Government" of Canada was vested in the Queen, and the Canadian Parliament was composed of the Queen, the Senate and the Commons; the provincial governments were to consist of the lieutenant-governor and one or two chambers. The governor general assented to legislation in the Queen's name, but the lieutenant-governors—though none did—were, by the Act, instructed to assent in the name of the governor general.[9]

On the other hand, the lieutenant-governor possessed a Great Seal, the instrument of sovereign authority, and was authorized by the Queen, in the governor general's Commission, to exercise "all powers lawfully belonging to Us." Unquestionably, the confederation architects viewed the lieutenant-governor (referred to once as Superintendent) as a federal officer who, Macdonald said during the debate on Confederation, "will be subordinate to the Representative of the Queen, and be responsible and report to him." Surprisingly, the drafters overlooked that, in practice, an exercise of legislative or administrative authority was, in theory, an exercise of prerogative powers by the Crown or its representative. Did the lieutenant-governor lose those prerogative powers? Did he possess only those prerogatives expressly conferred?

The subject arose during the drafting of the Act. The Quebec Resolutions provided that the prerogative of pardon "which belongs of right to the Crown, shall be administered by the Lieutenant-Governor of each Province in Council" subject to instructions from the federal government. The Governor General disapproved of the resolution because it gave "the *highest* exercise of the Royal Prerogative to the charge of officials, not even appointed by Her Majesty," and the Colonial Secretary categorically refused, for, "this duty belongs to the Representative of the Sovereign—and could not with propriety be devolved upon the Lieutenant-Governors." In London the Canadians pressed hard and had, thought Macdonald, "the best of the argument." But the Colonial Office, backed by the law officers, adamantly refused to alter its decision.

The issue was by no means academic. It became apparent at once that such matters as escheats, priority in the collection of debts, appointment of Queen's Counsel, and so on, depended in theory on the royal prerogative. If the lieutenant-governor did not possess these prerogatives, the authority would then rest with the central government. The question was soon before the Canadian courts and although the judges were clearly confused by the contradiction between status and function, their decisions denied the lieutenant-governor any prerogative powers not expressly stated in the constitution. Even the opinion of Canadian and British law officers that the provincial legislature could confer the appointment of Queen's Counsel on the lieutenant-governor was rejected by the Supreme Court of Canada.

Oliver Mowat refused to accept the decisions of the Canadian courts, and outlined his argument in a lengthy despatch to Ottawa over the Lieutenant-Governor's signature:

The position of my Government is, that the Lieutenant-Governor is entitled *virtute officii*, and without express statutory enactment, to exercise all prerogatives incident to Executive authority in matters over which the Provincial Legislatures have jurisdiction; as the Governor General is entitled *virtute officii* and without any statutory enactment, to exercise all prerogatives incident to Executive authority in matters within the jurisdiction of the Federal Parliament; that a Lieutenant-Governor has the administration of the Royal Prerogatives as far as they are capable of being exercised in relation to the Government of the Province, as the Governor General has the administration of them as far as they are capable of being exercised in relation to the Government assigned to the Dominion.

The B.N.A. Act does not expressly define all the powers either of the Governor General or of the Lieutenant-Governor. It is presumed that as a matter of law the Crown might delegate to either of these Officers any of the powers of the Crown for which express provision is not made by the B.N.A. Act, or by authorized Dominion or Provincial legislation. But in the absence of any such express delegation or legislation, my Government insists that the Governor General and Lieutenant-Governors have respectively under their Commissions, all powers incident to their respective offices, all powers necessary and proper for the administration of their respective governments, all powers usually given to or exercised by Colonial Governors.[10]

Explaining his position in the Ontario legislature, Mowat insisted that only an imperial statute could alter the impossible situation created by politicians, law officers, and courts.

There proved to be a much simpler and faster solution. With one magisterial sweep of the judicial pen in the *Liquidators* case in 1892 Lord Watson basically accepted Mowat's argument and declared that the lieutenant-governor "is as much the representative of Her Majesty, for all purposes of provincial government as the Governor General himself for all purposes of Dominion Government." Whatever may have been thought, or said, or written, Lord Watson wrote authoritatively in a famous *obiter dicta*, that the object of the 1867 constitution:

was neither to weld the provinces into one, nor to subordinate provincial governments to a central authority, but to create a federal government in which they should all be represented, entrusted with the exclusive administration of affairs in which they had a common interest, each province retaining its independence and autonomy. . . .[11]

A quarter of a century later, Haldane boasted that "whatever obscurity may at one time have prevailed as to the position of the Lieutenant-Governors has been dispelled by the decision of this Board,"[12] and in *Re Initiative and Referendum Act* he simply echoed Watson's words.

So direct was that representation of the Crown, in Haldane's view, that he ruled a Manitoba statute (providing for direct legislation as a result of the initiative and referendum procedures) unconstitutional because, in his judgment, it amounted to an amendment of the powers of the lieutenant-governor. Earlier opinion had been that the powers of the office had been protected, as the Ontario Court of Chancery had observed, "to keep intact the headship of the provincial Government, forming as it does, the link of federal power." For Haldane, however, the power of the provincial government to amend the constitution "except as regards the office of Lieutenant-Governor" seemed fitting because:

> his position as directly representing the Sovereign in the province, renders natural the exclusion of his office from the power conferred on the Provincial Legislature to amend the constitution of the Province. The analogy of the British Constitution is that on which the entire scheme is founded, and that analogy points to the impropriety, in the absence of clear and unmistakable language, of construing s. 92 as permitting the abrogation of any power which the Crown possesses through a person who directly represents it.

The power in this case was freedom of action in the legislative process, which ended with royal assent.[13]

HALDANE: THE STATE AND THE ROLE OF LAW

Interesting as Professor Wexler's analysis is, there are other avenues that perhaps offer more promise of understanding Haldane's construction of the Act and the reasoning behind his *obiter dicta*. There is no doubt that his view of the Canadian federation was shaped during his work for the provinces at Watson's bar, and his commitment to imperial unity and Irish home rule may well have, consciously or unconsciously, added to his apparent bias in favour of provincial rights and autonomy. But more important were the philosophical underpinnings which shaped his view of the nature of the state and the role of law and the courts.

In his eulogies of Watson, Lord Haldane made no attempt to argue that Watson had remained faithful to the logic or language of the 1867 Act. In fact, he boasted that in Watson,

> we have the ideal of what a judge of the empire ought to be. Whether he sits in the House of Lords or the Privy Council, a man in that position wields enormous influence. He not only decides particular cases. Such is the weight of the decision of this Court, that its spirit extends far beyond its letter, and it moulds and makes as well as interprets the law.

To look upon the Judicial Committee "as a mere means of declaring, without altering, the existing law and Constitution" Haldane dismissed as "a narrow view, and mischievous pedantry" for it was "law-changing functions" of the Court that had written important chapters in constitutional history.[14]

Haldane's view of the importance of the "law-changing functions" of the Court derived from his philosophic, rather than his juristic ideas. As a philosopher, he had reached conclusions about the nature of the state and about the relationship between the state and individuals which, as Jonathan Robinson has demonstrated so well, came largely from his study of Hegel. What matters here is not his understanding of Hegel, but his conclusions about the nature of sovereignty and the state, for these determined his view of the role of the jurist and of the courts. While sitting on the Judicial Committee, Haldane wrote:

> If the source of the power of the state and the reality of the state is the embodiment of common purposes entertained by the people who constitute it, that source can only be a general will...and the true source of sovereignty must be simply public or general opinion. Now general opinion is not easy to diagnose and ascertain. It has a history, and it often fluctuates rapidly. It may have entrusted a particular body of men with the duty of carrying its decisions into effect, and it may appear, say in the programme nominally endorsed at a general election, to have expressed itself and to have given authority for the execution of its decrees. But none the less it may not really have done so. One of the most delicate tasks confided to a newly elected Ministry is to determine what mandate has really been given. Not only may that mandate be really different from what it appeared to be from the language at the time employed by those who gave it, but it may be undergoing rapid and yet silent modification. This implies that it is the general opinion of the nation at the time when action has to be taken that is the ultimate source of authority, and that under a constitution like our own such opinion has to be interpreted, not as crystallised, but by continuous exegesis directed to ascertaining what it has become. . . .
>
> Thus there has always to take place a careful balancing of considerations, in order to determine the extent of a mandate that has been entrusted to the legislature. For the legislature does not really represent sovereign power. Sovereignty has its definite source, and even the highest institutions in the state may not be able to claim it.[15]

The state, Haldane wrote on another occasion,

> is no static unity...not an arbitrary creation....The stability of the state depends on continuity of broad national purpose, and, consistently with that continuity and stability resulting from it, there is room for infinite modification in internal institutions. The state is made, not by external acts, but by the continuous thought and action of the people who live its life. In this sense it is never perfect, for it is a process that remains always unbroken in creative activity.[16]

It follows that the law cannot be static, and that the courts must somehow keep the law abreast of that "unbroken creative activity" and in harmony with the general will of the people, as interpreted, presumably, by the judiciary. As Haldane wrote:

law is more than a mere command. It is this indeed, but it has a significance which cannot be understood apart from the history and spirit of the nation whose law it is. Larger conceptions than those of the mere lawyer are required for the appreciation of that significance, conceptions which belong to the past and which fall within the province of the moralist and the sociologist. Without these we are sometimes unable to determine what is and what is not part of the law....The laws contain general rules of conduct, expressed in objective form, and enforced by sanctions applied by the state. But they are not always to be found expressed in definite and unchanging form, and the tribunal which enforces them has to consider a context of a far-reaching character, a context which may have varied from generation to generation, and which may render even a written rule obsolete, or make it necessary to apply one that is unwritten and about which ethical judgments are at variance.[17]

As professor Robinson observed, Haldane clearly believed "that law *cannot* be practised without reference to more than the law itself" and he quotes Haldane's comment: "I am a lawyer whose almost daily practice is to ascertain the reasons why the law has become what it is, because unless I can do so, I am bound to fail in the interpretation of its scope and authority." Haldane made it clear, Robinson adds, that the "why" includes "more than legal reasons, and we must have knowledge of a context which includes the 'spirit of an age'...."[18]

Clearly, Watson had captured the spirit of the age, discovered the general will, followed the trend of the "unbroken creative activity" and with a mind "wholly free from any tendency to technicality" gave Canada the federal constitution it really wanted. Haldane was determined to do the same. He, too, would find the general will and with a mind free from any tendency to technicality would render constitutional decisions to give it effect. Given his philosophical assumptions, he could not do otherwise.

Not even Professor Robinson has been able to explain clearly the direct application of Haldane's philosophy to his Canadian decisions. Somehow, in his search for the source of sovereignty, for the general will or for public opinion, he seemed to find it in the provinces, as he had in an Ireland under British control. To allow that general will to find its full expression, the apparently oppressive hand of the federal government had to be removed. His decision in the Australian case (mentioned at the beginning of this essay) is revealing. The challenged statute of the Commonwealth government gave a Royal Commission the power to examine the sugar industry and secure information on production, costs, profits, dividends and salaries. Because the Commonwealth government had only the powers specified in the constitution, and because the power to impose "new duties on the subjects of, or people residing within, the individual States were, before federation, vested in the Legislatures of the States," he declared, the central government had to prove that the power was among those specified. "None of them relate to that general control over the liberty of the subject," he concluded, "which must be shewn to be transferred if it is to be regarded as vested in the Commonwealth."

Haldane showed the same concern for the "liberty of the subject" in his Canadian decisions, and found it neatly tucked into property and civil rights. A concern for the liberty of the subject is not surprising in a man who, despite his support as a politician for an activist state, found the source of sovereignty, the justification for the state itself, in the individuals who make up the community and ultimately form the general will. It is less obvious, however, why he should state in the *Board of Commerce* case that since "the regulation and restriction" of the civil rights of Canadians had been "exclusively confided" to the provinces it was "only under necessity in highly exceptional circumstances...that the liberty of the inhabitants of the Provinces may be restricted by the Parliament of Canada...." One is left with the conclusion that the liberty of Canadians, which would alone permit the general will to be manifested, had been assigned to the provinces and had to be protected against any encroachment by a distant and, if not a foreign, an almost dangerous power.

As Robinson concluded:

> It seems, then, that Hegelian philosophy played no small role in determining the nature of the government under which millions of Canadians were to live. Whether one regards this as the mark of Teutonic metaphysics clouding the clear air of the land of the maple leaf, or a rational view of the state which alone could have preserved that tenuous unity born at Quebec in 1864—these questions I leave to my readers.[19]

NOTES

1. Jonathan Robinson, "Lord Haldane and the British North America Act," *University of Toronto Law Journal* (1970), 55–69; Stephen Wexler, "The Urge to Idealize: Viscount Haldane and the Constitution of Canada," *McGill Law Journal* (1984), 609–47.

2. Cited in Wexler "Urge to Idealize," 638. Haldane appeared as counsel for the provinces in ten cases. He acted for Ontario in such important cases as *St. Catherines Milling* (1888), *Attorney-General of Ontario v. Attorney-General of Canada* (1894) and the *Local Prohibition* case in 1896.

3. *Attorney-General for the Commonwealth of Australia v. Colonial Sugar Refining Company Limited* [1914] A.C. 252–55.

4. *Parliamentary Debates*, 1900, vol. LXXXII, p. 98.

5. R. B. Haldane, *Education and Empire: Addresses on Certain Topics of the Day* (London, 1902), 137–39, 111–12.

6. *Education and Empire*, 131–35, 139.

7. [1919] A.C. 935 at 943.

8. Wexler, "Urge to Idealize," 611.

9. The following section on the lieutenant-governor is based on John T. Saywell, *The Office of Lieutenant-Governor: A Study in Canadian Government and Politics*, rev. ed. (Toronto, 1986), 9–15.

10. Quoted in Saywell, *Lieutenant-Governor*, 12.

11. *Liquidators of the Maritime Bank of Canada v. Receiver General of New Brunswick* [1892] A.C. 437 at 941–42.

12. *Bonanza Creek Gold Mine Company v. R* [1916] 1 AC 581.

13. Haldane found the constitutional position of the lieutenant-governor difficult to reconcile with the decision in *Liquidators* and his own view. He describes the power of the federal

government to appoint and dismiss the officer "a remarkable provision." As he wrote:

> But while to the legal principle of construction which the Privy Council established there is no real exception, a remarkable exception to the constitutional principle has, by the combined operation of the language of the Act and of the usages which it imported, been created in regard to that office of Lieutenant-Governor to which I have adverted.

It is, in fact, the 1867 Act which is wrong, not the construction of co-ordinate federalism placed on by Watson in *Liquidators* (Haldane, *Education and Empire*, 110–14).

14. Haldane, *Education and Empire*, 141. Soon after he became Lord Chancellor, Haldane noted in his diary: "I am sitting as president of the Supreme Tribunal of the Empire at the Privy Council—carrying out as well as I can the principle I advocated years ago in my little book *Education and Empire*." (Cited in Wexler, "Urge to Idealize," 630.)

15. R.B. Haldane, *The Reign of Relativity* (Toronto, 1921), 366 ff.

16. In the introduction to M.P. Follett, *The New State* (London, 1920), xii.

17. Haldane, *Reign of Relativity*, 351. In arguing that the "most elementary justification of the Privy Council rests on the broad sociological ground that the provincial bias which pervaded so many of its decisions was in fundamental harmony with the regional pluralism of Canada" and presumably with public opinion or the general will, Alan Cairns comes close to accepting Haldane's view of the role of the Court, (Alan C. Cairns, "The Judicial Committee and Its Critics," *Canadian Journal of Political Science* (September 1971), 320.

18. Robinson, "Lord Haldane," 65.

19. Robinson, "Lord Haldane," 68.

THE PRIVY COUNCIL AND THE SUPREME COURT: A JURISPRUDENTIAL ANALYSIS◇

MARK MACGUIGAN

◦

A legal positivist unfamiliar with Canadian constitutional law might well be pardoned for thinking that the *British North America Act* was the ideal constitution and the Judicial Committee of the Privy Council the ideal constitutional court. The constitutional document is ideologically neutral, embodying no lofty statements of ideals and parading no value judgments. In the words of Sir Ivor Jennings, "It contains no metaphysics, no political philosophy, and no party politics."[1] The constitutional court sat out its days in judicial seclusion an ocean removed from the colony-state, with no knowledge of the geographic, economic, social, and political conditions beyond what it might gather from the London newspapers; it did not know enough about the country to choose sides in Canadian controversies. Lord Haldane was merely giving utterance to the conventional positivistic wisdom when he wrote: "We sit there, perfectly impartial; we have no prejudices, either theological or otherwise."[2] Such a court, reading such a constitution, should have produced a perfect positivistic product, ninety-nine and forty-four one-hundredths per cent pure. That it did not, is arguably good for the country; that it could not, is incontestably fatal for positivism.

By way of contrast, a legal sociologist would wish to point to native judicial bodies that were keenly aware of the social conditions of the nation and contended nobly with the Privy Council for the more socially beneficial rule. But unfortunately for the sociologist, while there is some evidence to support such a thesis, there is far from enough to prove it. There are, in fact, only a handful of cases which display significant disagreement between Canadian courts and the imperial court.

There were two important cases involving *per saltum* appeals from the Ontario Court of Appeal to the Privy Council in which strong judgments of the Ontario

Court were reversed. In the *Voluntary Assignments Case* [3] in 1894 a four-to-nothing Court of Appeal decision holding that a section of the *Ontario Assignments and Preferences Act* was *ultra vires* as a transgression of the federal bankruptcy power was reversed by a Board speaking through Lord Herschell, who held that the legislation was supportable under the provincial power over property and civil rights. Again in *Toronto Electric Commissioners v. Snider*,[4] where an Ontario trial judge and four of five judges in the Appellate Division had held that the *Industrial Disputes Investigation Act* was *intra vires* the federal parliament under the peace, order and good government clause on the authority of *Russell v. The Queen*,[5] Lord Haldane's Razor decimated the federal general power to the profit of section 92(13). Similarly in *Lymburn v. Mayland* [6] a unanimous judgment of the Alberta Court of Appeal holding a provincial statute authorizing investigations into fraudulent practices *ultra vires* as infringing the criminal law power was reversed by the Judicial Committee through Lord Atkin.

There are also two important cases in which the Privy Council reversed the Supreme Court of Canada, but they were both three-to-two decisions in the Supreme Court. In the *Local Prohibition* case [7] in 1896 the Privy Council through Lord Watson upheld the constitutionality of a section of the *Ontario Liquor Licence Act* under either section 92(13) or section 92(16), and in 1916, in *Bonanza Creek Gold Mining Co. Ltd. v. The King*,[8] a Supreme Court judgment that an Ontario company had neither the power nor the capacity to carry on mining operations outside the Province was reversed by Lord Haldane. There are two further cases in which the Privy Council invalidated federal legislation where the Supreme Court had been evenly divided: *The Board of Commerce Act Reference* [9] in 1921 and the *Labour Conventions* case [10] in 1937.

It could be argued from the rarity of reversals that the Canadian Courts warmly endorsed the views of the Privy Council, but such a conclusion would not be warranted by the evidence. The Supreme Court of Canada adopted a strict rule of *stare decisis* in the 1909 case of *Stuart v. The Bank of Montreal*,[11] and insofar as its relationship with the Privy Council was concerned, was faithful to the spirit as well as to the letter of the rule. The early history of the Court, before the provincially oriented trend of Privy Council interpretation was firmly established, would also suggest the fallacy of identifying Supreme Court acceptance of the decision of a superior Court with enthusiastic assent. In its early "independent" period up to 1896 there was no doubt in the minds of the Supreme Court judges as to the supremacy of federal power, and the only question at issue was as to the validity of provincial legislation in the absence of federal legislation. In one of the last cases of this period Mr. Justice Sedgewick, making a plea for sociological interpretation, said: "In the *British North America Act* it was in a technical sense only that the Imperial Parliament spoke; it was there that in a real and substantial sense the Canadian people spoke, and it is to their language, as they understood it, that effect must be given."[12]

Moreover, in later years at least one Supreme Court judge, Chief Justice Anglin, made clear over a period of time his continuing disagreement with the Privy Council. In the *Insurance Act Reference* [13] in 1916 he advocated an interpretation of the general power in terms of "national concern": which on appeal fell afoul of Haldane's Razor. In the *Board of Commerce Act Reference* [14] in 1920 he took the view that the federal legislation there could be upheld under both the general power and the trade and commerce clause, but Lord Haldane took a contrary view. The Supreme Court had no opportunity to express an opinion in the *Snider* case, but in a later case the same year Chief Justice Anglin (dissenting) took strong exception to Haldane's "emergency doctrine" interpretation to the general power.[15]

However, if from the evidence one cannot read internal assent into the external compliance of the Supreme Court, still less can one conclude colonial judicial disaffection. Canadian courts themselves did not seem to be alive to sociological factors. Indeed, to take the fate of the Canadian "New Deal" legislation as an example, with the exception of the *Labour Conventions Acts* (on which there was a three-to-three split in the Supreme Court of Canada), the Privy Council decided the other references in the same way as had the Supreme Court, save that in three instances the Privy Council was slightly more favourable to the federal legislation than the Supreme Court had been. Moreover, the judge who is considered by many to be our greatest native jurist, Sir Lyman Duff, appeared not merely to follow in the footsteps of the Board but to break new ground for the benefit of provincial rights. In many instances his concepts were taken up by the Privy Council,[16] and Professor Laskin has not hesitated to pronounce that, "Sir Lyman showed, as early as the *Board of Commerce* case, that he had embarked on that course [of interpretation with respect to the general power] as much by his own choice as by the dictates of *stare decisis*."[17]

ESSENTIALISTIC NATURAL LAW APPROACH

To this point, it has been suggested, but not proved, that the approach of the Privy Council to the Canadian Constitution cannot be adequately explained either in terms of positivism or of sociologism. A third possibility might be raised: that their approach was essentially a natural-law one and that, as a converse to the establishing of this thesis, it was neither positivistic nor sociological.[18]

It is not necessary, in order to establish a natural-law approach, to demonstrate that the Board considered certain things to be taboo for both national and regional governments, though Dean Scott has drawn attention to the fact that generally the Board found *ultra vires* all statutes attempting to control trade and commerce, whether they were federal or provincial.[19] It is sufficient, however, to show that the Law Lords indulged in extensive judicial legislation, and that the source of their legislative wisdom was not the clamour of the colonial populace, nor even their own observation of the actual exigencies of the society, but rather an abstract and pre-existing concept of federalism which they applied like a procrustean bed to the ungainly limbs of the adolescent statute. Such an essentialistic use of natural-law theory is one toward which the contemporary natural lawyer feels no more kinship, than he does toward the *laissez-faire* natural law epoused by the U.S. Supreme Court a few decades ago; but he can hardly deny the validity of the technique, even if he quarrels with the content of the doctrine.

The introductory clause of Section 91, the so-called general power, gives the Parliament of Canada the right "to make laws for the Peace, Order, and good Government of Canada," and this is the only grant of legislative power given to

Parliament. However, "for greater certainty, but not so as to restrict the generality of the foregoing terms" Parliament is given exclusive legislative authority over twenty-nine enumerated classes of subjects. Section 92 then assigns to the Provincial legislatures legislative power over sixteen enumerated classes of subjects. The scheme of the Act clearly suggests the supremacy of federal power and that the peace, order, and good government clause is properly to be interpreted as a grant of residuary legislative power.

There can be no doubt that this was also the intention of the Fathers of Confederation. In the Confederation debate in the Parliament of Canada in 1865 John A. Macdonald maintained: "We have strengthened the general government. We have given the General Legislature all the great subjects of legislation."[20] In a similar vein Lord Carnarvon, the Secretary of State for the Colonies, told the House of Lords: "Just as the authority of the central Parliament will prevail whenever it may come into conflict with the local legislatures, so the residue of legislation, if any, unprovided for in the specific legislation . . . will belong to the central body."[21]

What the Privy Council did with the Constitution is another story.[22] In its early period, from 1873 (when the first Privy Council appeal from Canada was decided) until 1894, there was no strong trend in the direction of either the Provinces or the Dominion. The main desire of the Board seems to have been to uphold all legislation brought before it, though this undoubtedly implied a failure to emphasise the paramount position of the Federal Government to the extent intended by the Fathers. The most important cases in this period were *Russell v. The Queen*,[23] which upheld federal regulation of the liquor traffic under the general power, and *Hodge v. The Queen*,[24] in which provincial liquor legislation not essentially different from the federal legislation approved in the *Russell* case was upheld.

The next period, from 1894 to 1906, saw the dominance of Lord Watson in the years up to 1899. During that time he was a member of the Board in all nine constitutional cases and gave the opinion five times; Lord Herschell gave the opinion three times, and Lord Halsbury once. After 1899 Lord Halsbury gave the opinion in the only two constitutional cases. The most important case in this period is probably the *Local Prohibition* case [25] in 1896, in which Lord Watson began the whittling down of section 91, and especially of the general power.

The years 1907 to 1912 were transitional in terms of court personnel, and there were no crucial cases during this time. Then in 1912 Lord Haldane, who had been active as counsel in Canadian appeals since 1885, appeared for the first time, and from then until 1929 he was the dominant personality on the Board. In those years there were forty-one decisions on legislative power; Lord Haldane was present on thirty-two occasions and delivered the opinion nineteen times. Of the many important cases in this period only two will be mentioned: the *Board of Commerce Act Reference* [26] in 1921 and the *Snider* case [27] in 1925. By means of the *Board of Commerce Act* the Dominion was attempting to regulate retail prices, and endeavoured to sustain this regulation under both the general power and the trade and commerce clause. In the course of his opinion Lord Haldane said that the general power can justify interference with property and civil rights only "in highly exceptional circumstances."[28] He also held that the commerce clause could not of itself sustain legislation, but could merely have the effect of aiding jurisdiction under the general power; thus in fact it was denied independent existence as a head of section 91.

In the *Snider* case in striking down a federal act which had been in effect for nearly twenty years, Lord Haldane declared:

Their Lordships think that the decision in *Russell v. The Queen* can only be supported today . . . on the assumption of the Board, apparently made at the time of deciding the case of *Russell v. The Queen*, that the evil of intemperance at that time amounted in Canada to one so great and so general that at least for the period it was a menace to the national life of Canada so serious and pressing that the National Parliament was called on to intervene to protect the nation from disaster. An epidemic of pestilence might conceivably have been regarded as analogous.[29]

The next period, 1929 to 1935, coincides with the years of England's first Labour Government and the reign of Lord Sankey as Lord Chancellor. With his famous "living tree" metaphor in the *Edwards* case [30] Lord Sankey suggested the possibility of a new approach to the Constitution, and in the four following cases (the *P.A.T.A.* case,[31] the *Aeronautics* case,[32] the *Radio* case,[33] and the *British Coal Corporation* case)[34] the decisions went in favour of the federal government.

The late period of Privy Council activity, stretching from 1935 to 1953, began with 1937 New Deal references, in which the Board reverted to a limited view of federal power, and ended with a number of postwar cases in which the Board took a more benign view of federal power. Of the eight New Deal acts considered by the Privy Council, five were held completely *ultra vires*, one was held partly *ultra vires*, and two were upheld.[35] The statutes wholly struck down were the three *Labour Conventions Acts* passed to enable Canada to discharge her obligations under the Treaty of Versailles and related draft conventions, the *Employment and Social Insurance Act*, which established a national unemployment insurance scheme, and the *Natural Products Marketing Act*, which established a national marketing board to regulate marketing and distribution. The result respecting unemployment insurance was rectified by a 1940 amendment to the B.N.A. Act, but the disallowance of the other acts remained a serious blow to the National Government. In the *Natural Products Marketing Act Reference* [36] the Privy Council took the view that neither the peace, order, and good government power nor section 91(2) could sustain the legislation, and in the *Labour Conventions Reference* [37] it held that the acts could be based neither on the introductory clause of section 91 nor on section 132. In sum, the result of the cases to the beginning of World War II was that the commerce clause had no meaning at all, and that the general power gave Parliament the right to make laws only for the emergencies of war, famine, or pestilence, for the incorporation of companies having national objects, and for the regulation of communication by radio.

Subsequently in the 1946 *Canada Temperance Federation* case,[38] where the Privy Council was asked to consider again substantially the same statute approved in *Russell v. The Queen*, Viscount Simon refused to accept Lord Haldane's emergency doctrine and upheld the statute under the general power, stating "it is the nature of the legislation itself, and not the existence of emergency, that determines whether it is valid or not."[39] And in the *Reference re Privy Council Appeals*[40] the following year Viscount Jowitt, like Lord Sankey before him, chose to treat the *British North America Act* as a constitution rather than as an ordinary statute.

This has been too cursory a survey of the cases to establish any substantive point of constitutional law, but it serves perhaps to illustrate the method of interpretation. Twenty-five years ago Dean Kennedy argued that in not one case "has the *ratio decidendi* [of a Privy Council decision] depended on reasons external to the Act,"[41] but this is surely true only in a formal sense. The Privy Council no doubt always found words in the Act on which to rest its interpretation, but there was nothing inevitable about the solutions, not even in terms of the accumulated precedents. To take just two examples, the *Insurance Act Reference* and the *Labour Conventions Reference* could have been decided in the opposite way even by a court which genuinely accepted the precedents. (Indeed, in the former case Lord Haldane was himself unable to cite any precedent to support his drastic limitation of the general power). Moreover, the foregoing survey has shown that interpretation has varied with the composition of the Board, with some relief from provincial supremacy in the early thirties and in the middle forties.

Over the years the Privy Council established many doctrines to help them interpret the constitution: the paramountcy doctrine, the trenching doctrine, the ancillary powers doctrine, the occupied field doctrine, the pith and substance doctrine, and the aspect doctrine. But these doctrines were merely the implements of the lawyers' craft; they were the tools by which the Law Lords rationalized their conclusions, but they were not the instruments for reaching the conclusions. In essence what the Privy Council had to decide was what meaning and purpose to assign to the whole Act and what meaning and purpose to ascribe to the relevant parts of sections 91 and 92; neither of these tasks is at bottom predetermined by logic or precedent. The ultimate decision had to be a value judgment, or, if you prefer, a policy decision.

That the Privy Council itself had no illusions on this score is indicated by these words of Lord Haldane, spoken in 1921:

> At one time, after the *British North America Act* of 1867 was passed, the conception took hold of the Canadian courts that what was intended was to make the Dominion the centre of government in Canada, so that its statutes and its position should be superior to the statutes and position of the Provincial Legislatures. That went so far that there arose a great fight; and as the result of a long series of decisions Lord Watson put clothing upon the bones of the Constitution, and so covered them over with living flesh that the Constitution of Canada took a new form. The Provinces were recognized as of equal authority co-ordinate with the Dominion, and a long series of decisions were given by him which solved many problems and produced a new contentment in Canada with the Constitution they had got in 1867. It is difficult to say what the extent of the debt was that Canada owes to Lord Watson, and there is no part

of the Empire where his memory is held in more reverence in legal circles.[42]

Lord Haldane here proves himself a poor prognosticator: with the emergence of the law teaching profession and the consequent development of legal writing in Canada in the twenties and thirties, discontent with the Constitution proved almost boundless, and if there is any name less revered in Canadian legal circles than that of Lord Watson it is only that of Lord Haldane himself. But his statement is a frank enough admission of judicial legislation: the "new form" which Lord Watson gave the Canadian Constitution was painly in Lord Haldane's mind not dictated by the bare bones of the text, and in his opinion but for Lord Watson's heroic fattening job the Constitution might have remained a mere skeleton.

Fault can be found with the Watson–Haldane axis not on the score of judicial legislation, nor even primarily on the score of favouritism towards the provinces. Their failure was not *that* they legislated, nor even so much *what* they legislated, but rather *how* they legislated. Their failure was to view the Constitution too abstractly and therefore to rely on a formalistic and formularistic natural law.

Some years ago Professor Freund wisely remarked:

> If the first requisite of a constitutional judge is that he be a philosopher, the second requisite is that he be not too philosophical. Success in the undertaking requires absorption in the fact rather than deduction from large and rigidly held abstractions. The constitutional judge is an architect, one who tempers the vision of the artist with a reliable knowledge of the strengths and weaknesses and availability of materials.[43]

Lord Haldane more than once proclaimed his devotion to Hegelian dialectic, which is characterised not only by great abstractness, but also by the inevitability of historical process through a conflict of thesis and antithesis. In such an intellectual universe how easy it is to see the Dominion principle and the provincial principle as exclusive opposites plunged inevitably into dialectical struggle, how noble it is to feel the need to assist the weaker so that the eternal struggle could continue.

The result of the application of such an essentialistic natural-law doctrine to the Canadian Constitution was an insoluble dilemma for the Privy Council. On the one hand, by treating the B.N.A. Act as an ordinary statute and not as a constitutional document, by giving consideration neither to the historically documented intention of the Fathers nor to the exigencies of the present as revealed through such devices as Brandeis Briefs, by insisting that nothing can aid decision but the words of the statute itself, it deliberately thrust itself into a positivistic vacuum excluding everything but form and formula. But on the basis solely of such a process of pure textual interpretation it could not possibly have reached a result so far removed from the clearly expressed structure and meaning of the Act. Thus, to delineate the other horn of the dilemma, the Board found with experience that it did not really want to give merely a literal interpretation to the Act, even that it could not do so. Forced by the pressure of reality into making policy, it was at the same time compelled by the logic of its own position to make policy in complete abstraction from the socio-economic needs of the people; unable to feed on facts, it had to dine on transcendentals. In sum, even without the aid of the Bill of Rights, the Privy Council found it possible to give a natural-law cast to the Canadian Constitution, but unfortunately it was a dull, abstract, essentialistic natural law.

CANADIAN FEDERALISM

Thus far the substantive aspect of constitutional law held up for examination has been the question of distribution of legislative powers, which resolves itself into the policy issue whether the Court should favour the national power or the provincial powers. But more fundamental even than the distribution of legislative power is the conception of federalism which underlies it. Canadian Confederation was conceived in terms of classical federalism, which considered the national and regional governments as independent and autonomous entities—though in the Canadian case with the modification that the greater sovereignty should be given to the central government. The individualism and *laissez-faire* which gave birth to classic federalism assumed that, since there would be a minimum of government at both levels, there would be little prospect of collision, but the facts of life soon showed that this was an unrealistic expectation.

The Privy Council decided early to adopt the model of classical federalism—though without provision for federal dominance as intended by the Fathers. As early as 1883 it established the complete equality of status between Parliament and the Provincial legislatures, neither being inferior or subordinate to the other. As Lord Watson proclaimed in 1892: "The object of the Act was neither to weld the provinces into one, nor to subordinate the provincial governments to a central authority, but to create a federal government in which they should all be represented, entrusted with the exclusive administration of affairs in which they had a common interest, *each province retaining its independence and autonomy.*"[44]

Over the years their Lordships continued to assume a state of constant conflict between Parliament and the Legislatures (an assumption not entirely at variance with the facts), but the full effects of the fundamental principle were not seen until the *Natural Products Marketing Act Reference* in 1937. The Act in question there provided for the establishment of a national marketing board to regulate marketing and distribution, and it also provided for the exercise by the board of any powers that might be conferred upon it by provincial legislatures. The federal government, having accomplished the miraculous feat of surmounting the technical, legal, and political difficulties in the way of provincial co-operation, found itself faced with a Privy Council declaration of *ultra vires*, despite the fact that all nine provinces had supported the plan, and that all had actually enacted special legislation to confer powers on the federal marketing board. Verbally sympathetic to the concept of co-operation, the Court commented that the desired aim "will not be achieved by either party leaving its own sphere and encroaching upon that of the other."[45]

A sociological analysis of Canada in the thirties would, it is suggested, show the inutility of the Privy Council decisions at that time. The conduct of international relations by the federal government had been seriously interfered with; Canada actually had much less power to implement treaties by legislation than it had had under section 132 in the days when the Mother Country entered into all treaties on her behalf. Many matters of national importance had been placed beyond the legislative competence of Parliament. The Provinces, which had been the beneficiaries of the legislative bounty of the Privy Council, did not have the financial resources to deal effectively with the subjects under their jurisdiction. The results seemed so unfortunate at the time that one observer wrote, "Confederation itself may well have difficulty in surviving the disintegrating effect of the Court's judgments upon the B.N.A. Act."[46]

But co-operative federalism could not be stopped by the courts. The depression, the War, the increasing industrialization, the tax rental agreements, the new budgetary policy all pushed the country inexorably into co-operative federalism, and a large part of the work of the Supreme Court since 1949 has consisted in the *legal* establishment of the co-operative principle. In the economic field, when the question of dovetailing federal and provincial statutes came before the newly emancipated Court in 1951 in the *Nova Scotia Delegation Reference*,[47] it took the same narrowly legalistic approach as the Privy Council, holding that since both Parliament and the Provincial Legislature were sovereign bodies with exclusive jurisdiction, each was incapable of delegating to the other and of receiving delegated power from the other. Subsequently, however, in the *P.E.I. Potato Marketing Board* case [48] the Court felt able to approve the delegation of federal powers to a provincially created and controlled board, thus providing a solution to one of the problems of economic co-operation. In the field of criminal law, even before 1949 the Supreme Court showed a considerable tolerance of nearly identical legislation as in the *Egan* [49] case, and recent decisions such as *O'Grady v. Sparling*[50] promise a continuance of the same trend. It is submitted that this trend in criminal law is to be welcomed, and that it would be all to the good if a constitutional conference made criminal law constitutionally what it is in fact, viz. a field of concurrent federal and provincial jurisdiction, provided that this was accompanied by a clear recognition of federal jurisdiction over civil liberties.

At the outset co-operative federalism had a decided federal bias—not because of anything in the law, whether legislative or judicial, but rather because of the realities of economic and political power (which precede rather than follow the law). For this reason it is a bad word and a bad idea in the minds of many French-speaking Canadians.

But today co-operative federalism has in truth a decided provincial bias. The reasons are many: the political strength of the provincial governments, the political weakness of minority federal governments, the years of recession and of unbalanced federal budgets, the development of closer liaison between the provincial governments and the possible emergence of a third form of government, viz., the continuing Federal–Provincial Conference, and perhaps most of all the dynamism of the Quebec Revolution. The point is, however, that the bias in co-operative federalism will be taken care of by non-legal factors. The law should go on further than to reflect the desire of the people and the necessity of the times for co-operative federalism. It may be that as part of its task of umpiring the federal system the Court will be called upon to decide the boundaries in areas of conflict, but it should be slow to rush into economic controversies. If the Court adopts generally a hands-off

160 INVENTION AND CONSOLIDATION

policy in the economic area, it will find that most of the work of striking a balance is done for it by other forces.[51]

CONCLUSION

A discussion of the great question of constitutional reform is not within the scope of this article. The concern is not with the new Confederation Pact, but with what the Court will do with it, if it comes about. It too will age and require interpretation as all written documents are wont to do.

This article is almost concluded and very little has been said about the role of the Supreme Court of Canada. Yet implicitly, continuing reference has been made to it. The opinion advanced is that it should not continue the positivistic fiction of pretending that everything but the words of the constitution is irrelevant to its interpretation; and that it should embrace a sociological or a sociological natural-law approach and the means necessary for the success of such an approach. Only a contemporary-minded Court can keep a constitution contemporary, and a constitution which is not contemporary will prove to be merely temporary.

With a sociological approach there is, of course, the danger of bad policy judgments, which would probably be understood to mean ones with which we are not in sympathy. But is it preferable to have ultimate decisions made by a court without sociological knowledge which are sure (except for accidental coincidences) to be the wrong solutions, or is it preferable to have decisions made by a sociologically conscious court which have at least a possibility of being the best solutions? On the answer to this question will depend the future role of the Supreme Court.

NOTES

1. Sir Ivor Jennings, "Constitutional Interpretation: The Experience of Canada" (1937) 51 *Harv. L. Rev.* 1.

2. Haldane, *The Work for the Empire of the Judicial Committee of the Privy Council* (1922) 1 *Cam. L. Rev.* 143, at 153.

3. *A.-G. Ont. v. A.-G. Can.*, [1894] A.C. 189. Since the sociological criticism of the Privy Council is to the effect that the Board favoured Provincial power at a time when social conditions demanded a strengthening of federal power, I have cited only the cases which might support *this* criticism by showing a pro-provincial bias in the Board. There are a number of other cases, however, in which the Privy Council overruled Canadian courts in order to invalidate or limit provincial legislation. See, e.g., *Union Colliery of B.C. Limited v. Bryden*, [1899] A.C. 580; *:John Deere*

Plow Company Limited v. Wharton, [1915] A.C. 330; *Great West Saddlery Company, Limited v. The King*, [1921] A.C. 91.

4. [1925] A.C. 396. There was a second Ontario judge who thought the Act *ultra vires*—Orde J. before whom the case came on a motion for an interim injunction, which he granted.

5. (1882) 7 App. Cas. 829.

6. [1932] A.C. 318.

7. *A.-G. Ont. v. A.-G. Can.*, [1896] A.C. 348.

8. [1916] A.C. 566.

9. [1922] A.C. 191.

10. *A.-G. Can. v. A.-G. Ont.*, [1937] A.C. 326.

11. (1909) 41 S.C.R. 516.

12. In re Prohibiting Liquor Laws (1895) 24 S.C.R. 170 at 231.

13. (1916) 48 S.C.R. 260, at 310; [1916] 1 A.C. 588, at 595.

14. (1920) 60 S.C.R. 456; [1922] 1 A.C. 191.

15. The King v. Eastern Terminal Elevator Co., [1925] S.C.R. 434, at 438.

16. Several instances are cited by Bora Laskin (now Laskin J.A. of the Ontario Court of Appeal), "The Supreme Court of Canada: A Final Court of and for Canadians" (1951) 29 Can. Bar Rev. 1038, at 1067–69.

17. Laskin, "Peace, Order, and good Government Re-Examined" (1947) 25 Can. Bar Rev. 1054, at 1056.

18. But see Mark R. MacGuigan, "Sources of Judicial Decision Making and Judicial Activism" in Equality and Judicial Neutrality, ed. Sheilah L. Martin and Kathleen E. Mahoney (Toronto: Carswell, 1987), 36, note 36 in which he indicates a change in his thinking.

19. F. R. Scott, "The Consequences of the Privy Council Decisions" (1937) 15 Can. Bar Rev. 485, at 492.

20. The Confederation Debates, ed. Waite, 44 (1963).

21. Hansard, vol. 185, cols. 563, 566.

22. My review of Privy Council activity is based in part upon that of Jennings, "Constitutional Interpretation."

23. (1882) 7 App. Cas. 829.

24. (1883) 9 App. Cas. 117.

25. A.-G. Ont. v. A.-G. Can., [1896] A.C. 348.

26. [1922] 1 A.C. 191.

27. [1925] A.C. 396.

28. [1922] 1 A.C. 191, at 197.

29. [1925] A.C. 396, at 412.

30. Edwards v. A.-G. Can., [1930] A.C. 124, at 136.

31. Proprietory Articles Trade Assn. v. A.-G. Can., [1931] A.C. 310.

32. [1932] A.C. 54.

33. [1932] A.C. 304.

34. [1935] A.C. 500.

35. I am indebted to the complete analysis of the New Deal references in Vincent C. MacDonald, "The Canadian Constitution Seventy Years After" (1937) 15 Can. Bar Rev. 401.

36. A.-G. B.C. v. A.-G. Can., [1937] A.C. 377.

37. A.-G. Can. v. A.-G. Ont., [1937] A.C. 326.

38. A.-G. Ont. v. Canada Temperance Federation, [1946] A.C. 193.

39. Ibid., at 205.

40. A.-G. Ont. v. A.-G. Can., [1947] A.C. 127.

41. W.P.M. Kennedy, The Constitution of Canada, 2d ed. (1938), 550.

42. Jennings, "Constitutional Interpretation," 150.

43. P.A. Freund, "Umpiring the Federal System" (1954) 51 Col. L. Rev. 561, at 574.

44. The Liquidators of the Maritime Bank of Canada v. The Receiver-General of New Brunswick, [1892] A.C. 437, at 442 (emphasis added).

45. [1937] A.C. 377, at 390.

46. Scott, "The Consequences of the Privy Council Decisions," 494.

47. A.-G. N.S. v. A.-G. Can., [1951] S.C.R. 31.

48. [1952] S.C.R. 392.

49. [1941] S.C.R. 396.

50. [1960] S.C.R. 804.

51. I would, however, argue that it should adopt a much more active policy in defence of civil liberties, which I regard as having a preferred position among human liberties.

CRITICS OF THE JUDICIAL COMMITTEE: THE NEW ORTHODOXY AND AN ALTERNATIVE EXPLANATION[*]

FREDERICK VAUGHAN

A new and defensive orthodoxy has emerged as a result of the writings on the Judicial Committee of the Privy Council by Alan Cairns[1] and the late G.P. Browne.[2] That new orthodoxy—as seen in the writings of Peter Russell—defends the Judicial Committee vigorously and rejects impatiently criticisms of the law lords and what they wrought. My purpose in this article is to re-open the controversy by assessing the major influential writings that provide the foundation of this new orthodoxy and to offer an alternative explanation.

Alan Cairns referred to the longstanding debate over the Judicial Committee's interpretation of the *Constitution Act, 1867,* as "the most significant, continuing constitutional controversy in Canadian history." He suggested that the constitutional jurisprudence permeating the dispute remains crucial to an understanding of the development of our federal system. Indeed, he left the impression that the legitimacy of the present constitutional process is rooted in that jurisprudence. But Cairns's primary intention was not to draw attention to the controversy; it was to end it by silencing the critics of the Judicial Committee once and for all. The generally accepted view among many Canadian students of constitutional law is that Cairns has successfully achieved that ambition. His article on the critics of the Judicial Committee, published in 1971, has virtually become the indispensable background piece for the study of Canadian constitutional law.

Since the conclusions espoused by Cairns were prepared by G.P. Browne's book-length study of the Judicial Committee in 1967, it becomes necessary to begin with an assessment of that important work. There is no intention of implying that Cairns depended upon Browne; indeed, while they agree in their conclusions,

Canadian Journal of Political Science 19, 3 (September 1986): 495–519.

they are in total disagreement as to the means by which they reach those conclusions. Browne remains important, however, because several leading Canadian constitutional authorities rely on his book.

THE JURISPRUDENTIAL FOUNDATIONS

G.P. Browne's *The Judicial Committee and The British North America Act* remains the only book-length attempt to justify the Judicial Committee's understanding of the *British North America Act, 1867*. The central thesis of that book is the proposition that the Judicial Committee was correct in adopting a three-compartment view of the terms of our basic constitutional document. Browne's claim is that the critics of the Judicial Committee are trapped in a two-compartment view of the Act, and have failed to see how cogent and jurisprudentially sound the three-compartment view is.[3] He argues from a detailed examination of the Canadian constitutional cases decided by the Judicial Committee that the board adopted the position that the B.N.A. Act embodies three distinct bases of legislative power: one for the provincial legislatures and two for the federal parliament. Specifically, he claims that a careful reading of the Judicial Committee judgments reveals a consistent and jurisprudentially sound position in which the law lords established the three grants of legislative power—the head of section 91 (peace, order, and good government), the enumerated powers listed in section 91, and section 92 outlining the legislative powers of the provincial governments. As well, he argues that the Judicial Committee placed those grants of power in a certain jurisprudential order of priority. That order is: section 91, section 92, followed by "peace, order, and good government" (as an aid to the powers enumerated in section 91). In the course of establishing this fundamental proposition, Browne makes a distinction between those important decisions that support his thesis (he calls them "determinant" decisions)[4] and those other decisions where the "Judicial Committee was occasionally affected by the constituent statute argument." There are, in short, first- and second-class decisions. The first class includes those that support the three-compartment thesis; the second-class decisions do not support it. It is important to observe, at the outset, that Browne never engages directly the objections to the Judicial Committee's jurisprudence enunciated so forcefully over the years by leading Canadian constitutional authorities from W.P.M. Kennedy[5] to W.F. O'Connor,[6] Vincent MacDonald[7] and Bora Laskin.[8] He purports to refute them by building a case which by implication answers their objections.

On his own admission, Browne claims that his case rests on the theoretical foundations presented in the first two chapters. This response must, accordingly, begin with assessment of the arguments presented there. After tracing very briefly the establishment of the binding force of precedent as "the 'sacred principle' of English law," and asserting that the Judicial Committee followed precedent in practice, Browne concludes that the central point is how English jurists (including the law lords) exercised judicial self-restraint. In this context the author then discusses the problem of statutory interpretation. While agreeing with the "cardinal rule" that statutes "should be construed according to the intent of the Parliament which passed them,"[9] he concluded that the intent must be drawn from the words used. Browne's book is in all its particulars a literal interpretation of the terms of the B.N.A. Act. But he believes that judges in their quest for the intent of Parliament must on occasion "resort to extrinsic aids." If a literal interpretation would make the Act of Parliament "insensible," then "the court may reject words outright as surplusage." On the other hand, however, the use of extrinsic aids does not extend to the history of the Act; the intention of the legislature must not, Browne insists, be gathered from the debates that took place in the legislature. The words of the B.N.A. Act are the only legitimate means of achieving access to Parliament's intent.

Finally, Browne argues in chapter one that the Judicial Committee never accepted the invitation to view the B.N.A. Act as a constituent statute, as one creating not merely a law, but a state. The ordinary rules of statutory interpretation governing English courts of law prevailed in the Judicial Committee. Yet Browne concedes that it might be proper for a court to employ the constituent statute approach *sub rosa* in an effort "to safeguard the autonomy of one of the various legislative authorities in a federal constitution." In short, whenever it became convenient in the interest of pursuing certain desired ends, it was permissible for the Judicial Committee to use the constituent statute approach and deviate from the strict or literal meaning of the Act.

The task of showing that *stare decisis* played an important role even in constitutional cases is established by appeal to a select list of cases beginning in 1885 with an unreported case, the *McCarthy Act* reference; the author then moves to the *Aeronautics* case of 1932 and from there to the *Canada Temperance Act* judgment of 1946 and the *Margarine* reference of 1951. It is easy to see how this list of cases leaves out *Russell v. The Queen.* For there are, as we have seen earlier, two classes of authorities, the "determinant decisions" and all others. The fact that Browne does not treat *Russell* in the section of the chapter relating to the constituent statute approach is unfortunate because that case casts doubt upon his fundamental thesis.

Having shown in considerable detail that from time to time the Judicial Committee did indeed, in a number of cases, adopt the constituent statute approach, Browne concludes:

> Even so, the question is not whether the Judicial Committee was occasionally affected by the constituent statute argument, but whether it applied that argument in its "determinate" decisions. And this question is really undebatable. In by far the majority of cases, it was the approach adopted in *Bank of Toronto v. Lambe* (1887), rather than the one reflected in *Edwards v. Attorney-General for Canada* (1930), that prevailed. It was also this literal approach that led to the resolution, if not the formulation of the three major problems—Compartment, Ambit, and Consignment.[10]

This proposition would have added a greater credibility if Browne had confronted the earlier decision of *Russell v. The Queen* (1882). That judgment contained one of the most explicit statements on how the courts ought to read the terms of the B.N.A. Act. The author, however, never mentions it in this chapter; he refers to it only in passing in other parts of the book.

Chapter two concludes with a brief outline of the Judicial Committee's view of the federal principle. After a series of lengthy citations from a number of Judicial Committee judgments, Browne concludes that there is no conclusive evidence to prove that the law lords were motivated by an *a priori* view of federalism. The best one can say is that "it is not the only possible answer; for it is just as likely that the 'federal principle' was not imposed on the British North America Act, but derived from it." Browne gives the impression that the question of the degree of commitment to federalism in the Judicial Committee was relatively unimportant; that the "interpretative scheme" arose predominantly out of the language of the Act.

Chapter three contains, by far and away, the most important foundation for the thesis proposed throughout the book. That chapter contains the author's understanding of the terms of the *British North America Act*. But this understanding is not drawn from the Judicial Committee's judgments: it is Browne's exclusively. Yet it provides the main pillars upon which he erects his three compartments. The author begins by focussing attention on the terms of section 91. That section reads in full:

> 91. It shall be lawful for the Queen, by and with the Advice and Consent of the Senate and House of Commons, to make laws for the Peace, Order, and good Government of Canada, in relation to all Matters not coming within the Classes of Subjects by this Act assigned exclusively to the Legislatures of the Provinces; and for greater Certainty, but not so as to restrict the Generality of the foregoing Terms of this Section, it is hereby declared (notwithstanding anything in this Act) the exclusive Legislative Authority of the Parliament of Canada extends to all Matters coming within the Classes of Subjects next herein-after enumerated; that is to say [etc.]. . . .

After citing this head of section 91 and the head of section 92, Browne draws a conclusion from which he never retreats: "Section 91 accordingly consists of two 'parts': the 'Peace, Order, and good Government' clause (up to the first semi-colon in the 'introductory words'); and the thirty-one 'heads' (introduced by the phrase 'and for greater Certainty,' and rounded off by the 'deeming' paragraph, beginning 'And Matter')." He claims that the first problem for the reader is how to explain the relationship between these two parts. Browne argues that the solution lies in whether the classes of subjects listed in section 91 are either supplementary to or illustrative of the broad grant of authority to make laws for the "Peace, Order, and good Government of Canada." This question is central to the "three-compartment" thesis propounded. For, "if the second part of section 91 [the listed Classes of Subjects] is illustrative, there would be only two 'compartments'—section 91 (as a whole) and section 92." The remainder of the chapter is given over to an analysis of the language of the B.N.A. Act. The author leads the reader through an attempt to demonstrate that the listed Classes of Subjects in section 91 are meant to be supplementary. He does this by arguing that the grammatical structure of the head of section 91 severs the "Peace, Order, and good government" clause from the enumerated powers.

He begins the process by asserting the existence of two parts in section 91. This assertion is, however, unwarranted and, if unjustified, undermines his basic premise.

Browne supports the division of section 91 by avoiding the force of the phrase "but not so as to restrict the Generality of the foregoing Terms of this Section ['Peace, Order, and good Government']." This crucial connection between the general power and the enumerated Classes of Subjects is never discussed in this chapter. The exclusion cannot have been by oversight, given the careful attention the author gives to a semi-colon in section 91. Indeed at the very end of the book Browne contends that the semi-colon following "Provinces" in the head of section 91 "is employed, with grammatical significance, if nothing more to separate the two 'parts' of section 91." Yet the grammatically powerful clause "but not so as to restrict the Generality of the foregoing Terms of the Section" is ignored. The failure to consider this clause is crucial because it was the foundation for the Judicial Committee's judgment in *Russell*. Sir Barnes Peacock raised the issue explicitly on the second day of the hearings in May 1882. His and Sir Montague Smith's conclusion was that the enumerated items of section 91 were not to restrict the "peace, order, and good government" clause. No one on the board disagreed with this understanding.[11] On strictly grammatical grounds alone Browne's "two parts" view of section 91 would appear to fail.

Browne confronts directly the words "but not so as to restrict..." on the second last page of the book where he calls it a "caution" and claims that it "can be easily fitted to the other stipulations (by presuming a 'quantity' construction of the word 'restrict')." It is not clear what this means. In any event, how can one be sure that the Judicial Committee adopted Browne's "most natural reading of section 91"?

Two important supplementary issues, however, run throughout this chapter and could be said to be the main motive force in Browne's determination to establish "three compartments." Those issues are: fear of a dominant federal legislative power, and a conception of federalism that is alien to the terms of the B.N.A. Act. To consider the second issue first, it is significant that when Browne speaks in his own name he presents (on the authority of Wheare) a simple view of federalism, one in which "the federal principle of exclusive legislative spheres" dominates. The possibility that the conception of federalism embodied in the B.N.A. Act might be unique and incompatible with that simplistic view is never considered. Never once in this chapter does Browne allude to 92 (10)*c*, where the declaratory power of Parliament is unequivocally enunciated, to say nothing of the power of disallowance. Nor does he refer to section 94, which John A. Macdonald called one of the most important sections. He likewise does not note the strong centralising provisions relating to the appointment of judges from the county court level and above, or the powerful provisions relating to the appointment, instruction and dismissal of lieutenant-governors. Nor, finally, does he cite section 95 of the Act covering agriculture and immigration. These sections reinforce in specific terms the kind of federalism embodied in the B.N.A. Act.

The remainder of the book constitutes a review of the Judicial Committee judgments in which the author attempts to show that the law lords viewed the terms of the B.N.A. Act as he presented them in chapter three. From time to time throughout he is forced to acknowledge that the Judicial Committee viewed the Act as a "constituent statute." But on balance, he claims, the Judicial Committee supported his view of federalism and the "three-compartment" view of sections 91 and 92. These substantive chapters rest on the earlier discussion and hence stand or fall on the cogency of Browne's reading of the Act.

Many of the propositions stated emphatically earlier throughout the book become qualified in the concluding chapter. Indeed, the penultimate sentence is a curious disclaimer; it reads: "whatever its practical defects, the Judicial Committee's interpretative scheme for the British North America Act is both *fairly* certain and *generally* congruous." What was formerly stated with confidence is now hedged with qualification.

However critically Browne's book may have been received,[12] it provided a certain quiet foundation for later defenders of the Judicial Committee. One still finds references to it in footnotes in articles and books where the Judicial Committee's impact on Canadian federalism is praised.

THE SOCIOLOGICAL FOUNDATIONS

By far the most influential defence of the Judicial Committee in recent years came from the pen of Alan Cairns. It is not without significance that he is one of the leading exponents of the "province-building" thesis of Canadian federalism. Indeed Cairns was a central figure in a small group of political scientists who, in the 1960s, began to call for "a fresh perspective" on Canadian federalism and an end to "constitutional legalism."[13] By his own admission, Cairns's approach to the Judicial Committee is accordingly more sociological than legal. My purpose here is to examine the premises and conclusions of this highly acclaimed article on the critics of the Judicial Committee, beginning with the author's statement of purpose.

Cairns begins with the statement that his purpose is to assess "the quality of Canadian jurisprudence through an examination of the most significant, continuing constitutional controversy in Canadian history." He claims that in the course of achieving this end he will present "a more favourable evaluation of the Privy Council's conduct." But his overriding objective is to end the debate between the critics and the supporters of the Judicial Committee by an exhaustive review of their respective positions. This initial statement of purpose is, however, confounded when Cairns repeats his aim 43 pages later. At the end of the article the author reflects back on his objective in the following words:

> The purpose of this paper has been only to provide documentation for the minimum statement that a strong case can be made for the Judicial Committee, and to act as a reminder that the basic question was jurisprudential, a realm of discussion in which neither the Privy Council, its critics, nor its supporters proved particularly illuminating.[14]

The vagueness of the language used here in the concluding restatement of purpose betrays considerable ambiguity. In fairness to the author, we must postpone a final assessment of this matter until the end of this response.

After a brief introduction, the author proceeds to the substance of his case. Permeating it are several important themes. The first, which infuses the case against the critics of the Judicial Committee, is the important problem of intention, both of the founders and of the B.N.A. Act. The view of the Fathers of Confederation or their work presented throughout this article is not favourable; indeed, it is highly negative. We are told, for example, that they "lacked the gift of foresight," or that, when they did possess it, it was "restricted." We are encouraged to jettison any attempt to understand the intention of such men because it was inferior to "the more comprehensive understandings of their successors." They are dismissed collectively as "a small body of men in the 1860s." Neither their thought nor their works are worth our respect, for we are told they were the victims of a "completely static society."

Having attempted to establish the futility of any appeal to the intention of the founders, Cairns next proceeds to dismiss appeal to the intention of the legislature (the Imperial Parliament) contained in the language of the B.N.A. Act. What is noteworthy here is the absence of any discussion of the actual judgments of the Judicial Committee or of the terms of the Act. This stands in contrast to Browne. We are told that any appeal to the terms of the Act for the intention of the legislature is an intellectually sterile activity. The Judicial Committee, on the other hand, is praised for setting aside the language of the Act, for keeping abreast of "the trends of the times." At the same time, Cairns claims that the law lords of the Judicial Committee were victims of "the sterilities of the legal tradition [they] espoused." Despite these sterilities it possessed a "wisdom" which was "appropriate for the Canadian government," because it was "able to overcome some of the dangers caused by its own ignorance." Nevertheless it did its work "imperfectly." These points are not supported by appeal to Judicial Committee judgments.

The end result of Cairns's argument here is that members of the Judicial Committee were not especially intelligent, but that they possessed a wisdom when it came to Canadian affairs. Cairns excuses their failings as "inevitable for a body of men who adjudicated disputes emanating from the legal systems of a large part of the world, and who could not be expected to become specialists in the shifting socio-political contexts in which each legal system was embedded."[15] Yet we were told earlier that the Judicial Committee was responding to the sociological conditions throughout Canada. Even here, Cairns does not support the claims by references to what the law lords themselves said. There is one clear instance where Viscount Haldane alludes to the sociological conditions throughout Canada. In the *Snider* case, Haldane wrote that "the evil of intemperance at that time amounted in Canada to one so great and so general that at least for a period it was a menace to the national life of Canada so serious and pressing that the National Parliament was called on to intervene to protect the nation from disaster."[16] Haldane's foray into the "sociological realm" has continued to strike most readers of *Snider* as unpersuasive.

In the final analysis, the basic reason Cairns supports the Judicial Committee is that it contributed to "the evolution of Canadian federalism" in the direction he preferred, that is, in the direction of strong provinces. In short, his entire case is result-oriented constitutional jurisprudence. After dismissing the charges of the critics that the Judicial Committee did not take pre-Confederation events or history into account, Cairns lauds the judges for being sensitive to the "sociological" reality of Canada. That reality was the de facto existence, he asserts, of a "federal society."

The wisdom of the Judicial Committee was in seeing that the character of British North American society was "federal." They accordingly set out to give legal and constitutional support to that reality. Cairns writes: "The most elementary justification of the Privy Council rests on the broad sociological ground that the provincial bias which pervaded so many of its decisions was in fundamental harmony with the regional pluralism of Canada." We here learn that "federal society" means "regional pluralism" or diversity. But the Fathers of Confederation were perhaps as aware (if not more aware) of this "regional pluralism" as the Judicial Committee decades later. John A. Macdonald's thoughts on the inherent weakness of the federal form of government may not have been the last word on the subject, but they were expressed in full cognizance of the regional diversity of Canada.

Cairns's result-oriented jurisprudence forces him to expound, in a section on "The Weakness of the Judicial Committee," his view of the judicial function. The arguments contained here constitute the basis of his case against the critics as well as his support for the Judicial Committee. He asserts that it is "self-evident that no technical analysis of an increasingly ancient constitutional document can find answers to questions undreamt of by the Fathers." All judges of final appellate courts—not simply that unique body of law lords constituting the Judicial Committee—must rise above the terms of this statutory instrument and assume "a candid policy role" which "seems to be imperatively required in such conditions," such as those that confronted the emerging Canadian state. Judges must reject the simplistic canons of technical construction because "numerous legal writers" have affirmed that "the rules of statutory construction are little more than a grab bag of contradictions."

Having established the negative aspect of his view of the judicial function, Cairns proceeds to develop the positive side of that view. Here he favours policy-making judges: judges who are not bound by the intention of acts of parliament or by the language of constitutional statutes. He admires the "creative statesmanship" of the Judicial Committee. That "creative statesmanship" often took the form of silence, Cairns tells us. For example, he says that the law lords' most basic response to the obligation to exercise discretionary power "was silence, supplemented by isolated statements of principle dealing with the federal system." In short, Cairns embraces a judiciary not unduly fettered by "the doctrine of parliamentary supremacy." The active policy role of the Judicial Committee was required, Cairns claims, because the B.N.A. Act "was not subject to easy formal change by the amending process."

Cairns informs us that despite the drawbacks or jurisprudential restraints under which members of the Judicial Committee laboured, they broke out of them in the results they reached. But then we are told that the law lords remained captives of those restraints in the language of their explanations. The Judicial Committee, Cairns explains, "partially escaped from this dilemma by occasionally giving overt recognition to the need for a more flexible, pragmatic approach, and by covertly masking its actual policy choices behind the obfuscating language and precedents of statutory interpretation."

An important overriding implication that emerges from Cairns's article has to do with the perception of the judicial function in the final court of appeal. If we take seriously what he says about the way the Judicial Committee performed its task, and if he intends to apply this to any final court of appeal (as he clearly appears to do), then what we are left with is an invitation for our final appellate court to become an imperial judiciary. Cairns's views lead unequivocally to an activist Supreme Court, especially when armed, as it is now, with the Charter of Rights and Freedoms. What the justices of the Supreme Court of Canada should do, according to Cairns's view of the judicial function, is attempt to ascertain what the "sociological realities" of Canada are at any given time, and use the Charter (without being restricted by either the intention of Parliament or the language of the Act) as an instrument by which to give effect to their perceptions of those realities.

Another implication that flows from Cairns's support for the work of the Judicial Committee relates to federalism. It is surprising that the author who has made a major contribution to our understanding of federalism fails to assess how the Judicial Committee's judgments affected the institutional structure of our federal system. Our founders, and the people throughout British North America, conceived their federal system in the context of the Civil War raging at the time in the United States. They attempted to erect a federal system that would minimize the centrifugal political forces by locating the cementing force in the legislative division of powers. The federal or national legislature was given the dominant and residuary powers. When the Judicial Committee frustrated the development of the original federal dominance, it had the effect of ungluing the unique federal system designed by the Fathers of Confederation. As a result, we are left with a federal system that is seriously lacking an institutional body by which to bind the several provinces at the centre so as to ensure the continued existence of Canada as one nation.

It should be obvious, in conclusion, that Cairns's position is not identical to Browne's. Indeed, it is based on a fundamental disagreement with Browne. Cairns's case is that the Judicial Committee based its decentralising position in virtual defiance of the explicit terms of the Act. The board achieved this, Cairns affirms, by taking into account the extraneous evidence provided by the "social realities" of Canada. The main sociological reality was the "federal character" of Canadian society. Brown, on the other hand, claims that the Judicial Committee developed its conclusions in a vigorous jurisprudential manner without regard to the sociological realities. Little wonder that Cairns simply notes in passing the existence of Browne's book. He makes it clear that he does not need this "legal explanation" as an aid to his position. He implies that the legal approach to the problem leads nowhere; the only valid explanation is to be found in the realm of the "sociological realities." The chief defenders of the Judicial Committee are, therefore, in complete disagreement as to the basis for the jurisprudence adopted by the law lords.

THE JUDICIAL COMMITTEE FROM THE ANARCHIST PERSPECTIVE

If there is one prominent Canadian constitutional scholar who wishes that the controversy surrounding the Judicial Committee of the Privy Council had been settled by Browne and/or Cairns, it is Peter H. Russell. For Russell is one of the most inveterate defenders of provincial autonomy and supports the decentralising impact of the Judicial Committee. His main concern is to affirm the proposition that the Judicial Committee ruled wisely when it set about to deny a strong central power and to accord autonomy to the provinces. Due to the popularity of Russell's constitutional case book, this pro-Judicial Committee position has become the dominant view among many law professors and most political scientists. Unfortunately, Russell has never presented a thematic discussion of his views on the Judicial Committee. The principal source, of course, is his lengthy essay in *Leading Constitutional Decisions*.[17] As well, Russell reveals his views on the Judicial Committee in the brief comments preceding each case in the case book.

It is perhaps important to note that Russell was the only reviewer to find Browne's book persuasive. Russell accepted Browne's three-compartment case as "the most plausible way of understanding the relationship of the peace, order, and good government clause to the other parts of sections 91 and 92." This endorsement of Browne, however, does not prevent Russell from recommending to his students Cairns's article on the Judicial Committee. But Russell tends, at the same time, to dismiss Cairns along with what he calls "sociological natural law." Yet he concedes that the Judicial Committee had, on occasion, to break out of the "purely legalistic" mode of operating at least to the extent that it was required to say, for example, whether a national emergency existed. He is prepared to concede some measure of deference to the demands of the occasion without, however, adopting Cairns's view that the law lords kept abreast of the times. That would concede too much judicial activism for Russell, who is opposed to an activist judiciary.

Russell's defence of the Judicial Committee's decentralisation of the Canadian federal system forms the bedrock of his view of Canadian constitutional development. He is resolute in the determination to prevent a look back to the founding for legitimacy. He is firm in the conviction that the present and future hopes and aspirations of Canadians must never be fettered by the past. In this respect one is reminded of William Godwin, to whom Russell gives a quiet obeisance. Godwin wrote in *Political Justice*:

> The true state of man ... is not to have his opinions bound down in the fetters of an eternal quietism, but, flexible and unrestrained, to yield with facility to the impressions of accumulated observation and experience. That form of society will, of consequence, appear most eligible which is best founded in a principle of permanence .... The idea of giving permanence to what is called the constitution of any government, and rendering one class of laws, under the appellation of fundamental, less susceptible of change than another, must be founded in misapprehension and error.[18]

Russell implicitly concedes with Godwin that "the prevailing apprehensions of equity and truth"[19] must take precedence over the past conceptions.

Russell gives every impression in his writings that he prefers a constitutional order that allows for an ever-changing equilibrium rather than forms fixed by constitutional documents. With Godwin, Russell decries the tendency among men to find the basis of rights in "the records and charters of a barbarous age" rather than in "the great principles of morality" which are readily and presently available to men. Above all, with Godwin, Russell protests that "no man can be justified in setting up his judgment as a standard for others." The issues are far too important "to be left to appointed judges in the cloistered sanctuaries of judicial tribunals."[20]

In his most explicit overview of the Judicial Committee's work, it is clear that Russell attempts to strike a balanced position between the legalistic approach of Browne and the sociological position of Cairns. After acknowledging the "narrow legalistic approach to judicial review," Russell claims that the Judicial Committee occasionally recognized "the extraordinary significance attaching to the interpretation of a statute [the B.N.A. Act] which contained the written constitution of a large state and hence the need to treat it with some sensitivity to the actual milieu in which it originated and in which its terms must take effect." He commends, therefore, Lord Sankey's "living-tree" doctrine, where the Judicial committee announced that it was not its intention "to cut down the provisions of the Act by a narrow and technical construction, but rather to give it a large and liberal interpretation." For this reason, Russell continues, the law lords were required to go beyond the plain words of the Act. In sharp contrast to Browne in this connection, Russell claims that "the words alone would not yield answers to the constitutional questions that had to be decided." He claims further that one must not be misled into thinking that the Judicial Committee was adopting a narrow legalistic approach simply because its judgments were expressed in narrow legal terms. Russell applauds the tendency of the law lords to render the B.N.A. Act "internally consistent." He gives the clear impression that the justices of the early Supreme Court of Canada in their effort to interpret the terms of the Act turned "not to legal history but to political history, particularly to *their understanding* of the intentions of the Fathers of Confederation."[21]

This contrasting assessment of the work of the law lords and the justices of the Supreme Court of Canada conceals two fundamental issues. First, to say that the Judicial Committee attempted to render the terms of the Act "internally consistent" implies that they were not as stated, internally consistent. Russell's case is that the Judicial Committee rendered the terms consistent by raising the thirteenth item enumerated in section 92 ("Property and Civil Rights in the Province") to such prominence as to accord "independence" and "autonomy" to the provinces. In the process of reaching this "consistency" the law lords (correctly in Russell's view) reduced the scope of the federal "peace, order, and good government" power to a subsidiary or an ancillary role. As well, the Judicial Committee rendered completely void the agricultural part of section 95 since the newly prominent section 92 (13) had the effect of negating the force of federal "balanced federalism," one which reflected more realistically the "hopes and expectations than the very centralist position of the early Supreme Court."

Russell never claims that the Judicial Committee was seeking the intention of the Act (the Imperial Will) or that of the Fathers of Confederation (unknowable, in any event). What motivated the law lords was their own view of federalism. "Their commitment to classical federalism," says Russell, "as a fundamental principle of the Canadian constitution underlies most of their opinions and occasionally breaks through their legalistic prose." Russell applauds this commitment as a proper corrective to the strong centralist alternative. Browne, we will recall, explicitly rejected this proposition as lacking conclusive proof. In many respects on this point, Russell is closer to Cairns. But Russell, unlike Cairns, is concerned to show the jurisprudential soundness of the Judicial Committee's work; he accordingly applauds its judicial statesmanship.

What is not readily apparent in Russell's view here is his anarchistic bias. Central to the anarchist philosophy is the distrust of any central authority, whether intellectual or practical (political). Russell accordingly applauds the fragmentation of power wrought by the Judicial Committee. By mandating the existence of autonomous provinces, the Judicial Committee increased the authority of local power and reduced the force of the central power.

The second problem with Russell's contrasting assessment of the jurisprudence of the Judicial Committee and the Supreme Court of Canada has to do with the alleged use of political history by the Supreme Court. Russell emphasises that the Justices of the early Supreme Court of Canada imposed *"their understanding* of the intentions of the Fathers of Confederation." The implication from this charge is that the jurisprudence of the Supreme Court was based on a prejudicial foundation. This, according to Russell, undermines their jurisprudence. The extraneous commitment to classical federalism by the Judicial Committee is justified, or at least forgiven, but the alleged extraneous historical influence on the Supreme Court is condemned. Actually, Russell says that classical federalism was somehow contained in the basic constitutional document. He is careful not to say that *classical* federalism can be found in the letter of the Act; but he implies that it is consistent with the spirit of the Act.

But the question is: did the Supreme Court of Canada in the early years impose a prejudicial political history on the terms of the B.N.A. Act, as Russell asserts? This is the crucial question to which we must now turn. Russell claims that the "Judicial Committee's espousal of balanced federalism may better reflect the historical balance of hopes and expectations than the very centralist position of the early Supreme Court." But the "historical balance of hopes and expectations" is a euphemism for political history which he faults the Supreme Court for using. Furthermore, the justices of the early Supreme Court had greater and more immediate access to that "historical balance of hopes and expectations" than law lords sitting in isolation across a wide expanse of ocean. If, as Russell admits, that historical evidence is important, we should be quick to welcome it from those who experienced it most immediately. It is no unfair presumption to allege that justices of the Supreme Court experienced the historical events of their day closely. Many of them had been politically active before going to the bench. The judgments of the Supreme Court become, therefore, important sources for our understanding of the underlying issues in this debate. Especially is this true since the Judicial Committee constituted a court of appeal for many of the important cases.

There is another aspect to Russell's anti-historical posture that is in some respects more important than others. That is his tendency to minimize the importance of the influence of Sir John A. Macdonald. He insists that Macdonald "was not the only Father of Confederation," that "Macdonald was only one of the

Fathers of Confederation and that he belonged to the group who were most skeptical about federalism." That "group," in fact, constituted almost the entire body of men identified as the Fathers of Confederation. And their skepticism was rooted in a keen awareness of the natural weaknesses of the federal form of government. The anti-confederate forces did not include a group of federalists "who hoped that strong provincial governments could flourish under the new constitution."[22] The anti-confederates' major weakness was their failure to present an alternative plan of federal union. Those who opposed confederation did not present a unified response; they were comprised of several major factions, principally of those who believed that confederation would weaken the tie with Great Britain. The one main anti-confederate plan was for Imperial Union, not an alternative model of federalism, as Russell implies. If there is one thing that rings clearly throughout anti-confederate writings and speeches it was that federalism, pure and simple, was to be resisted. They were, in fact, more skeptical about federalism than the confederate forces. Alexander Galt, for example, attempted to calm the fears of anti-confederates by assuring them that the new constitution was only federal in name, that in "time the artificial boundaries which now separate us into provinces, will one day disappear."[23] The confederation plan clearly contained a deceptive constitutionalism by giving the impression that the new constitution embodied the federal principle in an effective manner. Christopher Dunkin exposed that deception more pointedly than anyone else. Dunkin reduced to ashes the Quebec scheme of confederation in a systematic attack on the alleged federal character of the plan. He contrasted the confederation plan, item for item, with the federal system of the United States. He revealed that the principle of centralisation contained in the plan destroyed any semblance of federalism. In order to give formal, legal effect to this centralised constitutionalism it is obvious that an authoritative judicial determination had to be obtained. This is why John A. Macdonald and the first government of the new nation set about almost immediately to establish a Supreme Court, one that would be composed of Canadian judges who knew at first hand the hopes and aspirations of the new nation.

Russell claims that it is a mistake to assume that because the Judicial Committee ignored political history in interpreting the B.N.A. Act it distorted the intentions of the Canadian founders. This kind of criticism, he asserts, ignores "the complex nature of the confederation settlement and the difficulty of finding documentary evidence strong enough to throw definitive light on the terms of the B.N.A. Act." The claim that there is insufficient evidence is Russell's ultimate "stopper." It represents the heart of his historical agnosticism.

In a certain sense, Russell is correct. There is little *secondary* material available on the formation of the terms of the *British North America Act*. The most prominent historical writings, to which Russell alludes, are Peter B. Waite's *Life and Times of Confederation* (1962), and Donald Creighton's *The Road to Confederation* (1964). There are other historical accounts pertaining to the role of individual provinces, such as F.W. Bolger's *Prince Edward Island and Confederation* (1964) and Kenneth Pryke's *Nova Scotia and Confederation* (1962), to which Russell does not explicitly refer. There is no reason to doubt, however, that he is aware of these sources. Unfortunately, none of these histories treats thematically the content of the federal form of government embodied in the confederation settlement. The closest one comes is Waite's *Life and Times of Confederation*, especially chapter 8. But that discussion is primarily concerned with the newspaper accounts of the confederation plan, not the legislative discussions.

Clifford Ian Kyer,[24] one of Russell's major authorities on this issue, claims that the terms of union were not formally discussed in the Maritime and Newfoundland legislatures; that the only legislature to discuss and adopt the confederation plan was the Legislature of the United Canadas in 1865. This alleged failure in the four colonial legislatures leads Kyer to claim that we cannot say with certainty how the terms of the B.N.A. Act were understood by the Fathers of Confederation in those other colonies. The fact is, however, that the terms of confederation were debated fully, both formally and informally in all the colonial legislatures. Kyer's reliance on the debates in the United Canadas in 1865, and his failure to consult the debates in the four colonies of New Brunswick, Nova Scotia, Prince Edward Island and Newfoundland, leads him to claim that we "lack a similar set of materials for the Maritime provinces which could be used to verify the interpretation given the Resolutions by the Canadians." If he had consulted the Prince Edward Island *Debates and Proceedings of the House of Assembly* (1865) he would have read Mr. Longworth, among many others, deride the Quebec resolutions for containing "novel principles, principles not hither to tested by the experience of any previous Confederation of which history makes mention. We are required to yield up our position of comparative dependence as a separate Colony and to reduce the scope of our legislative functions to the privileges of a local vestry in the Mother Country."[25] And Mr. Duncan in the same legislature complained that "The Local legislature, which the Quebec Report contemplates to leave us, would be little better than a town council."[26] Kyer might have found especially instructive the remarks of George Coles, a P.E.I. delegate to Quebec, on his reasons for refusing to sign the "Quebec Report."

As well, he might have found helpful the documents attached to the 1866 P.E.I. *Debates* relating to confederation. Both Legislative Assembly and the Legislative Council of the Island debated the Quebec scheme of confederation extensively throughout 1865 and 1866. The 1865 *Debates* in the Assembly are alone recorded in over 100 pages. There can be no misunderstanding from those *Debates* that the Islanders understood the Quebec scheme to constitute a powerful central government and weak provinces. The same kind of debates took place in the legislatures of the other colonies with the same understanding of the Quebec plan emerging.

The key to Kyer's case is his claim that the Quebec resolutions were not *formally* debated in the Maritime and Newfoundland legislatures. The Nova Scotia legislative debates for 1865 clearly reveal, however, why Tupper refused to submit the resolutions for formal approval. They were certain to be defeated. But the terms of the confederation plan were discussed and debated for many days in all the colonial legislatures. The fact that the debates and proceedings of the Maritime and Newfoundland legislatures are not as readily accessible as the Canadian debates is unfortunate. They are, however available and they contain detailed evidence of the understanding of the terms of union.

TOWARDS AN ALTERNATIVE EXPLANATION

But having made our way through this perplexing issue, we are left without an explanation for why the Judicial Committee emasculated the centralising terms of the *British North America Act*. For if Browne is wrong and if Cairns is wrong, it would appear that we are forced to side with the critics, such as V.C. MacDonald. But the critics say in effect that the law lords were either incompetent or perverse. That explanation is no more persuasive than the charge that the Fathers of Confederation were confused when they wrote the terms of the B.N.A. Act.

However reasonable the course taken by the Judicial Committee of the Privy Council now in retrospect appears, the prevailing explanations are not quite satisfactory. None takes into account certain fundamental problems of judicial construction. Sir Ivor Jennings claimed more than 40 years ago that the members of the board "never seriously wavered from the principle that it was their function to interpret the 'intention of Parliament' as laid down in the Act." Yet on several major occasions we find a judgment of the board claiming, as Sir Montague Smith did in the *Parsons* case when confronted with an instance where the B.N.A. Act clearly demanded federal dominance, that "the legislature [the Imperial Parliament] could not have intended that the powers exclusively assigned to the provincial legislature should be absorbed in those given to the dominion parliament." He reached this conclusion despite the clear language of the B.N.A. Act. Why could this not have been intended by the legislature? Especially when there are both specific and general provisions of the Act which point to this very possibility. The B.N.A. Act is not contradictory, as many have claimed. It is, however, crudely centralist. But his was not a result of shoddy draughtsmanship but the conscious effort of the framers of the Act.

The question is, therefore, how are we to understand the manner in which the Judicial Committee of the Privy Council interpreted the terms of our fundamental constitutional document so as to conclude that the terms of the Act were to be ensconced in "watertight compartments," that the provinces were to be "autonomous," that "peace, order, and good government" ("notwithstanding anything in the Act") were to be restricted to times of emergency? J.R. Mallory has offered an intriguing explanation in his *Social Credit and the Federal Power in Canada*.[27] Mallory suggested here that the law lords were motivated by a *laissez-faire* attitude, one that was inherently hostile to a collectivist alternative. This led them to resist energetically national government initiatives, especially in cases involving economic issues such as wages and hours of work. This is a fascinating suggestion, but unfortunately Mallory does not pursue it sufficiently to make it stand as anything more than an hypothesis. It clearly requires more support than is provided; it is especially in need of support in the judgments of Lord Watson. To my knowledge no one has yet attempted to provide this ideological explanation with the requisite support.

Perhaps the reason why the law lords ruled the way they did lies in how they viewed their function rather than in institutional self-interest, as Murray Greenwood has suggested. There is a consistent disposition throughout the literature on the subject to assume that the Judicial Committee was performing a *judicial* function. Indeed, all criticisms of the board take this for granted. Unfortunately, courts rarely if ever set out the terms under which they exercise their function. In the case of the Judicial Committee, however, we have several accounts which amount to statements on how the law lords viewed their judicial function. The first statements are contained in verbatim transcripts of proceedings before the Judicial Committee in two important constitutional cases: *Russell v. The Queen* (1882)[28] and the *Local Prohibition* case (1896),[29] cases in which the Judicial Committee set down major judicial doctrines. In addition to these judicial sources there is the significant nonjudicial statement by Viscount Haldane explaining the function of the Judicial Committee.

The first thing that becomes apparent from the proceedings in *Russell* and *Local Prohibition* is that the law lords viewed their function as essentially political, not as judicial. Watson went so far at one point in *Local Prohibition* to say that the Judicial Committee did not give judicial opinions. As well, there was a clear disposition on the part of all members of the board to side with the provinces against the claims of the federal Parliament. The transcript of proceedings in both *Russell* and *Local Prohibition* discloses that almost all the law lords viewed the federal dominance as *a priori* to be resisted, as essentially a threat to viable provinces. But what is even more astonishing from the questions and objections raised throughout these cases is the complete disregard for the intention of Parliament (that is, of the Imperial Parliament) as contained in the language of the B.N.A. Act. What they did attempt to do was to identify areas of provincial power and place them beyond the easy reach of the federal Parliament. Contrary to Browne, the law lords emerge as intent on giving effect to a conception of federalism which was clearly counter to that contained in the B.N.A. Act. This is why they viewed the function of the Judicial Committee as essentially political: their function was to correct the "deficiencies" of the B.N.A. Act; they viewed their function, therefore, as primarily legislative—to make up for or to correct the mistakes of the legislature (that is, the Imperial Parliament). What started as a not unreasonable judicial proposition— to determine the scope of Dominion and provincial powers—became a political mission, especially for Watson and later for Haldane.

By far and away the most interesting recent comment on Viscount Haldane and his influence on the Judicial Committee came from Stephen Wexler. Writing in the *McGill Law Journal*, Wexler presents a thorough and persuasive account of the main intellectual forces that moved Haldane to adopt a pro-provincial bias throughout his tenure as counsel before the Judicial Committee and later as a law lord.[30] Wexler's article confirms in intriguing detail that Haldane's perception of his function was not narrowly perceived as formally judicial. Haldane's passion for the British Empire and for Home Rule are presented as having a profound impact on how he viewed the status of the provinces within the Canadian federal state. Wexler presents a cogently reasoned and articulate account of how "Haldane was abe to misread the clear, unequivocal text of Canada's constitution."

But it is a mistake to view this matter simply through the eyes of Watson and Haldane. The *Local Prohibition* transcript makes it clear that other members of the board—especially Lord Herschell—were just as strong as Watson and Haldane in their determination to make the terms of the Act more consistent with a minimum federalism. In short, the overwhelming preoccupation of the law lords was with a conception of federalism, however ill-prepared they were by training and experience. Viscount Haldane confirmed this view in a speech he gave at Cambridge in November 1921 while he was still active on the board. On that occasion, Haldane said that the lords were appointed to the Judicial Committee of the Privy Council for their qualities of past experience, for their "statesmanlike outlook . . . The outlook which makes him remember that with a growing constitution things are always changing and developing, and that you cannot be sure that what was right ten years ago will be right today." These sentiments were elaborated upon five years later in an introduction to the British edition of Mary P. Follett's book, *The New State*.[31] Haldane wrote: "The form of the state and the meaning of the resulting sovereignty may vary, following general opinion at different periods and under different conditions, and so may the mode of expressing the imperative."[32] True to his fundamental Hegelianism, Haldane insisted that "the will is no static thing but is a form of the dynamic activity characteristic of mind." Above all, Haldane agreed with Follet when she claimed that "the true state does not demand a merely submissive allegiance, for it is the outcome of a spontaneous and instinctive process of unifying manifold interests." The state is, according to Haldane, "a process." "The state is made," he wrote, "not by external acts, but by the continuous thought and action of the people who live its life. In this sense it is never perfect for it is a process that remains always unbroken in creative activity." The art of statesmanship, even judicial statesmanship, is clearly to participate actively in that forward-looking process; there is no "submissive allegiance" to a founding vision.

Haldane praised Watson, a Scot ("who came to London knowing nothing [and] became a great English lawyer") for rendering:

> an enormous service to the Empire and to the Dominion of Canada by *developing* the Dominion ·onstitution. At one time, after the B.N.A. Act of 1867 was passed, the conception took hold of the *Canadian Courts* and *what was intended* was to make the Dominion the centre of government in Canada, so that its statutes and its position should be superior to the statutes and position of the Provincial Legislatures. That went so far that there arose a great fight, and as the result of a long series of decisions Lord Watson put clothing upon the bones of the Constitution, and so covered them over with living flesh that the constitution of Canada took a *new form*. The provinces were recognized as of *equal authority co-ordinate with the Dominion*, and a long series of decisions were given by him which solved many problems and produced a new contentment in Canada with the constitution they had got in 1867.[33]

On this foundation the Judicial Committee went out of its way to set straight the Supreme Court of Canada. It overruled no less than 50 per cent of appeals from the Supreme Court while overruling only 25 per cent of appeals from other Canadian courts. (This should be contrasted with the figures for all other self-governing colonies except Canada—33 per cent.)

The prior disposition or commitment to judicial statesmanship resulted in a political jurisprudence. And if one looks carefully at the judgments one sees, *by and large*, the following procedures emerge: The Judicial Committee almost always (in the crucial Watson years) drafted that if one "goes in" by way of 92 one will "come out" on the side of 92. If one approaches the subject at bar with the question: "Is this a matter relating to property and civil rights?" or "Is this a matter of a merely local or private nature?" the answer in most cases will be affirmative. The task then becomes to diminish the force of the inevitably conflicting provision in section 91. This is precisely the procedure Judah Benjamin recommended to the Judicial Committee in *Russell*. Benjamin pointed out that *Parsons* a year earlier had endorsed the procedure of determining an issue by first enquiring whether it is covered by one of the enumerated provincial powers in section 92. It was somewhat self-serving of Benjamin to say this because it was he who convinced the board to adopt that approach in *Parsons*. If one looks at the major constitutional judgments of the Judicial Committee one will find this happened. In *Russell*, Sir Montague Smith states his agreement with Benjamin's approach succinctly:

> According to the principle of construction there pointed out [in *Parsons*], the first question to be determined is, whether the Act now in question falls within any of the classes of subjects enumerated in section 92 and assigned exclusively to the Legislatures of the Provinces. If it does, then the further question would arise, viz., whether the subject of the Act does not also fall within one of the enumerated classes of subjects in section 91.

The transcripts of the Judicial Committee proceedings in *Russell* and *Local Prohibition* clearly confirm the political character of the board's perception as well as the general entrance via section 92. The law lords are frequently reported as saying in response to counsel for the federal government: "There must be some restraint on federal power." Watson, in *Local Prohibition*, for example, was disturbed at the prospects of "peace, order, and good government" overriding "nearly all the clauses giving jurisdiction" to the provinces.

Lord Herschell in *Local Prohibition* consistently worried about federal power intruding into local matters. Blake attempted to persuade the Committee that the federal Parliament had occupied the field. He attempted to convince the board that the B.N.A. Act contained mutually exclusive not concurrent powers. But Herschell resisted this and led the board in the defence of the provinces even more strongly than Watson. Herschell, it must be remembered, was co-counsel with Judah Benjamin in *Parsons*.

There can be no doubt, however, that Lord Watson was *the* principal proponent of "judicial statesmanship." As Haldane wrote of him in the *Juridical Review*: "He was an Imperial judge of the very first order. The function of such a judge, sitting in the supreme tribunal of the Empire, is to do more than decide what abstract and familiar legal conceptions should be applied to particular cases. His function is to be a statesman as well as a jurist, to fill in the gaps which Parliament has deliberately left in the skeleton constitution and laws that it had provided for the British Colonies."[34]

Looking at this matter from the Canadian point of view, that is, looking upon the Judicial Committee as a judicial body with a strict judicial function, Watson's conception is nothing short of outrageous. Little wonder Canadian writers as recently as Mark MacGuigan and others could recoil in shock at the "blatant judicial legislation" of the Judicial Committee.[35] But the Judicial Committee did not view its function simply as a judicial one. And if this is not sufficiently clear from the decisions of Watson we have merely to turn to Haldane. For Haldane the task of judicial statesmanship was even more compelling. The thoughtful article by Jonathon Robinson showing the influence of Hegelian political philosophy on Haldane is both impressive and persuasive.[36] Haldane clearly thought deeply about the issues and wrote about them. And there can be little doubt that his basic commitment to Hegelian political philosophy influenced him at the bar, as he himself admits. But it would be to overextend the influence of both Haldane and Hegel to accord more than minimal importance to this aspect of the matter, for Watson's perception was well established by the time Haldane came to the board. And we have no way of knowing what philosophical influences prompted Watson from adopting his view of the proper function of the Judicial Committee. Nor does Haldane's Hegelianism explain the view of Lord Herschell and others which was so compatible with Watson's view.

CONCLUSION

A problem nevertheless remains: having understood that the Judicial Committee viewed its function as part of the political or legislative function, can that be justified? Who are we, Canadians, at the time in a posture of colonial subservience, to say what the proper function of a British institution should be? The exercise of judicial statesmanship by the Judicial Committee was clearly consistent with the exercise of Imperial power over the colonies. And it must not be overlooked that Canada remained in a position of colonial dependence until 1931. Nor ought it to be overlooked that no opposition arose in the Imperial Government over the decisions of the Judicial Committee, that is, over a misuse of power. A succession of Canadian authorities might rail against the Judicial Committee, but there is no evidence to conclude that the Imperial government or Parliament was at any time critical of Judicial Committee judgments in Canadian cases. If any body had a right to object to the legislative function of the Judicial Committee, one would suppose that it would be the Imperial Parliament. In the absence of explicit objection, one must conclude that the Imperial Parliament concurred in the perception of the function as exercised by the Judicial Committee.

However foreign judicial legislating may now appear to us, in the nineteenth century it was a respectable doctrine. In the fifth edition of *The Province of Jurisprudence Determined*, published in 1885, John Austin wrote: "I cannot understand how any person who has considered the subject can suppose that society could possibly have gone on if judges had not legislated, or that there is any danger whatever in allowing them that power which they have in fact exercised, to make up for the negligence or the incapacity of the avowed legislator. That part of the law of every country which was made by judges has been far better made than that part which consists of statutes enacted by the legislative."[37]

Our attitude towards the judicial function has been influenced by the doctrine of the separation of powers. But there is no strict separation of power in Great Britain, where the Lord Chancellor, who often presides in the Judicial Committee, is a member of the House of Lords and a member of the cabinet. There can be no doubt that the Judicial Committee was always, and remains, an advisory committee of Her Majesty's Privy Council offering what in constitutional matters is political advice; and that advice has never been rejected.

Functioning thus as a branch of the legislative process, the Judicial Committee made up for the "negligence and incapacity" of the Imperial Parliament and the Canadian framers in 1867. More specifically, what the Judicial Committee did was to loosen the terms of the B.N.A. Act so as to accord a greater degree of autonomy to the provinces and thereby to make the Canadian system of government a more authentic federal system. In a certain sense, the Judicial Committee of the Privy Council restored a large measure of the self-government which the provinces had enjoyed before confederation, while at the same time preserving the integrity of the federal government and Parliament. In so doing the Judicial Committee became in fact the real fathers of Canadian confederation.

NOTES

1. "The Judicial Committee and Its Critics" (1971) 4 *Canadian Journal of Political Science (CJPS)*, 301–45.

2. G.P. Browne, *The Judicial Committee and the British North America Act* (Toronto: University of Toronto Press, 1967).

3. See for example his response to Laskin, ibid., 127 and 128.

4. Ibid., 28.

5. W.P.M. Kennedy, "The British North America Act: Past and Future" (1937) 15 *Canadian Bar Review (Can. Bar Rev.)*, 393.

6. W.F. O'Connor, *Report to the Senate of Canada* (Ottawa: King's Printer, 1939).

7. V.C. MacDonald, "Judicial Interpretation of the Canadian Constitution" (1935–1936) 1 *University of Toronto Law Journal*, 260.

8. Bora Laskin, " 'Peace, Order, and good Government' Re-examined" (1947) 25 *Can. Bar Rev.* 1054.

9. Browne depends almost exclusively on R. Cross, *Precedent in English Law* (Oxford: Oxford University Press, 1961).

10. Browne, *The Judicial Committee*, 28.

11. See *Argument in Privy Council, Russell v. The Queen* (London, 1882). This document is a printed version of the shorthand notes of the proceedings by Messrs. Martin and Meredith.

12. See Bora Laskin's review (1967) 10 *Canadian Public Administration* 514; Dale Gibson (1968) 44 *Can. Bar Rev.* 153; J.A. Corry (1968) 1 *CJPS*, 268; Pierre Blache (1968) 6 *Alberta Law Review* 146; and Peter Russell (1968) 48 *Canadian Historical Review* 66.

13. Edwin R. Black and Alan C. Cairns, "A Different Perspective on Canadian Federalism" (1966) 9 *Canadian Public Administration* 27.

14. Cairns, "The Judicial Committee and Its Critics," 344.

15. Ibid., 330.

16. *Toronto Electric Commissioners v. Snider* (1925) A.C. 396 [Olmsted II], 409.

17. Russell, *Leading Constitutional Decisions*, 3d ed. (Ottawa: Carleton University Press, 1982).

18. William Godwin, *Enquiry concerning Political Justice* (Oxford: Clarendon Press, 1971), 234.

19. Peter H. Russell, "A Democratic Approach to Civil Liberties," in *Contemporary Issues in Canadian Politics*, Frederick Vaughan et al., eds. (Scarborough: Prentice Hall, 1970), 95.

20. Russell, "A Democratic Approach," 97.

21. Russell, "Introduction," *Leading Constitutional Decisions*, 12. Emphasis in the original.

22. Russell, "Introduction," 13.

23. Alexander Galt, Sherbrook Speech, 1865, P.A.C. For a good discussion of John A. Macdonald's influence on the Canadian constitution, see Eugene Forsey, "Macdonald's Constitution" (1976) 3 *Dalhousie Law Journal* 529.

24. Clifford Ian Kyer, "Has History a Role to Play in Constitutional Adjudication? Some Preliminary Considerations" (1981) *The Law Society Gazette* 135.

25. P.E.I. *Debates* (1865), 60.

26. P.E.I. *Debates* (1865), 65.

27. J.R. Mallory, *Social Credit and the Federal Power in Canada* (Toronto: University of Toronto Press, 1954), 47ff.

28. Argument in *Privy Council: Russell v. The Queen* (Whitehall, 1882) [Transcript from the shorthand notes of Messrs. Martin and Meredith].

29. *The Liquor Prohibition Appeal* (1895), An Appeal from the Supreme Court of Canada to Her Majesty The Queen in Council (London: Wm. Brown & Co., 1895) [Transcript from the shorthand notes of Messrs. Martin and Meredith].

30. Stephen Wexler, "The Urge to Idealize: Viscount Haldane and the Constitution of Canada" (1984) 29 *McGill Law Journal* 609–50.

31. M.P. Follett, *The New State* (London: Longmans, Green, 1926).

32. Follett, "Introduction by Viscount Haldane," viii.

33. Viscount Haldane, "The Work for the Empire of the Judicial Committee of the Privy Council" (1923) *Cambridge Law Review* 148. Italics added.

34. Viscount Haldane, "Lord Watson" (1899) 11 *Juridical Review* 278.

35. Mark MacGuigan, "Precedent and Policy in the Supreme Court of Canada" (1967) 45 *Can. Bar Rev.* 627.

36. Jonathan Robinson, "Lord Haldane and the British North America Act" (1970) 20 *University of Toronto Law Journal* 55.

37. John Austin, *The Province of Jurisprudence Determined* (London: Weidenfeld and Nicholson, 1954), 191.

COMMENT ON "CRITICS OF THE JUDICIAL COMMITTEE: THE NEW ORTHODOXY AND AN ALTERNATIVE EXPLANATION"◇

ALAN C. CAIRNS

⟩

The 1982 Charter gives the contemporary Supreme Court enhanced responsibilities in the overall Canadian constitutional system. These novel responsibilities require a jurisprudence appropriate to the new relations between courts and legislatures for which our past has ill-prepared us. In addition to the Charter and the host of citizen-state relations which are thus placed on the Supreme Court agenda, the 1982 *Constitution Act*, s. 52 (1), establishes the supremacy of the constitution, which further underlines the growing significance of the judicial branch in our constitutional evolution, seeking to adapt the constitution as an instrument of government to emerging conditions, or are they largely to eschew such a role by employing varying strategies and philosophies of self-control, such as adhering as closely as possible to a more technical task definition, deferring wherever possible to legislatures, resisting the lure of judicial creativity as inappropriate to their appointed status, and throwing the burden of constitutional adaptation on other more overtly political institutions of government?

In answering these difficult questions, which involve assessments of judicial capacity and the political theory of a representative federal democracy now possessed of a Charter of Rights, one strategy is to explore the past, to search for answers or negative lessons from the experience of our predecessors. The expansion of the contemporary judicial role thus reopens past jurisprudential controversies as history is viewed through new lenses. One impressive example of this rethinking is the provocative article by Professor Vaughan, to which this note is a response. His task was to assess the analytical basis of support for the Judicial Committee's overall interpretation of the B.N.A. Act by G.P. Browne, Peter Russell and myself.

◇ *Canadian Journal of Political Science* 19, 3 (September 1986): 521–29.

It is worth noting that the Browne-Russell-Cairns position of which Vaughan is critical is itself a departure from the conventional criticism of the Judicial Committee which became dominant in the legal and nationalist circles of English Canada in the period leading up to the 1949 abolition of appeals. Indirectly, therefore, Vaughan is returning to a previous orthodoxy. To the extent that he succeeds in his task, the performance of the Judicial Committee will receive low marks[1] and those who formerly criticized it will have their reputations invigorated. It is also relevant to his task that Vaughan views his "opponents" as provincialists. Browne is described as fearing "a dominant federal legislative power" and as adhering to a "simplistic view" of federalism, based on Wheare, which is "incompatible" with "the conception of federalism embodied in the B.N.A. Act."[2] Russell is one of "the most inveterate defenders of provincial autonomy,"[3] and I am alleged to be a supporter of the Judicial Committee because I am an exponent of province-building, and the Judicial Committee's contribution to the evolution of Canadian federalism was congruent with my preferences.[4] The debate, therefore, is partly cast in centralist-provincialist terms with Vaughan donning the mantle of John A. Macdonald.

Vaughan has little difficulty in indicating that the three of us provide different, if partially overlapping, rationales for our evaluation of the performance of the Judicial Committee. In particular, G.P. Browne elaborated a highly technical defence of the law lords based on a three-compartment interpretation of sections 91 and 92. My position is correctly viewed as more sociological than Browne's, and as opposed to confining the debate to the terms of the 1867 Act or to the intentions of the Fathers. Peter Russell, who is separately responding to Vaughan's article, is described as drawing on both Browne and Cairns.

In my 1971 article I did not, as Vaughan claims, seek to silence the critics of the Judicial Committee "once and for all," and I do not identify with a new "orthodoxy . . . [which] . . . rejects impatiently criticisms of the law lords and what they wrought."[5] More generally, I take for granted that it is the fate of our always limited understandings to be modified and surpassed by subsequent scholarship. So I am pleased that Vaughan has decided to "re-open the controversy,"[6] which is not to say that I am in agreement with his basic position.

Initially, it is necessary to deal with Vaughan's alternative explanation of "why the Judicial Committee emasculated the centralising terms of the *British North America Act*."[7] His thesis is that the law lords viewed their function as "essentially political," which they translated into "giving effect to a conception of federalism which was clearly counter to that contained in the B.N.A. Act."[8] The Judicial Committee saw itself as part of the "legislative process" with the task of making up for the " 'negligence and incapacity' of the Imperial Parliament and the Canadian framers in 1867."[9] This is an alternative to Browne's technical three-compartment explanation of what drove the law lords in a provincialist direction. It is clear, however, that both Russell and I are in agreement with Vaughan that the Judicial Committee injected a decentralising impulse into the centralised federalism with which Canada began its existence.[10] The "alternative" in his explanation thus presumably refers to the political or legislative definition of their task which he asserts was held by the law lords.

Vaughan's section 4 ("Towards an Alternative Explanation") in which this position is elaborated, is, however, less than convincing on why an essentially political view of their task drove the Judicial Committee in a provincialist direction.[11] Vaughan accepts recent scholarship by Stephen Wexler and Jonathon Robinson as helpful in explaining Haldane's position, but he denies that the pro-provincial behaviour of other law lords was a byproduct of Haldane's beliefs or influence. In fact, he has no answer to the question of why the Privy Council had a particular conception of federalism that led them to throw their weight on the side of the provinces. His unwillingness to look at developments in Canadian society works against his acceptance of one plausible explanation—that they thought such a conception was appropriate to the realities of the country whose constitution they were interpreting.

In any event, Vaughan's alternative explanation of why the Judicial Committee did what it did is not a response to the question which concerned me—the adequacy of the criteria by which Canadian scholars, politicians and others had judged the overall tendency of its decisions. The major purpose of my article was to examine the Pavlovian-type criticisms of the Judicial Committee which had become a thought-stifling conventional wisdom in English-Canadian commentary. I documented almost ad nauseam the profound divide between the two main orientations found among the critics, which I labelled fundamentalist and constitutionalist, noted that they contradicted each other, and argued that neither was up to the task of providing convincing normative criteria to evaluate judicial performance.[12]

My major concern[13] in much of the remainder of this comment is with the criteria used to evaluate the judicial role in constitutional interpretation provided by Vaughan. Vaughan's position on how a final appeal court should perform its task of constitutional interpretation is scattered through his article. I risk doing an injustice to his thought by providing my interpretation of his answer to a question which he did not directly address. I interpret him as supporting a version of that espoused by the O'Connor Report in 1939[14]—that both the terms of the B.N.A. Act and the intentions which it reflected were clearly centralist, and that judges should simply give effect to those terms for they reflect a superior wisdom with which later generations, especially judges, should not tamper.

Vaughan's position may be reconstructed as follows:

1. The B.N.A. Act clearly established a highly centralised federal system.[15]

2. The debates in the legislatures of the four Atlantic colonies, as well as in the United Province of Canada, confirm that the federalism constructed was seen as, and was intended to be, highly centralised.[16]

3. The adoption of a centralist federalism was based on a particular understanding of the appropriate relation of the institutions of government to society, with which Vaughan is in agreement. A centralist federalism was constructed not in ignorance of centrifugal forces, but as a deliberate attempt to control them. In Vaughan's words:

> Our founders...attempted to erect a federal system that would minimize the centrifugal political forces by locating the cementing

force in the legislative division of powers. The federal or national legislature was given the dominant and residuary powers. When the Judicial Committee frustrated the development of the original federal dominance, it had the effect of ungluing the unique federal system designed by the Fathers of Confederation. As a result, we are left with a federal system that is seriously lacking an institutional body by which to bind the several provinces at the centre so as to ensure the continued existence of Canada as one nation.[17]

4. Given Vaughan's attribution of enduring wisdom to the constitutional design of the Fathers, the task of judicial interpretation was to protect that centralist structure by a literal, fundamentalist approach to the Act which embodies the intentions of the Fathers. In particular, Vaughan is hostile to a sociological jurisprudence which stresses the need to respond to provincially based diversities. Such an approach is a perversion of the originally understood relationship between the centre and the provinces. Equally, he opposes, for the same reason, the injection of a Wheare-type definition of federalism into the jurisprudence of the very different centralised Canadian federalism.[18]

5. Implicit in the Vaughan position is the assumption that the Judicial Committee and the Canadian courts subordinate to it could have sustained a highly centralised federal system simply by a faithful interpretation of the B.N.A. Act. Their failure to do so made the Canadian system more authentically federal, and thus made the law lords "the real fathers of Canadian confederation."[19]

Vaughan's basic constitutional philosophy is summed up in 3, although his abbreviated presentation may lend itself to misinterpretation. Exactly how a dominant national legislature would bind the several provinces at the centre is unclear. In more than a century of federalism we have seen several periods in which a strong centre could not maintain itself, and precipitated counter-tendencies to its own brief hegemonies.

Vaughan is not a fan of federalism. He refers positively to John A. Macdonald's "thoughts on the inherent weakness of the federal form of government,"[20] and he minimizes the federal element in the confederation settlement. In remarkably strong language he asserts that the "confederation plan clearly contained a deceptive constitutionalism by giving the impression that the new constitution embodied the federal principle in an effective manner."[21] He approvingly quotes Christopher Dunkin, who "revealed that the principle of centralisation contained in the plan destroyed any semblance of federalism."[22] This "centralised constitutionalism" was to be sustained by "authoritative judicial determination," to which end early efforts were directed to the establishment of a Supreme Court cognizant of "the hopes and aspirations of the new nation."[23]

Limitations of space preclude disentangling the multiple issues involved in the above position, in contrast to which the late Donald Creighton looks like a rampant provincialist. Silver's recent volume indicates clearly that in Quebec the confederation scheme was not seen in the way it is portrayed by Vaughan. In Quebec, "Confederationist propaganda . . . underlined the Quebec-centredness of French Canada's approach to Confederation, and the degree to which French Quebec's separateness and autonomy were central to French-Canadian acceptance of the new régime."[24]

Of more serious import than differences of historical interpretation, to found the judicial task on obeisance to a deceptive constitutionalism is unlikely to produce either a wholesome jurisprudence or a functionally necessary respect for the integrity of the judicial process. Presumably the original deception reflected the belief that clarity would have weakened the chances of getting agreement on the terms of confederation. Was the judicial task to continue with the deception, assuming of course that judges could clearly see through it, or was the unmasking to take place on the bench?[25] Neither role would seem capable of eliciting much judicial enthusiasm.

It is symptomatic of Vaughan's fundamentalist position that neither society nor post-confederation history enters into his analysis. Thus he avoids having to discuss whether post-confederation developments might have justified a departure, to which courts could properly have contributed, from the centralist intentions of the founders. He displays no apparent sympathy with the idea of a living constitution. By inference, the steel frame of a centralised constitutionalism could have both survived and tamed subsequent centrifugal pressures as the four-province Canada of 1867 expanded to ten provinces and as the country moved through eras of war and peace, of economic growth and stagnation. Vaughan does not, of course, explicitly support such a thesis, but the logic of his argument requires that he be able to do so. It is not an easy task which he has left undone. There is considerable academic support for the proposition, to which I subscribe, that the federalism of 1867 was too centralist for the underlying regionalism of the country, to which it subsequently responded.[26]

I am equally unable to support a thesis which attaches primary causal significance to judicial decisions for the subsequent evolution of Canadian federalism away from its 1867 beginnings. Judicial decisions are the product of judge and company, and there was a goodly company that supported the decentralising impulse that the Judicial Committee injected into Canadian federalism.[27] It is also undeniable, as previously argued,[28] that various instruments of centralisation fell into disuse for reasons unrelated to judicial pronouncements. It was not Watson or Haldane who rendered the disallowance power obsolete, or caused section 94 to be a dead letter. Further, it was not only judicial interpretation, but the accidents of history that made so many of the provincial responsibilities far more significant than they were originally intended to be.

The Vaughan position on the capacity of a faithful court to preserve the reality of a centralised federalism independently of developments external to the constitution, and conversely his affixing of the primary responsibility for the post-1867 decentralisation of Canadian federalism on the Judicial Committee, both reflect a primacy accorded to judicial power, and, relatedly, an attribution of capacity to institutions to shape society which is striking, even in an era in which political science is *Bringing the State Back In*.[29] My general sympathy with the perspective that institutions matter and that the state has significant moulding power falls short of the position I detect in the Vaughan analysis. This means that ultimately the differences in our evaluations of the Judicial Committee rest on prior differences of understanding of the way society works. I do not think that the role which Vaughan would have had the Judicial Committee perform would have been sufficient to "bind the several provinces at the centre so as to ensure the continued existence of Canada as one nation"[30] of the kind he seems to have in mind. Accordingly, I applaud rather than denigrate a court which can roll with the punches and respond to insistent pressure while preserving the basic constitutional structure of the polity.

If I infer Vaughan's position correctly, as hewing closely to the fundamentalist posture in jurisprudential discourse, I simply extend to his presentation the criticisms I applied to an earlier generation of fundamentalists in my 1971 article. My appraisal of the fundamentalist position, which is too lengthy to be repeated here,[31] is summed up in the critique by Evan Gray of the fundamentalist posture of the O'Connor Report, which is based on "the pretension . . . that by a miracle of understanding and foresight, the Canadian Fathers of Confederation provided in 1867 a constitution suitable to any future."[32]

My own position is close to that of K. N. Llewellyn:

> there is no quarrel to be had with judges *merely* because they disregard or twist Documentary language, or "interpret" it to the despair of original intent, in the service of what those judges conceive to be the inherent nature of our institutions. To my mind, such action is their duty. To my mind, the judge who builds his decision to conform with his conception of what our institutions must be if we are to continue, roots in the deepest wisdom.[33]

Two additional points in conclusion:

1. Although the opening statement of purpose and the concluding retrospective statement of purpose in my article employ different language and perhaps reflect different shadings of emphasis, I do not agree with Vaughan that my vagueness "betrays considerable ambiguity."[34] However, I will leave that judgment to others.

2. Vaughan asserts that the results-oriented jurisprudence which I allegedly espouse could, in the era of the Charter, produce a free-wheeling imperial judiciary imposing its perception of the "sociological realities" of Canada as an act of almost untrammelled freedom. I find this description of my position surprising. I explicitly argued that a developed jurisprudence had to come to grips with the particular institutional division of labour characteristic of the Canadian polity.[35] I continue to adhere to that position in the more complex division of labour which the Charter has brought in its wake. At a minimum, that division of labour imposes a particular style of reasoning on the judicial process and requires attention to the non-elected status of judges and a recognition that certainty and predictability are more essential virtues for courts than for legislatures.

It is nevertheless evident that the Charter—even given s. 33—enhances the relative significance of courts vis-à-vis legislatures in the overall constitutional system. This is a commonplace of contemporary discussion. There is, however, an openness and indeterminacy to the emerging judicial role. The chief justice, on many occasions, has not only underlined the new responsibilities of the Supreme Court, but has explicitly asked for the assistance of social scientists as well as the legal fraternity in the working out of that expanded role. He does not view the Charter as speaking with a clarity which removes from the Court a range of discretion which can be wisely or foolishly handled.[36]

The Charter once more highlights the basic question of constitutional jurisprudence facing a final appeal court, how it should apply the discretion it unavoidably possesses. In an earlier era, that was the question facing the Judicial Committee. To describe the judicial task in terms of the controlled exercise of discretion is to deny that in constitutional adjudication the task of judging is equivalent to historical discovery. It is to affirm the leadership role which lurks in courtrooms and which recurrently surfaces in situations of novelty and uncertainty. Peter Russell has said it well: "One of the overriding interests of political scientists who study judicial review should be to discover where pure legal analysis ends and judgments of legislative policy and constitutional principle, which cannot themselves be determined by such analysis, begins."[37]

Professor Vaughan may believe that this rejoinder is based on a misunderstanding and misinterpretation of his position, as I think his article is of mine. Fortunately, neither of us has the power to decide who is right. These exchanges indicate that in this kind of subject matter truth, our quarry, is approached but never captured.

NOTES

1. There is, however, an ambiguity in his position which, while generally critical of Judicial Committee performance, contains the odd statement, perhaps only rhetorical: "However reasonable the course taken by the Judicial Committee of the Privy Council now in retrospect appears..." (Frederick Vaughan, "Critics of the Judicial Committee: The New Orthodoxy and an Alternative Explanation" [1986] 19 *CJPS* 495–519, at 519.

2. Vaughan, "Critics of the Judicial Committee," 500.

3. Ibid., 506.

4. Ibid., 501–2, 503. In general, I do not accept the label provincialist and I deny that my attitude to the Judicial Committee is a product of a provincial perspective. In the article which I co-authored with Ed Black ("A Different Perspective on Canadian Federalism" [1966] 9 *Canadian Public Administration* 43), concern was

expressed over several possible negative consequences of province-building. Evidence is not lacking in my other writings of a centralist, nation-building perspective.

5. Vaughan, "Critics of the Judicial Committee," 495. For example, I am impressed with and sympathetic to the recent argument of Gordon Bale, which is highly critical of the Judicial Committee decisions in the Manitoba School cases in the 1890s ("Law, Politics and the Manitoba School Question: Supreme Court and Privy Council" [1985] 63 *Can. Bar Rev.* 462–518).

6. Vaughan, "Critics of the Judicial Committee," 495.

7. Ibid., 512.

8. Ibid., 514.

9. Ibid., 519.

10. Peter H. Russell, ed., *Leading Constitutional Decisions*, 3d ed.

(Ottawa: Carleton University Press, 1982), 8, 12; Alan C. Cairns, "The Judicial Committee and its Critics" (1971) 4 *CJPS* 323.

11. Somewhat paradoxically, at one point Vaughan reverses the sequence and suggests that "*why* they viewed...[their] function...as essentially political" was *because* they were "intent on giving effect to a conception of federalism which was clearly counter to that contained in the B.N.A. Act" (Vaughan, "Critics of the Judicial Committee," 514; italics added).

12. Cairns, "The Judicial Committee and its Critics," 302–12, 332–44.

13. Several small points may be relegated to an endnote. I disagree with Vaughan's assertion that my view of the Fathers or their work "is highly negative" (502). To say that they "lacked the gift of foresight" is not a criticism but a statement of the human condition. I did not say that they were "the victims of a 'completely static society,'" but that a fundamentalist approach to their creation was only plausible for "a completely static society, in which the original settlement was perfectly suited to existing social values and needs" (Cairns, "The Judicial Committee and its Critics," 335) and went on to make the point, that I have not heard denied, that post-confederation Canada was not a static society. I did not dismiss them as "a small body of men in the 1860s," but simply noted that is what they were. I do not worship the Fathers and their creation in every detail. Who does? I respect them and it.

14. *Report Pursuant to Resolution of the Senate to the Honourable the Speaker by the Parliamentary Counsel Relating to the Enactment of the British North America Act, 1867, any lack of consonance between its terms and judicial construction of them and cognate matters* (Ottawa, 1939).

15. Vaughan, "Critics of the Judicial Committee," 500–51.

16. Ibid., 511–12.

17. Ibid., 505. In light of the above I am unclear why Vaughan concludes that in

addition to strengthening the provinces, the Judicial Committee also "preserv[ed] the integrity of the federal government and Parliament" (ibid., 519). This sounds suspiciously like praise.

18. Ibid., 500.

19. Ibid., 519.

20. Ibid., 504.

21. Ibid., 510.

22. Ibid., 510–11.

23. Ibid., 511.

24. A. I. Silver, *The French-Canadian Idea of Confederation 1864–1900* (Toronto: University of Toronto Press, 1982), 50.

25. There is some tension, if not contradiction, between the argument that on the one hand the confederation plan embodied a "deceptive constitutionalism," which presumably provided a spurious appearance of federalism, and the thesis stated elsewhere that "The B.N.A. Act is not contradictory...[but]...crudely centralist...[reflecting]...the conscious effort of the framers of the Act" (Vaughan, "Critics of the Judicial Committee," 510, 513).

26. See Cairns, "The Judicial Committee and its Critics," 323, n. 99 for extensive references and quotations.

27. Ibid., 319–20.

28. Ibid., 322.

29. Peter B. Evans, Dietrich Rueschemeyer and Theda Skocpol, eds., *Bringing the State Back In* (Cambridge: Cambridge University Press, 1985).

30. Vaughan, "Critics of the Judicial Committee," 505. It is difficult to come to grips with Vaughan's position without a more elaborate understanding of what he means by "the continued existence of Canada as one nation."

31. Cairns, "The Judicial Committee and its Critics," 334–38.

32. Evan Gray, "'The O'Connor Report' on the British North America Act, 1867" (1939) 17 *Can. Bar Rev.* 334,

cited in Cairns, "The Judicial Committee and its Critics," 337, n. 148.

33. K. N. Llewellyn, "The Constitution as an Institution" (1934) 23 *Columbia Law Review*, 33, cited in Cairns, "The Judicial Committee and its Critics," 335, n. 140.

34. Vaughan, "Critics of the Judicial Committee," 502.

35. Cairns, "The Judicial Committee and its Critics," 342–43.

36. For one example, see "An Address by the Right Honourable Brian Dickson,

Closing Banquet, University of Ottawa Conference on the Supreme Court of Canada," 4 October 1985 (mimeo). See also the very impressive David B. Goodman Memorial Lectures delivered by Madame Justice Bertha Wilson at the University of Toronto, 26–27 November 1985 (mimeo), which subtly discusses four "tensions" in judicial decision making, and in the second lecture explicitly addresses the judicial role with respect to the Charter.

37. Russell, *Leading Constitutional Decisions*, 17.

COMMENT ON "CRITICS OF THE JUDICIAL COMMITTEE: THE NEW ORTHODOXY AND AN ALTERNATIVE EXPLANATION"◇

PETER H. RUSSELL

o

I appreciate the opportunity Professor Vaughan's article provides to clarify some of my thoughts on the Judicial Committee and constitutional interpretation.

Vaughan and I are in agreement on two broad points. First, the Judicial Committee of the Privy Council read a theory of classical federalism into the B.N.A. Act. This theory of divided sovereignty was expressed most clearly by Lord Watson in the *Maritime Bank* case.[1] Secondly, the B.N.A. Act's treatment of federalism is highly centralist, both in the division of powers and in the federal government's imperial powers over provincial governments. Both these points are contained in the following passage from my introduction: "In their anxiety to preserve a division of powers appropriate for 'classical federalism' and thereby resist the strongly centralising tendencies of the constitutional text, the Judicial Committee developed an acute sensitivity to the competing claims of the provinces and the federal government."[2] I think Professor Vaughan would agree with that statement.

Where we seem to differ is over how seriously the Judicial Committee distorted what I refer to as "the true intentions of Canada's Founding Fathers."[3] I see the Fathers of Confederation as a fragile political coalition within which there was a range of opinion on how strong the provinces should be in the Canadian federation. Sir John A. Macdonald was certainly at one end of the spectrum in wanting the weakest possible provinces. I believe, however, "There were others, especially from Lower Canada and the Maritimes, who hoped that strong provincial governments could flourish under the new constitution."[4] When I referred to "others" in the passage just quoted I was not, as Vaughan suggests, referring to the opponents of the confederation scheme. I was thinking of British North American politicians who supported confederation and forced Macdonald to abandon his preference for a

◇ *Canadian Journal of Political Science* 19, 3 (September 1986): 531–36.

legislative union. In the Confederation Debates Macdonald explained why he had to abandon that preference: "it would not meet the assent of the people of Lower Canada, because they felt that in their peculiar position—being in a minority, with a different language, nationality and religion from the majority—in case of a junction with the other provinces, their institutions and their laws might be assailed, and their ancestral associations...attacked and prejudiced."[5] He went on to explain that "there was as great a disinclination on the part of the various Maritime Provinces to lose their individuality, as separate political organizations, as we observed in the case of Lower Canada herself."[6] It is my assumption—and none of the historical evidence cited by Vaughan persuades me that it is a mistaken assumption—that these passages reflect a compromise within the confederation movement among politicians, some of whom wanted significantly stronger provinces than Macdonald hoped for.

Support for a federal division of powers which would secure significant powers for the provinces was not limited to members of the confederation coalition from Lower Canada and the Maritimes. Among "Reformers" in Upper Canada there was a strong desire to maintain a significant degree of autonomy for Ontario. Support for the confederation scheme on the part of some of Macdonald's colleagues from this reform tradition was contingent on the constitutionalization of the idea, as George Brown put it, that "local governments are to have control over local affairs."[7] The Judicial Committee's interpretation of the B.N.A. Act did not reverse the intentions of these Fathers of Confederation.

It may help to clarify my understanding of the confederation settlement by comparing it with the constitutional settlement of 1981. That too, was a compromise. Members of the Trudeau government and many of its supporters wanted to entrench rights and freedoms so deeply that judicial determinations of their meaning could be overcome only by the difficult process of constitutional amendment. A number of provincial leaders and their followers were reluctant to give judges so much power to overturn the decision of elected governments. The basic compromise which made possible an accord between politicians representing these two bodies of political sentiment was a constitutional charter with a legislative override. Underlying this accord are conflicting hopes and fears on how much power the judiciary will exert on decisions affecting rights and freedoms. This situation is analogous to what I was trying to get at when I stated that "The Judicial Committee's espousal of balanced federalism may better reflect the historical balance of hopes and expectations than the very centralist position of the early Supreme Court."[8]

The sentence just quoted pinpoints the difference between Vaughan and myself. I take it that he prefers the approach taken by the Supreme Court of Canada in *Severn v. The Queen*[9] to that of the Judicial Committee in *Citizens Insurance Co. v. Parsons*.[10] In *Severn* the Supreme Court was willing to treat the federal trade and commerce power as an unqualified power. In the words of Mr. Justice Henry, "Every constituent...of trade and commerce is...withdrawn from the consideration of the Local Legislatures." In Parsons, on the other hand, the Judicial Committee put forward the view that sections 91 and 92 of the B.N.A. Act must be read together, so that broad and general subjects in one list do not absorb and cancel out more specific subjects in the other list. Thus the federal trade and commerce power could not be treated as an unqualified power. A year later, in the *Russell* case, the Judicial Committee applied the same rationale in rejecting the widest possible interpretation of the most broadly phrased provincial power—property and civil rights.

Consider the implications had *Severn* rather than *Parsons* prevailed. The federal Parliament would be responsible for virtually every aspect of economic regulation no matter how local, no matter how closely tied to provincial responsibilities such as municipal zoning or the sale of public lands, or contract law. I cannot believe that such an outcome conforms with either the internal structure of the B.N.A. Act or the intentions of the confederation movement. According to Vaughan the language of the B.N.A. Act clearly provides for the absorption of exclusive federal powers. But surely this is wrong. It would have been ridiculous for the Fathers of Confederation to go to all the trouble of negotiating two lists of powers if all along they intended that some of the powers in the provincial list were "not for real" but were intended to be absorbed into federal powers. It is much more logical to assume, as Sir Montague Smith does in *Parsons*, that large and general subjects in one list (for instance "marriage and divorce") must be cut down to enable more specific subjects (for instance "solemnization of marriage") to survive in the other list. Vaughan may be thinking of the "deeming" paragraph at the end of section 91 as the language which clearly authorizes the extinguishment of subjects assigned exclusively to the provinces. If he is, he is wrong. That paragraph simply provides that where a legislative matter is deemed (presumably by the courts) to come within a class of subjects assigned to the federal Parliament it will not be considered to come within one of the provincial subjects. It is not a directive to the courts to absorb provincial subjects into federal subjects.

The members and supporters of the confederation movement gave both levels of government some significant economic powers: all forms of taxation, the regulation of trade and commerce, banking, interest and currency on the federal side; the sale of public lands, the ownership of natural resources, a board licensing power and the commercial law components of French civil law on the provincial side. Passages from the *bleu* newspapers in Canada East demonstrate how Macdonald's Quebec colleagues endeavoured to assure their supporters that the provinces would retain some significant powers, including some in the economic sphere. According to *Le Courier du Canada*, the central government "n'aurait pas le droit de venir mettre la main dans nos affaires locales qui resteraient sous le contrôle de notre législature locale; puisque la législature fédérale n'aurait pas le droit de toucher à l'économie interne de chaque province."[11] In a similar vein, *La Minerve* of Montreal stated that Lower Canada "aura son gouvernement particulier dont l'autorité s'étendra à tous les objets qui suivent le cours ordinaire des affaires, intéressant de la vie, la liberté et la prosperité des citoyens . . . ."[12] No doubt these newspapers exaggerated the significance of the powers allocated to the provinces under the confederation scheme. Still, an interpretation of the division of powers such as that offered by the Supreme Court in *Severn* denying the provinces *any* jurisdiction over commerce, however local it may be, would betray the hopes of Cartier, Taché and other Fathers of Confederation who believed the provinces should retain significant powers. Similarly, an interpretation such as that favoured by Vaughan, under which provincial powers could be absorbed in federal powers,

would be totally out of keeping with the expectations of those Fathers of Confederation who believed the provinces should endure as significant units of government.

Vaughan tends to treat courts and their commentators in rather categorical
terms. As a revisionist who does not believe the Privy Council was all bad, I am not
committed to thinking it was all good. Viscount Haldane's treatment of the trade
and commerce power as a subordinate, ancillary power was a pure judicial gloss on
the constitution. His emergency test for the circumstances under which peace,
order, and good government can be invoked was dangerously anti-centralist, just
as Viscount Simon's test of inherent national concern was dangerously centralist.
My inclination on the division of powers in Canadian federalism is not, as Vaughan
suggests, towards "an ever-changing equilibrium" but towards a balanced
federalism. I believe the Supreme Court since 1949 has done a better job in striking
that balance than did the Judicial Committee before 1949.[13]

But how should we assess a court's work in interpreting a constitution? That
is the crucial normative question in this field of study. For more than a generation
now this has been the central issue in American and Canadian constitutional
jurisprudence. Most commentators (Vaughan may be an exception) rule out one
possibility: that the answers to hard cases can be logically deduced from the
language of the constitution. Constitutions have to be interpreted. The question is
how should they be interpreted? In interpreting them, how much weight should be
given to history, how much to current needs and how much to the internal logic of
the constitutional text, or to the need to maintain consistency with previous judicial
decisions? If history should be taken into account (and surely it should) then what
history should count? How much weight should be given to the record of the
drafters' intentions? Who are to count as "drafters"? Should the judges attempt to
ascertain the broader historical forces and purposes behind the constitution? If the
judges are to show some concern for their country's contemporary exigencies (and
surely they must) by what standards and techniques should they gauge these needs?

These questions are difficult and will continue to preoccupy us as we consider
the work of our courts in interpreting Canada's new constitutional charter. In
dealing with these questions I have not found the categories of "activism" or
"self-restraint" to be very useful in assessing the quality of the reasons a court gives
for overriding or upholding challenged acts of government. That is why Professor
Vaughan is wrong to say I am opposed to an activist judiciary. If an "activist"
decision is based on good reasons (as, for instance, Chief Justice Duff's decision in
the *Alberta Press* case[14] was) then I will approve of it. Which, of course, brings us
back to the basic question of what constitutes "good reasons" for constitutional
decisions. I am doubtful that anyone can produce a completely satisfactory answer
to that question. The best I could do in my "Introduction" was to suggest that "All
that we can reasonably expect is that the judges might persuade us that their
decisions are based on principles which embody the wisdom of our collective
experience."[15]

This formulation, I must admit, is very sketchy. But it does point to some of
the elements of a good judicial decision on the constitution. Such decisions should
be principled. That is, they should not be simply acts designed to favour a particular
litigant or policy outcome, but should be based on a reading of the constitutional

text that is true to both its internal logic and its historical context. In identifying these principles, judges should consider the political ideals and objectives that animated those who established the constitution as well as the practical experience of the country in living with the various implications of the constitution. A good decision is more than the product of these considerations. Ideally it is the articulation of these considerations in reasons that are clearly and cogently expressed. These reasons must serve both as a guide to the legal community, which must advise citizens and governments on their constitutional rights and duties, and for the wider public as an exercise in practical reasoning on the best application of the country's constituent political values. For my money, the judicial opinion in my collection of leading constitutional decisions that comes closest to meeting this ideal is that of Justice Brian Dickson, as he then was, in *The Queen v. Hauser.*[16] Sadly, I must record, it was a dissenting opinion.

NOTES

1. *Liquidators of the Maritime Bank of Canada v. Receiver General of New Brunswick* (1892) A.C. 437. See, Frederick Vaughan, "Critics of the Judicial Committee: The New Orthodoxy and an Alternative Explanation" (1986) 19 *CJPS,* 495–519.

2. Peter H. Russell, "Introduction," *Leading Constitutional Decisions,* 3d ed. (Ottawa: Carleton University Press, 1982), 12.

3. Ibid., 12.

4. Ibid., 13.

5. P.B. Waite, ed., *Confederation Debates* (Toronto: McClelland and Stewart, 1963), 40–41.

6. Ibid., 41.

7. Quoted in Robert C. Vipond, "Constitutional Politics and the Legacy

of the Provincial Rights Movement in Canada" (1985) 18 *CJPS,* 271.

8. Russell, "Introduction," 13.

9. (1878), 2 S.C.R. 70.

10. (1881), 7 App. Cas. 96.

11. Quoted in P.B. Waite, *The Life and Times of Confederation* (Toronto: University of Toronto Press, 1962), 139.

12. Ibid.

13. See Russell, "The Supreme Court and Federal–Provincial Relations: The Political Use of Legal Resources" (1985) 11 *Canadian Public Policy,* 161.

14. [1938] S.C.R. 100.

15. Russell, "Introduction," 14.

16. [1979] 1 S.C.R. 984.

REPLY◇

FREDERICK VAUGHAN

◦

I would like to begin by thanking Alan Cairns and Peter Russell for responding to my article. Their comments have transformed the issues I have treated into a spirited debate.[1] My only regret is that I have been restricted to a brief reply. I should, especially, have liked more space to reply to Professor Cairns's pointed response. As a general defence, permit me to state that my article was originally much longer than the printed version; the editors insisted that it be substantially reduced. In my view, several of my points have suffered because of this surgery.

As a general observation to Professor Russell's comments, to which I will respond first, let me say that I think he errs when he equates the atmosphere of the 1980s with the 1860s. The meeting of Maritime politicians in Charlottetown was called for the purpose of discussing a legislative union, not a federal system. The general consensus was strongly against federalism. By the 1980s, of course, federalism had become a deep and permanent condition in Canadian political consciousness.

As for my understanding of the "deeming" paragraph at the end of s. 91, I do indeed understand that clause *when taken in the context provided by the head* of s. 91 as authorizing the extinguishment of subjects allegedly assigned exclusively to the provinces. The question is *what precisely* is assigned exclusively to the provinces? In the final analysis, very little. When a member of the P.E.I. Legislature reviewed the Quebec resolutions, he protested that the only thing left to the provinces was "the regulation of the running at large of swine." Section 95 of the *British North America Act* makes it clear that not even that was exclusively within provincial legislative jurisdiction. I believe that Act must be read together, each provision or section considered as a unit of instruction. It is wrong, in my view of the judicial function, for judges or courts to detach phrases or clauses from their context. This does not mean that judges ought to perform their function without regard to

◇*Canadian Journal of Political Science* 19, 3 (September 1986): 537–39.

changing needs and aspirations. My charge against the Judicial Committee is that the law lords gave insufficient consideration to the intention of the legislators. This is an issue I will return to in a moment when I reply to Cairns.

Finally, I do not quarrel with Russell when he states his preference for principled decisions. So do I. And I also agree with his praise of Chief Justice Dickson's judgments as examples of superb judicial reasoning.

Turning now to Cairns's comments, let me restate why I undertook to write the article. I have long been troubled by the implicit old charge that the law lords of the Judicial Committee were either fools or knaves. And I have been equally unpersuaded by Cairns's thesis that the Judicial Committee ruled in defiance of the centralised terms of the B.N.A. Act because they took into account the "sociological realities" of Canada. My point is that he presents no evidence to support this thesis. As well, I have never been convinced that the law lords were better informed of the "sociological realities" than our Fathers of Confederation. I was forced, therefore, to look for a plausible alternative explanation. I think I have found it in what members of the Judicial Committee have said in their judgments as well as in the verbatim transcripts of the proceedings in *Russell* (1882) and *Local Prohibition* (1896). I obviously have not persuaded Cairns or Russell.

And, by the way, I do not worship at the altar of the Fathers of Confederation; I certainly do not presume to robe myself in Sir John A. Macdonald's mantle. I do, however, defend the founders' right to a fair hearing. I do not say that their thoughts or reflections equal Solon's or Lycurgus'. But I do say that some of them—the leading ones—such as Macdonald, McGee, Galt and Dunkin, and a few others, pondered the debates on federalism provided in the published proceedings of the American constitutional convention. They also reflected on the *Federalist* papers. I pointed this out in my article. My judgment is, for what it is worth, that those reflections were at least as substantive as those of some members of the Canadian political science community writing one hundred years later. I restate a point: Cairns treats our founders with disdain. To do so, I think, is unfair. But our readers will have to decide for themselves.

I am especially pleased that Cairns took up the issue of the judicial function. The points he raises are central to my concern. Cairns may well have changed his mind since he wrote his article on the critics of the Judicial Committee, but I am persuaded that the account of the judicial function articulated in that article leads to what I have called the "imperial judiciary." Now I find that he too (along with Russell) applauds the judicial reasoning of Chief Justice Dickson. But there is no similarity between Dickson's reasoning (see for example his judgment in the recent *Big M Drug Mart* case) and what Cairns advocates in his article. Dickson anchors his reasoning in the intention of the legislature. The issue of the judicial function is clearly a debate over the duty of judges to attempt to accommodate new social conditions within the statutory instrument duly enacted by Parliament. I in no way believe, as Cairns claims, that "judges should simply give effect to those terms for they reflect a superior wisdom with which later generations, especially judges, should not tamper." Far from being a fundamentalist (if I understand what that means) I endorse the manner in which Dickson and Wilson (and others on our Supreme Court) exercise their judicial function. Cairns's portrayal of the judicial function in the Judicial Committee excludes the demand that judges seek out the legislative intent. It is on this point that we are in fundamental disagreement.

Secondly, far from being unsympathetic to federalism, as Cairns charges me, I am deeply concerned with it. To put the matter bluntly, I believe that the results for our federal system that flow from the Judicial Committee judgments have not been adequately considered by Cairns and other Canadian political scientists. It surprises me that Cairns does not respond to this particular issue. I believe that our federal system lacks an adequate central *institution* to accommodate the strains inherent in all federal systems.

Finally, Professor Cairns claims that I do not account adequately for the brand of federalism espoused by the Judicial Committee. In my view, the precise nature of federalism was not a problem for the law lords. They were not attempting to enter into or resolve a theoretical problem over the nature of federalism. The thrust of the discussions before the board and in the judgment of the Judicial Committee was towards finding some measure of exclusive legislative authority for the provinces. They cared little about whether observers called it "classical federalism" or not. Their chief or dominant concern was to enunciate the basis for provincial legislative authority.

NOTES

1. Alan C. Cairns, "Comment..." (1986) 19 *CJPS* 521–29; Peter H. Russell, "Comment..." (1986) 19 *CJPS* 531–36.

s e c t i o n

4

MADE IN CANADA: THE LAWS OF THE SUPREME COURT

1949 - 1989

o

he abolition, in 1949, of appeals to the Judicial Committee of the Privy Council made the Supreme Court the final arbiter of Canadian law. For all practical purposes, the Court already fulfilled this role in a number of areas. Not only had the Privy Council rarely heard criminal or civil appeals, it had also controlled its agenda, and its practice had been to hear appeals only when "the case [was] of gravity, involving matters of public interest of some important question of law . . . ."[1] The major result of the Court's promotion, then, was its new ability to determine constitutional law. For this reason, it is tempting to regard the abolition of appeals as a political expression of Canada's dissatisfaction with the Privy Council's federalist jurisprudence.[2] But the record is hardly this straightforward.

True, it was the outcome of the 1937 reference cases which inspired C.H. Cahan to introduce a private member's bill to abolish appeals, but his passion was not shared by the government, which referred the bill to the Supreme Court to determine its constitutionality.[3] When, two years after the Privy Council's final disposition of the matter in 1947, the Liberal government introduced the amendment to the *Supreme Court Act*, the debate in Parliament centred not on whether the Supreme Court should disregard Privy Council jurisprudence, but on whether the Court should be required by statute to follow precedent, or be free to do so of its own accord.[4] No express parliamentary mandate existed, then, for the Supreme Court to use its new status to re-fashion Canadian federalism. Postwar federal–provincial relations were not expected to be trouble free, but, as the failure to produce constitutional amendment showed, a redistribution of jurisdictional heads of power was not considered a solution.

A major reason for this was the changing concept of the scope and function of governmental activity after the war. Nineteenth-century statesmen could see government as primarily a body which legislated on certain discrete "matters." In such a view, private activity and state action are sharply distinguished. Citizens carry on their activities in a private realm; legislation is the exceptional response when the consequences of these activities are socially unacceptable.

Postwar policy makers did not share this view of government as an occasional actor. Monetary and fiscal policy, regulatory agencies and government corporations reflected an image of government as a permanent role-player. The objects of legislative activity, in turn, were becoming too diffuse and overlapping to fit into conceptually distinct matters. The boundaries between government and private activity became blurred, as did the jurisdictional boundaries between federal and provincial governments. Government initiatives defied classification into all in-clusive "watertight compartments." From the perspective of policy makers, the paradigm of federalism was shifting from the autonomy to the interdependence of jurisdictions.

It was in this political and intellectual context that the Supreme Court found itself in 1949. Whether it should disregard strict jurisdictional distinctions was, and in some ways still is, a central focus of legal debate. While the Court had no direct mandate to strike out on its own jurisprudential path, its members were part of a legal community which was rethinking the role of law in a modern federal state.

In 1951, Bora Laskin and Louis-Philippe Pigeon, both future Supreme Court Justices, reflected on the state of the constitution and the role of judicial review.[5]

Although not written in response to each other, their articles capture the conflicting views of law and federalism, and provide a context in which the Supreme Court's doctrinal contributions can be appreciated.

In "The Meaning of Provincial Autonomy," Pigeon embraced what he called the "autonomist conception of federation":

> federation implies a division of political authority so that the component states or provinces are free to define their general policy in their own sphere of activity, without being obliged to conform [to] any pattern set down by the central authority.[6]

Provincial autonomy was the right to be different. Pigeon saw this view as following from the concept of individual liberty: "Just as freedom means for the individual the right of choosing his own objective so long as it is not illegal, autonomy means for a province the privilege of defining its own policies."[7] In each case, the confines of legality are crucial for Pigeon. It is only when the law is clearly settled that an actor can be free. "It implies limitations," he wrote "but it also implies free movement within the area bounded by the limitations."[8] The role of the court, then, is to maintain these boundaries so that the provinces are capable of choosing their own policies within them. This has obvious implications for precedent and for the judicial response to the need for the co-ordination of federal and provincial policies.

Strict adherence to precedent is necessary so that new laws do not have retroactive effects for the subjects they touch. As for policy co-ordination, the judiciary should not be offended by the apparently incoherent national policies which result from provincial autonomy. Conceding that autonomy "allows the provinces on occasion to work at cross purposes," Pigeon nonetheless maintained that "it would be a grave mistake to assume that this is wrong in itself, or that it is necessarily against the national interest."[9] Not surprisingly, Pigeon approved of the Privy Council's legacy; by maintaining provincial autonomy "they are preserving the essential condition of the Canadian federation."[10]

Professor Bora Laskin (as he then was) did not share Pigeon's satisfaction with the Privy Council. In "The Supreme Court of Canada: A Final Court of and for Canadians," Laskin argued that the abolition of appeals provided the means to escape from Privy Council doctrine. For Laskin, provincial autonomy was based on nothing as eternal as individual liberty; the doctrine was founded upon "impermanent social and economic considerations which ... [were] rarely articulated." Indeed, as all legal reasoning was based on social and economic contingencies, there would be no reason for the Supreme Court to follow the approach of the Privy Council:

> It is hardly credible that the Supreme Court will seek to walk in the shadow of the Privy Council, asking itself not only what Privy Council decisions are controlling but striving to reflect the Privy Council's approach to problems of interpretation. Such a final court would be merely a judicial "zombie" without soul or character.[11]

As a further result of the contingency of judicial outcomes, Laskin, unlike Pigeon, did not relate settled precedent to the necessary bound of liberty. He mocked the notion that freedom entails activity within established precedent, referring to it as "will o' the wisp." The preferred approach, he said, "is to adopt a simple rule of adult behaviour and to recognise that law must pay tribute to life; and that in constitutional litigation, especially, *stare decisis* cannot be accepted as an inflexible rule of conduct."[12]

Laskin, when Chief Justice, repeated this view. Dissenting in a non-constitutional law decision, Chief Justice Laskin declined to follow a Supreme Court decision rendered five years earlier because this "Court, above all others, cannot be simply mechanistic about previous decisions, whatever be the respect it would pay to such decisions."[13] Not surprisingly, Pigeon J. concurred in the majority decision which adopted the following quotation from Cardozo's *The Nature of the Judicial Process*:

> The judge, even when he is free, is still not wholly free. He is not to innovate at pleasure. He is not a knight-errant, roaming at will in pursuit of his own idol of liberty or goodness. He is to draw his inspiration from consecrated principles.[14]

The two theories of legal reasoning and constitutional adjudication are thus clear. Pigeon's view that provincial autonomy is as basic as human freedom meant that the boundaries between federal and provincial governments must be strictly maintained, so that the latter are free to pursue their own ends. Laskin saw provincial autonomy as one of a number of possible results of a division of power. Breaking precedent is not legislating retroactively, but evidence of mature minds adapting legal concepts to new realities. Perhaps because such a stark contrast appeared between the two views, embracing either whole-heartedly was impossible for the Supreme Court.

Pigeon's exacting standards of legal clarity were well suited to the single voice of the Judicial Committee, but for a seven member court with a practice of issuing individual judgments, some differences of opinion would always complicate a decision. Moreover, with the provincial governments co-operating in joint programs it was less imperative—and impossible in practice, if not in law—for the Court to confine each government to its own sphere. Finally, even within their own jurisdictions, the provinces were experimenting with legislation that affected other provinces and the national government. Paradoxically, maintaining hard jurisdictional boundaries would restrict what the provinces regarded as an exercise of their own autonomy.

Equally, Laskin's easy dismissal of the importance of precedent would be resisted by the judges of the Supreme Court. Educated in a traditional legal fashion, they would be unlikely to accept the idea that legal decisions were mere reflections of social and economic conditions of the time. While Laskin pointed to the American Supreme Court as a model of a final court willing to depart from its past decisions, the Canadian Court was more likely to identify with the British House of Lords which, until 1966, was legally bound by precedent. Indeed, Laskin the judge, while attempting to reshape some aspects of Canadian federalism, felt the need to justify his opinions by relying on precedent.[15]

The court's inability to settle upon a firm jurisdictional direction, however, did not work a great hardship on the Canadian federal state. The decisions rendered by the Court were by no means immaterial, but the imperatives of postwar politics and public policy led governments to circumvent the "watertight" compartments and devise new ways, outside the written and judicially determined federal constitution, to achieve their objectives. If the quasi-federal system of 1867 had given way to classical federalism, that in turn was succeeded in the postwar period by a procedure that can only be described as *ad hoc*—the strange offspring of decades of political pragmatism, confrontation and co-operation, negotiation and improvisation.

The federal system that emerged after 1945 was a product of the Depression, the war, Lord Keynes, and of the politics and policies of the welfare state, or what Thomas Courchêne has appropriately called "the protected society."[16] The Rowell–Sirois Report brilliantly documented and analysed how the Depression revealed (but did not cause) variations in wealth and in vulnerability among regional provincial economies, and exposed the inequalities of provincial and personal income across the country.[17] The war demonstrated that the country could raise billions for defence; it could also, therefore, raise billions in peacetime to wage war against poverty and unemployment, sickness and destitution among the aged. Lord Keynes's view that governments could manage "aggregate demand" in the economy to offset the tendency of a capitalist economy to experience sharp fluctuations in the business cycle, was endorsed by the federal government in 1945.[18] Finally, Mackenzie King's government, pushed by more progressive minds in the party and the bureaucracy, and driven by the threat of the CCF on the left, emerged from the war with a "new national policy" of social programs and of economic and fiscal management.[19]

Canadian federalism, at least as it had been shaped by the courts, stood in the way of the implementation of the new national policy. Maintaining "a high and stable level of employment and income" by pursuing a counter-cyclical fiscal and public expenditure policy (as recommended by Keynes) demanded that fiscal policy be completely, or largely, in the hands of the central government. The provinces had rejected the Rowell–Sirois proposal that they abandon direct taxation in favour of a guaranteed income through a system of National Adjustment Grants. Although they had surrendered those taxes during the war, the provinces had the right to retake them after the war, and the intention of doing so. Moreover, the national social programs proposed by Ottawa in 1945, like most economic regulation, were firmly located within provincial jurisdiction.

In the summer of 1945 the federal government placed its proposals for postwar reconstruction before the provincial governments. Ottawa proposed that the provinces permanently relinquish personal and corporate income taxes and success-sion duties in return for an unconditional grant from Ottawa, its value tied to increases or decreases in the gross national product. Ottawa made other offers to pay half the cost of a provincially administered hospital insurance program, to assume full responsibility for universal old age pensions for those over 70, without a means test, to share 50–50 with the provinces an old age assistance program for those between 65 and 69 (with a provincially administered means test), and to assume complete responsibility for the unemployed who had exhausted their benefits under the unemployment insurance program which the federal government had established following a constitutional amendment in 1940. Ottawa also offered to share the cost of major provincial public works projects, provided the projects were undertaken when Ottawa deemed they were desirable for counter-cyclical reasons.[20]

The package of proposals represented a revolution in Canadian federalism. These proposals deserved the title of "new national policy" not only because it revealed that Ottawa had assumed new responsibilities for economic management, but also because it would mean a dramatic shift in the balance of power in the federal system.[21] Gone were the "watertight compartments," as the federal government planned a massive penetration of provincial jurisdiction. The provinces, in fact, were being asked to give up much of their fiscal independence in return for a guaranteed income. Moreover, in agreeing to the *shared-cost programs* previously mentioned, provinces were required to shape their social security programs according to federally determined priorities and guidelines, if not explicit regulations, in return for federal financial support. As Richard Bastien wrote:

> These proposals upset the whole conception of federalism on which relations between the two orders of government had been based up to that time. By expanding the number and value of shared-cost programs, the federal government was suggesting that the principle of exclusive responsibility and complete independence of action of each order of government was no longer valid. The programs also implied that economic and social policies had become closely intertwined. Furthermore, the federal recommendations required that the different sources of revenue no longer be considered from a purely constitutional point of view, but in terms of their usefulness as macro-economic management tools.[22]

The refusal of Quebec, and to a lesser extent of Ontario, to vacate the direct tax fields effectively killed the federal fiscal proposal. Negotiations over the next twenty years achieved some of the objectives and efficiencies of a centralised tax system, but today Ontario, Quebec and Alberta levy their own corporate income taxes, and Quebec levies its own personal income taxes. In the other provinces, personal income taxes are levied at the same rate as the federal tax and are collected by Ottawa, but each province levies its own income tax as a percentage of the federal tax payable. As might be expected, the poorer the province, the higher the taxes. In many ways, Canada returned to the tax jungle.

Despite the failure of the fiscal proposals, however, Ottawa continued to move forward, negotiating shared-cost programs in social security and welfare fields. The principles and financing of the postwar shared-cost programs were worked out in the political arena. Federal proposals were placed before the provinces, and negotiations were carried out at both the bureaucratic and the first ministers' level, a process Donald Smiley aptly labelled "executive federalism." By the late 1960s, shared-cost programs half funded by the federal government included hospital care, medicare, and the Canada Assistance Plan (for the elderly, the blind, the disabled, and the unemployed). In 1952, the federal government also began to support university education through grants-in-aid.[23]

Although Quebec threatened to challenge the shared-cost programs and the federal spending power in the courts, and other provinces grumbled that federal initiatives destroyed their autonomy by influencing, if not determining, their policy priorities, no province took legal action. Quebec persisted in attacking the programs in the political arena until, in 1965, the federal government permitted any province to "opt out" of most programs and take a financial equivalent if the province provided the same services. Only Quebec opted out. Finally, in 1977, faced with the spiralling costs of many programs but without the capacity to control costs, the federal government itself, in a sense, opted out. In the *Established Programs Financing Act* the federal government no longer paid roughly half of the costs of medicare, hospital insurance, and post-secondary education, but substituted an unconditional payment to the provinces, regardless of what they spent, which would increase with the growth of GNP. There have been no new major shared-cost programs since.[24]

Supreme Court decisions in the first quarter century of its independence did not represent ground-breaking federalist jurisprudence. While decisions and reasoning did show respect for *stare decisis*, there was also evident an attempt to rethink the Judicial Committee's approach to federalism. Although the Court did not explicitly refuse to follow precedent, it did chip away at the doctrinal legacy of the Judicial Committee, and it introduced elements of flexibility and dynamism into the abstract and rigid categorical reasoning which had come to characterise Canadian constitutional law.

The Supreme Court's opportunities were not long in coming. In 1951 the Court was asked to determine the constitutionality of a scheme whereby the federal and the Nova Scotian governments delegated some of their legislative authority to the other. This "inter-delegation" arrangement was rejected by the full court on the grounds that no such power was granted in the constitution. Chief Justice Rinfret adopted Lords Atkin's "watertight compartment" metaphor as a basis for confining each level of government to the heads of power distributed in 1867. Mr. Justice Rand, in arriving at the same conclusion, reasoned that legislative interdelegation was fundamentally inconsistent with the relationship of independent bodies: "Since neither is a creature nor a subordinate body of the other, the question is not only or chiefly whether one can delegate, but whether the other can accept." To accept a delegated power is to accept a subordinate position in relation to the delegator, Rand argued. "Would it be within constitutional propriety for the representatives both of the Sovereign and the people of Nova Scotia, to appropriate their legislative ritual to the enactment of a law not of Nova Scotia, but of Canada?" His answer was no.[25]

The decision was not universally accepted, and the reasoning appeared even more questionable the following year when the Court reached a seemingly different conclusion in another case. In this instance the federal government proposed to delegate its regulatory authority over the interprovincial and international marketing of potatoes to a marketing board established by the province of Prince Edward Island. Rand J. was faced with the argument he had used in the Nova Scotia case. If the province had no capacity to accept delegated authority, did it not follow that it could not create an entity which possessed that capacity? The Court decided that administrative delegation was somehow different from legislative delegation. With reference to the contested capacity of a single marketing board to undertake both federal and provincial responsibilities, Rand J. stated:

> We might just as logically conceive of it as a split personality with co-ordinate creators investing it with two orders of capacities. These metaphors and symbolisms are convenient devices to enable us to aggregate incidents or characteristics but carried too far they may threaten common sense.[26]

The two cases have been criticised as both dubious and inconsistent law. But they illustrate an apparent attempt by the court to introduce an element of flexibility into a rigid jurisprudential tradition, an element, perhaps, of "common sense."

An attempt to move away from the doctrinal purity of the Judicial Committee's decisions could be seen in the reasoning of a number of judges in the *Reference Re The Farm Products Marketing Act* in 1957. While the Court upheld the Ontario statute, provided that regulations under it would not deal with interprovincial trade, Mr. Justice Rand and others seized the occasion to reflect on the nature of trade and the difficulty of fitting a dynamic enterprise into somewhat rigid heads of power. The constitutional basis for provincial regulation had been its jurisdiction over property and civil rights; federal jurisdiction over trade and commerce did not encompass the regulation of rights arising out of contracts carried out within a single province. Rand J. rejected 92(13) as the authority for provincial regulation and located it instead in 92(16)—"Generally all matters of a merely local or private nature in the Province"—on the grounds that "The production and exchange of goods as an economic activity does not take place by virtue of positive law or civil rights; it is assumed as part of the residual free activity of men upon or around which law is imposed." Distinguishing insurance, on which the *Parsons* decision was based, Rand continued that

> the true conception of trade (in contradistinction to the static nature of rights, civil or property) is that of a dynamic, the creation and flow of goods from production to consumption or utilisation, as a individualized activity.[27]

By seeing trade as a dynamic flow rather than as a matter of contract, and by locating the regulation of local trade under 92(16), the extension of federal trade and commerce power became possible. In two notable decisions, the Court upheld national economic programs regulating both the trade and transportation of grain, and the regional division of the oil import market. That such regulations also affected property and civil rights was treated as a necessary feature of extraprovincial trade policy.

The Court continued to be troubled by the apparent conflict among jurisdiction and precedent, common sense, and the dynamics of trade. In *Carnation* the Court upheld a Quebec marketing plan for the sale of unpasteurised milk to

Carnation Co., although the bulk of the processed milk was clearly destined for interprovincial markets. Three years later, however, it struck down a Manitoba scheme contrived to regulate the marketing of eggs, on the grounds that its object was regulation of interprovincial trade in eggs. Finally, in 1978 it accepted as constitutional a federal–provincial scheme to control the production and marketing of eggs. One national and ten provincial marketing boards, each exercising powers delegated by the other, administered the plan.[28]

Scholarly commentators found it difficult to follow the reasoning in the decisions, in part because most judges issued separate opinions which often followed different paths though concurring in the result. Whatever the signs of a tentative rethinking of Canadian federalism, there was little that suggested a new and coherent theory of constitutional law. Nevertheless, the court's apparent recognition of a dynamic administrative interaction within a static source of legislative authority was neatly aligned with the prevailing acceptance of the practice of jurisdictional interdependence.

In the *Ontario Marketing Act* reference, Mr. Justice Rand also stepped outside the case to consider the doctrinal freedom which the Supreme Court possessed:

> The powers of this Court in the exercise of its jurisdiction are no less in scope than those formerly exercised in relation to Canada by the Judicial Committee. From time to time the Committee had modified the language used by it in the attribution of legislation to the various heads of ss. 91 and 92, and in its general interpretative formulations, and that incident of judicial power must, now, in the same manner and with the same authority, wherever deemed necessary, be exercised in revising or restating those formulations that have come down to us. This is a function inseparable from constitutional decision. It involves no distribution; it is rather a refinement of interpretation in application to the particularized and evolving features and aspects of matters which the intensive and extensive expansion of the life of the country inevitably presents.[29]

The Supreme Court also revised or restated the Judicial Committee's formulations in its early treatment of the federal government's residual power, contained in the peace, order and good government clause. In *Johannesson v. Rural Municipality of West St. Paul* in 1952, a provincial attempt—through a municipality—to regulate the location of an airport was found to conflict with federal jurisdiction over aeronautics, which fell under its residual power. Stating that the peace, order and good government clause was an enclave of federal power, Kellock J. argued in rather sweeping terms that

> Once the decision is made that a matter is of national interest and importance, so as to fall within the peace, order and good government clause, the provinces cease to have any legislative jurisdiction with regard thereto and the Dominion jurisdiction is exclusive.[30]

In *Munro v. National Capital Commission* (1966) the Court again used the residual clause as a basis for permitting the federal government to expropriate land for the establishment of a National Capital Region.[31]

Johannesson aroused little comment, for aeronautics had been placed within federal jurisdiction by the Judicial Committee, but *Munro* revealed to academic commentators that the Supreme Court was developing an original form of reasoning in approaching and locating a home for "matter." Professors Lyon and Atkey praised the court for not attempting to characterise the federal government's objective "until it had been fully examined in all its ramifications" and suggested that the "old fragmentary approach appears in this case to have been abandoned."

> Under that approach the judges would have begun by asking whether the subject matter of the legislation came within any of the heads of section 92, and, in a fragmentary view of the world the Act clearly relates to property in the provinces of Ontario and Quebec.... Then the Court would have had to ask whether the subject matter of the Act also came under a section 91 head or whether there were circumstances which made the subject matter a concern of Canada as a whole ... so as to displace it from section 92. That is, under the old, fragmentary approach there was virtually a built-in presumption of provincial competence with respect to matters of property and civil rights, and the very existence of the emergency doctrine for so long indicates the difficulty in displacing a statute from section 92 once it had found even tentative location there.[32]

Professors Whyte and Lederman took strong exception to the centralist implications of the Lyon–Atkey analysis:

> Does not the B.N.A. Act dictate the very approach that Lyon and Atkey stigmatize as old and fragmentary? Note that the Act contains two lists of enumerated powers and residuary powers. Why then, is a double-aspect approach to the legislation looked upon with such disfavour by the authors? Suppose the legislation purported to withdraw Ottawa from the Ottawa–Carleton regional government and to create a municipal government directly responsible to Parliament. Would single-aspect characterisation be quite so simple in that case?
> ... That is, if one were concerned with preserving a federal state is it not true that peace, order and good government would support legislation only in cases where provincial regulatory enactments were failing to meet a social or economic problem which threatened to undermine peace or order or good government in Canada?[33]

Clearly, the concern for provincial autonomy while the federal government expanded its power through the residual clause or through the enumerated heads of power was still occupying the minds of academics and those on the bench.

After almost two decades of independence, however, there seemed to be few signs that the federally appointed court was striking out on its own. Writing in 1968, Barry Strayer asked

> would the abolition of appeals bring real independence to the Supreme Court? Would the Court be free to take bold initiatives in developing the law, or would it be bound as before by its own past decisions and

those of the Imperial Tribunal? These questions cannot yet be answered with assurance.[34]

Writing in 1970, Donald Smiley observed that the courts had played a much more limited role than before in shaping the course of Canadian federalism, and he agreed with J.A. Corry that the "courts are retiring, or being retired, from their posts as the supervisors of the (federal) balance."[35] Smiley suggested that judicial review would probably continue to play a "relatively minor role" in the future.

> Most of the major issues between the federal and provincial governments seem not to be susceptible to judicial resolution. Business interests are less disposed than in the past to support judicial challenges to federal power. The machinery of intergovernmental consultation is becoming increasingly institutionalized and legitimized.... [O]ther "devices of adjustment"... offer alternative possibilities for constitutional adaptation. Judicial review results in the delineation of federal and provincial powers where the perceived needs of the federal system are for a more effective articulation of these powers. In general, the prospects are remote that the courts will reassume a major role as keepers of the federal balance.[36]

Professor Smiley's opinion was widely shared, but his dismissal of the Court's importance was premature. In the 1970s and 1980s, the Supreme Court played a central role in the political and policy disputes which characterised the end of "co-operative federalism." The provinces, business, unions, and the central government—in different combinations—brought disputes relating to economic regulation, resource development, the environment, and control of cable television to the judicial forum.

At the same time, the impartiality of the federally appointed Supreme Court was called into question. In 1973, Prime Minister Trudeau broke with almost fifty years of practice by passing over five more senior justices and promoting Bora Laskin to the position of Chief Justice. Although Trudeau, as Minister of Justice and later as Prime Minister, had also appointed Louis-Philippe Pigeon and Jean Beetz to the Court, the promotion of Laskin, noted for his criticism of the decentralising effect of Judicial Committee decisions, could not but give the appearance of stacking the court. Indeed, after some controversial decisions and with Laskin's appointment, Professor Peter Hogg felt it necessary to ask whether the Supreme Court was biased in constitutional cases, and to argue that it was not.[37]

The reason Smiley and others proved to be wrong, in part at least, was a remarkable change in the nature of federalism in the 1970s. A decade of negotiations over constitutional reform ended for a time when Quebec refused to accept the agreement negotiated at Victoria in 1971. The violence of the FLQ had exploded in the October 1970 crisis. The federal government under Prime Minister Trudeau faced the threat of the Parti Québécois, a threat which became more menacing with the party's electoral victory in 1976. The recession of the mid-1970s placed an increasing burden on all levels of government, and ultimately forced the

Trudeau government to introduce its controversial anti-inflation legislation. Governments seemed more inclined to regulate business, along a wide front, including the environment, and business more determined to challenge regulatory legislation. The soaring price of world oil and the energy crisis led to a confrontation between Ottawa and the oil-producing provinces, as the federal government attempted to devise an energy policy that would give it entry into the industry and enable it to capture some of the economic rents for national purposes. Finally, in 1975–76 the process of constitutional reform began again, and before the decade was out the Prime Minister was threatening to act unilaterally to secure constitutional patriation and a charter of rights if he could not secure provincial agreement. In most aspects of federal–provincial relations, unilateralism had replaced negotiation, and stubbornness was more evident than compromise.

It was inevitable under these changing conditions that there would be increasing recourse to the courts to resolve conflicts between governments or between the state and enterprise. As Patrick Monohan points out in the chapter of his book reprinted here, between 1950 and 1979 only 3.6 per cent of Supreme Court decisions were made on federalist cases (and many of them late in the 1970s); between 1980 and 1984 there were more cases than in the previous decade and 10.9 per cent were federalist cases. The dramatic increase in the number of reference cases and of interventions by both levels of government also suggests that governments were looking more often to the Supreme Court to resolve the problems of divided and contested jurisdiction.

Although the Supreme Court decisions on the Charter captured the headlines, there were a number of very important decisions in the late 1970s and the following decade. Politically, the period seemed to be one of growing provincial assertiveness, if not power, but the decisions of the Supreme Court in a number of key areas supported the assertion of federal jurisdiction. Federal jurisdiction was upheld in some areas of communication, including cable TV, and there the Court gave new scope to the federal trade and commerce power and the national dimension aspect of peace, order and good government.

In *General Motors v. City National Leasing*, (1989) the Court resuscitated the "general" federal power over trade and commerce. Ironically, the suggestion that there could be such a general trade power was first provided by the Judicial Committee in the case that has been relied upon to restrict that power: *Citizens Insurance Company v. Parsons* (1881). In that case, Sir Montague Smith restricted the federal power in stating that it did not extend to "the power to regulate by legislation the contracts of a particular business or trade." At the same time, His Lordship noted that "it may be" that s.91(2) "would include general regulation of trade affecting the whole Dominion."

This sentence remained a potential source of jurisdiction for over one hundred years. After being alluded to by Laskin C.J. in *MacDonald v. Vapor Canada* (1977) and used in a concurring judgment of Dickson J. in *A.G. Canada v. C.N. Transportation* (1983) this potential was finally actualized in *City National Leasing*. The decision provides not only an expansion of federal jurisdiction but a classical example of jurisprudential development. In a masterful style, Dickson, by then Chief Justice, melds together a century's worth of largely failed attempts to give effect to a general trade and commerce power which provides the federal government with a basis for legislation while at the same time limits its potential to destroy provincial jurisdiction over trade.

On another front, *R. v. Crown Zellerbach* (1988) provided an expansion of the national aspect of peace, order and good government. The judicial debate carried on between Le Dain and La Forest JJ. mirrored the classic Laskin C.J. and Beetz J. positions in the *Anti-Inflation Reference*. In *Crown Zellerbach*, however, ocean pollution was found to be a matter sufficiently distinct to satisfy a majority of the Court that it could fall within federal jurisdiction. Again, the majority decision painstakingly reviews and revises the doctrinal history in finding an expanded, but not unlimited, source of federal jurisdiction.

In federalism and Charter decisions the Supreme Court owed much to the analytical ability and refined literary skill of Chief Justice Brian Dickson. His retirement in 1990 ended another chapter in the history of judicial review. As the new decade dawns it remains to be seen whether the Court under the new leadership of Chief Justice Lamer will continue to break new ground in re-examining an old, but thanks to the courts, a continually evolving federal constitution.

NOTES

1. *Prince v. Gagnon* (1883), 8 A.C. 103 at 105.

2. See, for example, C.G. Pierson, *Canada and the Privy Council* (London, 1960).

3. For an account of Cahan's initiative see W.H. McConnell, "The Judicial Review of Prime Minister Bennett's 'New Deal,'" *Osgoode Hall Law Journal* (1968): 78–82.

4. Mark McGuigan, "Precedent and Policy in the Supreme Court of Canada," *Canadian Bar Review* 45 (1968): 627–38.

5. Louis-Philippe Pigeon, "The Meaning of Provincial Autonomy," *Canadian Bar Review* (1951): 1126–35; Bora Laskin, "The Supreme Court of Canada: A Final Court of and for Canadians," *Canadian Bar Review* 29 (1951): 1038–79.

6. Pigeon, "Meaning of Provincial Autonomy," 1127.

7. Ibid., 1133.

8. Ibid., 1132–33.

9. Ibid., 1133.

10. Ibid., 1135.

11. Laskin, "The Supreme Court of Canada," 1071.

12. Ibid., 1073.

13. *Harrison v. Carswell* [1976] 2 S.C.R. 200.

14. Cardozo, *The Nature of the Judicial Process* (1921), 141.

15. Katherine Swinton, "Bora Laskin and Federalism," *University of Toronto Law Journal* 35 (1981): 353.

16. Thomas J. Courchene, "Towards a Protected Society: The Politicization of Economic Life," *Canadian Journal of Economics* (November 1980).

17. Royal Commission on Dominion–Provincial Relations *Report*, Book II, *Recommendations* (Ottawa, 1940).

18. *Employment and Income with Special Reference to the Initial Period of Reconstruction* (Ottawa, 1945).

19. See J.L. Granatstein, *Canada's War: The Politics of the Mackenzie King Government 1939–1945* (Toronto, 1975), 249 ff.

20. Canada, *Dominion–Provincial Conference on Reconstruction* (Ottawa, 1945, 1946).

21. Vernon C. Fowke, "The National Policy Old and New," *Canadian Journal of Economics and Political Science* 18, 3 (August 1952): 271–86.

22. Richard Bastien, *Federalism and Decentralization: Where Do We Stand?* (Ottawa, 1981), 14.

23. Pierre Trudeau, then a professor, was one of the most outspoken opponents of the use of the federal spending power for purposes under provincial jurisdiction and supported Premier Duplessis in his refusal to accept federal aid to the universities. Trudeau cited Professor Corry who wrote that he found it "extraordinary that no one has challenged the constitutionality of the assumed spending power before the Supreme Court" and added:

> I share his wonderment; but I even find it more extraordinary that political scientists fail to see the eroding effect that the "power of the purse" will have on Canadian democracy if the present construction continues to prevail, and in particular what chaos will prevail if provincial governments borrow federal logic and begin using their own "power of the purse" to meddle in federal affairs.

Prime Minister Trudeau seemed to be less categorical in his advocacy of classical federalism than Professor Trudeau. (See "Federal Grants to Universities" and "The Practice and Theory of Federalism," reprinted in P.E. Trudeau, *Federalism and the French Canadians* (Toronto, 1968).)

24. The unrestricted spending power of the federal government remained a contentious issue, however, and while the Meech Lake/Langevin Block Accord recognized the legitimacy of the power, it also stated:

> The Government of Canada shall provide reasonable compensation to the government of a province that chooses not to participate in a national shared-cost program that is established by the Government of Canada after the coming into force of this section in an area of exclusive provincial jurisdiction, if the province carried on a program or initiative that is compatible with the national objectives.

25. *A.G. Nova Scotia v. A.G. Canada* [1951] S.C.R. 31.

26. *P.E.I. Marketing Board v. Willis* [1952] 2 S.C.R. 814. For a critique of the decisions see P.W. Hogg, *Constitutional Law of Canada*, 2d ed. (1985), 295 ff.

27. *Reference Re The Farm Products Marketing Act* [1957] S.C.R. 198.

28. *Carnation Co. v. Quebec Agricultural Marketing Board* [1968] S.C.R. 238; *A.G. Manitoba v. Manitoba Egg and Poultry Association* [1971] S.C.R. 689; *Re Agricultural Products Marketing Act* [1978] 2 S.C.R. 1198.

29. Reference [1957] *Ontario Marketing Act* 168 S.C.R. at 212–213.

30. *Johannesson v. Rural Municipality of West St. Paul* [1952] 1 S.C.R. 292.

31. *Munro v. National Capital Commission* [1966] S.C.R. 663.

32. J.M. Lyon and R.G. Atkey, *Canadian Constitutional Law in a Modern Perspective* (Toronto, 1970), 698–99.

33. J.D. Whyte and W.R. Lederman, *Canadian Constitutional Law* (Toronto, 1977), 7, 65–66.

34. Barry Strayer, *Judicial Review of Legislation in Canada* (Toronto, 1968), 27.

35. Donald V. Smiley, *Constitutional Adaptation and Canadian Federalism since 1945* (Ottawa, 1970), 39.

36. Ibid., 40.

37. Peter Hogg, "Is the Supreme Court Biased in Constitutional Cases?" *Canadian Bar Review* 57 (1979): 721–39.

INFLATION

REFERENCE RE ANTI-INFLATION ACT[◇]

The Canadian Parliament, with the political consent of the provinces, passed the *Anti-Inflation Act* in 1975. The Act authorized the federal government to control wages and prices in what it considered to be key economic sectors of private business, the federal public sector and the public sector of "opted in" provincial governments. The legislation was challenged by various Ontario public employees' unions and finally referred to the Supreme Court of Canada in 1976. The Court held, Beetz and de Grandpré dissenting, that the Act was *intra vires* the federal government.

LASKIN C.J. (Judson, Spence and Dickson JJ. concurring):
Chief Justice Laskin began his decision by reviewing the decisions of the Judicial Committee and the Supreme Court of Canada which addressed the federal government's "Peace, Order, and good Government" power.

What emerges from the lines of cases up to the *Snider* case are differences more of degree than of kind about the scope of the federal general power. It is true that neither the *Russell* case nor, indeed, Lord Watson's observations in the *Local Prohibition* case fitted into Viscount Haldane's emphasis on the need for exceptional circumstances, but even on that standard there was no preclusion against finding that a peacetime crisis would warrant resort to the general power in support of federal legislation.

Lord Watson's "national dimensions" proposition, which appears to have been studiously ignored by the Privy Council through to the *Snider* case, was mentioned by it in the *Labour Conventions* case, [1937] A.C. 326, where Lord Atkin said of Lord Watson's words that "they laid down no principle of constitutional law, and were cautious words intended to safeguard possible eventualities which no one at the time had any interest or desire to define." It is my view that a similar approach of caution is demanded even today, both against a loose and unrestricted scope of the general power and against a fixity of its scope that would preclude resort to it in circumstances now unforeseen. Indeed, I do not see how this Court can, consistently with its supervisory function in respect of the distribution of legislative

---

◇[1976] 2 S.C.R. 373.

power, preclude in advance and irrespective of any supervening situations a resort to the general power or, for that matter, to any other head of legislative authority. This is not to say that clear situations are to be unsettled, but only that a constitution designed to serve this country in years ahead ought to be regarded as a resilient instrument capable of adaptation to changing circumstances . . . .

Chief Justice Duff attempted in his extensive reasons in the *Natural Products Marketing Reference* a synthesis of the preceding case law touching the general power but, significantly, he began his discussion with the following prelude:

> . . . There is no dispute now that the exception which excludes from the ambit of the general power all matters assigned to the exclusive authority of the legislatures must be given its full effect. Nevertheless, it has been laid down that matters normally comprised within the subjects enumerated in section 92 may, in extraordinary circumstances, acquire aspects of such paramount significance as to take them outside the sphere of that section.

What followed was a reconciliation of Lord Watson's national dimensions approach with Viscount Haldane's notion of the extraordinary, by requiring that there be some crisis or peril to support federal legislation for the peace, order and good government of Canada, of which war, present of apprehended, was an example. This did not exclude peacetime crises . . . .

I come, finally, to the *Canada Temperance Federation* case. The Privy Council was fully entitled to overrule the *Russell* case and could have marshalled intervening observations in various cases to support it in doing so. But it felt, to use its own words, that "the decision now sought to be overruled has stood for over sixty years . . . and [it] must be regarded as firmly embedded in the constitutional law of Canada and it is impossible now to depart from it." The importance of Viscount Simon's reasons in the *Canada Temperance Federation* case lies not only in his rejection of the explanation of the *Russell* case given in the *Snider* case but also in his restatement of the scope of the federal general power without advertence either to the *Board of Commerce* case or to the *Fort Frances* case and even without reference to Lord Watson's observations in the *Local Prohibition* case. Of course, as I have already noted, general propositions must be viewed in the context of the facts and issues out of which they arise, and I emphasise again the point made earlier that it would be unwise to nail down any head of legislative power in such firm fashion as to make it incapable of application to situations as yet unforeseen.

The Attorney General of Canada, supported by the Attorney General of Ontario, put his position in support of the *Anti-Inflation Act* on alternative bases. He relied, primarily, on the *Canada Temperance Federation* case, contending that the Act, directed to containment and reduction of inflation, concerned a matter which went beyond local or private or provincial concern and was of a nature which engaged vital national interests, among them the integrity of the Canadian monetary system which was unchallengeably within exclusive federal protection and control. He urged, in the alternative, that there was an economic crisis amounting to an emergency or exceptional peril to economic stability sufficient to warrant federal intervention, and, if not an existing peril, there was a reasonable apprehension of an impending one that justified federal intervention through the legislation in question which was designed to support measures and policies of a fiscal and monetary character which were undoubtedly within Parliament's legislative authority....

Since there was, in general, a concession by those opposing the legislation that it would be valid if it were what I may call crisis legislation, and since the proponents of the legislation urged this as an alternative ground on which its validity should be sustained, it appears to me to be the wise course to consider first whether the *Anti-Inflation Act* can be supported on that footing. If it is sustainable as crisis legislation, it becomes unnecessary to consider the broader ground advanced in its support, and this because, especially in constitutional cases, Courts should not, as a rule, go any further than is necessary to determine the main issue before them.

The competing arguments on the question whether the Act is supportable as crisis legislation raised four main issues: 1. Did the *Anti-Inflation Act* itself belie the federal contention because of the form of the Act and, in particular because of the exclusion of the provincial public sector from its imperative scope, notwithstanding that it is framed as a temporary measure albeit subject to extension of its operation? 2. Is the federal contention assisted by the preamble to the statute? 3. Does the extrinsic evidence put before the Court, and other matters of which the Court can take judicial notice without extrinsic material to back it up, show that there was a rational basis for the Act as a crisis measure? 4. Is it a tenable argument that exceptional character could be lent to the legislation as rising beyond local or provincial concerns because Parliament could reasonably take the view that it was a necessary measure to fortify action in other related areas of admittedly federal authority, such as the monetary policy? . . .

The Attorney General of Canada relied upon the preamble to the *Anti-Inflation Act* both in respect of his primary argument and in respect of his alternative argument. He emphasized the words therein "that the containment and reduction of inflation has become a matter of *serious* national concern" and as well the following words that "to accomplish such containment and reduction of inflation it is *necessary* to restrain profit margins, prices, dividends and compensation" (the italicized words were especially emphasized). I do not regard it as telling against the Attorney General's alternative position that the very word "emergency" was not used. Forceful language would not carry the day for the Attorney General of Canada if the circumstances attending its use did not support the constitutional significance sought to be drawn from it. Of course, the absence of any preamble would weaken the assertion of crisis conditions, and I have already drawn attention to the fact that no preamble suggesting a critical economic situation, indeed no preamble at all was included in the legislation challenged in the *Board of Commerce* case.

The preamble in the present case is sufficiently indicative that Parliament was introducing a far-reaching program prompted by what in its view was a serious national condition. The validity of the *Anti-Inflation Act* does not, however, stand or fall on that preamble, but the preamble does provide a base for assessing the gravity of the circumstances which called forth the legislation.

This brings me to the third of the four issues above-mentioned, namely, the relevancy and weight of the extrinsic evidence and the assistance to be derived from judicial notice. When, as in this case, an issue is raised that exceptional circumstances underlie resort to the legislative power which may properly be invoked in such circumstances, the Court may be asked to consider extrinsic material bearing on the circumstances alleged, both in support of and in denial of the lawful exercise of legislative authority. In considering such material and assessing its weight, the Court does not look at it in terms of whether it provides proof of the exceptional circumstances as a matter of fact. The matter concerns social and economic policy and hence governmental and legislative judgment. It may be that the existence of exceptional circumstances is so notorious as to enable the Court, of its own motion, to take judicial notice of them without reliance on extrinsic material to inform it. Where this is not so evident, the extrinsic material need go only so far as to persuade the Court that there is a rational basis for the legislation which it is attributing to the head of power invoked in this case in support of its validity.

There is before this Court material from Statistics Canada, upon which the Court is justified in relying, which, proceeding from a base of 100 in 1971, shows that the purchasing power of the dollar dropped to 0.78 by September 1974 and to 0.71 in September 1975. On the same base, the cost of living index rose to 127.9 by September 1974 and 141.5 by September 1975, with food, taken alone, and weighted at 28 per cent of all the items taken into calculation, showing a rise to 147.3 in September 1974 and 166.6 in September 1975 . . . .

There is another consideration that arises from the submissions, particularly those of the Canadian Labour Congress, in opposition to the validity of the *Anti-Inflation Act* as a measure justified by crisis circumstances. The consideration I refer to is based on Professor Lipsey's study and on his conclusion that the policy adopted in the *Anti-Inflation Act* is not one that can, on the basis of experience elsewhere and on his appraisal as an economist, be expected to reduce the rate of inflation by more than one to two per cent. The answer to this submission is simple, and it is an answer that has been consistently given by the Courts, namely, that the wisdom or expediency or likely success of a particular policy expressed in legislation is not subject to judicial review. Hence, it is not for the Court to say in this case that because the means adopted to realize a desirable end, i.e., the containment and reduction of inflation in Canada, may not be effectual, those means are beyond the legislative power of Parliament . . . .

In my opinion, this Court would be unjustified in concluding, on the submissions in this case and on all the material put before it, that the Parliament of Canada did not have a rational basis for regarding the *Anti-Inflation Act* as a measure which, in its judgment, was temporarily necessary to meet a situation of economic crisis imperilling the well-being of the people of Canada as a whole and requiring Parliament's stern intervention in the interest of the country as a whole. That there may have been other periods of crisis in which no similar action was taken is beside the point.

The rationality of the judgment so exercised is, in my view, supported by a consideration of the fourth of the issues which I enumerated above. The fact that there had been rising inflation at the time federal action was taken, that inflation is regarded as a monetary phenomenon and that monetary policy is admittedly within exclusive federal jurisdiction persuades me that the Parliament of Canada was entitled, in the circumstances then prevailing and to which I have already referred, to act as it did from the springboard of its jurisdiction over monetary policy and, I venture to add, with additional support from its power in relation to the regulation of trade and commerce. The Government White Paper refers to a prices and incomes policy as one element in a four-pronged program of which the first engages its fiscal and monetary authority; and although the White Paper states that the Government rejects the use of severe monetary and fiscal restraints to stop inflation because of the alleged heavy immediate cost in unemployment and foregone output, it could seek to blend policies in those areas with a prices and incomes policy under the circumstances revealed by the extrinsic material.

Since no argument was addressed to the trade and commerce power I content myself with observing only that it provides the Parliament of Canada with a foothold in respect of "the general regulation of trade affecting the whole Dominion," to use the words of the Privy Council in *Citizens Insurance Co. v. Parsons* (1881). The *Anti-Inflation Act* is not directed to any particular trade. It is directed to suppliers of commodities and services in general and to the public services of governments, and to the relationship of those suppliers and of the public services to those suppliers and of the public services to those employed by and in them, and to their overall relationship to the public. With respect to some of such suppliers and with respect to the federal public service, federal legislative power needs no support from the existence of exceptional circumstances to justify the introduction of a policy of restraint to combat inflation.

The economic interconnection with other suppliers and with provincial public services, underlined by collective bargaining conducted by, or under the policy umbrella of trade unions with Canada-wide operations and affiliations, is a matter of public general knowledge of which the Court can take judicial notice. The extrinsic material does not reveal any distinction in the operation and effect of inflation in respect of those economic areas which are ordinarily within and those ordinarily outside of effective federal regulatory control. In enacting the *Anti-Inflation Act* as a measure for the peace, order and good government of Canada, Parliament is not opening an area of legislative authority which would otherwise have no anchorage at all in the federal catalogue of legislative powers but, rather, it is proceeding from legislative power bases which entitle it to wage war on inflation through monetary and fiscal policies and entitle it to embrace within the *Anti-Inflation Act* some of the sectors covered thereby but not all. The circumstances recounted above justify it in invoking its general power to extend its embrace as it has done.

For all the foregoing reasons, I would hold that the *Anti-Inflation Act* is valid legislation for the peace, order and good government of Canada and does not, in the circumstances under which it was enacted and having regard to its temporary character, invade provincial legislative jurisdiction . . . .

RITCHIE J. (Martland and Pigeon JJ. concurring):
I have had the privilege of reading the reasons for judgment of the Chief Justice and his comprehensive review of the authorities satisfies me that the answer to the question of whether or not the *Anti-Inflation Act* is *ultra vires* the Parliament of Canada, must depend upon whether or not the legislation was enacted to combat

a national economic emergency. I use the phrase "national emergency" in the sense in which I take it to have been used by Lord Wright in *Co-operative Committee on Japanese Canadians v. Attorney General of Canada*, (1947) and accepted by this Court in the *Reference as to the Validity of the Wartime Leasehold Regulations* (1950). In those cases the "emergency" was occasioned by war and the aftermath of war, but I see nothing to exclude the application of the principles there enunciated from a situation created by highly exceptional economic conditions prevailing in times of peace.

In my opinion such conditions exist where there can be said to be an urgent and critical situation adversely affecting all Canadians and being of such proportions as to transcend the authority vested in the legislatures of the provinces and thus presenting an emergency which can only be effectively dealt with by Parliament in the exercise of the powers conferred upon it by s. 91 of the *British North America Act* "to make laws for the peace, order and good government of Canada." The authority of Parliament in this regard is, in my opinion, limited to dealing with critical conditions and the necessity to which they give rise and must perforce be confined to legislation of a temporary character.

I do not consider that the validity of the Act rests upon the constitutional doctrine exemplified in earlier decisions of the Privy Council, to all of which the Chief Justice has made reference, and generally known as the "national dimension" or "national concern" doctrine. It is not difficult to envisage many different circumstances which could give rise to national concern, but at least since the *Japanese Canadians* case, I take it to be established that unless such concern is made manifest by circumstances amounting to a national emergency, Parliament is not endowed under the cloak of the "peace, order and good government" clause with the authority to legislate in relation to matters reserved to the Provinces under s. 92 of the *British North America Act*. In this regard I am in full agreement with the reasons for judgment prepared for delivery by my brother Beetz which I have had the advantage of reading, and I have little to add to what he said.

I should also say, however, that I cannot find that the authority of Parliament to pass legislation such as the present Act stems from any of the enumerated classes of subjects referred to in s. 91. The source of the federal power in relation to the *Anti-Inflation Act* must, in my opinion, be found in the peace, order and good government clause, and the aura of federal authority to which that clause relates can in my view only be extended so as to invade the provincial area when the legislation is directed to coping with a genuine emergency in the sense to which I have made reference . . . .

The provisions of the Act quite clearly reveal the decision of Parliament that exceptional measures were considered to be required to combat this emergency and it has not been seriously suggested that these provisions were colourably enacted for any other purpose.

I am accordingly satisfied that the record discloses that in enacting the *Anti-Inflation Act* the Parliament of Canada was motivated by a sense of urgent necessity created by highly exceptional circumstances and that a judgment declaring the Act to be *ultra vires* could only be justified by reliance on very clear evidence that an emergency had not arisen when the statute was enacted.

BEETZ J. (de Grandpré J. concurring) dissenting:
... Two submissions have been made in support of the validity of the *Anti-Inflation Act*. The first submission relates to a constitutional doctrine founded on judicial decisions and known as the national emergency doctrine.

The first submission made by Counsel for Canada and for Ontario is that the subject matter of the *Anti-Inflation Act* is the containment and the reduction of inflation. This subject matter, it is argued, goes beyond local provincial concern or interest and is from its inherent nature the concern of Canada as a whole and falls within the competence of Parliament as a matter affecting the peace, order and good government of Canada. It was further submitted that the competence of Parliament over the subject of inflation may be supported by reference to the following heads of s. 91 of the Constitution: [2, 3, 4, 14, 15]. . . .

If the first submission is correct, then it could also be said that the promotion of economic growth or the limits to growth or the protection of the environment have become global problems and now constitute subject matters of national concern going beyond local provincial concern or interest and coming within the exclusive legislative authority of Parliament. It could equally be argued that older subjects such as the business of insurance or labour relations, which are not specifically listed in the enumeration of federal and provincial powers and have been held substantially to come within provincial jurisdiction have outgrown provincial authority whenever the business of insurance or labour have become national in scope. It is not difficult to speculate as to where this line of reasoning would lead: a fundamental feature of the Constitution, its federal nature, the distribution of powers between Parliament and the Provincial Legislatures, would disappear not gradually but rapidly.

I cannot be persuaded that the first submission expresses the state of the law. It goes against the persistent trend of the authorities. It is founded upon an erroneous characterization of the *Anti-Inflation Act*. As for the cases relied upon by Counsel to support the submission, they are quite distinguishable and they do not, in my view, stand for what they are said to stand . . . .

I have no reason to doubt that the *Anti-Inflation Act* is part of a more general program aimed at inflation and which may include fiscal and monetary measures and government expenditure policies. I am prepared to accept that inflation was the occasion or the reason for its enactment. But I do not agree that inflation is the subject matter of the Act. In order to characterize an enactment, one must look at its operation, at its effects and at the scale of its effects rather than at its ultimate purpose where the purpose is practically all embracing. If for instance Parliament is to enact a tax law or a monetary law as a part of an anti-inflation program no one will think that such laws have ceased to be a tax law or a monetary law and that they have become subsumed into their ultimate purpose so that they should rather be characterized as "anti-inflation laws," an expression which, in terms of actual content, is not meaningful. They plainly remain and continue to be called a tax law or a monetary law, although they have been enacted by reason of an inflationary situation . . . . Similarly, the *Anti-Inflation Act* is, as its preamble states, clearly a law relating to the control of profit margins, prices, dividends and compensation, that is, with respect to the provincial private sector, a law relating to the regulation of local trade, to contract and to property and civil rights in the provinces, enacted as part of a program to combat inflation. Property and civil rights in the provinces are, for the greater part, the pith and substance or the subject matter of the *Anti-Inflation Act*. According to the Constitution, Parliament may fight inflation with the powers put at its disposal by the specific heads enumerated in s. 91 or by such powers as are outside of s. 92. But it cannot, apart from a declaration of national emergency or from a constitutional amendment, fight inflation with powers exclusively reserved to the provinces, such as the power to make laws in relation to property and civil rights. This is what Parliament has in fact attempted to do in enacting the *Anti-Inflation Act*.

The authorities relied upon by Counsel for Canada and Ontario in support of the first submission are connected with the constitutional doctrine that became known as the national concern doctrine or national dimension doctrine....

I fail to see how the authorities which so decide lend support to the first submission. They had the effect of adding by judicial process new matters or new classes of matters to the federal list of powers. However, this was done only in cases where a new matter was not an aggregate but had a degree of unity that made it indivisible, an identity which made it distinct from provincial matters and a sufficient consistence to retain the bounds of form. The scale upon which these new matters enabled Parliament to touch on provincial matters had also to be taken into consideration before they were recognized as federal matters: if an enumerated federal power designated in broad terms such as the trade and commerce power had to be construed so as not to embrace and smother provincial powers (*Parson's* case) and destroy the equilibrium of the Constitution, the Courts must be all the more careful not to add hitherto unnamed powers of a diffuse nature to the list of federal powers.

The "containment and reduction of inflation" does not pass muster as a new subject matter. It is an aggregate of several subjects some of which form a substantial part of provincial jurisdiction. It is totally lacking in specificity. It is so pervasive that it knows no bounds. Its recognition as a federal head of power would render most provincial powers nugatory....

It was argued that other heads of power enumerated in s. 91 of the Constitution and which relate for example to the regulation of trade and commerce, to currency and coinage, to banking, incorporation of banks and the issue of paper money may be indicative of the breadth of Parliament's jurisdiction in economic matters. They do not enable Parliament to legislate otherwise than in relation to their objects and it was not argued that the *Anti-Inflation Act* was in relation to their objects. The Act does not derive any assistance from those powers any more than the legislation found invalid in the *Board of Commerce* case.

For those reasons, the first submission fails.

The second submission made in support of the validity of the *Anti-Inflation Act* is that the inflationary situation was in October of 1975 and still is such as to constitute a national emergency of the same significance as war, pestilence or insurrection and that there is in Parliament an implied power to deal with the emergency for the safety of Canada as a whole; that such situation of exceptional necessity justified the enactment of the impugned legislation . . . .

Before I deal with this second submission I should state at the outset that I am prepared to assume the validity of the following propositions:

1. the power of Parliament under the national emergency doctrine is not confined to war situations or to situations of transition from war to peace; an emergency of the nature contemplated by the doctrine may arise in peace time;

2. inflation may constitute such an emergency;

3. Parliament may validly exercise its national emergency powers before an emergency actually occurs; a state of apprehended emergency or crisis suffices to justify Parliament in taking preventive measures including measures to contain and reduce inflation where inflation amounts to state of apprehended crisis.

In order to decide whether the _Anti-Inflation Act_ is valid as a national emergency measure, one must first consider the way in which the emergency doctrine operates in the Canadian Constitution; one must find, in the second place whether the _Anti-Inflation Act_ was in fact enacted on the basis that it was a measure to deal with a national emergency in the constitutional sense.

In referring to the emergency doctrine, the Judicial Committee has sometimes used expressions which would at first appear to indicate that there is no difference between the national dimension or national concern doctrine and the emergency doctrine, the latter being but an instance of the first, or that the distribution of powers between Parliament and the provincial legislatures is not altered by a state of emergency, or again that when Parliament deals with a matter which in normal times would be an exclusively provincial matter, it does so under a federal aspect or in a new relation which lies outside of s. 92 of the Constitution.

Counsel for Canada and for Ontario have relied upon them for the proposition that the difference between the national concern doctrine and the emergency doctrine is one of the semantics, which perhaps explains why the Ontario factum does not support the validity of the _Anti-Inflation Act_ on the basis of an emergency although Counsel for Ontario said that his position did not, because of that reason of semantics, differ from that of Counsel for Canada. The latter insisted that the difference between the two doctrines is only one of form but made two separate submissions based on each of the two doctrines.

I disagree with the proposition that the national concern or national dimension doctrine and the emergency doctrine amount to the same. Even if it could be said that "where an emergency exists it is the emergency which gives the matter its dimension of national concern or interest" . . . the emergency does not give the matter the same dimensions as the national concern doctrine applied for instance in the _Aeronautics_ case, in the _Johannesson_ case or in the _Munro_ case. The national concern doctrine illustrated by these cases applies in practice as if certain heads such as aeronautics or the development and conservation of the national capital were added to the categories of subject matters enumerated in s. 91 of the Constitution when it is found by the Courts that, in substance, a class of subjects not enumerated in either s. 91 or s. 92 lies outside the first fifteen heads enumerated in s. 92 and is not of a merely local or private nature. Whenever the national concern theory is applied, the effect is permanent although it is limited by the indentity of the subject newly recognized to be of national dimensions. By contrast, the power of Parliament to make laws in a great crisis knows no limits other than those which are dictated by the nature of the crisis. But one of those limits is the temporary nature of the crisis . . . .

Perhaps it does not matter very much whether one chooses to characterize legislation enacted under the emergency power as legislation relating to the emergency or whether one prefers to consider it as legislation relating to the particular subject matter which it happens to regulate. But if one looks at the practical effects of the exercise of the emergency power, one must conclude that it operates so as to give to Parliament for all purposes necessary to deal with the emergency, concurrent and paramount jurisdiction over matters which would normally fall within exclusive provincial jurisdiction. To that extent, the exercise of that power amounts to a temporary *pro tanto* amendment of a federal Constitution by the unilateral action of Parliament. The legitimacy of that power is derived from the Constitution: when the security and the continuation of the Constitution and of the nation are at stake, the kind of power commensurate with the situation "is only to be found in that part of the Constitution which establishes power in the State as a whole" (Viscount Haldane in the *Fort Frances* case).

The extraordinary nature and the constitutional features of the emergency power of Parliament dictate the manner and form in which it should be invoked and exercised. It should not be an ordinary manner and form. At the very least, it cannot be a manner and form which admits of the slightest degree of ambiguity to be resolved by interpretation. In cases where the existence of an emergency may be a matter of controversy, it is imperative that Parliament should not have recourse to its emergency power except in the most explicit terms indicating that it is acting on the basis of that power. Parliament cannot enter the normally forbidden area of provincial jurisdiction unless it gives an unmistakable signal that it is acting pursuant to its extraordinary power. Such a signal is not conclusive to support the legitimacy of the action of Parliament but its absence is fatal. It is the duty of the courts to uphold the Constitution, not to seal its suspension, and they cannot decide that a suspension is legitimate unless the highly exceptional power to suspend it has been expressly invoked by Parliament. Also, they cannot entertain a submission implicitly asking them to make findings of fact justifying even a temporary interference with the normal constitutional process unless Parliament has first assumed responsibility for affirming in plain words that the facts are such as to justify the interference. The responsibility of the Courts begins after the affirmation has been made. If there is no such affirmation, the Constitution receives its normal application. Otherwise, it is the Courts which are indirectly called upon to proclaim the state of emergency whereas it is essential that this be done by a politically responsible body.

We have not been referred to a single judicial decision, and I know of none, ratifying the exercise by Parliament of its national emergency power where the constitutional foundation for the exercise of that power had not been given clear utterance to. And, apart from judicial decision, I know of no precedent where it could be said that Parliament had attempted to exercise such an extraordinary power by way of suggestion or innuendo.

The use of the national emergency power enables Parliament to override provincial laws in potentially every field: it must be explicit....

...What is required from Parliament when it purports to exercise its extraordinary emergency power is any situation where a dispute could arise as to the existence of the emergency and as to the constitutional foundation of its action, is an indication, I would even say a proclamation, in the title, the preamble or the text of the instrument, which cannot possibly leave any doubt that, given the nature of the crisis, Parliament in fact purports to act on the basis of that power. The statutes of Canada and the Canada Gazette contain several examples of laws, proclamations and orders-in-council which leave room for no doubt that they have been enacted pursuant to the exceptional emergency power of Parliament, or issued or passed under the authority of an act of Parliament enacted by virtue of that power....

The *Anti-Inflation Act* fails in my opinion to pass the test of explicitness required to signal that it has been enacted pursuant to the national emergency power of Parliament.

The preamble has been much relied upon:

> WHEREAS the Parliament of Canada recognizes that inflation in Canada at current levels is contrary to the interests of all Canadians and that the containment and reduction of inflation has become a matter of serious national concern;
>
> AND WHEREAS to accomplish such containment and reduction of inflation it is necessary to restrain profit margins, prices, dividends and compensation;

The words "a matter of serious national concern" have been emphasised. I remain unimpressed.

The death penalty is a matter of national concern. So is abortion. So is the killing or maiming of innumerable people by impaired drivers. So is the traffic in narcotics and drugs. One can conceive of several drastic measures, all coming within the ordinary jurisdiction of the Parliament of Canada, and which could be preceded by a preamble reciting that a given situation had become a matter of serious national concern. I fail to see how the adding of the word "serious" can convey the meaning that Parliament has decided to embark upon an exercise of its extraordinary emergency power. The *Canada Water Act*, 1969–70 (Can.), c. 52 on the constitutionality of which, again, I refrain from expressing any view, contains a preamble where it is stated that pollution of the water resources of Canada has become "a matter of urgent national concern." Is the *Canada Water Act* an emergency measure in the constitutional sense? It does not seem to present itself as such. How is a matter of serious national concern to be distinguished from a matter of urgent national concern? I cannot read the preamble of the *Anti-Inflation Act* as indicating that the act was passed to deal with a national emergency in the constitutional sense.

ENERGY

CANADIAN INDUSTRIAL GAS & OIL LTD. v. GOVERNMENT OF SASKATCHEWAN ET AL.◇

The Government of Saskatchewan passed Bill 42 following the dramatic increase in world oil prices in 1973. As stated in the majority decision:

> The practical consequence of the application of this legislation is that the Government of Saskatchewan will acquire the benefit of all increases in the value of oil produced in that province above the set basic well-head price fixed by the statute and regulations, which is approximately the same as that which existed in 1973 before the increase in world prices for oil.

To achieve this purpose, the legislation imposed a royalty surcharge on all oil produced in that province. The Supreme Court of Canada held, Dickson and de Grandpré dissenting, that the Act was *ultra vires* the provincial government.

MARTLAND J. (Laskin C.J., Judson, Ritchie, Spence, Pigeon and Beetz JJ. concurring):

It is contended that the imposition of these taxes will not result in an increase in the price paid by oil purchasers, who would have been required to pay the same market price even if the taxes had not been imposed, and so there could be no passing on of the tax by the Saskatchewan producer to his purchaser. On this premise, it is argued that the tax is not indirect. This, however, overlooks the all important fact that the scheme of the legislation under consideration involves the fixing of the maximum return of the Saskatchewan producers at the basic well-head price per barrel, while at the same time compelling him to sell at a higher price. There are two components in the sale price, first the basic well-head price and second the tax imposed. Both are intended by the legislation to be incorporated into the price payable by the purchaser. The purchaser pays the amount of the tax as a part of the purchase price.

For these reasons it is my opinion that the taxation scheme comprising the mineral income tax and the royalty surcharge does not constitute direct taxation within the province and is therefore outside the scope of the provincial power under s. 92(2) of the *British North America Act*.

◇[1978] 2 S.C.R. 545.

REGULATION OF TRADE AND COMMERCE

In considering this issue the important fact is, or course, that practically all of the oil to which the mineral income tax or the royalty surcharge becomes applicable is destined for interprovincial or international trade. Some of this oil is sold by producers at the well-head and thereafter transported from the province by pipeline. Some of the oil is not sold at the well-head, but is produced by companies for their own purposes, and is likewise transported out of the province by pipeline. In either case the levy becomes applicable. The producer in the first case must, if he is to avoid pecuniary loss, sell at the well-head at the well-head value established. The company which has its own oil production transported from the province must, if it is to avoid pecuniary loss, ultimately dispose of the refined product at a price which will recoup the amount of the levy. Thus, the effect of the legislation is to set a floor price for Saskatchewan oil purchased for export by the appropriation of its potential incremental value in interprovincial and international markets, or to ensure that the incremental value is not appropriated by persons outside the province.

DICKSON J. (de Grandpré J. concurring) dissenting:

I would hold that, in its true nature and effect, the mineral income tax constitutes direct taxation within the province in order to the raising of a revenue for provincial purposes....

Counsel for appellant urged the Court to strike down the legislation as an infringement of Parliament's exclusive authority respecting the regulation of trade and commerce. Appellant says: "the tax and surcharge are established in a way which enables the Province of Saskatchewan to control the minimum price at which Saskatchewan crude oil is sold. This control is imposed on a commodity almost exclusively consumed outside of Saskatchewan, either in the Canadian or international marketplace." ...

Section 91, head 2 of the *British North America Act, 1867*, has undergone a jurisprudential renaissance during the past fifty years. Appellant asks the Court to extend that revivification to an unprecedented degree....

Implicit in the argument of the appellant is the assumption that federal regulatory power pursuant to s. 91(2) follows the flow of oil backward across provincial boundaries, back through provincial gathering systems and finally to the well-head. A secondary assumption is that sale at the well-head marks the start of the process of exportation. In the view I take of the case it is unnecessary to reach any conclusion as to the validity of either of these assumptions. It is, however, worth noting that neither American nor Canadian jurisprudence has ever gone that far.

I can find nothing in the present case to lead me to conclude that the taxation measures imposed by the Province of Saskatchewan were merely a colourable device for assuming control of extraprovincial trade. The language of the impugned statutes does not disclose an intention on the part of the province to regulate, or control, or impede the marketing or export of oil from Saskatchewan. "Oil produced and sold" means produced and sold within the provinces. "Well-head price" by definition means the price at the well-head of a barrel of oil produced in

Saskatchewan. The mineral income tax and the royalty surcharge relate only to oil produced within Saskatchewan. The transactions are well-head transactions. There are no impediments to the free movement of goods as were found objectionable in *Attorney General of Manitoba v. Egg and Poultry Association* ([1971] S.C.R. 689), and in *Burns Foods Ltd. v. Attorney General of Manitoba* ([1975] 1 S.C.R. 494).

Nor is there anything in the extraneous evidence to form the basis of an argument that the impugned legislation in its *effect* regulated interprovincial or international trade. The evidence is all to the contrary and that evidence comes entirely from witnesses called on behalf of the appellant. Production and export of oil increased after the legislative scheme was implemented. Sales of oil by the appellant were continued in 1974 as in 1973 and previously ....

The Province of Saskatchewan had a *bona fide*, legitimate and reasonable interest of its own to advance in enacting the legislation in question, as related to taxation and natural resources, out of all proportion to the burden, if there can be said to be a burden, imposed on the Canadian free trade economic unit through the legislation. The effect, if any, on the extraprovincial trade in oil is merely indirectly and remotely incidental to the manifest revenue-producing object of the legislation under attack.

o

CENTRAL CANADA POTASH CO. LTD. AND A.-G. CANADA v. GOVERNMENT OF SASKATCHEWAN*

In 1969 the governments of Saskatchewan and the state of New Mexico had met to settle various problems that arose from the sale of potash from Saskatchewan to that state. Following these negotiations, Saskatchewan passed regulations by order in council limiting the production of potash. Through subsequent amendments to these regulations, the Central Canada Potash Company found itself unable to meet its export commitments and challenged the province's authority to make what amounted to international trade agreements; the company was joined in its legal battle by the federal government. The Supreme Court of Canada unanimously decided in the company's favour.

LASKIN C.J. (for the court):

What is evident from the circumstances under which the Potash Conservation Regulations were promulgated, and from the terms of the directives and licences through which the ... schemes were instituted and administered, is that the Government of Saskatchewan had in view the regulation of the marketing of potash through the fixing of a minimum selling price applicable to the permitted production quotas. The only market for which the schemes had any significance was the

*[1979] 1 S.C.R. 42.

export market. There could be no suggestion that the schemes had any relation to the marketing of potash within the Province of Saskatchewan when there was hardly any Saskatchewan market for the mineral. There was no question here of any concluded transactions of sale and purchase in the province, as was the situation in the *Carnation* case. Out of province and offshore sales were the principal objects of the licences and directives . . . .

The present case reduces itself therefore to a consideration of "the true nature and character" of the prorationing and price stabilization schemes which are before us. This Court cannot ignore the circumstances under which the Potash Conservation Regulations came into being, nor the market to which they were applied and in which they had their substantial operation. In *Canadian Industrial Gas & Oil Ltd. v. Government of Saskatchewan* [1978] 2 S.C.R. 545, this Court, speaking in its majority judgment through Martland J., said that "provincial legislative authority does not extend to fixing the price to be charged or received in respect of the sale of goods in the export market." It may properly be said here of potash as it was said there of oil that "the legislation is directly aimed at the production of potash destined for export, and it has the effect of regulating the export price since the producer is effectively compelled to obtain that price on the sale of his product."

I do not agree with Chief Justice Culliton that the consequence of invalidating the provincial scheme in this case is to move to the Parliament of Canada the power to control production of minerals in the province and the price to be charged at the mine. There is no accretion at all to federal power in this case, which does not involve federal legislation, but simply a determination by this Court, in obedience to its duty, of a limitation on provincial legislative power. It is true, as he says that (with some exceptions, not relevant here) the *British North America Act* distributes all legislative power either to Parliament or to the provincial Legislatures, but it does not follow that legislation of a province held to be invalid may *ipso facto* be validly enacted by Parliament in its very terms. It is nothing new for this Court, or indeed, for any Court in this country seized of a constitutional issue, to go behind the words used by a Legislature and to see what it is that it is doing. It is especially important for Courts, called upon to interpret and apply a constitution which limits legislative power, to do so in a case where not only the authorizing legislation but regulations enacted pursuant thereto are themselves couched in generalities, and the bite of a scheme envisaged by the parent legislation and the delegated regulations is found in administrative directions.

Where governments in good faith, as in this case, invoke authority to realize desirable economic policies, they must know that they have no open-ended means of achieving their goals when there are constitutional limitations on the legislative power under which they purport to act. They are entitled to expect that the Courts, and especially this Court, will approach the task of appraisal of the constitutionality of social and economic programs with sympathy and regard for the serious consequences of holding them *ultra vires*. Yet, if the appraisal results in a clash with the constitution, it is the latter which must govern. That is the situation here.

In my opinion, the judgment of the Saskatchewan Court of Appeal on the constitutional question for this Court should be set aside and the declaration of invalidity by the trial judge should be restored.

BROADCASTING

CAPITAL CITIES COMMUNICATIONS INC.
v. CANADIAN RADIO-TELEVISION
COMMISSION◇

The Canadian Radio-Television Commission (C.R.T.C.) licenses Canadian cable operators. One of its policies was to encourage Canadian operators to replace non-Canadian commercials with domestic ones; accordingly, it authorized a Canadian company to delete commercials from an American broadcast and replace them with public service announcements. Capital Cities Communications of Buffalo claimed that the C.R.T.C. had no jurisdiction over cable television. Pigeon, Beetz, and de Grandpré JJ. dissented from the following decision.

LASKIN C.J. (Martland, Judson, Dickson, Ritchie and Spence JJ. concurring):

... The main argument of the appellants and of those in support of their position is that legislative jurisdiction is divided in respect of regulation of television signals received by cablevision companies. Exclusive federal jurisdiction is conceded so far as concerns the reception of foreign or domestic television signals at the antennae of the cablevision companies. It is contended, however, that once received at those antennae federal legislative power is exhausted, and any subsequent distribution of those signals, whether in the same or modified form, within a particular Province is a matter exclusively for that Province ....

I am unable to accept the submission of the appellants and of the Attorneys-General supporting them that a demarcation can be made for legislative purposes at the point where the cable distribution systems receive the Hertzian waves. The systems are clearly undertakings which reach out beyond the Province in which their physical apparatus is located; and, even more than the *Winner* case, they each constitute a single undertaking which deals with the very signals which come to each of them from across the border and transmit those signals, albeit through a conversion process, through its cable system to subscribers. The common sense of which the Privy Council spoke in the *Radio* case seems to me even more applicable here to prevent a situation of a divided jurisdiction in respect of the same signals or programs according to whether they reach home television sets and the ultimate viewers through Hertzian waves or through coaxial cable.

The fallacy in the contention of behalf of the Attorney General of Ontario and the Attorneys General of Quebec and of British Columbia, and, indeed, of the appellants, is in their reliance on the technology of transmission as a ground for shifting constitutional competence when the entire undertaking relates to and is dependent on extra-provincial signals which the cable system receives and sends on to subscribers. It does not advance their contentions to urge that a cable distribution system is not engaged in broadcasting. The system depends upon a telecast for

◇[1978] 2 S.C.R. 141.

its operation, and is no more than a conduit for signals from the telecast, interposing itself through a different technology to bring the telecast to paying subscribers.

I agree with the submission of counsel for the Attorney-General of Quebec that since the *Radio* reference was concerned with a general question of legislative jurisdiction it was not itself determinative of the validity of any specific legislation. The constitutional question posed in the present case is, however, in the context of particular legislation, the *Broadcasting Act* enacted in 1968, but constitutionality is posited on the basis that the Act authorizes the regulation of cable distribution systems which receive and distribute television signals. Such signals may, of course, come by Hertzian waves from within a particular Province as well as from without it. The contention appears to be that since there is a local character to the cable distribution system in its physical aspect, and it may be receiving signals intraprovincially, it does not fall under total federal legislative authority. I understood, however, that it was conceded that federal jurisdiction was exclusive in respect of the receipt of signals at the antenna of the cable distribution system, wherever be their point of emanation. If that be the case, I do not see how legislative competence ceases in respect of those signals merely because the undertaking which receives them and sends them on to its local subscribers does so through a different technology.

In addition to the foregoing submissions, which do not differ from those made by others opposing federal jurisdiction, counsel for the Attorney-General of Quebec denied federal authority over the content of cable television, at least at the point of distribution through the coaxial cables. This, however, simply rephrases the issue in the present case without changing its substance. What the reformulation suggests, however, is that the Parliament of Canada may regulate, perhaps by a licensing system, the equipment or machinery through which signals are received in international or interprovincial transmission but that is all. There was a time when licensing of receiving sets was prescribed by federal legislation; but if, as is alleged, there is no authority to regulate content, it is difficult to understand how there can be a constitutional basis for federal licensing of receiving sets in a Province, or even of transmitting apparatus which sends signals by way of international and interprovincial transmission. To put the matter in another perspective, it would be as if an interprovincial or international carrier of goods could be licensed for such carriage but without federal control of what may be carried or of the conditions of carriage.

This submission amounts to a denial of any effective federal legislative jurisdiction of what passes in interprovincial or international communication, whether by radio or television, and is in truth an invitation to this Court to recant from the *Radio* case. It would, presumably, leave federal authority in relation to "telegraphs" intact, although reducing the meaning of that head of power from the meaning attributed to it by the Privy Council in the *Radio* case.

Although this Court is not bound by judgments of the Privy Council any more than it is bound by its own judgments, I hold the view that the *Radio* case was correctly decided under the terms of ss. 91 and 92(10)*(a)*. Implicit in the objection raised to federal legislative authority in relation to the content of television programs as they are transmitted by cable distribution systems is an attenuation of the meaning of the words "undertaking . . . extending beyond the limits of the Province" in s. 92(10)*(a)* . . . .

I am therefore in no doubt that federal legislative authority extends to the regulation of the reception of television signals emanating from a source outside of Canada and to the regulation of the transmission of such signals within Canada. Those signals carry the programs which are ultimately viewed on home television sets; and it would be incongruous, indeed, to admit federal legislative jurisdiction to the extent conceded but to deny the continuation of regulatory authority because the signals are intercepted and sent on to ultimate viewers through a different technology. Program content regulation is inseparable from regulating the undertaking through which programs are received and sent on as part of the total enterprise.

○

PUBLIC SERVICE BOARD v. DIONNE[◇]

The Quebec Public Service Board was given the power to regulate cable television in the province. The Quebec Court of Appeal held that the regulations of the operations of cable distribution companies was beyond provincial jurisdiction. On appeal the Supreme Court of Canada upheld the decision 6 to 3. Chief Justice Laskin delivered the majority decision with Martland, Judson, Ritchie, Spence and Dickson JJ. concurring.

PIGEON J. (Beetz and de Grandpré JJ. concurring) dissenting:
In my view, the question in this case is whether the unchallengeable federal jurisdiction over radio communication involves exclusive legislative authority over all cable distribution systems making use of signals received by radio communication or whether such exclusive authority extends only to what I will call the radio communication aspect.

It is important at the outset to observe that federal jurisdiction over some activities or operations does not necessarily mean that any undertaking involved in such activities or operations automatically comes under federal jurisdiction. For instance under head 10 of s. 91 of the *British North America Act, 1867,* "Navigation and Shipping," are enumerated among the classes of subjects coming within exclusive federal authority. It would, however, be wrong to conclude that this means that all navigation undertakings come under federal jurisdiction, because head 13 includes only "Ferries between a Province and any British or Foreign Country or between Two Provinces." A ferry operating within the limits of a single Province is obviously a navigation operation. However, it is perfectly clear that, from a constitutional point of view, it is a "local," not a federal undertaking. This does not mean that it is not subject to federal jurisdiction but that it is subject to such jurisdiction only in respect of the navigation aspect. How far that may extend need not be considered, it is enough to say that it does not mean that the whole undertaking is subject to federal control. On the contrary, such an undertaking is subject to provincial control save in respect of what may properly be called the

---

[◇][1978] 2 S.C.R. 191.

navigation aspect. It is equally clear that the same is true of all shipping because in head 10 of s. 92 one finds that the following come under provincial legislative authority:

10. Local Works and Undertakings other than such as are of the following Classes:—

(a) Lines of Steam or other Ships, Railways, Canals, Telegraphs, and other Works and Undertakings connecting the Province with any other or others of the Provinces, or extending beyond the Limits of the Province:

(b) Lines of Steam Ships between the Province and any British or Foreign Country:

It must be stressed that by virtue of the above-noted provisions, provincial jurisdiction over all undertakings is the rule, federal jurisdiction being the exception. With reference to undertakings of the kind with which we are presently concerned, it is to be noted that telegraph lines are specially included among the undertakings under provincial jurisdiction because exception is made only of those which connect the Province with another or extend beyond its limits. At the time of Confederation, telegraph lines were the only known kind of lines used for communication at a distance by means of electrical impulses carried over wires. However, in *City of Toronto v. Bell Telephone Co. of Canada*, [1905], the Privy Council had no difficulty in coming to the conclusion that telephone lines should be considered as telegraph lines for constitutional purposes. Lord MacNaghten said:

It can hardly be disputed that a telephone company the objects of which as defined by its Act of incorporation contemplate extension beyond the limits of one province is just as much within the express exception as a telegraph company with like powers of extension.

It seems to me that the same should be said of coaxial cable lines as of telephone lines. Coaxial cables are nothing but a further development in the technology of using wires for the transmission of signals by means of electrical impulses. Morse telegraphy, as known in 1867, made use of long and short discrete impulses of direct current actuating a magnet at the receiving end. The telephone invented a few years later made use of an electrical current amplitude modulated at audio frequency by the human voice acting on a microphone at an end of the line. Instead of these low frequencies under 10 kilohertz, coaxial networks make use of very high frequencies in the range of 100 megahertz with a tremendous increase in the quantity of information that may be carried over a single cable, this is what makes it possible to transmit television images which, on the American standards require a band width of some 6 megahertz.

In support of federal jurisdiction over coaxial cable networks it is contended that the change of technology in transmission should make no difference. The fallacy of this argument is that it is inconsistent with the very basis of federal jurisdiction which is the use of hertzian waves. Let us not forget that the basic constitutional rule is provincial jurisdiction over local undertakings. Telegraph systems are specifically included in local undertakings. It is clear that these include all communication systems by electrical signals transmitted over wires as appears from the *Bell Telephone Co.* case. In *Re Regulation and Control of Radio Communication: A.-G. Que. v. A.-G. Can.*, [1931]...Smith, J., said:

> When a transmitter sends out into space these electro-magnetic waves, they are projected in all directions for the great distances referred to, and it is not possible for the transmitter to confine them within the bounds of a Province.

With respect to what was said by the Privy Council, it is important to bear in mind that the case was a reference dealing solely with "radio communications," that is transmissions by means of hertzian waves. The language used should be construed in the light of the question which was under consideration and should not be treated as applicable to an entirely different question.

I think it is of the utmost importance in this matter, to consider the tremendous extent to which communications transmitted by hertzian waves at one point or another are used by undertakings under provincial jurisdiction or conveyed by such undertakings. With the exception of the Bell Telephone Co. system which was established as an interprovincial undertaking and declared by Parliament to be a work for the general advantage of Canada, telephone companies generally come under provincial jurisdiction. It is a well known fact, of which we are entitled to take judicial notice, that they carry on their wires or cables not only telephone conversations but communications of all kinds, including radio network programs. No one has ever contended that, on that account, they have become undertakings subject to federal jurisdiction.

It appears from the record of the instant case that the provincial telephone company which provides the cables used for both Dionne's and D'Auteuil's systems, does use for the transmission of communications several microwave links. It would not be reasonable for the federal authorities to claim jurisdiction over the whole undertaking because it is making use of radio communications. Of course, this telephone company has to comply with the *Radio Act* concerning the technical aspects of its microwave links, but it would, in my view, be an usurpation of power on the part of the federal authorities to claim to exercise control over the whole undertaking because of this use of radio communications.

It is equally obvious to me that the federal authorities could not by virtue of their jurisdiction over radio communications claim to exercise general control over all users of such communications like truckers, taxi-cabs, police forces, power companies, etc. In fact the use of radio communications, both sending and receiving, has become so much a feature of daily life that it has been made generally available to the public on what is known as citizens band recently expanded to 40 channels. All those communications are undoubtedly subject to the federal licensing power and there is no specific limit to the possible extent of the conditions that may be appended to the licences. However, it seems clear to me that it would be an abuse of this licensing power to require that every undertaking obtaining a licence should become subject to federal jurisdiction. In so doing, the federal would exceed the limits of its authority over radio communications just as it would overstep the limits of its jurisdiction over navigation by requiring that all navigation undertakings, including ferries within a Province and intra-provincial carriers, become subject to federal control over their whole operations rather than in respect of navigation only . . . .

As presently operated, the two cable distribution systems with which we are concerned distribute nothing but TV programs broadcast by some four or five distant TV stations. These broadcasts are received over their aerials which are set up at a substantial distance from the area where the major part of their subscribers are residing. The distribution of locally produced programs was initially contemplated and could be accomplished without any change in the distribution network but it remains as a future possibility only. In those circumstances it is contended that the cable networks are nothing but an adjunct of TV broadcasting, that they are nothing but a means of bringing to the subscribers programs that the hertzian waves do not carry to them but that special antennae erected in favourable locations are able to receive and transmit to them in the form of electrical impulses carried over coaxial cable.

As against this, however, it must be considered that a cable distribution network has to be carried either in underground conduits, as is done only in some densely built urban areas, or, as in this case, carried over utility poles. Those utilities are, as a rule, under provincial jurisdiction as in these cases. In fact the cable networks are, in the main, the property of a provincial telephone company and the cable operators are only lessees. With respect to some parts they are not even exclusive lessees, the telephone company leasing only a certain number of channels or retaining the right to make use of a capacity not needed by the lessee. In the order of 13 September 1974 one reads (translation):

> The necessity of providing for joint use by Quebec Telephone of the coaxial cables that may be installed for the purposes of the proposed cable distribution undertakings is not called into question by the testimony in support of the applications.

It will thus be seen that from a physical point of view, with respect to the material set-up which is the essential feature of a cable system, the provincial aspect is by far predominant. The distinctive feature of a cable system, as opposed to radio broadcasting, is that its channels of communication are carried over metal cables strung on poles throughout the area served instead of being carried over what is commonly called "airwaves." The importance of the provincial aspect is therefore undeniable. However, when an aerial is the sole source of signals to be distributed over the cable network, it cannot be denied that this part is also essential. Nevertheless, in view of the considerations previously developed, I cannot agree that "common sense" dictates that on that account the whole undertaking should be under federal jurisdiction. I have already shown by several illustrations how exorbitant it would be for the federal to claim jurisdiction over all undertakings which make use of radio communication and for many of which such use is essential under present conditions.

I cannot agree that the federal authority over radio broadcasting must extend to all undertakings receiving radio broadcasts. In the *Radio* case it was held that federal authority must extend to radio receivers but this does not mean or imply that it must extend to all undertakings operating receivers. Hotels often have aerials and cable distribution networks feeding more receiving sets than many cable distribution undertakings, could this put them under federal control? It is true that for them it is accessory to their principal business. But cable distribution is a developing technology which may, in time, not only complement but even supplant radio broadcasting as a means of bringing television and some other programs to the public. Those undertakings are essentially localized and as is properly stressed in the Public Service Board decisions, they should be specially controlled for the purpose of serving the local needs of the particular area for which they are licensed and must, on account of practical consideration enjoy an exclusive franchise. In its order of 13 September 1974 the Board said (translation):

> Taken as a whole, the Regulation indicates that a primary objective to be attained is to give a voice to local communities; the organization and the laying out of the areas to be served must take this social and cultural objective into consideration. The Board should therefore promote the formation of public cable distribution companies whose owners, managers and organization are as closely related as possible to the communities they will be serving, so that on the one hand local vitality will be naturally led to express itself and on the other hand the company will always be sensitive to the social and cultural needs of the community and to the means of making cable distribution work to satisfy these needs.

The Board chose to ignore the problem arising out of federal jurisdiction over the broadcast receiving antenna. It is, however, an issue that must be faced. I cannot agree that it should be solved by saying that the federal should have full control over the undertaking so as to avoid the difficulties of divided jurisdiction. Divided jurisdiction is inherent in any federal system. Whatever may be the extent of the jurisdiction held to be included in the matters allocated to the federal, provincial powers will impinge at some point....

I have already pointed out that a great many undertakings and services under provincial authority require radio communication licences for a variety of purposes. There is no doubt that this implies complete federal control over technical aspects. In my view, it is equally clear that it does not involve control over economic aspects. This, I think, may be deduced from what was decided in *Carnation Co. Ltd. v. Quebec Agricultural Board et al.* (1968). Essentially, the decision was that extra-provincial economic repercussions would not remove a local matter from provincial authority. The issue was the validity of an order fixing the price of milk to be paid to producers by the owner of an evaporated milk plant. After processing, the major portion of the product was used "for export out of Quebec." It was held that the fact that the orders might thus have "some impact" upon interprovincial trade did not invalidate them.

Policy statements of the Canadian Radio-Television Commission which were brought before us on appeal from the Federal Court of Appeal judgment in *Re Capital Cities Communications Inc. et al. and Canadian Radio Television Com'n* (1975), show that the Commission was very much concerned with the economic repercussions of cable distribution on broadcasting station owners. It is, of course, obvious that where cable distribution brings a variety of programs into an area where there are only one or two broadcasting stations whose signals are readily available otherwise, there will be more competition for the available audience. However, a similar effect would result from programs distributed by cable and obtained otherwise than by receiving broadcast signals. In my view, the principle adopted in the construction of the Canadian constitution is, as exemplified by the *Carnation Milk* case, to reject economic repercussions as a basis for the allocation of legislative jurisdiction apart from emergency conditions such as in *Reference re Anti-Inflation Act* (1976).

o

A.-G. QUEBEC v. KELLOGG'S CO. OF CANADA[✦]

Regulations under the Quebec *Consumer Protection Act* were concerned with the content of "advertising intended for children" and prohibited the use of "cartoons" in such advertising. Kellogg's violated the provisions and, in defence, challenged the constitutionality of the legislation. The Supreme Court in a 6 to 3 decision upheld the legislation.

MARTLAND J. (Ritchie, Pigeon, Dickson, Beetz and de Grandpré JJ. concurring):

As its name indicates, the purpose of the *Consumer Protection Act* is the protection of consumers in Quebec by regulating the commercial conduct of persons engaged in the sale of goods in that Province. Part of this regulation involves the control of the advertising which is used in effecting such sales. Paragraph (*n*), under attack in this case, is one of several restrictions imposed in connection with advertising intended for children. It forbids the use of a particular kind of advertising considered to have a special appeal to children.

In my opinion this Regulation does not seek to regulate or to interfere with the operation of a broadcast undertaking. In relation to the facts of this case it seeks to prevent Kellogg from using a certain kind of advertising by any means. It aims at controlling the commercial activity of Kellogg. The fact that Kellogg is precluded from using televised advertising may, incidentally, affect the revenue of one or more television stations but it does not change the true nature of the Regulation. In this connection the case of *Carnation Co. Ltd. v. Quebec Agricultural Marketing Board* (1968) is analogous.

Kellogg is not exempted from the application of restriction upon its advertising practices because it elects to advertise through a medium which is subject to federal control. A person who caused defamatory material to be published by means of a televised program would not be exempted from liability under provincial law because the means of publication were subject to federal control. Further, he could

---

✦[1978] 2 S.C.R. 211.

be enjoined from repeating the publication. In my opinion the position of Kellogg in relation to this Regulation is analogous. It cannot justify conduct which has been rendered illegal because it is using the medium of television.

Throughout these reasons I have stressed the fact that it is Kellogg and not the television station which is sought to be enjoined. The question is whether Kellogg's conduct has been regulated by the provincial legislation. Whether the Regulation could be applied to the television station itself or whether an injunction against Kellogg would bind such station does not arise in this case and I prefer to express no opinion with respect to it.

In my opinion para. (*n*) is within the power of the Province to enact and applies to all persons who employ advertising as a means of selling their goods in the Province of Quebec.

A second argument raised by Kellogg is that which is stated in the second question defined by the Court. It is contended that because the television advertising used by Kellogg in Quebec was produced in Ontario the Regulation encroached upon the federal power to legislate in respect of interprovincial trade under s. 91(2) of the *British North America Act, 1867.* In my opinion this contention fails. The aim of para. (*n*) of the Regulation was certainly not to control interprovincial trade in television programs and it does not do so. The impact of the Regulation may affect such trade, but only indirectly. The case made by Kellogg on this issue is the same as that submitted unsuccessfully in the *Carnation* case and in the *Canadian Indemnity* case and in my opinion cannot succeed in the light of those decision.

LASKIN C.J. (Judson and Spence JJ. concurring) dissenting:

The issue in this case is whether a provincial statute and a Regulation thereunder relating to advertising intended for children may constitutionally be applied to preclude a manufacturing company from advertising its products on television through picture signals received in the Province from television stations in the Province . . . .

This Court established in two recent decisions that federal competence in relation to television, and in relation even to cablevision which relies on and retransmits television signals, embraces exclusive authority to deal with the content of television programs: *Capital Cities Communications Inc. et al. v. Canadian Radio-Television Com'n et al.* . . . *Re Public Service Board et al., Dionne et al. and A.-G. Can. et al.* . . . We are urged, however, to say that because the provincial statute and Regulation are invoked against the advertiser and not against the medium and that because the Province may control advertising in the Province by persons doing business there, where the business is subject to provincial regulatory control in the Province, there is no intrusion upon federal competence in relation to television . . . .

We are not concerned here with the use of advertising in any general sense or as related to some activity, whether it be a local trade or the practice of a profession, which is within provincial legislative jurisdiction . . . . We are concerned rather with the right to resort to a particular medium which is within exclusive federal competence, and the generality of the challenged provincial legislation and Regulation does not aid the Province in extending its prohibition of advertising to a medium which is outside of its legislative jurisdiction. The effect of the position taken by the appellant and by supporting intervenors is to uphold the provincial legislation and Regulation even if they expressly forbade an advertiser to use cartoon advertising on television, the theory being that it is the advertiser who is aimed at and not the television stations in the Province. I regard this as no less vulnerable than the by-law zoning land against use as an airport, which this Court struck down in *Johannesson et al. v. Rur. Mun. of West St. Paul.*

The principle espoused by the appellant in this case amounts to an assertion of some sort of ancillary power in the Province, an assertion that if the Province has a legislative power base in relation to some activity or trade in the Province it may constitutionally extend its authority to embrace objects which, strictly, are outside its competence. The argument would have the Court determine the aim or purpose of the provincial legislation and, finding it valid from a provincial point of view, would have the Court permit an extension into an otherwise forbidden field. This is not and has never been part of our constitutional prescriptions. Provincial powers are limited, and it has always been a canon of construction to interpret and confine provincial legislation to matters within its specified powers where its terms would, in their generality, support a wider compass . . . .

In so far as the *British North America Act, 1867* may be said to recognize an ancillary power or a power to pass legislation necessarily incidental to enumerated powers, such a power resides only in the Parliament of Canada: see *A.-G. Ont. v. A.-G. Can.*, [1894] A.C. 189. However, it has been made manifest by this Court that it is not invariably necessary for the Parliament of Canada to rely on an ancillary power to support its competent legislation. It may be supported in the ordinary way by evaluation of the thrust of the legislation . . . . Indeed, as was shown recently by the judgment of this Court in *MacDonald et al. v. Vapour Canada Ltd. et al.* [1977] 2 S.C.R. 134, the Parliament of Canada can no more trespass on a provincial field than can a Province encroach upon a federal field of legislative power. This cannot be done directly by expressly embracing matters outside of the competence of the legislating authority, nor can it be done indirectly by the silent approach, by refraining from explicit inclusion but then proceeding to an embracing application.

It is this indirect approach which is evident here and I would reject it.

This case, on its facts, does not raise an issue as to the power of a Province, under the legislation and Regulation now before us, to apply them to forbid an advertiser to use a telecast originating in another Province but seen in the legislating Province. That would be to reach into extraprovincial activity as well as into a medium which is within exclusive federal competence even in respect of purely intraprovincial operations. I put this situation simply to expose the assertion of the appellant herein for what it is, namely, an attempt to control the content of television programs. I do not think a rational distinction can be drawn between television programs which originate with the television station or come in from outside the Province and those which are bought and paid for by a commercial advertiser. Whether and in what circumstances he can use that medium is for its regulatory agency to determine under competent federal legislation.

o

IRWIN TOY LTD. v. QUEBEC◇

Irwin Toy, a toy manufacturer, challenged the constitutionality of ss. 248 and 249 of Quebec's *Consumer Protection Act*, R.S.Q. c. P–40.1 which prohibited advertising directed at children under 13 years of age. Irwin claimed that this prohibition violated both the *Constitution Act, 1867* and the *Charter*.

Although the challenged Act applied to all forms of advertising, regulations passed pursuant to the Act exempted some forms of written advertising from the prohibition. As a result, it was argued that the Act purported to regulate a broadcast undertaking within federal jurisdiction by virtue of ss.91(20) and 92(10) of the *Constitution Act, 1867*.

DICKSON C.J. (for the Court):

In the case at bar the respondent contended that the challenged provision of the *Consumer Protection Act*, when read together with the regulations to which they are made expressly subject and considered in the light of the evidence of their practical effect, exhibit a different purpose or object from that of the regulation that was in issue in *Kellogg's*. The respondent contends that when the challenged provisions are seen in the context of the regulations and the evidence it is clear that they are aimed essentially and primarily at television as a medium of children's advertising, a matter within exclusive federal jurisdiction. In support of this contention the respondent emphasises the relative importance of the prohibition of television advertising directed to persons under thirteen years of age, as indicated by the evidence and the extent of the exemptions provided by the regulations for other forms of children's advertising . . . .

The Attorney General of Quebec noted that there are other forms of children's advertising subject to the prohibition. On the whole, despite the fact that the relative impact on television advertising is much greater than it was in *Kellogg's*, we are of the opinion that ss. 248 and 249 of the Act, as modified by or completed by the regulations, can also be said to be legislation of general application enacted in relation to consumer protection, as in *Kellogg's*, rather than a colourable attempt, under the guise of a law of general application, to legislate in relation to television advertising. In other words, the dominant aspect of the law for purposes of characterisation is the regulation of all of advertising directed at persons under thirteen years of age rather than the prohibition of television advertising which cannot be said to be the exclusive or even primary aim of the legislation . . . .

The relative importance of television advertising and the other forms of children's advertising subject to exemption and prohibition is not in our opinion a sufficient basis for a finding of colourability. There is no suggestion that the children's advertising is a mere pretense or facade for a primary, if not exclusive, purpose of regulating television advertising. It is not the relative importance of these other forms of advertising but the *bona fide* nature of the legislative concern with them that is in issue on the question of colourability.

◇[1989] 1 S.C.R. 927.

The interveners Pathonic, as we understand their argument, did not contend, as did the respondent, that the challenged provisions of the *Consumer Protection Act* were distinguishable on their face in respect of the characterisation of their purpose or object from the provisions of the regulations that was considered in *Kellogg's*. They contended that the challenged provisions were rendered *ultra vires* or inoperative because of their effect on a television undertaking. They submitted that the prohibition of television advertising affected a vital part of the operation of such an undertaking and impaired the undertaking . . . .

The federal government has exclusive jurisdiction as regards "essential and vital elements" of a federal undertaking, including the management of such an undertaking, because those matters form the "basic, minimum and unassailable content" of the head of power created by operation of s. 91(29) and the exceptions in s. 92(10) of the *Constitution Act*, 1867. No provincial law touching on those matters can apply to a federal undertaking. However, where provincial legislation does not purport to apply to a federal undertaking, its incidental effect, even upon a vital part of the operation of the undertaking, will not normally render the provincial legislation *ultra vires*.

There is no doubt that television advertising is a vital part of the operation of a television broadcast undertaking. The advertising services of these undertakings therefore fall within exclusive federal legislative jurisdiction. It is well established that such jurisdiction extends to the content of broadcasting . . . and advertising forms a part of such content. However, ss. 248 and 249 of the *Consumer Protection Act* do not purport to apply to television broadcast undertakings. Read together with s. 252, it is clear that ss. 248 and 249 apply to the acts of an advertiser, not to the acts of a broadcaster. Nor did Pathonic contend that ss. 248 and 249 applied to television broadcasters. Indeed, it went so far as to submit that the province of Quebec was unable to regulate the advertising practices of television broadcasters because signals coming from outside the province and received directly by the public or re-distributed by a cable company could not be subject to the standards of the *Consumer Protection Act*. While this submission demonstrates that the Quebec government can only achieve partial success in controlling commercial advertising aimed at children, it also demonstrates that a province can aim to regulate provincial advertisers without applying its regulations to television broadcasters situate in the province. Therefore the provisions in question do not trench on exclusive federal jurisdiction by purporting to apply to a federal undertaking and, in so doing, affecting a vital part of its operation.

Do the provisions nevertheless have the effect of impairing the operation of a federal undertaking? The interveners adduced evidence showing the importance of advertising revenues in the operation of a television broadcast undertaking and that the prohibition of commercial advertising directed to persons under thirteen years of age affected the capacity to provide children's programs. This is not a sufficient basis on which to conclude that the effect of the provisions was to impair the operation of the undertaking, in the sense that the undertaking was "sterilized in all its functions and activities." The most that can be said, as in *Kellogg's* (at 225), is that the provisions "may, incidentally, affect the revenue of one or more television stations."

TRADE AND COMMERCE

MACDONALD v. VAPOR CANADA LTD.✧

Vapor sought and received an injunction preventing MacDonald from making use of confidential business information in violation of section 7(e) of the federal Trade Mark Act which provided that no person shall "do any other act or adopt any business practice contrary to honest industrial or commercial usage in Canada." MacDonald appealed the injunction on the grounds that section 7(e) was ultra vires for it attempted to regulate intraprovincial economic activity. The Federal Court had upheld the statute, including section 7(e), under 91(2). The Supreme Court found the section in question invalid as coming within property and civil rights.

LASKIN C.J. (Spence, Pigeon, Dickson and Beetz JJ. concurring):

...I think it fair to look upon s. 7 as embodying a scheme, one limited in scope perhaps but none the less embodying an array of connected matters. I shall come later to what appeared to be a fundamental underpinning of the respondent's position and that of the Attorney General for Canada, namely, that s. 7 or at least s. 7(e) must not be construed in vacuo, but must itself be brought into account as a segment or a piece of a tapestry of regulation and control of industrial and intellectual property.

It was not disputed that the common law in the Provinces outside of Quebec and the Civil Code of Quebec governed the conduct or aspects thereof now embraced by s. 7 and embraced earlier by s. 11 of the Act of 1932.

The Chief Justice then canvassed the common and civil law sanctions against various unfair trading practices.

It was emphasised again and again by counsel for the respondent that s. 7(e) deals with predatory practices in competition, in a competitive market, that it postulates two or more aspirants or competitors in business and that it involves misappropriation and a dishonest use, in competition, of information or documents so acquired. This may equally be said of the tort of conversion where it involves persons in business or in competition. The fact that Parliament has hived off a particular form of an existing tort or has enlarged the scope of the liability does not determine constitutionality. The relevant questions here are whether the liability is imposed in connection with an enterprise or an activity, for example, banking or bills of exchange, that is itself expressly within federal legislative power; or, if not, whether the liability is dealt with in such a manner as to bring it within the scope of some head of federal legislative power.

This depends not only on what the liability is, but as well on how the federal enactment deals with its enforcement. What is evident here is that the predatory

---

✧[1977] 2 S.C.R. 134.

practices are not under administrative regulation of a competent federally appointed agency, nor are they even expressly brought under criminal sanction in the statute in which they are prohibited. It is, in my opinion, difficult to conceive of them in the wide terms urged upon the Court by the respondent and by the Attorney General of Canada when they are left to merely private enforcement as a private matter of business injury which may arise, as to all its elements including damage, in a small locality in a Province or within a Province. I do not see any general cast in s. 7(e) other than the fact that it is federal legislation and unlimited (as such legislation usually is) in its geographic scope. Indeed, the very basis upon which s. 7(e) is analysed by the respondent, namely, that it postulates two or more competitors in business, drains it, in my opinion, of the generality that would have been present if the legislation had established the same prescriptions to be monitored by a public authority irrespective of any immediate private grievance as to existing or apprehended injury . . . .

I do not find anything in the case law on s. 91(2) that prevents this Court, even if it would retain a cautious concern for *stare decisis*, from taking the words of the Privy Council in the *Parsons* case, as providing the guide or lead to the issue of validity that arises here. I think the Federal Court of Appeal was correct in doing so, but I do not agree with its use of the *Parsons* criteria to sustain s. 7(e). I repeat the relevant sentence in the *Parsons* case . . . :

> . . . the words "regulation of trade and commerce" . . . would include political arrangements in regard to trade requiring the sanction of Parliament, regulation of trade in matters of interprovincial concern, and it may be that they would include general regulations of trade affecting the whole dominion.

It is the last-mentioned category that is to be considered here. I take it as it is phrased, or as paraphrased by Duff C.J., in the *Natural Products Marketing Act* reference, [1936] . . . where he spoke of "general regulations of trade as a whole or regulations of general trade and commerce within the sense of the judgment in *Parsons'* case."

The plain fact is that s. 7(e) is not a regulation, nor is it concerned with trade as a whole nor with general trade and commerce. In a loose sense every legal prescription is regulatory, even the prescriptions of the *Criminal Code*, but I do not read s. 91(2) as in itself authorizing federal legislation that merely creates a statutory tort, enforceable by private action, and applicable, as here, to the entire range of business relationships in any activity, whether the activity be itself within or beyond federal legislative authority. If there have been cases which appeared to go too far in diminution of the federal trade and commerce power, an affirmative conclusion here would, in my opinion, go even farther in the opposite direction.

What is evident here is that the Parliament of Canada has simply extended or intensified existing common and civil law delictual liability by statute which at the same time has prescribed the usual civil remedies open to an aggrieved person. The Parliament of Canada can no more acquire legislative jurisdiction by supplementing existing tort liability, cognizable in provincial Courts as reflective of provincial competence, than the provincial Legislatures can acquire legislative jurisdiction by supplementing the federal criminal law: see *Johnson v. A.-G. Alta.*, [1954] . . . .

One looks in vain for any regulatory scheme in s. 7, let alone s. 7(*e*). Its enforcement is left to the chance of private redress without public monitoring by the continuing oversight of a regulatory agency which would at least lend some colour to the alleged national or Canada-wide sweep of s. 7(*e*). The provision is not directed to trade but to the ethical conduct of persons engaged in trade or in business, and, in my view, such a detached provision cannot survive alone unconnected to a general regulatory scheme to govern trading relations going beyond merely local concern. Even on the footing of being concerned with practices in the conduct of trade, its private enforcement by civil action gives it a local cast because it is as applicable in its terms to local or intraprovincial competitors as it is to competitors in interprovincial trade . . . .

o

A.-G. CANADA v. C.N.
TRANSPORTATION LTD.[♦]

A number of railways were charged with conspiring to lessen competition in interprovincial transport in violation of section 32 (1)(*c*) of the *Combines Investigation Act*. The federally initiated prosecution was challenged as an invasion of provincial jurisdiction over the "Administration of Justice" 92(14). The majority opinion, written by Laskin C.J. with Ritchie, Estey and McIntyre JJ. concurring, upheld the prosecution under the criminal law power. A concurring opinion was written by Dickson J., with Beetz and Lamer JJ. While the narrow question raised by the case was the competence of the federal government to prosecute violations of the *Combines Investigation Act*, there were "much broader questions" involved "touching on the fundamental principles that govern the division of powers between the federal and provincial authorities in the areas of criminal justice and economic regulation." That in turn involved a discussion of the reach of 91(2) and began with the passage in *Parsons* where Sir Montague Smith construed the meaning of the words "trade and commerce."

DICKSON J.:

These passages from *Parsons* establish three important propositions with regard to the federal trade and commerce power: (i) it does not correspond to the literal meaning of the words "regulation of trade and commerce"; (ii) it includes not only arrangements with regard to international and interprovincial trade but "it may be that [it] would include general regulation of trade affecting the whole Dominion"; (iii) it does not extend to regulating the contracts of a particular business or trade. Subsequent jurisprudence on the meaning and extent of s. 91(2) is to a large extent an expansion and an explication of these three interrelated propositions . . . .

One possible indication of federal competence over economic regulation is its operation across and beyond provincial borders. In *Parsons* the Privy Council identified international and interprovincial trade as coming within the ambit of

[♦][1983] 2 S.C.R. 206.

s. 91(2) and much of the subsequent jurisprudence on the federal trade and commerce power has been devoted to a consideration of just how much or how little intraprovincial commerce could be validly swept into the flow of the interprovincial trade affected by a given enactment. In the present case, however, even on the most generous definition, s. 32(1)(c) of the *Combines Investigation Act* cannot be seen as a regulation of interprovincial trade and commerce. The appellant Attorney General of Canada concedes that if it is to be justified under s. 91(2), this enactment must fall within what has been called the "second branch" of the *Parsons* classification, namely, "the general regulation of trade affecting the whole Dominion."

Although in *Parsons* this second branch is presented as merely a possibility ("and it may be that they would include . . . "), the existence of a "general trade and commerce" power seems to have been widely assumed in subsequent cases. In *John Deere Plow Co. v. Wharton, supra*, the Privy Council held that the limits of powers of federally incorporated companies was "a question of general interest throughout the Dominion" and hence under federal competence pursuant to s. 91(2). In *A.-G. Ont. v. A.-G. Can. et al.* (Canada Standard Trade Mark), (1937), the Privy Council held that the creation of a national trade mark was within "the class of subjects enumerated in s. 91(2), the existence of such a "general" power seems not to have been put in doubt: see *Toronto Electric Com'rs v. Snider et al.*, [1925] *Reference re Natural Products Marketing Act*. In more recent cases, the existence of a "general" trade and commerce power has been affirmed by the Chief Justice in *MacDonald et al. v. Vapor Canada Ltd.* (1976), and by Estey J. in *Labatt Breweries of Canada Ltd. v. A.-G. Can. et al.*, (1970). Yet, despite all these affirmations, the *Wharton* and *Canada Standard Trade Mark* cases remain the only ones in which a final appellate court has actually applied the general trade and commerce power to validate federal legislation and the correctness of even these decisions has been widely doubted . . . . With these exceptions, the potential applicability of the general trade and commerce power has been considered and rejected in a string of final appellate court decisions beginning the year after *Wharton*'s case with *A.-G. Can. v. A.-G. Alta et al.* (Insurance Reference), through to and including both the *Vapor Canada* and *Labatt* cases.

One reason for this conspicuous lack of success is doubtless to be found in the test for the general trade and commerce power implicit in *Wharton*. If every economic issue that could be characterised as a "question of general interest throughout the Dominion" were to fall under federal competence by virtue of s. 91(2), then the extent of the power would hardly be narrower than it would on a literal reading of the words "regulation of trade and commerce" alone. There is hardly an economic issue which, if only by virtue of its recurrence in locations around the country, could not be characterised as a matter of general interest throughout the Dominion . . . .

Every general enactment will necessarily have some local impact, and if it is true that an overly literal conception of "general interest" will endanger the very idea of the local there are equal dangers in swinging the telescope the other way around. The forest is no less a forest for being made up of individual trees . . . .

The reason why the regulation of a single trade or business in the province cannot be a question of general interest throughout the Dominion, is that it lies at the very heart of the local autonomy envisaged in the *Constitution Act, 1867.* That a federal enactment purports to carry out such regulation in the same way in all the provinces or in association with other regulatory codes dealing with other trades or businesses does not change the fact that what is being created is an exact overlapping and hence a nullification of a jurisdiction conceded to the provinces by the Constitution. A different situation obtains, however, when what is at issue is general legislation aimed at the economy as a single integrated national unit rather than as a collection of separate local enterprises. Such legislation is qualitatively different from anything that could practically or constitutionally be enacted by the individual provinces either separately or in combination. The focus of such legislation is on the general, though its results will obviously be manifested in particular local effects any one of which may touch upon "property and civil rights in the province." Nevertheless, in pith and substance such legislation will be addressed to questions of general interest throughout the Dominion. The line of demarcation is clear between measures validly directed at a general regulation of the national economy and those merely aimed at centralised control over a large number of local economic entities . . . .

In approaching this difficult problem of characterisation it is useful to note the remarks of the Chief Justice in *MacDonald v. Vapor Canada Ltd.*, in which he cites as possible indicia for a valid exercise of the general trade and commerce power the presence of a national regulatory scheme, the oversight of a regulatory agency and a concern with trade in general rather than with an aspect of a particular business. To this list I would add what to my mind would be even stronger indications of valid general regulation of trade and commerce, namely (i) that the provinces jointly or severally would be constitutionally incapable of passing such an enactment, and (ii) the failure to include one or more provinces or localities would jeopardize successful operation in other parts of the country.

The above does not purport to be an exhaustive list, nor is the presence of any or all of these indicia necessarily decisive. The proper approach to the characterisation is still the one suggested in *Citizens Ins. Co. of Canada v. Parsons* (1881), a careful case-by-case assessment. Nevertheless, the presence of such factors does at least make it far more probable that what is being addressed in a federal enactment is genuinely a national economic concern and not just a collection of local ones.

It is with these considerations in mind that I turn to the question of whether s. 32(1)(c) can be said validly to depend on the federal trade and commerce power . . . .

Having found that s. 32(1)(c) is not an isolated provision, but rather part of a regulatory scheme, it still remains to assess whether this scheme is valid under the second branch of s. 91(2). The fact of forming part of such a scheme is but one indication of validity and not in itself determinate. A number of cases have found that the scheme embodied by the Act also displays such additional indicia as a national scope, a general application and a concern with trade as a whole rather than with a single business . . . .

I would also, however, mention an additional factor. A scheme aimed at the regulation of competition is in my view an example of the genre of legislation that could not practically or constitutionally be enacted by a provincial government. Given the free flow of trade across provincial borders guaranteed by s. 121 of the

246 *MADE IN CANADA*

Constitution Act, 1867, Canada is, for economic purposes, a single huge marketplace. If competition is to be regulated at all it must be regulated federally. This fact leads to the syllogism cited by Hogg and Grover, "The Constitutionality of the Competition Bill" at 200.

> [R]egulation of the competitive sector of the economy can be effectively accomplished only by federal action. If there is no federal power to enact a competition policy, then Canada cannot have a competition policy. The consequence of a denial of federal constitutional power is, therefore, in practical effect, a gap in the distribution of legislative powers.

It has been suggested that in *R. v. Eastern Terminal Elevator Co.,* (1925), Duff J., endorsed the existence of such a distributive gap when he identified as a "lurking fallacy" in a federal argument the proposition "that the Dominion has such power because no single Province, nor, indeed, all the Provinces acting together, could put into effect such a sweeping scheme." I am of the opinion that Duff J., was in this quote speaking of logistical or financial obstacles standing in the way of provincial action. If he intended to go beyond this and identify an area in which neither the federal nor the provincial government could constitutionally legislate then, with great respect, I believe him to have been in error. The same error would deny federal constitutional competence to legislate under the general trade and commerce power.

All these considerations lead to the conclusion that s. 32(1)*(c)* is valid federal legislation under s. 91(2) of the *Constitution Act 1867,* as well as s. 91(27). The Attorney-General of Canada also contends that s. 32(1)*(c)* is valid under the "Peace, Order, and good Government" power, but in view of the finding of validity under s. 91(2) it is unnecessary to pursue this contention.

o

CITY NATIONAL LEASING v. GENERAL MOTORS OF CANADA LTD.◇

City National Leasing purchased the majority of its vehicles from General Motors. It claimed that GM had violated a section of the *Combines Investigation Act* by giving preferential interest rates to its competitors. As a result, it brought an action for damages against GM as provided by section 31.1 of the Act. GM claimed that the institution of a private right of action was *ultra vires* the federal government. The central issue before the court was whether section 31.1 could be sustained under the general trade and commerce power. The Chief Justice, writing the decision for the court, began again with an analysis of *Parsons* as he did in *C.N. Transport.*

◇[1989] 1 S.C.R. 641.

DICKSON C.J. (for the Court):

In examining cases which have considered s. 91(2), it is evident that courts have been sensitive to the need to reconcile the general trade and commerce power of the federal government with the provincial power over property and civil rights. Balancing has not been easy. Following the initial articulation of the scope of the general trade and commerce power in *Parsons*, ... the Privy Council briefly adopted what might be regarded as an overly inclusive interpretation of the power in *John Deere Plow Co. v. Wharton*, ... before retreating to an overly restrictive stance to its interpretation in the *Board of Commerce* case. In *Wharton*, Viscount Haldane, speaking of federally incorporated companies, sketched in broad terms the federal power to regulate trade and commerce under the second branch of *Parsons*:

> ... if it be established that the Dominion Parliament can create such companies, then it becomes *a question of general interest throughout the Dominion* in what fashion they should be permitted to trade. [Emphasis added.]

In contrast, in the *Board of Commerce* case, the Privy Council rejected the trade and commerce power (without distinguishing between the two branches) as the basis for anti-combines legislation, holding that the trade and commerce power had no independent content and could only be invoked as ancillary to other federal powers ...

With respect, in my view, neither the position articulated in *Wharton* nor that advanced in the *Board of Commerce* case correctly assesses the balance to be struck between s. 91(2) and s. 92(13). *Wharton* is clearly overly expansive, sweeping all general economic issues into the grasp of s. 91(2). On the other hand, the residual interpretation articulated in the *Board of Commerce* case fails to breathe life into the trade and commerce power and fails to recognize that provincial powers are a subtraction from the federal powers. The true balance between property and civil rights and the regulation of trade and commerce must lie somewhere between an all pervasive interpretation of s. 91(2) and an interpretation that renders the general trade and commerce power to all intents vapid and meaningless.

This court took the first step towards delineating more specific principles of validity for legislation enacted under the general trade and commerce power in *Vapour Canada*.

In that case, s. 7(e) of the *Trade Marks Act*, R.S.C. 1970, c. T-10, was challenged as *ultra vires* Parliament ....

The court struck down the provision as *ultra vires*. Chief Justice Laskin, speaking for five members of the court, proposed three hallmarks of validity for legislation under the second branch of the trade and commerce power. First, the impugned legislation must be part of a general regulatory scheme. Second, the scheme must be monitored by the continuing oversight of a regulatory agency. Third, the legislation must be concerned with trade as a whole rather than with a particular industry. Each of these requirements is evidence of a concern that federal authority under the second branch of the trade and commerce power does not encroach on provincial jurisdiction. By limiting the means which federal legislators may employ to that of a regulatory scheme overseen by a regulatory agency, and by limiting the object of federal legislation to trade as a whole, these requirements attempt to maintain a delicate balance between federal and provincial power. On the basis of these criteria, Laskin C.J., then rejected the general trade and commerce power as the constitutional foundation for s. 7(*e*).

Three members of the court affirmed the *Vapor Canada* criteria in *Canadian National Transportation* . . . .

In reaching the conclusion that s. 32(1)(*c*) of the *Combines Investigation Act* was within the scope of the general trade and commerce power, and writing for the minority of the court, I adopted Laskin C.J.'s three criteria in *Vapor Canada, supra*, but added two factors that I considered indicia of the valid exercise of the general trade and commerce power: (i) the legislation should be of a nature that the provinces jointly or severally would be constitutionally incapable of enacting; and (ii) the failure to include one or more provinces or localities in the legislative scheme would jeopardize the successful operation of the scheme in other parts of the country. These two requirements, like Laskin C.J.'s three criteria, serve to ensure that federal legislation does not upset the balance of power between federal and provincial governments. In total, the five factors provide a preliminary checklist of characteristics, the presence of which in legislation is an indication of validity under the trade and commerce power. These indicia do not, however, represent an exhaustive list of traits that will tend to characterise general trade and commerce legislation. Nor is the presence or absence of any of these five criteria necessarily determinative . . . .

On any occasion where the general trade and commerce power is advanced as a ground of constitutional validity, a careful case by case analysis remains appropriate. The five factors articulated in *Canadian National Transportation* merely represent a principled way to begin the difficult task of distinguishing between matters relating to trade and commerce and those of a more local nature.

The Chief Justice then considered the approach to be taken when determining the constitutionality of legislation under 91 (2).

The steps in the analysis may be summarised as follows: First, the court must determine whether the impugned provision can be viewed as intruding on provincial powers, and if so to what extent (if it does not intrude, then the only possible issue is the validity of the act). Second, the court must establish whether the act (or a severable part of it) is valid; in cases under the second branch of s. 91(2) this will normally involve finding the presence of a regulatory scheme and then ascertaining whether that scheme meets the requirements articulated in *Vapor Canada*, and in *Canadian National Transportation*. If the scheme is not valid, that is the end of the inquiry. If the scheme of the regulation is declared valid, the court must then determine whether the impugned provision is sufficiently integrated with the scheme that it can be upheld by virtue of that relationship. This requires considering the seriousness of the encroachment on provincial powers, in order to decide on the proper standard for such a relationship. If the provision passes this integration test, it is *intra vires* Parliament as an exercise of the general trade and commerce power. If the provision is not sufficiently integrated into the scheme of regulation, it cannot be sustained under the second branch of s. 91(2). I note that in certain cases it may be possible to dispense with some of the aforementioned steps if a clear answer to one of them will be dispositive of the issue. For example, if the provision in question has no relation to the regulatory scheme then the question of its validity may be quickly answered on that ground alone. The approach taken in a number of past cases is more easily understood if this possibility is recognized.

The first step, therefore, in assessing the validity of s. 31.1 of the *Combines Investigation Act* is to determine whether the impugned provision can be seen as encroaching on provincial powers, and if so, to what extent. As s. 31.1 creates a civil right of action it is not difficult to conclude that the provision does, on its face, appear to encroach on provincial power to some extent. The creation of civil actions is generally a matter within provincial jurisdiction under s. 92(13) of the *Constitution Act, 1867*. This provincial power over civil rights is a significant power and one that is not lightly encroached upon. In assessing the seriousness of this encroachment, however, three facts must be taken into consideration. The first is that s. 31.1 is only a remedial provision; its purpose is to help enforce the substantive aspects of the act, but it is not in itself a substantive part of the act. By their nature, remedial provisions are typically less intrusive *vis à vis* provincial powers. The second important fact is the limited scope of the action. Section 31.1 does not create a general cause of action; its application is carefully limited by the provisions of the act. The third relevant fact is that it is well-established that the federal government is not constitutionally precluded from creating rights of civil action where such measures may be shown to be warranted. This court has sustained federally created civil actions in a variety of contexts . . . .

The Chief Justice next referred to a number of cases showing "that the inclusion of a private right of action in a federal enactment is not constitutionally fatal."

. . . The second step in determining the validity of s. 31.1 is to establish whether the act contains a regulatory scheme. The presence of a well-orchestrated scheme of economic regulation is immediately apparent on examination of the *Combines Investigation Act*. The existence of a regulatory scheme is in evidence throughout the entire act . . . .

From this overview of the *Combines Investigation Act* I have no difficulty in concluding that the act as a whole embodies a complex scheme of economic regulation. The purpose of the act is to eliminate activities that reduce competition in the marketplace. The entire act is geared to achieving this objective. The act identifies and defines anti-competitive conduct. It establishes an investigatory mechanism for revealing prohibited activities and provides an extensive range of criminal and administrative redress against companies engaging in behaviour that tends to reduce competition. In my view, these three components, elucidation of prohibited conduct, creation of an investigatory procedure, and the establishment of a remedial mechanism, constitute a well-integrated scheme of regulation designed to discourage forms of commercial behaviour viewed as detrimental to Canada and the Canadian economy.

Having discerned the presence of a regulatory scheme in the *Combines Investigation Act*, it is necessary to consider the validity of the scheme under the general trade and commerce power in light of the criteria established in *Canadian National Transportation*. . . . Four criteria remain to be examined: (1) whether the regulatory scheme operates under the oversight of an agency, (2) whether the act is concerned with trade in general, (3) whether the provinces would be constitutionally capable of enacting combines legislation, and finally, (4) whether the failure to include one or more provinces or localities would jeopardize the successful operation of the *Combines Investigation Act*.

The foregoing review of the *Combines Investigation Act* leaves no doubt that the scheme regulating anti-competitive activities operates under the watchful gaze of a regulatory agency. . . .

I am also of the view that the *Combines Investigation Act* meets the remaining three indicia of *Canadian National Transportation*. These criteria share a common theme: all three are indications that the scheme of regulation is national in scope and that local regulation would be inadequate. The act is quite clearly concerned with the regulation of trade in general, rather than with the regulation of a particular industry or commodity . . . .

Having found that the *Combines Investigation Act* contains a regulatory scheme, valid under s. 91(2) of the *Constitution [Act]*, the only issue remaining to be addressed is the constitutional validity of s. 31.1. As I have already noted, mere inclusion in a valid legislative scheme does not *ipso facto* confer constitutional validity upon a particular provision. The provision must be sufficiently related to that scheme for it to be constitutionally justified. The degree of relationship that is required is a function of the extent of the provision's intrusion into provincial powers. I have already discussed this issue and concluded that s. 31.1 intrudes, though in a limited way, on the important provincial power over civil rights. In this light, I do not think that a strict test such as "truly necessary" or "integral," is appropriate. On the other hand, it is not enough that the section be merely "tacked on" to admittedly valid legislation. The correct approach in this case is to ask whether the provision is functionally related to the general objective of the legislation, and to the structure and the content of the scheme. A similar test has been applied in other cases, as I have noted, and I think it is also the proper test for the circumstances of this appeal.

The nature of this relationship is addressed in this last stage of constitutional analysis. If s. 31.1 cannot be characterised as functionally related to the scheme of combines regulation, it will be *ultra vires*. Neither the respondent nor the Attorney General of Canada submitted that s. 31.1 could be sustained under a head of power other than s. 91(2).

I am of the opinion that the necessary link between s. 31.1 and the act exists. Section 31.1 is the integral, well-conceived component of the economic regulation strategy found in the *Combines Investigation Act*. Even if a much stricter test of fit were applied—for instance one of "necessarily incidental"—s. 31.1 would still pass the test. Under the test of "functionally related" the section is clearly valid.

ENVIRONMENT

INTERPROVINCIAL CO-OPERATIVES LTD. v. R.◇

The defendants were operators of chlor-alkali plants in Saskatchewan and Ontario which discharged mercury into waterways flowing into Manitoba. As required by section 2 of its *Fisherman's Assistance and Polluter's Liability Act*, the province of Manitoba provided compensation to Manitoba fishing enterprises harmed by water pollution. The Act also provided that the province could recover its losses through legal action even if the activity was permitted in the polluter's home jurisdiction. The defendants, who had complied with the laws of their provinces, claimed that Manitoba's attempt to recover losses from them amounted to regulation of enterprises in other provinces and was therefore, *ultra vires*. By a majority of four to three the Supreme Court held that Manitoba could not create a right of action against firms acting legally outside the province.

PIGEON J. (Martland and Beetz JJ. concurring):
... On its face s. 4(2) of the *Assistance Act* purports to destroy the effect of legislation passed in adjacent Provinces. It was agreed on all sides in argument that the question raised in this case is to be answered on the assumption that the appellants' activities complained of were properly licensed under the laws of the Province in which they were performed, but this essential provision of the *Assistance Act* declares that this will afford no defence to Manitoba's claim. Thus, the situation is that, although presumably the appellants' operations are authorized by the law of the Province where they are effected, they are sought to be enjoined under the laws of another Province by virtue of an enactment of that other Province.

In the circumstances of this case, I find it necessary to say that it does not appear to me that a Province can validly license on its territory operations having an injurious effect outside its borders so as to afford a defence against whatever remedies are available at common law in favour of persons suffering injury thereby in another Province ....

The legal situation would not be different if, instead of polluting plants, we were faced with dams flooding lands in an adjoining Province. It could certainly not be contended that the Province in which the dam was erected could validly license the flooding in the other ....

It has been determined in *Citizens Ins. Co. of Canada v. Parsons* (1881), that the power to regulate by legislation the contracts of a particular business or trade is within the scope of provincial legislative authority over property and civil rights. However, where business contracts affect interprovincial trade, it is no longer a question within provincial jurisdiction. The matter becomes one of federal jurisdiction. Such is the substance of our recent judgment in *Burns Foods Ltd. et al. v. A.-G. Man. et al.* (1973). In my opinion, the same view ought to be taken in respect of

---

◇[1976] 1 S.C.R. 477.

pollution of interprovincial waters as with respect to interprovincial trade. Even if the enumerated power, s. 91(12), "Sea Coast and Inland Fisheries," is not quite as explicit as s. 91(2), "The Regulation of Trade and Commerce," the paramount consideration is that the specific powers are only "for greater certainty," the basic rule is that general legislative authority in respect of all that is not within the provincial field is federal. The importance of this basic rule is such that, although s. 91(2) is in terms unlimited, it has in fact been construed as limited to interprovincial or international trade and commerce. Here, we are faced with a pollution problem that is not really local in scope but truly interprovincial . . . .

It seems clear that a Province, as owner of inland fisheries in its territory, is entitled to legislate for the protection of its property. However, in respect of injury caused by acts performed outside its territory, I cannot accede to the view that this can be treated as a matter within its legislative authority when those acts are done in another Province any more than when they are accomplished in another country. In my view, although the injurious acts cannot be justified by or under legislation adopted in the Province or State where the plants are operated, by the same token, Manitoba is restricted to such remedies as are available at common law or under federal legislation.

For those reasons, I would allow the appeals and restore the judgment of Matas J., with costs in this Court and in the Court of Appeal; there should be no costs to or against any of the intervenants.

LASKIN C.J. (Judson and Spence JJ. concurring) dissenting:

I do not see how it can be said that the Manitoba Act denies to the appellants any legal rights they acquired in Saskatchewan or in Ontario in respect of the operation there of their respective chlor-alkali plants. If, as is assumed for the purposes of this case, they are respectively licensed to discharge contaminants to the extent that they did, that licence, local to each of the Provinces, does not have an extra-territorial reach to entitle each of them with impunity to send their pollutants into the waters of another Province. That would be to assert against Manitoba an extra-territorial privilege and to use it as a basis for denying to Manitoba any local internal power to charge Ipco and Dryden with civil liability for damage produced in Manitoba to Manitoba property interests . . . .

Manitoba's predominant interest in applying its own law, being the law of the forum in this case, to the question of liability for injury in Manitoba to property interests therein is undeniable. Neither Saskatchewan nor Ontario can put forward as strong a claim to have their provincial law apply in the Manitoba action; in other words, the wrong in this case was committed, or the cause of action arose in Manitoba and not in Saskatchewan or in Ontario.

RITCHIE J.:

Ritchie J. agreed with Pigeon J. that the act was _ultra vires_ because it purported to permit Manitoba to invoke its laws in other provinces. He also commented on the jurisdiction of the federal government.

Mr. Justice Pigeon, as I understand his reasons, has reached the same conclusion on the ground that as the acts of the appellants necessarily have an interprovincial effect they are a subject matter within the exclusive authority of Parliament in accordance with its residual power over matters of interprovincial concern not specifically allocated to either federal or provincial authority under the *British North America Act, 1867*. He concludes therefore that the Provinces of Ontario and Saskatchewan were without authority to license the appellants' acts of contamination, and as a corollary to this reasoning, he concludes that the legislation in question is *ultra vires* the Province as involving the exclusively federal field of the pollution of interprovincial rivers. This argument was not advanced by either of the parties at any stage and it formed no part of the submissions made by any of the intervenants as all concerned proceeded throughout on the assumption that the acts of pollution were duly permitted by the appropriate regulatory authority having jurisdiction where they took place. I am unable to share the view of my brother Pigeon because I take the view that while the control of pollution of such rivers is a federal matter, the legislation here impugned has to do with its effect in damaging property within the Province of Manitoba and it only becomes inapplicable by reason of the extra-territorial aspect to which I have made reference. The action here was instituted by the Crown as assignee of the rights of private individuals and in my view the applicable law is that of the place where the acts complained of were done.

o

FOWLER v. R. [◇]

In his logging operation in Forbes Bay, British Columbia Fowler dragged logs across a small stream leaving a residue of branches and tree-tops. He was charged under section 33 of Canada's *Fisheries Act* which provides that "No person engaged in logging, lumbering . . . shall put or knowingly permit to be put, any slash, stumps or other debris into any water frequented by fish or that flows into such water. . . ." Fowler's defence was that the Act was *ultra vires* for the matter fell within provincial jurisdiction under public lands, local works, and/or property and civil rights. The federal government claimed jurisdiction under 91(12) "Sea Coast and Inland Fisheries." The stream, used by salmon for spawning, flowed into the coastal waters, and at trial a fishery officer testified that every time something was dumped into the stream it could have a far-reaching effect or little effect. The Supreme Court decided in Fowler's favour on the grounds that the prohibition was too broad and was not linked directly to "any likely" harm to the fisheries.

MARTLAND J. (for the Court):

The legislation in question here does not deal directly with fisheries, as such, within the meaning of those definitions. Rather, it seeks to control certain kinds of operations not strictly on the basis that they have deleterious effects on fish but, rather, on the basis that they might have such effects. *Prima facie* s. 33(3) regulates

---

◇[1980] 2 S.C.R. 213.

property and civil rights within a Province. Dealing, as it does, with such rights and not dealing specifically with "fisheries," in order to support the legislation it must be established that it provides for matters necessarily incidental to effective legislation on the subject matter of sea coast and inland fisheries . . . .

Counsel for the respondent supports the legislation on the ground that it is preventive legislation intended to protect and preserve fish. He contends that its validity does not depend on showing that the operations to which it relates cause actual harm to a fishery. . . .

The criteria for establishing liability under s. 33(3) are indeed wide. Logging, lumbering, land clearing and other operations are covered. The substances which are proscribed are slash, stumps and other debris. The amount of the substance which is deposited is not relevant. The legislation extends to cover not only water frequented by fish but also water that flows into such water, ice over any such water and any place from which slash, stumps and other debris are likely to be carried into such water.

Section 33(3) makes no attempt to link the proscribed conduct to actual or potential harm to fisheries. It is a blanket prohibition of certain types of activity, subject to provincial jurisdiction, which does not delimit the elements of the offence so as to link the prohibition to any likely harm to fisheries. Furthermore, there was no evidence before the Court to indicate that the full range of activities caught by the sub-section do, in fact, cause harm to fisheries. In my opinion, the prohibition in its broad terms is not necessarily incidental to the federal power to legislate in respect of sea coast and inland fisheries and is *ultra vires* of the federal Parliament.

I would allow the appeal, set aside the judgment of the Court of Appeal and the County Court and restore the judgment at trial. The appellant is entitled to his costs throughout.

o

NORTHWEST FALLING
CONTRACTORS LTD. v. R. ✧

Northwest Falling spilled diesel fuel into fish-inhabited waters and was charged under section 33 of Canada's *Fisheries Act* which stated that no "person shall deposit or permit the deposit of a deleterious substance of any type in water frequented by fish or in any place under any conditions where such deleterious substance or any deleterious substance that results from the deposit of such deleterious substance may enter any such water." Northwest claimed that the federal law invaded provincial jurisdiction over "property and civil rights." The Supreme Court rejected their argument.

MARTLAND J. (for the Court):

The appellant's main argument was that the legislation under attack is really an attempt by Parliament to legislate generally on the subject matter of pollution and

---

✧[1980] 2 S.C.R. 292.

thus to invade the area of provincial legislative power over property and civil rights. He points to the very broad definition of "water frequented by fish" in s. 33(11) which refers to "Canadian fisheries waters" which, under s. 2, includes "all waters in the territorial sea of Canada and all internal waters of Canada." He also refers to the broad scope of the definition of "deleterious substance." When these definitions are applied to s. 33(2), it is said that the sub-section is really concerned with the pollution of Canadian waters.

The charges laid in this case do not, however, effectively bring into question the validity of the extension of the reach of the sub-section to waters that would not, in fact, be fisheries waters "or to substances other than those defined in paragraph (*a*) of sub-section 33(11)." The charges relate to diesel fuel spilled into tidal waters. The task of the Court in determining the constitutional validity of s. 33(2) is to ascertain the true nature and character of the legislation. It is necessary to decide whether the sub-section is aimed at the protection and preservation of fisheries. In my opinion it is.

Basically, it is concerned with the deposit of deleterious substances in water frequented by fish, or in a place where the deleterious substance may enter such water. The definition of a deleterious substance is related to the substance being deleterious to fish. In essence, the sub-section seeks to protect fisheries by preventing substances deleterious to fish entering into waters frequented by fish. This is a proper concern of legislation under the heading of "Sea Coast and Inland Fisheries."

The situation in this case is different from that which was considered in *Fowler v. The Queen*, a judgment of this Court recently delivered.... That case involved the constitutional validity of s. 33(3) of the *Fisheries Act* and it was held to be *ultra vires* of Parliament to enact. Unlike s-s. (2), s-s. (3) contains no reference to deleterious substances. It is not restricted by its own terms to activities that are harmful to fish habitat....

In my opinion, s. 33(2) was *ultra vires* of the Parliament of Canada to enact. The definition of "deleterious substance" ensures that the scope of s. 33(2) is restricted to a prohibition of deposits that threaten fish, fish habitat or the use of fish by man.

o

R. v. CROWN ZELLERBACH LTD.✧

Crown Zellerbach was charged with dumping wood waste into the waters of Beaver Cove in British Columbia thus breaching the federal *Ocean Dumping Act* which permitted dumping only in accordance with the terms and conditions of a permit. The Company's defence was that the Act was *ultra vires* for it could not be shown that the prohibited dumping affected marine life. In a split 4 to 3 decision the Supreme Court found against the company.

✧[1988] 1 S.C.R. 401.

LE DAIN J. (Dickson C.J.C., McIntyre and Wilson JJ. concurring):
... Before considering the relationship of the subject matter of the Act to the possible bases of federal legislative jurisdiction something more should be said about the characterisation of that subject matter, according to the respective contentions of the parties. As I have indicated, the appellant contends that the Act is directed to the control or regulation of marine pollution, the subject matter of the Convention on the Prevention of Marine Pollution by Dumping of Wastes and other Matter. The respondent, on the other hand, contends that by its terms the Act is directed at dumping which need not necessarily have a pollutant effect. It prohibits the dumping of *any* substance, including a substance not specified in Sch. I or II, except in accordance with the terms and conditions of a permit. In my opinion, despite this apparent scope, the Act, viewed as a whole, may be properly characterised as directed to the control or regulation of marine pollution, in so far as that may be relevant to the question of legislative jurisdiction. The chosen, and perhaps only effective, regulatory model makes it necessary, in order to prevent marine pollution, to prohibit the dumping of any substance without a permit. Its purpose is to require a permit so that the regulatory authority may determine before the proposed dumping has occurred whether it may be permitted upon certain terms and conditions, having regard to the factors or concerns specified in ss. 9 and 10 of the Act and Sch. III. The Act is concerned with the dumping of substances which may be shown or presumed to have an adverse effect on the marine environment. The Minister and not the person proposing to do the dumping must be the judge of this, acting in accordance with the criteria or factors indicated in ss. 9 and 10 and Sch. III of the Act. There is no suggestion that the Act purports to authorize the prohibition of dumping without regard to perceived adverse effect or the likelihood of such effect on the marine environment. The nature of the marine environment and its protection from adverse effect from dumping is a complex matter which must be left to expert judgment ....

Le Dain J. then reviewed the court's decisions in *Fowler* and *Northwest Falling*. He concluded that the Act made no attempt to link the prohibited conduct to fisheries and, as a result, could not be supported as legislation in relation to "Sea Coast and Inland Fisheries." He then reviewed the decisions of the Judicial Committee and the Supreme Court relating to the national dimensions or national concern doctrine (as it is now generally called) of the federal peace, order, and good government power in its application to marine water pollution.

From this survey of the opinion expressed in this court concerning the national concern doctrine of the federal peace, order, and good government power I draw the following conclusions as to what now appears to be firmly established:

1. The national concern doctrine is separate and distinct from the national emergency doctrine of the peace, order, and good government power, which is chiefly distinguishable by the fact that it provides a constitutional basis for what is necessarily legislation of a temporary nature.

2. The national concern doctrine applies to both new matters which did not exist at Confederation and to matters which, although originally matters of a local

or private nature in a province, have since, in the absence of national emergency, become matters of national concern.

3. For a matter to qualify as a matter of national concern in either sense it must have a singleness, distinctiveness and indivisibility that clearly distinguishes it from matters of provincial concern and a scale of impact on provincial jurisdiction that is reconcilable with the fundamental distribution of legislative power under the Constitution.

4. In determining whether a matter has attained the required degree of singleness, distinctiveness and indivisibility that clearly distinguishes it from matters of provincial concern it is relevant to consider what would be the effect on extra-provincial interests of a provincial failure to deal effectively with the control or regulation of the intraprovincial aspects of the matter.

This last factor, generally referred to as the "provincial inability" test and noted with apparent approval in this court in *Labatt, Schneider* and *Wetmore*, was suggested, as Professor Hogg acknowledges, by Professor Gibson in his article, "Measuring 'National Dimensions,'" (1976) 7 *Man. L.J.* 15, as the most satisfactory rationale of the cases in which the national concern doctrine of the peace, order and good government power has been applied as a basis of federal jurisdiction. As expounded by Professor Gibson, the test would appear to involve a limited or qualified application of federal jurisdiction. As put by Professor Gibson at 34–35:

> By this approach, a national dimension would exist whenever a significant aspect of a problem is beyond provincial reach because it falls within the jurisdiction of another province or of the federal Parliament. It is important to emphasise however that the *entire* problem would not fall within federal competence in such circumstances. Only that aspect of the problem that is beyond provincial control would do so. Since the "P.O. & G.G." clause bestows only residual powers, the existence of a national dimension justifies no more federal legislation than is necessary to fill the gap in provincial powers. For example, federal jurisdiction to legislate for pollution of interprovincial waterways or to control "pollution price wars" would (in the absence of other independent sources of federal competence) extend only to measures to reduce the risk that citizens of one province would be harmed by the non-co-operation of another province or provinces.

To similar effect, he said in his conclusion at 36:

> Having regard to the residual nature of the power, it is the writer's thesis that "national dimensions" are possessed by only those aspects of legislative problems which are beyond the ability of the provincial legislatures to deal because they involve either federal competence or that of another province. Where it would be possible to deal fully with the problem by co-operative action of two or more legislatures, the "national dimension" concerns only the risk of non-co-operation, and justifies only federal legislation addressed to that risk.

This would appear to contemplate a concurrent or overlapping federal jurisdiction which, I must observe, is in conflict with what was emphasised by Beetz J. in the *Anti-Inflation Act* reference—that where a matter falls within the national concern doctrine of the peace, order and good government power, as distinct from the emergency doctrine, Parliament has an exclusive jurisdiction of a plenary nature to legislate in relation to that matter, including its intraprovincial aspects.

As expressed by Professor Hogg in the first and second editions of his *Constitutional Law of Canada*, the "provincial inability" test would appear to be adopted simply as a reason for finding that a particular matter is one of national concern falling within the peace, order and good government power: that provincial failure to deal effectively with the intraprovincial aspects of the matter could have an adverse effect on extraprovincial interests. In this sense, the "provincial inability" test is one of the indicia for determining whether a matter has that character of singleness or indivisibility required to bring it within the national concern doctrine. It is because of the interrelatedness of the intraprovincial and extraprovincial aspects of the matter that it requires a single or uniform legislative treatment. The "provincial inability" test must not, however, go so far as to provide a rationale for the general notion, hitherto rejected in the cases, that there must be a plenary jurisdiction in one order of government or the other to deal with any legislative problem. In the context of the national concern doctrine of the peace, order and good government power, its utility lies, in my opinion, in assisting in the determination whether a matter has the requisite singleness or indivisibility from a function as well as a conceptual point of view . . . .

Le Dain J. continued with a review of the decision in *Interprovincial Co-Operatives* and noted that three of the four justices in the majority found interprovincial waterways to be a matter of peace, order and good government.

Marine pollution, because of its predominantly extraprovincial as well as international character and implications, is clearly a matter of concern to Canada as a whole. The question is whether the control of pollution by the dumping of substances in marine waters, including provincial marine waters, is a single, indivisible matter, distinct from the control of pollution by the dumping of substances in other provincial waters. The *Ocean Dumping Control Act* reflects a distinction between the pollution of salt water and the pollution of fresh water. The question, as I conceive it, is whether that distinction is sufficient to make the control of marine pollution by the dumping of substances a single, indivisible matter falling within the national concern doctrine of the peace, order and good government power.

Marine pollution by the dumping of substances is clearly treated by the Convention of the Prevention of Marine Pollution by Dumping of Wastes and other Matter as a distinct and separate form of water pollution having its own characteristics and scientific considerations. This impression is reinforced by the United Nations Report of the Joint Group of Experts on the Scientific Aspects of Marine Pollution, Reports and Studies No. 15, *The Review of the Health of the Oceans* (UNESCO 1982) (hereinafter referred to as the "United Nations Report"), which forms part of the materials placed before the court in the argument. It is to be noted, however, that, unlike the *Ocean Dumping Control Act*, the Convention does not require regulation of pollution by the dumping of waste in the internal marine waters of a state. Article III, para. 3, of the Convention defines the "sea" as "all marine waters other than the internal waters of the States." The internal marine waters of a state are those which lie landward to the baseline of the territorial sea, which is determined in accordance with the rules laid down in the United Nations Convention on the Law of the Sea, 1982. The limitation of the undertaking in the Convention, presumably for reasons of state policy, to the control of dumping in the territorial sea and the open sea cannot, in my opinion, obscure the obviously close relationship, which is emphasised in the United Nations Report, between pollution in coastal waters, including the internal marine waters of a state, and pollution in the territorial sea. Moreover, there is much force, in my opinion, in the appellant's contention that the difficulty of ascertaining by visual observation the boundary between the territorial sea and the internal marine waters of a state creates an unacceptable degree of uncertainty for the application of regulatory and penal provisions. This, and not simply the possibility or likelihood of the movement of pollutants across that line, is what constitutes the essential indivisibility of the matter of marine pollution by the dumping of substances.

There remains the question whether the pollution of marine waters by the dumping of substances is sufficiently distinguishable from the pollution of fresh waters by such dumping to meet the requirement of singleness or indivisibility. In many cases the pollution of fresh waters will have a pollutant effect in the marine waters into which they flow, and this is noted by the United Nations Report, but that report, as I have suggested, emphasises that marine pollution, because of the differences in the composition and action of marine waters and fresh waters, has its own characteristics and scientific considerations that distinguish it from fresh water pollution. Moreover, the distinction between salt water and fresh water as limiting the application of the *Ocean Dumping Control Act* meets the consideration emphasised by a majority of this court in the *Anti-Inflation Act* reference—that in order for a matter to qualify as one of national concern falling within the federal peace, order and good government power it must have ascertainable and reasonable limits, in so far as its impact on provincial jurisdiction is concerned.

For these reasons I am of the opinion that s. 4(1) of the *Ocean Dumping Control Act* is constitutionally valid as enacted in relation to a matter falling within the national concern doctrine of the peace, order and good government power of the Parliament of Canada, and, in particular, that it is constitutional in its application to the dumping of waste in the waters of Beaver Cove . . . .

LA FOREST J. (Beetz and Lamer JJ. concurring) dissenting:
La Forest considered, and rejected, a number of possible bases for federal jurisdiction to enact the *Ocean Dumping Act* including heads 10, 12, 13 and 27 of Section 91 and the federal treaty power.

. . . However widely one interprets the federal power to control ocean pollution along the preceding line of analysis, it will not serve to support the provision impugned here, one that, as in the *Fowler* case, . . . is a blanket prohibition against depositing *any* substance in waters without regard to its nature or amount, and one moreover where there is, in Martland J.'s words, at p. 226 S.C.R. of that case, "no attempt to link the proscribed conduct to actual or potential harm" to what is sought to be protected; in *Fowler*, the fisheries, here, the ocean. As in *Fowler*, too, there is no evidence to indicate that the full range of activities caught by the provision cause the harm sought to be prevented . . . .

Why Parliament should have chosen to enact a prohibition in such broad terms is a matter upon which one is left to speculate. It may be that, in view of the lack of knowledge about the effects of various substances deposited in water, it may be necessary to monitor all such deposits. We have no evidence on the extent to which it is necessary to monitor all deposits into the sea to develop an effective regime for the prevention of ocean pollution. A system of monitoring that was necessarily incidental to an effective legislative scheme for the control of ocean pollution could constitutionally be justified. But here not only was no material advanced to establish the need for such a system, the Act goes much further and prohibits the deposit of any substance in the sea, including provincial internal waters. If such a provision were held valid, why would a federal provision prohibiting the emission of any substance in any quantity into the air, except as permitted by federal authorities, not be constitutionally justifiable as a measure for the control of ocean pollution, it now being known that deposits from the air are a serious source of ocean pollution?

Counsel for the appellant did not, of course, frame the issue in the manner in which I have thus far discussed it. I have examined it in this way, however, to show that on a more traditional approach to the underlying issues than he suggests Parliament has very wide powers to deal with ocean pollution, whether within or outside the limits of the province, but that even if one stretches this traditional approach to its limits, the impugned provision cannot constitutionally be justified. It requires a quantum leap to find constitutional justification for the provision, one, it seems to me, that would create considerable stress on Canadian federalism as it has developed over the years. What he urges for, we saw, is that the dumping of any substance in the sea beginning, apparently, from the coasts of the provinces and the mouths of provincial rivers falls exclusively within the legislative jurisdiction of Parliament as being a matter of national concern or dimension even though the seabed is within the province and whether or not the substance is noxious or potentially so.

Le Dain J. has in the course of his judgment discussed the cases relating to the development of the "national concern or dimension" aspect of the peace, order and good government clause, and I find it unnecessary to review that development in any detail. It is sufficient for my purpose to say that this development has since the 1930s particularly been resorted to from time to time to bring into the ambit of federal power a number of matters, such as radio (*Re Regulation & Control of Radio Communication*, (1932)) aeronautics (*Johannesson v. Rural Municipality of West St. Paul*, (1951)), and the national capital region (*Munro v. National Capital Com'n* (1966)), that are clearly of national importance. They do not fit comfortably within provincial power. Both in their workings and in their practical implications they have predominantly national dimensions. Many of these subjects are new and are obviously of extraprovincial concern. They are thus appropriate for assignment to the general federal legislative power. They are often related to matters intimately tied to federal jurisdiction. Radio (which is relevant to the power to regulate interprovincial undertakings) is an example. The closely contested issue of narcotics control (cf. *R. v. Hauser* (1979), and *Schneider v. The Queen* (1982), *per* Laskin C.J.C.) is intimately related to criminal law and international trade. The need to make such characterisations from time to time is readily apparent. From this necessary function, however, it is easy but, I say it with respect, fallacious to go further, and, taking a number of quite separate areas of activity, some under accepted constitutional values within federal, and some within provincial legislative capacity, consider them to be a single indivisible matter of national interest and concern lying outside the specific heads of power assigned under the Constitution. By conceptualizing broad social, economic and political issues in that way, one can effectively invent new heads of federal power under the national dimensions doctrine, thereby incidentally removing them from provincial jurisdiction or at least abridging the provinces' freedom of operation. This, as I see it, is the implication of the statement made by my colleague, then Professor Le Dain, in his article, "Sir Lyman Duff and the Constitution," 12 *Osgoode Hall L.J.* 261 (1974). He states, at p. 293:

> As reflected in the *Munro* case, the issue with respect to the general power, where reliance cannot be placed on the notion of emergency, is to determine what are to be considered to be single, indivisible matters of national interest and concern lying outside the specific heads of jurisdiction in sections 91 and 92. It is possible to invent such matters by applying new names to old legislative purposes. There is an increasing tendency to sum up a wide variety of legislative purposes in single, comprehensive designations. Control of inflation, environmental protection, and preservation of the national identity or independence are examples.

Professor Le Dain was there merely posing the problem; he did not attempt to answer it. It seems to me, however, that some of the examples he gives, notably the control of inflation and environmental protection, are all-pervasive, and if accepted as items falling within the general power of Parliament, would radically alter the division of legislative power in Canada. The attempt to include them in the federal general power seems to me to involve fighting on another plane the war that was lost on the economic plane in the Canadian New Deal cases. My colleague Beetz J. has, in *Reference re Anti-Inflation Act,* ... fully supported this way of viewing things in rejecting the control of inflation as a proper subject for incorporation into the peace, order and good government clause under the national dimension doctrine ....

What was there said by Beetz J. seems to me to apply, *a fortiori*, to the control of the environment, a subject more germane to the present issue. All physical activities have some environmental impact. Possible legislative responses to such activities cover a large number of the enumerated legislative powers, federal and provincial. To allocate the broad subject matter of environmental control to the federal government under its general power would effectively gut provincial legislative jurisdiction. As I mentioned before, environment protection, of course, encompasses far more than environmental pollution, which is what we are principally concerned with here. To take an example from the present context, wood waste in some circumstances undoubtedly pollutes the environment, but the very depletion of forests itself affects the ecological balance and, as such, constitutes an environmental problem. But environmental pollution alone is itself all-pervasive. It is a by-product of everything we do. In man's relationship with his environment, waste is unavoidable. The problem is thus not new, although it is only recently that the vast amount of waste products emitted into the atmosphere or dumped in water has begun to exceed the ability of the atmosphere and water to absorb and assimilate it on a global scale. There is thus cause for concern and governments of every level have begun to deal with the many activities giving rise to problems of pollution. In Canada, both federal and provincial levels of government have extensive powers to deal with these matters. Both have enacted comprehensive and specific schemes for the control of pollution and the protection of the environment. Some environmental pollution problems are of more direct concern to the federal government, some to the provincial government. But a vast number are interrelated, and all levels of government actively co-operate to deal with problems of mutual concern; for an example of this, see the Great Lakes study in *I.J.C. Report*.

To allocate environmental pollution exclusively to the federal Parliament would, it seems to me, involve sacrificing the principles of federalism enshrined in the Constitution. As Professor William R. Lederman has indicated in his article, "Unity and Diversity in Canadian Federalism: Ideals and Methods of Moderation" (1975), 53 *Can. Bar Rev.* 597, p. 610, environmental pollution "is no limited subject or theme, [it] is a sweeping subject or theme virtually all-pervasive in its legislative implications." If, he adds, it "were to be enfranchised as a new subject of federal power by virtue of the federal general power, then provincial power and autonomy would be on the way out over the whole range of local business, industry and commerce as established to date under the existing heads of provincial powers." And I would add to the legislative subjects that would be substantially eviscerated the control of the public domain and municipal government. Indeed, as Beetz J. in *Reference re Anti-Inflation Act*, stated of the proposed power over inflation, there would not be much left of the distribution of power if Parliament had exclusive jurisdiction over this subject. For similar views that the protection of environmental pollution cannot be attributed to a single head of legislative power, see P.W. Hogg, *Constitutional Law of Canada*, 2nd ed. (1985), pp. 392, 598; Gérald Beaudoin, "La protection de l'environnement et ses implications en droit constitutionnel", 23 *McGill L.J.* 207 (1977).

PATRIATION

A.-G. MANITOBA ET AL. v. A.-G. CANADA
(PATRIATION REFERENCE)◇

The Supreme Court of Canada, by way of appeal from reference cases put to the Manitoba Court of Appeal, the Newfoundland Court of Appeal and the Quebec Court of Appeal, was to decide whether by law or by constitutional convention,

---

◇[1981] 1 S.C.R. 753.

the government of Canada required provincial consent in requesting the Parliament of the United Kingdom to amend the *British North America Act* in such a way as would affect matters of provincial jurisdiction. The amendment here included an amending formula, a Charter of Rights and Freedoms, and a recognition of regional fiscal equalization. On the question of law the Court held, Martland and Ritchie JJ. dissenting, that Parliament needed no such consent. On the question of convention, the Court held, Laskin, C.J. and Estey and McIntyre JJ. dissenting, that "a substantial measure of [provincial] consent" was required.

THE QUESTION OF LAW

LASKIN C.J. AND DICKSON, BEETZ, ESTEY, MCINTYRE, CHOUINARD AND LAMER JJ.:

... The submission of the eight provinces which invites this Court to consider the position of the British Parliament is based on the Statute of Westminster, 1931 in its application to Canada. The submission is that the effect of the Statute is to qualify the authority of the British Parliament to act on the federal Resolution without previous provincial consent where provincial powers and interests are thereby affected, as they plainly are here. This issue will be examined later in these reasons.

Two observations are pertinent here. First, we have the anomaly that although Canada has international recognition as an independent, autonomous and self-governing state, as, for example, a founding member of the United Nations, and through membership in other international associations of sovereign states, yet it suffers from an internal deficiency in the absence of legal power to alter or amend the essential distributive arrangements under which legal authority is exercised in the country, whether at the federal or provincial level. When a country has been in existence as an operating federal state for more than a century, the task of introducing a legal mechanism that will thereafter remove the anomaly undoubtedly raises a profound problem. Secondly, the authority of the British Parliament or its practices and conventions are not matters upon which this Court would presume to pronounce.

The proposition was advanced on behalf of the Attorney General of Manitoba that a convention may crystallize into law and that the requirement of provincial consent to the kind of Resolution that we have here, although in origin political, has become a rule of law. (No firm position was taken on whether the consent must be that of the Governments or that of the Legislatures.)

In our view, this is not so. No instance of an explicit recognition of a convention as having matured into a rule of law was produced. The very nature of a convention, as political in inception and as depending on a consistent course of political recognition by those for whose benefit and to whose detriment (if any) the convention developed over a considerable period of time, is inconsistent with its legal enforcement.

A contrary view relied on by provincial appellants is that expressed by Professor W.R. Lederman in two published articles, one entitled "Process of Constitutional Amendment in Canada" (1967) *McGill Law Journal* 371, and the second entitled "Constitutional Amendment and Canadian Unity" (1978) *Law Society of Upper Canada Lectures*, 17. As a respected scholar, Professor Lederman's views deserve more than cursory consideration. He himself recognized that there are contrary views, including those of an equally distinguished scholar, Professor F.R. Scott, *Essays on the Constitution* (1977), pp. 144, 169, 204–205, 245, 370–371, 402. There is also the contrary view of Professor Hogg, already cited.

Professor Lederman relies in part on a line of cases that has already been considered, especially the reasons of Sir Lyman Duff in the *Labour Conventions* case. The leap from convention to law is explained almost as if there was a common law of constitutional law, but originating in political practice. That is simply not so. What is desirable as a political limitation does not translate into a legal limitation, without expression in imperative constitutional text or statute. The position advocated is all the more unacceptable when substantial provincial compliance or consent is by him said to be sufficient. Although Professor Lederman would not give a veto to Prince Edward Island, he would to Ontario or Quebec or British Columbia or Alberta. This is an impossible position for a Court to manage. Further reference to this is made later in these reasons . . . .

Turning now to the authority or power of the two federal Houses to proceed by Resolution to forward the address and appended draft statutes to Her Majesty the Queen for enactment by the Parliament of the United Kingdom. There is no limit anywhere in law, either in Canada or in the United Kingdom (having regard to s. 18 of the *British North America Act*, as enacted by 1875 (U.K.), c. 38, which ties the privileges, immunities and powers of the federal Houses to those of the British House of Commons) to the power of the House to pass resolutions . . . .

For the moment, it is relevant to point out that even in those cases where an amendment to the *British North America Act* was founded on a Resolution of the federal Houses after having received provincial consent, there is no instance, save in the *British North America Act, 1930* where such consent was recited in the Resolution. The matter remained, in short, a conventional one within Canada, without effect on the validity of the Resolution in respect of United Kingdom action . . . .

This Court is being asked, in effect, to enshrine as a legal imperative a principle of unanimity for constitutional amendment to overcome the anomaly—more of an anomaly today than it was in 1867—that the *British North America Act* contained no provision for effecting amendments by Canadian action alone. Although Saskatchewan has, alone of the eight provinces opposing the federal package embodied in the Resolution, taken a less stringent position, eschewing unanimity but without quantifying the substantial support that it advocates, the provinces, parties to the References and to the appeals here, are entitled to have this Court's primary consideration of their views . . . .

The stark legal question is whether this Court can enact by what would be judicial legislation a formula of unanimity to initiate the amending process which would be binding not only in Canada but also on the Parliament of the United Kingdom with which amending authority would still remain. It would be anomalous indeed, overshadowing the anomaly of a Constitution which contains no provision for its amendment, for this Court to say retroactively that in law we have had an amending formula all along, even if we have not hitherto known it; or, to say, that we have had in law one amending formula, say from 1867 to 1931, and a second amending formula that has emerged after 1931. No one can gainsay the desirability of federal–provincial accord of acceptable compromise. That does not, however, go to legality. As Sir William Jowitt said, and quoted earlier, we must operate the old machinery perhaps one more time . . . .

At bottom, the challenge to the competency in law of the federal Houses to seek enactment by the Parliament of the United Kingdom of the statutes embodied in the Resolution is based on the recognized supremacy of provincial legislatures in relation to the powers conferred upon them under the *British North America Act*, a supremacy *vis-à-vis* the federal Parliament. Reinforcement, or perhaps the foundation of this supremacy is said to lie in the nature or character of Canadian federalism.

The supremacy position, taken alone, needs no further justification than that found in the respective formulations of the powers of Parliament and the provincial Legislatures in ss. 91 and 92 of the *British North America Act*. Federal paramountcy is, however, the general rule in the actual exercise of these powers. This notwithstanding, the exclusiveness of the provincial powers (another way of expressing supremacy and more consonant with the terms of the *British North America Act*) cannot be gainsaid. The long list of judicial decisions, beginning with *Hodge v. The Queen* . . . and carrying through such cases as *Liquidators of the Maritime Bank v. Receiver General of New Brunswick*, . . . and the *Labour Conventions* case where the Privy Council expressed its "watertight compartment view" of legislative power . . . provide adequate support for the principle of exclusiveness or supremacy but, of course, within the limits of the *British North America Act*.

Although there are what have been called unitary features in the *British North America Act*, involving overriding powers (to be distinguished from paramountcy of legislation) in the federal Parliament and Government, their modification of exclusive provincial authority does not detract from that authority to any substantial degree. Thus, the federal declaratory power under s. 92(10)(*c*) has a limited operation; reservation and disallowance of provincial legislation, although in law still open, have, to all intents and purposes, fallen into disuse. The fact of appointment of the Lieutenant-Governors of the provinces by the central government does not, as a practical matter, have any significance for provincial powers when, under the law, the Lieutenant-Governor is as much the personal representative of the Crown as is the Governor General. In each case, the representation is, of course, in respect of the powers respectively assigned to Parliament and the legislatures. Moreover, since there is an international, a foreign relations aspect involved in the relationship of Canada and Great Britain, any formal communication between a province and its Lieutenant-Governor with the United Kingdom Government or with the Queen, must be through the federal government or through the Governor General.

It is important in this connection to emphasise that the Government of Canada had, by 1923, obtained recognition internationally of its independent power to enter into external obligations when it negotiated the Halibut Treaty with the United States. Great Britain understood this by that time as did the United States. The subsequent Imperial Conferences added confirmation, sanctified by the Statute of Westminster which also put internal independence from Great Britain on a legal foundation. The remaining badge of subservience, the need to resort to the British Parliament to amend the *British North America Act*, although preserved by the Statute of Westminster, did not carry any diminution of Canada's legal right in international law, and as a matter of Canadian constitutional law, to assert its independence in external relations, be they with Great Britain or other countries. The matter is emphasised by the judgment of this Court in *Reference re Offshore Mineral Rights*, [1967] S.C.R. 792, at p. 816. This is a relevant consideration in the appeals which are before this Court.

What is put forward by the provinces which oppose the forwarding of the address without provincial consent is that external relations with Great Britain in this respect must take account of the nature and character of Canadian federalism. It is contended that a legal underpinning of their position is to be found in the Canadian federal system as reflected in historical antecedents, in the pronouncements of leading political figures and in the preamble to the *British North America Act*.

The arguments from history do not lead to any consistent view or any single view of the nature of the *British North America Act*. . . . So, too, with pronouncements by political figures or persons in other branches of public life. There is little profit in parading them . . . .

There is not and cannot be any standardized federal system from which particular conclusions must necessarily be drawn. Reference was made earlier to what were called unitary features of Canadian federalism and they operate to distinguish Canadian federalism from that of Australia and that of the United States. Allocations of legislative power differ as do the institutional arrangements through which power is exercised. This Court is being asked by the provinces which objected to the so-called federal "package" to say that the internal distribution of legislative power must be projected externally, as a matter of law, although there is no legal warrant for this assertion . . . .

At bottom, it is this distribution, it is the allocation of legislative power as between the central Parliament and the provincial Legislatures that the provinces rely on as precluding unilateral federal action to seek amendments to the *British North America Act* that affect, whether by limitation or extension, provincial legislative authority. The Attorney General of Canada was pushed to the extreme by being forced to answer affirmatively the theoretical question whether in law the federal government could procure an amendment to the *British North America Act* that would turn Canada into a unitary state. That is not what the present Resolution envisages because the essential federal character of the country is preserved under the enactments proposed by the Resolution.

That, it is argued, is no reason for conceding unilateral federal authority to accomplish, through invocation of legislation by the United Kingdom Parliament, the purposes of the Resolution. There is here, an unprecedented situation in which the one constant since the enactment of the *British North America Act* in 1867 has been the legal authority of the United Kingdom Parliament to amend it. The law knows nothing of any requirement of provincial consent, either to a resolution of the federal Houses or as a condition of the exercise of United Kingdom legislative power.

MARTLAND AND RITCHIE JJ.:

...The effect of the position taken by the Attorney General of Canada is that the two Houses of Parliament have unfettered control of the triggering mechanism by means of which they can cause the B.N.A. Act to be amended in any way they desire. It was frankly conceded in argument that there were no limits of any kind upon the type of amendment that could be made in this fashion. In our opinion, this argument in essence maintains that the provinces have since, at the latest 1931, owed their continued existence not to their constitutional powers expressed in the B.N.A. Act, but to the federal parliament's sufferance. While the federal Parliament was throughout this period incompetent to legislate in respect of matters assigned to the provinces by s. 92, its two Houses could at any time have done so by means of a resolution to the Imperial Parliament, procuring an amendment to the B.N.A. Act.

The Attorney General of Canada, in substance, is asserting the existence of a power in the Houses of Parliament to obtain amendments to the B.N.A. Act which could disturb and even destroy the federal system of constitutional government in Canada. We are not aware of any possible legal source for such a power.... In our opinion, the two Houses lack legal authority, of their own motion, to obtain constitutional amendments which would strike at the very basis of the Canadian federal system, i.e., the complete division of legislative powers between the Parliament of Canada and the provincial legislatures. It is the duty of this Court to consider this assertion of rights with a view to the presentation of the Constitution.

This Court, since its inception, has been active in reviewing the constitutionality of both federal and provincial legislation. This role has generally been concerned with the interpretation of the express terms of the B.N.A. Act. However, on occasions, this Court has had to consider issues for which the B.N.A. Act offered no answer. In each case, this Court had denied the assertion of any power which would offend against the basic principles of the Constitution....

The federal position in these appeals can be summarised in these terms. While the federal Parliament lacks legal authority to achieve the objectives set out in the Resolution by the enactment of its own legislation, that limitation upon its authority can be evaded by having the legislation enacted by the Imperial Parliament at the behest of a resolution of the two Houses of the federal Parliament. This is an attempt by the federal Parliament to accomplish indirectly that which is it legally precluded from doing directly by perverting the recognized resolution method of obtaining constitutional amendments by the Imperial Parliament for an improper purpose. In our opinion, since it is beyond the power of the federal Parliament to enact such an amendment, it is equally beyond the power of its two Houses to effect such an amendment through the agency of the Imperial Parliament.

THE QUESTION OF CONVENTION

MARTLAND, RITCHIE, DICKSON, BEETZ, CHOUINARD AND LAMER JJ.:

In these questions, the phrases "Constitution of Canada" and "Canadian Constitution" do not refer to matters of interest only to the federal government or federal juristic unit. There are clearly meant in a broader sense and embrace the global system of rules and principles which govern the exercise of constitutional authority in the whole and in the same broad sense in these reasons . . . .

Those parts of the Constitution of Canada which are composed of statutory rules and common law rules are generically referred to as the law of the Constitution. In cases of doubt or dispute, it is the function of the courts to declare what the law is and since the law is sometimes breached, it is generally the function of the courts to ascertain whether it has in fact been breached in specific instances and, if so, to apply such sanctions as are contemplated by the law, whether they be punitive sanctions or civil sanctions such as a declaration of nullity. Thus, when a federal or a provincial statute is found by the courts to be in excess of the legislative competence of the legislature which has enacted it, it is declared null and void and the courts refuse to give effect to it. In this sense it can be said that the law of the Constitution is administered or enforced by the courts.

But many Canadians would perhaps be surprised to learn that important parts of the Constitution of Canada, with which they are the most familiar because they are directly involved when they exercise their right to vote at federal and provincial elections, are nowhere to be found in the law of the Constitution. For instance it is a fundamental requirement of the Constitution that if the Opposition obtains the majority at the polls, the Government must tender its resignation forthwith. But fundamental as it is, this requirement of the Constitution does not form part of the law of the Constitution.

A federal constitution provides for the distribution of powers between various legislatures and governments and may also constitute a fertile ground for the growth of constitutional conventions between those legislatures and governments. It is conceivable for instance that usage and practice might give birth to conventions in Canada relating to the holding of federal–provincial conferences, the appointment of lieutenant-governors, the reservation and disallowance of provincial legislation . . . .

The main purpose of constitutional conventions is to ensure that the legal framework of the Constitution will be operated in accordance with the prevailing constitutional values or principles of the period. For example, the constitutional value which is the pivot of the conventions stated above and relating to responsible government is the democratic principle: the powers of the state must be exercised in accordance with the wishes of the electorate; and the constitutional value or principle which anchors the conventions regulating the relationship between the members of the Commonwealth is the independence of the former British colonies.

Being based on custom and precedent, constitutional conventions are usually unwritten rules. Some of them however may be reduced to writing and expressed in the proceedings and documents of imperial conferences, or in the preamble of statutes such as the Statute of Westminster, 1931, or in the proceedings and documents of federal–provincial conferences. They are often referred to and recognized in statements made by members of governments.

The conventional rules of the Constitution present one striking peculiarity. In contradistinction to the laws of the Constitution, they are not enforced by the courts. One reason for this situation is that, unlike common law rules, conventions are not judge-made-rules. They are not based on judicial precedents but on precedents established by the institutions of government themselves. Nor are they in the nature of statutory commands which it is the function and duty of the courts to obey and enforce. Furthermore, to enforce them would mean to administer some formal sanction when they are breached. But the legal system from which they are distinct does not contemplate formal sanctions for their breach.

Perhaps the main reason why conventional rules cannot be enforced by the courts is that they are generally in conflict with the legal rules which they postulate and the courts are bound to enforce the legal rules. The conflict is not of a type which would entail the commission of any illegality. It results from the fact that legal rules create wide powers, discretions and rights which conventions prescribe should be exercised only in a certain limited manner, if at all.

It should be borne in mind however that, while they are not laws, some conventions may be more important than some laws. Their importance depends on that of the value or principle which they are meant to safeguard. Also they form an integral part of the Constitution and of the constitutional system. The come within the meaning of the word "Constitution" in the preamble of the *British North America Act, 1867*:

> Whereas the Provinces of Canada, Nova Scotia and New Brunswick have expressed their Desire to be federally united...with a Constitution similar in principle to that of the United Kingdom . . .

That is why it is perfectly appropriate to say that to violate a convention is to do something which is unconstitutional although it entails no direct legal consequence. But the words "constitutional" and "unconstitutional" may also be used in a strict legal sense, for instance with respect to a statute which is found *ultra vires* or unconstitutional. The foregoing may perhaps be summarised in an equation: constitutional conventions plus constitutional law equal the total Constitution of the country . . . .

WHETHER THE CONVENTION EXISTS

It was submitted by counsel for Canada, Ontario and New Brunswick that there is no constitutional convention that the House of Commons and Senate of Canada will not request Her Majesty the Queen to lay before the Parliament of Westminster a measure to amend the Constitution of Canada affecting federal–provincial relationships, etc., without first obtaining the agreement of the provinces . . . .

Requirements for establishing a convention

The requirements for establishing a convention bear some resemblance with those which apply to customary law. Precedents and usage are necessary but do not suffice. They must be normative. We adopt the following passage of Sir W. Ivor Jennings in *The Law and the Constitution* (5th ed. 1959, p. 136):

> We have to ask ourselves three questions: first, what are the precedents; secondly, did the actors in the precedents believe that they were bound by a rule; and thirdly, is there a reason for the rule? A single precedent with a good reason may be enough to establish the rule. A whole string

270 MADE IN CANADA

of precedents without such a reason will be of no avail, unless it is perfectly certain that the persons concerned regarded them as bound by it.

i) *The precedents*

An account of the statutes enacted by the Parliament of Westminster to modify the Constitution of Canada is found in a White Paper published in 1965 under the authority of the Honorable Guy Favreau, then Minister of Justice for Canada, under the title of "The Amendment of the Constitution of Canada." This account is quoted in the *Senate Reference* ... but we find it necessary to reproduce it here for convenience ....

Of these twenty-two amendments or groups of amendments, five directly affected federal–provincial relationships in the sense of changing provincial legislative powers: they are the amendment of 1930, the Statute of Westminster, 1931, and the amendments of 1940, 1951 and 1964.

These five amendments are the only ones which can be viewed as positive precedents whereby federal–provincial relationships were directly affected in the sense of changing legislative powers.

Every one of these five amendments was agreed upon by each province whose legislative authority was affected.

In negative terms, no amendment changing provincial legislative powers has been made since Confederation when agreement of a province whose legislative powers would have been changed was withheld.

There are no exceptions.

Furthermore, in even more telling negative terms, in 1951, an amendment was proposed to give the provinces a limited power of indirect taxation. Ontario and Quebec did not agree and the amendment was not proceeded with. (*Commons Debates*, 1951, pp. 2682 and 2726 to 2743.)

The Constitutional Conference of 1960 devised a formula for the amendment of the Constitution of Canada. Under this formula, the distribution of legislative powers could have been modified. The great majority of the participants found the formula acceptable but some differences remained and the proposed amendment was not proceeded with.

In 1964, a conference of first ministers unanimously agreed on an amending formula that would have permitted the modification of legislative powers. Quebec subsequently withdrew its agreement and the proposed amendment was not proceeded with.

Finally, in 1971, proposed amendments which included an amending formula were agreed upon by the federal government and eight of the ten provincial governments. Quebec disagreed and Saskatchewan which had a new government did not take a position because it was believed the disagreement of Quebec rendered the question academic. The proposed amendments were not proceeded with.

The accumulation of these precedents, positive and negative, concurrent and without exception, does not of itself suffice in establishing the existence of the convention; and it unmistakedly points in its direction. Indeed, if the precedents stood alone, it might be argued that unanimity is required ....

Each of those five constitutional amendments effected a limited change in legislative powers, affecting one head of legislative competence such as unemployment insurance. Whereas if the proposed Charter of Rights became law, every head of provincial (and federal) legislative authority could be affected. Furthermore, the Charter of Rights would operate retrospectively as well as prospectively with the result that laws enacted in the future as well as in the past, even before Confederation, would be exposed to attack if inconsistent with the provisions of the Charter of Rights. This Charter would thus abridge provincial legislative authority on a scale exceeding the effect of any previous constitutional amendment for which provincial consent was sought and obtained.

Finally, it was noted in the course of argument that in the case of four or five amendments mentioned above where provincial consent effectively had been obtained, the statutes enacted by the Parliament of Westminster did not refer to this consent. This does not alter the fact that consent was obtained.

ii) The actors treating the rule as binding

The Justices then considered the principles regarding constitutional amendment found in the White Paper issued under the name of the federal minister of justice in 1965. The fourth general principle is as follows:

> that the Canadian Parliament will not request an amendment directly affecting federal–provincial relationships without prior consultation and agreement with the provinces. This principle did not emerge as early as others but since 1907, and particularly since 1930, has gained increasing recognition and acceptance. The nature and the degree of provincial participation in the amending process, however, have not lent themselves to easy definition.

The text which precedes the four general principles makes it clear that it deals with conventions. It refers to the laws and conventions by which a country is governed and to constitutional rules which are not binding in any strict sense (that is in a legal sense) but which have come to be recognized and accepted in practice as part of the amendment process in Canada. The first three general principles are statements of well-known constitutional conventions governing the relationships between Canada and the United Kingdom with respect to constitutional amendments.

In our view, the fourth general principle equally and unmistakedly states and recognizes as a rule of the Canadian Constitution the convention referred to in the second question of the Manitoba and Newfoundland References as well as in question B of the Quebec Reference, namely that there is a requirement for provincial agreement to amendments which change provincial legislative powers.

It would not be appropriate for the Court to devise in the abstract a specific formula which would indicate in positive terms what measure of provincial agreement is required for the convention to be complied with. Conventions by their nature develop in the political field and it will be for the political actors, not this Court, to determine the degree of provincial consent required.

It is sufficient for the Court to decide that at least a substantial measure of provincial consent is required and to decide further whether the situation before the Court meets with this requirement. The situation is one where Ontario and New Brunswick agree with the proposed amendments whereas the eight other provinces oppose it. By no conceivable standard could this situation be thought to pass muster. It clearly does not disclose a sufficient measure of provincial agreement. Nothing more should be said about this.

iii) A reason for the rule

The reason for the rule is the federal principle. Canada is a federal union . . . .

The purpose of this conventional rule is to protect the federal character of the Canadian Constitution and prevent the anomaly that the House of Commons and Senate could obtain by simple resolutions what they could not validly accomplish by statute.

It was contended by counsel for Canada, Ontario and New Brunswick that the proposed amendments would not offend the federal principle and that, if they become law, Canada would remain a federation. The federal principle would even be reinforced, it was said, since the provinces would as a matter of law be given an important role in the amending formula.

It is true that Canada would remain a federation if the proposed amendments became law. But it would be a different federation made different at the instance of a majority in the House of the federal Parliament acting alone. It is this process itself which offends the federal principle . . . .

CONCLUSION

We have reached the conclusion that the agreement of the provinces of Canada, no views being expressed as to its quantification, is constitutionally required for the passing of the "Proposed Resolution for a joint Address to Her Majesty respecting the Constitution of Canada" and that the passing of this Resolution without such agreement would be unconstitutional in the conventional sense.

LASKIN C.J. (Estey and McIntyre concurring) dissenting:

. . . A convention requires universal recognition by the actors in a scheme and this is certainly so where, as here, acceptance of a convention involves the surrender of a power by a sovereign body said to be a party to the convention. Furthermore, in recognizing uncertainty in specifying the degree of provincial participation, it denies the existence of any convention including that suggested by the Province of Saskatchewan. If there is difficulty in defining the degree of provincial participation, which there surely is, it cannot be said that any convention on the subject has been settled and recognized as a constitutional condition for the making of an amendment. It is the very difficulty of fixing the degree of provincial participation which, while it remains unresolved, prevents any formation or recognition of any convention. It robs any supposed convention of that degree of definition which is necessary to allow for its operation . . . .

It was also argued that Canada was formed as a federal union and that the existence of a legal power of the central government to unilaterally change the

Constitution was inimical to the concept of federalism. The convention then, it was argued, arose out of the necessity to restrain such unilateral conduct and preserve the federal nature of Canada. In this connection, it must be acknowledged at once that, in a federal union, the powers and rights of each of the two levels of government must be protected from the assault of the other. The whole history of constitutional law and constitutional litigation in Canada since Confederation has been concerned with this vital question. We are asked to say whether the need for the preservation of the principles of Canadian federalism dictates the necessity for a convention, requiring consent from the provinces as a condition of the exercise by the federal government of its legal powers, to produce amendment to the Canadian Constitution. If the convention requires only partial consent, as is contended by Saskatchewan, it is difficult to see how the federal concept is thereby protected for, while those provinces favouring amendment would be pleased, those refusing consent could claim coercion. If unanimous consent is required (as contended by the other objecting provinces), while it may be said that in general terms the concept of federalism would be protected it would only be by overlooking the special nature of Canadian federalism that this protection would be achieved. The B.N.A. Act has not created a perfect or ideal federal state. Its provisions have accorded a measure of paramountcy to the federal Parliament. Certainly this has been done in a more marked degree in Canada than in many other federal states. For example, one need only look to the power of reservation and disallowance of provincial enactments; the power to declare works in a province to be for the benefit of all Canada and to place them under federal regulatory control; the wide powers to legislate generally for the peace, order and good government of Canada as a whole; the power to enact the criminal law of the entire country; the power to create and admit provinces out of existing territories and, as well, the paramountcy accorded federal legislation. It is this special nature of Canadian federalism which deprives the federalism argument described above of its force. This is particularly true when it involves the final settlement of Canadian constitutional affairs with an external government, the federal authority being the sole conduit for communication between Canada and the Sovereign and Canada alone having the power to deal in external matters. We therefore reject the argument that the preservation of the principles of Canadian federalism requires the recognition of the convention asserted before us . . . .

THE LAW AND POLITICS OF FEDERALISM: AN OVERVIEW[◊]

PATRICK MONOHAN

o

There is little doubt that public awareness and interest in the Supreme Court has been awakened in the past decade primarily because of the enactment of the *Canadian Charter of Rights and Freedoms*. . . . [T]he *Charter* is thought to have heralded the triumph of values of law and legality over those of unbridled political power. But it is not the *Charter* alone that has spawned a perception that Canadian political life is becoming increasingly judicialized. The politics of Canadian federalism appear to be increasingly dominated by the courts in general and the Supreme Court in particular. With the demise of "co-operative federalism" and the heightening of intergovernmental tensions,[1] as well as the loosening of traditional limits on standing,[2] the courts rather than the political backrooms have apparently become a primary stage for federal politics. In this theatre, lawyers and judges rather than bureaucrats or ministers block and direct the action.

Of course, the most visible and memorable instance of this was the protracted dispute over the patriation of the constitution, in which the Courts became the forum for a bitter struggle by the provinces to resist the unilateralism of the federal government. But numerous other high profile federal–provincial disputes, including those over oil revenues, the ownership of the off-shore, Senate reform and incomes policy all ended up in the Supreme Court, often at the instance of governments themselves. As one provincial government put it: "These are fundamental federal–provincial issues and they are being resolved by an institution not in the mainstream of the political processes."[3] By the middle of the 1980s, it seemed obvious, if somewhat troubling, that the Canadian judiciary had assumed centre stage in the politics of Canadian federalism.

. . . In this chapter, I offer an extremely crude overview of the evolution of federalism in Canada since 1945. I then examine the Court's federalism workload

---

◊Patrick Monohan, *Politics and the Constitution* (Toronto: Carswell, 1987), 141–53.

over the past ten years, indicating the extent to which its presence and influence in this area has grown. The Court has been deciding more federalism cases in the past decade than ever before, and it has become increasingly activist in its decisions . . . .

In general terms, I argue that the federalism jurisprudence of the Court in the past decade has been just as "political" as any of its decisions under the *Charter*. But I also suggest that there has been a tendency to exaggerate the instrumental impact of the Court's federalism decisions. Although many of the Court's decisions have received considerable public attention and criticism, I argue that much of this attention has probably been unwarranted. If governments are unhappy with particular judicial results, there are often alternative regulatory instruments which can be employed to substitute around that result. This suggests that there would be little point in attempting to revise significantly or limit the federalism jurisdiction of the Supreme Court.

THE SETTING: THE EVOLUTION OF FEDERALISM 1945–1985

The 1940s represented a watershed for Canadian federalism. Prior to 1940, Canada had been premised on an essentially classical model of federalism. Governments possessed authority over "spheres" of jurisdiction. While there was undeniably considerable consultation and co-ordination, each level of government regarded it as legitimate to act independently of the other within its allotted sphere. Moreover, there was an intelligible and widely understood line of demarcation between the responsibilities of Ottawa and the provinces. This was the era of "constitutionalism"—the notion that a legally enforceable document should define the society's federal institutions and establish standards for their evaluation.[4]

The last four decades have witnessed the demise of constitutionalism. By 1940, it was apparent that the division of responsibilities expressed in the *British North America Act* had not merely become irrelevant; these "watertight compartments" now constituted a costly obstacle in the public policy process, particularly in terms of the evolution of the welfare state in the postwar era.

Canada was faced with a fundamental political choice. On the one hand, it could recut the federal–provincial deck of cards, redealing the "spheres" or jurisdiction so that they more closely conformed with the functions and demands of government in the mid-twentieth century. The first option represented a continued commitment to the morality of constitutionalism. Alternatively, the players could have ostensibly continued to play their existing hands, while simply dealing themselves more cards from a second deck in order to strengthen their weak suits. This pragmatic, flexible alternative would have appeared to leave the terms of the federal–provincial deal undisturbed. In fact, it would have amounted to a fundamental transformation in the rules of the game. With each player free to add more cards to his hand at will, at some point the hands of the players would become virtually indistinguishable from each other. The terms of the original deal would be little more than a distant and irrelevant trifle. In fact, the central notion which gave the game its integrity in the first place—the idea that each player should be restricted to holding only certain suits or cards—would eventually seem a mindless and absurd limitation.

Canada in the postwar era chose the second alternative over the first, with precisely these predictable consequences. Rather than seek a fundamental redistribution of "spheres" of jurisdiction, the whole notion of discrete and identifiable spheres of legislative authority was itself abandoned. Converts to modernism, Canadian policy makers now espoused the dogma that all things were inextricably related to all other things. The trouble with the "watertight compartments" view was not so much that it was undesirable; more precisely, it was unattainable, the product of a naïve and simplistic world view. Rather than "spheres of jurisdiction," the reconstituted federalism was to be organized around the notion of "levels" of government defending "interests." Each level of government was now concerned with virtually the whole range of public policy issues. The hands of the players had indeed become indistinguishable from each other. The only way to differentiate the players from each other was to identify the various social, economic and political interests they represented at any given moment. Having banished considerations of principle, federalism was essentially just another form of _Realpolitik_.

One important indication of the new federalism was the growth of federal transfer payments to the provinces.[5] In 1949, federal cash transfers to the provinces (excluding tax-rental payments) amounted to 5.9 per cent of federal spending; by the 1957–62 period, transfers had nearly doubled, to 10.2 per cent of federal spending; by 1971–72, transfers had doubled again, to 23 per cent of federal spending. In effect, nearly one-quarter of all federal spending in 1970 was being directed to objectives nominally within provincial jurisdiction.

At the same time, provincial governments were becoming increasingly dependent on federal transfers for revenue. Whereas federal transfers to provinces had amounted to 13.4 per cent of provincial revenues in 1949–52, the proportion had increased to slightly over 25 per cent by 1971–72. Moreover, these transfers increasingly took the form of conditional grants as opposed to unconditional transfers; at their peak in 1967, conditional grants represented 83 per cent of federal payments to provinces.[6]

It would be mistaken to suppose that these developments necessarily implied greater centralization of power. First, the very fact that the postwar growth of government was taking place in areas of traditional provincial jurisdiction meant that the federal government increasingly required the co-operation of the provinces in order to achieve what were styled "national" policy objectives. Moreover, beginning in the early 1960s and led by the Lesage administration in Quebec, provincial governments became committed to explicit programs of regional economic development.[7] The Lesage program included policies with respect to regional economic development, vocational training, the exploitation of natural resources, cultural affairs, and the channelling of private savings into provincial economic development. In short, Quebec now regarded itself as being responsible for developing an autonomous and distinct provincial community, not only in cultural, but in economic terms. Moreover, the province was no longer willing to play the subordinate role that had been envisaged by the federal drafters of the New

National Policy in the 1940s. By the mid-1960s, the other provincial governments began committing themselves to similar programs of comprehensive economic development. Already, the new phenomenon had a name: "province building."[8]

The terms of the debate had now changed. The discourse was no longer about "rights," but about "interests." Co-operation and consultation was not simply required when one government pursued policies in areas nominally under the jurisdiction of the other, such as shared-cost programs. Collaboration was seen as essential in any case in which the policies of one government had effects on those of another. Premier Lesage of Quebec defined the new assumptions at the federal–provincial conference of 1965, when he argued that "a government may not do exactly as it pleases simply because it has legal authority in a given field."[9] Even when a government was legislating in fields that fell within its own jurisdiction, "it must see that its actions are compatible with those of the other legislative authorities, and do not infringe on their rights and privileges."[10]

The notion that governments exercised "exclusive jurisdiction" over "classes of subjects" as set out in the B.N.A. Act had become a kind of meaningless sham. Anyone who actually believed or asserted such claims to exclusivity was not merely foolish, but rude. Thus, when Premier Lesage had informed an earlier federal–provincial conference in the 1960s that Quebec intended to pursue its "rights" in the courts, this was widely interpreted as a challenge to the federal system itself.[11] Lesage was attempting to pay heed, rather than mere lip service to the discredited values of constitutionalism. The power of a new orthodoxy was reflected in the fact that Lesage was roundly criticized, not just by the federal government, but by the other provinces, for his betrayal of the understandings surrounding the new federalism.

Indeed, it was only in Quebec that voices were raised in defence of constitutionalism, most notably by Pierre Elliott Trudeau. In his brilliant essay, "The practice and theory of federalism,"[12] Trudeau documented the "sometimes subtle, sometimes brazen, and usually tolerated encroachments by one government upon the jurisdiction of the other."[13] Trudeau was particularly critical of the use of the federal spending power in order to ensure that the provinces were properly exercising the rights they held under the constitution. The provisions of the B.N.A. Act had become an illusory constraint: "it almost seems as though whenever an important segment of the Canadian population needs something badly enough, it is eventually given to them by one level of government or the other, regardless of the constitution."[14] The trouble with this federal practice, according to Trudeau, was that it undermined democratic values. When one government intervened in an area falling under the other's jurisdiction, it blurred accountability to the electorate and retarded democratic debate and argument.[15]

Yet Trudeau's arguments went unheeded, even after he had become leader of the federal Liberals and Prime Minister. By the 1970s, the era of "co-operative federalism" had given way to "executive federalism,"[16] but the basic assumptions regarding overlapping of jurisdictions remained the same. It was only in the late 1970s and early 1980s that serious efforts were made to "disentangle" federal and provincial responsibilities. In large part, this effort at disentanglement came at the initiative of the federal government. For a variety of reasons, the federal government had lost faith in the established system of federal–provincial collaboration.[17] The federal government claimed that executive federalism had given the provinces power to irresponsibly block reforms which were clearly in the interests of all Canadians. The constitutional "straightjacket" was cited as an exemplary instance of this provincial veto power. It was also thought that the federal government had become isolated from individual citizens. The provinces were able to claim exclusive political credit for the delivery of goods and services which had been partly financed by federal money.

The re-election of the Liberal government in 1980 signalled the beginning of an era of unilateralism by the federal government. Unilateralism was pursued simultaneously on a number of fronts, including the constitution, energy policy and the fiscal arrangements. The defining characteristic of the federal strategy was that it embraced policy areas in which federal–provincial co-operation and agreement had become the accepted norm. In the constitutional area, there was a widespread understanding that provincial legislative powers would not be disturbed without prior provincial consent.[18] Energy policy throughout the 1970s had been formulated through bilateral pricing agreements between the federal government and the energy-producing provinces. Fiscal transfers to the provinces had been the subject of extensive federal–provincial bargaining dating back to the tax-rental agreements of 1947. In all of these crucial policy areas, the federal government now asserted the right and responsibility to act unilaterally.[19] Such action was legitimate, according to the federal government, because the national government was the voice of the national interest. Transcending the parochialism of the provincial premiers, Ottawa alone could "speak for Canada."

Yet this era of federal unilateralism did not signal a return to the prewar classical federalism of watertight compartments. Instead, it merely confirmed the extent to which the classical orthodoxy had before outdated. On all fronts, the provinces moved to block the federal initiatives, often through recourse to the courts. Thus, rather than a return to classical federalism, the developments of the past decade signalled the emergence of what one commentator has termed "double unilateralism."[20] Under this model, both levels of government continue to act in the same general policy areas, but in an antagonistic rather than co-operative fashion. The issue for federalism in the eighties is "not whether the two levels of government will be involved [in the same areas of public policy] but whether they act unilaterally or will collaborate in one fashion or another."[21] The prevailing view is captured by the Royal Commission on the Economic Union and Development Prospects For Canada (the MacDonald Commission), which reports that there is no merit to efforts to restore a classic model of watertight compartments.[22] Overlapping of authority and *de facto* concurrence are "not only inevitable but also desirable."[23] Shared responsibility makes governments compete with one another to respond to citizens' problems, which in turn will temper the self-interest of state officials. To require governments to adhere to an incoherent and outdated set of categories contained in the B.N.A. Act would be to frustrate this competition for public support. The MacDonald Commission's realism both epitomizes and legitimizes the current discourse about federalism.

THE EVOLUTION OF JUDICIAL REVIEW

With constitutionalism losing its legitimacy, commentators in the 1960s became convinced that judicial review was becoming an increasingly marginal activity. Governments seemed less willing to have their disputes resolved by the courts, with the most contentious areas of federal and provincial conflicts being resolved without resort to the judiciary. Business interests were apparently less inclined than in the past to support judicial challenges to federal power. Judicial review had been supplanted by political processes of adjustment and compromise, as courts were "being retired" from their posts as supervisors of the federal balance.[24] The prevailing view in the late 1960s was captured by Donald Smiley: "Judicial review results in a delineation of federal and provincial powers where the perceived needs of the federal system are for a more effective articulation of these powers. In general, the prospects are remote that the courts will reassume a major role as keepers of the federal balance."[25]

A mere fifteen years after Professor Smiley issued this confident prognosis, he appears to have been hopelessly mistaken. All of the indicators which suggested that judicial review was declining in importance have now dramatically reserved themselves. The norms of negotiation and compromise, so widely accepted in the 1960s, had been largely repudiated by the late 1970s and early 1980s. The federal government pursued a policy of unilateralism on the constitution and energy rents, matters which had formerly been the subject of collaboration. The response of the provinces was to attempt to block the federal initiatives through resort to the courts. This thrust the Supreme Court centre stage in crucial federal–provincial conflicts over constitutional amendment and energy policy.

Nor did private interests appear reluctant about invoking federalism arguments in order to avoid state regulation. A recent and prominent instance of this is the private challenge to the federal *Canada Health Act*,[26] litigation which has profound implications for the tangled edifice of intergovernmental transfers that has been the bedrock of the new federalism since 1945. Finally, the courts themselves appear to be assuming an increasingly activist stand, more willing to invoke federalism norms to limit state activity. Particularly in the *Patriation Appeals*, the Supreme Court cast itself as the guardian of the federal character of the constitution against encroachments by the central government. All of these developments have induced scholars to revise their assessments about the marginality, if not about the legitimacy, of judicial review. The new conventional wisdom asserts that the courts are assuming an increasingly critical role in the evolution of federalism.

These claims about increasing judicial involvement in federalism matters are confirmed by the figures in Table 1. In the 5-year period ending in 1985, the Court decided almost as many federalism cases as in the decade between 1970 and 1980. Perhaps more significant is the increase in the percentage of the Court's time spent on federalism matters in the past decade. In the 1960s, only one out of every 30 cases decided by the Supreme Court raised a federalism issue. This ratio remained relatively stable throughout the 1970s, despite the change in the leave to appeal procedures instituted in 1974. By the early 1980s, one out of every nine opinions written by the Court was decided on federalism grounds. It is important to remember that these figures do not take into account the impact of the *Charter of Rights* on the Court's workload. With *Charter* cases just beginning to reach the Court in the 1984–85 term, the Court's workload will likely become even more dominated by constitutional issues in the future.

TABLE 1   *FEDERALISM CASES DECIDED BY THE SUPREME COURT 1950–1984*[+]

	Federalism cases	Total cases	Ratio (%)
1950–59	30	651	4.6
1960–69	36	1161	3.1
1970–79	54	1464	3.7
1980–84	57	524	10.9

[+]Includes cases reported to 31 December 1984.

Source: Reported cases, S.C.R.s 1950–85—includes cases in which constitutional arguments raised, even if case decided on non-constitutional grounds.

Not only is the Court deciding more constitutional cases than in the past, it also appears to be assuming a more "activist" stance. As table 2 indicates, the Court today is more likely to strike down a statute on federalism grounds than at any time in the past 20 years. What is equally significant is the changing attitude of the Court towards federal statutes. In the 1950s and 1960s, the Court appears to have regarded federal laws as virtually immune constitutionality; of 20 challenges to federal laws, only two were successful.[27] In the 1980–84 period there were 28 challenges to federal law that reached the Supreme Court and in 12 instances the challenge was successful. This indicates that more challenges to federal laws are reaching the Supreme Court, and with greater success. The extent of the change is indicated by the fact that over the 30-year period ending in 1980, the Court's constitutional docket was dominated by challenges to provincial laws; approximately two-thirds of all federalism cases involved such challenges. In the past five years, this historic relationship has been altered, with federalism challenges now being directed equally towards federal and provincial legislation and with virtually identical success.

TABLE 2   *STATUTES HELD TO BE ULTRA VIRES*[+]
         (on federalism grounds)

	Federal statutes	Provincial statutes	Total	Percentage of decisions
1950–59	2/11	11/19	13/30	43
1960–69	0/9	7/27	7/36	20
1970–79	4/20	17/34	21/54	39
1980–84	12/28[++]	12/30	24/57	42

[+] Includes statutes held to be inapplicable to private activity on constitutional grounds.

[++] *McEvoy v. A.G. N.B.* is attributed to both federal and provincial totals: *ultra vires* in both instances.

Of course, this heightened judicial activism does not necessarily imply a more aggressive attitude on the part of the Supreme Court. It is possible that judicial attitudes have remained constant but that other variables have fluctuated, with the effect of multiplying the number of statutes declared *ultra vires*. We can examine at least two such variables: the nature of the statutes being considered by the Court, as well as the attitudes of government towards judicial review itself.

Over the past decade, many of the received understandings surrounding federal–provincial relations were challenged or abandoned. The federal government in particular rejected the norms of negotiation and compromise in favour of greater competition and scope for unilateral action. The national energy program and the constitutional initiative exemplified the national government's new concern with building more direct ties with Canadian citizens rather than with simply financing the provision of goods and services by the provinces. Moreover, the federal government disputed the claim that provincial co-operation should be secured before acting within areas which were nominally within federal jurisdiction. This more aggressive stance on the part of the national government, rather than judicial activism, may well account for the increase in the numbers of federal laws being ruled *ultra vires*. As the federal government pursues policies which intrude onto areas of established provincial turf, the Court will function as a conservative, checking mechanism, seeking to maintain the existing equilibrium. The predictable result would be that federal statutes would be challenged with greater frequency and success. In effect, the mere act of preserving the constitutional *status quo* would make the Court falsely appear to be adopting a more hostile stance towards federal laws.

The difficulty is that the available evidence fails to support this hypothesis. The cases in which the Court has ruled against the federal government cannot be characterized as responses to aggressive federal initiatives such as the national energy program or the constitutional reform package. With one or two notable exceptions, the Court has been striking down provisions that have either been in place for many years or are similar to provisions which previously have been upheld in an almost perfunctory manner.[28] For instance, in *McEvoy*,[29] the Court ruled against a joint federal–provincial attempt to restructure the criminal courts, applying the structures of s. 96 to the federal government for the first time; in *Boggs*,[30] the Court struck down a provision in the *Criminal Code* which made it an offence to drive while one's licence was suspended under provincial law; in *Labatt Breweries*,[31] the Court declared that federal standards for "lite" beer could not be applied to the beer industry, since this would constitute regulation of a "local trade." These federal laws, as well as others which met a similar fate, were hardly symbolic of constitutional hubris on the part of the federal government. Clearly, there is nothing in the character of the laws themselves which adequately explains the about-face performed by the Court with respect to federal legislation.

The other possibility is that the Court has been responding to changing attitudes on the part of government towards constitutional adjudication. In the 1960s, governments consciously attempted to avoid judicial resolution of federal–provincial disputes. Rather than play the zero-sum game of court challenges, governments practised the politics of a positive sum, bargaining to a result which advanced their collective and individual interests.

To a significant degree, this aversion towards constitutional litigation has now disappeared. Governments have increasingly assumed the role of catalysts of constitutional litigation, both in terms of referring cases to the courts and intervening in private litigation. While the vast bulk of constitutional cases still originate through private litigation, there were as many reference cases reaching the Supreme Court in the 1980–84 period as in the previous 20 years. More telling of increased governmental litigiousness is the degree to which governments now intervene in private litigation. As table 3 indicates, during the 1950s and 1960s, most governments devoted only minimal resources towards constitutional litigation. Indeed, the federal government and the provinces of Ontario and Quebec accounted for more than half of the interventions during the 1950–1970 period. This pattern reversed itself in the 1970s, with virtually all governments participating vigorously in constitutional litigation. This was particularly so of the western provinces. By the 1980s, the province of Alberta was the most frequent intervener in federalism cases, surpassing even the federal government.

TABLE 3   *INTERVENTIONS BY GOVERNMENT 1950–1984*

Government	1950–59	1960–69	1970–79	1980–84	Total
Canada	14	18	29	23	84
Ontario	8	14	22	17	61
Quebec	8	12	21	21	62
Newfoundland	2	1	4	8	15
Nova Scotia	1	1	5	11	18
New Brunswick	3	2	8	18	31
P.E.I.	2	1	2	4	9
Manitoba	2	2	6	11	21
Saskatchewan	2	5	13	17	37
Alberta	4	8	29	26	67
British Columbia	2	2	18	18	40
Total	48	66	157	174	
No. of cases	30	36	54	57	
Interventions per case	1.6	1.8	3.0	3.0	

There does appear to be some link between reference cases and rulings of *ultra vires*. Of the fifteen references that have reached the Supreme Court since 1970, the Court has made a ruling of *ultra vires* in ten of them; contrast this with the fact that of the 96 private challenges reaching the Court over the same period, the Court was twice as likely to make a declaration of invalidity in a reference case as in a case initiated by a private litigant. Nor can this result be explained by the fact that the reference cases were being initiated by governments hostile to the legislation in question. In the four instances in which a government referred legislation enacted by the other level of government, the Court declared the legislation to be invalid only once. It was precisely in those cases in which a government was referring its own legislation to the Court that rulings of *ultra vires* were most common. The startling thing about this result is that it appears to contradict the common claim that private interests use federalism arguments to escape regulation.[32] The Court appears most receptive to federalism arguments when government, rather than private interest, has instituted the litigation.

There are a variety of reasons why this might be so. The first is that governments tend to refer legislation which is politically highly contentious; this means that there will be well-organized and financed interests willing to mount a concerted lobby against the legislation when it reaches the Court. Secondly, the very act of referring a statute to the Court may act as an implicit signal to the judiciary that the legislation is constitutionally suspect. Whatever the reasons, the increasing willingness on the part of government to refer legislation to the courts cannot itself account for the increased judicial activism of recent years. Both the absolute and the relative number of reference cases is small and the Supreme Court's constitutional docket remains overwhelmingly dominated by private litigation.

This brings us to a consideration of the impact of the dramatic increase in interventions by governments in private constitutional challenges. It might be assumed that when a government intervenes in a private challenge to legislation, the challenge is more likely to succeed; the intervention changes the complexion of the case, transforming a purely private attempt to escape regulation into a choice between competing conceptions of the public good. In fact, a particular provincial complaint during the 1970s was the frequency of hostile federal interventions in constitutional cases. For instance, following the Supreme Court's decisions in *Canadian Industrial Gas & Oil (CIGOL)*[33] and *Central Canada Potash*[34] in 1978, the province of Saskatchewan was "disturbed" by the fact that the government of Canada had supported the private litigants in the cases.[35] The participation of the federal government had given legitimacy to the challenge; it was no longer purely private interests opposing the province, but the "national" interests as represented by the government of Canada. Premier Blakeney regarded the federal action as a "betrayal" of previous understandings between the two governments on the energy issue.

Yet when one examines a broader range of outcomes, there is little evidence to support the hypothesis that intervention by government makes private challenges to legislation more likely to succeed. In the 1950s and 1960s, the outcomes in cases in which there were no interventions are virtually indistinguishable from those in which governments did intervene.[36] In the 1970s and 1980s, the cases in which there were interventions by government did have a slightly larger proportion of holdings of *ultra vires*.[37] Yet even here it is difficult to draw a causal link between the government's decision to intervene and a judicial holding of *ultra vires*. In many cases, governments intervened in support of legislation rather than against it. Moreover, even when governments intervened to support private challenges, it may well be that they did so when the issue was particularly contentious and thus, there was an antecedent likelihood that the Court would find in favour of the challenge.

In any event, this focus on the increase in total interventions tends to exaggerate the impact of the change in government behaviour. While it is true that governments have demonstrated an increasing interest in constitutional litigation, the proportion of cases in which governments intervene has remained fairly constant. Since the 1950s, there has been an intervention by at least one government in roughly four out of every five federalism cases reaching the Supreme Court.[38] The only change is that, whereas in the 1950s there would be only one or two intervenors in a given case, now there may be four or five. It is difficult to see how a change of this order could have a significant impact on the outcomes of federalism cases.

Thus, while these various factors may well be linked in some marginal way with the increasing judicial activism of recent years, they offer, at best, a partial explanation. One is ultimately led to the conclusion that the increasing activism in federalism cases is primarily a consequence of changed judicial attitudes. These evolving attitudes, which can be detected throughout the recent pronouncements of the Court, at bottom depend upon a particular conception of the judicial role. At the heart of the Court's vision is the belief that judges and lawyers constitute a central pillar in the defence of constitutional government in Canada. The paradigm is premised on private decision making, constrained at the margins by traditional models of adjudication, rather than through managerial or administrative approaches to the economy.

There are numerous illustrations of the paradigm. Perhaps the most obvious exemplar is the judgment of the Court in the *Patriation Appeals*. The Court revealed a willingness to accept primary responsibility for preserving the federal political tradition. The conventions of the constitution, matters which had always been left to the vagaries of the political process, were now regarded as too important to be left in such a fluid state. It was time to usher these amorphous understandings under the protective robes of legal supervision. The claim that conventions remained legally unenforceable was the height of legal formalism, disguising the transformation in their juridical character. The same general themes can be detected in the s. 96 cases, in which the Court ensures that decision making on "jurisdictional" grounds will be reviewable. This serves to protect traditional models of adjudication against what the Court regards as the excesses of the regulatory state. The decision of the Court in *Jabour*, while ostensibly aimed at preserving provincial autonomy, simultaneously emphasises the autonomy and importance of the legal profession.

The point of citing these developments is not to suggest that the Court has suddenly embarked on a policy-making frolic and that it should return to an apolitical, neutral role. The argument is more systemic. My claim is that these recent cases are simply a more overt and measurable manifestation of the policy making which pervades legal decision making. The judiciary cannot return to some neutral or objective state of nature, since such objectivity never existed.

These observations have important implications for the continuing debate over the "objectivity" of legal reasoning. Drawing on analogies to literary theory, Ronald Dworkin has argued that judges have a duty to "interpret" legal texts and materials, rather than to "change" them.[39] Judges are like writers who are each asked to write a chapter in a "chain" novel; the novelists are expected to create a single, unified novel rather than a series of independent short stories whose characters happen to have the same names. Each must interpret the work of the earlier members of the chain. They must assess what the characters are "really" like, identify "the" theme of the novel, and establish what the novel amounts to. Dworkin claims that judges stand in a similar position; "he *must* interpret what has gone before because he has a responsibility to advance the enterprise in hand rather than strike out in some new direction of his own."[40]

Yet the recent evolution of judicial review in Canada belies the claim that a sharp distinction can be drawn between "interpreting" legal materials and "changing" them. The recent federalism decisions of the Supreme Court were simultaneously an interpretation as well as a change of what had gone before. They represented an "interpretation" in the sense that the arguments were framed within the parameters established by the existing constitutional jurisprudence. They were simultaneously a "change" in the sense that the outcomes of the cases were significantly different from those in the 1950s and 1960s. This exemplifies Stanley Fish's observation that "paradoxically, one can be faithful to legal history only by revising it, by redescribing it in such a way as to accommodate and render manageable the issues raised by the present."[41]

The more general point that emerges is that the very dichotomy between objectivity and subjectivity which has fueled debates over judicial review is itself suspect.[42] Building on the "hermeneutic insight"—the view that "a sharp distinction cannot be drawn between understanding the text in its own terms and reading the interpreter's concerns into it"[43]—it becomes unnecessary to discover some independent, apolitical ground for legal reasoning. In this view, the only meaningful use of the term "objectivity" is "the view which would be agreed upon as a result of argument undeflected by irrelevant considerations."[44] Legal reasoning, along with other forms of political argument, is accordingly best understood as contingent yet constrained. It is constrained in the sense that legal argument must interpret and advance the aspirations and ideals which exemplify the political tradition. Yet it is contingent in the sense that the very act of interpreting those ideals changes them; the past is redescribed in order to accommodate the issues raised by the present.[45]

THE IMPACT OF ACTIVISM

Acknowledging the political character of constitutional adjudication does little to address the critical, if elusive, issue of the impact of this heightened judicial activism. It is tempting to conclude that the more federalism cases decided by the Court, the greater the impact of the Court's work on federal–provincial relations. But even a cursory analysis of recent federal–provincial disputes suggests that the empirical significance of many of these decisions has been minor. In the energy field, for example, the province of Alberta turned to the courts in an attempt to block the federal government's proposed tax on exported natural gas. But before the Supreme Court could rule on the matter, the federal government signed an agreement with the province of Alberta in which it renounced its plans for the tax. In the constitutional reform process, to take a second example, the Supreme Court decision in September 1981 essentially threw the initiative back into the political arena; the accord of November 1981 was acceptable to all parties except Quebec, whose subsequent legal challenge was dismissed by the Supreme Court. This particularistic analysis, in itself, proves little. But it does suggest that merely citing figures about numbers of federalism cases will not support claims about the impact and significance of constitutional adjudication.

One of the central contributions of Ronald Coase was his insight that individuals will seek to bargain around legal rules in order to achieve more efficient results.[46] Of course, there are a whole series of obstacles militating against such bargaining in the federalism context. Chief amongst these is the sheer complexity and cost of any bargaining that might occur. Before we can even contemplate bargaining *between* government, there must be bargaining *within* government, as the respective polities try to make up their "minds" about the best bargaining strategy to pursue. Despite these obstacles, we can expect that governmental elites will continually attempt to limit the effect of judicial rulings which run contrary to what they perceive to be their best interests.

The point can be illustrated by considering the response of federal and provincial governments to the decision of the Supreme Court of Canada in the *Nova Scotia Inter-delegation* case.[47] In this case, the Court ruled that an attempt by one level of government to delegate its power to the other was prohibited by the constitution. It was clearly in the interests of both levels of government to limit the effect of this rule. Translated into market terms, the effect of the ruling was to prevent the various governments from trading their "assets." All governments stood to gain from removing such restraints on alienation; an asset that can be traded is worth more than an asset that must remain in the hands of its legal owner. It is thus hardly surprising to observe that governments subsequently were able largely to nullify the effect of this legal rule. The nullification received Court sanction two years later in *P.E.I. Potato Marketing Board v. H.B. Willis Inc.*[48] Here, the Court declared that the constitution did not prevent one level of government from delegating power to an administrative body created by the other. This device, combined with the technique of "incorporation by reference,"[49] meant that it was now possible to trade legislative powers.

This produces the central law of the federalism equation: it is *always* possible to do indirectly what you cannot do directly. The *Nova Scotia Inter-delegation* case neatly illustrates in a single instance the two primary ways in which such indirection can be accomplished. First, the case illustrates the potential to utilize inter-governmental agreement in order to evade judicially imposed limitations. Second, the case simultaneously provides an example of governments using an alternative regulatory instrument in place of an instrument or technique that has been ruled invalid. Having discovered that the courts would not countenance direct transfers of jurisdiction, the various governments devised an alternative mechanism which achieved the same result, albeit indirectly.

Given that in virtually any case it is possible to achieve indirectly what you cannot do directly, the interesting question is the extent to which governments actually resort to these various devices. One hypothesis would be that such substitution will occur whenever this would produce the "efficient" result. Yet we can immediately see why this hypothesis will turn out to be false. The most obvious reason is the one suggested by Coase himself; parties will bargain to the most efficient result only when transaction costs are zero. In the real world, and certainly in the context of federalism, transaction costs are never zero. In fact, the transaction costs appear virtually insurmountable, since the "parties" to the agreement are not merely the governments themselves but the millions of constituents who must indirectly feature in the calculations of the governments. Even the rigid party discipline of parliamentary government cannot eliminate the difficulty of achieving the required consensus.

There is a second difficulty. This is with the underlying assumption that, even in the absence of transaction costs, the parties will bargain towards "efficient" results. The difficulty stems from the fact that the parties to any such agreement are governments rather than private economic actors. Governments certainly have some interest in the goal of technical efficiency. But there are numerous other factors which influence the shape of government regulation. Governments have a desire to select policies that will result in their re-election.[50] Their policies may thus be directed towards certain powerful interest groups or to an identifiable group of marginal voters. They may opt for policies that provide benefits in concentrated form, so that their visibility is enhanced, and impose costs in dispersed form, so that their visibility is disguised. They may select policies that have a heavy bureaucratic orientation over decentralised forms of resource allocation.[51] This does not mean that considerations of technical efficiency will be irrelevant to the policy process. The more limited point is that technical efficiency is merely one out of a number of competing goals influencing public choice.

Thus, we would expect to observe governments bargaining around the effects of judicial decisions only when these various "political" factors pointed in that direction. It is likely that many of the results would be "inefficient" from the standpoint of technical efficiency. But this is more a product of the political system that any failing on the part of the judiciary. Even if, by some fantastic coincidence, the courts were able to select the result that was efficient from a technical point of view, we would expect to see governments bargaining around the result when there were significant political gains available. There would be little point, therefore, in instructing courts to choose the "efficient" result, even if such an instruction were capable of being executed.[52]

It is possible to advance a hypothesis regarding the extent to which judicial review constrains the ability of government to regulate the economy. Stated simply, this hypothesis is that judicial review constitutes a minimal and marginal constraint on the behaviour of government. Moreover, we would expect that constitutional limitations will be significant only when they are reinforced by the various political factors outlined above. Constitutional limitations standing on their own can be avoided by governments in virtually all cases.

One basis for such a hypothesis is the fact that certain forms of governing instruments play almost no role in constitutional adjudication. Consider that of the 177 federalism cases decided since 1949, there were no challenges to the spending power, one case dealing with state enterprise and four cases challenging a government's proprietary interest. The vast majority of cases have dealt with what might be termed command and control regulation.[53] Thus, it would be very surprising indeed if judicial review constituted a major obstacle to government regulation of economic activity. While certain forms of regulation may be impermissible, others will always be available. Moreover, many of the most important forms of economic regulation appear to be virtually immune from constitutional scrutiny. On the federal level, for example, the instruments of fiscal and monetary policy are largely free of constitutional constraint. The federal government can set macroeconomic policy without having to cast an eye backward on the Supreme Court.

While there seems to be a sound basis for supposing that such a hypothesis regarding the role of judicial review would turn out to be valid, it can only be tested through a detailed consideration of actual government behaviour in response to judicial decisions . . . .

NOTES

1. See D. Smiley, *Canada in Question: Federalism in the Eighties*, 3d ed. (1980), which details the rise of what he terms "executive federalism" in the 1970s, in which federal–provincial relations became the prerogative of elected, political actors rather than of members of the bureaucracy. Smiley suggests that this development has led to increased tensions between the respective levels of government, since the political actors are less likely to seek compromise and are less likely to view disputes as mere technical issues which can be resolved in a neutral, apolitical manner.

2. *Min. of Justice, Can. v. Borowski*, [1981] 2 S.C.R. 575 (S.C.C.); *Thorson v. A.G. Can.*, [1975] 1 S.C.R. 138 (S.C.C.).

3. "Reform of the Supreme Court of Canada," *British Columbia's Constitutional Proposals* (Paper No. 4, October 1978) at 45.

4. See G. Schochet, "Constitutionalism, Liberalism and the Study of Politics," in J. Pennock and J. Chapman, eds., *Constitutionalism* (1979) at 1, 4. Of course I do not mean to imply that this ethic of constitutionalism dominated all aspects of political discourse at the time. My point is limited to the realm of federal–provincial relations. Nor do I mean to suggest that there were not features and practices of federalism at the time that did not fit within the assumptions of constitutionalism. My point is merely that the federal tradition largely conformed to this ethic in the period prior to 1940.

5. The figures in this paragraph are taken from K. Dowd and A. Sayeed, "Federal–Provincial Fiscal Relations: Some Background" in T. Courchene, D. Conklin and G. Cook, eds., *Ottawa and the Provinces: The Distribution of Money and Power* 2 (1985) at table 9, 253, 268.

6. See generally Royal Commission on the Economic Union and Development Prospects for Canada, *Report* III (1985) at 237–47.

7. For a description and analysis of these trends, see D. Smiley, *Constitutional Adaptation and Canadian Federalism Since 1945* (Royal Commission on Bilingualism and Biculturalism, 1970) at 29–32.

8. See Smiley, *Canada in Question*.

9. J. Lesage, "Opening Statement" (Federal–Provincial Conference, July 1965), quoted in Smiley, *Constitutional Adaptation* at 83.

10. Ibid.,

11. Ibid., at 40.

12. See M. Oliver, ed., *Social Purpose for Canada* (1961) at 371.

13. Ibid., at 382.

14. Ibid.

15. To give but one example: from the Quebec point of view, the most serious objection to federal grants to universities was obviously not that the universities had enough money or that the federal money had a particular odour; it was that once the universities had their bellies filled with federal grants they would see no reason to oppose that provincial government which had persistently failed in its constitutional duties by leaving

leaving education in such an impoverished state; and Quebeckers would chalk up another failure in their struggle to master the art of self-government.

Ibid. at 384.

16. These are the terms used by Smiley, *Canada in Question*. According to Smiley, "co-operative federalism" was characterised by collaboration on specific programs on an *ad hoc* basis; the governments tended to be represented by technical officials, who shared a common set of values and program objectives. The move to executive federalism replaced these program officials with politicians or high-ranking bureaucrats, who were much less likely to share any common set of values or assumptions. Smiley argues that executive federalism is more likely to promote conflict, since the individuals involved come to the bargaining table with fundamentally contradictory goals and visions of the country.

17. The federal critiques of executive federalism are summarized in McRoberts, "Unilateralism, Bilateralism and Multilateralism: Approaches to Canadian Federalism" in *Intergovernmental Relations* 63, ed. R. Simeon (Royal Commission on the Economic Union Research Studies, 1985). The arguments outlined in the following paragraph are drawn from McRoberts' account.

18. The Supreme Court of Canada, in its judgment on the patriation of the constitution in September 1981, concluded that there was a "convention," or political norm, requiring provincial consent in cases where provincial legislative powers were to be altered. See *Ref. re Amendment of the Constitution of Can. (Nos. 1, 2, 3)* (1981), 125 D.L.R. (3d) 1 (S.C.C.).

19. In October 1980, the federal government tabled a joint resolution in the House of Commons which sought an amendment to the *British North America Act* without the consent of the provinces; in October 1980, the federal government announced the National Energy Policy, which sought to alter the

distribution of economic rent from the energy sector; in the spring of 1983, under Bill C-150, the federal government separated the cash contribution for the hospital insurance and medical care programs, and then imposed "six and five" restraint limits on transfers for post-secondary education.

20. McRoberts, "Unilateralism," at 93.

21. Ibid.

22. See *Final Report* III, at 254–58.

23. Ibid., at 256.

24. J.A. Corry and J.E. Hodgetts, *Democratic Government and Politics* (1959) at 557–79.

25. D. Smiley, *Constitutional Adaptation* at 40.

26. *Canada Health Act*, S.C. 1984, c. 6.

27. In one case, the Court ruled the statute to be *ultra vires*, while in the other, the Court ruled that the statute could not be applied to the activity in question.

28. According to my calculations, of the twelve cases in which the Court ruled a federal law to be invalid since 1980, only two of these can be attributed to attempts by the federal government to intrude onto established provincial turf: these two instances are the *Ref. re Exported Natural Gas* (1982), 42 N.R. 361 (S.C.C.); and *A.G. Can. v. L.S.U.C.; A.G. Can. v. Jabour*, [1982] 2 S.C.R. 307 (S.C.C.). Of course, the federal constitutional reform package was ruled to be legally valid in the Court's decision in the *Patriation Appeals*, [1981] 1 S.C.R. 753 (S.C.C.).

29. *Re Ct. of Unified Criminal Jurisdiction; McEvoy v. A.G. N.B.*, [1983] 1 S.C.R. 704 (S.C.C.).

30. *R. v. Boggs; Boggs v. R.*, [1981] 1 S.C.R. 49 (S.C.C.).

31. *Labatt Breweries of Can. Ltd. v. A.G. Can.*, [1980] 1 S.C.R. 914 (S.C.C.).

32. For instances of this line of argument, see P. Weiler, *In the Last Resort* (1974) at 155–85. I argue only that the results "appear" to contradict the claim regarding private interests and

federalism litigation. Of course, even in reference cases there are often private interests opposing the legislation and thus, a ruling of *ultra vires* may be indirectly of benefit to these interests. But, at the very least, the data suggest that the Court is not pursuing any conscious policy of assisting private interests in its federalism jurisprudence.

33. *Cdn. Industrial Gas & Oil (CIGOL) v. Saskatchewan*, [1977] 2 S.C.R. 545 (S.C.C.).

34. *Central Can. Potash Co. v. Saskatchewan*, [1979] 1 S.C.R. 42 (S.C.C.).

35. See Letter from the Premier of Saskatchewan, Allan Blakeney, to the Prime Minister of Canada, Pierre E. Trudeau, 10 October 1978. Saskatchewan was particularly upset by the fact that the government of Canada had become a co-plaintiff in the *Central Can. Potash* case.

36. In the 1950s, there were a total of eighteen private challenges to legislation on federalism grounds. The twelve cases in which there were intervenors split evenly, private litigants winning six; the six cases in which there were no intervenors also split evenly, the private litigants winning three. In the 1960s, there were 31 private challenges. Of the 22 in which there were interventions, the private litigants won only four, while in the nine in which there were no interventions, the private litigants won four.

37. In the 1970s, there were 49 private challenges. Of the 38 cases in which there were interventions, the challenges succeeded fourteen times; in the eleven cases in which there were no interventions, the challenges succeeded three times. In the 1980s, there were 47 private challenges. Of the 36 cases in which there were interventions, the challenges fifteen times; in the eleven cases in which there were no interventions, the challenges succeeded three times.

38. Cases in which governments have intervened, by decade:
   1950s: 23/30 cases
   1960s: 27/36 cases
   1970s: 43/54 cases
   1980s: 45/57 cases

39. R. Dworkin, "How Law Is Like Literature" in *A Matter of Principle* (1985) at 146.

40. Ibid., at 159.

41. S. Fish, "Working on the Chain Gang: Interpretation in Law and Literature," (1982) 60 *Tex. L. Rev.* 551, 559.

42. An attack on the objective–subjective dichotomy, as well as other "liberal antinomies," has been a prime element in the "total critique" of the so-called "critical legal studies movement" in America. See generally, R. Unger, *Knowledge and Politics* (1975). Surprisingly, mainstream legal theories have recently shown an impatience with the continuing search for objective legal standards. See L. Tribe, *Constitutional Choices* (1985) at 1–10.

43. D. Hoy, "Interpreting the Law: Hermeneutical and Post Structural Perspectives," (1985) 58 *S. Cal. L. Rev.* 136, 137.

44. R. Rorty, *Philosophy and the Mirror of Nature* (1979) at 383.

   What we need...is the ability to think about science in such a way that its being a "value-based enterprise" occasions no surprise. All that hinders us from doing so is the ingrained notion that "values" are "inner," whereas "facts" are "outer" and that it is as much a mystery how, beginning with values, we could produce bombs as how, beginning with private inner episodes, we could avoid bumping into things.

   Ibid., at 341–42.

45. For an account of interpretation along these lines, see Fish "Working on the Chain Gang."

46. R. Coase, "The Problem of Social Cost," (1961) 3 *Journ. of Law and Econ.* 1.

47. *A.G.N.S. v. A.G. Can.*, [1951] S.C.R. 31 (S.C.C.).

48. *P.E.I. Potato Marketing Board v. H.B. Willis Inc.*, [1952] 2 S.C.R. 392 (S.C.C.).

49. Here, one jurisdiction simply incorporates the rules or laws in force in another jurisdiction, without repeating those rules. This can be done in an "anticipatory" manner. Not only are the current rules adopted, but any amendments to those rules in the future by the original enacting jurisdiction are automatically deemed to be included in the laws of the incorporating jurisdiction. See *Coughlin v. Ont. Highway Transport Bd.*, [1968] S.C.R. 569 (S.C.C.).

50. This theory of "political rationality" governing instrument choice is developed in M.J. Trebilcock et al., *The Choice of Governing Instrument* (Economic Council of Canada, 1982) at 27.

51. For a discussion of the various reasons for such choices, see Trebilcock et al., ibid. at 33.

52. See Posner, *Economic Analysis of Law* (1977), whose claim is that courts should choose the efficient result, the result which the parties themselves would have selected in the absence of transaction costs. In effect, Posner's instruction to courts is to try to mimic the market. Posner's argument appears largely irrelevant in the context of federalism.

53. For a discussion of the various types of governing instruments, see Trebilcock et al., *The Choice of Governing Instrument*.

section

5

THE SUPREME COURT AND THE CHARTER

T he Charter will prove to be Pierre Elliott Trudeau's most important, memorable, and controversial legacy. When the constitutional debate began about 1960, the issues on the agenda were an amending formula and patriation of the constitution. Over the next few years the redistribution of legislative and fiscal powers were added. But when Trudeau appeared on the scene, first as Minister of Justice in the Pearson cabinet, and then as Prime Minister, the question of rights became part of the federal agenda. In the 1971 *Victoria Charter*, the rights were limited to language rights, largely at the federal level, and the political rights which ultimately became sections 2 and 3 of the 1982 Charter. But when Prime Minister Trudeau began to force the pace of constitutional reform with the *Time for Action* and Bill C-60 in 1978, the federal package included a full-blown Charter of Rights and Freedoms, which immediately became the most important and controversial issue in the negotiations.[1]

Trudeau's advocacy of a charter of rights had a long history. As early as 1955, Trudeau had proposed that Quebec accept a "declaration of human rights in the constitution on the condition that the rights of disallowance and reservation be done away with." A decade later, just before entering politics, he proposed a bill of rights "to limit the powers that legal authorities have over human rights in Canada. In addition to protecting traditional political and social rights, such a bill would specifically put the French and English languages on an equal basis before the law." And the subject of one of his first major speeches after becoming Minister of Justice in 1967 was "A Constitutional Declaration of Rights."[2]

Speaking to the Canadian Bar Association, Trudeau observed that although Canada had passed a Bill of Rights in 1960 and a number of provinces had similar bills, these were ordinary statutory enactments which did not "preclude future encroachments on those rights by Parliament or the Legislatures."[3] What was urgently needed as the basis for all constitutional reform, he argued, was a bill of rights, much broader in scope and including language rights, which was entrenched in the constitution and could not be modified by the ordinary legislative process. Obviously, Trudeau had not secured provincial agreement to the broad statement of rights he wanted by 1971. By 1978, however, he began the pursuit of a broader bill with that stubborn determination that marked his career whenever he was passionately committed to a cause. Advocating the Charter was also astute politically, for, in attempting to secure provincial agreement to his constitutional package of an amending formula, patriation, and the Charter, he could argue that the issue was the rights of the people versus the power of the state.[4]

There was widespread opposition to the idea of an entrenched Charter, and the intergovernmental and public debate was long and bitter. Opposition came from all sides—from left and right, radicals and traditionalists, from those who said it went too far or not far enough.[5] There were, however, four major arguments that dominated the debate. Those responsible for law enforcement argued that the guarantee of legal rights would inevitably hamper their work and would, if not protect the guilty, certainly make it more difficult to detect, arrest and prosecute. On the other side were those who argued that the Charter was too limited in its scope because it said nothing about economic rights or economic equality. Indeed, the very emphasis on political and legal rights, and on procedural rights, would make the achievement of greater economic equality more difficult. In a similar vein ran the argument that it was too limited, because it guaranteed protection only against encroachments by government, and excluded the abuse of civil liberties and of equality rights through the exercise of private powers.

Other critics argued that a Charter was either unnecessary or an illusion as a guarantee of fundamental rights and freedoms. Some maintained that the principles and practices of the common law were far more effective than an abstract statement of rights in a constitution. Common law presumed that freedom extended to everything that was not expressly prohibited by law, and rights which were amply protected by the "due process" of law were far more effective than an abstract statement of rights in a constitution. It was not difficult to demonstrate that the record in Britain and Canada was much better than in many countries, including the United States, where rights were entrenched in the constitution. In the long run, civil liberties depended upon the determination to protect the values of a free and democratic society.

Perhaps the most pervasive, if not persuasive, criticism of the idea of the Charter was that it represented a denial of Parliamentary supremacy, indeed of the democratic process. It placed into the hands of the judiciary the ultimate determination not only of rights and freedoms but also the breadth of the criminal law and the nature of social policy. Judicial review replaced legislative supremacy at the apex of the Canadian political system. The result was a limitation not an extension of freedom, said Allan Blakeney, the premier of Saskatchewan:

> Canadians ought not to have taken away from them[selves] the fundamental right to participate in political choices, in particular they ought not to have eroded, under the guise of advancing their freedoms, their right to make important social choices, and to participate in those decisions.[6]

Other critics added that governments would hide behind the Charter and the courts in order to avoid making difficult policy decisions.

It was not difficult to argue that eleven elected governments were far more likely to reflect Canadian values than the nine men and women on the Supreme Court of Canada whose decisions on rights, freedoms, and all that these meant, would be final and conclusive. Members of the legal profession and professors of law were the most outspoken critics of judicial supremacy. While few still held the view that the judges were not political actors, but only neutral and independent interpreters of the law, there was an understandable and justifiable belief that courts were not the proper forum for working out a balance of political and social interests, an inevitable result of the Charter. Neither training nor experience equipped the men and women who sat on the bench to give substantive content to the abstract expressions in the Charter, and in effect to engage in what could only be described as policy making.

Radical critics went further. By training, lawyers and judges were defenders of the status quo, well-to-do if not always wealthy members of the possessing class, whose decisions would inevitably reflect their social and economic bias. Moreover, litigation was an expensive exercise, always more feasible for the wealthy and powerful who would use the Charter to protect their interests. The result would be, as Professor Michael Mandel argues it has become, "legalised" politics, where instead of politicians accountable to electorates, the courts, accountable to no one, arbitrate conflicting interests and shape the nature of Canadian society.[7]

Although Trudeau was adamantly opposed to any weakening of the Charter, he was forced to compromise in the last hours of desperate negotiations that led to the acceptance of the Charter and patriation of the constitution. The compromise was section 33 of the Charter, the famous *non obstante* clause, which provided that

> Parliament of the legislature of a province may expressly declare in an Act of Parliament or of the legislature, as the case may be, that the Act or a provision thereof shall operate notwithstanding a provision included in section 2 or sections 7 to 15 of this Charter.

Such a declaration, however, would cease to have effect after five years unless re-enacted. Naturally, the *non obstante* clause was—and still is—denounced by those who felt it weakened the Charter; and it was praised—and still is—by those critics, radical and conservative alike, who preferred that in the last analysis supremacy should reside with the legislature rather than the courts.

The Charter presented the judiciary with a clean chalkboard on which it could write a new prescription for individual rights and freedoms and define new boundaries between the individual and the state. How the courts—above all the Supreme Court—viewed their role would determine whether the Charter would help recast Canadian society or leave it much as it was. Would the judiciary fulfil the worst fears of the traditionalists by adopting an activist point of view and seizing the opportunity to shape Canadian society in its own image? Would that image reflect the views of the social class to which judges were said to belong? Or would the court exercise judicial restraint and defer whenever possible to the supremacy of the legislative process? Would the courts feel more comfortable—and perhaps less restrained—with questions of legal rights, procedural fairness, and of police behaviour than with social, ethical and philosophical questions such as the right to life or the freedom of conscience? Would the existence of an entrenched Charter make Canadians more aware of their rights and those of others? Would the emphasis on individual rights, as many feared, outweigh social or collective goals when the two conflicted? Would the emphasis on individual rights be gender-neutral? Would governments seize upon the notwithstanding provision to limit guaranteed rights and freedoms, and even to override decisions of the Supreme Court?

NOTES

1. The Canadian Charter of Rights and Freedoms is Part I of the *Constitution Act, 1982*. Part II deals with aboriginal rights, Part III with equalization; Part IV provides for future constitutional conferences, and Part V is the amending formula. Section 52, in Part VII, entrenches the Charter as part of the constitution: "The Constitution of Canada is the supreme law of Canada, and any law that is inconsistent with the provisions of the Constitution is, to the extent of the inconsistency, of no force or effect." A comprehensive account of the negotiations between 1976 and 1981, written by participants is Roy Romanow, John Whyte and Howard Lesson, *Canada... Notwithstanding:*

296 SUPREME COURT AND THE CHARTER

The Making of the Constitution 1976–1982 (Toronto, 1984). For the views of other actors see Leonard Cohen, Patrick Smith and Paul Warwick, *The Vision and the Game: Making the Canadian Constitution* (Calgary, 1987).

2. Pierre Elliott Trudeau, "Quebec and the Constitutional Problem" and "A Constitutional Declaration of Rights," reprinted in *Federalism and the French Canadians* (Toronto, 1968). When the Charter emerged in Bill C-60 it applied only to the federal government, but a province could opt in, and if it did, Ottawa would give up its powers of reservation and disallowance for that province.

3. On the protection provided by the common law and the Canadian Bill of Rights see Peter Hogg, *Constitutional Law of Canada* (Toronto, 1985), 627 ff; Walter S. Tarnopolsky, *The Canadian Bill of Rights* (Toronto, 1975); *Discrimination and the Law in Canada* (Toronto, 1982); and R. St. J. Macdonald and J.P. Humphrey, *The Practice of Freedom* (Toronto, 1979).

4. The federal strategy of emphasising the "People's Package" as opposed to the "Package on Government Power and Institutions" argued that judges were more impartial than self-seeking politicians and likely to be more concerned about personal rights than about state power. The famous Kirby memorandum of 30 August 1980 outlined the strategy:

The strategy on the People's Package is really very simple. The federal position on the issues within the package clearly is very popular with the Canadian public and should be presented on television in the most favourable light possible. The Premiers who are opposed should be put on the defensive very quickly and should be made to appear that they prefer to trust politicians rather than impartial and non-partisan courts in the protection of the basic rights of citizens in a democratic society. It is evident that the Canadian people prefer their rights protected by judges rather than politicians.

The memorandum is reprinted in Cohen, Smith and Warwick, *The Vision and the Game*, 113–27.

5. An excellent analysis and commentary on the criticisms of the Charter is R.A. Macdonald, "Postscript and Prelude—The Jurisprudence of the Charter: Eight Theses," *Supreme Court Law Review* 4 (1982): 321–50.

6. On Blakeney's position see Romanow, Whyte, and Leeson, *Canada... Notwithstanding: The Making of the Constitution 1976–1982*, 110.

7. Michael Mandel, *The Charter of Rights and the Legalization of Politics in Canada* (Toronto, 1989).

INTERPRETING THE CHARTER

R. v. BIG M DRUG MART◊

DICKSON C.J.:

In my view, both purpose and effect are relevant in determining constitutionality; either an unconstitutional purpose or an unconstitutional effect can invalidate legislation. All legislation is animated by an object the legislature intends to achieve. This object is realised through the impact produced by the operation and application of the legislation. Purpose and effect respectively, in the sense of the legislation's object and its ultimate impact, are clearly linked, if not indivisible. Intended and actual effects have often been looked to for guidance in assessing the legislation's object and thus, its validity.

Moreover, consideration of the object of legislation is vital if rights are to be fully protected. The assessment by the courts of legislative purpose focusses scrutiny upon the aims and objectives of the legislature and ensures they are consonant with the guarantees enshrined in the Charter. The declaration that certain objects lie outside the legislature's power checks governmental action at the first stage of unconstitutional conduct. Further, it will provide more ready and more vigorous protection of constitutional rights by obviating the individual litigant's need to prove effects violative of Charter rights. It will also allow courts to dispose of cases where the object is clearly improper, without inquiring into the legislation's actual impact.

In short, I agree with the respondent that the legislation's purpose is the initial test of constitutional validity and its effects are to be considered when the law under review has passed or, at least, has purportedly passed the purpose test. If the legislation fails the purpose test, there is no need to consider further its effects, since it has already been demonstrated to be invalid. Thus, if a law with a valid purpose interferes by its impact, with rights or freedoms, a litigant could still argue the effects of the legislation as a means to defeat its applicability and possibly its validity. In short, the effects test will only be necessary to defeat legislation with a valid purpose; effects can never be relied upon to save legislation with an invalid purpose.

WILSON J.:

It is, of course, trite law that the analytic starting point in a division of powers case is the determination of the "pith and substance" of the challenged enactment. In the words of Professor Bora Laskin (as he then was) the Court endeavours to achieve a "distillation of the constitutional value represented by the challenged legislation . . . and its attribution to a head of power . . . ."

The division of powers jurisprudence is repleat with instances where the analytic focal point in determining whether a given piece of legislation is *ultra vires* the enacting legislature is the purpose or primary function of the legislation. Only when the effects of the legislation so directly impinge on some other subject matter as to reflect some alternative or ulterior purpose do the effects themselves take on analytic significance. . . .

In my view, the constitutional entrenchment of civil liberties in the Canadian Charter of Rights and Freedoms necessarily changes the analytic approach the courts must adopt in such cases. . . .

While it remains perfectly valid to evaluate the purpose underlying a particular enactment in order to determine whether the legislature has acted within its constitutional authority in division of powers terms, the Charter demands an evaluation of the impingement of even *intra vires* legislation on the fundamental rights and freedoms of the individual. It asks not whether the legislature has acted for a purpose that is within the scope of the authority of that tier of government, but rather whether in so acting it has had the effect of violating an entrenched individual right. It is in other words, first and foremost an effects-oriented document. . . .

In my view, so long as a statute has such an actual or potential effect on an entrenched right, it does not matter what the purpose behind the enactment was. . . .

o

HUNTER v. SOUTHAM[◆]

DICKSON J.:

The task of expounding a constitution is crucially different from that of construing a statute. A statute defines present rights and obligations. It is easily enacted and as easily repealed. A constitution, by contrast, is drafted with an eye to the future. Its function is to provide a continuing framework for the legitimate exercise of government power and, when joined by a Bill or a Charter of Rights, for the unremitting protection of individual rights and liberties. Once enacted, its provision cannot easily be repealed or amended. It must, therefore, be capable of growth and development over time to meet new social, political and historical realities often unimagined by its framers. The judiciary is the guardian of the constitution and must, in interpreting its provisions, bear these considerations in mind. Professor Paul Freund expressed this idea aptly when he admonished the American courts "not to read the provisions of the Constitution like a last will and testament lest it become one."

[◆][1984] 2 S.C.R. 145.

The Rights Protected: Section 2(a)

2. Everyone has the following fundamental freedoms: (a) freedom of conscience and religion. . . .

R. v. BIG M DRUG MART◇

Big M Drug Mart was charged with violating the Federal Government's *Lord's Day Act* for operating on Sunday; the store defended itself by claiming that the prohibition was unconstitutional.

DICKSON C.J. (Beetz, McIntyre, Chouinard and Lamer JJ. concurring):

. . . A truly free society is one which can accommodate a wide variety of beliefs, diversity of tastes and pursuits, customs and codes of conduct. A free society is one which aims at equality with respect to the enjoyment of fundamental freedoms and I say this without any reliance on s. 15 of the *Charter*. Freedom must surely be founded in respect for the inherent dignity and the inviolable rights of the human person. The essence of the concept of freedom of religion is the right to entertain such religious beliefs as a person chooses, the right to declare religious beliefs openly and without fear of hindrance or reprisal, and the right to manifest religious belief by worship and practice or by teaching and dissemination. But the concept means more than that.

Freedom can primarily be characterised by the absence of coercion or restraint. If a person is compelled by the state or the will of another to a course of action or inaction which he would not otherwise have chosen, he is not acting of his own volition and he cannot be said to be truly free. One of the major purposes of the *Charter* is to protect, within reason, from compulsion or restraint. Coercion includes not only such blatant forms of compulsion as direct commands to act or refrain from acting on pain of sanction, coercion includes indirect forms of control which determine or limit alternative courses of conduct available to others. Freedom in a broad sense embraces both the absence of coercion and constraint, and the right to manifest beliefs and practices. Freedom means that, subject to such limitations as are necessary to protect public safety, order, health, or morals or the fundamental rights and freedoms of others, no one is to be forced to act in a way contrary to his beliefs or conscience.

What may appear good and true to a majoritarian religious group, or to the state acting at their behest, may not, for religious reasons, be imposed upon citizens who take a contrary view. The *Charter* safeguards religious minorities from the threat of "the tyranny of the majority."

To the extent that it binds all to a sectarian Christian ideal, the *Lord's Day Act* works a form of coercion inimical to the spirit of the *Charter* and the dignity of all non-Christians. In proclaiming the standards of the Christian faith, the *Act* creates a climate hostile to, and gives the appearance of discrimination against, non-Christian

---

◇[1985] 1 S.C.R. 295.

Canadians. It takes religious values rooted in Christian morality and, using the force of the state, translated them into a positive law binding on believers and non-believers alike. The theological content of the legislation remains as a subtle and constant reminder to religious minorities within the country of their differences with, and alienation from, the dominant religious culture.

Non-Christians are prohibited for religious reasons from carrying out activities which are otherwise lawful, moral and normal. The arm of the state requires all to remember the Lord's day of the Christians and to keep it holy. The protection of one religion and the concomitant non-protection of others imports disparate impact destructive of the religious freedom of the collectivity. I agree with the submission of the respondent that to accept that Parliament retains the right to compel universal observance of the day of rest preferred by one religion is not consistent with the preservation and enhancement of the multicultural heritage of Canadians. To do so is contrary to the expressed provisions of s. 27, which as earlier noted reads:

> This *Charter* shall be interpreted in a manner consistent with the preservation and enhancement of the multicultural heritage of Canadians . . .

If I am a Jew or a Sabbatarian or a Muslim, the practice of my religion at least implies my right to work on a Sunday if I wish. It seems to me that any law purely religious in purpose, which denies me that right, must surely infringe my religious freedom . . . .

The ability of each citizen to make free and informed decisions is the absolute prerequisite for the legitimacy, acceptability, and efficacy of our system of self-government. It is because of the centrality of the rights associated with freedom of individual conscience both to basic beliefs about human worth and dignity and to a free and democratic political system that American jurisprudence has emphasised the primacy or "firstness" of the First Amendment. It is this same centrality that in my view underlies their designation in the *Canadian Charter of Rights and Freedoms* as "fundamental." They are the *sine qua non* of the political tradition underlying the *Charter*.

Viewed in this context, the purpose of freedom of conscience and religion becomes clear. The values that underlie our political and philosophic traditions demand that every individual be free to hold and to manifest whatever beliefs and opinions his or her conscience dictates, provided *inter alia* only that such manifestations do not injure his or her neighbours or their parallel rights to hold and manifest beliefs and opinions of their own. Religious belief and practice are historically prototypical and, in many ways, paradigmatic of conscientiously held beliefs and manifestations and are therefore protected by the *Charter*. Equally protected, and for the same reasons, are expressions and manifestations of religious non-belief and refusals to participate in religious practice. It may perhaps be that freedom of conscience and religion extends beyond these principles to prohibit other sorts of governmental involvement in matters having to do with religion. For the present case it is sufficient in my opinion to say that whatever else freedom of conscience and religion may mean, it must at the very least mean this: government may not coerce individuals to affirm a specific religious belief or to manifest a specific religious practice for a sectarian purpose . . . .

In my view, the guarantee of freedom of conscience and religion prevents the government from compelling individuals to perform or abstain from performing otherwise harmless acts because of the religious significance of those acts to others. The element of religious compulsion is perhaps somewhat more difficult to perceive (especially for those whose beliefs are being enforced) when, as here, it is non-action rather than action that is being decreed, but in my view compulsion is nevertheless what it amounts to.

I would like to stress that nothing in these reasons should be read as suggesting any opposition to Sunday being spent as a religious day; quite the contrary. It is recognized that for a great number of Canadians, Sunday is the day when their souls rest in God, when the spiritual takes priority over the material, a day which, to them, gives security and meaning because it is linked to Creation and the Creator. It is a day which brings a balanced perspective to life, and opportunity for man to be in communion with man and with God. In my view, however, as I read the *Charter*, it mandates that the legislative preservation of a Sunday day of rest should be secular; diversity of belief and non-belief, the diverse socio-cultural backgrounds of Canadians make it constitutionally incompetent for the federal Parliament to provide legislative preference for any one religion at the expense of those of another religious persuasion.

In an earlier time, when people believed in the collective responsibility of the community towards some duty, the enforcement of religious conformity may have been a legitimate object of government, but since the *Charter*, it has become the right of every Canadian to work out for himself or herself what his or her religious obligations, if any, should be and is not for the state to dictate otherwise. The state shall not use the criminal sanctions at its disposal to achieve a religious purpose, namely, the uniform observance of the day chosen by the Christian religion as its day of rest.

On the authorities and for the reasons outlined, the true purpose of the *Lord's Day Act* is to compel the observance of the Christian Sabbath and I find the *Act*, and especially s. 4 thereof, infringes upon the freedom of conscience and religion guaranteed in s. 2(*a*) of the *Charter* . . . .

The Chief Justice also found that the Act was not saved by section 1 of the *Charter*. Wilson J. wrote a concurring judgment.

○

EDWARDS BOOKS AND ART LTD. v. R.◇

Section 2 of the *Retail Business Holidays Act of Ontario* prohibited the carrying on of a retail business on government designated holidays. Sections 3 and 4 provided a number of exceptions (as stated by Dickson C.J.):

Most "corner store" operations are exempted by subs. 3(1). Pharmacies, gas stations, flower stores, and during the summer

---

◇[1986] 2 S.C.R. 713.

months, fresh fruit and vegetable stores or stands are excluded by subs. 3(2) and 3(3). Subsection 3(6) exempts educational, recreational or amusement services. Prepared meals, laundromat services, boat and vehicle rentals and service are permitted under subs. 3(7). Subsection 3(8) and s. 4 allow a municipality to create its own scheme of exemptions where necessary for the promotion of the tourist industry.

Subsection 3(4) provided an exemption for "Saturday observers":

3(4) Section 2 does not apply in respect of the carrying on of a retail business in a retail business establishment on a Sunday where,

   (a) the retail business establishment was closed to the public and no goods or services were sold or offered for sale therein during a period of twenty-four consecutive hours in the period of thirty-two hours immediately preceding the Sunday; and

   (b) the number of persons engaged in the service of the public in the establishment on the Sunday does not at any time exceed seven; and

   (c) the total area used for serving the public or for selling or displaying to the public in the establishment on the Sunday is less than 5000 square feet.

A number of retailers, charged with violation of the Act, challenged its constitutionality.

DICKSON C.J. (Chouinard and Le Dain JJ. concurring):

The first question is whether indirect burdens on religious practice are prohibited by the constitutional guarantee of freedom of religion. In my opinion indirect coercion by the state is comprehended within the evils from which s. 2(a) may afford protection. The Court said as much in the *Big M Drug Mart* case and any more restrictive interpretation would, in my opinion, be inconsistent with the Court's obligation under s. 27 to preserve and enhance the multicultural heritage of Canadians . . . .

It matters not, I believe, whether a coercive burden is direct or indirect, intentional or unintentional, foreseeable or unforeseeable. All coercive burdens on the exercise of religious beliefs are potentially within the ambit of s. 2(a).

This does not mean, however, that every burden on religious practices is offensive to the constitutional guarantee of freedom of religion. It means only that indirect or unintentional burdens will not be held to be outside the scope of *Charter* protection on that account alone. Section 2(a) does not require the legislatures to eliminate every minuscule state-imposed cost associated with the practice of religion. Otherwise the *Charter* would offer protection from innocuous secular legislation such as a taxation act that imposed a modest sales tax extending to all products, including those used in the course of religious worship. In my opinion, it is unnecessary to turn to s.1 in order to justify legislation of that sort. The purpose of s. 2(a) is to ensure that society does not interfere with profoundly personal beliefs that govern one's perception of oneself, humankind, nature, and in some cases, a higher or different order of being. These beliefs, in turn, govern one's conduct and practices. The Constitution shelters individuals and groups only to the extent that religious beliefs or conduct might reasonably or actually be threatened. For a state-imposed cost or burden to be proscribed by s. 2(*a*) it must be capable of interfering with religious belief or practice. In short, legislative or administrative action which increases the cost of practising or otherwise manifesting religious beliefs is not prohibited if the burden is trivial or insubstantial . . . .

The Chief Justice then considered whether s. 3(4) of the Act provided a reasonable limit in accordance with section 1 of the *Charter*; and noted that New Brunswick legislation provided for the issuance of permits to "Saturday Observers." American legislation lacking any such exemptions was referred to also.

In this context, I note that freedom of religion, perhaps unlike freedom of conscience has both individual and collective aspects. Legislatures are justified in being conscious of the effect of legislation on religious groups as a whole, as well as on individuals. In some circumstances, it is open to balance the religious freedoms of the many members of any particular religious group against those of the few when differential treatment is based on a criterion, such as the size of one's retail business, which is not in itself offensive to constitutional provisions, principles, and purposes.

Nevertheless, while the number of detrimentally affected retailers may be small, no legislature in Canada is entitled to do away with any of the religious freedoms to which these or any other individuals are entitled without strong reason. In my view, the balancing of the interest of more than 7 employees to a common pause day against the freedom of religion of those affected constitutes justification for the exemption scheme selected by the Province of Ontario, at least in a context wherein any satisfactory alternative scheme involves an inquiry into religious beliefs.

I might add that I do not believe there is any magic in the number seven as distinct from, say, five, ten, or fifteen employees as the cut-off point for eligibility for the exemption. In balancing the interests of retail employees to a holiday in common with their family and friends against the s. 2(*a*) interests of those affected the legislature engaged in the process envisaged by s. 1 of the *Charter*. A "reasonable limit" is one which, having regard to the principles enunciated in *Oakes*, it was reasonable for the legislature to impose. The courts are not called upon to substitute judicial opinions for legislative ones as to the place at which to draw a precise line.

LA FOREST J. (concurring in part):

. . . In seeking to achieve a goal that is demonstrably justified in a free and democratic society . . . a legislature must be given reasonable room to manoeuvre to meet these conflicting pressures. Of course, what is reasonable will vary with the context. Regard must be had to the nature of the interest infringed and to the legislative scheme sought to be implemented. In a case like the present, it seems to me, the Legislature is caught between having to let the legislation place a burden on people who observe a day of worship other than Sunday or create exemptions which in their practical workings may substantially interfere with the goal the Legislature seeks to advance and which themselves result in imposing burdens on

Sunday observers and possibly on theirs as well. That being so, it seems to me that the choice of having or not having an exemption for those who observe a day other than Sunday must remain, in essence, a legislative choice. That, barring equality considerations, is true as well of the compromises that must be made in creating religious exemptions. These choices require an in-depth knowledge of all the circumstances. They are choices a court is not in a position to make . . . .

While, like the Chief Justice, I favour the making of whatever exemptions are possible to accommodate minority groups, I am of the view that the nature of the choices and compromises that must be made in relation to Sunday closing are essentially legislative in nature. In the absence of unreasonableness or discrimination, courts are simply not in a position to substitute their judgment for that of the Legislature . . . .

BEETZ J. (McIntyre J. concurring in result):

. . . In my respectful opinion, the impugned legislation does not violate the freedom of conscience and religion guaranteed by s. 2(*a*) of the *Charter* and, accordingly, is of full force and effect without any need to rely on s. 1 of the *Charter* . . . .

The economic harm suffered by a Saturday observer who closes shop on Saturdays is not caused by the *Retail Business Holidays Act*. It is independent from this Act. It results from the deliberate choice of a tradesman who gives priority to the tenets of his religion over his financial benefit. It is accordingly erroneous to suggest that the effect of the *Act* is to induce a Saturday observer to choose between his religion and the requirements of business competition.

Wilson J. dissented on the grounds that granting a common pause day to one group of workers while denying it to others violated section 1 of the *Charter*.

o

The Rights Protected: Section 2(b)

2. Everyone has the following fundamental freedoms: (b)freedom of thought, belief, opinion and expression, including freedom of the press and other media of communication . . . .

FORD v. A.-G. QUEBEC[◇]

Ford, among a number of people, was charged with violating section 58 of the *Charter of the French Language* which required that all public signs and commercial advertising be only in French as well as section 69 which provided that only a French version of a firm name be used. Upon prosecution, Ford claimed that the law was unconstitutional. It was also claimed that it violated section 3 of the *Quebec Charter of Human Rights and Freedoms* which provides:

[◇][1988] 2 S.C.R. 712.

Every person is the possessor of the fundamental freedoms, including freedom of conscience, freedom of religion, freedom of opinion, freedom of expression, freedom of peaceful assembly and freedom of association.

THE COURT:

Whether the Freedom of Expression Guaranteed by s. 29(*b*) of the *Canadian Charter of Rights and Freedoms* and by s. 3 of the Quebec *Charter of Human Rights and Freedoms* includes the freedom to express oneself in the language of one's choice:

In so far as this issue is concerned, the words "freedom of expression" in s. 2(*b*) of the Canadian *Charter* and s. 3 of the Quebec *Charter* should be given the same meaning. As indicated above, both the Superior Court and the Court of Appeal held that freedom of expression includes the freedom to express oneself in the language of one's choice. After indicating the essential relationship between expression and language by reference to dictionary definitions of both, Boudreault J. in the Superior Court said that in the ordinary or general form of expression there cannot be expression without language. Bisson J.A. in the Court of Appeal said that he agreed with the reasons of Boudreault J. on this issue and expressed his own view in the form of the following question: "Is there a purer form of freedom of expression than the spoken language and written language?" He supported his conclusions by quotation of the following statement of this Court in *Reference re Manitoba Language Rights*, [1985] 1 S.C.R. 721, at p. 744: "The importance of language rights is grounded in the essential role that language plays in human existence, development and dignity. It is through language that we are able to form concepts; to structure and order the world around us. Language bridges the gap between isolation and community, allowing humans to delineate the rights and duties they hold in respect of one another, and thus to live in society."

The conclusion of the Superior Court and the Court of Appeal on this issue is correct. Language is so intimately related to the form and content of expression that there cannot be true freedom of expression by means of language if one is prohibited from using the language of one's choice. Language is not merely a means or medium of expression; it colours the content and meaning of expression. It is, as the preamble of the *Charter of the French Language* itself indicates, a means by which a people may express its cultural identity. It is also the means by which the individual expresses his or her personal identity and sense of individuality. That the concept of "expression" in s. 2(*b*) of the Canadian *Charter* and s. 3 of the Quebec *Charter* goes beyond mere content is indicated by the specific protection accorded to "freedom of thought, belief [and] opinion" in s. 2 and to "freedom of conscience" and "freedom of opinion" in s. 3. That suggests that "freedom of expression" is intended to extend to more than the content of expression in its narrow sense.

The Court then turned to the issue of whether commercial speech was protected under the two *Charters*.

It is apparent to this Court that the guarantee of freedom of expression in s. 2(b) of the Canadian *Charter* and s. 3 of the *Charter* cannot be confined to political expression, important as that form of expression is in a free and democratic society. The pre-*Charter* jurisprudence emphasised the importance of political expression because it was a challenge to that form of expression that most often arose under the division of powers and the "implied bill of rights," where freedom of political expression could be related to the maintenance and operation of the institutions of democratic government. But political expression is only one form of the great range of expression that is deserving of constitutional protection because it serves individual and societal values in a free and democratic society.

In order to address the issues presented by this case it is not necessary for the Court to delineate the boundaries of the broad range of expression deserving of protection under s. 2(b) of the Canadian *Charter* or s. 3 of the Quebec *Charter*. It is necessary only to decide if the respondents have a constitutionally protected right to use the English language in the signs they display, or more precisely, whether the fact that such signs have a commercial purpose removes the expression contained therein from the scope of protected freedom.

In our view, the commercial element does not have this effect. Given the earlier pronouncements of this Court to the effect that the rights and freedoms guaranteed in the Canadian *Charter* should be given a large and liberal interpretation, there is no sound basis on which commercial expression can be excluded from the protection of s. 2(b) of the *Charter*. It is worth noting that the courts below applied a similar generous and broad interpretation to include commercial expression within the protection of freedom of expression contained in s. 3 of the Quebec *Charter*. Over and above its intrinsic value as expression, commercial expression which, as has been pointed out, protects listeners as well as speakers plays a significant role in enabling individuals to make informed economic choices, an important aspect of individual self-fulfillment and personal autonomy. The Court accordingly rejects the view that commercial expression serves no individual or societal value in a free and democratic society and for this reason is undeserving of any constitutional protection.

Rather, the expression contemplated by ss. 58 and 69 of the *Charter of the French Language* is expression within the meaning of both s. 2(b) of the Canadian *Charter* and s. 3 of the Quebec *Charter*. This leads to the conclusion that s. 58 infringes the freedom of expression guaranteed by s. 3 of the Quebec *Charter* and s. 69 infringes the guaranteed freedom of expression under both s. 2(b) of the Canadian *Charter* and s. 3 of the Quebec *Charter*. Although the expression in this case has a commercial element, it should be noted that the focus here is on choice of language and on a law which prohibits the use of a language. We are not asked in this case to deal with the distinct issue of the permissible scope of regulation of advertising (for example to protect consumers) where different governmental interests come into play, particularly when assessing the reasonableness of limits on such commercial expression pursuant to s. 1 of the Canadian *Charter* or to s. 9.1 of the Quebec *Charter*. It remains to be considered whether the limit imposed on freedom of expression by ss. 58 and 69 is justified under either s. 1 of the Canadian *Charter* or s. 9.1 of the Quebec *Charter*, as the case may be.

In considering whether the sections could be saved by section 1 of the Canadian *Charter*, the Court also considered the terms of section 9.1 of the *Quebec Charter of Rights and Freedoms* which provides:

> In exercising his fundamental freedoms and rights, a person shall maintain a proper regard for democratic values, public order and the general well-being of the citizens of Quebec.
> In this respect, the scope of the freedoms and rights, and limits to their exercise, may be fixed by law.

...The section 1 and s. 9.1 materials establish that the aim of the language policy underlying the *Charter of the French Language* was a serious and legitimate one. They indicate the concern about the survival of the French language and the perceived need for an adequate legislative response to the problem. Moreover, they indicate a rational connection between protecting their French language and assuring that the reality of Quebec society is communicated through the "*visage linguistic.*" The section 1 and s. 9.1 materials do not, however, demonstrate that the requirement of the use of French only is either necessary for the achievement of the legislative objective or proportionate to it. That specific question is simply not addressed by the materials. Indeed, in his factum and oral argument the Attorney General of Quebec did not attempt to justify the requirement of the exclusive use of French. He concentrated on the reasons for the adoption of the *Charter of the French Language* and the earlier language legislation, which, as was noted above, were conceded by the respondents. The Attorney General of Quebec relied on what he referred to as the general democratic legitimacy of Quebec language policy without referring explicitly to the requirement of the exclusive use of French. In so far as proportionality is concerned, the Attorney General of Quebec referred to the American jurisprudence with respect to commercial speech, presumably as indicating the judicial deference that should be paid to the legislative choice of means to serve an admittedly legitimate legislative purpose, at least in the area of commercial expression. He did, however, refer in justification of the requirement of the exclusive use of French to the attenuation of this requirement reflected in ss. 59 to 62 of the *Charter of the French Language* and the regulations. He submitted that these exceptions to the requirement of the exclusive use of French indicate the concern for carefully designed measures and for interfering as little as possible with commercial expression. The qualifications of the requirement of the exclusive use of French in other provisions of the *Charter of the French Language* and the regulations do not make ss. 58 and 69 any less prohibitions of the use of any language other than French as applied to the respondents. The issue is whether any such prohibition is justified. In the opinion of this Court it has not been demonstrated that the prohibition of the use of any language other than French in ss. 58 and 69 of the *Charter of the French Language* is necessary to the defence and enhancement of the status of the French language in Quebec or that it is proportionate to that legislative purpose. Since the evidence put to us by the government showed that the predominance of the French language was not reflected in the "*visage linguistic*" of Quebec, the governmental response could well have been tailored to meet that specific problem and to impair freedom of expression minimally.

Thus, whereas requiring the predominant display of the French language, even its marked predominance, would be proportional to the goal of promoting and maintaining a French "*visage linguistic*" in Quebec and therefore justified under the Quebec *Charter* and the Canadian *Charter*, requiring the exclusive use of French has not been so justified. French could be required in addition to any other language or it could be required to have greater visibility than that accorded to other languages. Such measures would ensure that the "*visage linguistic*" reflected the demography of Quebec: the predominant language is French. This reality should be communicated to all citizens and non-citizens alike, irrespective of their mother tongue. But exclusivity for the French language has not survived the scrutiny of a proportionality test and does not reflect the reality of Quebec society. Accordingly, we are of the view that the limit imposed on freedom of expression by s. 58 of the *Charter of the French Language* respecting the exclusive use of French on public signs and posters and in commercial advertising is not justified under s. 9.1 of the Quebec *Charter*. In like measure, the limit imposed on freedom of expression by s. 69 of the *Charter of the French Language* respecting the exclusive use of the French version of a firm name is not justified under either s. 9.1 of the Quebec *Charter* or s. 1 of the Canadian *Charter*....

o

REFERENCE RE SS. 193 AND 195.1(1)(C) OF THE CRIMINAL CODE (MANITOBA PROSTITUTION REFERENCE)◊

Section 195.1(1)(c) of the *Criminal Code* prohibits soliciting for the purposes of prostitution. The Lieutenant-Governor of Manitoba referred the constitutionality of the section to the Manitoba Court of Appeal. A majority of the Court held that the section did not violate s. 2 of the Charter. The following excerpt deals with the Court's disposition of the section 2(b) argument.

WILSON J. (L'Heureux-Dubé J. concurring, and Dickson C.J., La Forest and Sopinka JJ. concurring on section 2(b) but dissenting on section 1):

... Rather than deal directly with the variety of harmful consequences which the Attorney General of Canada and others submit ultimately flow from the communication act, s. 195.1(1)(c) prohibits the communication act itself in the hope that this will put an end to such consequences. To paraphrase this Court's observation in *Irwin Toy*, this is not a case in which the government has sought to control the physical consequences of certain human activity regardless of the meaning being conveyed. Rather, this is a case where the government's purpose is to restrict the content of expression by singling out meanings that are not to be conveyed in the hope that this will deal with the physical consequences emanating from expressive activity that carries the prohibited meaning.

◊(1990) Forthcoming in S.C.R.

This approach has obvious weaknesses. Section 195.1(1)(*c*) does not make clear the harmful consequences that it is designed to control. Nor does it limit the range of instances in which the expressive activity will be prohibited by requiring a link between the expressive activity and the harmful consequences. More precisely, s. 195(1)(*c*) does not require that the Crown show that the expressive act in a given case is in fact likely to lead to undesired consequences such as noise or traffic congestion. Instead, the provision prohibits *all* communicative acts for the purpose of engaging in prostitution or obtaining the sexual services of a prostitute that take place in public regardless of whether a given communicative act gives rise to harmful consequences or not.

The provision prohibits persons from engaging in expression that has an economic purpose. But economic choices are, in my view, for the citizen to make (provided that they are legally open to him or her) and, whether the citizen is negotiating for the purchase of a Van Gogh or a sexual encounter, s. 2 (*b*) of the *Charter* protects that person's freedom to communicate with his or her vendor. Where the statute is concerned about the harmful consequences that flow from communicative activity with an economic purpose and where, rather than address those consequences directly, the content of communicative activity is proscribed, then the provision must, in my view, be justified as a reasonable limit under s. 1 of the *Charter* if it is to be upheld.

Wilson J. found that the object of preventing street solicitation was a pressing and substantial concern; she also found that the section's prohibition against soliciting was rationally related to that concern. The next issue under s. 1 is whether the legislation is proportionate to that objective.

. . . The Attorney General of Canada described the legislation as "time and place regulation" and emphasised that many trades and businesses are subject to government regulation in the public interest. He argued that the net effect of the legislation is merely to remove the transaction of the business of prostitution from public places. It is no different, he submitted, from regulating the condition under which other businesses must operate. The Attorney General further submitted that no business enterprise should be free to pre-empt a public place for its own commercial gain without regard to the nuisance it may create for the surrounding community. The Attorney General submitted (rather surprisingly, I think, in light of the impact on s. 193 of the *Criminal Code* on attempts to engage in prostitution from private premises) that one of the purposes of s. 193 is to diffuse the activities associated with prostitution and ensure that prostitutes, like retailers and consumers, conduct their activities on private premises and in a way which will avoid the creation of a nuisance to others.

I believe, with respect, that the Attorney General has overlooked a number of significant aspects of the impugned legislation which go directly to the question of its proportionality. The first is that it criminalizes communication or attempted communication for the prohibited purpose in any public place or place open to public view. "Public place" is then expanded in subs. (2) to include any place to which the public have access as of right or by invitation express or implied. In other words, the prohibition is not confined to places where there will necessarily be lots of people to be offended or inconvenienced by it. The prohibited communication may be taking place in a secluded area of a park where there is no one to see or hear it. It will still be a criminal offence under the section. Such a broad prohibition as to the locale of the communication would seem to go far beyond a genuine concern over the nuisance caused by street solicitation in Canada's major centres of population. It enables the police to arrest citizens who are disturbing no one, solely because they are engaged in communicative acts concerning something not prohibited by the *Code*. It is not reasonable, in my view, to prohibit *all* expressive activity conveying a certain meaning that takes place in public simply because in *some* circumstances and in *some* areas that activity *may* give rise to a public or social nuisance.

I note also the broad scope of the phrase "in any manner communicates or attempts to communicate." It would seem to encompass every conceivable method of human expression. Indeed, it may not be necessary for the prostitute to say anything at all in order to be found to be "communicating" or "attempting to communicate" for the purpose of prostitution. The proverbial nod or wink may be enough. Perhaps more serious, a hapless citizen may be picked up for soliciting when he or she has nothing more pressing in mind than hailing a taxi! While it is true that he or she may subsequently be let go as lacking the necessary intent for the offence, the experience of being arrested is not something the ordinary citizen would welcome. Some definitional limits would appear to be desirable in any activity labelled as criminal.

Directly relevant to the issue of proportionality, it seems to me, is the fact already referred to that under para. (*c*) no nuisance or adverse impact of any kind on other people need be shown, or even be shown to be a possibility, in order that the offence be complete. Yet communicating or attempting to communicate with someone in a public place with respect to the sale of sexual services does not automatically create a nuisance any more than communicating or attempting to communicate with someone on the sidewalk to promote a candidate for municipal election. Moreover, as already mentioned, prostitution is itself a perfectly legal activity and the avowed objective of the legislature was not to make it illegal but only, as the Minister of Justice emphasised at the time, to deal with the nuisance created by street solicitation. It seems to me that to render criminal the communicative acts of persons engaged in a lawful activity which is not shown to be harming anybody cannot be justified by the legislative objective advanced in its support. The impugned provision is not sufficiently tailored to that objective and constitutes a more serious impairment of the individual's freedom than the avowed legislative objective would warrant. Section 195.1(1)(*c*) therefore fails to meet the proportionality test in *Oakes*.

DICKSON C.J. (La Forest and Sopinka JJ. concurring):

Dickson C.J. for the majority agreed with Wilson J. that s. 185 violated freedom of expression; he then turned to s. 1. After finding that the governmental objective of taking solicitation out of public view was pressing and substantial and that the measures taken were rationally related to that objective, Dickson C.J. considered the issue of proportionality.

I start by considering the nature of the expression and the nature of the infringing legislation. Freedom of expression is fundamental to a democratic society. Parliament, through s. 195(1)(c) of the *Criminal Code*, has chosen to use the criminal justice system to prosecute individuals on the basis of the exercise of their freedom of expression. When a *Charter* freedom has been infringed by state action that takes the form of criminalization, the Crown bears the heavy burden of justifying that infringement. Yet, the expressive activity, as with any infringed *Charter* right, should also be analysed in the particular context of the case. Here, the activity to which the impugned legislation is directed in expression with an economic purpose. It can hardly be said that communications regarding an economic transaction of sex for money lie at, or even near, the core of the guarantee of freedom of expression.

The legislation aims at restraining communication or attempts at communication for the purpose of engaging in prostitution. That communication must occur in "a public place or in any place open to public view." It is argued that the legislation is over-broad because it is not confined to places where there will *necessarily* be many people, or, in fact, *any* people, who will be offended by the activity. The objective of this provision, however, is not restricted to the control of actual disturbances or nuisances. It is broader, in the sense that it is directed at controlling, in general, the nuisance-related problems identified above that stem from street soliciting. Much street soliciting occurs in specified areas where the congregation of prostitutes and their customers amounts to a nuisance. In effect, the legislation discourages prostitutes and customers from concentrating their activities in any particular location. While it is the cumulative impact of individual transactions concentrated in a public area that effectively produces the social nuisance at which the legislation in part aims, Parliament can only act by focussing on individual transactions. The notion of nuisance in connection with street soliciting extends beyond interference with the individual citizen to interference with the public at large, that is with the environment represented by streets, public places and neighbouring premises.

The appellants' argument that the provision is too broad and therefore cannot be found to be appropriately tailored also focusses on the phrase "in any manner communicate or attempt to communicate." The communication in question cannot be read without the phrase "for the purpose of engaging in prostitution or of obtaining the sexual services of a prostitute" which follows and qualifies it. In my opinion, the definition of communication may be, and indeed is, very wide, but the need for flexibility on the part of Parliament in this regard must be taken into account. Certain acts or gestures in addition to certain words can reasonably be interpreted as attracting customers for the purposes of prostitution or as indicating a desire to procure the services of a prostitute. This provides the necessary delineation of the scope of the communication that may be criminalized by s. 195.1(1)(c)....

Can effective yet less intrusive legislation be imagined? The means used to attain the objective of the legislation may well be broader than would be appropriate were actual street nuisance the only focus. However, as I find the objective to extend to the general curtailment of visible solicitation for the purposes of prostitution, it is my view that the legislation is not unduly intrusive.

The Rights Protected: Section 2(d)

2. Everyone has the following fundamental freedoms: (d) freedom of association.

REFERENCE RE PUBLIC SERVICE EMPLOYEE RELATIONS ACT◇

The Province of Alberta introduced bills prohibiting striking among public service employees, police officers, fire fighters and hospital workers; the Acts instituted compulsory arbitration as the means of settling industrial disputes. They were referred to the Alberta Court of Appeal where a four to one majority found them not to infringe on the employees' freedom of association. This decision was appealed to the Supreme Court of Canada.

LE DAIN J. (Beetz and La Forest JJ. concurring):

... In considering the meaning that must be given to freedom of association in s. 2(*d*) of the *Charter* it is essential to keep in mind that this concept must be applied to a wide range of associations or organizations of a political, religious, social or economic nature, with a wide variety of objects, as well as activity by which the objects may be pursued. It is in this larger perspective, and not simply with regard to the perceived requirements of a trade union, however important they may be, that one must consider the implications of extending a constitutional guarantee, under the concept of freedom of association, to the right to engage in particular activity on the ground that the activity is essential to give an association meaningful existence.

In considering whether it is reasonable to ascribe such a sweeping intention to the *Charter* I reject the premise that without such additional constitutional protection the guarantee of freedom of association would be a meaningless and empty one. Freedom of association is particularly important for the exercise of other fundamental freedoms, such as freedom of expression and freedom of conscience and religion. These afford a wide scope for protected activity in association. Moreover, the freedom to work for the establishment of an association, to belong to an association, to maintain it, and to participate in its lawful activity without penalty or reprisal is not to be taken for granted. That is indicated by its express recognition and protection in labour relations legislation. It is a freedom that has been suppressed in varying degrees from time to time by totalitarian regimes.

What is in issue here is not the importance of freedom of association in this sense, which is the one I ascribe to s. 2(*d*) of the *Charter*, but whether particular activity of an association in pursuit of its objects is to be constitutionally protected or left to be regulated by legislative policy. The rights for which constitutional protection is sought—the modern rights to bargain collectively and to strike, involving correlative duties or obligations resting on an employer—are not fundamental rights or freedoms. They are the creation of legislation, involving a balance of competing interests in a field which has been recognized by the courts

---

◇[1987] 1 S.C.R. 313.

as requiring a specialized expertise. It is surprising that in an area in which this court has affirmed a principle of judicial restraint in the review of administrative action we should be considering the substitution of our judgment for that of the legislature by constitutionalizing in general and abstract terms rights which the legislature has found it necessary to define and qualify in various ways according to the particular field of labour relations involved. The resulting necessity of applying s. 1 of the *Charter* to a review of particular legislation in this field demonstrates in my respectful opinion the extent to which the court becomes involved in a review of legislative policy for which it is really not fitted.

MCINTYRE J.:

... In considering the constitutional position of freedom of association, it must be recognized that while it advances many group interests and, of course, cannot be exercised alone, it is nonetheless a freedom belonging to the individual and not to the group formed through its exercise. While some provisions in the *Constitution* involve groups, such as s. 93 of the *Constitution Act, 1867* protecting denominational schools, and s. 25 of the *Charter* referring to existing aboriginal rights, the remaining rights and freedoms are individual rights; they are not concerned with the group as distinct from its members. The group or organization is simply a device adopted by individuals to achieve a fuller realisation of individual rights and aspirations. People, by merely combining together, cannot create an entity which has greater constitutional rights and freedoms than they, as individuals, possess. Freedom of association cannot therefore vest independent rights in the group.

McIntyre J. then went on to outline six theories upon which freedom of association had been supported:

1. The right is attached to individuals who decide to associate: "neither the objects nor the actions of the group are protected by freedom of association."

2. It is an individual right which attaches to a group once there has been an association: "the freedom to engage collectively in those activities which are constitutionally protected for each individual."

3. It is an individual right which remains with the individual when he joins a group: "an individual is entitled to do in concert with others that which he may lawfully do alone."

4. The freedom recognized "activities which may be fundamental to our culture and traditions and which by common assent are deserving of protection."

5. The freedom "extends constitutional protection to all activities which are essential to the lawful goals of the association."

6. Freedom of association constitutionally protects "all acts done in association, subject only to limitation under s. 1 of the Charter."

... It follows from this discussion that I interpret freedom of association in s. 2(*d*) of the *Charter* to mean that *Charter* protection will attach to the exercise in association of such rights as have *Charter* protection when exercised by the individual. Furthermore, freedom of association means the freedom to associate for the purposes of activities which are lawful when performed alone. But, since the fact of association will not by itself confer additional rights on individuals, the association does not acquire a constitutionally guaranteed freedom to do what is unlawful for the individual.

When this definition of freedom of association is applied, it is clear that it does not guarantee the right to strike. Since the right to strike is not independently protected under the *Charter*, it can receive protection under freedom of association only if it is an activity which is permitted by law to an individual. Accepting this conclusion, the appellants argue that freedom of association must guarantee the right to strike because individuals may lawfully refuse to work. This position, however, is untenable for two reasons. First, it is not correct to say that it is lawful for an individual employee to cease work during the currency of his contract of employment . . . .

The second reason is simply that there is no analogy whatever between the cessation of work by a single employee and a strike conducted in accordance with modern labour legislation. The individual has, by reason of the cessation of work, either breached or terminated his contract of employment. It is true that the law will not compel the specific performance of the contract by ordering him back to work as this would reduce "the employee to a state tantamount to slavery" (I. Christie, *Employment Law in Canada* (1980), p. 268). But, this is markedly different from a lawful strike. An employee who ceases work does not contemplate a return to work, while employees on strike always contemplate a return to work. In recognition of this fact, the law does not regard a strike as either a breach of contract or a termination of employment. Every province and the federal Parliament has enacted legislation which preserves the employer–employee relationship during a strike . . . .

It is apparent, in my view, that interpreting freedom of association to mean that every individual is free to do with others that which he is lawfully entitled to do alone would not entail guaranteeing the right to strike . . . .

This conclusion is entirely consistent with the general approach of the *Charter* which accords rights and freedoms to the individual but, with a few exceptions noted earlier, does not confer group rights. It is also to be observed that the *Charter*, with the possible exception of s. 6(2) (*b*) (right to earn a livelihood in any province) and s. 6(4), does not concern itself with economic rights. Since trade unions are not one of the groups specifically mentioned by the *Charter*, and are overwhelmingly, though not exclusively, concerned with the economic interests of their members, it would run counter to the overall structure and approach of the *Charter* to accord by implication special constitutional rights to trade unions.

Labour relations and the development of the body of law which has grown up around that subject have been for many years one of the major preoccupations of legislators, economic and social writers, and the general public. Strikes are commonplace in Canada and have been for many years. The framers of the Constitution must be presumed to have been aware of these facts . . . .

Furthermore, it must be recognized that the right to strike accorded by legislation throughout Canada is of relatively recent vintage. It is truly the product of this century and, in its modern form, is in reality the product of the latter half of this century. It cannot be said that it has become so much a part of our social and historical traditions that it has acquired the status of an immutable, fundamental right, firmly embedded in our traditions, our political and social philosophy. There is then no basis, as suggested in the fourth approach to freedom of association, for implying a constitutional right to strike. It may well be said that labour relations have become a matter of fundamental importance in our society, but every incident of that general topic has not. The right to strike as an element of labour relations has always been the subject of legislative control. It has been abrogated from time to time in special circumstances and is the subject of legal regulation and control in all Canadian jurisdictions. In my view, it cannot be said that at this time it has achieved status as a fundamental right which should be implied in the absence of specific reference in the *Charter....*

DICKSON C.J. (Wilson J. concurring) dissenting:

A wide variety of alternative interpretations of freedom of association has been advanced in the jurisprudence summarised above and in argument before this court.

At one extreme is a purely constitutive definition whereby freedom of association entails only a freedom to belong to or form an association. On this view, the constitutional guarantee does not extend beyond protecting the individuals's status as a member of an association. It would not protect his or her associational actions....

In my view, while it is unquestionable that s. 2(*d*), at a minimum, guarantees the liberty of persons to be in association or belong to an organization, it must extend beyond a concern for associational status to give effective protection to the interests to which the constitutional guarantee is directed....

I am also unimpressed with the argument that the inclusion of s. 2(*d*) with freedoms of a "political" nature requires a narrow or restrictive interpretation of freedom of association. I am unable to regard s. 2 as embodying purely political freedoms. Paragraph (a), which protects freedom of conscience and religion, is quite clearly not exclusively political in nature. It would, moreover, be unsatisfactory to overlook our Constitution's history of giving special recognition to collectivities or parties. Sections 93 and 133 of the *Constitution Act, 1867* and sections 16–24, 25, 27 and 29 of the *Charter*, dealing variously with denominational schools, language rights, aboriginal rights, and our multicultural heritage implicitly embody an awareness of the importance of various collectivities in the pursuit of educational, linguistic, cultural and social as well as political ends. Just as the individual is incapable of resisting political domination without the support of persons with similar values, so too is he or she, in isolation, incapable of resisting domination, over the long term, in many other aspects of life.

Freedom of association is protected in s. 2(*d*) under the rubric of "fundamental" freedoms. In my view, the "fundamental" nature of freedom of association relates to the central importance to the individual of his or her interaction with fellow human beings. The purpose of the constitutional guarantee of freedom of association is, I believe, to recognize the profoundly social nature of human endeavours and to protect the individual from state-enforced isolation in the pursuit of his or her ends....

However, it is not in my view correct to regard this proposition as the exclusive touchstone for determining the presence or absence or a violation of s.2(*d*). Certainly, if a legislature permits an individual to enjoy an activity which it forecloses to a collectivity, it may properly be inferred that the legislature intended to prohibit the collective activity because of its collective or associational aspect. Conversely, one may infer from a legislative proscription which applies equally to individuals and groups that the purpose of the legislation was a bona fide prohibition of a particular activity because of detrimental qualities inhering in the activity (e.g. criminal conduct), and not merely because of the fact that the activity might sometimes be done in association. The proposition articulated by Chief Justice Belzil is therefore a useful test of legislative purpose in some circumstances. There will, however, be occasions when no analogy involving individuals can be found for associational activity, or when a comparison between groups and individuals fails to capture the essence of a possible violation of associational rights. This is precisely the situation in this case. There is no individual equivalent to a strike. The refusal to work by one individual does not parallel a collective refusal to work. The latter is qualitatively rather then quantitatively different. The overarching consideration remains whether a legislative enactment or administrative action interferes with the freedom of persons to join and act with others in common pursuits. The legislative purpose which will render legislation invalid is the attempt to preclude associational conduct because of its concerted or associational nature.

I wish to refer to one further concern. It has been suggested that associational activity for the pursuit of economic ends should not be accorded constitutional protection. If by this it is meant that something as fundamental as a person's livelihood or dignity in the workplace is beyond the scope of constitutional protection, I cannot agree. If, on the other hand, it is meant that concerns of an exclusively pecuniary nature are excluded from such protection, such an argument would merit careful consideration. In the present case, however, we are concerned with interests which go far beyond those of a merely pecuniary nature.

Work is one of the most fundamental aspects in a person's life, providing the individual with a means of financial support and, as importantly, a contributory role in society. A person's employment is an essential component of his or her sense of identity, self worth and emotional well-being. Accordingly, the conditions in which a person works are highly significant in shaping the whole compendium of psychological, emotional and physical elements of a person's dignity and self-respect ....

The role of association has always been vital as a means of protecting the essential needs and interests of working people. Throughout history, workers have associated to overcome their vulnerability as individuals to the strength of their employers. The capacity to bargain collectively has long been recognized as one of the integral and primary functions of associations of working people. While trade unions also fulfill other important social, political and charitable functions, collective bargaining remains vital to the capacity of individual employees to participate in ensuring fair wages, health and safety protections, and equitable and humane working conditions.

I am satisfied, in sum, that whether or not freedom of association generally extends to protecting associational activity for the pursuit of exclusively pecuniary ends—a question on which I express no opinion—collective bargaining protects important employee interests which cannot be characterised as merely pecuniary in nature. Under our existing system of industrial relations, effective constitutional protection of the associational interests of employees in the collective bargaining process requires concomitant protection of their freedom to withdraw collectively their services, subject to s. 1 of the *Charter.*

APPLICATION TO THE ALBERTA LEGISLATION

All three enactments prohibit strikes and, as earlier stated, define a strike as a cessation of work or refusal to work by two or more persons acting in combination or in concert or in accordance with a common understanding. What is precluded is a collective refusal to work at the conclusion of a collective agreement. There can be no doubt that the legislation is aimed at foreclosing a particular collective activity because of its associational nature. The very nature of a strike, and its *raison d'être*, is to influence an employer by joint action which would be ineffective if it were carried out by an individual. Professor Harry Arthurs refers, correctly in my respectful opinion, to the "notion of collective action" as "the critical factor" in the definition of "strike": *The Right to Strike in Ontario and the Common Law Provinces of Canada* (1967), Proceedings of the Fourth International Symposium on Comparative Law, University of Ottawa, at p. 187. It is precisely the individual's interest in joining and acting with others to maximize his or her potential that is protected by s. 2(d) of the *Charter.*

The Chief Justice found that the acts were too broad in their definition of "essential services" and that the compulsory arbitration scheme formed by it gave too much discretion to the province and was not, therefore, a reasonable limit on the freedom to associate.

○

The Rights Protected: Section 7

7. Everyone has the right to life, liberty and security of the person and the right not to be deprived thereof except in accordance with the principles of fundamental justice.

R v. OPERATION DISMANTLE◇

Operation Dismantle, a peace activist group, challenged the federal cabinet's decision to allow the testing of American cruise missiles in Canada. The claim was dismissed at a pre-trial hearing as disclosing no reasonable cause of action—that is, even if the facts alleged were proved to be true, no interference with the right could be shown. The dismissal was appealed to the Supreme Court.

◇[1985] 1 S.C.R. 441.

Dickson C.J. dismissed the appeal (as shown below). Wilson J. concurred in the decision but elaborated on the role of the courts to decide on "political questions."

WILSON J.:

... [C]ourts should not be too eager to relinquish their judicial review function simply because they are called upon to exercise it in relation to weighty matters of state. Equally, however, it is important to realise that judicial review is not the same thing as substitution of the court's opinion on the merits for the opinion of the person or the body to whom discretionary decision-making power has been committed.... The question before us is not whether the government's defence policy is sound but whether or not it violates the appellants' rights under s. 7 of the *Charter of Rights and Freedoms*. This is a totally different question. I do not think there can be any doubt that this is a question for the courts. Indeed, s. 24(1) of the *Charter*, also part of the Constitution, makes it clear that the adjudication of that question is the responsibility of "a court of competent jurisdiction." While the court is entitled to grant such remedy as it "considers appropriate and just in the circumstances," I do not think it is open to it to relinquish its jurisdiction either on the basis that the issue is inherently non-justiciable or that it raises a so-called "political question" ....

I would conclude, therefore, that if we are to look at the Constitution for the answer to the question whether it is appropriate for the courts to "second guess" the executive on matters of defence, we would conclude that it is not appropriate. However, if what we are being asked to do is to decide whether any particular act of the executive violates the rights of the citizens, then it is not only appropriate that we answer the question; it is our obligation under the *Charter* to do so.

DICKSON C.J. (Estey, McIntyre, Chouinard, and Lamer JJ. concurring):

As a preliminary matter, it should be noted that the exact nature of the deprivation of life and security of the person that the appellants rely upon as the legal foundation for the violation of s. 7 they allege is not clear. There seem to be two possibilities. The violation could be the result of actual deprivation of life and security of the person that would occur in the event of a nuclear attack on Canada, or it could be the result of general insecurity experienced by all people in Canada as a result of living under the increased threat of nuclear war ... I am prepared to accept that the appellants intended both of these possible deprivations as a basis for the violation of s. 7. It is apparent, however, that the violation of s. 7 alleged turns upon an actual increase in the risk of nuclear war, resulting from the federal cabinet's decision to permit the testing of the cruise missile. Thus, to succeed at trial, the appellants would have to demonstrate, *inter alia*, that the testing of the cruise missile would cause an increase in the risk of nuclear war. It is precisely this link between the cabinet decision to permit the testing of the cruise and the increased risk of nuclear war which, in my opinion, they cannot establish. It will not be necessary therefore to address the issue of whether the deprivations of life and security of the person advanced by the appellants could constitute violations of s. 7 ....

I do not believe that action impugned in the present case can be characterised as contrary to the duties of the executive under the *Charter*. Section 7 of the *Charter* cannot reasonably be read as imposing a duty on the government to refrain from those acts which might lead to consequences that deprive or threaten to deprive individuals of their life and security of the person. A duty of the federal cabinet cannot arise on the basis of speculation and hypothesis about possible effects of government action. Such a duty only arises, in my view, where it can be said that a deprivation of life and security of the person could be proven to result from the impugned government act.

The principles governing remedial action by the courts on the basis of allegations of future harm are illustrative of the more general principle that there is no legal duty to refrain from actions which do not prejudice the legal rights of others. A person, whether the government or a private individual, cannot be held liable under the law for an action unless that action causes the deprivation, or threat of deprivation, of legal rights. And an action cannot be said to cause such deprivation where it is not provable that the deprivation will occur as a result of the challenged action. I am not suggesting that remedial action by the courts will be inappropriate where future harm is alleged. The point is that remedial action will not be justified where the link between the action and the future harm alleged is not capable of proof....

The approach which I have taken is not based on the concept of justiciability. I agree in substance with Madame Justice Wilson's discussion of justiciability and her conclusion that the doctrine is founded upon a concern with the appropriate role of the courts as the forum for the resolution of different types of disputes. I have no doubt that disputes of a political or foreign policy nature may be properly cognizable by the courts. My concerns in the present case focus on the impossibility of the court finding, on the basis of evidence, the connection, alleged by the appellants, between the duty of the government to act in accordance with the *Charter of Rights and Freedoms* and the violation of their rights under s. 7. As stated above, I do not believe the alleged violation—namely, the increased threat of nuclear war—could ever be sufficiently linked as a factual matter to the acknowledged duty of the government to respect s. 7 of the *Charter*.

꙳

REFERENCE RE SECTION 94(2) OF THE MOTOR VEHICLE ACT (B.C.)꙳

Section 94 of the *Motor Vehicle Act* created a mandatory seven day imprisonment penalty for everyone found driving while their licence was suspended. By subsection (2), the provision created "an absolute liability offence in which guilt is established by proof of driving, whether or not the defendant knew of the prohibition or suspension..." The constitutionality of the act was referred to the Supreme Court of Canada.

꙳[1985] 2 S.C.R. 486.

LAMER J. (Dickson C.J., Beetz, Chouinard, Le Dain JJ. concurring):

...The novel feature of the *Constitution Act*...is not that it has suddenly empowered courts to consider the content of legislation. This the courts have done for a good many years when adjudicating upon the *vires* of legislation ....

The truly novel features of the *Constitution Act, 1982* are that it has sanctioned the process of constitutional adjudication and has extended its scope so as to encompass a broader range of values. Content of legislation has always been considered in constitutional adjudication. Content is now to be equally considered as regards to constitutional issues. Indeed, the values subject to constitutional adjudication now pertain to the rights of individuals as well as the distribution of governmental powers. In short, it is the scope of constitutional adjudication which has been altered rather than its nature, at least, as regards the right to consider the content of legislation.

In neither case, be it before or after the *Charter*, have the courts been enabled to decide upon the appropriateness of policies underlying legislative enactments. In both instances, however, the courts are empowered, indeed required, to measure the content of legislation against the guarantees of the Constitution ....

...Yet...[there] have sprung warnings of the dangers of a judicial "super-legislature" beyond the reach of Parliament, the provincial legislatures and the electorate. The Attorney General for Ontario, in his written argument, stated that,

> ...the judiciary is neither representative of, nor responsive to the electorate on whose behalf, and under whose authority policies are selected and given effect in the laws of the land.

This is an argument which was heard countless times prior to the entrenchment of the *Charter* but which has in truth, for better or for worse, been settled by the very coming into force of the *Constitution Act, 1982*. It ought not to be forgotten that the historic decision to entrench the *Charter* in our constitution was taken not by the courts but by the elected representatives of the people of Canada. It was those representatives who extended the scope of constitutional adjudication and entrusted the courts with this new and onerous responsibility. Adjudication under the *Charter* must be approached free of any lingering doubts as to its legitimacy ....

The concerns with the bounds of constitutional adjudication explain the characterisation of the issue in a narrow and restrictive fashion, i.e., whether the terms "principles of fundamental justice" have a substantive or merely procedural content. In my view, the characterisation of the issue in such fashion pre-empts an open-minded approach to determining the meaning of "principles of fundamental justice."

The substantive/procedural dichotomy narrows the issue almost to an all-or-nothing proposition. Moreover, it is largely bound up in the American experience with substantive and procedural due process. It imports into the Canadian context American concepts, terminology and jurisprudence, all of which are inextricably linked to problems concerning the nature and legitimacy of adjudication under the U.S. Constitution. That Constitution, it must be remembered, has no s. 52 nor has it the internal checks and balances of sections 1 and 33. We would, in my view, do our own Constitution a disservice to simply allow the American debate to define the issue for us, all the while ignoring the truly fundamental structural differences between the two constitutions. Finally, the dichotomy creates its own set of difficulties by the attempt to distinguish between two concepts whose outer boundaries are not always clear and often tend to overlap. Such difficulties can and should, when possible, be avoided.

The overriding and legitimate concern that courts ought not to question the wisdom of enactments, and the presumption that the Legislator could not have intended same, have to some extent distorted the discussion surrounding the meaning of "principles of fundamental justice." This has led to the spectre of a judicial "super-legislature" without a full consideration of the process of constitutional adjudication and the significance of sections 1, 33 and 52 of the *Constitution Act, 1982*. This in turn has also led to a narrow characterisation of the issue and to the assumption that only a procedural content to "principles of fundamental justice" can prevent the courts from adjudicating upon the merits or wisdom of enactments. If this assumption is accepted, the inevitable corollary, with which I would have to then agree, is that the Legislator intended that the words "principles of fundamental justice" refer to procedure only.

But I do not share that assumption. Since way back in time and even recently the courts have developed the common law beyond procedural safeguards without interfering with the "merits or wisdom" or enactments . . . .

The task of the Court is not to choose between substantive or procedural content per se but to secure for persons "the full benefit of the *Charter's* protection" (Dickson C.J. in *R. v. Big M Drug Mart Ltd.*, [1985] 1 S.C.R. 295 at 344), under s. 7, while avoiding adjudication of the merits of public policy. This can only be accomplished by a purposive analysis . . . .

It is clear that s. 7 surely protects the right not to be deprived of one's life, liberty and security of the person when that is done in breach of the principles of fundamental justice. The outcome of this case is dependent upon the meaning to be given to that portion of the section which states "and the right not to be deprived thereof except in accordance with the principles of fundamental justice." On the facts of this case it is not necessary to decide whether, absent a breach of the principles of fundamental justice, there still can be, given the way the section is structured, a violation of one's rights to life, liberty and security of the person under s. 7. Furthermore, because of the fact that only deprivation of liberty was considered in these proceedings and that no one took issue with the fact that imprisonment is a deprivation of liberty, my analysis of s. 7 will be limited, as was the course taken by all, below and in this Court, to determining the scope of the words life or security of the person.

In the framework of a purposive analysis, designed to ascertain the purpose of the s. 7 guarantee and "the interests it was meant to protect" (*R. v. Big M Drug Mart Ltd.* . . .), it is clear to me that the interests which are meant to be protected by the words "and the right not to be deprived thereof except in accordance with the principles of fundamental justice" of s. 7 are the life, liberty and security of the person. The principles of fundamental justice, on the other hand, are not a protected interest, but rather a qualifier of the right not to be deprived of life, liberty and security of the person.

Given that, as the Attorney General for Ontario has acknowledged, "when one reads the phrase 'principles of fundamental justice,' a single incontrovertible meaning is not apparent," its meaning must, in my view, be determined by reference to the interests which those words of the section are designed to protect and the particular role of the phrase within the section. As a qualifier, the phrase serves to establish the parameters of the interests but it cannot be interpreted so narrowly as to frustrate or stultify them. For the narrower the meaning given to "principles of fundamental justice" the greater will be the possibility that individuals may be deprived of these most basic rights. This latter result is to be avoided given that the rights involved are as fundamental as those which pertain to life, liberty and security of the person, the deprivation of which "has the most severe consequences upon an individual": *Re Cadeddu and The Queen* (1982) . . . .

For these reasons, I am of the view that it would be wrong to interpret the term "fundamental justice" as being synonymous with natural justice as the Attorney General of British Columbia and others have suggested. To do so would strip the protected interests of much, if not most, of their content and leave the "right" to life, liberty and security of the person in a sorely emaciated state. Such a result would be inconsistent with the broad, affirmative language in which those rights are expressed and equally inconsistent with the approach adopted by this Court toward the interpretation of Charter rights in *Law Society of Upper Canada v. Skapinker* . . . and *Hunter v. Southam Inc.*

It would mean that the right to liberty would be narrower than the right not to be arbitrarily detained or imprisoned (s.9), that the right to security of the person would have less content than the right to be secure against unreasonable search or seizure (s.8). Such an interpretation would give the specific expressions of the "right to life, liberty and security of the person" which are set forth in ss. 8 to 14 greater content than the general concept from which they originate.

Sections 8 to 14, in other words, address specific deprivations of the "right" to life, liberty and security of the person in breach of the principles of fundamental justice, and as such, violations of s.7. They are designed to protect, in a specific manner and setting, the right of life, liberty and security of the person set forth in s.7. It would be incongruous to interpret s.7 more narrowly than the rights in ss. 8 to 14. The alternative, which is to interpret all of ss. 8 to 14 in a "[n]arrow and technical" manner for the sake of congruity, is out of the question: *Law Society of Upper Canada v. Skapinker* . . . .

Absolute Liability and Fundamental Justice in Penal Law

It has from time immemorial been part of our system of laws that the innocent not be punished. This principle has long been recognized as an essential element of a system for the administration of justice which is founded upon a belief in the dignity and worth of the human person and on the rule of law. It is so old that its first enunciation was in Latin, *actus non facit reum nisi mens sit rea*.

As Glanville Williams said:

There is no need here to go into the remote history of *mens rea*; suffice it to say that the requirement of a guilty state of mind (at least for the more serious crimes) had been developed by the time of Coke, which is as far back as the modern lawyer needs to go. "If one shoot at any wild fowl upon a tree, and the arrow killeth any reasonable creature afar off, without any evil intent in him, this is *per infortunium*."

This view has been adopted by this Court in unmistakable terms in many cases[;] ... [it] is predicated upon a certain number of postulates one of which, given the nature of the rules it elaborates, has to be to the effect that absolute liability in penal law offends the principles of fundamental justice. Those principles are, to use the words of Dickson J., to the effect that "there is a generally held revulsion against punishment of the morally innocent." ...

He also stated ... that the argument that absolute liability "violated fundamental principles of penal liability" was the most telling argument against absolute liability and one of greater force than those advanced in support thereof.

In my view, it is because absolute liability offends the principles of fundamental justice that this Court created presumptions against Legislatures having intended to enact offenses of a regulatory nature falling within that category. This is not to say, however, and to that extent I am in agreement with the Court of Appeal, that, as a result, absolute liability *per se* offends s. 7 of the Charter.

A law enacting an absolute liability offence will violate s. 7 of the Charter only if and to the extend that it has the potential of depriving of life, liberty or security of the person.

Obviously, imprisonment (including probation orders) deprives persons of their liberty. An offence has that potential as of the moment it is open to the judge to impose imprisonment. There is no need that imprisonment, as in s. 94(2) be made mandatory.

I am therefore of the view that the combination of imprisonment and of absolute liability violates s. 7 of the Charter and can only be salvaged if the authorities demonstrate under s. 1 that such a deprivation of liberty in breach of those principles of fundamental justice is, in a free and democratic society, under the circumstances, a justified reasonable limit to one's rights under s. 7.

Because the Attorney General offered no justification under section 1, Lamer J. found that the Act could not be saved by that section. McIntyre and Wilson JJ. wrote concurring opinions.

꙳

R. v. MORGANTALER[◇]

Dr. Henry Morgantaler was charged with violating s. 251(1) of the *Criminal Code* which made it an indictable offence to procure a miscarriage. By s. 521(4), the above provision did not apply where a qualified medical practitioner, acting upon

---

◇[1988] 1 S.C.R. 30.

the recommendation of a separate hospital committee, procures a miscarriage to prevent danger to the life or health of the woman. In Morgantaler's defence, it was claimed that the required procedure violated the "principles of fundamental justice" guaranteed by section 7 of the *Charter*.

DICKSON C.J. (Lamer J. concurring):

... At the most basic, physical and emotional level, every pregnant woman is told by the section that she cannot submit to a generally safe medical procedure that might be of clear benefit to her unless she meets criteria entirely unrelated to her own priorities and aspirations. Not only does the removal of decision-making power threaten women in a physical sense; the indecision of knowing whether an abortion will be granted inflicts emotional stress. Section 251 clearly interferes with a woman's bodily integrity in both a physical and emotional sense. Forcing a woman, by threat of criminal sanction, to carry a foetus to term unless she meets certain criteria unrelated to her own priorities and aspirations, is a profound interference with a woman's body and thus a violation of security of the person ...

Although this interference with physical and emotional integrity is sufficient in itself to trigger a review of s. 251 against the principles of fundamental justice, the operation of the decision-making mechanism set out in s. 251 creates additional glaring breaches of security of the person. The evidence indicates that s. 251 causes a certain amount of delay for women who are successful in meeting its criteria. In the context of abortion, any unnecessary delay can have profound consequences on the woman's physical and emotional well-being.

The Chief Justice then outlined how the delays caused by the procedural requirements lead to increased physical and emotional stress for a woman attempting to end a pregnancy.

In summary, s. 251 is a law which forces women to carry a foetus to term contrary to their own priorities and aspirations and which imposes serious delay causing increased physical and psychological trauma to those women who meet its criteria. It must, therefore, be determined whether that infringement is accomplished in accordance with the principles of fundamental justice, thereby saving s. 251 under the second part of s. 7.

THE PRINCIPLES OF FUNDAMENTAL JUSTICE

Although the "principles of fundamental justice" referred to in s. 7 have both a substantive and a procedural component (*Re B.C. Motor Vehicle Act*, at p. 499), I have already indicated that it is not necessary in this appeal to evaluate the substantive content of s. 251 of the *Criminal Code*. My discussion will therefore be limited to various aspects of the administrative structure and procedure set down in s. 251 for access to therapeutic abortions.

The Chief Justice then turned to the practical workings of the section's administrative requirements. He noted that the requirement of a three member committee's approval for a fourth doctor to perform an abortion left the practice unavailable in almost one quarter of Canadian hospitals; as well, the requirement of an "accredited" or "approved" hospital left the discretion to approve a hospital to a provincial minister of health; the same requirement specified services which were unavailable in 58.5 per cent of Canadian hospitals and provided no obligations upon those hospitals that were eligible to provide abortion services. Finally, the "health" requirement of subsection (4) was not defined in the *Code* and as well "therapeutic abortion committees appl[ied] widely differing definitions of health."

. . . The combined effect of all of these problems with the procedure stipulated in s. 251 for access to therapeutic abortions is a failure to comply with the principles of fundamental justice. In *Re B.C. Motor Vehicle Act*, Lamer J. held, at p. 503, that "the principles of fundamental justice are to be found in the basic tenets of our legal system." One of the basic tenets of our system of criminal justice is that when Parliament creates a defence to a criminal charge, the defence should not be illusory or so difficult to attain as to be practically illusory. The criminal law is a very special form of governmental regulation, for it seeks to express our society's collective disapprobation of certain acts and omissions. When a defence is provided, especially a specifically tailored defence to a particular charge, it is because the legislator had determined that the disapprobation of society is not warranted when the conditions of the defence are met . . . .

I conclude that the procedures created in s. 251 of the *Criminal Code* for obtaining a therapeutic abortion do not comport with the principles of fundamental justice. It is not necessary to determine whether s. 7 also contains a substantive content leading to the conclusion that, in some circumstances at least, the deprivation of a pregnant women's right to security of the person can never comport with fundamental justice. Simply put, assuming Parliament can act, it must do so properly. For the reasons given earlier, the deprivation of security of the person caused by s. 251 as a whole is not in accordance with the second clause of s. 7. It remains to be seen whether s. 251 can be justified for the purposes of s. 1 of the *Charter*.

SECTION 1 ANALYSIS

. . . The appellants contended that the sole purpose of s. 251 of the *Criminal Code* is to protect the life and health of pregnant women. The respondent Crown submitted that s. 251 seeks to protect not only the life and health of pregnant women, but also the interests of the foetus. On the other hand, the Crown conceded that the Court is not called upon in this appeal to evaluate any claim to "foetal rights" or to assess the meaning of "the right to life." I expressly refrain from so doing. In my view, it is unnecessary for the purpose of deciding this appeal to evaluate or assess "foetal rights" as an independent constitutional value. Nor are we required to measure the full extent of the state's interest in establishing criteria unrelated to the pregnant woman's own priorities and aspirations. What we must do is evaluate the particular balance struck by Parliament in s. 251, as it relates to the priorities and aspirations of pregnant women and the government's interests in the protection of the foetus.

Section 251 provides that foetal interests are not to be protected where the "life or health" of the woman is threatened. Thus, Parliament itself has expressly stated in s. 251 that the "life or health" of pregnant women is paramount. The procedures of s. 251(4) are clearly related to the pregnant woman's "life or health" for that is the very phrase used by the subsection. As McIntyre J. states in his reasons (at p. 155), the aim of s. 251(4) is "to restrict abortion to cases where the continuation of the pregnancy would, or would likely, be injurious to the life or health of the woman concerned, not to provide unrestricted access to abortion." I have no difficulty in concluding that the objective of s. 251 as a whole, namely, to balance the competing interests identified by Parliament, is sufficiently important to meet the requirements of the first step in the *Oakes* inquiry under s. 1. I think the protection of the interests of pregnant women is a valid governmental objective, where life and health can be jeopardized by criminal sanctions. Like Beetz and Wilson JJ., I agree that protection of foetal interests by Parliament is also a valid governmental objective. It follows that balancing these interests, with the lives and health of women a major factor, is clearly an important governmental objective. As the Court of Appeal stated at p. 366, "the contemporary view [is] that abortion is not always socially undesirable behaviour."

I am equally convinced, however, that the means chosen to advance the legislative objectives of s. 251 do not satisfy any of the three elements of the proportionality component of *R. v. Oakes*. The evidence has led me to conclude that the infringement of the security of the person of pregnant women caused by s. 251 is not accomplished in accordance with the principles of fundamental justice. It has been demonstrated that the procedures and administrative structures created by s. 251 are often arbitrary and unfair. The procedures established to implement the policy of s. 251 impair s. 7 rights far more than is necessary because they hold out an illusory defence to many women who would *prima facie* qualify under the exculpatory provisions of s. 251(4). In other words, many women whom Parliament professes not to wish to subject to criminal liability will nevertheless be forced by the practical unavailability of the supposed defence to risk liability or to suffer other harm such as a traumatic late abortion caused by the delay inherent in the s. 251 system. Finally, the effects of the limitation upon the s. 7 rights of many pregnant women are out of proportion to the objective sought to be achieved. Indeed, to the extent that s. 251(4) is designed to protect the life and health of women, the procedures it establishes may actually defeat that objective. The administrative structures of s. 251(4) are so cumbersome that women whose health is endangered by pregnancy may not be able to gain a therapeutic abortion, at least without great trauma, expense and inconvenience.

I conclude, therefore, that the cumbersome structure of subs. (4) not only unduly subordinates the s. 7 rights of pregnant women but may also defeat the value Parliament itself has established as paramount, namely, the life and health of the pregnant woman. As I have noted, counsel for the Crown did contend that one purpose of the procedures required by subs. (4) is to protect the interests of the foetus. State protection of foetal interests may well be deserving of constitutional recognition under s. 1. Still, there can be no escape from the fact that Parliament has failed to establish either a standard or a procedure whereby any such interests might prevail over those of the woman in a fair and non-arbitrary fashion.

Section 251 of the *Criminal Code* cannot be saved, therefore, under s. 1 of the *Charter*. . . .

MCINTYRE J. (La Forest J. concurring) dissenting:

*THE RIGHT TO ABORTION AND S. 7
OF THE CHARTER*

The judgment of my colleague, Wilson J., is based upon the proposition that a pregnant woman has a right, under s. 7 of the *Charter*, to have an abortion. The same concept underlies the judgment of the Chief Justice. He reached the conclusion that a law which forces a woman to carry a foetus to term, unless certain criteria are met which are unrelated to her own priorities and aspirations, impairs the security of her person. That, in his view, is the effect of s. 251 of the *Criminal Code*. He has not said in specific terms that the pregnant woman has the right to an abortion, whether therapeutic or otherwise. In my view, however, his whole position depends for its validity upon that proposition and that interference with the right constitutes an infringement of her right to security of the person. It is said that a law which forces a woman to carry a foetus to term unless she meets certain criteria unrelated to her own priorities and aspirations interferes with security of her person. If compelling a woman to complete her pregnancy interferes with security of her person, it can only be because the concept of security of her person includes a right not to be compelled to carry the child to completion of the pregnancy. This, then, is simply to say that she has a right to have an abortion. It follows, then, that if no such right can be shown, it cannot be said that security of her person has been infringed by state action or otherwise.

All laws, it must be noted, have the potential for interference with individual priorities and aspirations. In fact, the very purpose of most legislation is to cause such interference. It is only when such legislation goes beyond interfering with priorities and aspirations, and abridges rights, that courts may intervene. If a law prohibited membership in a lawful association it would be unconstitutional, not because it would interfere with priorities and aspirations, but because of its interference with the guaranteed right of freedom of association under s. 2(*d*) of the *Charter*. Compliance with the *Income Tax Act* has, no doubt, frequently interfered with priorities and aspirations. The taxing provisions are not, however, on that basis unconstitutional, because the ordinary taxpayer enjoys no right to be tax free. Other illustrations may be found. In my view, it is clear that before it could be concluded that any enactment infringed the concept of security of the person, it would have to infringe on some underlying right included in or protected by the concept. For the appellants to succeed here, then, they must show more than an interference with priorities and aspirations; they must show the infringement of a right which is included in the concept of security of the person.

The proposition that women enjoy a constitutional right to have an abortion is devoid of support in the language of s. 7 of the *Charter* or any other section. While some human rights documents, such as the *American Convention on Human Rights, 1969* (Article 4(1)), expressly address the question of abortion, the *Charter* is entirely silent on the point. It may be of some significance that the *Charter* uses specific language in dealing with other topics, such as voting rights, religion, expression and such controversial matters as mobility rights, language rights and minority rights, but remains silent on the question of abortion which, at the time the *Charter* was under consideration, was as much a subject of public controversy as it is today . . . .

PROCEDURAL FAIRNESS

I now turn to the appellant's argument regarding the procedural fairness of s. 251 of the *Criminal Code*. The basis of the argument is that the exemption provisions of subs. (4) are such as to render illusory or practically illusory any defence arising from the subsection for many women who seek abortions. It is pointed out that therapeutic abortions are available only in accredited or approved hospitals, that hospitals so accredited or approved may or may not appoint abortion committees, and that "health" is defined in vague terms which afford no clear guide to its meaning. Statistically, it was said that abortions could be lawfully performed in only twenty per cent of all hospitals in Canada. Because abortions are not generally available to all women who seek them, the argument goes, the defence is illusory, or practically so, and the section therefore fails to comport with the principles of fundamental justice . . . .

It would seem to me that a defence created by Parliament could only be said to be illusory or practically so when the *defence is not available in the circumstances in which it is held out as being available*. The very nature of the test assumes, of course, that it is for Parliament to define the defence and, in so doing, to designate the terms and conditions upon which it may be available. The Chief Justice has said in his reasons, at p. 70:

> The criminal law is a very special form of governmental regulation, for it seeks to express our society's collective disapprobation of certain acts and omissions. When a defence is provided, especially a specifically tailored defence to a particular charge, it is because the legislator has determined that the disapprobation of society is not warranted when the conditions of the defence are met.

From this comment, I would suggest it is apparent that the Court's role is not to second-guess Parliament's policy choice as to how broad or how narrow the defence should be. The determination of when "the disapprobation of society is not warranted" is in Parliament's hands. The Court's role when the enactment is attacked on the basis that the defence is illusory is to determine whether the defence is available in the circumstances in which it was intended to apply. Parliament has set out the conditions, in s. 251(4), under which a therapeutic abortion may be obtained, free from criminal sanction. It is patent on the face of the legislation that the defence is circumscribed and narrow. It is clear that this was the Parliamentary intent and it was expressed with precision. I am not able to accept the contention that the defence has been held out to be generally available. It is, on the contrary, carefully tailored and limited to special circumstances. Therapeutic abortions may be performed only in certain hospitals and in accordance with certain specified provisions. It could only be classed as illusory or practically so if it could be found that it does not provide lawful access to abortions in circumstances described in the section. No such finding should be made upon the material before this Court. The evidence will not support the proposition that significant numbers of those who meet the conditions imposed in s. 251 of the *Criminal Code* are denied abortions.

It is evident that what the appellants advocate is not the therapeutic abortion referred to in s. 251 of the *Code*. Their clinic was called into being because of the perceived inadequacies of s. 251. They propose and seek to justify "abortion on demand." The defence in s. 251(4) was not intended to meet the views of the appellants and provide a defence at large which would effectively repeal the operative subsection of s. 251. Some feel strongly that s. 251 is not adequate in today's society. Be that as it may, it does not follow that the defence provisions of s. 251(4) are illusory. They represent the legislative choice on this question and, as noted, it has not been shown that therapeutic abortions have not been available in cases contemplated by the provision.

WILSON J:

At the heart of this appeal is the question whether a pregnant woman can, as a constitutional matter, be compelled by law to carry the foetus to term. The legislature has proceeded on the basis that she can be so compelled and, indeed, has made it a criminal offence punishable by imprisonment under s. 251 of the *Criminal Code*, R.S.C. 1970, c. C-34, for her or her physician to terminate the pregnancy unless the procedural requirements of the section are complied with.

My colleagues, the Chief Justice and Justice Beetz, have attacked those requirements in reasons which I have had the privilege of reading. They have found that the requirements do not comport with the principles of fundamental justice in the procedural sense and have concluded that, since they cannot be severed from the provisions creating the substantive offence, the whole of s. 251 must fall.

With all due respect, I think that the Court must tackle the primary issue first. A consideration as to whether or not the procedural requirements of obtaining or performing an abortion comport with fundamental justice is purely academic if such requirements cannot as a constitutional matter be imposed at all . . . .

It seems to me, therefore, that to commence the analysis with the premise that the s. 7 right encompasses only a right to physical and psychological security and to fail to deal with the right to liberty in the context of "life, liberty and security of the person" begs the central issue in the case. If either the right to liberty or the right to security of the person or a combination of both confers on the pregnant woman the right to decide for herself (with the guidance of her physician) whether or not to have an abortion, then we have to examine the legislative scheme not only from the point of view of fundamental justice in the procedural sense but in the substantive sense as well. I think, therefore, that we must answer the question: what is meant by the right to liberty in the context of the abortion issue? Does it, as Mr. Manning suggests, give the pregnant woman control over decisions affecting her own body? If not, does her right to security of the person give her such control? I turn first to the right to liberty.

(a) The Right to Liberty

In order to ascertain the content of the right to liberty we must, as Dickson C.J. stated in *R. v. Big M Drug Mart Ltd.*, [1985] 1 S.C.R. 295, commence with an analysis of the purpose of the right.... We are invited, therefore, to consider the purpose of the Charter in general and of the right to liberty in particular.

The *Charter* is predicated on a particular conception of the place of the individual in society. An individual is not a totally independent entity disconnected from the society in which he or she lives. Neither, however, is the individual a mere cog in an impersonal machine in which his or her values, goals and aspirations are subordinated to those of the collectivity. The individual is a bit of both. The *Charter* reflects this reality by leaving a wide range of activities and decisions open to legitimate government control while at the same time placing limits on the proper scope of that control. Thus, the rights guaranteed in the *Charter* erect around each individual, metaphorically speaking, an invisible fence over which the state will not be allowed to trespass. The role of the courts is to map out, piece by piece, the parameters of the fence ....

The question then becomes whether the decision of a woman to terminate her pregnancy falls within this class of protected decisions. I have no doubt that it does. This decision is one that will have profound psychological, economic and social consequences for the pregnant woman. The circumstances giving rise to it can be complex and varied and there may be, and usually are, powerful considerations militating in opposite directions. It is a decision that deeply reflects the way the woman thinks about herself and her relationship to others and to society at large. It is not just a medical decision; it is a profound social and ethical one as well. Her response to it will be the response of the whole person.

It is probably impossible for a man to respond, even imaginatively, to such a dilemma not just because it is outside the realm of his personal experience (although this is, of course, the case) but because he can relate to it only by objectifying it, thereby eliminating the subjective elements of the female psyche which are at the heart of the dilemma. As Noreen Burrows, lecturer in European Law at the University of Glasgow, has pointed out in her essay on "International Law and Human Rights: the Case of Women's Rights," in *Human Rights: From Rhetoric to Reality* (1986), the history of the struggle for human rights from the eighteenth century on has been the history of men struggling to assert their dignity and common humanity against an overbearing state apparatus. The more recent struggle for women's rights has been a struggle to eliminate discrimination, to achieve a place for women in a man's world, to develop a set of legislative reforms in order to place women in the same position as men (pp. 81–82). It has *not* been a struggle to define the rights of women in relation to their special place in the societal structure and in relation to the biological distinction between the two sexes. Thus, women's needs and aspirations are only now being translated into protected rights. The right to reproduce or not to reproduce which is in issue in this case is one such right and is properly perceived as an integral part of modern woman's struggle to assert *her* dignity and worth as a human being.

Given then that the right to liberty guaranteed by s. 7 of the *Charter* gives a woman the right to decide for herself whether or not to terminate her pregnancy, does s. 251 of the *Criminal Code* violate this right? Clearly it does. The purpose of the section is to take the decision away from the woman and give it to a committee. Furthermore, as the Chief Justice correctly points out, at p. 56, the committee bases its decision on "criteria entirely unrelated to [the pregnant woman's] own priorities and aspirations." The fact that the decision whether a woman will be allowed to terminate her pregnancy is in the hands of a committee is just as great a violation of the woman's right to personal autonomy in decisions of an intimate and private nature as it would be if a committee were established to decide whether a woman should be allowed to continue her pregnancy. Both these arrangements violate the woman's right to liberty by deciding for her something that she has the right to decide for herself. . . .

THE SCOPE OF THE RIGHT UNDER S. 7

I turn now to a consideration of the degree of personal autonomy the pregnant woman has under s. 7 of the *Charter* when faced with a decision whether or not to have an abortion or, to put it into the legislative context, the degree to which the legislature can deny the pregnant woman access to abortion without violating her s. 7 right. This involves a consideration of the extent to which the legislature can "deprive" her of it under the second part of s. 7 and the extent to which it can put "limits" on it under s. 1 . . . .

I believe . . . that a deprivation of the s. 7 right which has the effect of infringing a right guaranteed elsewhere in the *Charter* cannot be in accordance with the principles of fundamental justice.

In my view, the deprivation of the s. 7 right with which we are concerned in this case offends s. 2(*a*) of the *Charter*. I say this because I believe that the decision whether or not to terminate a pregnancy is essentially a moral decision, a matter of conscience. I do not think there is or can be any dispute about that. The question is: whose conscience? Is the conscience of the woman to be paramount or the conscience of the state? I believe, for the reasons I gave in discussing the right to liberty, that in a free and democratic society it must be the conscience of the individual. Indeed, s. 2(*a*) makes it clear that this freedom belongs to "everyone," i.e., to each of us individually . . . .

It seems to me, therefore, that in a free and democratic society "freedom of conscience and religion" should be broadly construed to extend to conscientiously held beliefs, whether grounded in religion or in a secular morality. Indeed, as a matter of statutory interpretation, "conscience" and "religion" should not be treated as tautologous if capable of independent, although related, meaning. Accordingly, for the state to take sides on the issue of abortion, as it does in the impugned legislation by making it a criminal offence for the pregnant woman to exercise one of her options, is not only to endorse but also to enforce, on pain of a further loss of liberty through actual imprisonment, one conscientiously held view at the expense of another. It is to deny freedom of conscience to some, to treat them as means to an end, to deprive them, as Professor MacCormick puts it, of their "essential humanity." Can this comport with fundamental justice? Was Blackman J. not correct when he said in *Thornburgh* . . .

A woman's right to make that choice freely is fundamental. Any other result . . . would protect inadequately a central part of the sphere of liberty that our law guarantees equally to all.

Legislation which violates freedom of conscience in this manner cannot, in my view, be in accordance with the principles of fundamental justice within the meaning of s. 7.

SECTION 1 OF THE CHARTER

. . . In my view, the primary objective of the impugned legislation must be seen as the protection of the foetus. It undoubtedly has other ancillary objectives, such as the protection of the life and health of pregnant women, but I believe that the main objective advanced to justify a restriction on the pregnant woman's s. 7 right is the protection of the foetus. I think this is a perfectly valid legislative objective.

Miss Wein submitted on behalf of the Crown that the Court of appeal was correct in concluding at p. 378 that "the situation respecting a woman's right to control her own person becomes more complex when she becomes pregnant, and that some statutory control may be appropriate." I agree. I think s. 1 of the *Charter* authorizes reasonable limits to be put upon the woman's right having regard to the fact of the developing foetus within her body. The question is: at what point in the pregnancy does the protection of the foetus become such a pressing and substantial concern as to outweigh the fundamental right of the woman to decide whether or not to carry the foetus to term? At what point does the state's interest in the protection of the foetus become "compelling" and justify state intervention in what is otherwise a matter of purely personal and private concern? . . .

Section 251 of the *Criminal Code* takes the decision away from the woman at *all* stages of her pregnancy. It is a complete denial of the woman's constitutionally protected right under s. 7, not merely a limitation on it. It cannot, in my opinion, meet the proportionality test in *Oakes*. It is not sufficiently tailored to the legislative objective and does not impair the woman's right "as little as possible." It cannot be saved under s. 1. Accordingly, even if the section were to be amended to remedy the purely procedural defects in the legislative scheme referred to by the Chief Justice and Beetz J. it would, in my opinion, still not be constitutionally valid.

One final word. I wish to emphasise that in these reasons I have dealt with the existence of the developing foetus merely as a factor to be considered in assessing the importance of the legislative objective under s. 1 of the *Charter*. I have not dealt with the entirely separate question whether a foetus is covered by the word "everyone" in s. 7 so as to have an independent right to life under that section. The Crown did not argue it and it is not necessary to decide it in order to dispose of the issues on this appeal.

Beetz J., on behalf of Estey J., delivered a concurring opinion in which he found that the administrative procedures of the Act resulted in unnecessary risk to the health of pregnant women who qualified for an abortion thereby violating the principles of fundamental justice; for the same reason, the Act was not saved by section 1 of the *Charter*.

The Rights Protected: Section 8

8. Everyone has the right to be secure against unreasonable search or seizure.

HUNTER v. SOUTHAM INC.◇

Subsection 10(1) of the *Combines Investigation Act* allowed the Act's Director of Investigation and Research to authorize entry into business premises and to seize any documents that the Director believed may be relevant to an inquiry under the Act. Southam Inc., the defendant, challenged a search carried out under this subsection on the grounds that it violated s. 8 of the *Charter*.

DICKSON J. (for the Court):

... It is clear that the meaning of "unreasonable" cannot be determined by recourse to a dictionary, nor for that matter, by reference to the rules of statutory construction. The task of expounding a constitution is crucially different from that of construing a statute. A statute defines present rights and obligations. It is easily enacted and as easily repealed. A constitution, by contrast, is drafted with an eye to the future. Its function is to provide a continuing framework for the legitimate exercise of governmental power and, when joined by a *Bill* or a *Charter of Rights*, for the unremitting protection of individual rights and liberties. Once enacted, its provisions cannot easily be repealed or amended. It must, therefore, be capable of growth and development over time to meet new social, political and historical realities often unimagined by its framers. The judiciary is the guardian of the constitution and must, in interpreting its provisions, bear these considerations in mind. Professor Paul Freund expressed this idea aptly when he admonished the American courts "not to read the provisions of the Constitution like a last will and testament lest it become one." ...

... Since the proper approach to the interpretation of the *Charter of Rights and Freedoms* is a purposive one, before it is possible to assess the reasonableness or unreasonableness of the impact of a search or of a statute authorizing a search, it is first necessary to specify the purpose underlying s. 8: in other words, to delineate the nature of the interests it is meant to protect.

... The guarantee of security from *unreasonable* search and seizure only protects a *reasonable* expectation. This limitation on the right guaranteed by s. 8, whether it is expressed negatively as freedom from "unreasonable" search and seizure, or positively as an entitlement to a "reasonable" expectation of privacy, indicates that an assessment must be made as to whether in a particular situation the public's interest in being left alone by government must give way to the government's interest in intruding on the individual's privacy in order to advance its goals, notably those of law enforcement.

The question that remains, and the one upon which the present appeal hinges, is how this assessment is to be made. When is it to be made, by whom and on what basis? Here again, I think the proper approach is a purposive one.

◇[1984] 2 S.C.R. 145.

334   *SUPREME COURT AND THE CHARTER*

A) *When Is the Balance of Interests to be Assessed?*

... A requirement of prior authorization, usually in the form of a valid warrant, has been a consistent prerequisite for a valid search and seizure both at common law and under most statutes. Such a requirement puts the onus on the state to demonstrate the superiority of its interest to that of the individual. As such it accords with the apparent intention of the *Charter* to prefer, where feasible, the right of the individual to be free from state interference to the interests of the state in advancing its purposes through such interference . . . .

B) *Who Must Grant the Authorization?*

The purpose of a requirement of prior authorization is to provide an opportunity, before the event, for the conflicting interests of the state and the individual to be assessed, so that the individual's right to privacy will be breached only where the appropriate standard has been met, and the interests of the state are thus demonstrably superior. For such an authorization procedure to be meaningful it is necessary for the person authorizing the search to be able to assess the evidence as to whether that standard has been met in an entirely neutral and impartial manner.

... The person performing this function need not be a judge, but he must at a minimum be capable of acting judicially.

C) *On What Basis Must the Balance of Interests be Assessed?*

... Requiring the authorizing party to satisfy himself as to the legality of the inquiry and the reasonableness of the Director's belief in the possible existence of relevant evidence, would have the advantage of substituting an objective standard for an amorphous one, but would, in my view, still be inadequate. The problem is with the stipulation of a reasonable belief that evidence *may* be uncovered in the search. Here again it is useful, in my view, to adopt a purposive approach. The purpose of an objective criterion for granting prior authorization to conduct a search or seizure is to provide a consistent standard for identifying the point at which the interests of the state in such intrusions come to prevail over the interests of the individual in resisting them. To associate it with an applicant's reasonable belief that relevant evidence *may* be uncovered by the search, would be to define the proper standard as the *possibility* of finding evidence. This is a very low standard which would validate intrusion on the basis of suspicion, and authorize fishing expeditions of considerable latitude. It would tip the balance strongly in favour of the state and limit the right of the individual to resist, to only the most egregious intrusions. I do not believe that this is a proper standard for securing the right to be free from unreasonable search and seizure.

Anglo-Canadian legal and political traditions point to a higher standard. The common law required evidence on oath which gave "strong reason to believe" that stolen goods were concealed in the place to be searched before a warrant would issue. Section 443 of the *Criminal Code* authorizes a warrant only where there has been information upon oath that there is "reasonable ground to believe" that there is evidence of an offence in the place to be searched. The American *Bill of Rights* provides that "no Warrants shall issue, but upon probable cause, supported by Oath or affirmation . . . . " The phrasing is slightly different but the standard in each of these formulations is identical. The state's interest in detecting and preventing crime begins to prevail over the individual's interest in being left alone at the point where credibly based probability replaces suspicion. History has confirmed the appropriateness of this requirement as the threshhold for subordinating the expectation of privacy to the needs of law enforcement. Where the state's interest is not simply law enforcement as, for instance, where state security is involved, or where the individual's interest is not simply his expectation of privacy as, for instance, when the search threatens his bodily integrity, the relevant standard might well be a different one. That is not the situation in the present case. In cases like the present, reasonable and probable grounds, established upon oath, to believe that an offence has been committed and that there is evidence to be found at the place of the search, constitutes the minimum standard, consistent with s. 8 of the *Charter*, for authorizing search and seizure. In so far as subss. 10(1) and 10(3) of the *Combines Investigation Act* do not embody such a requirement, I would hold them to be further inconsistent with s. 8 ....

o

R . v . D U A R T E ◇

Section 178.11(1) of the *Criminal Code* makes it an offence to electronically intercept private communications. As a result, police interception could only be accomplished by way of a judicially granted search warrant. Subsection 178.11(2)(9) of the *Code*, however, permits interception with either the sender's or the intended recipient's consent. The defendant Duarte was charged for his role in a narcotics operation as a result of a police investigation which made use of a recording of his conversation with an intended purchaser. Duarte claimed that this warrantless interception violated section 8 of the *Charter*.

LA FOREST J. (for the Court):

The principal issue in this appeal is whether the commonly styled "consent" or "participant" surveillance—i.e., electronic surveillance in which one of the parties to a conversation, usually an undercover police officer or a police informer, surreptitiously records it—infringes the right under s. 8 of the *Charter* to be secure against unreasonable search and seizure. This raises the subsidiary issues of whether such infringement is justifiable under s. 1 of the *Charter* and whether the recorded conversation can nonetheless be admitted into evidence against an accused. I should at the outset note that "consent surveillance" is an unhappy term to describe a practice where only one party to a conversation has agreed to have it recorded. As put by the United States Supreme Court in *Katz v. United States*, 389 U.S. 347 (1967), at p. 358: "the very nature of electronic surveillance precludes its use pursuant to the suspect's consent." I shall, therefore, use the term "participant surveillance." ...

◇[1990] 1 S.C.R. 30.

By contrast to the general provisions on electronic surveillance, the *Code* places no restriction on participant surveillance. The police may employ this practice in their absolute discretion, against whom they wish and for whatever reasons they wish, without any limit as to place or duration. There is a total absence of prior judicial supervision of this practice.

I am unable to see any logic to this distinction between third party electronic surveillance and participant surveillance. The question whether *unauthorized* electronic surveillance of private communications violates a reasonable expectation of privacy cannot, in my view, turn on the location of the hidden microphone. Whether the microphone is hidden in the wall or concealed on the body of a participant to the conversation, the assessment whether the surreptitious recording trenches on a reasonable expectation of privacy must turn on whether the person whose words were recorded spoke in circumstances in which it was reasonable for that person to expect that his or her words would only be heard by the persons he or she was addressing. As I see it, where persons have reasonable grounds to believe their communications are private communications in the sense defined above, the *unauthorized* surreptitious electronic recording of those communications cannot fail to be perceived as an intrusion on a reasonable expectation of privacy.

The *Charter* standard just described must, in my view, apply on a uniform basis. To have any meaning, it must be taken to afford protection against the arbitrary recording of private communications every time we speak in the expectation that our words will only be heard by the person or persons to whom we direct our remarks. Section 8 of the *Charter* guarantees the right *to be secure* against unreasonable search or seizure. Our perception that we are protected against arbitrary interceptions of private communications ceases to have any real basis once it is accepted that the state is free to record private communications, without constraint, provided only that it has secured the agreement of one of the parties to the communication. Since we can never know if our listener is an informer, and since if he proves to be one, we are to be taken to be tacitly consenting to the risk that the state may be listening to and recording our conversations, we should be prepared to run this risk every time we speak . . . .

Section 1 Justification

It is necessary to make only brief mention of possible justification under s. 1 of the police action in this case. The question whether participant surveillance constitutes a reasonable limit on the right to be secure against unreasonable search or seizure takes one back to the point that the appellant is in no way arguing that the police should be denied the right to use informers or to intercept communications themselves once they have gained the confidence of a suspect. The sole thrust of his argument is that judicial supervision of the practice should exist, just as it exists in the case of third party surveillance. In a word, there is no justification for warrantless searches once it is accepted that the police could employ the same investigatory tool with or without a warrant. This simple fact (and I find no argument by the respondent refuting the notion that the police could have attended before a judge to secure an authorization for participant surveillance) destroys, in my view, any argument that participant surveillance can be upheld as a reasonable limit to the right to be secure from unreasonable search and seizure.

To conclude, the *Charter* is not meant to protect us against a poor choice of friends. If our "friend" turns out to be an informer, and we are convicted on the strength of his testimony, that may be unfortunate for us. But the *Charter* is meant to guarantee the right to be secure against unreasonable search and seizure. A conversation with an informer does not amount to a search and seizure within the meaning of the *Charter.* Surreptitious electronic interception and recording of a private communication does. Such recording, moreover, should be viewed as a search and seizure in all circumstances save where *all* parties to the conversation have expressly consented to its being recorded. Accordingly the constitutionality of "participant surveillance" should fall to be determined by application of the same standard as that employed in third party surveillance, i.e., by application of the standard of reasonableness enunciated in *Hunter v. Southam Inc.,* .... By application of that standard, the warrantless participant surveillance engaged in by the police here was clearly unconstitutional.

o

R. v. MCKINLEY TRANSPORT LTD.✧

Section 231(3) of the *Income Tax Act* permits the Minister of Revenue to order any person whose income tax returns are being audited to produce, on oath, any documents or records relating to the tax return. The defendant, McKinley Transport Ltd., claimed that the order violated s. 8 of the *Charter* because it did not require the Minister to show reasonable grounds for believing that the defendant's original income tax return was incorrect.

WILSON J. (Lamer, La Forest, L'Heureux-Dubé JJ. concurring):

A chief source of revenue for the federal government is the collection of income tax. The legislation scheme which has been put in place to regulate the collection of tax is the *Income Tax Act.* The Act requires taxpayers to file annual returns and estimate their tax payable as a result of calculations made in these returns. Moreover, the Act requires various third parties such as employers, corporations and banks to file information on wages, dividends, interest payments and the like ... In essence, the system is a self-reporting and self-assessing one which depends upon the honesty and integrity of the taxpayers for its success.

... The Act could have provided that each taxpayer submit all his or her records to the Minister and his officials so that they might make the calculations necessary for determining each person's taxable income. The legislation does not so provide, no doubt because it would be extremely expensive and cumbersome to operate such a system. However, a self-reporting system has its drawbacks. Chief among these is that it depends for its success upon the taxpayers' honesty and integrity in preparing their returns. While most taxpayers undoubtedly respect and comply with the system, the facts of life are that certain persons will attempt to take advantage of the system and avoid their full tax liability.

✧[1990] 1 S.C.R. 627.

Accordingly, the Minister of National Revenue must be given broad powers in supervision this regulatory scheme to audit taxpayers' returns and inspect all records which may be relevant to the preparation of these returns. The Minister must be capable of exercising these powers whether or not he has reasonable grounds for believing that a particular taxpayer has breached the Act. Often it will be impossible to determine from the face of the return whether any impropriety has occurred in its preparation. A spot check or a system of random monitoring may be the only way in which the integrity of the tax system can be maintained. If this is the case, and I believe that it is, then it is evident that the *Hunter* criteria are ill-suited to determine whether a seizure under s. 231(3) of the *Income Tax Act* is reasonable. The regulatory nature of the legislation and the scheme enacted require otherwise. The need for random monitoring is incompatible with the requirement in *Hunter* that the person seeking authorization for a search or seizure have reasonable and probable grounds, established under oath, to believe that an offence has been committed. If this *Hunter* criterion is inapplicable, then so too must the remaining *Hunter* criteria since they all depend for their vitality upon the need to establish reasonable and probable grounds. For example, there is no need for an impartial arbiter capable of acting judicially since his central role under *Hunter* is to ensure that the person seeking the authorization has reasonable and probable grounds to believe that a *particular* offence has been committed, that there are reasonable and probable grounds to believe that the authorization will turn up something relating to that *particular* offence, and that the authorization only goes so far as to allow the seizure of documents relevant to that *particular* offence.

This is not to say that any and all forms of search and seizure under the *Income Tax Act* are valid. The state interest in monitoring compliance with the legislation must be weighed against an individual's privacy interest. The greater the intrusion into the privacy interests of an individual, the more likely it will be that safeguards akin to those in *Hunter* will be required. Thus, when the tax officials seek entry onto the private property of an individual to conduct a search or seizure, the intrusion is much greater than a mere demand for production of documents. The reason for this is that, while a taxpayer may have little expectation of privacy in relation to his business records relevant to the determination of his tax liability, he has a significant privacy interest in the inviolability of his home.

In my opinion, s. 231(3) provides the least intrusive means by which effective monitoring of compliance with the *Income Tax Act* can be effected. It involves no invasion of a taxpayer's home or business premises. It simply calls for the production of records which may be relevant to the filing of an income tax return. A taxpayer's privacy interest with regard to these documents *vis-à-vis* the Minister is relatively low. The Minister has no way of knowing whether certain records are relevant until he has had an opportunity to examine them. At the same time, the taxpayer's privacy interest is protected as much as possible since s. 241 of the Act protects the taxpayer from disclosure of his records or the information contained therein to other persons or agencies.

For these reasons I conclude that the seizure contemplated by s. 231(3) of the *Income Tax Act* is reasonable and does not violate s. 8 of the *Charter*. That being so, it is unnecessary for me to consider whether the section is justified under s. 1 of the *Charter*. I would dismiss the appeal and make no order as to costs.

The Rights Protected: Section 10

10. Everyone has the right on arrest or detention

(a) to be informed promptly of the reasons therefor;

(b) To retain and instruct counsel without delay and to be informed to that right; and

(c) to have the validity of the detention determined by way of *habeus corpus* and to be released if the detention is not lawful.

R v. CLARKSON◇

Mrs. Clarkson was intoxicated on the night her husband was shot to death. The police arrested her and, after taking her to the hospital, began to question her. Mrs. Clarkson's sister, present at the interrogation, instantly warned Mrs. Clarkson not to answer questions without the presence of a lawyer. Mrs. Clarkson, who had been informed of her s. 10 right, said that it would be of "no use" to see a lawyer and continued to answer the police's questions.

WILSON J. (Estey, Lamer, Le Dain and La Forest JJ. concurring; McIntyre and Chouinard JJ. did not answer the constitutional question):

The question whether the appellant's right to counsel has been violated may well provide an acceptable ... approach to the problem posed by the police extraction of an intoxicated confession. This right, as entrenched in s. 10 (*b*) of the *Canadian Charter of Rights and Freedoms* is clearly aimed at fostering the principles of adjudicative fairness ....

This constitutional provision is clearly unconcerned with the probative value of any evidence obtained by the police but rather, in the words of Le Dain J. in *Therens* pp. 641–42, its aim is "to ensure that in certain situations a person is made aware of the right to counsel" where he or she is detained by the police in a situation which may give rise to a "significant legal consequence."

Given the concern for fair treatment of an accused person which underlies such constitutional civil liberties as the right to counsel in s. 10(*b*) of the *Charter*, it is evident that any alleged waiver of this right by an accused must be carefully considered and that the accused's awareness of the consequences of what he or she was saying is crucial ....

Whether or not one goes as far as requiring an accused to be tuned in to the legal intricacies of the case before accepting as valid a waiver of the right to counsel, it is clear that the waiver of the s. 10(*b*) right by an intoxicated accused must pass some form of "awareness of the consequences" test. Unlike the confession itself, there is no room for an argument that the court in assessing such a waiver should only be concerned with the probative value of the evidence so as to restrict the test to the accused's mere comprehension of his or her own words. Rather, the purpose

◇[1986] 1 S.C.R. 383.

of the right, as indicated by each of the members of this Court writing in *Therens*, is to ensure that the accused is treated fairly in the criminal process. While this constitutional guarantee cannot be forced upon an unwilling accused, any voluntary waiver in order to be valid and effective must be premised on a true appreciation of the consequences of giving up the right.

The trial judge found as a fact that the appellant's confession could not pass the "awareness of the consequences" test and, if such is the case, then presumably neither could the waiver of the s. 10(*b*) right to counsel. Accordingly, the test for a valid and effective waiver of the right was not met and the continued questioning of the appellant constituted a violation of s. 10(*b*) of the *Charter*. At the very minimum it was incumbent upon the police to delay their questioning and the taking of the appellant's statement until she was in a sufficiently sober state to properly exercise her right to retain and instruct counsel or to be fully aware of the consequences of waiving this right. Accordingly, regardless of the view one takes of the admissibility of the intoxicated confession per se, the conclusion that the appellant's confession was improperly obtained is inescapable.

)

R . v. M A N N I N E N◇

In October 1982 a Mac's Milk store was robbed. Acting upon eyewitness information, the police located R.C. Manninen at the garage where his stolen car was being repaired. He was told that he was being charged with armed robbery and was read his rights. He stated that he wanted to see a lawyer. The police then asked him where the knife was that he had used in the robbery. He replied: "He's lying. When I was in the store I only had the gun. The knife was in the tool box in the car." The questioning continued until Manninen refused to answer further questions. He did not see his lawyer until he was at the police station later that evening. At trial he was convicted on the basis of the statements made in response to the police questioning. The Ontario Court of Appeal unanimously allowed his appeal and ordered a new trial; the Crown appealed to the Supreme Court of Canada.

LAMER J. (for the Court):
It is not disputed that the respondent was informed of his right to retain and instruct counsel without delay. Further, the sufficiency of the communication is not challenged.

The respondent's comment on being informed of his right to counsel was

> Prove it. I ain't saying anything until I see my lawyer. I want to see my lawyer.

Since there could hardly be a clearer assertion of the desire to exercise the right to counsel, it is not necessary in this appeal to decide whether an arrested or

---

◇[1987] 1 S.C.R. 1233.

detained person is required to positively assert his right to counsel before a correlative obligation is imposed on the police.

In my view, s. 10(*b*) imposes at least two duties on the police in addition to the duty to inform the detainee of his right. First, the police must provide the detainee with a reasonable opportunity to exercise the right to retain and instruct counsel without delay. The detainee is in the control of the police and he cannot exercise his right to counsel unless the police provide him with a reasonable opportunity to do so.

In my view, this aspect of the right to counsel was clearly infringed in this case. The respondent clearly asserted his right to remain silent and his desire to consult his lawyer. There was a telephone immediately at hand in the office, which the officers used for their own purposes. It was not necessary for the respondent to make an express request to use the telephone. The duty to facilitate contact with counsel included the duty to offer the use of the telephone. Of course, there may be circumstances in which it is particularly urgent that the police continue with an investigation before it is possible to facilitate a detainee's communication with counsel. There was no urgency in the circumstances surrounding the offenses in this case.

Further, s. 10(*b*) imposes on the police the duty to cease questioning or otherwise attempting to elicit evidence from the detainee until he has had a reasonable opportunity to retain and instruct counsel. The purpose of the right to counsel is to allow the detainee not only to be informed of his rights and obligations under the law but, equally if not more important, to obtain advice as to how to exercise those rights. In this case, the police officers correctly informed the respondent of his right to remain silent and the main function of counsel would be to confirm the existence of that right and then to advise him as to how to exercise it. For the right to counsel to be effective, the detainee must have access to this advice before he is questioned or otherwise required to provide evidence . . . .

This aspect of the respondent's right to counsel was clearly infringed in the circumstances of this case. Immediately after the respondent's clear assertion of his right to remain silent and his desire to consult his lawyer, the police officer commenced his questioning as if the respondent had expressed no such desire. Again, there may be circumstances in which it is particularly urgent that the police proceed with their questioning of the detainee before providing him with a reasonable opportunity to retain and instruct counsel, but there was no such urgency in this case.

The Crown contends that there was no infringement of the right to counsel because the respondent had waived his right by answering the police officer's questions. While a person may implicitly waive his rights under s. 10(*b*), the standard will be very high . . . . In my view, the respondent's conduct did not constitute an implied waiver of this right to counsel. It seems that he did not intend to waive his right, as he clearly asserted it at the beginning and at the end of the questioning. Rather, the form of the questioning was such as to elicit involuntary answers. The police have ignored his request and have proceeded to question him, he is likely to feel that his right has no effect and that he must answer. Finally, the respondent had the right not to be asked questions, and he must not be held to have implicitly waived that right simply because he answered the questions. Otherwise, the right not to be asked questions would only exist where the detainee refused to answer and thus where there is no need for any remedy or exclusionary rule.

For these reasons, I would conclude that the respondent's rights under s. 10(*b*) were infringed.

o

The Rights Protected: Section 11(d)

11. Any person charged with an offence has the right: (*d*) to be presumed innocent until proven guilty according to law in a fair and public hearing by an independent and impartial tribunal.

R. v. OAKES[*]

David Edwin Oakes was arrested with eight one-ounce vials of hashish oil in his possession. At trial he called no evidence to defeat this charge. According to s. 8 of the *Narcotic Control Act*, an accused found guilty of possession would also be found guilty of trafficking in a narcotic unless he could prove otherwise; the trial judge, therefore, also found him guilty of the more serious offence.

DICKSON C.J. (for the Court):
The Chief Justice found that the Act violated s. 11 (*d*), and went on to consider whether the violation was saved by s. 1.

It is important to observe at the outset that s. 1 has two functions: first, it constitutionally guarantees the rights and freedoms set out in the provisions which follow; and, second, it states explicitly the exclusive justificatory criteria (outside of s. 33 of the *Constitution Act, 1982*) against which limitations on those rights and freedoms must be measured. Accordingly, any s. 1 inquiry must be premised on an understanding that the impugned limit violated constitutional rights and freedoms—rights and freedoms which are part of the supreme law of Canada . . . .

A second contextual element of interpretation of s. 1 is provided by the words "free and democratic society." Inclusion of these words as the final standard of justification for limits on rights and freedoms refers the Court to the very purpose for which the *Charter* was originally entrenched in the Constitution: Canadian society is to be free and democratic. The Court must be guided by the values and principles essential to a free and democratic society which I believe embody, to name but a few, respect for the inherent dignity of the human person, commitment to social justice and equality, accommodation of a wide variety of beliefs, respect for cultural and group identity, and faith in social and political institutions which enhance the participation of individuals and groups in society. The underlying values and principles of a free and democratic society are the genesis of the rights

---

[*][1986] 1 S.C.R. 103.

and freedoms guaranteed by the *Charter* and the ultimate standard against which a limit on a right or freedom must be shown, despite its effect, to be reasonable and demonstrably justified.

The rights and freedoms guaranteed by the *Charter* are not, however, absolute. It may become necessary to limit rights and freedoms in circumstances where their exercise would be inimical to the realisation of collective goals of fundamental importance.

For this reason, s. 1 provides criteria of justification for limits on the rights and freedoms guaranteed by the *Charter*. These criteria impose a stringent standard of justification, especially when understood in terms of the two contextual considerations discussed above, namely, the violation of a constitutionally guaranteed right or freedom and the fundamental principles of a free and democratic society.

The onus of proving that a limit on a right or freedom guaranteed by the *Charter* is reasonable and demonstrably justified in a free and democratic society rests upon the party seeking to uphold the limitation. It is clear from the text of s. 1 that limits on the rights and freedoms enumerated in the *Charter* are exceptions to their general guarantee. The presumption is that the rights and freedoms are guaranteed unless the party invoking s. 1 can bring itself within the exceptional criteria which justify their being limited. This is further substantiated by the use of the word "demonstrably" which clearly indicates that the onus of justification is on the party seeking to limit: *Hunter v. Southam Inc.* . . . .

The standard of proof under s. 1 is the civil standard, namely, proof by a preponderance of probability. The alternative criminal standard, proof beyond a reasonable doubt, would, in my view, be unduly onerous on the party seeking to limit. Concepts such as "reasonableness," "justiciability," and "free and democratic society" are simply not amenable to such a standard. Nevertheless, the preponderance of probability test must be applied rigorously. Indeed, the phrase "demonstrably justified" in s. 1 of the *Charter* supports this conclusion. Within the broad category of the civil standard, there exist different degrees of probability depending on the nature of the case . . . .

Having regard to the fact that s. 1 is being invoked for the purpose of justifying a violation of the constitutional rights and freedoms the *Charter* was designed to protect, a very high degree of probability will be, in the words of Lord Denning, "commensurate with the occasion." Where evidence is required in order to prove the constituent elements of a s. 1 inquiry, and this will generally be the case, it should be cogent and persuasive and make clear to the Court the consequences of imposing or not imposing the limit. . . . A court will also need to know what alternative measures for implementing the objective were available to the legislators when they made their decisions. I should add, however, that there may be cases where certain elements of the s. 1 analysis are obvious or self-evident.

To establish that a limit is reasonable and demonstrably justified in a free and democratic society, two central criteria must be satisfied. First, the objective, which the measures responsible for a limit on a *Charter* right or freedom are designed to serve, must be "of sufficient importance to warrant overriding a constitutionally protected right or freedom": *R. v. Big M Drug Mart Ltd.* The standard must be high in order to ensure that objectives which are trivial or discordant with the principles integral to a free and democratic society do not gain s. 1 protection. It is necessary, at a minimum, that an objective relate to concerns which are pressing and substantial in a free and democratic society before it can be characterised as sufficiently important.

Second, once a sufficiently significant objective is recognized, then the party invoking s. 1 must show that the means chosen are reasonable and demonstrably justified. This involves "a form of proportionality test": *R. v. Big M Drug Mart Ltd.*, *supra*. Although the nature of the proportionality test will vary depending on the circumstances, in each case courts will be required to balance the interests of society with those of individuals and groups. There are, in my view, three important components of a proportionality test. First, the measures adopted must be carefully designed to achieve the objective in question. They must not be arbitrary, unfair or based on irrational considerations. In short, they must be rationally connected to the objective. Second, the means, even if rationally connected to the objective in this first sense, should impair "as little as possible" the right or freedom in question: *R. v. Big M Drug Mart Ltd.* Third, there must be a proportionality between the effects of the measures which are responsible for limiting the *Charter* right or freedom, and the objective which has been identified as of "sufficient importance."

With respect to the third component, it is clear that the general effect of any measure impugned under s. 1 will be the infringement of a right or freedom guaranteed by the *Charter*; this is the reason why resort to s. 1 is necessary. The inquiry into effects must, however, go further. A wide range of rights and freedoms are guaranteed by the *Charter*, and an almost infinite number of factual situations may arise in respect of these. Some limits on rights and freedoms protected by the *Charter* will be more serious than others in terms of the nature of the right or freedom violated, the extent of the violation, and the degree to which the measures which impose the limit trench upon the integral principles of a free and democratic society. Even if an objective is of sufficient importance and the first two elements of the proportionality test are satisfied, it is still possible that, because of the severity of the deleterious effects of a measure on individuals or groups, the measure will not be justified by the purposes it is intended to serve. The more severe the deleterious effects of a measure, the more important the objective must be if the measure is to be reasonable and demonstrably justified in a free and democratic society . . . .

The Chief Justice then applied these principles to the case before it.

The objective of protecting our society from the grave ills associated with drug trafficking, is, in my view, one of sufficient importance to warrant overriding a constitutionally protected right or freedom in certain cases. Moreover, the degree of seriousness of drug trafficking makes its acknowledgement as a sufficiently important objective for the purposes of s. 1, to a large extent, self-evident. The first criterion of a s. 1 inquiry, therefore, has been satisfied by the Crown.

The next stage of inquiry is a consideration of the means chosen by Parliament to achieve its objective. The means must be reasonable and demonstrably justified in a free and democratic society. As outlined above, this proportionality test should begin with a consideration of the rationality of the provision: is the reverse onus clause in s. 8 rationally related to the objective of curbing drug trafficking? At a minimum, this requires that s. 8 be internally rational; there must be a rational connection between the basic fact of possession and the presumed fact of possession for the purpose of trafficking. Otherwise, the reverse onus clause could give rise to unjustified and erroneous convictions for drug trafficking of persons guilty only of possession of narcotics.

In my view, s. 8 does not survive this rational connection test. As Martin J.A. of the Ontario Court of Appeal concluded, possession of a small or negligible quantity of narcotics does not support the inference of trafficking. In other words, it would be irrational to infer that a person had an intent to traffic on the basis of his or her possession of a very small quantity of narcotics. The presumption required under s. 8 of the *Narcotic Control Act* is over-inclusive and could lead to results in certain cases which would defy both rationality and fairness. In light of the seriousness of the offence in question, which carries with it the possibility of imprisonment for life, I am further convinced that the first component of the proportionality test has not been satisfied by the Crown.

Having concluded that s.8 does not satisfy this first component of proportionality, it is unnecessary to consider the other two components.

‍

The Rights Protected: Section 12

12. Everyone has the right not to be subject to any cruel and unusual punishment.

R. v. SMITH◇

E. D. Smith was found guilty of importing 7 ounces of cocaine contrary to s. 5(1) of the *Narcotic Control Act*; s. 5(2) of that act provided the following sentence: "Imprisonment for life but not less than seven years." The trial judge found the minimum sentence requirement to be an infringement of s. 12 of the Charter and therefore unconstitutional. He nevertheless sentenced Smith to eight years imprisonment. The sentence was appealed to the British Columbia Court of Appeal where it was dismissed and the trial judge's constitutional finding was overturned. Smith then appealed to the Supreme Court of Canada.

LAMER J. (Dickson C.J. concurring):

. . . A minimum mandatory term of imprisonment is obviously not in and of itself cruel and unusual. The legislature may, in my view, provide for a compulsory term of imprisonment upon conviction for certain offenses without infringing the rights protected by s. 12 of the *Charter*. For example, a long term of penal servitude for he or she who has imported large amounts of heroin for the purpose of trafficking would certainly not contravene s. 12 of the *Charter*, quite the contrary. However, the seven year minimum prison term of s. 5(2) is grossly disproportionate when examined in light of the wide net cast by s. 5(1).

◇[1987] 1 S.C.R. 1045.

As indicated above, the offence of importing enacted by s. 5(1) of the *Narcotic Control Act* covers numerous substances of varying degrees of dangerousness and totally disregards the quantity of the drug imported. The purpose of a given importation, such as whether it is for personal consumption or for trafficking, and the existence or nonexistence of previous convictions for offenses of a similar nature or gravity are disregarded as irrelevant. Thus, the law is such that it is inevitable that, in some cases, a verdict of guilt will lead to the imposition of a term of imprisonment which will be grossly disproportionate.

This is what offends s. 12, the certainty, not just the potential. Absent the minimum, the section still has the potential of operating so as to impose cruel and unusual punishment. But that would only occur if and when a judge chose to impose, let us say, seven years or more on the "small offender." Remedy will then flow from s. 24. It is the judge's sentence, but not the section, that is in violation of the *Charter*. However, the effect of the minimum is to insert the certainty that, in some cases, as of conviction the violation will occur. It is this aspect of certainty that makes the section itself a *prima facie* violation of s. 12, and the minimum must, subject to s.1, be declared of no force or effect.

In its factum, the Crown alleged that such eventual violations could be, and are in fact, avoided through the proper use of prosecutorial discretion to charge for a lesser offence.

In my view the section cannot be salvaged by relying on the discretion of the prosecution not to apply the law in those cases where, in the opinion of the prosecution, its application would be a violation of the *Charter*. To do so would be to disregard totally s. 52 of the *Constitution Act, 1982* which provides that any law which is inconsistent with the Constitution is of no force or effect to the extent of the inconsistency and the courts are duty bound to make that pronouncement, not to delegate the avoidance of a violation to the prosecution or to anyone else for that matter. Therefore, to conclude, I find that the minimum term of imprisonment provided for by s. 5(2) of the *Narcotic Control Act* infringes the rights guaranteed by s. 12 and, as such, is a *prima facie* violation of the *Charter*. Subject to the section's being salvaged under s. 1, the minimum must be declared of no force or effect . . . .

This Court has already had occasion to address s. 1 . . . . [It has been] indicated that once there has been a *prima facie* violation of the *Charter* the burden rests upon the authorities to salvage the legislative provision in question . . . .

In the present appeal, the Crown had but one argument. It urged upon us that the imposition of severe punishments on drug importers will discourage the perpetration of such a serious crime. Those non-users, who import and traffic in such noxious drugs as heroin, are slave masters and responsible not only for the destruction of numerous human beings, but also for the very extensive criminal activity which is spawned by the drug trade. In my view, the fight against the importing and trafficking of hard drugs is, without a doubt, an objective "of sufficient importance to warrant overriding a constitutionally protected right or freedom."

This then brings us to the next phase of the test, the proportionality of the means chosen to reach that "important" result. Of course, the means chosen do "achieve the objective in question." The certainty that all those who contravene the prohibition against importing will be sentenced to at least seven years in prison will surely deter people from importing narcotics. Therefore, rationality, the first prong of the proportionality test, has been met. But the Crown's justification fails the second prong, namely minimum impairment of the rights protected by s. 12. Clearly there is no need to be indiscriminate. We do not need to sentence the small offenders to seven years in prison in order to deter the serious offender. Indeed, the net cast by s. 5(2) for sentencing purposes need not be so wide as that cast by s. 5(1) for conviction purposes. The result sought could be achieved by limiting the imposition of a minimum sentence to the importing of certain quantities, to certain specific narcotics of the schedule, to repeat offenders, or even to a combination of these factors. But the wording of the section and the schedule is much broader. I should add that, in my view, the minimum sentence also creates some problems. In particular, it inserts into the system a reluctance to convict and thus results in acquittals for picayune reasons of accused who do not deserve a seven year sentence, and it gives the Crown an unfair advantage in plea bargaining as an accused will be more likely to plead guilty to a lesser or included offence. For these reasons, the minimum imprisonment provided for by s. 5(2) breaches s. 12 of the *Charter* and this breach has not been justified under s. 1.

MCINTYRE J. (dissenting):

... The formation of public policy is a function of Parliament. It must decide what the aims and objectives of social policy are to be, and it must specify the means by which they will be accomplished. It is true that the enactments of Parliament must now be measured against the *Charter* and, where they do not come within the provisions of the *Charter* they may be struck down. This step, however, must not be taken by the courts merely because a court or a judge may disagree with a Parliamentary decision but only where the *Charter* has been violated. Parliament has the necessary resources and facilities to make a detailed inquiry into relevant considerations in forming policy. It has the capacity to make a much more extensive inquiry into matters concerning social policy than has the Court. It may test public opinion, review and debate the adequacy of its programs, and make decisions based upon wider considerations, and infinitely more evidence, than can ever be available to a court . . . .

In view of the careful and extensive consideration given this matter by Parliament and the lack of evidence before this Court suggesting that an adequate alternative to the minimum sentence exists which would realise the valid social aim of deterring the importation of drugs, I cannot find that the minimum sentence of seven years goes beyond what is necessary for the achievement of a valid social aim, having regard to the legitimate purposes of punishment and the adequacy of possible alternatives.

Wilson, Le Dain and La Forest JJ. wrote separate concurring decisions.

The Rights Protected: Section 15

15(1) Every individual is equal before and under the law and has the right to the equal protection and equal benefit of the law without discrimination and, in particular, without discrimination based on race, national or ethnic origin, colour, religion, sex, age or mental or physical disability.

15(2) Subsection (1) does not preclude any law, program or activity that has as its object the amelioration of conditions of disadvantaged individuals or groups including those that are disadvantaged because of race, national or ethnic origin, colour, religion, sex, age or mental or physical disability.

ANDREWS v. LAW SOCIETY OF BRITISH COLUMBIA ✧

Andrews, a landed immigrant, was refused admission to the Law Society of British Columbia after completing his articles and Bar Admission course. The Law Society relied upon section 42 of the *Barristers and Solicitors Act* which provided that only Canadian citizens may be called to the bar. Andrews challenged the constitutionality of the section which, in effect, prohibited him from practising law in British Columbia. That Province's Court of Appeal found that the section violated s. 15(1) of the *Charter* and that it was not saved by s. 1; the Law Society appealed to the Supreme Court.

MCINTYRE J. (Dickson C.J. and Lamer, Wilson and L'Heureux-Dubé JJ. concurred in this part of the decision; a majority of Dickson C.J. and Wilson and L'Heureux-Dubé JJ. disagreed with McIntyre J.'s disposition of the section 1 issue):

The Concept of Equality

Section 15(1) of the *Charter* provides for every individual a guarantee of equality before and under the law, as well as the equal protection and equal benefit of the law without discrimination. This is not a general guarantee of equality; it does not provide for equality between individuals or groups within society in a general or abstract sense, nor does it impose on individuals or groups an obligation to accord equal treatment to others. It is concerned with the application of the law . . . .

In simple terms . . . it may be said that a law which treats all identically and which provides equality of treatment between "A" and "B" might well cause inequality for "C," depending on differences in personal characteristics and situations. To approach the ideal of full equality before and under the law—and in human affairs an approach is all that can be expected—the main consideration must be the impact of the law on the individual or the group concerned. Recognizing that there will always be an infinite variety of personal characteristics, capacities,

---

✧[1989] 1 S.C.R. 143.

entitlements and merits among those subject to a law, there must be accorded, as nearly as may be possible, an equality of benefit and protection and no more of the restrictions, penalties or burdens imposed upon one than another. In other words, the admittedly unattainable ideal should not because of irrelevant personal differences have a more burdensome or less beneficial impact on one than another.

It is not every distinction or differentiation in treatment at law which will transgress the equality guarantees of s. 15 of the *Charter*. It is, of course, obvious that legislatures may—and to govern effectively—must treat different individuals and groups in different ways. Indeed, such distinctions are one of the main preoccupations of legislatures. The classifying of individuals and groups, the making of different provisions respecting such groups, the application of different rules, regulations, requirements and qualifications to different persons is necessary for the governance of modern society. As noted above, for the accommodation of differences, which is the essence of true equality, it will frequently be necessary to make distinctions. What kinds of distinctions will be acceptable under s. 15(1) and what kinds will violate its provisions? . . .

Discrimination

The right to equality before and under the law, and the rights to the equal protection and benefit of the law contained in s. 15, are granted with the direction contained in s. 15 itself that they be without discrimination. Discrimination is unacceptable in a democratic society because it epitomizes the worst effects of the denial of equality, and discrimination reinforced by law is particularly repugnant. The worst oppression will result from discriminatory measures having the force of law. It is against this evil that s. 15 provides a guarantee . . . .

I would say . . . that discrimination may be described as a distinction, whether intentional or not but based on grounds relating to personal characteristics of the individual or group, which has the effect of imposing burdens, obligations, or disadvantages on such individual or group not imposed upon others, or which withholds or limits access to opportunities, benefits, and advantages available to other members of society. Distinctions based on personal characteristics attributed to an individual solely on the basis of association with a group will rarely escape the charge of discrimination, while those based on an individual's merits and capacities will rarely be so classed.

The Court in the case at bar must address the issue of discrimination as the term is used in s. 15(1) of the *Charter*. In general, it may be said that the principles which have been applied under the Human Rights Acts are equally applicable in considering questions of discrimination under s. 15(1). Certain differences arising from the difference between the *Charter* and the Human Rights Acts must, however, be considered. To begin with, discrimination in s. 15(1) is limited to discrimination caused by the application or operation of law, whereas the Human Rights Acts apply also to private activities. Furthermore, and this is a distinction of more importance, all the Human Rights Acts passed in Canada specifically designate a certain limited number of grounds upon which discrimination is forbidden. Section 15(1) of the *Charter* is not so limited. The enumerated grounds in s. 15(1) are not exclusive and the limits, if any, on grounds for discrimination which may be established in future cases await definition. The enumerated grounds do, however, reflect the most common and probably the most socially destructive and historically practised bases of discrimination and must, in the words of s. 15(1), receive particular attention. Both the enumerated grounds themselves and other possible grounds of discrimination under s. 15(1) must be interpreted in a broad and generous manner, reflecting the fact that they are constitutional provisions not easily repealed or amended but intended to provide for a "continuing framework for the legitimate exercise of governmental power" and at the same time, for the "unremitting protection" of equality rights; see *Hunter v. Southam Inc....*

Relationship between s. 15(1) and s. 1 of the Charter

...The Analysis of discrimination in this approach must take place within the context of the enumerated grounds and those analogous to them. The words "without discrimination" require more than a mere finding of distinction between the treatment of groups or individuals. Those words are a form of qualifier built in s. 15(1) itself and limit those distinctions which are forbidden by the section to those which involve prejudice or disadvantage....

The ... "enumerated and analogous grounds" approach most closely accords with the purposes of s. 15 and the definition of discrimination outlined above and leaves questions of justification to s. 1. However, in assessing whether a complainant's rights have been infringed under s. 15(1), it is not enough to focus only on the alleged ground of discrimination and decide whether or not it is an enumerated or analogous ground. The effect of the impugned distinction or classification on the complainant must be considered. Once it is accepted that not all distinctions and differentiations created by law are discriminatory, then a role must be assigned to s. 15(1) which goes beyond the mere recognition of a legal distinction. A complainant under s. 15(1) must show not only that he or she is not receiving equal treatment before and under the law or that the law has a differential impact on him or her in the protection or benefit accorded by law but, in addition, must show that the legislative impact is discriminatory.

Where discrimination is found a breach of s. 15(1) has occurred and—where s. 15(2) is not applicable—any justification, any consideration of the reasonableness of the enactment; indeed, any consideration of factors which could justify the discrimination and support the constitutionality of the impugned enactment would take place under s. 1. This approach would conform with the directions of this Court in earlier decisions concerning the application of s. 1 and at the same time would allow for the screening out of the obviously trivial and vexatious claim. In this, it would provide a workable approach to the problem.

It would seem to me apparent that a legislative distinction has been made by s. 42 of the *Barrister and Solicitors Act* between citizens and non-citizens with respect to the practice of law. The distinction would deny admission to the practice of law to non-citizens who in all other respects are qualified. Have the respondents, because of s. 42 of the Act, been denied equality before and under the law or the equal protection of the law? In practical terms it should be noted that the citizenship requirement affects only those non-citizens who are permanent residents. The permanent resident must wait a minimum of three years from the date of establishing permanent residence status before citizenship may be acquired. The distinction therefore imposes a burden in the form of some delay on permanent residents who have acquired all or some of their legal training abroad and is, therefore, discriminatory.

The rights guaranteed in s. 15(1) apply to all persons whether citizens or not. A rule which bars an entire class of persons from certain forms of employment, solely on the grounds of a lack of citizenship status and without consideration of educational and professional qualifications or the other attributes or merits of individuals in the group, would, in my view, infringe s. 15 equality rights. Non-citizens, lawfully permanent residents of Canada, are—in the words of the U.S. Supreme Court in *United States v. Carolene Products Co....*—a good example of a "discrete and insular minority" who come within the protection of s. 15.

Section 1

...The essence of s. 1 is found in the expression "reasonable" and it is for the Court to decide if s. 42 of the *Barristers and Solicitors Act* of British Columbia is a reasonable limit. In reaching the conclusion that it is, I would say that the legislative choice in this regard is not one between an answer that is clearly right and one that is clearly wrong. Either position may well be sustainable and...the Court is not called upon to substitute its opinion as to where to draw the line. The Legislature in fixing public policy has chosen the citizenship requirement and, unless the Court can find that choice unreasonable it has no power under the *Charter* to strike it down or, as has been said, no power to invade the legislative field and substitute its views for that of the Legislature. In my view, the citizenship requirement is reasonable and sustainable under s. 1. It is chosen for the achievement of a desirable social goal: one aspect of the due regulation and qualification of the legal profession. This is an objective of importance and the measure is not disproportionate to the object to be attained. The maximum delay imposed upon the non-citizen from the date of acquisition of permanent resident status is three years. It will frequently be less. No impediment is put in the way of obtaining citizenship. In fact the policy of the Canadian government is to encourage the newcomer to become a citizen. It is reasonable, in my view, to expect that the newcomer who seeks to gain the privileges and status within the land and the right to exercise the great powers that admission to the practice of law will give should accept citizenship and its obligations as well as its advantages and benefits. I would therefore allow the appeal....

Wilson J. agreed with McIntyre's analysis of s. 15 and his conclusions in that regard; she disagreed with his conclusion under s. 1.

WILSON J. (Dickson C.J. and L'Heureux-Dubé J. concurring):

...The appellant Law Society submitted that the Court of Appeal erred in its consideration of the citizenship requirement by failing to accord proper recognition to the role of the legal profession in the governmental process of the country in failing to consider that Canadian citizenship could reasonably be regarded by the legislature as a requirement for the practice of law. The respondents, on the other hand, argued that the Court of Appeal was right in concluding that there was not a sufficiently rational connection between the required personal characteristic of citizenship and the governmental interest in ensuring that lawyers in British Columbia are familiar with Canadian institutions, are committed to Canadian society, and are capable of playing a role in our system of democratic government....

To my mind, even if lawyers do perform a governmental function, I do not think the requirement that they be citizens provides any guarantee that they will honourably and conscientiously carry out their public duties. They will carry them out, I believe, because they are good lawyers and not because they are Canadian citizens.

In my view, the reasoning advanced in support of the citizenship requirement simply does not meet the tests in *Oakes* for overriding a constitutional right particularly, as in this case, a right designed to protect "discrete and insular minorities" in our society. I would respectfully concur in the view expressed by McLachlin J.A....that the citizenship requirement does not "appear to relate closely to those ends, much less to have been carefully designed to achieve them with minimum impairment of individual rights"....

○

Remedies: Section 24

24. (1) Anyone whose rights or freedoms, as guaranteed by this Charter, have been infringed or denied may apply to a court of competent jurisdiction to obtain such remedy as the court considers appropriate and just in the circumstances.

   (2) Where, in proceedings under subsection (1), a court concludes that evidence was obtained in a manner that infringed or denied any rights or freedoms guaranteed by this Charter, the evidence shall be excluded if it is established that, having regard to all the circumstances, the admission of it in the proceedings would bring the administration of justice into disrepute.

R. v. COLLINS⬦

Mrs. Collins, sitting in a booth in a bar, was grabbed by the throat and wrestled to the ground by a police constable. The "throat hold" was common practice in narcotic searches as a method of preventing dealers from swallowing condoms holding viles of heroin. Mrs. Collins was, in fact, in possession of heroin. Prior to the search, however, the constable did not, as required by s. 10(1)(a) of the *Narcotic Control Act*, have "reasonable grounds" for this belief; the search was therefore an "unreasonable" one as proscribed by s. 8 of the *Charter*. Having found the search to be unreasonable, the trial judge declined to exclude the

---

⬦[1987] 1 S.C.R. 265.

evidence under s. 24(2) of the *Charter*. The British Columbia Court of Appeal upheld this decision. Collins appealed to the Supreme Court of Canada.

LAMER J. (Dickson C.J., Wilson and La Forest JJ. concurring):

At the outset, it should be noted that the use of the phrase "if it is established that" places the burden of persuasion on the applicant, for it is the position which he maintains which must be established. Again, the standard of persuasion required can only be the civil standard of the balance of probabilities. Thus, the applicant must make it more probable than not that the admission of the evidence would bring the administration of justice into disrepute.

It is whether *the admission of the evidence* would bring the administration of justice into disrepute that is the applicable test. Misconduct by the police in the investigatory process often has some effect on the repute of the administration of justice, but s. 24(2) is not a remedy for police misconduct, requiring the exclusion of the evidence if, because of this misconduct, the administration of justice was brought into disrepute. Section 24(2) could well have been drafted in that way, but it was not. Rather, the drafters of the *Charter* decided to focus on the admission of the evidence in the proceedings, and the purpose of s. 24(2) is to prevent having the administration of justice brought into *further disrepute* by the admission of the evidence in the proceedings. This further disrepute will result from the admission of evidence that would deprive the accused of a fair hearing, or from judicial condonation of unacceptable conduct by the investigatory and prosecutorial agencies. It will also be necessary to consider any disrepute that may result from the exclusion of the evidence. It would be inconsistent with the purpose of s. 24(2) to exclude evidence if its exclusion would bring the administration of justice into greater disrepute than would its admission.

The concept of disrepute necessarily involves some element of community views, and the determination of disrepute thus requires the judge to refer to what he conceives to be the views of the community at large. This does not mean that evidence of the public's perception of the repute of the administration of justice, which Professor Gibson suggested could be presented in the form of public opinion polls . . . will be determinative of the issue . . . . The position is different with respect to obscenity, for example, where the court must assess the level of tolerance of the community, whether or not it is reasonable, and may consider public opinion polls . . . . It would be unwise, in my respectful view, to adopt a similar attitude with respect to the *Charter*. Members of the public generally become conscious of the importance of protecting the rights and freedoms of accused only when they are in some way brought closer to the system either personally or through the experience of friends or family . . . .

The *Charter* is designed to protect the accused from the majority, so the enforcement of the *Charter* must not be left to that majority.

The approach I adopt may be put figuratively in terms of the reasonable person test proposed by Professor Yves-Marie Morissette in his article *The Exclusion of Evidence under the Canadian Charter of Rights and Freedoms: What to Do and What Not to Do* (1984), 29 *McGill L.J.* 521, at p. 538. In applying s. 24(2), he suggested that the relevant question is: "Would the admission of the evidence bring the administration of justice into disrepute in the eyes of the reasonable man, dispassionate and fully apprised of the circumstances of the case?" The reasonable person is usually the average person in the community, but only when that community's current mood is reasonable.

The decision is thus not left to the untrammelled discretion of the judge. In practice, as Professor Morissette wrote, the reasonable person test is there to require of judges that they "concentrate on what they do best: finding within themselves, with cautiousness and impartiality, a basis for their own decisions, articulating their reasons carefully and accepting review by a higher court where it occurs." It serves as a reminder to each individual judge that his discretion is grounded in community values, and, in particular, long term community values. He should not render a decision that would be unacceptable to the community when that community is not being wrought with passion or otherwise under passing stress due to current events. In effect, the judge will have met this test if the judges of the Court of Appeal will decline to interfere with his decision, even though they might have decided the matter differently, using the well-known statement that they are of the view that the decision was not unreasonable.

In determining whether the admission of evidence would bring the administration of justice into disrepute, the judge is directed by s. 24(2) to consider "all the circumstances." The factors which are to be considered and balanced have been listed by many courts in the country . . . .

The factors that the courts have most frequently considered include:

- what kind of evidence was obtained?

- what *Charter* right was infringed?

- was the *Charter* violation serious or was it of a merely technical nature?

- was it deliberate, wilful or flagrant, or was it inadvertent or committed in good faith?

- did it occur in circumstances of urgency or necessity?

- were there other investigatory techniques available?

- would the evidence have been obtained in any event?

- is the offence serious?

- is the evidence essential to substantiate the charge?

- are other remedies available?

I do not wish to be seen as approving this as an exhaustive list of the relevant factors, and I would like to make some general comments as regards these factors.

As a matter of personal preference, I find it useful to group the factors according to the way in which they affect the repute of the administration of justice. Certain of the factors listed are relevant in determining the effect of the admission of the evidence on the fairness of the trial. The trial is a key part of the administration of justice, and the fairness of Canadian trials is a major source of the repute of the system and is now a right guaranteed by s. 11(*d*) of the *Charter*. If the admission of the evidence in some way affects the fairness of the trial, then the admission of the evidence would *tend* to bring the administration of justice into disrepute and, subject to a consideration of the other factors, the evidence generally should be excluded.

It is clear to me that the factor relevant to this determination will include the nature of the evidence obtained as a result of the violation and the nature of the right violated and not so much the manner in which the right was violated. Real evidence that was obtained in a manner that violated the *Charter* will rarely operate unfairly for that reason alone. The real evidence existed irrespective of the violation of the *Charter* and its use does not render the trial unfair. However, the situation is very different with respect to cases where, after a violation of the *Charter*, the accused is conscripted against himself through a confession or other evidence emanating from him. The use of such evidence would render the trial unfair, for it did not exist prior to the violation and it strikes at one of the fundamental tenets of a fair trial, the right against self-incrimination. Such evidence will generally rise in the context of an infringement of the right to counsel . . . .

The use of self-incriminating evidence obtained following a denial of the right to counsel will generally go to the very fairness of the trial and should generally be excluded. Several Courts of Appeal have also emphasised this distinction between pre-existing real evidence and self-incriminatory evidence created following a breach of the *Charter*.

. . . It may also be relevant, in certain circumstances, that the evidence would have been obtained in any even without the violation of the *Charter*.

There are other factors which are relevant to the seriousness of the *Charter* violation and thus to the disrepute that will result from judicial acceptance of evidence obtained through that violation . . . .

I should add that the availability of other investigatory techniques and the fact that the evidence could have been obtained without the violation of the *Charter* tend to render the *Charter* violation more serious. We are considering the actual conduct of the authorities and the evidence must not be admitted on the basis that they could have proceeded otherwise and obtained the evidence properly. In fact, their failure to proceed properly when that option was open to them tends to indicate a blatant disregard for the *Charter*, which is a factor supporting the exclusion of the evidence.

The final relevant group of factors consists of those that relate to the effect of excluding the evidence. The question under s. 24(2) is whether the system's repute will be better served by the admission or the exclusion of the evidence, and it is thus necessary to consider any disrepute that may result from the exclusion of the evidence. In my view, the administration of justice would be brought into disrepute by the exclusion of evidence essential to substantiate the charge, and thus the acquittal of the accused, because of a trivial breach of the *Charter*. Such disrepute would be greater if the offence was more serious . . . .

I hasten to add, however, that if the admission of the evidence would result in an unfair trial, the seriousness of the offence could not render that evidence admissible. If any relevance is to be given to the seriousness of the offence in the context of the fairness of the trial, it operates in the opposite sense: the more serious the offence, the more damaging to the system's repute would be an unfair trial . . . .

The evidence obtained as a result of the search was real evidence, and, while prejudicial to the accused as evidence tendered by the Crown usually is, there is nothing to suggest that its use at the trial would render the trial unfair. In addition, it is true that the cost of excluding the evidence would be high: someone who was found guilty at trial of a relatively serious offence will evade conviction. Such a result could bring the administration of justice into disrepute. However, the administration of justice would be brought into greater disrepute, at least in my respectful view, if this Court did not exclude the evidence and dissociate itself from the conduct of the police in this case which, always on the assumption that the officer merely had suspicions, was a flagrant and serious violation of the rights of an individual. Indeed, we cannot accept that police officers take flying tackles at people and seize them by the throat when they do not have reasonable and probable grounds to believe that those people are either dangerous or handlers of drugs. Of course, matters might well be clarified in this case if and when the police officer is offered at a new trial an opportunity to explain the grounds, if any, that he had for doing what he did. But if the police officer does not then disclose additional grounds for his behaviour, the evidence must be excluded.

MCINTYRE J. (dissenting):

I have had the advantage of reading the reasons for judgment prepared in this appeal by my colleague, Justice Lamer. I accept and adopt his statement of facts. I accept as well his statement of the question for decision, that is, was the search conducted by the police officer unreasonable and, if so, having regard to all the circumstances, would the admission of the evidence bring the administration of justice into disrepute? I am unable, however, with deference to my colleague's views, to reach the same conclusion.

For the purposes of this appeal, I will accept with some hesitation the finding of the trial judge that the search was unreasonable. It then becomes necessary to decide whether the evidence obtained by the search should have been admitted or rejected under the provisions of s. 24(2) of the *Canadian Charter of Rights and Freedoms*. In deciding this question, I am content to adopt the judgment of Seaton J.A., in the Court of Appeal in the case at bar, now reported in (1983), 5 C.C.C. (3d) 141. In my view, he has correctly stated the principles upon which this issue must be decided. I would accordingly, adopt his result and dismiss the appeal.

With the exception of his conclusion, there is little, if anything, inconsistent in the judgment of Seaton J.A., with what my colleague, Lamer J., has said up to the point where he discusses his approach to the question of how a court should determine, in accordance with s. 24(2) of the *Charter*, whether the admission of evidence would bring the administration of justice into disrepute. It is with respect to that aspect of my colleague's judgment that a divergence in our views appears. With the very greatest deference to my colleague, I would not approve of a test so formulated. I would prefer the less formulated approach of Seaton J.A., who said at p. 151:

> Disrepute in whose eyes? That which would bring the administration of justice into disrepute in the eyes of a policeman might be the precise action that would be highly regarded in the eyes of a law teacher. I do not think that we are to look at this matter through the eyes of a

policeman or a law teacher, or a judge for that matter. I think that it is the community at large, including the policeman and the law teacher and the judge, through whose eyes we are to see this question. It follows, and I do not think this is a disadvantage of the suggestion, that there will be a gradual shifting. I expect that there will be a trend away from admission of improperly obtained evidence.

I do not suggest that the courts would respond to public clamour or opinion polls. I do suggest that the views of the community at large, developed by concerned and thinking citizens, ought to guide the courts when they are questioning whether or not the admission of evidence would bring the administration of justice into disrepute.

In this, I take it that Seaton J.A., in deciding the question has adopted an approach similar to that of the reasonable man, so well known in the law of torts. This is by no means a perfect test, but one which has served well and which has, by its application over the generations, led to the development of a serviceable body of jurisprudence from which has emerged a set of rules generally consistent with what might be termed social attitudes. I would suggest that such an approach, developing rules and principles on a case-by-case basis, will produce an acceptable standard for the application of s.24 (2) of the *Charter* . . . .

I do not suggest that we should adopt the "community shock" test or that we should have recourse to public opinion polls and other devices for the sampling of public opinion. I do not suggest that we should seek to discover some theoretical concept of community views or standards on this question. I do suggest that we should adopt a method long employed in the common law courts and, by whatever name it may be called, apply the standard of the reasonable man . . . .

Applying this test to the case at bar, I am led to the conclusion that the administration of justice would not fall into disrepute by the admission of this evidence. This is not a case where the search revealed a concealed capsule or two of heroin, such as one might have for personal use. Here, the appellant, with heroin in her hand contained in a balloon, was found in a public bar among other people. In my view, the admission of this evidence on a trial for possession of narcotics for the purpose of trafficking would not—in the eyes of a reasonable man, dispassionate and fully apprised of the circumstance of the case—bring the administration of justice into disrepute.

Le Dain J. wrote a concurring opinion.

o

Application: Sections 32 and 52

32. (1) This Charter applies

   (a) to the Parliament and government of Canada in respect of all matters within the authority of Parliament including all matters relating to the Yukon and Northwest Territories; and *(b)* to the legislature and government of each province in respect of all matters within the authority of the legislature of each province . . . .

52. (1) The Constitution of Canada is the supreme law of Canada, and any law that is inconsistent with the provisions of the Constitution is, to the extent of the inconsistency, of no force or effect.

RETAIL, WHOLESALE AND DEPARTMENT STORE UNION v. DOLPHIN DELIVERY[◇]

The Retail, Wholesale and Department Store Union, Local 580, was on strike against Purolator Courier. The latter had an arrangement with Dolphin Delivery whereby Dolphin had made deliveries for Purolator that were in Dolphin's delivery area. When Purolator closed its operations during the strike, the union claimed that a new company, Supercourier, was a subterfuge for Purolator; it then advised Dolphin that it would be picketed if it carried out deliveries for Super-courier as it had for Purolator. Dolphin sought, and was granted, an injunction against the picketing. In the British Columbia Court of Appeal, the union claimed that the granting of the injunction was unconstitutional in that it denied the union freedom of expression. A majority there held that picketing was not a constitutionally protected right; the union appealed to the Supreme Court of Canada. After finding that picketing was protected under "freedom of expression" (s. 2(*b*)), the Court considered whether the *Charter* applied in this case.

MCINTYRE J. (for the Court):

DOES THE CHARTER APPLY TO THE COMMON LAW?

In my view, there can be no doubt that it does apply. Section 52(1) of the *Constitution Act, 1982* provides:

52.(1) The Constitution of Canada is the supreme law of Canada, and any law that is inconsistent with the provisions of the Constitution is, to the extent of the inconsistency, of no force or effect.	52.(1) La Constitution du Canada est la loi suprême du Canada; elle rend inopérantes les dispositions incompatibles de toute autre règle de droit.

The English text provides that "any law that is inconsistent with the provisions of the Constitution is, to the extent of the inconsistency, of no force or effect." If this language is not broad enough to include the common law, it should be observed as well that the French text adds strong support to this conclusion in its employment of the words "*elle rend inopérantes les dispositions incompatibles de tout autre règle de droit.*" (Emphasis added.) To adopt a construction of s. 52(1) which

---

would exclude from _Charter_ application the whole body of the common law which in great part governs the rights and obligations of the individuals in society, would be wholly unrealistic and contrary to the clear language employed in s. 52(1) of the Act.

DOES THE CHARTER APPLY TO PRIVATE LITIGATION?

This question involves consideration of whether or not an individual may found a cause of action or defence against another individual on the basis of a breach of a _Charter_ right. In other words, does the _Charter_ apply to private litigation divorced completely from any connection with Government? . . .

In my view, s. 32 of the _Charter_, specifically dealing with the question of _Charter_ application, is conclusive on this issue . . . .

Section 32(1) refers to the Parliament and Government of Canada and to the legislatures and governments of the Provinces in respect of all matters within their respective authorities. In this, it may be seen that Parliament and the Legislatures are treated as separate or specific branches of government, distinct from the executive branch of government, and therefore where the word "government" is used in s. 32 it refers not to government in its generic sense—meaning the whole of the governmental apparatus of the state—but to a branch of government. The word "government," following as it does the words "Parliament" and "Legislature," must then, it would seem, refer to the executive or administrative branch of government. This is the sense in which one generally speaks of the Government of Canada or of a province. I am of the opinion that the word "government" is used in s. 32 of the _Charter_ in the sense of the executive government of Canada and the Provinces. This is the sense in which the words "Government of Canada" are ordinarily employed in other sections of the _Constitution Act, 1867_. Sections 12, 16 and 132 all refer to the Parliament and the Government of Canada as separate entities. The words "Government of Canada," particularly where they follow a reference to the word "Parliament," almost always refer to the executive government.

It is my view that s. 32 of the _Charter_ specifies the actors to whom the _Charter_ will apply. They are the legislative, executive and administrative branches of government. It will apply to those branches of government whether or not their action is invoked in public or private litigation. It would seem that legislation is the only way in which a legislature may infringe a guaranteed right or freedom. Action by the executive or administrative branches of government will generally depend upon legislation, that is, statutory authority. Such action may also depend, however, on the common law, as in the case of the prerogative. To the extent that it relies on statutory authority which constitutes or results in an infringement of a guaranteed right or freedom, the _Charter_ will apply and it will be unconstitutional. The action will also be unconstitutional to the extent that it relies for authority or justification on a rule of the common law which constitutes or creates an infringement of a _Charter_ right or freedom. In this way the _Charter_ will apply to the common law, whether in public or private litigation. It will apply to the common law, however, only in so far as the common law is the basis of some governmental action which, it is alleged, infringes a guaranteed right or freedom.

The element of governmental intervention necessary to make the *Charter* applicable in an otherwise private action is difficult to define. We have concluded that the *Charter* applies to the common law but not between private parties. The problem here is that this is an action between private parties in which the appellant resists the common law claim of the respondent on the basis of a *Charter* infringement. The argument is made that the common law, which is itself subject to the *Charter*, creates the tort of civil conspiracy and that of inducing a breach of contract. The respondent has sued and has procured the injunction which has enjoined the picketing on the basis of the commission of these torts. The appellants say the injunction infringes their *Charter* right of freedom of expression under s. 2(*b*). Professor Hogg meets this problem when he suggests, at p. 677 of his text, after concluding that the *Charter* does not apply to private litigation, that:

> Private action is, however, a residual category from which it is necessary to subtract those kinds of action to which s. 32 does make the Charter applicable.

He added:

> The Charter will apply to any rule of the common law that specifically authorizes or directs an abridgement of a guaranteed right.

and he concluded by saying, at p. 678:

> The fact that a court order is governmental action means that the Charter will apply to a purely private arrangement, such as a contract or proprietary interest, but only to the extent that the Charter will preclude judicial enforcement of any arrangement in derogation of a guaranteed right.

Professor Hogg, at p. 678, rationalized his position in these words:

> In a sense, the common law authorizes any private action that is not prohibited by a positive rule of law. If the Charter applied to the common law in that attenuated sense, it would apply to all private activity. But it seems more reasonable to say that the common law offends the Charter only when it crystallizes into a rule that can be enforced by the courts. Then, if an enforcement order would infringe a Charter right, the Charter will apply to preclude the order, and, by necessary implication, to modify the common law rule.

I find the position thus adopted troublesome and, in my view, it should not be accepted as an approach to this problem. While in political science terms it is probably acceptable to treat the courts as one of the three fundamental branches of Government, that is, legislative, executive, and judicial, I cannot equate for the purposes of *Charter* application the order of a court with an element of governmental action. This is not to say that the courts are not bound by the *Charter*. The courts are, of course, bound by the *Charter* as they are bound by all law. It is their duty to apply the law, but in doing so they act as neutral arbiters, not as contending parties involved in a dispute. To regard a court order as an element of governmental intervention necessary to invoke the *Charter* would, it seems to me, widen the scope of *Charter* application to virtually all private litigation. All cases must end, if carried to completion, with an enforcement order and if the *Charter* precludes the making of the order, where a *Charter* right would be infringed, it would seem that all private litigation would be subject to the *Charter*. In my view, this approach will not provide the answer to the question. A more direct and a more precisely defined connection between the element of government action and the claim advanced must be present before the *Charter* applies.

An example of such a direct and close connection is to be found in *Re Blainey and Ontario Hockey Association* . . . . In that case, proceedings were brought against the hockey association in the Supreme Court of Ontario on behalf of a twelve year old girl who had been refused permission to play hockey as a member of a boys' team competing under the auspices of the Association. A complaint against the exclusion of the girl on the basis of her sex alone had been made under the provisions of the *Human Rights Code, 1981,* S.O. 1981, c. 53, to the Ontario Human Rights Commission. It was argued that the hockey association provided a service ordinarily available to members of the public without discrimination because of sex, and therefore that the discrimination against the girl contravened this legislation. The Commission considered that it could not act in the matter because of the provisions of s. 19(2) of the *Human Rights Code,* which are set out hereunder:

> 19.—(1) . . .
>
> (2) The right under section 1 to equal treatment with respect to services and facilities is not infringed where membership in an athletic organization or participation in an athletic activity is restricted to persons of the same sex.

In the Supreme Court of Ontario it was claimed that s. 19(2) of the *Human Rights Code* was contrary to s. 15(1) of the *Charter* and that it was accordingly void. The application was dismissed. In the Court of Appeal, the appeal was allowed (Dubin, Morden JJ.A., Finlayson J.A. dissenting). Dubin J.A., writing for the majority, stated the issue in these terms at [D.L.R., p. 735]:

> Indeed, it was on the premise that the ruling of the Ontario Human Rights Commission was correct that these proceedings were launched and which afforded the status to the applicant to complain now that, by reason of s. 19(2) of the *Human Rights Code* she is being denied the equal protection and equal benefit of the *Human Rights Code* by reason of her sex, contrary to provisions of s. 15(1) of the *Canadian Charter of Rights and Freedoms* (the "Charter").

He concluded that the provisions of s. 19(2) were in contradiction of the *Charter* and hence of no force or effect. In the *Blainey* case, a law suit between private parties, the *Charter* was applied because one of the parties acted on the authority of a statute, i.e., s. 19(2) of the Ontario *Human Rights Code* which infringes the *Charter* rights of another. *Blainey* then affords an illustration of the manner in which *Charter* rights of private individuals may be enforced and protected by the courts, that is, by measuring legislation—government action—against the *Charter*.

As has been noted above, it is difficult and probably dangerous to attempt to define with narrow precision that element of governmental intervention which will suffice to permit reliance on the *Charter* by private litigants in private litigation. Professor Hogg has dealt with this question . . . where he said:

> . . . the Charter would apply to a private person exercising the power of arrest that is granted to "any one" by the Criminal Code, and to a private railway company exercising the power to make by-laws (and impose penalties for their breach) that is granted to a "railway company" by the Railway Act; all action taken in exercise of a statutory power is covered by the Charter by virtue of the references to "Parliament" and "legislature" in s. 32. The Charter would also apply to the action of a commercial corporation that was an agent of the Crown, by virtue of the reference to "government" in s. 32.

It would also seem that the *Charter* would apply to many forms of delegated legislation, regulations, orders in council, possibly municipal by-laws, and by-laws and regulations of other creatures of Parliament and the Legislatures. It is not suggested that this list is exhaustive. Where such exercise of, or reliance upon, governmental action is present and where one private party invokes or relies upon it to produce an infringement of the *Charter* rights of another, the *Charter* will be applicable. Where, however, private party "A" sues private party "B" relying on the common law and where no act of government is relied upon to support the action, the *Charter* will not apply. I should make it clear, however, that this is a distinct issue from the question whether the judiciary ought to apply and develop the principles of the common law in a manner consistent with the fundamental values enshrined in the Constitution. The answer to this question must be in the affirmative. In this sense, then, the *Charter* is far from irrelevant to private litigants whose disputes fall to be decided at common law. But this is different from the proposition that one private party owes a constitutional duty to another, which proposition underlies the purported assertion of *Charter* causes of action or *Charter* defences between individuals.

Can it be said in the case at bar that the required element of government intervention or intrusion may be found? In *Blainey*, s. 19(2) of the Ontario *Human Rights Code*, an Act of a legislature, was the factor which removed the case from the private sphere. If in our case one could point to a statutory provision specifically outlawing secondary picketing of the nature contemplated by the appellants, the case—assuming for the moment an infringement of the *Charter*—would be on all fours with *Blainey* and, subject to s. 1 of the *Charter*, the statutory provision could be struck down. In neither case, would it be, as Professor Hogg would have it, the order of a court which would remove the case from the private sphere. It would be the result of one party's reliance on a statutory provision violative of the *Charter*.

In the case at bar, however, we have no offending statute. We have a rule of the common law which renders secondary picketing tortious and subject to injunctive restraint, on the basis that it induces a breach of contract. While, as we have found, the *Charter* applies to the common law, we do not have in this litigation between purely private parties any exercise of or reliance upon governmental action which would invoke the *Charter*. It follows then that the appeal must fail. The appeal is dismissed . . . .

o

THE RHETORIC OF RIGHTS: THE SUPREME COURT AND THE CHARTER[◊]

MARC GOLD

᠈

The Supreme Court of Canada's initial interpretations of the *Canadian Charter of Rights and Freedoms*[1] were as broad and liberal as could possibly have been expected. Invoking the metaphor of the constitution as a living tree and dismissing concerns about the legitimacy of its expanded role, the Court upheld the Charter arguments in the majority of the cases it decided during this first period.[2] Even in those cases where the claim was denied, the Court made it clear that the Charter was to be taken very seriously.[3] No one could mistake the Court's message: the Charter was to be liberally interpreted and enthusiastically applied.

This paper examines the rhetoric used by the Supreme Court of Canada in its first applications of the Charter. Part one reviews the basic principles of the rhetorical analysis of law and sets out the context within which the rhetoric of the Court must be situated. Part two examines various ways in which the Court attempts to legitimate the broad role it has assumed under the Charter, while Part three analyses the rhetoric of the Court used to justify particular case results. I conclude with some brief observations on the judicial activism of the Court as manifested in these early cases, and I comment on the direction that future work on Charter rhetoric should take.

THE RHETORICAL CONTEXT

RHETORICAL ANALYSIS OF LAW

The study of rhetoric currently enjoys a Renaissance in a variety of disciplines.[4] No longer pejoratively considered to be ornamental and usually misleading speech, rhetoric is now understood to be an indispensible and inescapable tool of practical

◊ *Osgoode Hall Law Journal* 25, 2 (1987): 375–410.

reason in all domains of human activity. Indeed, there is a growing literature on law and rhetoric that offers the interested reader a number of useful case studies and introductions to rhetorical analysis as applied to law.[5] This obviates the need for more than a few words of introduction to this way of looking at the law.

There are two related foci of rhetorical analysis. The first is based upon the Aristotelian definition of rhetoric as the faculty of discovering the available means of persuasion in a given case.[6] Rhetorical analysis thus conceived involves the analysis of the means used to persuade the audience that the result in a given case or set of cases was justified. The second dimension to rhetorical analysis is based upon a conception of rhetoric as the way in which we constitute ourselves as a community through language.[7] Understood in this way, a rhetorical analysis of Charter cases would concentrate on the political visions expressed by these judgments.

This paper pursues both aspects of rhetorical analysis, but for reasons more practical than theoretical, it concentrates more on the means of persuasion than on the political visions articulated by the Court. Because this study examines only a very limited set of cases, any evaluation of the Court's overall political vision risks being incomplete and ultimately misleading. For example, although it will be suggested later that the Court projects a highly individualistic image of Canadian society in its initial opinions, it would seem premature to conclude that this image will persist without qualification as the Court proceeds through its docket. A complete and balanced analysis of this dimension of the court's rhetoric must therefore be based upon a larger set of cases decided over a longer period of time, and must await another occasion.

To understand the rhetoric of the Court, one must examine what Lloyd Bitzer has called "the rhetorical situation," that is, the concrete situation confronting the Court, the audiences to whom the court's opinions are directed, and the constraints imposed on the Court by the expectations of those audiences.[8] The following section addresses the audiences of the Court and the expectations they had regarding the Charter's interpretation.

THE AUDIENCES AND THEIR EXPECTATIONS

The Supreme Court has a variety of audiences to whom its opinions may be directed: the parties to the case, Parliament, legislatures and other governmental institutions, the bench, the bar, the academic community, the public, and the media.[9] When the Court first embarked upon its interpretations of the Charter, it is striking that there appeared to be a consensus amongst the various audiences that the Charter ought to be interpreted in a liberal and activist fashion. At the same time, there was an expectation that the Court would decide the cases in a judicial, and not political manner. These two expectations significantly influenced the rhetoric of the Court.

There can be little doubt that a large number of groups both wanted and expected the Court to give a large and liberal interpretation to the Charter. The public favoured the entrenchment of the Charter, influenced in this respect by the large-scale advertising program initiated by the federal government to promote its virtues. Presented as a way in which the citizen would be protected from the abuses of government, the idea of the Charter was popular amongst Canadians.

At the same time, there was no substantial or sustained debate on the merits of entrenching the Charter and the increase in judicial power that would accompany it. At the political level, the three federal parties supported the idea of entrenchment notwithstanding the opposition of the Conservatives and some New Democrats to the unilateralism of the process. At the provincial level, it was the process that dominated the debate.[10] A number of provincial premiers, notably Premiers Lyon of Manitoba and Blakeney of Saskatchewan, expressed their opposition to the idea of an entrenched Charter, but they proved unable to influence the debate significantly. By ridiculing them as politicians representing narrow and parochial interests, who were prepared to trade individual rights for fish, Prime Minister Trudeau and his colleagues succeeded in delegitimating their principled arguments against the Charter. As a result, the public bought the idea of entrenchment without worrying very much about the question of the enhanced powers of the courts.

As for the expectations of the academic community, most commentators desired to see the Court play an activist role in interpreting the Charter.[11] In this regard, it is impossible to overstate the influence of the *Canadian Bill of Rights*[12] on both the Court and the academic community. It was generally agreed that the Court had failed miserably in its application of the Bill of Rights, and the main thrust of most commentary was to encourage the Court to take a more active and liberal role in the protection of rights. Similarly, most of the academic writing on the Charter supported a broad role for the Court.[13] In any event, most commentators assumed that the fact of entrenchment, reinforced by the provisions of sections 24 and 52, would incline the Supreme Court to take a broader view of the Charter than it had of the Bill of Rights.[14] There was thus an appearance of consensus on how the Court would and should approach the interpretation of the Charter.

Also worth underlining was the role played by the various individuals and groups who testified before the Special Joint Committee of the House of Commons and Senate. Those who favoured both the idea of entrenchment and an expanded role for the courts had the largest influence on the final drafting of the Charter.[15] Not only did these "pro-Charter" groups influence the Charter's final text, they also influenced the general political climate surrounding it. It was thus possible to believe that the issues surrounding the Charter had been completely mooted and that a social consensus had crystallized around the idea of an expanded role for the courts.

This appearance of a consensus would not have influenced the Supreme Court were it not compatible with its own view of itself as an institution. For some time, however, the Court has seen itself as an increasingly important actor on the political scene.[16] Combined with the expectations of its various audiences, this self-image rendered the idea of an activist and liberal court in Charter matters virtually irresistible.

Also important was the particular judicial context in which the Supreme Court delivered its initial decisions. The Charter had been interpreted by lower courts for some years before the Supreme Court released its own first opinion, and radically different positions had been taken by various courts on virtually every issue that could arise.[17] More specifically, the courts were divided on the question of the extent to which the entrenchment of the Charter had altered the basic principles of Canadian constitutional law. Accordingly, one of the initial tasks of the Supreme Court was to provide guidance to both bench and bar regarding the basic perspective that should be taken in Charter argument and interpretation. The Court clearly believed that the text and history of the Charter required that it be interpreted generously, and that that message had to be conveyed clearly and unambiguously to both bench and bar.

Nevertheless, there existed an important constraint on the ability of the Court to apply the Charter liberally, a constraint flowing from both the expectations of the Court's audiences and the self-image of the Court itself. Simply put, it was expected that the Court would interpret the Charter in a non-political, judicial manner. Accordingly, it was important for the Court to find ways to interpret the Charter generously without putting into question the legitimacy of its role as an adjudicative body. Before considering such matters, however, it is necessary to say a few words about constitutional interpretation in order to provide a benchmark against which the Court's rhetoric may be evaluated.

CONSTITUTIONAL INTERPRETATION

There is a vast literature on the subject of constitutional interpretation, and I do not intend to summarise it (were that possible) or offer any prescriptions about how the Charter ought to be interpreted.[18] Instead, I wish only to describe what necessarily takes place when a text like the Charter is being interpreted.

Let me begin rather dogmatically. The meaning of the Charter is exclusively a function of its interpretation. There is no sense in which the meaning inheres intrinsically in the words of the text, in the minds of the drafters, or anywhere else for that matter, in a manner that is independent from the interpretive process.[19] Accordingly, the judges are responsible for the meaning given to the rights and freedoms set out in the Charter, however much they may tie their interpretations to the views of others. Moreover, the meaning to be given to a particular phrase or text will vary with the interpreter's conception of both the nature of the text and the purposes to be served by its interpretation.

This general view of the relationship between meaning and interpretation is consistent with the way in which the Supreme Court has treated its earlier decisions under the Bill of Rights when interpreting analogous clauses of the Charter. For example, the Court has refused to follow the definition of freedom of religion it had previously adopted under the Bill of Rights, arguing that the narrow interpretation it gave to the Bill of Rights was a function of the Court's view of its non-constitutional nature.[20] Thus the Court recognizes that the meaning of a text is a function of the relationship between the text and the interpreter, not something that inheres naturally in the text, and that in the process of interpretation one is inevitably influenced by one's view of that text's nature and status.

It is also the case that the materials that judges bring to bear on their interpretation of the Charter necessarily go beyond strictly legal considerations. The very act of understanding engages the personal values, experience, and prejudices of the interpreter.[21] We simply cannot understand anything without relying upon our accumulated stock of knowledge, much of which is tacit rather than explicit. It follows that no judge can ever be aware of all of the forces influencing the interpretations given to the Charter, much less set them out on paper. In this respect, written reasons for judgment are necessarily incomplete.

In giving meaning to the Charter the Court works with a relatively discrete set of argumentative conventions, by which I mean forms of argument through which the interpretation of the Charter is effected. As has been discussed elsewhere, one can identify six basic kinds of arguments in our constitutional jurisprudence: textual, historical, structural, doctrinal, prudential, and ethical.[22] Although all are legitimate in the sense that they can all claim some plausible link with certain features of the Charter, no one form of argument can claim an *a priori* superiority over the others. What can be said, however, is that different forms of argument suggest different images of the Court as consitutional interpreter. For example, arguments based upon the text of the Charter, its history, or on judicial precedents tend to suggest an image of interpretation that minimizes, if not obscures, the creative role of the Court in giving the Charter meaning. On the other hand, the remaining forms of argument more clearly implicate the Court's responsibility for the interpretations rendered.[23]

Just as there are a number of argumentative conventions available to a Court, so too are there a number of different functions that a Court performs in reviewing the constitutionality of legislation. They include the functions of policing the boundaries of governmental power set out in the constitution, legitimating the exercise of such power within its limits, "cueing" other institutions of government, and expressing through its opinions its conception of the basic values underlying Canadian society.[24] These functions appear to flow inevitably from the role assumed by the Supreme Court in our constitutional system.

None of this is meant to suggest that the interpretation of the Charter is necessarily subjective or arbitrary, or that the text exercises no influence on the interpreter. Indeed, to put it in such terms implies that there is some "objective" way to interpret a text that could somehow escape the influence of these factors. Such is not the case.[25] What is important is the rhetorical force of appeals to objectivity in interpretation, because the legitimacy of the judicial role depends to no small extent on the perception that the judiciary is applying rules and principles of the law, rather than deciding cases based on personal political preferences. Thus we can distinguish between different styles of opinion writing and different images projected by the Court as an institution.

The more traditional style can be termed formalistic in the sense that decisions are portrayed as following from the impartial application of pre-existing rules. The image of the Court implied by this style is that of a neutral, reactive institution. It engages what Abram Chayes has called the classical image of adjudication.[26] The competing style portrays adjudication not as a matter of applying rules, but as a matter of balancing competing interests: the Court appears actively and personally involved in the resolution of the issues, and does not pretend simply to apply the will of others in resolving the case. Chayes has termed this the public law image of adjudication and one could also call it a political image of adjudication.[27]

These admittedly rough distinctions between judicial styles will prove useful in evaluating the Court's rhetoric. To legitimate judicial review under the Charter, the Court tended to invoke the rhetoric of the classical image, thereby avoiding the appearance that the Court itself was playing a major political role. In this way the Court responded to the central expectations of its audiences: that it interpret the Charter generously without moving from the judicial arena to the political.

THE RHETORIC OF LEGITIMACY

ESTABLISHING THE LEGITIMACY OF JUDICIAL REVIEW

As important as it was for the Court to set out the basic principles of Charter interpretation in the early cases, it was equally important for the Court to establish the legitimacy of the broad interpretive role it had chosen for itself. To this end, the Court invoked a series of arguments based upon the text and history of the Charter, the main thrust of which were to show that the Court had no choice but to assume the role imposed upon it.

The Court's reliance upon the provisions of section 24 of the Charter and section 52 of the *Constitution Act, 1982* to justify judicial review under the Charter was predictable and appropriate. Entrenchment of the Charter, reflected in section 52, was the principal reason cited by the academic commentators in defence of a broad role for the courts, and section 24 makes it clear that the courts possess a broad remedial authority with regard to Charter breaches. Nevertheless, it is illuminating that the Court chose to rely upon textual arguments to support its new role. By so doing, the Court appears to have exercised no choice in the matter, and to have acted simply as the constitutional text dictated.

In this respect, consider how the Court used these textual arguments to reject any limitations to the exercise of its mandate for judicial review. For example, in *Operation Dismantle*, counsel for the federal government argued that the issues raised were inherently non-justiciable and were outside the ambit of judicial review by virtue of their political nature. Madame Justice Wilson relied upon section 24 of the Charter not only to reject these arguments, but to reject as inappropriate the notion that doctrines of non-justiciability and "political questions" ought to be part of the jurisprudence of the Charter. Characterising the issue as whether or not the government's defence policy violates section 7 of the Charter, she wrote:

> I do not think there can be any doubt that this is a question for the courts. Indeed, s.24(1) of the *Charter*...makes it clear that the adjudication of that question is the responsibility of "a court of competent jurisdiction." While the court is entitled to grant such remedy as it "considers appropriate and just in the circumstances," I do not think it is open to it to relinquish its jurisdiction either on the basis that the issue is inherently non-justiciable or that it raises a so-called "political question"....[28]

By invoking the text of the Charter, Madame Justice Wilson secured a large role for the courts without appearing in any way responsible for the assumption of that role. It was the Charter itself, we are told, that obliged the Court to respond to the questions posed in the case.[29]

Historical arguments also figured prominently in the early cases. For example, in *Reference Re Section 94(2) of the Motor Vehicle Act (B.C.)*, Mr. Justice Lamer justified a broad interpretation of section 7 by drawing a parallel between judicial review under the Charter and judicial review of the division of legislative powers in the Constitution: "[i]t is the scope of constitutional adjudication which has been altered rather than its nature, at least, as regards the right to consider the content of legislation."[30] By establishing a continuity between its role before and after entrenchment, the Court attempted to legitimate judicial review under the Charter by minimizing its novelty.

In any event, the Court tells us, it had no choice but to assume the role thrust upon it. As Mr. Justice Lamer wrote:

> It ought not to be forgotten that the historic decision to entrench the *Charter* in our Constitution was taken not by the courts but by the elected representatives of the people of Canada. It was those representatives who extended the scope of constitutional adjudication and entrusted the courts with this new and onerous responsibility. Adjudication under the *Charter* must be approached free of any lingering doubts as to its legitimacy.[31]

It is true, of course, that the "historic decision" was taken by elected officials and not by the Court. At the same time, one should not forget the important role played by the Court in the patriation process, a role that legitimated the entrenchment of the Charter itself.[32] Just as textual argument can obscure the Court's responsibility for the result reached, this historical argument avoids reference to the Court's pre-entrenchment role.

The rhetorical significance of all these arguments is two-fold. First, the Court uses those forms of argument that place the responsibility for the Court's expanded role on others, and portrays itself as merely responding to the will of others. Although this positivist image contrasts sharply with what the Court actually has done in the exercise of judicial review, it does function to legitimate the Court's role in the eyes of its audiences, notably those in the legal community.

Second, the Court's concern with removing any doubts about the legitimacy of its role is telling. This goal was pursued in a number of additional ways. One recurring technique was to invoke a distinction between proper and improper approaches to constitutional interpretation in order to reassure its audiences that the Court was following the proper and legitimate approach. This is the subject of the following section.

"COURTS DO NOT QUESTION THE WISDOM OF LEGISLATION."[33]

In virtually all of its decisions, the Court insisted on the distinction between assessing the constitutionality and questioning the wisdom of legislation. Indeed, this is invoked in the first paragraph of the first case decided by the Court under the Charter.[34]

This distinction cannot be maintained in any strong sense with regard to Charter interpretation. To the extent that the distinction implies only that a judge does not decide a case explicitly on the basis of his or her personal preferences, it is possible to believe that judges can and do honour it. It seems to me, however, that the Court invokes this distinction in a stronger and more controversial sense than this. The core idea appears to be that there is something intrinsically different about judging the wisdom of legislation and assessing its constitutionality so that the former role is entrusted to the political branches of government while the latter is ultimately a matter for the courts.[35] The maintenance of this distinction is necessary in order to legitimate the Court's role.

Consider the opinion of Mr. Justice Lamer in *Reference Re Section 94(2) of the Motor Vehicle Act (B.C.)*, where the absolute liability provisions of the *Motor Vehicle Act*[36] were held to violate section 7 of the Charter and were not justified under section 1 as being necessary to keep bad drivers off the road. Having invoked the distinction between the constitutionality and wisdom of legislation at least four times in the course of his reasons for judgment, Mr. Justice Lamer wrote:

> I do not take issue with the fact that it is highly desirable the "bad drivers" be kept off the road. I do not take issue either with the desirability of punishing severely bad drivers who are in contempt of prohibitions against driving. The bottom line of the question to be addressed here is: whether the Government of British Columbia has demonstrated as justifiable that the risk of imprisonment of a few innocent is, given the desirability of ridding the roads of British Columbia of bad drivers, a reasonable limit in a free and democratic society. That result is to be measured against the offence being one of strict liability open to a defence of due diligence, the success of which does nothing more than let those few who did nothing wrong remain free.[37]

One might be tempted to argue that Mr. Justice Lamer was not questioning the wisdom of the legislation inasmuch as he accepted the objectives underlying it and only questioned the means chosen by which to realise them. Nonetheless, by drawing the comparison between absolute and strict liability, he is saying that it was unwise to have opted for a regime of absolute liability in this case. If this is so, wherein lies the distinction between the wisdom and the constitutionality of legislation?

Simply put, the distinction cannot be maintained in the face of section 1 of the Charter. According to the Chief Justice in *R. v. Oakes*, section 1 addresses both the objectives of legislation and the means used to achieve those objectives. Regarding the former, the objective must relate to "concerns which are pressing and substantial in a free and democratic society before it can be characterised as sufficiently important."[38] But how can a court decide that an objective is sufficiently important without putting into question the wisdom of the legislation itself? It seems obvious that the wisdom of legislation is a function, in part, of what it tries to accomplish. For a court to weigh this on its scale is to question its wisdom.

Even if one takes the rather dubious position that the wisdom of legislation is exclusively a function of the legislative means chosen, and not of the ends pursued, the result is the same. According to *Oakes*, the test to be applied with regard to the legislative means is one of proportionality: "in each case courts will be required to balance the interests of society with those of individuals and groups."[39] More specifically, there must be a rational connection between means and ends, the legislation must not impose upon constitutional rights to a greater extent than is necessary to achieve the objective pursued, and one must balance the importance of the governmental objective against the importance and degree of violation of the constitutional right at issue.[40]

How can it be said that this does not involve the Court in questioning the wisdom of legislation? When legislators consider the enactment of a given law, they ask themselves whether the ends to be realised by the law are justified by the costs entailed by the legislation. Responsible legislators consider the impact on rights as one such cost in their evaluation of the wisdom of their legislation; the fact that legislation has been passed is evidence that the legislators believed that the benefits outweighed the costs and that the balance of interests struck in the legislation was justified. Is that not what we mean when we talk of the wisdom of a law? And yet, this is precisely what is entailed in the application of the proportionality test under section 1.

Lest this be misunderstood, I am not suggesting that the Court is aware that it is invoking a distinction that is impossible to maintain. On the contrary, I have no doubt that the Court sincerely believes that it can exercise judicial review under the Charter without questioning the wisdom of legislation. Nevertheless, the Court's good faith cannot transform an illusory distinction into a real one.

What is real, of course, is the rhetorical function of invoking the distinction. By drawing a line between permissible and impermissible approaches to constitutional interpretation, the Court reassures its audiences (and itself) that it is acting judicially and not politically. As suggested earlier, it is the legitimacy of judicial review itself that is ultimately at stake. Unless the role of the judge can be distinguished from that of legislator, the power of the courts under the Charter cannot easily be justified in a democratic society.

LIMITING THE APPEARANCE OF BALANCING INTERESTS

To the extent that a court appears to be deciding cases by defining legal rights and applying legal rules, it acts consistently with the traditional image of adjudication. In the eyes of much of the legal community, this rather formalistic style needs no elaborate defence—it is itself a legitimating ideal of adjudication. Where a court appears to be engaged in a process of openly balancing competing interests, however, the image of adjudication becomes much more political and, amongst many, more controversial.[41] The purpose of this section is to show how the Court depoliticised its early interpretations of the Charter by limiting the extent to which it had to balance interests openly.

The most striking example is provided by the Court's opinion in *Quebec Association of Protestant School Boards v. A.G. Quebec (No. 2)*. Having set out the conflicts between the provisions of Quebec's *Charter of the French Language*[42] (Bill 101) and section 23 of the Charter, the Court held that it was unnecessary to consider any of the arguments submitted by Quebec under section 1. The Court reasoned that the drafters of the Charter clearly had Quebec's legislation in mind when they drafted section 23, thereby intending to limit the scope of Quebec's language legislation as it related to the language of instruction in schools. Accordingly, the drafters could not have contemplated that section 1 could save the legislation.[43]

For a Court determined to give a liberal interpretation to the Charter while maintaining its image as a judicial and non-political body, the avoidance of any analysis of section 1 in this case was a brilliant stroke of rhetorical strategy. If one recalls the lengthy reasons for judgment written by Chief Justice Deschênes of the Superior Court of Quebec in that case, one can appreciate why the Supreme Court was eager to avoid a similar analysis.[44] Simply put, to have entered into a section 1 analysis would have required the Court to pass judgment on the conflicting evidence concerning demographic trends in the province, and more to the point, on the importance of promoting French in Quebec as compared with the burden on minority language rights imposed by Bill 101. To observe that these are matters of intense political importance in Quebec understates the obvious: no other issue is as potentially explosive as language. In my view, the Court did not want to be seen as responsible for a decision adverse to the government of Quebec.[45] Far better to have a judgment—and an anonymous one at that—that allowed the Court to say as little as possible, and which placed the responsibility for the decision squarely on the drafters of the Charter and not on the Court.

There are other examples, albeit less highly charged, where the Court limited the circumstances under which it will be forced, in future, to balance interests openly. For example, in *Re Singh and Minister of Employment and Immigration*, Madame Justice Wilson held that the lack of an oral hearing for the adjudication of refugee claims under the *Immigration Act, 1976*[46] violated section 7 of the Charter. The government argued, *inter alia*, that the procedures were justified under section 1, given that the Immigration Appeal Board had too many cases and too few resources to be able to accord an oral hearing in each case. Rejecting this argument, Madame Justice Wilson expressed her doubts that such "utilitarian consideration[s]" could support the limitation of constitutional rights under section 1.[47] By dismissing arguments of this kind as illegitimate, Madame Justice Wilson avoided having to weigh the competing interests in the case.

The opinions of Madame Justice Wilson provide an example of another way in which the need to balance interests overtly is minimized. For example, in both *Operation Dismantle* and the *Reference Re Section 94(2) of the Motor Vehicle Act (B.C.)*, Madame Justice Wilson defined the concept of liberty as set out in section 7 in non-absolute terms, thus recognizing limits to liberty without having to employ the rather political language of section 1.[48] To be sure, this general approach to the conception of rights and their limits has a very respectable philosophical pedigree.[49] Moreover, it may be that the very same considerations enter into the analysis regardless of whether one defines rights absolutely and limits them through section 1, or defines the rights more narrowly without reference to section 1. At the rhetorical level, however, there is a difference between the two approaches: the process of defining rights appears paradigmatically judicial, whereas balancing interests appears more political.

Consider finally the conception of legislative purpose as advanced by the Chief Justice in the *Big M Drug Mart* case. Having affirmed that legislative purpose is constitutionally relevant, the Chief Justice rejected the idea that the purpose might change over time.[50] To the extent that legislation can be struck down on the basis of an original legislative purpose found to contravene the Charter, as was the case in *Big M Drug Mart* itself, this tends to limit the need to balance interests overtly.

Moreover, the reasons given for rejecting the notion of a shifting legislative purpose illuminate the Court's rhetorical design:

> No legislation would be safe from a revised judicial assessment of purpose. Laws assumed valid on the basis of persuasive and powerful authority could, at any time, be struck down as invalid. Not only would this create uncertainty in the law, but it would encourage re-litigation of the same issues and, it could be argued, provide the courts with a means by which to arrive at a result dictated by other than legal considerations.[51]

By invoking the dangers of uncertainty and instability, the Chief Justice addresses the deep concerns of his audiences, notably the legal community.[52] Indeed, by raising the spectre of decisions "dictated by other than legal considerations," he suggests the distinction between permissible and impermissible approaches to constitutional interpretation—between judging the wisdom of legislation as opposed to its constitutionality. Although it is unclear why the "shifting purpose" approach raises this danger more in this than in any other case, the reference to the danger reassures the reader that the decision reached by the Court was based upon proper considerations.

INVOKING AND REJECTING THE INTENT OF THE DRAFTERS

The final matter to be considered here is the role played by the concept of the drafters' intentions. In the great majority of cases considered here, the Court appealed to an assumed drafters' intention to justify the interpretations given to the Charter. For example, in *A.G. Quebec v. Quebec Association of Protestant School Boards* the Court relied upon the drafters' intent to justify the avoidance of a section 1 analysis.[53] In other cases the Court invoked what might be termed a negative intention of the drafters in support of its Charter interpretation. For example, in *R. v. Therens*, Mr. Justice Le Dain justified his definition of the term "detention" in section 10 by observing that it was unreasonable to assume that the drafters intended that the term be defined in the same way as it had been by the courts under the Bill of Rights.[54] Similarly, in *Reference Re Section 94(2) of the Motor Vehicle Act (B.C.)*, Mr. Justice Lamer invoked the intention of the drafters to reject an interpretation of section 7 that would have equated it with the principles of natural justice as understood in administrative law.

> It is, in my view, that precise and somewhat narrow meaning that the legislator avoided, clearly indicating thereby a will to give greater content to the words "principles of fundamental justice," the limits of which were left for the courts to develop . . . .[55]

In light of all of these allusions, it is easy to conclude that the drafters' intentions were to govern the Court's interpretations of the Charter. Nothing, however, is quite so simple. Every time that the drafters' intentions were established through evidence, the Court refused to consider them.[56] The clearest example of this is also the most telling.

In *Reference Re Section 94(2) of the Motor Vehicle Act (B.C.)*, counsel for British Columbia provided evidence of the testimony of the Minister of Justice, the Deputy Minister, and the Assistant Deputy Minister, Public Law, before the Special Joint Committee on the Constitution, to the effect that section 7 was intended to refer to procedure only. Notwithstanding his reliance on the assumed intent of the drafters when rejecting the argument that would define section 7 in terms of natural justice, Mr. Justice Lamer ignored the submitted testimony by giving it virtually no probative value whatsoever.[57] As a result, section 7 was defined in terms much broader than appears to have been intended by those who drafted the clause, thereby increasing the range of circumstances in which it could be used to strike down legislation.

The rhetorical perspective provides the key to what would otherwise appear as a logical contradiction, for there is indeed a rhetorical logic to the way that the Court treats the question of the drafters' intent. The rejection of the evidence of the Minister and his colleagues was a response to the expectation that the Charter be interpreted liberally by the Court. After all, in a judicial world view dominated by the image of the living tree, there is little allure in the idea of tying constitutional interpretations to the original intent of the drafters. At the same time, rhetorical considerations explain why the reasons for judgment so regularly invoke the drafters' intentions to justify the interpretations given. This is not only a convention of style, but is rooted in our positivist legal culture.[58] By appealing to the intentions of others, the Court distances itself from responsibility for the interpretations actually given, thereby invoking a traditional and non-political image of itself—the Court is not making interpretive choices at all, but merely deferring to the will of others. At the level of rhetoric, who can say that the Court lacks finesse?

THE RHETORIC OF ACTIVISM

The preceding part suggested that the Court invoked the traditional image of itself as an adjudicative institution in order to legitimate its expanded role under the Charter. The Court had to do more, however, than merely convince its audiences of the legitimacy of judicial review in general. First, it had to persuade its audiences that its decisions in particular cases were correct and appropriate; second, it had to satisfy the pervasive expectation that the Charter would be an instrument used for the vigorous protection of individual rights. Beginning with the latter, the following sections consider some of the ways in which the Court pursued these objectives.

THE RHETORIC OF INDIVIDUALISM

Given both the expectations surrounding the Charter and the need to provide guidance to its audiences, the Court quickly set out to establish its preferred approach to Charter interpretation. Advancing the general principle that the Charter must be interpreted "purposively," both with respect to the nature of the interests underlying a particular section of the Charter and to the "character and the larger objects of the *Charter* itself,"[59] the Court made it clear that the Charter would not suffer the same fate as had the Bill of Rights.

Two complementary conceptions of the Charter underlie the Court's opinions in these early cases. The first is the image of the Charter as a living tree, and the second is the idea that the Charter was designed for "the unremitting protection of individual rights and liberties."[60] These two conceptions function rhetorically to support those readings of the Charter that favour and expand the protection of rights over those which would limit the scope of the rights protected. For example, in *Reference Re Section 94(2) of the Motor Vehicle Act (B.C.)*, Mr. Justice Lamer invoked the living tree metaphor to deny probative value to the statements of the government officials concerning the meaning of section 7,[61] and he reinforced his preferred interpretation with the argument that a broader reading of section 7 is to be preferred over a narrower one.[62] Similar considerations informed the opinion of Mr. Justice Le Dain in *Therens* where he rejected the definition of "detention" advanced by the Court under the Bill of Rights as inappropriately narrow for the Charter.[63] Indeed, even when Mr. Justice Beetz resuscitated the Bill of Rights in the *Singh* case, he justified it by observing that it would serve the "better protection of rights and freedoms."[64] The Court clearly has based its jurisprudence on the proposition that the interpretation that best promotes rights is the one to be preferred.[65]

Informing this jurisprudence is a highly individualistic, almost classical liberal vision of the Charter and of Canadian society. By classical liberalism I refer to a tradition of social thought that is constituted by a number of related ideas: the primacy of the individual over community and the State, the mistrust of if not hostility toward a broad role for government, and a general faith in judges and the Rule of Law as protection against the collectivist pretensions of modern democratic government.[66] All of these ideas can be found prominently in the cases.

The dominant tone in the judgments is highly individualistic. For example, in *Hunter v. Southam*, notwithstanding that it was a corporation which invoked the protection against unreasonable search or seizure as guaranteed by section 8 of the Charter, the reasons for judgment are dominated by references to individual rights to privacy and so on.[67] Similarly, in the *Big M Drug Mart* case, the Chief Justice wrote at length about respect for human dignity and the valuation of individual conscience, notwithstanding that it was a corporation that brought the action challenging the *Lord's Day Act*. Through the constant affirmation of the virtues and values of individual rights, the Court not only adds to the persuasive force of its opinions, it also encourages us to see ourselves as rights-holders, thereby transforming the language of political discourse in Canada.[68]

Consistent with the classical liberal tradition, the Court defines individual rights in opposition to the interests and claims of government. For example, freedom is defined as the absence of coercion or constraint, but it is government, typically, that is presented as the enemy of freedom.[69] Even the Court's conception of democracy is tied to notions of individual rights. As the Chief Justice wrote:

> It should also be noted, however, that an emphasis on individual conscience and individual judgment also lies at the heart of our democratic political tradition. The ability of each citizen to make free and informed decisions is the absolute prerequisite for the legitimacy, acceptability, and efficacy of our system of self-government.[70]

More generally, the opinions can be read as evidencing a general antipathy towards government. For example, to limit rights under section 1 the government must satisfy the very stringent test as set out in the *Oakes* case, including the requirement that the governmental objective relate to "concerns which are pressing and substantial in a free and democratic society before it can be characterised as sufficiently important."[71] Moreover, the Court offers a fairly individualistic interpretation in setting out the values and principles essential to a free and democratic society, the values said to govern the evaluation of government's submissions under section 1:

> ...respect for the inherent dignity of the human person, commitment to social justice and equality, accommodation of a wide variety of beliefs, respect for cultural and group identity, and faith in social and political institutions which enhance the participation of individuals and groups in society.[72]

Finally, the nature of the governmental interests at stake in the cases are rarely elaborated with the same precision or detail as are the individual interests affected. The best example may be found in *Hunter v. Southam*, where the Court characterised the government's interest in the *Combines Investigation Act* as "simply law enforcement."[73] In all of this we can see the suspicious attitude towards government that lies at the heart of classical liberal thought.

The individualistic thrust of the Court's rhetoric is reinforced by what appears to be a deontological conception of individual rights that appears in some of the cases.[74] For example, as noted earlier, Madame Justice Wilson appears to reject the idea that arguments of efficiency or administrative convenience can be invoked legitimately in order to limit rights set out in the Charter,[75] and in *Big M Drug Mart*, Chief Justice Dickson dismissed one of the government's submissions under section 1 as "no more than an argument of convenience and expediency."[76] Even when it is acknowledged that arguments of administrative convenience can possibly justify the limitation of rights, the circumstances are narrowly conceived. As Mr. Justice Lamer put it, such arguments could justify absolute liability offenses (in the face of section 7 of the Charter) "only in cases arising out of exceptional conditions, such as natural disasters, the outbreak of war, epidemics, and the like."[77]

Finally, consistent with the liberal faith in courts and mistrust of other governmental institutions, the decisions affirm the priority of the judicial world view. In *Hunter v. Southam* the Court insisted on a quasi-judicial regime for the authorization of searches under the *Combines Investigation Act*,[78] notwithstanding rather compelling arguments that this would impair the effectiveness of the legislation as enforced. Similarly, in the *Singh* case, the Court required that there be an open hearing for the redetermination of refugee claims, notwithstanding the burden that this imposed on the entire system. Are these not examples of the traditional antipathy of judges to administrative processes, informed by a sense that the judicial way is the best way?[79]

The Court's individualistic rhetoric is easily explained. The idea of a constitutional Bill of Rights limiting government is paradigmatically a liberal one, reflecting a vision of society in which the individual is central. Moreover, it is fair to say that most judges, by virtue of their professional training and experience, are rather comfortable with a liberal conception of the world and would find the basic premises of classical liberalism to be almost self-evident. Finally, generations of legal scholars have been pleading with the Court to take individual rights more seriously, and once the Court decided to apply the Charter generously, it had to communicate that message strongly and unequivocally to its various audiences. Whatever one's views on such matters, it should be acknowledged that the Court is doing essentially what we asked and apparently desired it to do.

Given the popular and professional understanding of the Charter as designed to protect individuals from the excesses of government, the Court's individualistic rhetoric performed a legitimating function for its activism in these early cases. The Court also deployed other rhetorical techniques in combination with the rhetoric of individualism to enhance the persuasiveness of its opinions in particular cases. These techniques are the subject of the following sections.

THE RHETORIC OF FACTS

It is a commonplace among experienced counsel that the manner in which one presents the facts of the case can be crucial to the success of one's cause. Experienced judges are no less sensitive to the rhetorical dimension of how the facts are presented, as is illustrated by the reasons for judgment in *Hunter v. Southam.*

The offices of the Edmonton *Journal* were the object of a search authorized under section 10 of the *Combines Investigation Act.*[80] Of the authorization for the search, Mr. Justice Dickson (as he then was) wrote:

> The authorization has a breath-taking sweep; it is tantamount to a licence to roam at large on the premises of Southam Inc. at the stated address "and elsewhere in Canada". . . .
>
> [The officials] declined to give the name of any person whose complaint had initiated the inquiry, or to say under which section of the Act the inquiry had been begun. They also declined to give more specific information as to the subject matter of the inquiry than that contained in the authorization to search.[81]

What do these passages mean? They cannot mean that it was the scope of the authorization or the behaviour of the officials that rendered the law unconstitutional, for Mr. Justice Dickson insisted otherwise:

> At the outset it is important to note that the issue in this appeal concerns the constitutional validity of a statute authorizing a search and seizure. It does not concern the reasonableness or otherwise of the manner in which the appellants carried out their statutory authority. It is not the conduct of the appellants, but rather the legislation under which they acted, to which attention must be directed.[82]

The rhetorical perspective provides the key to the meaning of these passages. The exposition of the facts suggest the dangers associated with administrative regimes and implies that a judicial process would not have produced such a sweeping authorization. Moreover, the description of the actions of the officials invites the reader to view the entire process in a bad light. Why did the officials fail to divulge the name of the complainant? Why did they fail to specify the section of the Act, or to provide "more specific information as to the subject matter of the inquiry than that contained in the authorization"? Let us leave aside any questions about their obligation to provide such information, for in the absence of any such obligation, they were only doing their job, however ungraciously. The rhetorical object was to describe the administrative process in as negative terms as possible, in order to persuade us that the Court was right to strike it down.

Another example is provided by *Big M Drug Mart* where the Court struck down those provisions of the *Lord's Day Act* [83] that prohibited commercial activity on Sunday. As in *Hunter v. Southam*, the particular facts of the case were irrelevant; it was the law itself that was impugned. Nevertheless, early in his opinion Chief Justice Dickson wrote that the police who were in the store on Sunday "witnessed several transactions including the sale of groceries, plastic cups and a bicycle lock."[84] Except to confirm the fact that the store was open on Sunday, these facts are beside the point. From the rhetorical perspective, however, the recitation of these facts suggest the banality of the law as it is applied. Imagine, for a moment, that the transactions did not involve the sale of some plastic cups, but rather the sale of pornographic magazines, or of some other material deemed offensive. Would the Court have been so quick to specify the nature of the transactions in such a case?[85]

THE RHETORIC OF CHARACTERISATION

Students of constitutional law quickly appreciate that the way in which a judge characterises legislation under review can determine whether it will be upheld or struck down.[86] To illustrate the rhetorical dimension of the characterisation of legislation, consider the opinion of Chief Justice Dickson in the *Big M Drug Mart* case.

At the beginning of his opinion the Chief Justice presents the *Lord's Day Act* in fairly neutral terms, as legislation prohibiting commercial activity on Sundays.[87] The tone begins to shift as a subsequent passage speaks of the "acknowledged purpose of the *Lord's Day Act* [as] the compulsion of sabbatical observance."[88] As the reasons develop, the characterisations become increasingly harsh, so that by the end of the opinion, the Act has been characterised in terms so exceptionally negative that one has no doubt that it must offend the Charter:

> To the extent that it binds all to a sectarian Christian ideal, the *Lord's Day Act* works a form of coercion inimical to the spirit of the *Charter* and the dignity of all non-Christians. In proclaiming the standards of the Christian faith, the Act creates a climate hostile to, and gives the appearance of discrimination against, non-Christian Canadians. It takes religious values rooted in Christian morality and, using the force of the state, translates them into a positive law binding on believers and non-believers alike ... The arm of the State requires all to remember the Lord's day of the Christians and to keep it holy. The protection of one religion and the concomitant non-protection of others imports disparate impact destructive of the religious freedom of the collectivity ....[89]

and

> ... [T]he true purpose of the *Lord's Day Act* is to compel the
> observance of the Christian Sabbath .... [90]

These characterisations are reinforced by the terms used to describe the Act.
For example, count the number of times the terms coercion, compulsion, and
constraint appear in the opinion. These terms have a negative connotation in our
language, so much so that they have been dubbed "vice words" by Professor
Western.[91] Given that the Court adopted a definition of freedom as the absence of
coercion or constraint, every invocation of such a negative term as "coercion" tends
to suggest that its opposite concept, freedom, is being infringed. This tends to
enhance the persuasiveness of the result.

Given all of this, the conclusion that the *Lord's Day Act* offends the freedom
of religion guaranteed by section 2 of the Charter seems unimpeachable. At the
same time, one might question the accuracy of the Chief Justice's latter descriptions
of the Act—that it requires one to keep the Christian Sabbath holy, and so on. In
fact, nothing in the law requires one to keep Sunday holy or otherwise to compel
the observance of the Sabbath. Nevertheless, from the rhetorical point of view,
however accurate or overstated one might judge these characterisations of the Act
to be, the way in which they are structured is most effective.

THE RHETORIC OF DENIGRATION

A successful judicial opinion persuades its readers that the arguments accepted by
the court were superior to those rejected. Typically this is achieved by arguments
directed specifically to the merits of the opposing positions, but judges sometimes
pursue the task of persuasion in less direct if not unconscious ways. This section
considers two techniques by means of which the force of the rejected arguments
can be blunted: the manner in which the issue is posed, and the manner in which
the losing party is portrayed.

Experienced trial counsel appreciate that the way one asks a question can have
a significant influence on the answer provided.[92] Judges know this too, as is
evidenced by Madame Justice Wilson's opinion concerning section 1 of the Charter
in *Singh*.

To justify the lack of a hearing before the Immigration Appeal Board as a
reasonable limit to the rights guaranteed by section 7, the government argued that
the Canadian procedures had been approved of by the office of the United Nations
High Commissioner for Refugees, that it was common in western countries to deal
with such matters administratively without hearings, and that the volume of cases
before the Immigration Appeal Board was so large that it was impossible to accord
a hearing in each case. In response, Madame Justice Wilson characterised the
question raised by section 1 in the following terms:

> The issue in the present case is not simply whether the procedures set
> out in the *Immigration Act, 1967* for the adjudication of refugee claims
> are reasonable; it is whether it is reasonable to deprive the appellants of
> the right to life, liberty and security of the person by adopting a system

for the adjudication of refugee status claims which does not accord with the principles of fundamental justice.[93]

At the semantic and doctrinal level, there does not appear to be any difference between the two ways of posing the question. Whether or not the procedure is reasonable is a function not only of the financial costs associated with holding hearings, but of the consequences to the individuals affected by the process. After all, the nature of the individual interests at stake is one of the relevant factors courts consider when determining the content of "natural justice" applicable in the circumstances.[94] If this is so, it would seem that both of the ways in which the question was posed by Madame Justice Wilson oblige us to consider the very same factors.

At the rhetorical level, however, there is a considerable difference between the two formulations. The first directs our attention towards the law and the governmental interests underlying it, while the second focusses our attention on the individuals who have been denied their rights. Moreover, the way Madame Justice Wilson states the issue implies that the decision to establish the impugned procedure was taken in full knowledge that it was contrary to the principles of fundamental justice, when it is just as plausible to assume that the drafters honestly believed that it was both reasonable and just to proceed administratively. By posing the question as she did, Madame Justice Wilson directs our attention to those features of the issue that support her ultimate conclusions.

Another technique of reinforcing one's own position is to denigrate the character or competence of those who advanced the opposing arguments. Consider the way that Chief Justice Dickson introduced the appellant's (ultimately unsuccessful) arguments in the *Operation Dismantle* case:

> As a preliminary matter, it should be noted that the exact nature of the deprivation of life and security of the person that the appellants rely upon as the legal foundation for the violation of s.7 they allege is not clear.[95]

Later in the opinion he writes:

> I believe that we are obliged to read the statement of claim as generously as possible and to accommodate any inadequacies in the form of the allegations which are merely the result of drafting deficiencies.[96]

The contrast between the implicit image of the appellants and that of the Court is striking. The appellants failed to argue their position clearly; the Court must make a considerable effort to understand their argument. Moreover, there was certainly a lack of clarity, if not error, in their pleadings. Can it not be said that this suggests a lack of professionalism on their part? In contrast, the Court presents itself as generous and accommodating, ready to go to whatever lengths necessary to understand the appellant's arguments. In this way we are encouraged to view those arguments as weak, and those of the Court as well founded.[97] Moreover, by putting the responsibility for losing on the appellant's counsel, the Court invokes the classical image of adjudication, thereby legitimating the decision and reinforcing its persuasiveness.

CONCLUSION

It remains only to conclude with three brief observations on the analysis presented here. The first concerns the benefits of taking a rhetorical perspective on the judicial opinion. It is not only that we gain insights into our legal culture by attending to the argumentative practices that make up that culture: a rhetorical analysis also can provide a perspective through which we can understand what would otherwise appear paradoxical or contradictory. For example, it has been said of the *Skapinker* decision that it "displays a curious disharmony in reasoning and approach" in that it combines broad statements of principle with an approach that is very text-bound.[98] From the rhetorical perspective, however, there is nothing at all curious about the blend of these two styles. The expansive rhetoric on the nature of constitutional interpretation that begins the opinion was a response to the audience's expectations that the Charter would be interpreted liberally, as well as a signal to bench, bar, and government that the Court was taking the Charter seriously. At the same time, given that the Court did not uphold the Charter argument in *Skapinker*, its text-bound rhetoric can be understood as a response to the expectation that decisions should be rendered in a judicial and non-political manner.

The second observation concerns the role of the Court as revealed in the cases analysed. As suggested earlier, the Court's activism can be understood in terms of the rhetorical situation facing the Court: it had to communicate its view of the Charter unequivocally and unambiguously to its various audiences. It will be appreciated, however, that cases subsequent to those analysed here reveal the Court to have moderated its position somewhat. The Court's cautious interpretations of the language rights guarantees,[99] the upholding of Ontario's Sunday closing legislation,[100] and the jurisdictional scope of the Charter[101] suggest a Court searching for a more balanced approach to its role than its activism in the early cases would have suggested. It may be that future analyses of the Court and the Charter will bracket these initial cases as but the first of many phases through which the Court will have passed.

This leads me to my final point, and it relates to the direction that future work of this kind should take. If the general thrust of this paper has been descriptive and explanatory, it is not to suggest that this exhausts the ways in which rhetorical analysis can or should be practiced. On the contrary, critical evaluation of the political visions expressed in the cases is of central importance to a comprehensive treatment of the Court's rhetoric. It bears repeating, however, that any such analysis should be based upon a representative sample of cases if it is not to be misleading and ultimately irrelevant. Moreover, the issues raised are complex and difficult, and any responsible treatment of them necessarily must be a lengthy one if it is to avoid facile labels and undefended premises.

In this respect, it would be relatively easy to mount a critique against the societal vision expressed in the initial cases, inasmuch as it appears vulnerable to all of the criticisms made against classical liberal theory.[102] To the extent that the Court tempers its individualistic liberalism with a recognition of the claims of government and community, however, a rhetorical analysis of the jurisprudence will engage a richer and more defensible version of the liberal vision.[103] Important as these matters are, my consideration of them must await another occasion.

NOTES

1. *Canadian Charter of Rights and Freedoms*, Part I of the *Constitution Act, 1982*, being Schedule B of the *Canada Act 1982* (U.K.), 1982, c.11, ss.1–34 (hereinafter the Charter).

2. The following cases are considered in this paper: *The Law Society of Upper Canada v. Skapinker* (1984), [1984] 1 S.C.R. 357, 11 C.C.R. (hereinafter *Skapinker*); *A.G. Quebec v. Quebec Association of Protestant School Boards* (1984), [1984] 2 S.C.R. 66, 10 D.L.R. (4th) 321; *Hunter v. Southam Inc.* (1984), [1984] 2 S.C.R. 145, 11 D.L.R. (4th) 641 (hereinafter *Hunter v. Southam*); *Re Singh and Minister of Employment and Immigration* (1985), [1985] 1 S.C.R. 177, 58 N.R. 1 (hereinafter *Singh*); *R. v. Big M Drug Mart Ltd.* (1985), [1985] 1 S.C.R. 295, 18 D.L.R. (4th) 321 hereinafter *Big M Drug Mart*); *Staranchuk v. R.* (1985), [1985] 1 S.C.R. 439, 22 D.L.R. (4th) 480; *Operation Dismantle Inc. v. R.* (1985), [1985] 1 S.C.R. 441, 18 D.L.R. (4th) 481 (hereinafter *Operation Dismantle*); *R.v. Therens* (1985), [1985] 1 S.C.R. 613, 18 D.L.R. (4th) 655; *Trask v. R.* (1985), [1985] 1 S.C.R. 655, 19 D.L.R. (4th) 123; *Rahn v. R.* (1985), [1985] 1 S.C.R. 659, 19 D.L.R. (4th) 126; *Krug v. R.* (1985), [1985] 2 S.C.R. 255, 21 D.L.R. (4th) 161; *Spencer v. R.* (1985), [1985] 2 S.C.R. 278, 21 D.L.R. (4th) 756; *Dubois v. R.* (1985), [1985] 2 S.C.R. 350, 23 D.L.R. (4th) 503; *Reference Re Section 94(2) of the Motor Vehicle Act (B.C.)* (1985), [1985] 2 S.C.R. 486, 24 D.L.R. (4th) 536; *Valente v. R.* (1985), [1985] 2 S.C.R. 673, 24 D.L.R. (4th) 161; and *R. v. Oakes* (1986), [1986] 1 S.C.R. 103, 26 D.L.R. (4th) 200 (hereinafter *Oakes*).

3. For example, although denying the Charter claim in *Skapinker*, the opinion of Mr. Justice Estey is replete with references to the need to interpret the Charter broadly. *Skapinker*, 365–67. Similarly, in *Operation Dismantle*, the Court affirmed the application of the Charter to exercises of the royal prerogative, and dismissed as inappropriate the limiting doctrines of non-justiciability and "political questions," all in the context of rejecting the Charter argument on its merits.

4. In philosophy, a rhetorical perspective underlies the work of Richard Rorty. See, for example, R. Rorty, *Philosophy and the Mirror of Nature* (Princeton: Princeton University Press, 1979); R. Rorty, "Epistemological Behaviourism and the De-Transcendentalization of Analytic Philosophy" in *Hermeneutics and Praxis*, ed. R. Hollinger (Notre Dame, Ind.: Notre Dame University Press, 1985), 89. Indeed, it has been observed that modern hermeneutics is predicated upon the theoretical tools of rhetoric. See Hans Georg Gadamer, "On the Scope and Function of Hermeneutical Reflection" in *Philosophical Hermeneutics*, ed. H.G. Gadamer, trans. D.E. Linge (Berkely: University of California Press, 1976), 18 at 24. Recently, rhetorical analysis has been applied to modern economic theory: see Donald N. McCloskey, *The Rhetoric of Economics* (Madison, Wis.: University of Wisconsin Press, 1985). For an examination of the role of rhetoric in the natural sciences, see Stephen Toulmin, "The Construal of Reality: Criticism in Modern and Postmodern Science," in *The Politics of Interpretation*, ed. W.J. Thomas

Mitchell (Chicago: University of Chicago Press, 1983), 99. See also S. Toulmin, *The Uses of Argument* (Cambridge, Eng.: Cambridge University Press, 1958).

5. For a variety of perspectives on the relationship of rhetoric to law see Chaim Perelman, *Logique juridique* 2d ed. (Bruxelles: Etablissements Emile Bruylant, Société anonyme d'éditions juridiques et scientifiques, 1979); J. White, *Heracles Bow: Essays on the Rhetoric and Poetics of the Law* (Madison, Wis: University of Wisconsin Press, 1985); M. Ball, *Lying Down Together: Law, Metaphor, and Theology* (Madison, Wis.: University of Wisconsin Press, 1985); P. Goodrich, *Reading the Law* (Oxford: Basil Blackwell, 1986). For case studies of judicial rhetoric, see L. LaRue, "The Rhetoric of Powell's *Bakke*," (1981) *Wash. & Lee L. Rev.* 43; Erwin Chemerinsky, "Rationalizing the Abortion Debate: Legal Rhetoric and the Abortion Controversy" (1982) 31 *Buffalo L. Rev.* 85; M. Gold, "The Mask of Objectivity: Politics and Rhetoric in the Supreme Court of Canada" (1985) 7 *Sup. Ct. L. Rev.* 455.

6. Aristotle, *Rhetoric*, trans. W. Rhys Roberts (New York: Modern Library, 1954) at 1355. On rhetoric generally, see C. Perelman and L. Olbrechts-Tyteca, *The New Rhetoric: Treatise on Argumentation* (Notre Dame, Ind.: University of Notre Dame, 1958); Kenneth Burke, *A Rhetoric of Motives* (New York: Braziller, 1955); Maurice Nathanson and Henry W. Johnstone, Jr., eds., *Philosophy, Rhetoric and Argumentation* (University Park: Pennsylvania State University Press, 1965); Lloyd F. Bitzer and Edwin Black, eds., *The Prospect of Rhetoric* (Englewood Cliffs, N.J.: Prentice-Hall, 1971); Thomas R. Nilsen, ed., *Essays on Rhetorical Criticism* (New York: Random House, 1968); and E. Black, *Rhetorical Criticism: A Study in Method* (New York: Macmillan, 1965).

7. See White, *Heracles Bow*. This conception of rhetoric can be seen as a subset or outgrowth of the more traditional conception outlined above. See Gold, "The Mask of Objectivity," 459–60.

8. L. Bitzer, "The Rhetorical Situation" (1968) 1 *Philosophy & Rhetoric* 1.

9. On the audiences of the Court, see Gold, "The Mask of Objectivity" at 460–61.

10. On the history preceding patriation, see D. Milne, *The New Canadian Constitution* (Toronto: Lorimer, 1982); K. Banting and R. Simeon, eds., *And No One Cheered: Federalism, Democracy and the Constitutional Act* (Toronto: Methuen, 1983); R. Sheppard and M. Valpy, *The National Deal: The Fight for a Canadian Constitution* (Toronto: Fleet Books, 1982); and E. McWinney, *Canada and the Constitution 1979–1982: Patriation and the Charter of Rights* (Toronto: University of Toronto Press, 1982).

11. It would appear that the Court is increasingly sensitive and responsive to the views of legal academics. See, for example, Hon. Mr. Brian Dickson, "The Public Responsibility of Lawyers" (1983) 13 *Man. L.J.* 175 at 179–80.

12. R.S.C. 1970, App. III (hereinafter the Bill of Rights).

13. To be sure, there were some dissenting voices, but they were clearly in the minority. Moreover, some of the most articulate arguments against the Charter were offered by political scientists and not lawyers. See, for example, Peter H. Russell, "The Effect of a Charter of Rights on the Policy-Making Role of Canadian Courts" (1985) 25 *Can. Pub. Admin.* 1; D. Smiley, "A Dangerous Deed: The Constitution Act, 1982" in *And No One Cheered*, ed. Banting and Simeon, 74. For those who believe that lawyers understand issues of constitutional rights better than anyone else—and there are a fair

number within the legal community—the criticisms of non-lawyers may have been somewhat easy to ignore.

14. See, for example, W.S. Tarnopolsky and G.A. Beaudoin, eds., *The Canadian Charter of Rights and Freedoms: Commentary* (Toronto: Carswell, 1982). There were some who argued that the fact of entrenchment would not, in and of itself, alter the conservative approach of the Court. See, for example, B. Hovius and R. Martin, "The Canadian Charter of Rights and Freedoms in the Supreme Court of Canada" (1983) 61 *Can. Bar Rev.* 354. Nevertheless, this clearly went against the grain of most of the academic writing on the subject.

15. Milne, *The New Canadian Constitution*, 86–89.

16. For some examples, see M. Gold, "The Rhetoric of Constitutional Argumentation" (1985) 35 *U. of Toronto L.J.* 154, notes 3–6.

17. See F.L. Morton and M.J. Withey, *Charting the Charter, 1982–1985: A Statistical Analysis* (Calgary: Research Unit for Socio-Legal Studies, Faculty of Social Sciences, University of Calgary, 1986) and P.J. Monahan, "A Critic's Guide to the Charter" in *Charter Litigation*, ed. R.J. Sharpe (Toronto: Butterworths, 1987) at 383–408.

18. For my views concerning the interpretation of the equality rights guarantees in the Charter, see M. Gold, "A Principled Approach to Equality Rights: A Preliminary Inquiry" (1982) 4 *Sup. Ct. L.R.* 131; M. Gold, "Moral and Political Theories in Equality Rights Adjudication" in *Litigating the Values of a Nation: The Canadian Charter of Rights and Freedoms*, ed. J. Weiler and R. Elliot (Toronto: Carswell, 1968) 85. On constitutional interpretation more generally, see Gold, "The Rhetoric of Constitutional Argumentation."

19. See generally H.G. Gadamer, *Truth and Method*, trans. G. Barden and J. Cumming (New York: Crossroad, 1985). For a useful account of

hermeneutical theories, see Richard Palmer, *Hermeneutics* (Evanston Il.: Northwestern University Press, 1969).

20. *Big M Drug Mart*, at 342–44. See also *R. v. Therens*, at 638.

21. On the centrality of one's prejudices, see Gadamer, *Truth and Method* at 238ff.

22. Gold, "The Rhetoric of Constitutional Argumentation." This taxonomy was adopted from P. Bobbitt, *Constitutional Fate* (New York: Oxford University Press, 1982).

23. Gold, "The Rhetoric of Constitutional Argumentation."

24. On the functions of the Court see Gold, "The Rhetoric of Constitutional Argumentation." For a more complete account, see Bobbit, *Constitutional Fate.*

25. Gold, "The Rhetoric of Constitutional Argumentation."

26. A. Chayes, "Foreword: Public Law Litigation and the Burger Court" (1982) 96 *Harv. L. Rev.* 4. For a fuller account, see Gold, "The Mask of Objectivity."

27. Chayes, ibid.

28. *Operation Dismantle* at 472.

29. "It is therefore, in my view, not only appropriate that we decide the matter; it is our constitutional obligation to do so." Ibid., 473–74.

30. *Reference Re Section 94(2) of the Motor Vehicle Act (B.C.)* at 496.

31. *Reference Re Section 94(2) of the Motor Vehicle Act (B.C.)* at 497.

32. See *Reference Re Amendment to the Constitution of Canada (Nos. 1, 2 and 3)* (1981), [1981] 1 S.C.R. 753, [1981] 1 W.W.R. 1; *Re A.G. Quebec and A.G. Canada* (1982), [1982] 2 S.C.R. 793, 140 D.L.R. (3d) 385.

33. *Amax Potash Ltd. v. Saskatchewan* (1976), [1977] 2 S.C.R. 576 at 590, [1976] 6 W.W.R. 61.

34. "At the outset, let it be emphasized in the clearest possible language that the issue before this Court in this appeal is not whether it is or is not in the interest of this community to require Canadian citizenship as a precondition to membership in the bar. Rather, the only issue is whether s.. 289(*c*) of the *Law Society Act*, is inconsistent with s. 6(2)(*b*) of the *Canadian Charter of Rights and Freedoms.*" *Skapinker* at 359–60.

35. Madame Justice Wilson appears to embrace this conception of the distinction when she states, in *Operation Dismantle* at 472: "[I]f the court were simply being asked to express its opinion on the wisdom of the executive's exercise of its defence powers in this case, the court would have to decline. It cannot substitute its opinion for that of the executive to whom the decision-making power is given by the Constitution." For a similar view of the impossibility of maintaining the distinction between wisdom and constitutionality, see Patrick J. Monahan and Andrew Petter, "Developments in Constitutional Law: The 1985–86 Term" (1987) 9 *Sup. Ct. L. Rev.* 69.

36. R.S.B.C. 1979, c. 288, s. 94, amended by *Motor Vehicle Amendment Act, 1982*, S.B.C. 1982, c. 36, s. 19. The Act contemplated a minimum period of imprisonment for those who drove without a valid driver's licence or who drove while their licence was under suspension.

37. *Reference Re Section 94(2) of the Motor Vehicle Act (B.C.)* at 521.

38. *R. v. Oakes* at 138–39.

39. Ibid. at 139.

40. Ibid.

41. See Gold, "The Mask of Objectivity."

42. R.S.Q. 1977, c. C-11.

43. *Quebec Association of Protestant School Boards* at 79–84. The Court also reasoned that the impugned provisions of Quebec's legislation, if upheld, would amount in effect to an amendment of section 23. Amend-

ments must be pursued through the amending formulae set out in the constitution and cannot be effected via the terms of section 1 of the Charter. Ibid at 86–88.

44. *Quebec Association of Protestant School Boards v. A.G. Que. (No. 2)* (1982), 140 D.L.R. (3d) 33, 3 C.R.R. 114 (Que. Sup. Ct.).

45. On this issue, an analogy can be drawn between this case and the second patriation case concerning Quebec's putative veto over constitutional change. See Gold, "The Mask of Objectivity."

46. S.C. 1976–77, c. 52, ss. 2 and 71.

47. *Singh*, at 218–19.

48. *Operation Dismantle* at 488; *Reference Re Section 94(2) of the Motor Vehicle Act (B.C.)* at 529.

49. See, for example, Joel Feinberg, *Social Philosophy* (Englewood Cliffs, N.J.: Prentice-Hall, 1973).

50. "Purpose is a function of the intent of those who drafted and enacted the legislation at the time, and not of any shifting variable." *Big M Drug Mart* at 335.

51. *Big M Drug Mart* at 334–35.

52. This passage gestures towards a set of values associated with the ideal of the Rule of Law. See, for example, J. Raz, "The Rule of Law and its Virtue" (1977) 93 *L.Q. Rev.* 195. The Rule of Law remains an ideal around which the legal community is organized and will rally. See generally A. Hutchinson and P. Monahan, eds., *The Rule of Law: Ideal of Ideology?* (Toronto: Carswell, 1987).

53. *Quebec Association of Protestant School Boards* at 82, 84, 87–88.

54. *R. v. Therens* at 639–40. He applied the same form of reasoning in interpreting section 24 of the Charter, holding that it was not intended that evidence could be excluded pursuant to section 24(1). Ibid. at 647–48.

55. *Reference Re Section 94(2) of the Motor Vehicle Act (B.C.)* at 504.

56. In *Skapinker* at 382, Mr. Justice Estey stated that it was unnecessary to consider the legislative history of section 6. See also *R. v. Therens,* at 647.

57. *Reference Re Section 94(2) of the Motor Vehicle Act (B.C.)* at 507–509. There are a number of compelling reasons for rejecting the intent of the drafters as a decisive, or even weighty, element in constitutional interpretation. These are well known and need not be rehearsed here. See P. Brest, "The Misconceived Quest for the Original Understanding" (1980) 60 *Bos. U.L. Rev.* 204 and R. Dworkin, *A Matter of Principle* (Cambridge: Harvard University Press, 1985) at 33–71.

58. The core idea is that the Charter is valid, and hence to be applied, only because of the process through which it came to be enacted, and not because of any transcendant correspondence between it and natural law. See H.L.A. Hart, *The Concept of Law* (Oxford: Clarendon Press, 1961). It would appear to be a short step from this positivist foundation to the proposition that a court ought to be following the views of those who brought the Charter into being.

59. *Big M Drug Mart* at 344.

60. *Hunter v. Southam* at 155.

61. "If the newly planted 'living tree' which is the *Charter* is to have the possibility of growth and adjustment over time, care must be taken to ensure that historical materials, such as the Minutes of Proceedings and Evidence of the Special Joint Committee, do not stunt its growth." *Reference Re Section 94(2) of the Motor Vehicle Act (B.C.).*

62. Ibid. at 500–502.

63. *Therens* at 638–40.

64. *Singh* at 224.

65. See, for example, *Big M Drug Mart* at 331, where Chief Justice Dickson defends the independent relevance of legislative purpose in Charter adjudication, by arguing that rights will be better protected in this way.

66. See, for example, F.A. von Hayek, *The Constitution of Liberty* (Chicago: University of Chicago Press, 1960) and Hayk, *Law, Legislation and Liberty* (London: Routledge & K. Paul, 1973; Chicago: University of Chicago Press, 1976; and Chicago: University of Chicago Press, 1979).

67. For a critique of the individualistic tenor of the case, see A. Petter, "The Politics of the Charter" (1986) 8 *Sup. Ct. L. Rev.* 473.

68. See J. White, *When Words Lose Their Meaning* (Chicago: University of Chicago Press, 1984) 218.

69. See, for example, the opinion of Madame Justice Wilson in *Operation Dismantle* at 488. See also Mr. Justice Dickson's opinion in *Hunter v. Southam* 156: the Charter "is intended to constrain governmental action inconsistent with those rights and freedoms."

70. *Big M Drug Mart* at 346.

71. *Oakes* at 138–39.

72. *Oakes* at 136.

73. *Hunter v. Southam* at 168. See Petter, "The Politics of the Charter."

74. Within the liberal tradition one can distinguish between deontological and utilitarian conceptions of rights. A deontological conception admits that rights may be limited in the interest of securing the rights of others, but denies that it is appropriate to limit individual rights in the name of general societal welfare. John Rawls, *A Theory of Justice* (Cambridge: Belnap Press of Harvard University Press, 1971). A sophisticated form of utilitarianism is advanced in R.M. Hare, *Freedom and Reason* (Oxford: Clarendon Press, 1963). In the context of constitutional interpretation, the conception of rights chosen will determine what kinds of arguments are deemed legitimate and which are to be rejected as inadmissible. See M. Gold, "Equality before the Law in the Supreme Court of Canada: A Case Study" (1980) 18 *Osgoode Hall L.J.* 336 at 364–66.

75. *Singh* at 218–19.

76. *Big M Drug Mart* at 352.

77. *Reference Re Section 94(2) of the Motor Vehicle Act (B.C.)* at 518.

78. R.S.C. 1970, c. C-23.

79. See H. Arthurs, "Rethinking Administrative Law: A Slightly Dicey Business" (1979) 17 *Osgoode Hall L.J.* 1. It is not surprising that the Court appears to favour judicial models to administrative ones. The Charter itself is a testament to the faith we have that judges can and will decide issues of rights not only in a fair way, but in a way that is superior to legislative or administrative bodies.

80. R.S.C. 1970, c. C-23. The Court held that the provisions authorizing the search violated the right to be secure against unreasonable search or seizure as guaranteed by section 8 of the Charter.

81. *Hunter v. Southam* at 150.

82. Ibid. at 154.

83. R.S.C. 1970, c. L-13.

84. *Hunter v. Southam* at 301.

85. The case also provides an example of another technique analogous to the rhetoric of facts. Speaking of the *Lord's Day Act*, the Chief Justice wrote: "It is important to note that any person may be exempted from the operation of ss. 4, 6, and 7 by provincial legislation or municipal charter." *Big M Drug Mart* at 302. Why was it important to note these exemptions? In terms of the strict holding of the case, it would appear irrelevant. But from the point of view of rhetoric, it encourages the reader to wonder if the social purpose underlying the law can be so important given the possibility of so many exemptions from the law. Accordingly, how much of value really is being lost when the Court strikes down the law?

86. P. Hogg, *Constitutional Law of Canada*, 2d ed. (Toronto: Carswell, 1985) at 313–14.

87. *Big M Drug Mart* at 301.

88. Ibid. at 333.

89. Ibid. at 337.

90. Ibid. at 351.

91. P. Westen, "'Freedom' and 'Coercion'—Virtue Words and Vice Words" [1985] *Duke L.J.* 541.

92. This underlies the general rule limiting the leading of witnesses in direct examination. See S.A. Schiff, *Evidence in the Litigation Process,* 2d ed., vol. 1 (Toronto: Carswell, 1983) at 178–86.

93. *Singh* at 218.

94. See, for example, J.M. Evans, ed., *de Smith's Judicial Review of Administrative Action,* 4th ed. (London: Stevens, 1980) at 156–240.

95. *Operation Dismantle* at 450.

96. Ibid. at 451.

97. A similar denigration of the opposing viewpoint can be seen in Mr. Justice Lamer's opinion in *Reference Re Section 94(2) of the Motor Vehicle Act (B.C.)* at 498, where those who would interpret section 7 procedurally are depicted as viewing the issue in a "narrow and restrictive fashion," while those (including the Court) who take a broader view of section 7 are adopting "an open-minded approach."

98. H. Scott Fairley, "Developments in Constitutional Law: The 1983–84 Term" (1985) 7 *Sup. Ct. L. Rev.* 63 at 120.

99. *Bilodeau v. A.G. Manitoba* (1986), [1986] 1 S.C.R. 449, 27 D.L.R. (4th) 39; *MacDonald v. City of Montreal* (1986), [1986] 1 S.C.R. 460, 27 D.L.R. (4th) 321; *Société des Acadiens du Nouveau-Brunswick Inc. v. Association of Parents for Fairness in Education* (1986), [1986] 1 S.C.R. 549, 27 D.L.R. (4th) 406.

100. *Edwards Books and Art Ltd. v. R.,* (1986), [1986] 2 S.C.R. 713, 71 N.R. 161.

101. On the scope of the Charter, see *Retail, Wholesale and Department Store Union, Local 580 v. Dolphin Delivery Ltd.* (1986), [1986] 2 S.C.R. 573, 71 N.R. 83. On the question of

Charter, see *Mills v. R.* (1986), [1986] 1 S.C.R. 863, 67 N.R. 241.

102. One would argue that the individualistic focus in the cases obscures the extent to which we as individuals are constituted socially, that the liberal vision renders other more communal forms of human association less legitimate and less realisable, and so on. See, for example, Mr. Sandel, *Liberalism and the Limits of Justice* (New York: Cambridge University Press, 1982). In my earlier analysis of these cases I was tempted by such a critique. See M. Gold, "La Rhetorique des droits constitutionnels" (1988) 22 *Themis* 1. I am now of the view that such a critique was premature.

103. See, for example, J. Rawls, "Justice as Fairness: Political not Metaphysical" (1985) 14 *Philosophy & Public Affairs* 223. On certain problems with the communitarian perspective, see A. Gutmann, "Communitarian Critics of Liberalism" (1985) 14 *Philosophy & Public Affairs* 308.

DOES THE CHARTER APPLY
TO PRIVATE PERSONS?[*]

BRIAN SLATTERY

Charter of Rights and Freedoms—Does It Bind Private Persons—I am a Canadian of Estonian origins, born in Alberta. I have applied for membership in a local social club with excellent sports facilities. I am a fitness addict, and nothing else is available in the neighbourhood. The club turns me down. They say that the club is intended solely for persons of Irish extraction. It is a club for the advancement of Irish culture in Canada. If my name were O'Brien or Mulroney or even Slattery, I would be welcome. In the circumstances, they regret that they cannot offer me membership and hope that I understand.

I do not understand. In fact, I am rather annoyed. I know that the Charter of Rights and Freedoms (the Charter)[1] prohibits racial and ethnic discrimination,[2] and want to find out if I can invoke it.

The lawyer I approach is doubtful. She says that the Charter probably does not apply to relations among private individuals and groups. It only deals with people's rights *vis-à-vis* the government. Since the club I have applied to is private, the Charter may be irrelevant. However, she notes that writers have expressed differing opinions on the question, and offers her services for a modest hourly fee.

Is my lawyer right? Does the Charter only bind governments and legislatures, or does it also bind private individuals? The Charter is surprisingly unclear on the issue and lends itself to different interpretations.[3]

STANDARD VIEWS

At first sight, section 32(1) of the Charter appears to provide a definite answer. The section states:

[*]*Canadian Bar Review* 63 (1985): 148–61.

This Charter applies

(a) to the Parliament and government of Canada in respect of all matters within the authority of Parliament including all matters relating to the Yukon Territory and Northwest Territories; and

(b) to the legislature and government of each province in respect of all matters within the authority of the legislature of each province.

It can be argued that this section makes a comprehensive statement of the Charter's application. It identifies the full range of persons and institutions governed by its terms. A plea that one's rights under the Charter have been violated can only succeed where the alleged violator falls within section 32(1). The section mentions only governments and legislatures, and not private persons. So, when a Charter right is infringed by a private party, the Charter gives no protection.

This interpretation is supported by another argument. A constitution ordinarily serves to identify governmental institutions and define their powers; it does not deal with relations among private persons. So the Charter, in setting out a range of rights and freedoms held by private persons, only aims to circumscribe the powers of government over such persons. What might appear, at first blush, to be individual rights maintainable against the whole world are, on closer inspection, merely restrictions on governments.

Not all commentators, however, have accepted this viewpoint. Some have pointed out that section 32(1) does not actually say that the Charter applies *exclusively* to the bodies listed there, merely that the Charter does in fact apply to those bodies. Moreover, the section obviously does not give a complete description of the Charter's application. The Charter vests rights in private persons, and in that sense clearly applies to them, notwithstanding the fact that they are not mentioned in the section. On this alternate view, section 32(1) serves to indicate that the governments and legislatures of both Canada and the provinces are bound by the Charter, but does not purport to give a complete list of the persons and bodies affected. It confirms the amplitude of the Charter's scope in areas mentioned without narrowing its scope in other areas.

But why should the Charter bother to single out governments and legislatures in section 32(1) if not to indicate that these entities alone are bound by the Charter? Under a standard maxim of statutory interpretation, the specific mention of one thing impliedly excludes similar things left unmentioned.

Adherents of the second view give the following reply. So far as governments are concerned, it was necessary to mention them specifically because under standard rules of interpretation the Crown is not bound by a statute in the absence of explicit words.[4] As for legislatures, it was prudent to mention them in order to indicate clearly that the principle of Parliamentary supremacy did not apply. After all, the Constitution also contains sections allocating legislative powers between the federal and provincial governments.[5] Section 32(1) serves to make it clear that the Charter takes precedence over such sections. This function is not adequately performed by the supremacy clause in section 52(1), which makes the Constitution as a whole paramount to ordinary laws, without indicating the order of priority among the various parts of the Constitution itself.

What conclusions emerge from this exchange? I wish to argue here, not that one or the other view of section 32(1) is correct, but that the debate on this point is misguided. If we consider the underlying issue more closely, we can see that in the end if does not matter which view of section 32(1) we take: the result is much the same.

CLARIFYING THE ISSUE

The issue, as it is normally stated, is whether or not the Charter binds only governments and legislatures, or whether it also binds private persons. Yet, this way of framing the issue obscures the real problem. It suggests that the first alternative is a feasible one, that it would be *possible* to hold that the only function of the Charter is to curtail legislative and governmental powers. But a moment's reflection shows that the Charter has another important function: it lays down new law governing the rights and remedies of individuals. This is at the heart of the problem.

The dual functions of the Charter become clearer on comparison with several familiar types of legal provisions. The first type is one that imposes restrictions on the powers of federal or provincial legislatures, but does not otherwise affect the existing rights and obligations of ordinary people. An example is furnished by sections 91 and 92 of the *Constitution Act, 1867*, which define and restrict the powers of Parliament and the provincial legislatures by reference to a specified range of subject matters. Although these sections empower the legislatures to deal with private rights and obligations in the areas designated, they do not directly affect those rights.

The second type of legal provision is the reverse of the first. It affects the existing rights and obligations of people but does not restrict the ability of legislatures to alter those rights in future. Most ordinary Canadian statutes fall into this category. Examples would include a provincial act prohibiting racial discrimination in the rental of housing, and a federal act lowering the voting age. Such acts can be repealed in the ordinary manner.

The third and final type of legal provision combines the positive features of the first two types without sharing their limitations. It affects the existing rights or obligations of ordinary persons and at the same time shields those rights from future legislative intrusion. A good example is provided by section 93(2) of the *Constitution Act, 1867*, which in its terms grants the supporters of certain denominational schools in Quebec all the rights held by Catholic school supporters in Upper Canada at Confederation. This provision ostensibly enlarges educational rights in Quebec, and simultaneously prevents the provincial legislature from attacking those rights in the future.[6]

How should we classify the Charter? We know that it places permanent restrictions on the powers of Parliament and the provincial legislatures.[7] In this respect it resembles the first type of provision rather than the second. But it also has important changes in existing laws. A person previously denied the right to vote under federal or provincial law may now possess the right under section 3, while under section 2(c) the right to demonstrate peacefully in public, formerly restricted or denied under a municipal by-law, may now be extended. Even where the right granted by the Charter already existed under current law, the Charter provides a new basis for that right and arms it with a new set of remedies.[8]

So the Charter belongs in our third category of legal provisions. Like section 93(2) of the 1867 Act, which in its terms both enlarges and entrenches educational rights in Quebec, the Charter has dual functions. It is the source of new law governing the rights and remedies of ordinary people, and at the same time it protects those rights from future legislative interference.

If we consider only the second function, the entrenchment of rights, it seems true to say that the Charter applies exclusively to governments and legislatures and not to private persons, because the former bodies are the only ones potentially capable of amending the Charter. The real issue concerns the Charter's first function: does the new law laid down by the Charter regarding individual rights and remedies only affect relations between private persons and governmental bodies, or does it also affect relations among private persons themselves?

EFFECTS ON LAWS GOVERNING PRIVATE RELATIONS

Suppose that at the time the Charter took effect, a provincial statute directed private employers to give preference in hiring to applicants with ten years' residency in the province, and gave civil remedies to unsuccessful applicants. The statute, we note, governs the relations between two groups of private persons, namely employers and prospective employees, and establishes certain reciprocal rights and obligations.

Section 6 of the Charter states that every Canadian citizen has the right to move to and pursue the gaining of a livelihood in any province, subject to laws of general application in a province, other than those that discriminate among persons primarily on the basis of past or present residency. Does this section apply to the provincial statute?

Prima facie, the statute violates the Charter provision and may be struck down by the courts.[9] The statute seemingly will not escape scrutiny simply because it governs relations between private persons. Section 6 confers on private persons the right to pursue the gaining of a livelihood in any province, and explicitly excludes laws that discriminate on the basis of residency. The section, on its most natural reading, applies to laws regulating the relations between private employers and employees and is not confined to laws governing the public sector.

This example suggests, then, that a Charter provision may affect the legal relations between private persons when the law governing those relations differs from the terms of the Charter. But a single example, suggestive as it may be, hardly proves the point. A broader analysis is necessary.

When the Charter came into force, the entire field of relations among private individuals was governed by laws of one sort or another, permitting, ordaining, or forbidding certain conduct towards other people, or attaching certain legal consequences to such conduct. As we have seen the Charter is the source of new law governing the rights and remedies of individuals and amends all laws inconsistent with its terms. This flows in part from section 52(1) of the *Constitution Act, 1982*, which provides:

The Constitution of Canada is the supreme law of Canada, and any law that is inconsistent with the provisions of the Constitution is, to the extent of the inconsistency, of no force or effect.

There is nothing in this section to suggest that laws regulating private relations constitute a special group, uniquely shielded from the Constitution's impact. It follows that whenever laws governing those relations are inconsistent with rights guaranteed by the Charter, the Charter takes precedence. The effect holds true of both statutes and the common law, for section 52(1) makes the Constitution paramount to all forms of law, not merely statutes.

If we return now to section 32(1), we can see that it produces the same result, even on the assumption that the narrow interpretation of the section is correct. In providing that the Charter applies to the various governments and legislatures of Canada, the section effectively mandates the courts to give full effect to Charter rights, notwithstanding contrary provisions of statutes or the common law, including those governing private relations.[10]

Section 32(1) does not explicitly refer to the courts, but it plainly covers them. Courts owe their authority either to statutes passed by legislatures or prerogative acts issued by the Crown on behalf of a government. Yet a legislature or government bound by the Charter cannot create or maintain subordinate bodies that are free from the Charter's constraints. The act governing such a body is necessarily subject to the Charter, which limits the authority conferred.

Other considerations point to the same conclusion. Several substantive Charter provisions clearly apply to the courts, such as the provision governing self-in-crimination of witnesses (section 13), or that forbidding cruel and unusual punishment (section 12).[11] Moreover, section 24 mandates the courts to supply appropriate remedies for Charter violations, and section 52(1) implicitly instructs them to strike down laws inconsistent with the Charter.

If the Charter applies to the courts, it must apply not only to statutes enforced by the courts but also to the common law generated and administered there. Were the courts free to develop and apply common law rules that violated Charter rights, the supremacy of the Constitution would be undermined. It follows that, where a common law rule is inconsistent with a right granted by the Charter, the common law is superseded. Nothing in section 32(1) suggests that laws governing relations among private individuals are immune from this process.

Our analysis indicates, then, that the rights and remedies conferred by the Charter take precedence over both existing and future laws that regulate relations among private persons. It is worthwhile considering for a moment what this conclusion actually entails. It does not mean, of course, that each and every provision of the Charter necessarily affects private relations. It means only that where a Charter provision, on its true interpretation, confers rights that affect the interaction of private persons, the courts are mandated under section 32(1) to give it full effect.

In short, no uniform answer can be given to the question whether the Charter regulates private relations. All that can be said is that the Charter does not contain a general rule exempting them from its effects. The true issue, then, is not whether

Charter rights en bloc affect such relations but whether specific Charter rights do so. It may be that certain Charter rights, on their proper interpretation, do not have a significant impact on private relations. That is a matter for argument. But the argument should be addressed to the particular provision in question, and not to the abstract (and ultimately unanswerable) issue of the Charter's scope as a whole.

SOME ILLUSTRATIONS

A few examples may clarify the point. Suppose that a Chinese person declines to rent his house to a non-Chinese person on grounds of race. Does section 15(1) of the Charter[12] affect the common law right of the house-owner to rent to whomever he chooses?

Section 15(1) provides that every individual is equal before and under the law and has the right to the equal protection and equal benefit of the law without discrimination on grounds *(inter alia)* of race. The common law, on the other hand, simply holds that an owner may or may not rent out his property as he sees fit. His ownership of the building entitles him to lease it to another person. If he does lease it, and certain legal conditions are satisfied, the courts will enforce the lease at the instance of either party.

Is the common law on this point inconsistent with section 15(1)? The answer is arguably negative. The prospective non-Chinese tenant has the same legal power to secure a lease as anybody else. The law does not oblige the owner to accept his offer; but the law does not prevent the owner from accepting the offer, or direct him to accept anyone else's offer in similar circumstances. True, the common law fails to instruct the owner to disregard the applicant's race; but it does not oblige him to take race into account either. In short, the common law merely empowers the owner and the applicant to conclude a lease if they both agree. It does not compel that agreement, or direct either party to advert to or ignore the other party's complexion.

Arguably, then, the common law treats applicants of all races in an equal fashion. Obviously, the *owner*, in this instance, does not treat Chinese and non-Chinese equally, and his behaviour is reprehensible and possibly illegal under other laws, such as a provincial human rights code. But section 15(1) of the Charter does not directly regulate the owner's actions, or guarantee equal treatment at his hands. Rather, it applies to the *law* that governs his relations with prospective tenants. So long as the law itself does not discriminate racially, it is not affected by section 15(1).

Nevertheless, it could be contended that the common law contravenes section 15(1) in that it *permits* the owner to practise racial discrimination in renting out his house. The section nullifies any laws that discriminate on the basis of race; arguably, it must also nullify any laws that allow private persons to discriminate. This is a strong argument. But it is not entirely convincing.

A law that affords a benefit or protection to persons of one race but not those of another plainly contravenes section 15(1). But it is not clear that a law permitting landlords to take into account the race of prospective tenants confers an unequal benefit or protection. The "benefit" conferred here is the power to rent to whomsoever one wishes. The law gives the same power to everyone, regardless of race. To put the proposition in its most paradoxical form, the law permits persons of all races to take race into account in renting out housing. This is an undesirable state of affairs. But the remedy probably does not lie with section 15(1).

It could be argued, to the contrary, that the prospective tenant has been denied the equal benefit of the law in that the benefit of obtaining a lease (as provided for by law) has been withheld on racial grounds. In other words, section 15(1) ensures not only equality in legal form, but also equal *treatment* under the law. Now it seems arguable that where the law gives a person the right to do something (such as to vote, or to walk freely on the streets) and another private person tries to stop him from exercising that right on racial grounds, section 15(1) of the Charter might in some cases be invoked.[13] But here the prospective tenant has the right to sign a lease *only if the other party agrees*. The landlord's refusal does not violate or deny the right of the prospective tenant. The law simply empowers the latter to make a lease; it does not compel anyone to make a lease with him.

Let us suppose, however, that the owner lets out his house to another Chinese person, and the lease gives the tenant the power to sub-let, subject to the undertaking that he not rent to a non-Chinese. Is this clause affected by section 15(1)? Here, the answer seems to be affirmative. The reason is that section 15(1) strikes down any laws that discriminate on grounds of race. The lease is law between the parties, in the sense that the law renders it binding and enforceable in the courts. But under section 32(1) the courts cannot enforce a provision that violates a Charter right, in this case a clause requiring a tenant to practice racial discrimination. Insofar as the lease purports to oblige the tenant to discriminate against non-Chinese persons it is invalid, unless the clause can be justified under section 1, which seems unlikely.

What, then, is the position of a non-Chinese person who applies to sub-let the house in the example above and is refused by the existing tenant on grounds of race? Here, the answer is less clear-cut. The racially restrictive clause in the lease is invalid, and the applicant presumably may obtain a court declaration to that effect.[14] If the clause is the only reason the tenant refused to sub-let, the applicant will now be in a better position, at least theoretically. But under section 15(1) of the Charter, a court probably cannot *oblige* the tenant to sub-let to the non-Chinese applicant, or to treat applicants of all races on an equal basis. The tenant has the same rights in this respect as the original owner. He may or may not sub-let the house as he sees fit. If he discriminates racially in choosing among applicants, he is a poor citizen and perhaps violates other laws, but section 15(1) arguably does not affect him.

We have been discussing how section 15(1) interacts with the common law regulating private relations. But the same considerations apply to statutes. Take the following example, which recalls the problem posed at the start of this paper. A provincial statute provides that every person has the right to equal treatment with respect to services, goods and facilities, without discrimination on grounds of race. Persons suffering discrimination are supplied with various civil remedies. But the statute also states that the right in question is not infringed where membership in a religious, philanthropic, educational, or social organization is restricted to persons of a particular race, if the organization is primarily engaged in serving the interests of persons of that race.

Here we have a statute that explicitly authorizes certain organizations to exclude applicants on racial grounds. In this respect, the statute merely replicates the common law. Yet under arguments considered above, the common law does not violate section 15(1) in authorizing organizations to select members on whatever basis they wish, including race. Does the fact that the authorization is found in a statute alter the position? I suggest that it probably does not. The way in which we resolve the issue at common law determines our views of the statute and *vice versa*.

It would be surprising if this were not the case. The statutory exemption of racially based organizations merely preserves a freedom they already held at common law. Yet if the common law does not violate section 15(1) of the Charter in allowing organizations to select members on a racial basis (as can be argued), it is hard to see why the statutory enactment of the same rule in a narrower form should itself trigger a violation of the section.

Any distinction between statutes and the common law in this respect would result in an odd disparity between the common law provinces and Quebec, where relations among private persons are presumptively governed by the Quebec Civil Code, in the absence of other provisions. It seems unreasonable to suppose that rules which escape the Charter's scrutiny in common law provinces are covered in Quebec simply because they are found in the Code.

To return to our example, the mere fact that the rule exempting ethnic organizations takes a statutory form does not bring it within the Charter's reach. But organizations that restrict membership to persons of a specific race may find themselves in conflict with section 15(1) for another reason. If the restrictions are embodied in rules that are legally binding on officers and members of the organization, then those by-laws will themselves be subject to review under the section. *Prima facie*, a by-law that confined membership in a club to Irish or Italians or blacks would violate section 15(1), and require justification under section 1. Such a justification might, however, be given successfully, particularly in light of section 27, which provides that the Charter shall be interpreted so as to preserve and enhance the multicultural heritage of Canada.

To sum up, it seems probable that section 15(1) does not affect laws that merely *permit* private persons or bodies to engage in certain activities, so long as the laws themselves do not discriminate among persons on a proscribed basis. But where the law empowers private persons or bodies to alter the rules binding on themselves or others, as by making contracts, deeds, wills, or by-laws, the rules created in this fashion will themselves be subject to review under section 15(1) and may be struck down for inconsistency with its terms.

While these observations may hold true for section 15(1), they do not necessarily apply to other sections of the Charter. Take, for example, section 20(2), which provides that any New Brunswick resident has the right to communicate with the government or legislature of the province in English or French. Would this section prevent a private person from attempting to restrain another person from exercising this right?

To take a slightly fanciful example, suppose that the zealous principal of a private Francophone boarding school forbids students to communicate in English on school premises. A student is found writing a letter to a government department in English, and is expelled. Could she obtain a remedy against the school under section 20(2)?

If the principal, apart from the Charter, is within her rights in forbidding the use of English, this must be so because the common law or a statute permits her to do this. But, as seen earlier, the Charter is paramount to both statutes and the common law. Insofar as the law permits a private person to interfere with the right of communication guaranteed by section 20(2), the law is arguably superseded, unless section 1 can be brought in support. The fact that the law is merely permissive, and does not itself forbid the use of English on school premises does not seem to affect the question here, as it might in a case under section 15(1). The reason is that the right under section 20(2), while if affects primarily the New Brunswick government and legislature, apparently also has the incidental effect of restraining other persons from interfering with the right granted.

Our examples have shown, then, that certain Charter provisions may affect relations among private persons where there is a law that either directs or authorizes a private person to act in a manner violating the Charter right of another. This is a significant conclusion. It shows that, even on the assumption that section 32(1) gives an exhaustive list of persons and bodies bound, certain provisions of the Charter may have important effects on relations among ordinary persons. The process is clearest, perhaps, where there is a statute that governs some aspect of private relations. But the same effect may hold where the offending rule is embodied in the common law, or a binding instrument such as a contract, deed, will, or by-law.

THE FUNCTION OF A CONSTITUTION

I have argued that no uniform response can be given to the question whether the Charter governs private relations. The extent to which they are affected depends on the scope of the Charter's individual provisions, which must be interpreted on a case basis. This conclusion, however, allows for different views about the manner in which these provisions should *normally* be interpreted.

Here, an argument mentioned earlier comes into play. This maintains that a constitution serves to identify governmental institutions and regulate their powers; it does not ordinarily deal with relations among private individuals. The Charter should be read with this fact in mind and its individual provisions construed as presumptively regulating relations with governmental agencies only.

One drawback of this argument is that it relies heavily on a stereotype. It may be true that many written constitutions deal mainly with the powers of governmental bodies. The extent to which a particular constitution follows this pattern, however, can only be determined by examining its terms. If certain provisions of the Charter of Rights, on their true interpretation, affect relations among private persons, that fact is not affected by what other constitutions may or may not do. The claim that a particular horse has five legs is settled, not by reading the dictionary definition of a horse, but by counting the legs.

In any case, the stereotype is historically inaccurate. Consider some of our earliest constitutional documents in Canada. The Royal Proclamation of 1763,[15] issued by the Crown shortly after the cession of New France, laid down a constitution for the new colony of Quebec, in the course of which it provided for the introduction of English law. So doing, it ostensibly modified the French private law formerly obtaining in the colony.[16] The implications for legal relations among ordinary individuals were profound. So great was the resulting confusion and controversy that when a new constitution was granted to the colony in the *Quebec Act of 1774*,[17] French law was restored in matters pertaining to property and civil rights (virtually the whole of private law). Section 8 of the Act specifies that the inhabitants of Quebec shall enjoy their property relations because they appeared in a constitution.

The Proclamation of 1763 also contained detailed clauses governing relations between Indians and private persons in the settler communities. In particular, it forbade such persons to purchase any lands held by the Indians or to settle on them.[18] At the same time, it opened the Indian trade to all private individuals, on the condition of obtaining a licence. These provisions, which clearly affect relations among private individuals and groups, are mixed in with other provisions directed at public officials, such as a clause prohibiting colonial Governors to grant away Indian lands prior to their purchase by public authorities. If there be any impropriety in the juxtaposition of public and private matters in a constitutional document, the thought did not occur to the Proclamation's authors.

Looking farther afield in the old British Empire, we find other examples of constitutional provisions affecting private relations. The British Crown frequently laid down a basic legal standard governing the laws of an overseas colonial territory, repugnance to which entailed nullity. Such standards were supplied not only for local statutes (usually requiring conformity with English law),[19] but also for unwritten bodies of law such as local custom. The provisions governing customary law commonly excluded rules that were repugnant to "justice, equity and good conscience."[20] Such provisions were constitutional in the accepted sense that they defined the powers and functions of local courts. At the same time they affected laws governing relations among private individuals.

Similarly, the standard rule governing the reception of law in a settled colony holds that English law is introduced into the colony as of the time of settlement, but only insofar as it is applicable in the new circumstances of the territory.[21] Local courts are thus empowered to reject English statutes or common law rules that are unsuited to local conditions, and this power has frequently been exercised. The courts, of course, have not confined their scrutiny to laws regulating relations between the government and private persons.

These examples suggest, then, that there is nothing unusual or aberrant in the view that certain Charter provisions supply basic standards guiding Canadian courts in the application of statutes and the common law, regardless whether they concern relations among private persons or between a private person and the government. To the contrary, as seen above, Canadian and Commonwealth history provides notable instances of similar standards being applied by the courts without any sense of constitutional indecorum.

Underlying the arguments just reviewed are two opposing conceptions of the Charter of Rights. The first, which is inspired by the American Bill of Rights, views the Charter as designed to prevent unwarranted encroachments by governments on the rights and freedoms of citizens. This conception is rooted in a political philosophy that views unrestrained government as a major threat to the well-being of a society, and places great value on the freedom of the individual, even when the exercise of that freedom may affect other persons adversely. To oversimplify, this political philosophy views legal restraints on government more favourably than it does restraints on private activity. It seems fair to say that this philosophy has not hitherto played a major role in the shaping of Canada.

The second conception of the Charter views it as laying down certain principles that are fundamental to our idea of Canadian society, and that operate as standards for the conduct of private persons and public bodies alike. This conception is not rooted in any particular antagonism to governments. It assumes that actions threatening the basic values of a society are as likely to proceed from private persons as from government. It sees no great danger in subjecting the laws governing private relations to limited judicial scrutiny. This view harmonizes well with the wording and spirit of the Charter, and with our political traditions. Better a five-legged horse than a Trojan one.

NOTES

1. Part 1, *Constitution Act 1982*, Schedule B to the *Canada Act 1982*, c. 11 (U.K.). Unless otherwise indicated subsequent references to sections are to sections of the Charter.

2. Sections 15(1) and 32(2). The subsections read as follows:

   15(1) Every individual is equal before and under the law and has the right to the equal protection and equal benefit of the law without discrimination and, in particular, without discrimination based on race, national or ethnic origin, colour, religion, sex, age or mental or physical disability.

   32(2) Notwithstanding subsection (1), section 15 shall not have effect until three years after this section comes into force.

3. For a range of differing views, see: Michael R. Doody, "Freedom of the Press," "The Canadian Charter of Rights and Freedoms," and a "New Category of Qualified Privilege" (1983) 61 *Can. Bar Rev.* 124, at 136–39; Dale Gibson, "The Charter of Rights and the Private Sector" (1982) 12 *Man. L.J.* 213; Dale Gibson, "Distinguishing Governors from the Governed: The Meaning of 'Government' under Section 32(1) of the Charter" (1983) 13 *Man. L.J.* 505; Peter Hogg, "Canada Act 1982 Annotated" (1982), 76–77; Katherine Swinton, "Application of the Canadian Charter of Rights and Freedoms," in *The Canadian Charter of Rights and Freedoms: Commentary* ed. Walter S. Tarnopolsky and Gérald A. Beaudoin (1982), 41.

4. For a parallel clause, see the *Canadian Human Rights Act*, S.C. 1976–77, c. 33, s. 63; see also the discussion in Gibson. The Charter of Rights and the Private Sector, ibid., at pp. 214–215.

5. See e.g., sections 91–95, *Constitution Act, 1867*; and also sections 50–51, *Constitution Act, 1982*, which add new provisions to the *Constitution Act, 1867* dealing with non-renewable natural resources, forestry resources and electrical energy.

6. Whether the section actually adds anything to the rights Quebecers already possessed is another question.

7. Under sections 32(1) and 52(1), subject to justifiable limitations within the meaning of section 1, and "notwithstanding" clauses enacted under section 33.

8. Under section 24(1), which provides that anyone whose rights or freedoms, as guaranteed by the Charter, have been infringed or denied may apply to a court of competent jurisdiction to obtain such remedy as the court considers appropriate and just in the circumstances.

9. Unless the exception in section 6(4) applies, or the law is justifiable under section 1.

10. Subject always to section 1.

11. See also sections 11, 14, and 19.

12. Which came into effect on 17 April 1985.

13. It may be noted, however, that in most instances a remedy would already exist under the common law or statute, and that it would be available regardless of whether or not the right was denied on racial grounds.

14. Under section 24(1) of the Charter, which empowers courts to grant appropriate remedies where a person's Charter rights have been denied.

15. R.S.C. 1970, Appendices, p. 123.

16. There has been disagreement regarding how far French private law was actually affected. See, e.g., the varying views

expressed in *Stuart v. Bowman* (1852) 2 L.C.R. 369 (L.C.S.C.); (1853), 3 L.C.R. 309 (L.C.Q.B.); *Wilcox v. Wilcox* (1858), 8 L.C.R. 34 (L.C.Q.B.).

17. 14 Geo. III, c. 83, s. 8 (U.K.).

18. For discussion, see Brian Slattery, "The Hidden Constitution: Aboriginal Rights in Canada" (1984) 32 *A.J. Comp. L.* 361, at 368–72.

19. See, for example, the clause in Cornwallis' Commission as Governor of Nova Scotia in 1749, stating that statutes passed by the local assembly "are not to be repugnant, but as near as may be agreeable, to the Laws and Statutes of this our Kingdom of Great Britain," in W.P.M. Kennedy, *Statutes, Treaties and Documents of the Canadian Constitution, 1713–1929* 2d ed. (1930), 6 at 7. Repugnancy to English law, as distinct from imperial statutes extending to a colony, was later generally eliminated as a ground for nullity by section 3 of the *Colonial Laws Validity Act, 1865,* 28–29 Vict., c. 63, s. 3 (U.K.).

20. See Kenneth Roberts-Wray, *Commonwealth and Colonial Law* (1966), 534–35, 575–79; M.B. Hooker, *Legal Pluralism: An Introduction to Colonial and Neo-Colonial Laws* (1975), 129–35.

21. See, e.g., Elizabeth G. Brown, "British Statutes in the Emergent Nations of North America: 1606–1949" (1963) 7 *A.J. Leg. His.* 95; J.E. Coté, "The Reception of English Law" (1977) 15

FURTHER READING

o

Many of the books and articles listed below range over much of the period since 1867. They are located here in the first section in which they are important.

General

R.I. Cheffins and P.A. Johnson, *The Revised Canadian Constitution: Politics as Law* (Toronto, 1986).

W.R. Lederman, ed., *The Courts and the Canadian Constitution* (Toronto, 1964).

Peter W. Hogg, *Constitutional Law of Canada* (Toronto, 1985).

W.H. McConnell, *Commentary on the British North America Act* (Toronto, 1977).

F.L. Morton, ed., *Law, Politics and the Judicial Process in Canada* (Calgary, 1989).

Peter H. Russell, *The Judiciary in Canada: The Third Branch of Government* (Toronto, 1987).

Peter H. Russell, "Overcoming Legal Formalism: The Treatment of the Constitution, the Courts and Judicial Behaviour in Canadian Political Science," *Canadian Journal of Law and Society* 1 (1986): 5–33.

Barry L. Strayer, *The Canadian Constitution and the Courts* (Toronto, 1983).

Section 1

G.P. Browne, ed., *Documents on the Confederation of British North America* (Toronto, 1969).

G.P. Browne, *The Judicial Committee and the British North America Act* (Toronto, 1967).

W.R. Lederman, "Unity and Diversity in Canadian Federalism: Ideals and Methods of Moderation," *Canadian Bar Review* 53 (1975): 597–620.

K. Lysyk, "Constitutional Reform and the Introductory Clause of Section 91: Residual and Emergency Law-Making Authority," *Canadian Bar Review* 57 (1979): 531–74.

Rod Preece, "The Political Wisdom of Sir John A. Macdonald," *Canadian Journal of Political Science* (September 1984), 459–81.

The Senate of Canada, *Report to the Honourable the Speaker Relating to the Enactment of the B.N.A. Act 1867* (Ottawa, 1939). This extremely useful and controversial study is usually referred to as the O'Connor Report.

A.I. Silver, *The French-Canadian Idea of Confederation 1864–1900* (Toronto, 1982).

Robert C. Vipond, "1787 and 1867: The Federal Principle and Canadian Confederation Reconsidered," *Canadian Journal of Political Science* (March 1989), 3–26.

Section 2

Christopher Armstrong, *The Politics of Federalism: Ontario's Relations with the Federal Government, 1867–1942* (Toronto, 1981).

Alan C. Cairns, "The Judicial Committee and Its Critics," *Canadian Journal of Political Science* (September 1971), 301–45.

E.R. Cameron, "The House of Lords and the Judicial Committee," *Canadian Bar Review* (1923), 223–31.

Ramsay Cook, *Provincial Autonomy, Minority Rights and the Compact Theory* (Ottawa, 1969).

Martha Fletcher, "Judicial Review and the Division of Powers" in *Canadian Federalism: Myth or Reality?* ed. J. Peter Meekison (Toronto, 1968), 140–58.

Viscount Haldane, "The Work for the Empire of the Judicial Committee of the Privy Council," *Cambridge Law Journal* 1 (1922): 143–55.

Bruce W. Hodgins, "Disagreement at the Commencement: Divergent Ontarian Views of Federalism," in *Oliver Mowat's Ontario*, ed. Donald Swainson (Toronto, 1972), 52–68.

Bora Laskin, " 'Peace, Order, and good Government' Re-examined," *Canadian Bar Review* (1947), 1054–87, reprinted in Lederman, *The Courts and the Constitution*, 66–99.

Bora Laskin, "The Supreme Court of Canada: A Final Court of Appeal of and for Canadians," *Canadian Bar Review* 29 (1951), 1038–42, 1057–76. Reprinted in Lederman, *The Courts and the Constitution*, 125–51.

Bora Laskin, "Tests for the Validity of Legislation: What Is the Matter," *University of Toronto Law Journal* (1955–56), 114–27.

V.C. MacDonald, "The Privy Council and the Canadian Constitution," *Canadian Bar Review* 29 (1951), 1024–37.

Patrick Macklem, "Constitutional Ideologies" *Ottawa Law Review* 20 (1988): 117–56.

D.W. Mundell, "Test for Validity of Legislation under the British North America Act," *Canadian Bar Review* (October 1954) 813–43.

R.A. Olmsted, *Decisions of the Judicial Committee of the Privy Council relating to the British North America Act, 1867 and the Canadian Constitution 1867–1954* (Ottawa, 1954), 3 vols.

Jennifer Smith, "The Origins of Judicial Review," *Canadian Journal of Political Science* (March 1983), 115–34.

James G. Snell, and Frederick Vaughan, *The Supreme Court of Canada: The History of the Institution* (Toronto, 1985).

Section 3

Christopher Armstrong, "Federalism and General Regulation: The Case of the Canadian Insurance Industry," *Canadian Public Administration* (Spring 1976), 88–101.

C. Baggaley, *The Emergence of the Regulatory State*, Technical Report no. 15., Economic Council of Canada (Ottawa, 1981).

Donald Fouts, "The Supreme Court of Canada," in *Comparative Judicial Behaviour*, ed. Glendon Scubert and David Danelski (Oxford, 1969).

Gerald Le Dain, "Sir Lyman Duff and the Constitution," *Osgoode Hall Law Journal* (1974), 261–338.

J.R. Mallory, *Social Credit and the Federal Power* (Toronto, 1956).

W. Ivor Jennings, "Constitutional Interpretation: The Experience of Canada," *Harvard Law Review* (November 1937), 1–39.

W.H. McConnell, "The Judicial Review of Prime Minister Bennett's 'New Deal,' " *Osgoode Hall Law Journal* (1968), 39–86. *The Canadian Bar Review* (June 1937) is devoted to academic articles largely on the significance of the New Deal decisions.

Jonathan Robinson, "Lord Haldane and the British North America Act," *University of Toronto Law Journal* (1970), 55–69.

R.J.S. Schultz, *Federalism and the Regulatory Process* (Montreal, 1979).

Stephen Wexler, "The Urge to Idealize: Viscount Haldane and the Constitution of Canada," *McGill Law Journal* (1984), 609–47.

David R. William, *Duff: A Life in the Law* (Vancouver, 1984).

Section 4

R. Balcome, E. McBride and D. Russell, *Supreme Court of Canada Decision-Making: The Benchmarks of Rand, Kerwin and Martland* (Toronto, 1990).

Ivan Bernier, and Andrée Lajoie, eds., *The Supreme Court of Canada as an Instrument of Political Change* (Toronto, 1985).

R.I. Cheffins, "The Supreme Court of Canada: The Quiet Court in an Unquiet Country," *Osgoode Hall Law Journal* (1966), 259–75.

Peter Hogg, "Federalism and the Jurisdiction of Canadian Courts," *University of New Brunswick Law Journal* (1981), 9–25.

Peter Hogg, "Is the Supreme Court of Canada Biased in Constitutional Cases?" *Canadian Bar Review* (1979), 721–39.

A.W. Johnson, "The Dynamics of Federalism in Canada," *Canadian Journal of Political Science* (1968), 18–39.

R.S. Kay, "Courts as Constitution Makers in Canada and the United States," *Supreme Court Law Review* (1982), 23–41.

W.R. Lederman, *Continuing Constitutional Dilemmas* (Toronto, 1981).

W.R. Lederman, "Some Forms and Limitations of Co-operative Federalism," *Canadian Bar Review* (1967), 409–36.

M.R. MacGuigan, "Precedent and Policy in the Supreme Court," *Canadian Bar Review* (1967), 627–65.

Patrick Monohan, *Politics and the Constitution: The Charter, Federalism and the Supreme Court of Canada* (Toronto, 1987).

W.D. Moull, "Natural Resources: The Other Crisis in Canadian Federalism," *Osgoode Hall Law Journal* (1980), 2–48.

W.D. Moull, "Natural Resources and Canadian Federalism: Reflections of a Turbulent Decade," *Osgoode Hall Law Journal* (1987), 411–29.

S.R. Peck, "The Supreme Court of Canada, 1958–66: A Search for Policy through Scalogram Analysis," *Canadian Bar Review* (1967), 666–725.

A. Petter, "Federalism and the Myth of the Federal Spending Power," *Canadian Bar Review* (1989), 448–79.

K. Swinton, "Bora Laskin and Federalism," *University of Toronto Law Journal* (1985), 353–91.

F. Vaughan, "The Canadian Courts and Policy Making: The Case of Justice Emmett Hall," *Saskatchewan Law Review* (1974), 357.

P. Weiler, *In the Last Resort* (Toronto, 1974).

Section 5

E.R. Alexander, "The Supreme Court of Canada and the Canadian Charter of Rights and Freedoms," *University of Toronto Law Journal* (1990), 1–73.

A.F. Bayefsky, "The Judicial Function under the Canadian Charter of Rights and Freedoms," *McGill Law Journal* (1986–87), 791–833.

David Beatty, *The Canadian Production of Constitutional Review: Talking Heads and the Supremes* (Toronto, 1990).

L.E. Weinrib, "The Supreme Court of Canada and Section 1 of the Charter," *Supreme Court Law Review* (1988), 469–513.

J. Fudge, "The Public/Private Distinction: The Possibilities and the Limits to the Use of Charter Litigation to further Feminist Struggles," *Osgoode Hall Law Journal* (1987), 485–554.

R. Knopff, "What Do Constitutional Equality Rights Protect Canadians Against?" *Canadian Journal of Political Science* (1987), 265–86.

N. Lyon, "An Essay on Constitutional Interpretation," *Osgoode Hall Law Journal* (1988), 95–126.

R.A. Macdonald, "Postscript and Prelude—The Jurisprudence of the Charter: Eight Theses," *Supreme Court Law Review* (1982), 321–50.

Michael Mandel, *The Charter of Rights and the Legalization of Politics in Canada* (Toronto, 1989).

C.P. Manfredi, "Adjudication, Policy Making and the Supreme Court of Canada: Lessons from the Experience of the United States," *Canadian Journal of Political Science* (1989), 313–35.

B. Slattery, "A Theory of the Charter," *Osgoode Hall Law Journal* (1987), 701–47.

Barry Strayer, "Life under the Charter: Adjusting the Balance between Legislatures and Courts," *Public Law* (1988), 347–69.

Bertha Wilson, "The Making of a Constitution: Approaches to Judicial Interpretation," *Public Law* (1988), 370–84.